THE ROUTLEDGE HANDBOOK OF THE PHILOSOPHY OF CHILDHOOD AND CHILDREN

Childhood looms large in our understanding of human life, as a phase through which all adults have passed. Childhood is foundational to the development of selfhood, the formation of interests, values and skills and to the lifespan as a whole. Understanding what it is like to be a child, and what differences childhood makes, is thus essential for any broader understanding of the human condition. *The Routledge Handbook of the Philosophy of Childhood and Children* is an outstanding reference source for the key topics, problems and debates in this crucial and exciting field, and is the first collection of its kind. Comprising over thirty chapters by a team of international contributors, the *Handbook* is divided into five parts:

- Being a child
- Childhood and moral status
- Parents and children
- Children in society
- Children and the state.

Questions covered include: What is a child? Is childhood a uniquely valuable state and, if so, why? Can we generalize about the goods of childhood? What rights do children have, and are they different from adults' rights? What (if anything) gives people a right to parent? What role, if any, ought biology to play in determining who has the right to parent a particular child? What kind of rights can parents legitimately exercise over their children? What roles do relationships with siblings and friends play in the shaping of childhoods? How should we think about sexuality and disability in childhood, and about racialized children? How should society manage the education of children? How are children's lives affected by being taken into social care?

The Routledge Handbook of the Philosophy of Childhood and Children is essential reading for students and researchers in philosophy of childhood, political philosophy and ethics, as well as those in related disciplines such as education, psychology, sociology, social policy, law, social work, youth work, neuroscience and anthropology.

Anca Gheaus is a Ramon y Cajal researcher at the Universitat Pompeu Fabra, Spain.

Gideon Calder is Senior Lecturer in Social Sciences and Social Policy at Swansea University, UK.

Jurgen De Wispelaere is Political Economy Research Fellow with the Independent Social Research Foundation (ISRF) and a Policy Fellow at the Institute for Policy Research, University of Bath, UK.

ROUTLEDGE HANDBOOKS IN PHILOSOPHY

Routledge Handbooks in Philosophy are state-of-the-art surveys of emerging, newly refreshed, and important fields in philosophy, providing accessible yet thorough assessments of key problems, themes, thinkers, and recent developments in research.

All chapters for each volume are specially commissioned, and written by leading scholars in the field. Carefully edited and organized, *Routledge Handbooks in Philosophy* provide indispensable reference tools for students and researchers seeking a comprehensive overview of new and exciting topics in philosophy. They are also valuable teaching resources as accompaniments to textbooks, anthologies, and research-orientated publications.

Also available:

The Routledge Handbook of Collective Intentionality
Edited by Marija Jankovic and Kirk Ludwig

The Routledge Handbook Scientific Realism
Edited by Juha Saatsi

The Routledge Handbook of Pacifism and Non-Violence
Edited by Andrew Fiala

The Routledge Handbook of Consciousness
Edited by Rocco J. Gennaro

The Routledge Handbook of Philosophy and Science of Addiction
Edited by Hanna Pickard and Serge Ahmed

The Routledge Handbook of Moral Epistemology
Edited by Karen Jones, Mark Timmons, and Aaron Zimmerman

For more information about this series, please visit: https://www.routledge.com/Routledge-Handbooks-in-Philosophy/book-series/RHP

THE ROUTLEDGE HANDBOOK OF THE PHILOSOPHY OF CHILDHOOD AND CHILDREN

Edited by Anca Gheaus, Gideon Calder and Jurgen De Wispelaere

LONDON AND NEW YORK

First published 2019
by Routledge
2 Park Square, Milton Park, Abingdon, Oxon OX14 4RN

and by Routledge
711 Third Avenue, New York, NY 10017

Routledge is an imprint of the Taylor & Francis Group, an informa business

© 2019 selection and editorial matter, Anca Gheaus, Gideon Calder and Jurgen De Wispelaere; individual chapters, the contributors

The right of Anca Gheaus, Gideon Calder and Jurgen De Wispelaere to be identified as the authors of the editorial material, and of the authors for their individual chapters, has been asserted in accordance with sections 77 and 78 of the Copyright, Designs and Patents Act 1988.

All rights reserved. No part of this book may be reprinted or reproduced or utilised in any form or by any electronic, mechanical, or other means, now known or hereafter invented, including photocopying and recording, or in any information storage or retrieval system, without permission in writing from the publishers.

Trademark notice: Product or corporate names may be trademarks or registered trademarks, and are used only for identification and explanation without intent to infringe.

British Library Cataloguing-in-Publication Data
A catalogue record for this book is available from the British Library

Library of Congress Cataloging-in-Publication Data
A catalog record has been requested for this book

ISBN: 978-1-138-91597-8 (hbk)
ISBN: 978-1-351-05598-7 (ebk)

Typeset in Bembo
by Sunrise Setting Ltd, Brixham, UK

Printed and bound by CPI Group (UK) Ltd, Croydon, CR0 4YY

As editors, we dedicate this handbook to

My father Puiu and the memory of my mother Doina (Anca)
My siblings Rachel, Gowan and Douglas (Gideon)
My late mother, Yvette (Jurgen)

CONTENTS

List of contributors   xi

    Introduction   1
    Anca Gheaus

PART I
Being a child   11

1 Epistemology: knowledge in childhood   13
    Fabrice Clément and Melissa Koenig

2 Language and communication: evidence from studying children   23
    M. J. Cain

3 The science of the adolescent brain and its cultural implications   33
    Suparna Choudhury and Nancy Ferranti

4 Art and creativity   45
    Jonathan Fineberg

5 Philosophical thinking in childhood   53
    Jana Mohr Lone

PART II
Childhood and moral status — 65

6 The moral status of children — 67
   Agnieszka Jaworska and Julie Tannenbaum

7 The value of childhood — 79
   Patrick Tomlin

8 Children and well-being — 90
   Anthony Skelton

9 Children's rights — 101
   Robert Noggle

10 Childhood and autonomy — 112
   Sarah Hannan

11 Paternalism towards children — 123
   Kalle Grill

12 The age of consent — 134
   David Archard

PART III
Parents and children — 145

13 Reasons to have children – or not — 147
   Christine Overall

14 The right to parent — 158
   Anca Gheaus

15 The good parent — 169
   Colin M. Macleod

16 Parental partiality — 180
   Jonathan Seglow

17 The composition of the family — 191
   Daniela Cutas

18 Parental licensing and discrimination — 202
   Carolyn McLeod and Andrew Botterell

19	Ethical challenges for adoption regimes *Jurgen De Wispelaere and Daniel Weinstock*	213
20	Gender and the family *Amy Mullin*	225
21	Filial duties *Diane Jeske*	236

PART IV
Children in society — 247

22	Childhood and race *Albert Atkin*	249
23	Childhood and disability *Gideon Calder and Amy Mullin*	260
24	Childhood and sexuality *Jennifer Epp and Samantha Brennan*	271
25	Children and animals *Sue Donaldson and Will Kymlicka*	282
26	What's wrong with child labor? *Philip Cook*	294
27	The vulnerable child *Mianna Lotz*	304

PART V
Children and the state — 315

28	Childhood and the metric of justice *Lars Lindblom*	317
29	Children and political neutrality *Matthew Clayton*	328
30	The costs of children *Serena Olsaretti*	339
31	Schooling *Gina Schouten*	351

32 Children and the care system   362
    Gideon Calder

33 Children and health   373
    Havi Carel, Gene Feder and Gita Gyorffy

34 Children and the right to vote   384
    Ludvig Beckman

35 Children, crime and punishment   395
    Christopher Bennett

36 Children and war   406
    Cécile Fabre

Index   416

LIST OF CONTRIBUTORS

David Archard is Professor of Philosophy at Queen's University, Belfast, UK, having previously taught at the Universities of Ulster, St Andrews and Lancaster. He has published extensively in applied ethics, political philosophy and philosophy of law.

Albert Atkin is a Senior Lecturer in Philosophy and member of the Centre for Agency, Values and Ethics (CAVE) at Macquarie University in Sydney, Australia. He is interested in race and racism, pragmatism, language and epistemology. He is the author of numerous articles and two books: *The Philosophy of Race* (Routledge, 2012) and *Peirce* (Routledge, 2015).

Ludvig Beckman is Professor of Political Science, Stockholm University, Sweden and research director at the Institute for Futures Studies in Stockholm. His current research projects concern the boundary problem in democratic theory and the nature of popular sovereignty as expressed in national constitutions.

Christopher Bennett is Reader in Philosophy at the University of Sheffield, UK. He is the author of a book on punishment (*The Apology Ritual*, Cambridge, 2008) as well as of numerous articles in journals and edited collections. He is currently the Chief Editor of the *Journal of Applied Philosophy*.

Andrew Botterell is Associate Professor of Law and Philosophy at Western University, Canada. His primary teaching and research interests are in philosophy of law, metaphysics and the ethics of parenthood and procreation.

Samantha Brennan is Dean of the College of Arts, University of Guelph. Her main research interests lie in the area of contemporary normative ethics, applied ethics and feminist philosophy. She is President of the Canadian Philosophical Association and a co-editor of *Feminist Philosophy Quarterly*.

M. J. Cain is Reader in Philosophy at Oxford Brookes University, UK. He specializes in the philosophy of mind and language and has written two books, the most recent being *The Philosophy of Cognitive Science*, published in 2015 by Polity.

List of contributors

Gideon Calder is Senior Lecturer in Social Sciences and Social Policy at Swansea University, UK. He is author or editor of ten books, most recently *How Inequality Runs in Families* (Policy Press, 2016), and co-edits the Routledge journal *Ethics and Social Welfare*.

Havi Carel is Professor of Philosophy at the University of Bristol, UK. She is currently a Wellcome Trust Senior Investigator (www.lifeofbreath.org). She is the author of *Phenomenology of Illness* (2016), *Illness* (2013) and *Life and Death in Freud and Heidegger* (2006).

Suparna Choudhury is Assistant Professor at the Division of Social and Transcultural Psychiatry, McGill University, Canada. She studies the developing brain at the intersection of anthropology and cognitive neuroscience. She is co-editor of *Critical Neuroscience: A Handbook of the Social and Cultural Contexts of Neuroscience*.

Matthew Clayton is Professor of Political Theory at the University of Warwick, UK. He is the author of *Justice and Legitimacy in Upbringing* (Oxford University Press, 2006) and has co-edited *The Ideal of Equality* (Palgrave Macmillan, 2000) and *Social Justice* (Blackwell, 2004).

Fabrice Clément is Full Professor at the Cognitive Science Centre of the University of Neuchâtel, Switzerland. His research at the intersection of developmental psychology, anthropology and philosophy of mind has been published in journals including *Psychological Science*, *Child Development* and *Mind and Language*.

Philip Cook is Lecturer in Political Theory in the School of Social and Political Science, University of Edinburgh, UK. He is also joint Editor-in-Chief of the journal *Res Publica*.

Daniela Cutas is Associate Professor of Practical Philosophy at Umeå University and the University of Gothenburg. She is a co-editor of the volumes 'Families – Beyond the Nuclear Ideal' (2012), and 'Parental Responsibility in the Context of Neuroscience and Genetics' (2017).

Jurgen De Wispelaere is a Political Economy Research Fellow with the Independent Social Research Foundation (ISRF) and a Policy Fellow at the Institute for Policy Research, University of Bath, UK. His research interests are at the intersection of political theory and public policy.

Sue Donaldson is a Research Associate in the Department of Philosophy at Queen's University, Canada, and co-coordinator of the Animals in Philosophy, Politics, Research and Ethics (APPLE) research group. She has authored three books, including *Zoopolis: A Political Theory of Animal Rights* (with Will Kymlicka).

Jennifer Epp teaches Philosophy and Women's Studies at Western University and Huron University College in London, Ontario, Canada. She received her PhD from Western University. Her dissertation was called, "Testimony as Significance Negotiation".

Cécile Fabre is Senior Research Fellow in Politics at All Souls College, University of Oxford, UK. She has written extensively on distributive justice, the rights we have over our own bodies and just war theory. Her most recent research monographs, *Cosmopolitan War* and *Cosmopolitan Peace*, came out with Oxford University Press in 2012 and 2016 respectively. She is currently finishing a book on the ethics of economic statecraft.

List of contributors

Gene Feder is a General Practitioner in Bristol and Professor of Primary Care at the University of Bristol. He leads research programmes on the health care response to domestic violence and on the management of chronic cardiac and respiratory conditions.

Nancy Ferranti is an undergraduate at McGill University, Canada, studying Cognitive Science, with specialities in philosophy, neuroscience and anthropology. Her research focuses on the social determinants of psychosis as well as cross-cultural and critical approaches to neuroscience, particularly with regard to adolescent development.

Jonathan Fineberg is Director of the PhD at University of the Arts in Philadelphia, USA, and author of more than 30 books and catalogues, including *When We Were Young: New Perspectives on the Art of the Child and Art Since 1940*.

Anca Gheaus is a Ramon y Cajal researcher at the Universitat Pompeu Fabra, Spain. She has published numerous articles on childrearing and gender justice and has recently edited a special issue of the *Journal of Applied Philosophy* on the nature and value of childhood.

Kalle Grill is Associate Professor of Philosophy at Umeå University, Sweden. His research mainly concerns paternalism and related issues, such as nudging, respect for preferences and various issues in public health policy. He also works on population ethics.

Gita Gyorffy works as a Consultant General Paediatrician at Gloucester Royal Hospital, UK, and is a mother of two.

Sarah Hannan is an Assistant Professor of Political Theory at The University of Manitoba, Canada. Sarah has published on the value of childhood and the morality of procreation and parenting. She is co-editor of *Permissible Progeny?* (Oxford University Press, 2015).

Agnieszka Jaworska is Associate Professor of Philosophy at University of California, Riverside, USA. Her research at the intersection of bioethics, ethical theory and moral psychology has been published in journals including *Ethics*, *Philosophy and Phenomenological Research* and *Philosophy and Public Affairs*.

Diane Jeske is Professor of Philosophy at the University of Iowa, USA. She is the author of *Rationality and Moral Theory: How Intimacy Generates Reasons* (Routledge, 2008) and has published widely on the nature of special obligations to friends and family.

Melissa Koenig is Professor of Child Psychology at the Institute of Child Development, University of Minnesota, USA. Her research is at the intersection of cognitive development, social epistemology and cultural learning. She has published in journals including *Psychological Science*, *Cognition* and *Proceedings of the National Academy of Sciences*.

Will Kymlicka is the Canada Research Chair in Political Philosophy at Queen's University in Kingston, Canada. His books include *Contemporary Political Philosophy*, *Multicultural Citizenship* and (with Sue Donaldson) *Zoopolis: A Political Theory of Animal Rights*.

Lars Lindblom is Associate Professor at Umeå University, Sweden. He works on issues at the intersection between social science and philosophy, and has published on whistleblowing, risk, education, the market, work and equality.

List of contributors

Mianna Lotz is Senior Lecturer in Philosophy at Macquarie University, where she teaches in Ethics and Applied Ethics. Her research focuses on vulnerability; reproductive technologies (including uterus transplantation); the family; parents' rights, interests and liberties; children's welfare; and adoption.

Carolyn McLeod is Professor of Philosophy and Women's Studies and Feminist Research at Western University, Canada. Her philosophical interests lie in the areas of applied ethics and feminist philosophy. She has a long-standing interest in the ethics of procreation and parenthood.

Colin M. Macleod is Professor of Philosophy and Law at the University of Victoria, Canada. His most recent book, co-authored with Ben Justice, is *Have A Little Faith: Religion, Democracy and the American Public School* (University of Chicago Press, 2016).

Jana Mohr Lone is Director of the Center for Philosophy for Children at the University of Washington, USA, author of *The Philosophical Child* (2012), co-author of *Philosophy in Education: Questioning and Dialogue in Schools* (2016) and co-editor of *Philosophy and Education: Introducing Philosophy to Young People* (2012).

Amy Mullin is Professor of Philosophy at the University of Toronto, Canada. She is especially interested in questions about children's capacities and responsibilities.

Robert Noggle is Professor of Philosophy at Central Michigan University, USA. His research interests include moral issues relating to children, personal autonomy, the limits of moral obligation, philosophical psychopathology and the ethics of manipulation and influence.

Serena Olsaretti is an ICREA Research Professor at the Department of Law, Universitat Pompeu Fabra, Spain. She has published work on liberty, desert, well-being, equality, responsibility and is recently focusing on questions concerning justice and the family.

Christine Overall is Professor Emerita of Philosophy at Queen's University, Kingston, Canada. Her most recent books are *Why Have Children? The Ethical Debate* (MIT Press, 2012) and *Pets and People: The Ethics of Our Relationships with Companion Animals* (Oxford University Press, 2017).

Gina Schouten is Assistant Professor of Philosophy at Harvard University, USA. Her research interests include gender justice, educational justice and political legitimacy, including especially questions about whether political liberalism can constitute an adequate theory of legitimacy.

Jonathan Seglow is Reader (Associate Professor) in Political Theory at Royal Holloway, University of London, UK. He is the author of *Defending Associative Duties* (Routledge, 2014) and is currently working on issues of free speech, religious accommodation and the relationship between self-respect and social justice.

Anthony Skelton is Associate Professor in the Department of Philosophy at the University of Western Ontario, Canada. He researches in ethics and the history of ethics. His work has appeared in the journals *Ethics*, *Journal of the History of Philosophy* and *Utilitas*.

List of contributors

Julie Tannenbaum, Associate Professor at Pomona College, USA, received her doctorate in philosophy from the University of California, Los Angeles and did postdoctoral work at the Department of Bioethics at the National Institutes of Health. She publishes in bioethics, ethical theory and metaethics.

Patrick Tomlin is an Associate Professor in Political Philosophy at the University of Reading, UK. He works on a variety of issues in political, legal and moral philosophy, including moral uncertainty, just war theory, crime and punishment, children and aggregation.

Daniel Weinstock holds the James McGill Chair in the Faculty of Law at McGill University. He has published extensively in moral, legal and political philosophy, particularly on issues to do with the management of ethno-cultural and religious diversity in liberal democracies, and on the issues that arise within such societies in the relations between parents and children.

INTRODUCTION

Anca Gheaus

A burgeoning field

Children and childhood have, until recently, been largely neglected as philosophical topics. In a way, this is puzzling: we all start life as children and childhood spreads over a very significant proportion of the typical human life. It is during childhood that we change most, and acquire the physical and mental characteristics that individuate us. Moreover, many people tend to think that having a good childhood is very important for leading a successful life.

The scarcity of philosophical reflection on children and childhood can perhaps be explained through the belief that childhood is a state of being inferior to adulthood (Brennan 2014). Philosophers have always worked with a model of the human being that is adult and, at times, have explicitly defended this choice (Slote 1983). Their remarks about children have most often assumed that the latter are merely in-progress, unfinished, versions of the former. Further, philosophers have traditionally assumed that children's moral status is clearly inferior to that of adults: it is not only that children's lack of full autonomy disqualifies them from the same level of moral responsibility that we attribute to adults, and, therefore, denies them the same level of authority concerning their choices. These are fairly uncontroversial beliefs, especially with respect to infants and young children. But children have also been seen as individuals whose moral status cannot prevent adults – usually parents – from using them in order to further their own interests. Legal regimes have often sanctioned this view, with the most extreme illustrations being parents' right to expose or sell their children. Such legal rights are, thankfully, old history, but many social and legal arrangements, including parental powers, continue to allow us to use children as means to promoting adults' projects and goals. Thus, some philosophers claim that the legacy of the children-as-property view is still with us (Brennan and Noggle 1997; Archard and Macleod 2002; Brighouse and Swift 2014). This traditional representation of children and childhood also justifies a host of existing limitations on children's moral, social and legal entitlements, freedoms and powers, and liability.

But the traditional representation of children and childhood has been rapidly changing, first in law – where the principle of the child's best interests is now frequently used as a guideline – and, more recently, in philosophy. In moral and political philosophy, the literature on childrearing, and especially on the parent–child relationship, has been multiplying at an exponential rate during the past four decades, starting with an influential collection by Onora O'Neill and

William Ruddick (1979) and Jefferey Blustein's 1982 monograph, and continuing with the groundbreaking work of David Archard (1993). These days, numerous articles, collections and monographs on childrearing are being published on a regular basis. The question of children's moral status – of their fundamental rights and duties – is, implicitly, at the core of these investigations: today the prevalent belief is that children have full moral status – that is, that their interests have the same weight as the interest of adults. At the same time, in the philosophy of education, several authors have noted that before puberty children are more capable to ask deep, competent philosophical questions than adults who are not professional philosophers (Matthews 1980). On average, children's interest in philosophy – and in epistemic pursuits more generally – is less clouded by conventionalism and less dampened by the responsibilities of life than adults'. These, as well as other goods to which children seem to have better, maybe even unique, access, have been recently called "the special goods of childhood" and have been drawing increasing attention (Macleod 2010; Brennan 2014; Brighouse and Swift 2014). If these goods are indeed very weighty, then childhood is not entirely a predicament, but also a privilege insofar as it is a state of life when we display higher abilities to experiment, learn, enjoy and relate to others in trustful and spontaneous ways (Gheaus 2015; Alexandrova 2017). In this case, children are more than deficient adults.

Some philosophers reject the above, neo-romantic, representation of children (Hannan 2018). Whatever the truth about the value of childhood, it is uncontroversial that children are uniquely vulnerable to the actions – and inactions – of adults. Moreover, it is now generally accepted that children are recipients of duties of justice, although there is much debate with respect to the exact content of children's rights and the identification of duty-bearers.

Bringing children to the forefront of philosophical investigation is, therefore, a natural development. Some of this interest has been centred around the question, "what is a child?", where "child" is to be understood in terms of biological facts – as an individual who is at a stage of development in human life where they have not yet reached biological maturity. What are the unique characteristics of children, and what, if any, special abilities do they have? Answers to these questions bear directly on the issue of what the value of childhood is. In turn, axiological issues bear on the more practical ones concerning how we – as individuals and as society – ought to treat children. Finally, there is the fascinating matter of how thinking about children may challenge theories designed with the model of the adult in mind. If we give systematic philosophical attention to children and childhood, will this lead us to revise some of our views concerning values, morality, political institutions and even knowledge?

This handbook is a result of the growing interest in philosophical analyses of children and childhood. It introduces readers to various debates about the nature of childhood, children's moral status and its direct implications, duties owed to children by various agents and the ways in which society ought to treat children. Our aim is not merely to present the state of the art, but also to draw attention to the many issues that are still under-explored and, therefore, to encourage future research. Most of the handbook discusses children in general, although children of different ages are, obviously, very different in their abilities and level of autonomy; these differences have normative and practical significance. Some chapters address these differences, and one of them focuses exclusively on adolescents. Across the handbook, our aim has been to stay true to the diversity of childhood phases.

The philosophy of children and childhood spans across several sub-fields such as axiology, ethics, political philosophy, aesthetics, epistemology and feminist philosophy. It also bears on research in other fields, such as psychology, neuropsychology and neurolinguistics, anthropology, sociology, social policy, medicine and law. Readers from these disciplines are likely to find some of the chapters directly relevant.

The structure and content of the handbook

The handbook has a thematic structure. A number of chapters cover some ground in the history of philosophy, but many do not. All chapters offer an overview of the current debates. Most authors position themselves within these debates; some spend a fair amount of time defending their views, but a minority of chapters take a more encyclopaedic approach, and do not argue for a particular thesis.

Part I: Being a child

The first section of the handbook is about foundational matters concerning the nature of childhood. It opens with a chapter by Fabrice Clément and Melissa Koenig, drawing on developmental psychology in order to discuss knowledge in childhood. Thinking about children as knowers poses the following problem: we usually attribute some knowledge to very young children. According to the classical theory, knowledge is a species of true belief. We cannot, however, attribute proper beliefs to very young children. Clément and Koenig's solution is to defend a metacognitive understanding of knowledge.

The second chapter, by Mark Cain, addresses children's acquisition of their first language. The chapter is an overview of the long-standing debate on whether or not this process is explained by the existence of a substantial innate basis that is specific to language. Cain argues that it is.

In chapter 3, Suparna Choudhury and Nancy Ferranti critically introduce findings from the science of adolescent brains. The "teen brain" has been enjoying much attention from academics, the media and the educated public, because understanding its peculiarities is key to the well-being of adolescents and those around them. Yet, the authors argue that we ought to interpret the scientific findings by situating them in the social and cultural context that produced them, which sometimes casts doubt on their objectivity and universality. All of the first three chapters rely substantially on literature from neighbouring sciences that study children's brains and children's cognitive processes.

By contrast, the fourth chapter, written by Jonathan Feinberg, focuses on children's artistic abilities. It provides an analysis – much informed by historical knowledge – of the questions of what child art is and what its value is. Following some artists and art theorists, Feinberg believes that children can make real art; as artists, children don't merely emulate what adults do.

The last chapter of the first section is about doing philosophy with children. This is a large and expanding field, and, like many of its founders, and against some critics, Jana Mohr Lone argues that children can engage in genuinely philosophical inquiries. Children's sense of wonder and epistemic openness makes them natural philosophers and adults' tendency to discount their voices can represent a form of epistemic injustice; this, she thinks, is our as well as their loss.

Part II: Childhood and moral status

In the opening chapter of part 2, Agnieszka Jaworksa and Julie Tannenbaum explain the difficulty of accounting for the belief that children have full moral status without thereby concluding that there is no difference in moral status between human children and numerous animals. Their own theory of moral status gets around this difficulty by claiming that individuals have full moral status in virtue of incompletely realizing a cognitively sophisticated activity.

The next chapter, by Patrick Tomlin, analyses the value of childhood, proceeding through a number of distinctions between ways in which childhood can be valuable – intrinsically, and instrumentally – compared with non-existence or compared to adulthood, for the child herself or for others, etc. This is largely unexplored territory. One part of the chapter is on the question of whether childhood is valuable for the individual who is experiencing this stage of life and whether it would be rational for her to skip it or speed it up, if possible; some of this discussion also introduces the recent literature on the goods and bads of childhood. A closely related chapter is written by Anthony Skelton on the topic of childhood and well-being. It discusses in depth one of the questions identified by Tomlin, namely the nature of children's well-being: How should we account for how well a child's life is going from the point of view of the child living it? Skelton proposes that the nature of a child's well-being changes over the course of childhood and, therefore, theories of well-being must be differential and developmental.

Robert Noggle's chapter introduces the topic of children's rights. Noggle proceeds by explaining the advantages of thinking about obligations toward children in terms of rights and then examines the ways in which the two main theories of rights – the will theory and the interests theory – apply to children. This chapter also discusses some of the specific rights attributed to children and the contribution that the child liberationist movement made to thinking about children's rights.

In her chapter about children's autonomy, Sarah Hannan explains how the most influential accounts of autonomy entail that children can display it to a smaller or larger extent. She argues that autonomy develops in domain-specific degrees; Hannan, like other authors in the handbook, concludes that the current level of interference with children's choices is not always justified. In a similar vein, the chapter by Kalle Grill shows why it is wrong to assume that paternalism towards children is always and obviously justified. By contrast, Grill believes that instances of benevolent interference with children are in need of justification; most likely, paternalistic behaviour towards children can be justified to the extent to which children are less prudent than adults and less harmed when subjected to paternalism.

The final chapter in the section about children's moral status, by David Archard, is about consent. We think that children lack the power to render permissible what is otherwise impermissible by the communication of words or actions – that is, by giving consent. Archard defends a duty on the part of adults to give children a voice – if not necessarily final say – on matters that concern them, in proportion to the child's level of developed autonomy. He also examines particular cases to which children's limited ability to give consent is particularly relevant – including political legitimation, sexual relationships, medical treatment and research involving children, and the conditions necessary for securing children's open future. To the extent to which children lack the power of giving consent, adults' choices ought to be guided by children's interests.

Part III: Parents and children

This section, one of the largest in the handbook, is dedicated in its entirety to parenting; this is where most of the action in the philosophy of childhood has taken place. Christine Overall's chapter on reasons to have children (or not) investigates objectively good reasons for procreating and rearing. Overall takes seriously the main anti-natalist argument, which points to the inevitable suffering involved in any human life, and criticizes as unsound the most frequently invoked reasons to have children. Yet, she thinks that the goods of the parent–child relationships are capable of justifying the decision to bear and rear children.

My own chapter is an analysis of the different questions that are at stake in discussions about the right to parent: Should there be parents at all rather than institutional childrearing of some kind? What are the grounds for holding a right to parent in general? And what are the grounds for acquiring the right to parent a particular child? I explain how these questions are answered by theories that appeal to the child's interest, by those that appeal to the prospective parent's interest and by hybrid theories that appeal to both. It is generally believed that one of the duties we have towards children is to ensure they have good parents.

Colin Macleod writes about several aspects of good parenting. He argues that genetic ties and sexual orientation do not make a difference to the quality of parenting. Further, Macleod engages with the recently much-discussed issue of whether parents have a duty to love their children, with the parents' duty to promote their children's autonomy, with the limits of legitimate parental paternalism and with the question of whether good parents must strive for perfection. Next, Jonathan Seglow looks at one particular feature of good parenting, namely partiality. There is a long-recognized conflict between ethical theory – which usually requires impartiality – and our tendency to be partial, in particular towards our own children. On the one hand, parental partiality is valuable, and even praiseworthy; on the other hand, given the inequality of resources between different parents, it seems to unavoidably upset fair equality of opportunities. The best answer to the practical problem raised by parental partiality is to curb its expression by putting limits on how many resources parents pass on to their children and, concomitantly, to enact more egalitarian public policies.

Not all parents are their children's procreators; Jurgen De Wispelaere and Daniel Weinstock write about the special issues raised by children in need of adoption, and by the process of adoption itself. First, is the question of whether children have a moral right to be adopted rather than raised in institutions or foster homes, and the correlative duties of prospective parents to prefer adoption over procreation as a means to satisfying their desire to parent. Second, is the question of how to best design policies and regulations that are sensitive to the messy realities of international adoption and of potential parents' preferences for certain kinds of children.

Introducing licenses for parents is another topic that has received much attention from philosophers. The chapter by Andrew Botterell and Carolyn McLeod analyses the suggestion that parents be licensed in the same way in which we license those who engage in high-risk activities. This proposal draws support from the fact that we do, indeed, require adoptive parents to have licenses for the sake of their prospective children's well-being. Alternatively, given the reasons to oppose the licensing of natural parents, we should stop requiring licenses on the part of adoptive parents. Botterell and McLeod assess proposals to introducing parental licensing with an eye on the risks of discrimination against adoptive and fostering families, and prospective parents who are already subject to racism, classism, homophobia and ableism.

Daniela Cutas looks at the importance of family shape for children's well-being. The dominant view has been that rearing children by their heterosexual procreators is best for them, and the debate between the proponents and the critics of this view has often been hidden behind the apparently semantic question of what a family really is. Cutas examines the debate, introduces the readers to the intricate realities of contemporary family formation and presents evidence that children's well-being is primarily influenced by how good the care is that they receive and by the quality of the relationships between the adults who raise them. She also addresses the question of whether the presence of dependent children is necessary for something to count as a family.

In her chapter on parenting and gender, Amy Mullin discusses parental responses to children whose identities and preferences deviate from gender norms and who face particular difficulties in allowing their children to flourish in societies that are hostile towards their deviance. The second focus of the chapter is on parents' gendered behaviour and on their beliefs and implicit associations about gender roles. Parental endorsement of traditional gender norms tends to perpetuate unfairness towards women. This happens partly by directly reinforcing a gendered division of labour – for instance, when girls alone are trained to perform unpaid domestic work – and partly by encouraging gendered aspirations in children and, in girls, higher levels of responsibility for those in need of care.

The section ends with a chapter about filial duties, written by Diane Jeske. Most people share a strong intuition that grown-up children owe special duties to their parents; yet, philosophers have found it difficult to account for this. Jeske presents – and vividly illustrates – some of the most prominent and plausible accounts of filial duties, based on gratitude, friendship and the existence of special goods within parent–child relationships. She also provides an account of what theory of filial duty should be able to do in order to be adequate.

Part IV: Children in society

This part of the handbook concerns the ways in which children are being influenced and shaped by society more generally. Race is one shaping factor, analysed in Albert Atkin's chapter. All children learn their society's norms governing race and some are racialized as minorities. Atkin explores the ways in which children acquire these beliefs and deal with racial identity and race-based prejudice – and pays close attention to the issues raised by racial inequalities in schooling and by transracial adoption.

Disability is another factor that impacts the life of some children to a very significant degree. Gideon Calder and Amy Mullin's chapter discusses the nature of disability – including the debate between competing ways of understanding disability – and the main normative issues raised by children's disability. One of the particular subjects they discuss is how to understand parental love and care – one of the most important goods in any child's life – in the context of raising disabled children. Other important questions addressed in the chapter concern the moral status of children with cognitive disabilities; the normative aspects of the relationship between disabled parents and the children they raise; and what we owe to disabled children by way of education.

Yet another way in which children are shaped by their social environment comes from the beliefs about children's sexuality, which is the topic of Samantha Brennan and Jennifer Epp's chapter. Like most topics covered in Part 4, this is an area so far neglected by philosophers. Brennan and Epp note that children's sexuality is usually discussed in the context of their undeveloped autonomy, special vulnerability and need for protection. But children are also developing sexual agents, and the interest in their sexuality should go beyond the negative aim of protecting them from damaging predators. The authors make the case that we need more research into the nature of childhood sexuality. An important question in this respect concerns the relationship between children's sexuality and their innocence – one of the so-called goods of childhood. Other important questions concern children's budding autonomy as sexual agents and their ability to give consent in a number of respects.

Sue Donaldson and Will Kymlicka contribute a chapter on children and animals. Individuals from both groups have been traditionally represented as innocent and particularly vulnerable, features that both entitle them to care and exclude them from the rights of citizenship. However, recent developments in the philosophy of children – and, in particular, amongst advocates of children's citizenship – stress that we should give proper weight to children's capabilities, their developing moral responsibility and compassion. Children, too, contribute to society and, therefore, are entitled to some degree of agency as well as protection. Donaldson and Kymlicka note that this view of children's agency puts pressure on rethinking the political status of animals; in particular, they believe that interspecies sociability is unduly suppressed by our current legal and political order and argue that empowering children and animals would create a better world.

Philip Cook's chapter invites us to think about children's labour and, in doing this, to appreciate the various possible conflicts between attending to children's current and future well-being and between allowing them full exercise of their present agency versus nourishing their future opportunities for autonomy and well-being. Such conflicts are particularly stark in non-ideal circumstances of injustice or serious scarcity. We are used to thinking that child labour is an instance of, or at least in the vicinity of, violations of children's rights. Yet, older children are able to work in paying jobs and some children's labour is essential to their and their families' survival; in certain circumstances, allowing children to work, and directing efforts at improving the conditions in which they do so, is the best practical decision. Cook explores the limitations of objections to child labour, which appeal to harm, to failing to benefit children and to exploitation. He concludes that one of the best ways to contain the exploitation of children is to empower them *qua* workers.

The last chapter, written by Mianna Lotz, deals with children's special vulnerability. Lotz explains the unique ways in which children are vulnerable; this vulnerability puts them at special risk, but it also makes possible the enjoyment of some of the special goods of childhood. She argues that protectionist duties do not exhaust the scope of parents' and other adults' vulnerability-related obligations towards children in their care; some of these duties are facilitative and ameliorative.

Part V: Children and the state

The final part of the handbook covers the large question of how we ought to discharge our collective duties towards children through state institutions and policies. Its opening chapter, authored by Lars Lindblom, raises the general question of how to think about the metric of justice towards children: What is it that we owe them? Since they cannot be expected to take full moral responsibility for their choices, it appears that we owe children more than we owe adults: not only opportunities, but also security in the enjoyment of certain goods. In addition, if certain goods significantly contribute to how well children's – but not adults' – lives are going, it is likely that they feature as part of the metric of justice towards children; this, however, poses a challenge to the view that states should remain neutral with respect to their (reasonable) citizens' conceptions of the good life.

Political neutrality is the topic of the subsequent chapter, by Matthew Clayton. He argues that children have a right against being directed towards particular ethical or religious conceptions, irrespective of whether those who are in charge with children's education are their parents or state-employed teachers. This argument relies on the ideal of political neutrality, which, according to Clayton, applies to children as well as to adults, in virtue of children's development into autonomous individuals. The fully autonomous individuals they will one day become could refuse retrospective consent to having been enrolled into particular ethical or religious views.

The next question, addressed by Serena Olsaretti, is whether the costs of having and rearing children should be borne by parents alone or should be socially shared. One strand in luck egalitarianism has advanced the first answer, by pointing to two facts: that procreators avoidably bring into existence new individuals; and that parents usually see their child-rearing activities as a way of pursuing their own conception of the good life rather than a way of benefitting others. Yet, this position has been contested from different corners and Olsaretti shows how implausible it is when we push it to its logical conclusion. She also shows that any answer to the question of who should pay the costs of having and rearing children bears directly on one's theory of distributive justice.

Not all children have sufficiently good parents. Gideon Calder's chapter addresses the question of how we ought to take collective responsibility for the care of children whose parents prove to be inadequate. Even when the parent–child relationship has gone significantly wrong, its interruption is risky; yet, it is also risky to leave children in the care of abusive or neglectful parents. Calder explores the questions of how to determine when the state should intervene in the relationship between children and inadequate parents, what makes such interventions legitimate and how to balance, in this process, the interests of all those concerned: children, their parents and the wider society. Moreover, children who are raised in institutions tend to be at significant disadvantage compared to children who are raised by adequate parents. The way in which we should settle these questions depends on the weight we give to children's interests and to the ideal of moral equality in childrearing.

Two of the duties owed to children that we generally believe should be discharged *via* state institutions concern children's education and their access to healthcare. The chapter by Gina Schouten focuses on the first. Schouten distinguishes between education and schooling, arguing that the latter is pervasively coercive and seeks to determine what, if anything, could justify the coercion involved in schooling. Such justification, she thinks, must point to the goods provided by schooling and explains how these can make schooling legitimate to children, parents and taxpayers. Healthcare – the subject of the second duty that states owe to children – is discussed in the chapter by Havi Carel, Gene Feder and Gita Gyorffy. They adopt a phenomenological approach, trying to uncover what is specific to children's experience of being subjects of medical care. The most salient experiences of children in this context, they argue, have to do with their particular way of being embodied – experiencing constant and relatively rapid change, with change generated by their development rather than by illness or disfunction alone, as in the case of old people; by their limited agency, given that adults tend to make most decisions on their behalf; and by being part of families on whom they necessarily depend for the satisfaction of most of their interests. All these particularities raise specific ethical challenges; like many other authors in this handbook, Carel, Feder and Gyorffy support the conclusion that children should be given more power to participate in decision-making on issues that are of direct concern to them – in this case, medical procedures and treatments.

Traditionally, children have been disenfranchised (although the voting age varies across jurisdictions.) This is justified by appeal to several reasons to exclude children from having political rights, many of which have been recently contested. In his chapter about children's right to vote, Ludvig Beckman investigates several grounds for disenfranchising older children – grounds which have to do with children's well-being, with improving the results of the democratic process and with the claim that excluding children is, in itself, undemocratic.

Christopher Bennett looks at some of the distinctive issues posed by thinking about children in the context of criminal justice. Children grow up in environments shaped by particular criminal systems; often, these systems perpetuate forms of economic and racial injustice. Children are sometimes – albeit rarely – the direct targets of criminal justice; but even when they aren't, their lives are impacted by the criminalization of their parents and other significant adults. Of special interest, for Bennett, is the way in which the philosophy of childhood shapes the philosophy of criminal justice, by providing particular answers to questions about children's abilities, the proper length of childhood and the special goods that make childhoods go well.

Our final chapter is on children and war, written by Cecile Fabre. Children are frequent victims of war, but sometimes they are also its agents: they are often being enrolled as soldiers and, sometimes, perpetuate war crimes. Fabre argues that the victimization of children in the context of war, whether intentional or not, is a more serious wrong than the victimization of adults; further, she defends the standard prohibition against enlisting children as combatants, but also the permissibility to kill, in self- or other-defence, children who have been enlisted and who have engaged in wrongful killings. Fabre stresses that, unlike adults, children are always wronged by war – even when they end up as combatants on the side who inflicts an unjust war.

Together, the thirty-six chapters collected in this handbook provide a general overview of the contemporary field of the philosophy of childhood and children. Of course, there have been difficult editorial choices to be made. Further topics might have been included: childhood is relevant to almost any aspect of any branch of philosophy, and while the handbook covers the key terrain, we have not pursued every possible such direction of analysis. Meanwhile, we have made a conscious decision to include chapters on issues which are important, but which have been paid relatively little philosophical attention – such as child labour, children and race, and children and war. Our aim is to draw attention and interest to these under-explored areas. Doubtless there are other such areas that will become more prominent in time, in a rich and fast-developing field. Overall, we expect that the philosophy of childhood – already thriving, as we see from this volume – will continue to grow and deepen.

References

Alexandrova, A. 2017. *A Philosophy for the Science of Well-Being*. Oxford: Oxford University Press.
Archard, D. 1993. *Children: Rights and Childhood*. New York, NY: Routledge.
Archard, D., and Macleod, C. (eds.). 2002. *The Moral and Political Status of Children: New Essays*. Oxford: Oxford University Press.
Brennan, S. 2014. "The Goods of Childhood, Children's Rights, and the Role of Parents as Advocates and Interpreters," in F. Baylis and C. McLeod (eds.), *Family-making: Contemporary Ethical Challenges*. Oxford: Oxford University Press.
Brennan, S., and Noggle, R. 1997. "The Moral Status of Children: Children's Rights, Parents' Rights, and Family Justice," *Social Theory and Practice* 23(1): 1–26.
Brighouse, H., and Swift, A. 2014. *Family Values: The Ethics of Parent-Child Relationships*. Princeton, NJ and Oxford: Princeton University Press.
Blustein, J. 1982. *Parents and Children: The Ethics of the Family*. Oxford: Oxford University Press.
Gheaus, A. 2015. "Unfinished Adults and Defective Children: On the Nature and Value of Childhood," *Journal of Ethics and Social Philosophy* 9(1): 1–21.
Hannan, S. 2018. "Why Childhood is Bad for Children," *Journal of Applied Philosophy* 35(S1): 11–28.
Macleod, C. 2010. "Primary Goods, Capabilities, and Children," in I. Robeyns and H. Brighouse (eds.), *Measuring Justice. Primary Goods and Capabilities*. Cambridge: Cambridge University Press.
Matthews, G. 1980. *Philosophy and the Young Child*. Cambridge, MA and London: Harvard University Press.
O'Neill, O., and Ruddick, W. (eds.). 1979. *Having Children: Philosophical and Legal Reflections on Parenthood*. New York, NY: Oxford University Press.
Slote, M. 1983. *Goods and Virtues*. Oxford: Clarendon Press.

PART I

Being a child

1
EPISTEMOLOGY

Knowledge in childhood

Fabrice Clément and Melissa Koenig

Introduction

The word *infant* comes from the Latin *in-* (not) and *fant-* (speaking); the noun *infans* referred to a child who had not yet learned to talk. Therefore, almost by definition, young children have long been conceived as devoid of knowledge. This conception is not limited to Western civilization. The Vezo of Madagascar, for instance, consider that it is not worth explaining anything to children before they are about seven (Astuti 1995) – an age also considered as the age of reason by the Roman Cicero. From this perspective, children can only move from an absence of knowledge to its progressive acquisition through learning. Rousseau, for instance, thought that we are born "capable of learning, knowing nothing, perceiving nothing" (Rousseau, *L'Emile*, quoted in Kessen 1965: 76–77). It is now generally accepted that children learn from a very early age, but the famous phrase from James that the mental life of babies is "a blooming buzzing confusion" (James 1981: 462) would not surprise many contemporary Westerners.

Here we examine various notions of knowledge as they have been studied in young children by developmental science, and as young children apply them to others. In the first section, we review scientific conceptions of child knowledge, from Piaget's account to current theoretical approaches. In the second section, we discuss normative notions of knowledge and belief from contemporary epistemology and their implications for understanding children's knowledge. In the third section, we discuss children's own concepts of knowledge as expressed in their learning decisions, and we conclude with thoughts on how descriptive and normative projects might inform one another.

Notions of knowledge in child development

Faithful to the long tradition described above, Piaget's ambition was to understand how the child constructs knowledge from very meagre beginnings. On the long road to reason and knowledge, Piaget grants the baby only minimal initial equipment: some reflexes (like the sucking reflex) and her first actions on the environment. These first interactions with the world give rise to *schemes*, i.e. proto-conceptual frameworks which, once developed, assimilate new patterns of stimulation with configurational resemblances. When assimilation is impossible, the scheme will *accommodate* the novel situation and change (Piaget 1952). The famous case of "object permanence" illustrates this constructivist process. Piaget discovered that six-month-old babies interrupted an ongoing search as soon as an object was occluded (Piaget 1954). At around eight to nine months, babies revealed a rather puzzling pattern of search activity: the "A, not-B" error. They often searched at the location where they have previously found a hidden object (location A), even when they intently watched as it was hidden at a second location (location B). Piaget interpreted this error as evidence that infants viewed the object as an extension of their own action, the schema of the object and the schema of the action being not completely separated from one another. For Piaget, it was not before 12 to 18 months that children constructed a stable representation of an object as being "detached" from their own activities. Once this representational insight of the permanent object is achieved, the child can persist in searching under any number of screens, showing that she constantly maintains an image of the invisible object in mind throughout the searching period.

This vision of babies as empirical constructivists, who start with little but slowly build more and more abstract knowledge "by a process of elaboration essentially based on the activity of the child" (Inhelder 1962: 20), has been placed in a constant state of revision by a large number of studies indicating that babies may possess, from a very early age, basic or core concepts that support their expectations about how things work (Carey 2009; Spelke 1994; for a contemporary review, see Barner and Baron 2016). This type of research was made possible by the use of a specific methodology to study infants: habituation. It is known that organisms gradually cease to respond to a stimulus after repeated presentations. Thanks to this basic attentional mechanism, it is possible to study how young babies "make sense" of different aspects of their environment. Infants' *surprise* in response to a modified stimulus introduced after a period of habituation can be interpreted as a sign that babies expected something different to happen, or detected novelty in the test stimulus relative to what was presented during the habituation phase. This is how Renée Baillargeon and Elizabeth Spelke discovered infants' expectations about objects in a series of experiments. In one of their initial studies, they first familiarized infants with a screen whose top rotated toward and away from them a full 180°. They then laid the screen flat toward the infant and placed an object (a box) behind the pivot line of the screen. In the "possible" condition, the top rotated away from the infant, hiding first the box and then reaching the position where it reached the box and stopped. In the "impossible" condition, the screen continued to rotate a full 180°, invading the space that was occupied by the box. The results showed that 3.5-month-old infants looked longer when presented with the impossible event, indicating by the reaction that they were surprised by what was presented to them. In other words, infants expected the screen to stop when it reached the invisible box, demonstrating an implicit understanding of some of the physical properties of the object (Baillargeon, Spelke, and Wasserman 1985).

Since then, a wave of experimental research has demonstrated infants' precocious understanding of physical entities and their properties (for a synthesis, see Baillargeon 2004; Baillargeon et al. 2011). In parallel, comparable research challenging Piaget's account has revealed infants' basic expectations about other domains of their environment. For instance, young children understand many entities in terms of their essence: they conceive of many categories (i.e., "lion", "rabbit", "boy", "girl") as having an underlying reality that defines the properties of its members (Gelman 2003). Children have also demonstrated basic expectations about sets of small numbers (Wynn 1992), moral behaviors (Turiel 1983; Hamlin, Wynn, and Bloom 2007) or social relationship and membership (Kaufmann and Clément 2014; Kinzler, Dupoux, and Spelke 2007; Thomsen, Frankenhuis, Ingold-Smith, and Carey 2011). However, the most prolific area for the study of early cognitive competences have been in "naïve psychology", i.e. the ability to attribute mental states to others in order to compute their likely behaviors in terms of beliefs and desires (Baron-Cohen, Leslie, and Frith 1985; Wellman 1990, 2014). For a long time, it has been thought that the ability to represent others' mental states developed relatively late, i.e. at around four or five years of age (Wimmer and Perner 1983; Perner 1991). However, recent – and still discussed – studies indicate that an implicit understanding of others' epistemic states exists at a much earlier age (Onishi and Baillargeon 2005).

This burgeoning field of research on children's so-called "naïve theories" are closely linked with the development of evolutionary psychology. Darwin himself, notably in *The Expressions of the Emotions in Man and Animals*, suggested that many mental abilities emerge through a process of natural selection. This idea recently gave rise to a model insisting on the fact that we inherited not only physiological organs but also psychological "modules" that constituted advantages in our species' evolutionary past (Tooby and Cosmides 1990). From an evolutionary perspective, it is not surprising to discover that babies are endowed with certain basic conceptual knowledge. In developmental psychology, Elizabeth Spelke and Susan Carey refer to infants' early conceptual competences as *core knowledge* (Carey 2009; Spelke and Kinzler 2007). These early emerging knowledge systems are seen as "mechanisms for representing and reasoning about particular kinds of ecologically important entities and events" (Spelke 2000: 1233). These specific systems filter and detect the relevant entities and, due to the set of domain-specific principles that govern these entities, they support inferences about how such entities behave.

It is possible to position most contemporary researchers on a scale that goes from strict empiricism (all knowledge is dependent upon sense experience) to strong nativism (sense experience is structured by innate constraints). The core knowledge hypothesis, by specifying our conceptual primitives, would definitely fall on the nativist side. On the other hand, interesting developmental proposals insist on specifying the constructivist processes of cognitive development. For various neuroconstructivists, for instance, the human neocortex is characterized by its flexibility. Therefore, it has to be conceived as a changing organ with dynamic, back-propagating interactions between different levels – genes, brain, cognition, behavior and environment (Karmiloff-Smith 2009). This position is not incompatible with the existence of some genetic constraints, responsible for the general structures of the brain; nor with some conceptual constraints, responsible for basic constraints on human knowledge. But if neuroconstructivism is compatible with nativism, it is only in a weak sense because the focus is on epigenesis, i.e. on the developing interactions between genes and the environment. For the neuroconstructivists, genetic mechanisms are only responsible for a general starting point: processing certain kinds of information with increasing proficiency leads to a gradual specialization of parts of the brain, that become domain *specific* by progressive modualization. In other words, the dynamic development of our brain plays a role in the way information is channeled and processed, such that those parts of the brain that become specialized for processing language, or human behavior, for example, emerge relatively late in development (Karmiloff-Smith 1998; see also ch. 2, ch. 3).

Another contemporary position, strongly influenced by empiricism, attempts to understand the rapid and effortless learning competencies of children by investigating their ability to build and elaborate their *causal* knowledge. In this perspective, what is essential for the child is to generate from sensory inputs causal "maps of how the world works" (Gopnik 2009: 21). To this end, babies are endowed with a specific system, largely innate, that helps them detect the causal structures of the world so that they can then generate new expectations or hypotheses and anticipate what will happen next. These causal learning systems enable children to infer causal relations from patterns of correlation, a procedure that can be modeled as Bayesian networks (Gopnik et al. 2004). This perspective can be considered a midway between empiricism and nativism, with babies functioning like little scientists by formulating testable hypotheses or questions, conducting experiments, analyzing statistics and forming theories to account for their observations. In the long run, this will lead to the creation of different theories, according to the specific causal structure of a given domain (naïve physics, psychology, etc.) that will be unveiled by children.

Of course, the exact ways in which children develop knowledge during their early development is still a matter of considerable debate. Globally, almost everyone agrees that strict empiricism is difficult to sustain, and that some representational vocabulary is necessary to account for conceptual developments observed in infancy. However, the nature of these biologically inherited structures and the way they interact with the environment and the developing mind to support knowledge acquisition still characterizes a primary set of research questions in cognitive development since Piaget.

What is the nature of children's knowledge?

In the study of knowledge development, it is implicitly admitted that something like "knowledge" is present in some form as children grow up, and that their knowledge changes over time. However, it is not easy to specify the nature of infants' epistemic states or concepts, nor the nature of the changes that occur (Carey 2009; Margolis and Laurence 1999). Furthermore, these challenges are compounded by the tendency of Western philosophy to see knowledge as requiring an analysis in terms of necessary and sufficient conditions, conditions that determine which of our true beliefs count as knowledge. In this tradition, knowledge is considered a species of *belief* that, through appropriate evidence and/or reflection, becomes well *justified* and, in effect, *true*. This traditional conception, however, does not fit well with certain empirical challenges faced by developmental psychologists. On the one hand, knowledge is often attributed by developmental psychologists after acknowledging the mastery of certain systematic *competencies*. For instance, to assess that babies possess knowledge about the nature of physical objects, experimentalists measure the surprise they express when looking at a physical impossible event; it is common to say that they were surprised because they *believed* that the course of events would be different. However, from the infants' cognitive processes perspective, speaking of belief *stricto sensu* for these anticipations could well be an exaggeration. As Wittgenstein put it, a belief expresses a relation between a person and a proposition; on the contrary, knowing something is more "direct" and expresses a relation between the person and a fact (Wittgenstein 1968: §90). And the "mental distance" between a proposition and its content that is typical of a belief is something that is hard to attribute to young children (Perner 1991).

During the first four years of their life, children are well known for their ineptitude in disentangling reality from its representation. This difficulty exists for assessing their own beliefs as well as others' beliefs. For instance, three-year-olds were put in a situation where they discovered that a candy "Smarties" box actually contained small pencils; when asked about what they had thought was inside the box before opening it, most children answered "pencils". Only five-year-olds were able to recognize that they had changed their representation and that they initially entertained a "false belief" (Gopnik and Astington 1988). Many other tasks designed to exhibit the understanding that a belief can be false (for oneself or for others) have shown similar results (Wellman Cross, and Watson 2001). Given children's difficulty in disentangling mental representation from reality, it makes little sense to describe cognitive development as a progressive shift from beliefs to knowledge. On the contrary, children's developmental trajectory suggests the other way around: children shift from what can be seen, from a first-person perspective, as tacit *knowledge*, to a more distanced psychological attitude that corresponds to what *beliefs* are about.

Indeed, data suggest that children are much more comfortable with the concept of *knowledge* than with the concept of belief. For instance, while mental state utterances, including verbs like "think" or "believe", tend to appear only during the third year of life (Shatz, Wellman, and Silber

1983), utterances with the verb "to know" already appear during the second year of life (Harris, Yang, and Cui 2017). Moreover, by 16 months, infants reject speakers' statements when such statements contradict what they already know (Koenig and Echols 2003; Pea 1982). Finally, in their second year, infants understand that someone who can *see* where an object is *knows* where it is, compared to a situation where the object is occluded for that person (Moll and Tomasello 2007; Scott and Baillargeon 2013). Interestingly, this link between perceptual access and knowledge seems to be also understood by chimpanzees (Bräuer, Call, and Tomasello 2007; Povinelli, Nelson, and Boysen 1990). In summary, it seems that the distinction between knowledge and ignorance is much easier to understand that the notion of false belief (Call and Tomasello 2008). Young children are aware of the difference between having and not having *access* to information. This access can be acknowledged in another person by observing that there is a direct perceptual direct link between her and an object or event. With respect to the self, children are able to assess whether or not they have access to a given piece of information – assessment that children as young as two years of age communicate by utterances like "I know" or "I don't know" (Harris et al. 2018).

The literature in comparative and developmental psychology, therefore, calls into question the classic epistemic route going from ignorance to knowledge via justified beliefs. This position is obviously provocative because it implies that young children would not initially have "beliefs" *stricto sensu*. One could argue, analogously to a famous philosophical argument, that it is not necessary to have the concept of arthritis to suffer from this disorder (Burge 1979). In other words, is it not possible to entertain beliefs without having the concept of belief? This can be seen as a definitional issue but, if we accept that the concept of belief entails the possibility of entertaining a doubt, i.e. a "mental gap" between a psychological attitude (the *belief*) and its object (its intentional *content*), it is not very surprising that only older children can form beliefs *per se* because beliefs are by nature *metarepresentational*. Knowledge seems, therefore, to be a more "primitive" epistemic state that works in a dichotomous fashion (as a "possession" that we have, or do not have), at least when knowing involves a simple relation between individuals and the informational content they have access to.

Interestingly, some contemporary epistemologists resist defining knowledge by way of a conceptual analysis that "reduces" knowledge to justified and true beliefs. Timothy Williamson, in particular, defends the idea that the difference between knowledge and ignorance is central to the way in which we evaluate our epistemic states, and is irreducible to any concept of belief (Williamson 2002). Jennifer Nagel agrees with this view, thinking that attributions of belief are much harder and more complex than attributions of knowledge, which refer to a direct relation with the environment, unmediated by a state of belief. Knowledge refers, therefore, to a more primitive form of epistemological "contact" with reality that is conceived as an automatic correspondence between the person and her environment. Mastering knowledge is easier than belief because "knowledge is a state that essentially involves matching how things are, whereas belief is essentially a state that may or may not match reality" (Nagel 2016: 29). It seems, therefore, reasonable to think that children are rapidly endowed with a sense of what knowledge is, at least in the weak sense of "possessing" an informational content. This sense of knowledge does not have to be reflexive because it refers to a simple information access that is dichotomic: you have it or not and it is not a matter of degree. Moreover, it is important to possess this kind of ability early because it lets the individual know whether or not she can act given the information at her disposal. To avoid any confusion, it could be useful to specify this sort of knowledge, for instance, by calling it, following Russell, "knowledge by acquaintance" (Russell 1959: ch. 5). This sense of knowledge (close to the French *savoir*) cannot be considered as justified true belief, contrary to a more elaborate sense of knowledge that develops with reflexive thought (*connaître*).

Children's learning from others: concepts of knowledge in action

As mentioned above, Piaget's scientific aim was to understand how the child constructs knowledge from scratch. This led Piaget, and the scientific tradition that he instigated, to neglect the vast stores of knowledge children gain from other people. As a result, the child as a lone scientist – forming and testing hypotheses, making discoveries on her own, drawing logical inferences from data – characterizes a long-standing model in cognitive development for how knowledge acquisition begins and proceeds. Recent interest in correcting this standard characterization of the child learner (Callanan 2006; Harris and Koenig 2006; Rogoff 2003) has instigated research on the cognitive, conceptual and cultural mechanisms by which children gain knowledge from others, while protecting against various risks of misinformation (Harris et al. 2018; Sperber et al. 2010) and on the important implications this kind of knowing has for children's cognitive development.

Why is it important to consider children's use of social sources of knowledge? First, the knowledge to be gained purely from first-hand observation is very, very limited. Even the most self-directed learning (e.g., particles seen through a microscope, seeing a Dalmatian dog in the distance) has a hidden layer of testimonial or cultural input that we typically take for granted (e.g., seeing the Dalmatian recruits our capacity to apply a culturally acquired concept) (Harris and Koenig 2006). Second, if knowledge acquisition were reduced to first-hand observations, human development would consist of each generation making the same recapitulated set of discoveries. However, part of what accounts for the accumulation of cultural, scientific and historical knowledge over time is the socially stored knowledge that we provide to our children through our actions and testimony. Finally, if we neglected to study the cultural, linguistic and social practices that lead to knowledge in childhood, we would miss countless opportunities to examine the epistemic, cultural and interpersonal standards that children bring to their interactions with others. As Piaget was right to stress, there is certainly value in learning how to figure things out for oneself, how to experiment and to reason about the evidence. However, there is as much value in learning how to discern whom to trust about which matters – such decisions are just as much a rational skill (Koenig and McMyler 2018).

Given that children acquire a great deal of knowledge from others, it becomes important to examine children's developing concepts of knowledge. Presumably, such concepts, which are linguistically and culturally variable, will be useful in flagging appropriate sources of information for a learner. Indeed, in *Knowledge and the State of Nature*, Edward Craig argues that any investigation into our concepts of knowledge should specify what such concepts do for us – namely, what roles they serve. Craig suggests that one central function served by our concepts of knowledge is the identification of good sources of information (Craig 1991). If this proposal is correct, and one primary function of our knowledge concept is to identify knowledgeable informants, what might such concepts be like? Just as an infant's object concept undergoes developmental change and is used to reason about objects (Baillargeon et al. 2011), an infant's knowledge concepts undergo developmental change and are used to reason about human agents. Questions such as these are partly normative, partly conceptual and partly empirical. Characterizing children's epistemic concepts involves open, empirical hypotheses concerning how children identify knowledgeable, competent or rational others; it also involves conceptual analyses of things like agents, trust and knowledge, as well as normative hypotheses that concern the kinds of reasoning that might be required by our conceptual understanding. Inroads into the empirical questions – for example, what are children's concepts of knowledge like? – began with some of the research on children's social cognition surveyed above (Astington and Gopnik 1991; Wellman 2014) in tasks that present children with agents who have certain positional advantages to information (Onishi and Baillargeon 2005; Kovàcs, Tèglàs, and Endress 2010). As an example, consider two agents: one who has access and one who lacks access to a baited container (Pillow 1989; Pratt and Bryant 1990). When children are asked, "Who knows where the toy is?", they typically credit knowledge to the agent with appropriate access. The very existence of "purely positional advantages" like these (Williams 2002), or any differences in perceptual experience that can exist between two agents, might instigate a need for a primitive concept of knowledge. Without a concept of knowledge, how does anyone make sense of two agents who have different experiences of the same object? Infants' and young children's ability to correctly attribute knowledge based on positional advantages suggests their use of epistemic concepts early in development (e.g., Kovàcs, Tèglàs, and Endress 2010).

How might testimony indicate a speaker's knowledge to child listeners? Intuitively, naïve listeners might bring different epistemic criteria to testimony relative to expert listeners who possess more knowledge about a given topic. Indeed, in one recent project, when shown pictures of an unfamiliar exotic animal (e.g., pangolins), children and adults were asked to estimate a speaker's knowledge based on their singular statements (Koenig, Cole, Meyer, Ridge, Kushnir, and Gelman 2015). Before age 7–8, young children credited knowledge to speakers who verifiably discussed the animal's perceptual characteristics that were depicted in a picture ("Pangolins have little eyes"); and increasingly with age, children and adults credited knowledge to speakers making generic claims regardless of whether the claim matched what was seen in the picture (e.g., "Pangolins have scales") or not (e.g., "Pangolins live in Africa"). Thus, the early epistemic value that young children placed on verifiability shifted gradually to general, less-verifiable claims, and suggests that a listener's knowledge estimates are deeply tied to what she knows about the domain being discussed (see also Keil 2006).

Perhaps whenever we lack domain knowledge and encounter a speaker who discusses this poorly understood domain (e.g., medicine, epigenetics, evolution), we prefer sources whose claims confirm what little we know. And conversely, as we acquire domain knowledge, along with ideas about what it takes to be knowledgeable, we relax our requirements on verifiability, and this changes the epistemic standards we bring to what others say. In other words, when we have very little prior knowledge to apply, we may value those claims that confirm what little we do know, treating them as reassuring indicators of knowledge; and as we become increasingly knowledgeable ourselves, we gain a broader set of epistemic tools for extending our knowledge, and for discerning knowledgeable from less knowledgeable sources in a given domain. One important implication of these findings is that in so far as epistemic criteria are tied to changes in a domain-specific knowledge base, developmental changes in those criteria will not run in a serial developmental sequence but, rather, concurrently and in parallel. This helps clarify how any child or adult, regardless of age, who studies a new subject, learns a new language or lives in a new community with its own rules and conventions will repeatedly find themselves in a new "developmental" phase, using epistemic criteria appropriate to that state of knowledge, to distinguish good from less good informants (Craig 1991; Vygotsky 1962).

Conclusions

The notion of knowledge can be used in more or less restrictive ways. Philosophers are very much concerned with normative issues and one of their objectives is to highlight the different pathways leading to truth. Historically, they have insisted on the conditions, like justification and appropriate access, that enable certain states of mind to "qualify" as knowledge. Psychologists are much more concerned with individual competencies and understanding how children perform a certain task or anticipate a given course of events; each of which signal that children possess a certain form of knowledge.

A distinction, very popular these days, between what is processed implicitly (System 1) and what needs to be explicitly represented by the cognitive system (System 2) could bring these two perspectives on knowledge closer together (Apperly and Butterfill 2009; Stanovich and West 2000). In the case of young children, the genesis of specific expectations most likely relies on implicit cognitive processes, whether domain specific or based on statistical learning. This is not to say that children are not sensitive to the level of certainty that is associated with their epistemic states. But recent studies show that this epistemic evaluation does not have to be conscious or metarepresentational; it can be essentially *procedural*, most likely based on the felt fluency of their cognitive processes (Bernard, Proust, and Clément 2014; Proust 2013). In other words, the ease and speed with which a representation can be accessed is associated with a feeling of fluency that is automatically processed by the subject as a cue indicating the reliability of its content (Koriat 1993; Koriat and Levy-Sadot 1999). With time comes doubt, and the possibility of explicitly meta-representing a content of thought in order to evaluate its fallibility (Sperber 2000). Once this process of inquiry is pursued personally as well as collectively (Moshman 1998), a new kind of knowledge emerges, much closer to what philosophers have in mind when they speak of justified beliefs.

References

Apperly, I. A., and Butterfill, S. A. 2009. "Do Humans have Two Systems to Track Beliefs and Belief-Like States?" *Psychological Review* 116(4): 953.
Astington, J. W., and Gopnik, A. 1991. "Theoretical Explanations of Children's Understanding of the Mind," *British Journal of Developmental Psychology* 9(1): 7–31.
Astuti, R. 1995. *People of the Sea*. Cambridge: Cambridge University Press.
Baillargeon, R. 2004. "Infants' Physical World," *Current Directions in Psychological Science* 13(3): 89–94.
Baillargeon, R., Li, J., Gerner, Y., and Wu, D. 2011. "How do Infants Reason about Physical Events?," in U. Goswami (ed.), *The Wiley-Blackwell Handbook of Childhood Cognitive Development*, 2nd edn. Oxford: Blackwell.
Baillargeon, R., Spelke, E. S., and Wasserman, S. 1985. "Object Permanence in Five-Month-Old Infants," *Cognition* 20: 191–208.
Barner, D., and Baron, A. S. (eds.) 2016. *Core Knowledge and Conceptual Change*. Oxford: Oxford University Press.
Baron-Cohen, S., Leslie, A. M., and Frith, U. 1985. "Does the Autistic Child have a 'Theory of Mind'?" *Cognition* 21: 37–46.
Bernard, S., Proust, J., and Clément, F. 2014. "The Medium Helps the Message: Early Sensitivity to Auditory Fluency in Children's Endorsement of Statements," *Frontiers in Psychology* 5: 219.
Bräuer, J., Call, J., and Tomasello, M. 2007. "Chimpanzees Really Know What Others Can See in a Competitive Situation," *Animal Cognition* 10(4): 439–448.
Burge, Tyler. 1979. "Individualism and the Mental," in P. A. French, T. E. Uehling, and H. K. Wettstein (eds.), *Midwest Studies in Philosophy IV*. Minneapolis, MN: University of Minnesota Press.
Call, J., and Tomasello, M. 2008. "Does the Chimpanzee have a Theory of Mind? 30 Years Later," *Trends in Cognitive Sciences* 12(5): 187–192.
Callanan, M. A. 2006. *"Cognitive Development*, Culture, and Conversation: Comments on Harris and Koenig's 'Truth in Testimony: How Children Learn about Science and Religion,'" *Child Development* 77(3): 525–530.
Carey, S. 2009. *The Origin of Concepts*. Oxford: Oxford University Press.
Craig, E. 1991. *Knowledge and the State of Nature: An Essay in Conceptual Synthesis*. New York, NY: Oxford University Press.
Gelman, S. A. 2003. *The Essential Child*. Oxford: Oxford University Press.
Gopnik, A. 2009. *The Philosophical Baby: What Children's Minds Tell Us About Truth, Love and the Meaning of Life*. New York, NY: Farrar Strauss and Giroux.

Gopnik, A., and Astington, J. W. 1988. "Children's Understanding of Representational Change and Its Relation to the Understanding of False Belief and the Appearance-Reality Distinction," *Child Development* 59(1): 26.
Gopnik, A., Glymour, C., Sobel, D. M., Schulz, L. E., Kushnir, T., and Danks, D. 2004. "A Theory of Causal Learning in Children: Causal Maps and Bayes Nets," *Psychological Review* 111(1): 3–32.
Hamlin, J. K., Wynn, K., and Bloom, P. 2007. "Social Evaluation by Preverbal Infants," *Nature* 450(7169): 557–559.
Harris, P. L., and Koenig, M. A. 2006. "Trust in Testimony: How Children Learn about Science and Religion," *Child development* 77(3): 505–524.
Harris, P., Koenig, M., Corriveau, K., and Jaswal, V. 2018. "Cognitive Foundations of Learning from Testimony," *Annual Review of Psychology* 69: 251–273.
Harris, P. L., Yang, B., and Cui, Y. 2017. "'I don't know': Children's Early Talk about Knowledge," *Mind and Language* 32: 283–307.
Inhelder, B. 1962. "Some Aspects of Piaget's Genetic Approach to Cognition," *Monographs of the Society for Research in Child Development* 27(2): 19–40.
James, W. 1981 (orig. 1990). *Principles of Psychology*. Cambridge, MA: Harvard University Press.
Karmiloff-Smith, A. 1998. "Development Itself is the Key to Understanding Developmental Disorders," *Trends in Cognitive Sciences* 2(10): 389–398.
Karmiloff-Smith, A. 2009. "Nativism versus Neuroconstructivism: Rethinking the Study of Developmental Disorders," *Developmental Psychology* 45(1): 56–63.
Kaufmann, L., and Clément, F. 2014. "Wired for Society: Cognizing Pathways to Society and Culture," *Topoi* 33(2): 459–475.
Keil, F. C. 2006. "Doubt, Deference and Deliberation: Understanding and Using the Division of Cognitive Labor," in J. Hawthorne and T. Gendler (eds.), *Oxford Studies in Epistemology*. Oxford: Oxford University Press.
Kessen, W. 1965. *The Child*. New York, NY: Wiley.
Kinzler, K. D., Dupoux, E., and Spelke, E. S. 2007. "The Native Language of Social Cognition," *Proceedings of the National Academy of Sciences* 104(30): 12577–12580.
Koenig, M. A., Cole, C. A., Meyer, M., Ridge, K. E., Kushnir, T., and Gelman, S. A. 2015. "Reasoning about Knowledge: Children's Evaluations of Generality and Verifiability," *Cognitive Psychology* 83: 22–39.
Koenig, M. A., and Echols, C. H. 2003. "Infants' Understanding of False Labeling Events: The Referential Roles of Words and the Speakers Who Use Them," *Cognition* 87(3): 179–208.
Koenig, M. A., and McMyler, B. 2018. "Testimonial Knowledge: Understanding the Evidential, Uncovering the Interpersonal", in M. Fricker, P. Graham, D. Henderson, N. Pedersen, and J. Wyatt (eds.), *The Routledge Handbook of Social Epistemology*. New York, NY: Routledge.
Koriat, A. 1993. "How Do We Know That We Know? The Accessibility Model of The Feeling of Knowing," *Psychological Review* 100(4): 609–639.
Koriat, A. and Levy-Sadot, R. 1999. "Processes Underlying Metacognitive Judgments: Information-based and Experience-based Monitoring of One's Own Knowledge," in S. Chaiken, S. and Y. Trope (eds.), *Dual-Process Theories in Social Psychology*. New York, NY: Guilford Press.
Kovács, Á. M., Téglás, E., and Endress, A. D. 2010. "The Social Sense: Susceptibility to Others' Beliefs in Human Infants and Adults," *Science* 330(6012): 1830–1834.
Margolis, E., and Laurence, S. (eds.). 1999. *Concepts: Core Readings*. London: Bradford.
Moll, H., and Tomasello, M. 2007. "How 14- and 18-Month-Olds Know What Others Have Experienced," *Developmental Psychology* 43(2): 309.
Moshman, D. 1998. "Cognitive Development Beyond Childhood," in D. Kuhn, R. Siegler, and W. Damon (eds.), *Handbook of Child Psychology Volume 2*, 5th edn. New York, NY: Wiley.
Nagel, J. 2016. "Knowledge as Mental States," *Oxford Studies in Epistemology*: 1–37.
Onishi, K. H., and Baillargeon, R. 2005. "Do 15-Month-Old Infants Understand False Beliefs?," *Science* 308(5719): 255–258.
Pea, R. D. 1982. "Origins of Verbal Logic: Spontaneous Denials by Two- and Three-Year Olds," *Journal of Child Language* 9(3): 597–626.
Perner, J. 1991. *Understanding the Representational Mind: Learning, Development, and Conceptual Change*. Cambridge, MA: MIT Press.
Piaget, J. 1952. *The Origins of Intelligence in Children*. New York, NY: Norton.
Piaget, J. 1954. *The Construction of Reality in the Child*. New York, NY: Basic Books.
Pillow, B. H. 1989. "Early Understanding of Perception as a Source of Knowledge," *Journal of Experimental Child Psychology* 47(1): 116–129.

Povinelli, D. J., Nelson, K. E., and Boysen, S. T. 1990. "Inferences about Guessing and Knowing by Chimpanzees (Pan Troglodytes)," *Journal of Comparative Psychology* 104(3): 203–210.

Pratt, C., and Bryant, P. 1990. "Children Understand That Looking Leads to Knowing (So Long as They Are Looking into a Single Barrel)," *Child Development* 61: 973–982.

Proust, J. 2013. *The Philosophy of Metacognition*. Oxford: Oxford University Press.

Rogoff, B. 2003. *The Cultural Nature of Human Development*. New York, NY: Oxford University Press.

Russell, B. 1959 (orig. 1912). *The Problems of Philosophy*. Oxford: Oxford University Press.

Scott, R. M., and Baillargeon, R. 2013. "Do Infants Really Expect Agents to Act Efficiently? A Critical Test of the Rationality Principle," *Psychological Science* 24(4): 0956797612457395–474.

Shatz, M., Wellman, H. M., and Silber, S. 1983. "The Acquisition of Mental Verbs: A Systematic Investigation of the First Reference to Mental State," *Cognition* 14(3): 301–321.

Spelke, E. 1994. "Initial Knowledge: Six Suggestions," *Cognition* 50(1–3): 431–445.

Spelke, E. S. 2000. "Core Knowledge," *American Psychologist* 55(11): 1233–1243.

Spelke, E. S., and Kinzler, K. D. 2007. "Core Knowledge," *Developmental Science* 10(1): 89–96.

Sperber, D. (ed.). 2000. *Metarepresentations: A Multidisciplinary Perspective*. Oxford: Oxford University Press.

Sperber, D., Clément, F., Heintz, C., Mascaro, O., Mercier, H., Origgi, G., and Wilson, D. 2010. "Epistemic Vigilance," *Mind & Language* 25(4): 359–393.

Stanovich, K. E., and West, R. F. 2000. "Advancing the Rationality Debate," *Behavioral Brain Science* 23(5): 701–717.

Thomsen, L., Frankenhuis, W. E., Ingold-Smith, M., and Carey, S. 2011. "Big and Mighty: Preverbal Infants Mentally Represent Social Dominance," *Science* 331(6016): 477–480.

Tooby, J., and Cosmides, L. 1990. "The Past Explains the Present: Emotional Adaptations and the Structure of Ancestral Environments," *Ethology and Sociobiology* 11(4–5): 375–424.

Turiel, E. 1983. *The Development of Social Knowledge*. Cambridge: Cambridge University Press.

Vygotsky, L. 1962. *Thought and Language*. Cambridge, MA: MIT Press.

Wellman, H. M. 1990. *The Child's Theory of Mind*. Cambridge, MA: Bradford Books.

Wellman, H. M. 2014. *Making Minds: How Theory of Mind Develops*. Oxford: Oxford University Press.

Wellman, H. M., Cross, D., and Watson, J. 2001. "Meta-Analysis of Theory-of-Mind Development: The Truth about False Belief," *Child Development* 72(3): 655–684.

Williams, B. A. O. 2002. *Truth and Truthfulness: An Essay in Genealogy*. Princeton, NJ: Princeton University Press.

Williamson, T. 2002. *Knowledge and its Limits*. Oxford: Oxford University Press on Demand.

Wimmer, H., and Perner, J. 1983. "Beliefs about Beliefs: Representation and Constraining Function of Wrong Beliefs in Young Children's Understanding of Deception," *Cognition* 13(1): 103–128.

Wittgenstein, L. 1968. *On Certainty*. Oxford: Blackwell.

Wynn, K. 1992. "Addition and Subtraction by Human Infants," *Nature* 358(6389): 749–750.

2
LANGUAGE AND COMMUNICATION

Evidence from studying children

M. J. Cain

Introduction

At birth, human individuals do not speak any language but the developmental process leading to full linguistic mastery is rapid, leading some scholars to say that we ordinarily have a full mastery of language (barring vocabulary limitations) by the age of four or five (Pinker 1994). The development of language is one of the most important cognitive developments that humans undergo and that raises the question of how it takes place. For example, is learning central to the process or are there bodies of language-specific innate knowledge that obviate the need for learning? One particular aspect of this question will be the ultimate focus of this chapter: how do children come to grasp the meanings of the words that belong to their vocabularies?

Knowledge of language

One natural way of viewing linguistic mastery is to see it as being based on knowledge of language (Chomsky 1986). For example, I am able to communicate by means of English sentences because I possess the relevant knowledge of English, and this includes semantic, syntactic, morphological, phonological and pragmatic knowledge. How do children develop such linguistic knowledge? Recent decades have seen an explosion in the empirical study of language development (see Ambridge and Lieven (2011) for a helpful comprehensive survey). A key aspect of the debate has concerned the question of whether language is something that is learned by means of domain-general learning mechanisms or whether it has a substantial innate basis that is specific to language.

The concept of innateness looms large in debates about language acquisition, and this raises the question of what it is for something to be innate (see ch. 1). Unfortunately, the traditional characterisation of innateness in terms of presence at birth is problematic for two reasons. First, there are characteristics that are innate that are not present at birth but emerge in the course of development, such as secondary sexual characteristics like pubic hair and breasts. Second, the notion of *in utero* learning is hardly incoherent. In fact, there is evidence that the developing foetus is sensitive to language spoken by its mother and learns on the basis of this. For example, in an experiment conducted by DeCasper and Spence (1986), pregnant women repeatedly read aloud a particular story. After birth the children of these women were played recordings of their mother reading that very story. They were also played recordings of their mother reading new stories of a similar length and intonation pattern. The children displayed a clear preference for the story that their mother had read whilst pregnant, suggesting that they had a familiarity with it gained from before they were born. This preference was indicated by their sucking whilst breastfeeding more enthusiastically when listening to the story that their mother had read whilst pregnant.

In light of this, how should we characterise innateness? As a rough and ready characterisation, for something to be innate is for it *not* to be learned and for it to be a feature of the organism at the beginning of its existence or for it to emerge reliably from that initial state in the normal course of development.

Syntax

The most prominent debate in the recent study of language development relates to the development of syntactic knowledge – knowledge of how to put together words to build more complex structures such as phrases and sentences. The most prominent contribution to that debate is constituted by the work of Noam Chomsky who, since the late 1950s, has been developing and defending a theory according to which our knowledge of syntax has a substantial innate basis. (See Chomsky (2016) for a recent accessible statement of his perspective.)

For Chomsky, the mind-brain is made up of a number of functionally distinct yet interacting components that are akin to the internal organs of the body. These components are part of our biological endowment and they develop in a manner that is constrained and directed by our shared genetic makeup. One such component is the language faculty – a mental system that underlies language development and use. The initial state of the language faculty, its state before being subject to any linguistic input, encodes Universal Grammar (UG for short). UG is a system of syntactic rules or principles common to all human languages. It constitutes a template for language and constrains the form that any human language can take. That is not to say that all human languages are syntactically indistinguishable and, as a consequence, children do not have an innate knowledge of any particular spoken language. However, a child's language-specific knowledge at birth is such that she only requires quite limited information to acquire a full knowledge of the local language she ends up speaking – a knowledge that is encoded in the mature state of her language faculty.

Chomsky's primary argument for this nativist perspective is the "poverty of the stimulus" argument. According to this argument, children typically acquire a complete knowledge of the syntax of their first language by the age of four or five. However, the experiences they have of language in the first few years of their lives are far too impoverished to have facilitated learning from scratch, so they must have had language-specific innate knowledge to aid the developmental process. Their linguistic experiences are impoverished in several respects. First, the language that they hear contains many grammatical errors (Chomsky 1972). Second, many of the sentences that a child would need to hear to learn the syntactic rules of her language, particularly complex sentences, are rarely encountered. Third, children don't generally receive negative data – that is, explicit information that the ungrammatical sentences that they produce are ungrammatical (Pinker 1989).

Chomsky's views have dominated linguistics and cognitive science for several decades, but recent years have seen something of a backlash. Probably the most prominent contemporary alternative to Chomsky's linguistic nativism is constituted by an approach known as the usage-based theory, the key champion of which is Michael Tomasello. For Tomasello (2003, 2008) language is a system of communication that is both used and learned in a social context; for him, there is no such thing as the language faculty or UG.

Tomasello is committed to an approach in linguistics known as construction grammar. A construction is a "symbolic unit with meaning" (Tomasello 2003: 160). Hence, any concrete word or sentence, such as "aardvark" or "the aardvark ate a termite", is a construction. But as concrete sentences exemplify more abstract forms, the following are also constructions:

- X ate a termite
- X ate Y
- TRANSITIVE-SUBJECT TRANSITIVE-VERBed TRANSITIVE-OBJECT

Tomasello regards a language as an inventory of constructions that is learned in a gradual and piecemeal manner, beginning with concrete words and sentences and moving on to increasingly abstract constructions. Constructions, even the most abstract ones, differ from the rules and principles that lie at the heart of Chomsky's vision in that they are inherently meaningful; for example, "the pattern *X VERBed Y the Z* is a construction of English that signifies some transfer of possession (either literal or metaphorical)" (Tomasello 2003: 99). Thus, Tomasello's approach doesn't involve drawing a firm distinction between syntax and semantics and, accordingly, accounts for semantic development just as much as syntactic development.

For Tomasello the language-learning process begins at about age one when the child has developed certain key perceptual and cognitive capacities. The first of these involves the possession of basic concepts and the ability to represent a viewed scene in terms of those concepts. This capacity would be utilised when, for example, seeing a person throw a ball to someone else, a child conceptualises the scene as having three participants (two people and a ball) and involving one of the people acting on the ball so as to transfer its possession to the other. The second capacity is that of recognising patterns exemplified in items of data that differ at the concrete level. The third capacity is that of having sophisticated mind-reading skills. This capacity involves being able to discern the higher-order mental states of other people, where a higher-order mental state is a mental state the having of which involves attributing a mental state to someone (as when you believe that I believe that aardvarks eat termites and when I believe that you believe that I believe that aardvarks eat termites). Higher-order mental states are central to the phenomenon of joint attention when two people are not only attending to the same thing but are mutually aware that they share that attention.

The key thing about these capacities is that they can be brought together so as to facilitate the learning of language in the following manner. From infancy children participate in routinised activities with their carers such as being fed, being dressed, playing, and so. In this context, the child and carer will often jointly attend to an element of the viewed scene and employ language. For example, suppose a child in the early stages of language learning and an adult are playing with a ball and the adult hides the ball behind her back and says, "ball gone". The fact that the pair have been jointly attending to the ball whilst playing a familiar game and that they mutually know that the ball has disappeared from view enables the child to work out that the adult intends to say that the ball has disappeared. Now suppose a cat that has been sleeping in the corner of the room noisily stirs and slinks out of the room. The adult looks at the cat, turns to the child and then returns to watching the cat, thereby establishing joint attention of the cat with the child. The adult then says, "cat gone". Given the evidence, the child can easily work out that this phrase means that the cat has disappeared.

At this stage the child knows the meaning of two distinct sentences but doesn't appreciate the connections between them. This changes when she applies her pattern recognition skills to the sentences; she recognises that both sentences talk about something disappearing and contain the component "gone". This enables her to work out that "gone" relates to disappearance and, in a similar manner, she can work out the meaning of "cat" and "ball". Moreover, by reflecting on the similarities between distinct sentences she can recognise that distinct sentences can exemplify a common pattern. For example, both "ball gone" and "cat gone" have the form "X gone". Realising this, the child stores the construction "X gone", representing it as meaning that X, whatever it is, has disappeared. This construction can then be used in building and understanding sentences that the child has not encountered once she has learned the meaning of further words such as "dog", "man" and the like. In this manner the child can gradually add more constructions to her store of linguistic knowledge, moving towards increasingly abstract constructions. What is noteworthy about this process is that learning the meaning of words and that of larger abstract structures goes hand in hand and is mutually supportive.

Vocabulary development

Chomsky's nativism relates to syntax and it might seem that there is no mileage in extending a nativist perspective to vocabulary development for several reasons. First, suppose that we adopt the standard view that a word is a pairing of a sound and a meaning so that when a person has a particular word in their vocabulary they know that the relevant sound–meaning pairing holds in their linguistic community. Clearly, languages vary widely in how they pair sounds and meanings. It seems uncontentious that such sound–meaning pairings need to be learned if they are to be known. Second, vocabulary development is a much longer process than syntactic development and cannot plausibly be characterised as complete by age five. This seems to leave plenty of time for learning, thereby suggesting that poverty-of-the-stimulus considerations are not at work. Third, although adult speakers of any given language will have vocabularies that overlap, there will also be a lot of divergence reflecting differences in experience.

Nevertheless, I think that there is something important that is innate with respect to vocabulary development and this has to do with the meaning side of the sound–meaning pairing. To appreciate this, it is necessary to take a step back and reflect on the question of what meanings are and on the challenge that children face when working out the meaning of a newly encountered word.

Concepts are the ingredients of thoughts. For example, one cannot entertain the thought that all aardvarks eat termites unless one has the concepts ALL, AARDVARK, EAT and TERMITE. As thoughts exist in the mind then so do concepts. Concepts correspond to categories, be they categories of thing, event, state, process or whatever. A concept is at least partly individuated in terms of the particular category that it corresponds to and it serves to pick out or represent that category. Accordingly, the content of a concept is at least partly a matter of which category it represents. Hence, for example, the concept AARDVARK has the content *aardvark* because it picks out or represents the category of aardvarks.

There is a close relationship between language and thought: we use sentences to communicate our thoughts and come to appreciate what others think on the basis of understanding the sentences that they produce. For this to be the case there needs to be a close relationship between the contents of our thoughts and the meaning of the sentences that we use to express them.

Thought is compositional in that the content of a thought is determined by the content of its component concepts and the way that they are put together. Similarly, linguistic meaning is compositional in that the meaning of a sentence is determined by the meaning of its component words and how they are put together. The implication of this is that the meaning of the words we use in communicating our thoughts must align with the contents of the concepts that make up those thoughts. From this insight it is a small step to the conclusion that word meanings are concepts in the respect that the meaning of a word for an individual is a matter of the identity of the concept the individual associates with the sound half of the sound–meaning pairing that constitutes the word. So, for example, "aardvark" means *aardvark* for me (or my linguistic community) because I (or most members of my linguistic community) associate the sound I vocalise when I say "aardvark" with the concept AARDVARK.

Associating a sound with a concept is itself a mental state. This mental state of associating a particular sound with a particular concept involves employing a mental representation of the sound in question and the mental representation that constitutes the concept in question. Linguists sometimes label this in-head store of an individual's knowledge of the words of her language, how they sound and what they mean, a mental lexicon (Aitchison 2012). Thus, vocabulary development involves adding items to the mental lexicon.

Many researchers of language development refer to a thought experiment developed by the philosopher W. V. O. Quine (1960) to show that children face a substantial challenge in learning new words (Bloom 2000). Quine imagined a linguist attempting to translate the language of an isolated tribe. He witnesses a member of the tribe utter "gavagai" whilst pointing at a rabbit. How should "gavagai" be translated? Quine points out that there are many competing hypotheses that are equally consistent with the evidence. For example, for all the linguist can tell, "gavagai" could mean *rabbit, undetached part of a rabbit, time slice of a rabbit, rabbit flea* or any one of infinitely many other possibilities. Quine ultimately draws the conclusion that words don't have determinate meanings, but that is not the moral that psychologists and linguists have tended to draw from his reflections. Rather, they have assumed that children do succeed in learning words and so somehow overcome the challenge that Quine so vividly describes.

This raises the question of how children manage to overcome Quine's challenge as the empirical evidence suggests that they do so from an early age. For a long time, a child's comprehension of the words of her language lags behind production (Griffiths 1986), but even if we focus on production it is evident that vocabulary development proceeds at a heady rate. Most children produce their first word at about one year of age, and by the time they are two they typically have a productive vocabulary of between 200 and 300 words. This vocabulary is dominated by nouns that pick out categories of objects (such as "dog", "milk", and so on), but it also includes verbs, adjectives and other types of words (Bloom, Tinker, and Margulis 1993). From this age, children acquire on average 3.6 words per day, giving rise to a vocabulary of over 2000 words at four years of age. Some researchers have claimed that at this age children are capable of fast mapping – that is, learning a word on the basis of a single exposure to that word (Carey 1978).

In explaining how children overcome Quine's challenge, some researchers have attributed to them biases that lead to them ruling out certain hypotheses that are, in principle, consistent with the data. These biases are often conceived as being innate, but only operative in the early stages of language development. For example, Woodward and Markman (1998) postulate a whole object bias whereby children assume that nouns refer to whole objects rather than parts. Operating with this assumption would enable a child in Quine's situation to discount *undetached rabbit part* as a possible meaning for "gavagai".

Even if children have biases to help them narrow down the possible meanings of new words they encounter, they still need appropriate concepts in order to represent any possibilities they consider. This is clear from Tomasello's account of language learning: the child attempting to learn what "ball" or "ball gone" means in the manner he describes must have a prior grasp of concepts that enable her to represent the communicative intentions of the adult producing those words. That raises the question of how those concepts are acquired: are they learned or are they innate? Suppose that we have to learn what the words of our language mean (what sound–meaning pairings hold in our linguistic community). It is still consistent with this that the concepts that we combine with sounds in building our vocabularies are innate. I'm not suggesting that all of the concepts for which we have words are innate; no doubt we learn plenty of them. However, I will argue that there is a stock of abstract concepts needed to make language learning possible that belong to our innate endowment.

Abstract concepts

The term "abstract" is ambiguous. In one respect, an abstract concept is one that is general rather than just referring to a particular; for example, the concept AARDVARK is abstract in that it applies to many distinct particular things (Gauker 2011; Laurence and Margolis 2012). There is a question about how we acquire concepts that are abstract in this sense as our experiences are always of particulars; I experience particular aardvarks rather than aardvarkness in general. In the second respect, an abstract concept is one that refers to something that cannot directly be perceived, something that doesn't have a characteristic look, sound, taste, smell or feel. Arguably, the concept CAUSE is abstract in this sense. We might perceive a particular scene involving distinct objects, states or events and conceptualise them as being causally related. For example, I might perceive a striking of a match followed by a lighting of that match and take the former to be the cause of the latter. But I don't perceive any causation; rather, I apply the concept of causation in interpreting the nature of the relationship between the events I do perceive.

My concern is with concepts that are abstract in this second sense. We have many abstract concepts and words in our vocabularies that have such concepts as their meaning. As well as the concept CAUSE, concepts of mental states such as those of BELIEF, DESIRE and INTENTION are abstract. For, not only can we not directly perceive the mental states of another person, but many of our own mental states are unconscious. Even when we do introspect one of our own mental states we do so indirectly via an awareness of their internal effects such as their in-head vocalisation (Jackendoff 2002, 2012). Another important abstract concept is that of an object in general – that is, the concept of something that continues to exist when it is not being perceived. Moral concepts such as RIGHT, WRONG, FAIR, UNJUST, and so on, are also abstract.

How do we acquire abstract concepts? Within the empiricist tradition such concepts are generally portrayed as appearing relatively late in development, with the implication that an infant's conceptual scheme is very different from that of a typical adult being much less intellectually sophisticated. For example, Jean Piaget (1952, 1954), the founding father of developmental psychology, portrayed a child's development as passing through several distinct stages of increasing sophistication that begins from a very meagre base such that a child in her early years would not even possess the concept of an object or be capable of logical thought.

In recent years, much work in developmental psychology has served to undermine Piaget's views by suggesting that infants have a sophisticated perspective on reality as part of their innate endowment. For example, Elizabeth Spelke (1994), Susan Gelman (2003) and Susan Carey (2009) have argued that infants carve the world into distinct domains and utilise different abstract concepts and knowledge involving those concepts to deal with each of those domains. These domains include those of inanimate physical objects, minded agents and biological entities. For example, Spelke (1994) argues that we have a core system of concepts and knowledge for dealing specifically with inanimate physical objects. Such concepts and knowledge are in place before a child has had any chance to learn them on the basis of her experiences, suggesting that they are innate.

A classic experiment supporting this kind of view was conducted by Karen Wynn (1992). Wynn's experiment on five-month-old infants involved a stage, two puppets and a screen. At first, one puppet was placed on the stage in full view of the infants. Then a screen was introduced to hide the puppet from view, and a second puppet was placed behind the screen, with the infants seeing this manoeuvre. Then the screen was lowered, sometimes revealing one puppet and sometimes revealing two, with each participating infant seeing both of these scenarios. Wynn employed measures of looking time to determine which of these scenarios most surprised or violated the expectations of the infants (the assumption being that if an infant looked longer at one of the scenarios than the other then that indicated that she was more surprised by it). Wynn found that the infants were more surprised when only one puppet was revealed rather than two. From this she concluded that the infants had an innate concept of an object as something that continues to exist over time when not being perceived, and innate knowledge that the world is populated by such objects.

In addition to inanimate physical objects, children have to deal with other people who are minded and act on the basis of their mental states. To do this they need a theory of mind that is made up of a body of concepts for mental states and knowledge about how mental states causally relate to one another, to external stimulation and to behaviour (Bloom 2004). There is considerable evidence that infants draw a distinction between people and inanimate physical objects very early in life and have different expectations concerning how they behave. For example, infants express surprise when an inanimate physical object moves without something external making contact with it but become disconcerted when a face that was mobile suddenly becomes still (Tronick et al. 1978). Such data leads many psychologists to attribute to us an innate theory of mind (Spelke 2003; Baillargeon, Scott, and He 2010).

Even with respect to putatively concrete concepts such as DOG and WATER, there is evidence that children take an abstract perspective on them. In particular, children are essentialists with respect to many of the categories for which they have concepts. That is, they regard the items that belong to such categories as being bound together in virtue of having a hidden essence, a collection of properties that makes them what they are and is causally responsible for their perceivable features (Keil 1989). Susan Gelman (2003) argues that children adopt this essentialist viewpoint before they begin school, suggesting that it is part of an innate perspective on reality.

Moral concepts are also abstract, and research suggests that infants morally evaluate behaviour before the age of one. For example, Hamlin, Wynn, and Bloom (2007) showed infants a little under one year of age a puppet show in which a duck tries to open a toy box with a heavy lid. Two bears then appear, one of which attempts to help the duck open the box whilst the other attempts to hinder the duck. After the show the infants were given the opportunity to play with the bears and almost all of them chose to play with the kind bear, suggesting that they had morally evaluated the behaviour of the bears and preferred one to the other on that basis.

In short, there is considerable evidence that children have a body of innate abstract concepts and knowledge involving those concepts and that this is part and parcel of a metaphysical picture that carves the external world into different domains that work in different ways.

How do such abstract concepts relate to vocabulary development? Many of these concepts do get lexicalised and the words corresponding to them enter the vocabularies of most speakers in the form of a relevant sound–meaning pairing. Now there is a respect in which that sound–meaning pairing will have to be learned. For example, I had to learn how the concepts of CAUSATION and BELIEF are conventionally expressed in English. But in order to learn this I didn't have to learn the concepts, CAUSATION and BELIEF.

If the abstract concepts that I have highlighted are innate, then there is another implication with respect to vocabulary development that can be brought out by returning to Tomasello's theory of language learning. Tomasello portrays language learning from the beginning as drawing upon the child's ability to mind-read and to conceive of the viewed scene in a manner that lines up with that of the adults with whom she is interacting. This requires having a metaphysical picture akin to that attributed to children by the developmental psychologists discussed above. In particular, it requires drawing a distinction between inanimate physical objects and minded individuals and conceiving of both of these in terms of abstract concepts such as that of an object that continues to exist when not perceived and of numerous psychological concepts. This metaphysical perspective and the concepts that are bound up with it is both needed to get the language-learning process off the ground and central to all further attempts to learn elements of language. In short, it is not a peripheral aspect of a child's world view.

Is it possible to learn abstract concepts?

Is it possible that the kinds of abstract concepts that I have portrayed as being innate are in actual fact learned? There are some prominent attempts to explain how we can learn abstract concepts on the basis of our experiences and I will now consider two of these.

Jesse Prinz (2002) has developed an influential theory of concepts – the proxytype theory – according to which all concepts are constructed out of perceptual primitives. He addresses head-on the challenge that this theory cannot deal with abstract concepts. He argues that on anyone's account we apply abstract concepts to phenomena that we can perceive and do so on the basis of how we perceive them to be. This implies that perceivable properties correlate with abstract properties so that the instantiation of the latter can be detected on the basis of the instantiation of the former. He thinks that the upshot of this is that abstract properties can be expressed or encoded by means of perceptual representations.

My objection to Prinz's line of thought runs as follows. Suppose that we concede that a particular abstract property reliably correlates with certain perceptual ones. It wouldn't follow from this that the abstract property could be expressed or encoded by means of perceptual representations. This is because the mere correlation of two properties x and y does not imply that in representing an object as a y one is thereby representing it as an x; in addition, one needs a distinct representation that facilitates representing the object as an x *as such*. This can be seen by considering a simple example. Suppose a person is familiar with a particular species of bird for which she has a concept. She notices that members of this species come in two colours, namely, black and brown. Unbeknownst to her the colour of the birds correlates with their sex, the black ones being male and the brown ones being female. Because of her lack of knowledge of the link between colour and sex she does not represent a bird of this species as being female in representing it as being brown. In other words, the mere correlation of sex and colour does not imply that in representing a bird as having a particular colour one is thereby representing its sex. Consequently, in order to represent a bird's sex, one needs a representation distinct from representations of colour. This undermines Prinz's line of thought by suggesting that one cannot represent something as having a particular abstract property by merely perceptual means, even if there is a correlation between that abstract property and certain perceptual properties. Therefore, Prinz has not shown how abstract concepts can be built out of perceptual resources, and thus learned on the basis of perception.

A second attempt to explain how we learn abstract concepts on the basis of concrete concepts is suggested by George Lakoff and Mark Johnson's treatment of metaphor (Lakoff and Johnson 1980; Lakoff 1987). In cases of metaphor we understand a concept or word on the basis of analogy with some more concrete concept. For example, suppose a colleague says that they cannot join me for a coffee because they are currently bogged down answering a backlog of emails. I won't understand them as been literally stuck in a bog and unable to move whilst on a walk through the countryside. But I will understand their situation as being analogous to that in that they are currently unable to extract themselves from their office until they have answered a large volume of emails.

For Lakoff and Johnson not all of our concepts are metaphorical; rather, there is a stock of concepts that form the basis of our metaphors, providing the analogies in terms of which the metaphors are understood. Such basic concepts relate to our perceptual experiences of the outside world and to our bodily experiences. For example, we often conceive of mental states in spatial and postural terms, as when we say such things as:

"I'm feeling down today" to attribute a state of depression or a lack of enthusiasm.

"She is walking with a spring in her step" to attribute a state of confidence, happiness or enthusiasm.

"You should walk tall after your recent successes" to tell someone they should be proud of their achievements.

This treatment of metaphor suggests one way of dealing with the charge that abstract concepts cannot be learned. The suggestion is that we learn such concepts on analogy with more concrete concepts relating to perceptual and bodily experiences. So, for example, an individual could learn concepts for psychological states on the basis of a prior understanding of spatial concepts and concepts relating to the posture and manner of locomotion.

I accept that metaphor is commonplace in language and that when we appreciate the aptness of a metaphorical expression we often do so by noting an analogy between two distinct domains. However, I am sceptical of the claim that metaphorical extension provides a reliable way of acquiring new abstract concepts. The basic problem is that one can only appreciate the aptness of the metaphor when one has a prior grasp of the concept expressed in metaphorical terms. For example, I appreciate the aptness of the expression "walk tall" as a term meaning *proud* because of my understanding that people who are proud often hold themselves very upright as opposed to those who are ashamed who often slouch. Similarly, I appreciate the aptness of "down" as a term for depression as I know that depressed people typically do not hold themselves upright and spend a large proportion of their time lying or sitting down and are difficult to coax into activity that involves them being physically up and active. In short, I have a theory about such psychological states and how they manifest themselves in behaviour and this theory enables me to understand and appreciate the metaphorical expressions. But having such a theory requires having the psychological concepts in question. In other words, prior possession of the target concept is necessary for appreciating the aptness of its metaphorical expression. Thus, if one didn't have the target concept, the metaphorical expression would appear opaque. This suggests that one cannot learn abstract concepts on the basis of a prior possession of more concrete concepts; without a grasp of the target abstract concepts, one would simply not be able to appreciate the relevant analogy.

Conclusion

Acquiring knowledge of language is one of the most important cognitive developments that we undergo as children. A key element of this development involves building a vocabulary, each item of which consists of a pairing of a sound and a meaning that is represented in the mental lexicon. In this chapter I have discussed the question of how we acquire the meaning side of these pairings and have assumed that such meanings are constituted by concepts. I have argued that although learning does play an important role in vocabulary development in that we have to learn the conventions governing sound–meaning pairings that hold in our home linguistic communities, such learning is only possible because we have a battery of abstract concepts and an associated metaphysical perspective on the world that is part of our innate endowment.

References

Aitchison, J. 2012. *Words in the Mind: An Introduction to the Mental Lexicon*, 4th edn. Oxford: Wiley-Blackwell.
Ambridge, B., and Lieven, E. V. M. 2011. *Child Language Acquisition: Contrasting Theoretical Approaches*. Cambridge: Cambridge University Press.
Baillargeon, R., Scott, R. M., and He, Z. 2010. "False-belief Understanding in Infants," *Trends in Cognitive Sciences* 14: 110–118.
Bloom, L., Tinker, E., and Margulis, C. 1993. "The Words Children Learn: Evidence Against a Noun Bias in Early Vocabularies," *Cognitive Development* 8: 431–450.
Bloom, P. 2000. *How Children Learn the Meaning of Words*. Cambridge, MA: MIT Press.
Bloom, P. 2004. *Descartes' Baby: How Child Development Explains What Makes US Human*. London: William Heinemann.
Carey, S. 1978. "The Child as World Learner," in M. Halle, G. Miller, and J. Bresnan (eds.), *Linguistic, Theory and Psychological Reality*. Cambridge, MA: MIT Press.
Carey, S. 2009. *The Origin of Concepts*. New York, NY: Oxford University Press.
Chomsky, N. 1972. *Language and Mind*. New York, NY: Harcourt Brace Jovanavich.
Chomsky, N. 1986. *Knowledge of Language*. Westport, CT: Praeger.
Chomsky, N. 2016. *What Kind of Creatures Are We?* New York, NY: Columbia University Press.
DeCasper, A. J., and Spence, M. J. 1986. "Prenatal Maternal Speech Influences Newborns' Perception of Speech Sounds," *Infant Behaviour and Development* 9: 133–150.
Gauker, C. 2011. *Words and Images: An Essay on the Origins of Ideas*. Oxford: Oxford University Press.
Gelman, S. 2003. *The Essential Child*. New York, NY: Oxford University Press.
Griffiths, P. 1986. "Early Vocabulary," in P. Fletcher and M. Garman (eds.), *Langague Acquisition: Studies in First Language Development*, 2nd edn. Cambridge: Cambridge University Press.
Hamlin, J. K., Wynn, K., and Bloom, P. 2007. "Social Evaluation by Preverbal Infants," *Nature* 450: 557–559.
Jackendoff, R. 2002. *Foundations of Language*. Oxford: Oxford University Press.
Jackendoff, R. 2012. *A User's Guide to Thought and Meaning*. Oxford: Oxford University Press.
Keil, F. 1989. *Concepts, Kinds, and Cognitive Development*. Cambridge, MA: MIT Press.
Lakoff, G. 1987. *Women, Fire and Dangerous Things: What Categories Reveal About the Mind*. Chicago, IL: University of Chicago Press.
Lakoff, G., and Johnson, M. 1980. *Metaphors We Live By*. Chicago, IL: University of Chicago Press.
Laurence, S., and Margolis, E. 2012. "Abstraction and the Origin of General Ideas," *Philosophers' Imprint* 12: 1–22.
Piaget, J. 1952. *The Origins of Intelligence in Children*. New York, NY: Harcourt Brace.
Piaget, J. 1954. *The Construction of Reality in the Child*. New York, NY: Basic Books.
Pinker, S. 1989. *Learnability and Cognition: The Acquisition of Argument Structure*. Cambridge, MA: MIT Press.
Pinker, S. 1994. *The Language Instinct: The New Science of Language and Mind*. London: Penguin.
Prinz, J. 2002. *Furnishing the Mind: Concepts and their Perceptual Basis*. Cambridge, MA: MIT Press.
Quine, W. V. O. 1960. *Word and Object*. Cambridge, MA: MIT Press.
Spelke, E. 1994. "Initial Knowledge: Six Suggestions," *Cognition* 50: 435–445.
Spelke, E. 2003. "What Makes Us Smart? Core Knowledge and Natural Language," in D. Gentner and S. Goldin-Meadow (eds.), *Language in Mind*. Cambridge, MA: MIT Press.
Tomasello, M. 2003. *Constructing a Language: A Usage Based Theory of Language Acquisition*. Cambridge, MA: MIT Press.
Tomasello, M. 2008. *Origins of Human Communication*. Cambridge, MA: MIT Press.
Tronick, E., Als, H., Adamson, L., Wise, S., and Brazelton, T. B. 1978. "Infants' Response to Entrapment Between Contradictory Messages in Face-to-Face Interaction," *Journal of the American Academy of Child and Adolescent Psychiatry* 17: 1–13.
Woodward, A. L., and Markman, E. M. 1998. "Early Word Learning," in W. Damon, D. Kuhn and R. Seigler (eds.), *Handbook of Child Psychology, Volume 2: Cognition, Perception and Language*. New York, NY: Wiley.
Wynn, K. 1992. "Addition and Subtraction by Human Infants," *Nature* 358: 749–750.

3
THE SCIENCE OF THE ADOLESCENT BRAIN AND ITS CULTURAL IMPLICATIONS

Suparna Choudhury and Nancy Ferranti

Introduction

Scientific developments during the past two decades have ushered in new and widespread interest in the neuroscience of adolescent development, and what has come to be known popularly as the "teen brain". Clinicians, policy makers, educators, parents and youth are increasingly informed by emerging scientific insights into the adolescent brain's malleability and its sensitivity to environmental input from puberty through early adulthood. These findings have been made possible by the relatively recent availability of non-invasive neuroimaging techniques that have allowed researchers to attempt to identify the "neural underpinnings" of behavioral differences between adolescents, adults and children (Choudhury 2010). The rapid growth of a research domain dedicated to adolescent brain development has challenged the older assumption of brain rigidity after late childhood in developmental science (Fuhrmann, Knoll, and Blakemore 2015) and has given rise to an increasingly neuroscientifically informed and brain-centered understanding of adolescence in wider culture. As such, there has been widespread appeal for applying the view of the adolescent brain as a *different brain* – from the adult and child brain – to several societal domains of everyday life of youth. In this chapter, we describe the development of this emerging science, the implications for policy and public engagement, and the controversies therein. Finally, we discuss the importance of understanding this new science in its cultural contexts.

State of the science on adolescent brain development

The recent neuroimaging (magnetic resonance imaging (MRI)) and functional MRI (fMRI) studies support earlier, smaller-scale postmortem studies from the 1970s in suggesting that "sensitive periods" of development of the human brain may be more protracted than previously thought (Huttenlocher 1979). The adolescent brain is now frequently described as "a work in progress" to emphasize the structural remodeling and neuronal reconfiguring that occurs as the child brain transitions to the mature adult structure. This growing body of research has shown functional and structural changes in the brain during adolescence, hypothesized to correspond with behavioral changes during this period (Nelson, Jarcho, and Guyer 2016). The two major changes identified during adolescence are linear increases of white matter volume, which is implicated in more rapid transmission and processing of neural information, and non-linear decreases of grey matter volume, which is hypothesized to represent synaptic pruning – the process of eliminating and "rewiring" synapses to maximize the efficiency of neuronal communication (Vijayakumar et al. 2016).

Data depicting white and grey matter development have generally been interpreted as processes of experience-dependent synaptic reorganization and increased myelination of nerve projections in several parts of the brain. The synaptic reorganization that takes place in adolescence is a function of the highly plastic nature of the adolescent cortex. Cortical plasticity refers to the brain's ability to reorganize and adjust its neural connections in response to environmental stimuli. "Experience-dependent" plasticity reflects the brain's reaction to life experiences, lays the foundation for human brain function, and is responsible for all learning and persists at a baseline level throughout life. In contrast, "experience-expectant" plasticity gives rise to distinct "sensitive periods" during the life span in which specific experiences must occur for typical development (Fuhrmann, Knoll, and Blakemore 2015). Human studies of sensitive periods have largely focused on early childhood (Kuhl 2010), demonstrating highly plastic periods of language development and sensitive periods that underlie sensory capacities like sound categorization (Blakemore and Choudhury 2006; see also ch. 2). Researchers have begun to hypothesize that adolescence is a second period of intense neuronal plasticity, characterized by experience-expectant periods, specifically sensitive to experiential input affecting executive functions and social cognition (Blakemore and Mills 2014).

Empirical research has demonstrated extensive structural and functional changes in the brain during adolescence, particularly in regards to the frontal, parietal and temporal regions of the brain, but there has been much debate over the interpretation and findings of these studies (Tamnes et al. 2013). Discrepancies, in part, arise from difficulties characteristic to the logic of neuroimaging methodology. Functional imaging studies provide correlational information but cannot provide causal certainty, leaving the links between neuroanatomical development and changes in behavior and brain function unclear (Weber and Thompson-Schill 2010). In addition, variability of age range and pubertal status used to denote periods of "adolescence", "childhood" and "adulthood" leading to differing sample characteristics (Pfeifer and Allen 2016), difficulties in extrapolating across different neuroimaging paradigms, techniques and loci of study in the brain across studies are just some reasons why researchers in the field hold disparate views (Richards, Plate, and Ernst 2013).

The adolescent brain beyond the lab

These nuances and limitations remain under-debated while the appetite for the science in the public sphere and policy context has become increasingly strong. The appeal is clear: this research offers state-of-the-art scientific investigations into the brain basis of behaviors that are often anecdotally or stereotypically associated with teenagers, particularly in Western societies, and offers potential avenues for intervention. For example, neuroimaging studies explain why adolescents make "poorer" decisions than adults (Galvan et al. 2007) and reveal the neural correlates of "high-risk behaviors" associated with adolescence such as increased sensation-seeking behavior and heightened impulsivity (Brown et al. 2015). Stereotypical teen behaviors are thus explained, and validated, by experimentally detected changes in the brain. The prefrontal cortex (PFC) undergoes the most dramatic changes during adolescence. This is particularly significant, especially to researchers seeking to apply brain science to evidence-based policy-making and to inform young people about their brain health and personal identity, because this brain area is implicated in high-level cognitive capacities. The PFC is associated with capacities for behavioral control like decision-making, working memory and multitasking, emotional regulation and social cognitive skills such as empathy, perspective-taking, self-awareness and emotional recognition – the very capacities at stake in the debates about the relevance of the developing brain for education, law, psychiatry and child-rearing.

These developing abilities are characteristic of this ongoing developmental phase frequently referred to as a period of "vulnerabilities and opportunities" (Dahl 2004); adolescent neuroplasticity is thought to be both a source of risk (for onset of mental illness as well as problem behaviors in the healthy population) and at the same time a resource that can be tapped to harness the brain's potential through various behavioral interventions. Such findings are thus increasingly sought by policy makers at a moment in which neuroscientific discourse is continually becoming more influential to the health and everyday lives of teenagers. Despite the widespread uptake and influence on policy and popular discourse, there are several important methodological limitations, epistemological dilemmas and ethical questions surrounding the translation of new brain data into areas of society involved in the health and management of adolescent behaviors (see ch. 33).

For example, the drive to produce applications of neuroscience and the trend towards evidence-based education sparked the field of "neuroeducation". This research agenda aims to build educational strategies that improve academic achievement and social development of young people, reframing curricula to reflect current research on the developing brain. These strategies are presented as science-based and implicate ambitious assumptions of what programs that aim to capitalize on brain plasticity can accomplish. Despite the preliminary nature of research data, findings from neuroeducation have begun to trickle directly into schools in the form of new customized teaching methods built around interpretations of data about social cognitive development and neurocognitive plasticity (Ansari, De Smedt, and Grabner 2012). These methods aim predominantly to improve children and adolescents' regulations of actions, impulses and emotions, and to provide a biological foundation for working with developmental disorders like dyslexia in the classroom (Howard-Jones 2009).

This swift translation is not without controversy. Earlier attempts to bridge brain science and education through high-profile commercial projects such as Baby Einstein, Baby Mozart and educational programs premised on left brain/right brain lateralization have been widely discredited (Maxwell and Racine 2012), raising the need for greater scrutiny in the transfer of research to policy and educational practice. A primary critique of the commercialization and oversimplification of neuroscience is the emergence of "neuromyths", a term that gained prevalence with the "Brain and Learning" report by the OECD in 2002, defined as "a misconception generated by a misunderstanding, a misreading, or a misquoting of facts scientifically established (by brain research) to make a case for use of brain research in education and other contexts" (OECD 2002). While researchers caution policy makers about the "seductive allure" (Weisberg et al. 2008) of "neuromythology" (Rose 2005) and the risks of applying preliminary findings too soon, critical reflection on the brain data and interpretations outside the lab remain understudied.

Similarly, hopes for the role of this new brain science of adolescence in mental health have been set high, particularly in recent years since the recent reorientation of the National Institute of Mental Health (NIMH) research towards biological taxonomies (Insel and Lieberman 2013). The goal of many researchers is to apply the logic of neurobiological markers of mental disorders into the context of adolescent psychiatry (Croarkin and Ameis 2016). Imaging data on adolescent brain development and the potential for biomarkers in the clinic has been highlighted in the context of attention deficit hyperactivity disorder (ADHD) – a common disorder in school-age children characterized by inattention, impulsivity and hyperactivity (Sun et al.

2012). Despite enthusiasm to import these methods among some in the clinical community, it is important to assess whether neuroimaging in its current state can play an appropriate role. How reliable are these as biomarkers in the clinical context? Can neuroimaging be used to diagnose ADHD? What might be some of the commercial, societal and cultural drivers behind the investment in neuroimaging as a purportedly more objective tool for psychiatric diagnosis?

Bioethicists and social scientists speculate that a rapid translation into clinical settings could occur through the creation of algorithms that combine neurobiomarkers with heredity, environmental and social risk factors to predict the probability that a single individual has or could develop the illness (Singh 2008). These advances would mark the foundation of a re-engineering of the health care system that would assure novel streams of care especially designed for adolescents, a period when mental illnesses are considered to be increasing in incidence (McGorry et al. 2011). Researchers in neuroscience, psychiatry and health policy – as well as clinicians and policy makers – have significant roles in shaping research programs directed towards the discovery and use of brain-based biomarkers in adolescence.

Critical neuroscience offers a reflexive and interdisciplinary framework to examine political, cultural and social contexts of neuroscience, while considering ways to integrate these contexts into the experimental study of the adolescent brain (Choudhury and Slaby 2012). On the one hand, critical neuroscience draws on the notion of styles of reasoning to explore how knowledge, models and beliefs about adolescent behaviors are produced and communicated within the neuroscience community. Styles of reasoning refer to the ideas, practices, technologies and tacit knowledge drawn on when making a judgement (Young 2000). On the other hand, critical neuroscience seeks to bring into view multiple methodologies and approaches to study the human mind, without privileging the biological level of inquiry. In this way, it aspires to enrich experimental paradigms and broaden the interpretive possibilities about behaviors and possible routes to intervention.

The "teen brain" as a unique brain in popular culture

The interpretation of brain data showing that the "teen brain" is different has gained increasing visibility outside the neuroscience community in the media, resonating strongly with current cultural conceptions of teenagers in Western societies. The popular model of the "teen brain" offers a new scientific explanation of developmental challenges, while simultaneously providing a new vocabulary and set of metaphors to frame and interpret developmental challenges arising from normal development and illness. This is largely a result of the growing impetus for public engagement, or knowledge translation, activities that promote "neurotalk". In health-promotion literatures, including government websites, pamphlets and awareness videos, adolescence is understood as a paradoxical period of brain development during which teens undergo a phase of inevitable and normal "pathological" behavior which results from their "disorganized", "underdeveloped" or "maturing" cortex simultaneous with increased risk for the onset of mental illness (Dahl 2004). In other words, the typically developing brain is seen as "at risk".

Since the 1990s, neuroscientific explanations about the "teen brain" have been central in newspaper, magazine and television reports claiming to solve the "secret" or "mystery" of risky, sullen and rebellious teenage behavior in Canada, the USA and the UK. Brain-scanning studies provided salient explanations, for instance, about risk-taking, emotional immaturity and "suboptimal decisions" (Casey, Getz, and Galvan 2008). Scientific arguments about the adolescent brain continue to penetrate the public domain, in the form of public lectures, popular science books and television programs. These popularized neurological explanations for stereotypical adolescent behavior tend to result in explanations – often directed to parents and educators – that "blame the brain" (Morgan 2005).

Dissemination of public health information regarding the teen brain has shifted from exclusively targeting caregivers to engaging teens themselves as well (Choudhury, McKinney, and Merten 2012). Public engagements have included interactive exhibitions, books, multimedia projects and television programs. In the popular book *Blame My Brain*, Morgan (2005) explains different facets of teen life, like sleep and drug use, in terms of the immaturity of the developing teenage brain. PBS's video series, "Inside the Teenage Brain" (PBS 2002), advertises "finding new explanations for why adolescents behave the way they do".[1]

Although well-intentioned, empirical research with UK-based students aged 13–14 years old (Choudhury, McKinney, and Merten 2012) demonstrates how neurocentric public engagement has the potential to strip away teenagers' subjective experiences, while simultaneously creating new spaces to exact social control. The New Yorker article, *The Terrible Teens* (2015), quotes Frances Jensen, researcher and author of *The Teenage Brain: A Neuroscientist's Survival Guide to Raising Adolescents and Young Adults*, advising parents: "You need to be your teens' frontal lobes until their brains are fully wired". According to young people, being defined by neuroscience and this style of rhetoric inspired by neuroscientific discourse creates new ways of stigmatizing adolescents that reifies their lower societal status and essentializes long-standing societal tropes about teenagers (Choudhury, McKinney, and Merten 2012). There has been limited investigation into the effects of public engagement and knowledge translation initiatives on the "teen brain" among various audiences. Further, research should investigate the possible implications to young people's own self-understanding that result from these initiatives which widely circulate brain-centered views of adolescence and regard adolescents' brains as "different", "in construction", "incomplete" and associated with notions of poor decision-making, emotional volatility, impulsivity and risk-taking.

Situating the adolescent brain: historical, social and cultural contexts

In this section, we aim to emphasize that new insights about the central role of brain development, particularly since the "neuroscientific turn" (Littlefield and Johnson 2012), require an understanding of the brain as a cultural organ (Kirmayer 2006). In other words, the human brain is the organ of culture which allows us to adapt to varied and demanding social contexts and environments. This emphasis on social and cultural contexts of the developing brain is crucial to understanding a period of development during the lifespan that is as much defined and shaped by social and cultural transitions as it is by biological maturation. When reviewing this active and rapidly expanding body of brain research and applications for adolescents, then, researchers must acknowledge that the characteristics and experience of adolescence are variable and dependent upon the social and cultural environment to a degree that cannot be ignored. While the understanding of the brain as bathed in its environment at multiple levels is increasingly assumed by neuroscientists, recent research (Casey, Galvan, and Somerville 2016) clearly demonstrates that the integral role of the social context is lost in dissemination drives, ignored by policy makers and, at times, insidiously shielded (Fine 2010).

Models described in the growing body of neuroscience research that acknowledge the importance of social context and environment can be taken further by engaging with socio-environmental factors at a more elemental level. Paradigms that subordinate environmental effects to the course of neurological processes should be replaced by models that consider environmental effects as significant and fundamental as biological mechanisms. The intrinsic role of environment in brain development can be demonstrated by advances in epigenetics, which have been especially influential in fueling major shifts in scientific thinking about the relationship between the body and its environment (Szyf 2013). Research on epigenetics has begun to reveal how interactions between the genome and the environment throughout development lead to tissue-specific structural changes in, for example, the DNA methylation patterns that regulate cellular function. There is compelling evidence, for example, that early parenting experiences and social adversity alter the regulation of stress response systems for the life of the organism (McGowan 2013). Such studies provide biological evidence that lived experience, developmental histories, dynamic interactions and cultural contexts are all fundamentally bound up with biological processes as "low level" as gene expression. Through the case of adolescence, we explore the importance of a more integrative approach that considers brain, body and world, in which no process is uni-casual or firmly nested in another, but all equally mold and modify each other and themselves to a significant degree.

The historical construction of adolescence

Explanations that situate brain and cognitive function within the social and cultural environment of the person are increasingly called for from within neuroscience and psychiatry to develop multilevel theories of diseases and their etiologies (Kendler 2008). We add that to situate the brain in its social context, the historical contingencies of categories naturalized by neuroscience must be acknowledged. The category of "adolescence" has a well-documented history. Contrary to the way in which brain science of adolescent development is often interpreted, adolescence is not simply a naturally occurring period of development, or a consequence of brain changes or hormonal transitions. Indeed, it has long been argued by scholars in the humanities that adolescence is a cultural construction (Lesko 1996). There is an extensive sociological literature documenting the social, cultural and economic factors – such as changes in American family life, urbanization, employment changes and the introduction of full-time schooling – that are understood to have shaped the lived experience of adolescence in Western Europe and the USA, and the way in which this period of the lifespan was categorized (Lesko 1996). Concepts of adolescence in popular culture and theories of adolescent behavior in modern science have been characterized by notions of turmoil and a sense of a troubled transition, and likely have their origins in early 20th-century psychological science. Most notably, psychologist G. Stanley Hall popularized the concept of adolescence, putting forth influential theories of adolescence as an inevitable period of "storm and stress".

Researchers have demonstrated that the scientific model of adolescence was imbued with the cultural values of a certain historical moment at the turn of the 20th century. Hall's characterization of adolescence was guided by his evolutionary approach based on Ernst Haeckel's theory of recapitulation, which links stages of individual development to those of species evolution (Choudhury 2010). A popular theory in scientific and sociological discourses at the time, this view assumed that intellectual and moral evolution of individuals and cultures reflect each other, and adolescence as a developmental stage represented the transition from primitive to civilized. Researchers have, therefore, argued that the category of adolescence was a vehicle through which those in power could address their fears surrounding "savages" and the emasculating and de-civilizing influence of "others", including women and colonized peoples (Lesko 1996). In other words, the shaping of "adolescence" as an age category during the early 20th century was deeply contingent on the cultural and socio-economic concerns of the time.

Hall's 1904 book, *Adolescence*, explained that adolescents are driven to be emotionally labile, prone to delinquency, seeking intense sensations, liable to experiment with sex and alcohol, peer-oriented and in constant conflict with parents. These ideas continue to be reproduced in contemporary Western discourse, shaping every stage of scientific practice – from influencing the questions researchers ask to the ways in which researchers interpret results. Neuroscience interprets adolescent behaviors through the "storm and stress" framework and as natural consequences of adolescents' asynchronous brain, cognitive and hormonal development. For example, across the literature concerning risk-taking in adolescence, researchers are often biased to interpret certain behaviors as "risky" rather than considering alternative explanations, like those that posit higher reward-seeking behaviors as more reflective of social rewards and social learning.

Adolescence as a cultural phenomenon

Following the work of Margaret Mead (1928), many anthropologists and psychologists have investigated cultural variances in adolescence, challenging the universal conclusions advanced under neuroscience. Mead, when studying the relatively smooth and problem-free coming-of-age period in Samoa, first argued that "storm and stress" is just a function of certain cultural determinants and does not translate across all cultures. Although neuroscience demonstrates a specific set of neural changes during adolescence, this period is defined by social transitions, beginning with puberty and ending with a stable adult role (Schlegel and Barry 1991). The expression, onset and duration of this period is embedded in cultural definitions of childhood and adulthood, and is dependent on the individual ecology of the young person. For example, studies suggest that psychological turmoil only occurs in cultures where there is an extended gap between childhood and adulthood (Saraswathi 2002). Additionally, ethnographic work has linked longer periods of adolescence to societies whose training for adult roles is more complex (Schlegel and Barry 1991). Further, certain characteristics of adolescence proposed as universal – like youth propensity for risk-taking and its subsequent decline with age – may actually be particular, and subject to the affordances of local environments. A recent paper found that harsher living environments were associated with raised liability for risk-taking and reduced differences for risk-taking between genders and between younger and older individuals (Mata, Josef, and Hertwig 2016).

The interface of history, culture and neuroscience

Despite its historical and cultural shaping, it is generally accepted that adolescence defined as "any social stage intervening between childhood and adulthood in the passage through life" exists as a transitional stage worldwide (Dasen 2000: 25). Anthropologists Schlegel and Barry (1991) have published robust ethnographic evidence of this in an extensive work surveying 175 traditional (pre-industrial) societies, indicating a ubiquitous socially marked stage of adolescence. What, then, is the relevance of the historical and cultural context of adolescence to the neuroscience which demonstrates that a unique stage of brain development occurs during adolescence? Neuroscience's engagement with the adolescent brain assumes universality of findings, and interpretations of results tend to be consistent with this assumption, given that the brain is often believed to confer universality. However, cognitive neuroscience paradigms (including questionnaires and tasks completed in the imaging scanner) are created under the architecture of Western understanding and have largely been administered to, and standardized on, specific groups of participants deemed to represent the "norm". This norm or standard, though, has recently been demonstrated to represent "White, Educated, Industrialized, Rich and Democratic" ("WEIRD") societies (Henrich, Heine, and Norenzayan 2010), even though these groups are frequently unusual and not representative of large-scale human populations.

Similarly, conclusions drawn about adolescence in mainstream developmental psychology and cognitive neuroscience have been extrapolated from very specific samples of teenagers, resulting in the classical "storm and stress" model applicable to certain Euro-American adolescents (Dasen

2000). To illustrate, as of 2015 there exists only one study comparing brain development between Asian and North American youth. The dangers of extrapolating findings across diverse populations is evident from the study's results which reported differences in morphological brain development between the two populations, which could implicate functional differences (Xie et al. 2014).

To integrate findings from neuroscience, psychology and anthropology, and situate the adolescent brain in its environment, it is also important to unearth the relevant meaning of various developmental goals and processes associated with adolescence across cultures. For example, in investigating self-processing, a key interest of cognitive neuroscientists, researchers must consider a culture's definition and experience of self-construal that influences the individual's own understanding and experience of "self" (Ma and Han 2010). The investigation of meaning will help us understand varying first-person experiences of adolescence – for example, how individualistic and collectivist cultures differently experience and value the achievement of "autonomy" (Oyserman, Coon, and Kemmelmeier 2002; see also ch. 10). Several contemporary psychological theories and practices regarding the development and treatment of psychiatric disorders are founded on the assumption of autonomy achievement. For example, researchers have identified individuation and autonomy as critical components in understanding the development of substance-use disorders in teenagers. It is important to explore the role and centrality of autonomy achievement across cultures to understand the relevance of recommended interventions to clinical practitioners that result from such theories.

To make relevant and appropriate conclusions from neuroscientific findings, biological processes in the adolescent brain and body must be explored in relation to the context of the adolescent lifeworld, rather than in isolation. Furthermore, since neuroscientific inquiry has had enormous appeal beyond the laboratory in recent years, and is arguably giving rise to new forms of identity construction and ways of being, it is crucial to critically examine the development of neuroscientific models of categories of people (Hacking 1995). Critical reflection is imperative during the impressionable, plastic period of adolescence, where individuals undergo profound developments in self-concept and, consciously or not, take up and embody popular conceptions linked to the "adolescent brain" (Choudhury, McKinney, and Merten 2012).

Sociocultural and biological forces are inextricably entwined and mutually shape brain development and activity. Many studies demonstrate differences in neural activity across cultures and cultural effects on low-level attentional and perceptual neural processes, like those involved in object recognition, as well as on neural processes involved in high-level cognitive, emotional and social capacities like language, mental attribution and self-awareness (Domínguez Duque et al. 2010). The fundamental influence of context is also highlighted by epidemiological studies, such as the wide body of literature documenting adverse health consequences associated with current and early-life urban living, whereby certain health risks – such as for schizophrenia, which develops in adolescence – increase linearly with the degree of "urbanicity" (Ferranti and Rollins 2017). The environmental and socio-cultural constituents of the urban environment manifest in the brain, illustrated by fMRI studies that demonstrate unique neural social stress processing in individuals who currently reside, or were raised, in cities (Lederbogen et al. 2011). Reductionist accounts of the brain obscure the wider entanglements of biology, environment, culture and history. A critical interdisciplinary approach, however, can situate adolescent behavior and cognition in its ecological niche, and acknowledge the multiple levels at which developmental change is occurring.

Conclusions

The appeal of the neurobiology of adolescent development for translational applications is increasingly evident in areas of education, psychiatry and, though controversial, has been influential at the level of the US Supreme Court in the law (Steinberg 2013). Applications of developmental cognitive neuroscience in society are premised on the finding from non-invasive neuroimaging techniques that middle childhood to late adolescence represents a "sensitive period" of malleability – or neuroplasticity – during which environmental input can have particularly profound effects on development (Ansari, De Smedt, and Grabner 2012).

Despite some neuroscientists' warnings about the swift application of novel brain data to social applications, adolescent brain research is characteristic of a growing relationship between brain science and policy. Brain-based models of adolescence hold enormous appeal to multiple audiences, offering a biological explanation for challenging behaviors, mental disorders and stereotypical propensities. Parents, teachers and psychiatrists may find in these models a physical substrate that provides the hope for opportunities for educative, spiritual and medical remediation, and pre-emptive intervention. Moreover, brain-based models of adolescence provide a substrate that confers a "de-responsibilizing" effect – directing attention to the body of the adolescent rather than the familial, social, cultural or economic context in which she lives (Choudhury and Moses 2016).

The power of the brain-based model of adolescence to stigmatize young people as incomplete, immature or in turmoil, along with researchers' evidence of the dangerously "seductive allure" of neuroscientific explanations (Skolnik-Weisberg et al. 2008), gives reason to turn to approaches that situate the developing brain in its ecological context. Recent trends in cognitive neuroscience suggest that the timing is right to integrate multiple levels of inquiry into investigations and explanations of adolescent behaviors. For example, social neuroscience demonstrates that the human brain is a fundamentally social brain, adapted for social learning, interaction and the transmission of culture (Frith and Frith 2010). Moreover, the brain's structural malleability is understood to be experience-dependent and long-lasting, opening avenues for incorporating the study of the interaction of brain, cognition and environment. A critically oriented cultural neuroscience that is devoted to investigating the brain in the cultural context may represent a corrective to universalizing trend in neuroscience. Whereas mainstream neuroscience often assumes the universality of its findings, cultural neuroscience highlights the idea that cultural and social environments may be a source of variability in the functional architecture and activity of the brain. Some areas of cultural neuroscience draw on the tools of neuroscience in combination with methods in anthropology, to conduct research that takes seriously the notion that human brains are highly responsive to cultural input (Seligman and Brown 2010). Because they allow the collection of real-time data on neural function, as well as ethnographic methods, such techniques represent powerful tools for understanding how brains become encultured (Downey, Lende, and Brains 2012).

The techniques of neuroscience currently have immense rhetorical potency within both scientific and popular contexts. To avoid the pitfalls of neuromythology, a situated view of the adolescent brain studied within a critical neuroscience framework can actively work against pervasive forms of biological reductionism (Kirmayer and Gold 2012).

Note

1 http://www.pbs.org/wgbh/pages/frontline/shows/teenbrain.

References

Ansari, D., De Smedt, B., and Grabner, R. H. 2012. "Neuroeducation: A Critical Overview of an Emerging Field," *Neuroethics* 5(2): 105–117.

Blakemore, S. J., and Choudhury, S. 2006. "Development of the Adolescent Brain: Implications for Executive Function and Social Cognition," *Journal of Child Psychology and Psychiatry* 47(3–4): 296–312.

Blakemore, S. J., and Mills, K. L. 2014. "Is Adolescence a Sensitive Period for Sociocultural Processing?," *Annual Review of Psychology* 65: 187–207.

Brown, M. R. G. et al. 2015. "fMRI Investigation of Response Inhibition, Emotion, Impulsivity, and Clinical High-Risk Behavior in Adolescents," *Frontiers in Systems Neuroscience* 9: 124.

Casey, B. J., Galván, A., and Somerville, L. H. 2016. "Beyond Simple Models of Adolescence to an Integrated Circuit-Based Account: A Commentary," *Developmental Cognitive Neuroscience* 17: 128–130.

Casey, B. J., Getz, S., and Galvan, A. 2008. "The Adolescent Brain," *Developmental Review* 28(1): 62–77.

Choudhury, S. 2010. "Culturing the Adolescent Brain: What Can Neuroscience Learn from Anthropology?," *Social Cognitive and Affective Neuroscience* 5(2–3): 2–3.

Choudhury, S., and Moses, J. M. 2016. "Mindful Interventions: Youth, Poverty, and the Developing Brain," *Theory & Psychology* 26(5): 591–606.

Choudhury, S., McKinney, K. A., and Merten, M. 2012. "Rebelling Against the Brain: Public Engagement with the Neurological Adolescent," *Social Science and Medicine* 74(4): 565–573.

Choudhury, S., and Slaby, J. 2012. *Critical Neuroscience: A Handbook of the Social and Cultural Contexts of Neuroscience*. Chichester: Wiley-Blackwell.

Colbert, E. 2015. "The Terrible Teens," *The New Yorker*, August 31. Retrieved from http://www.newyorker.com/magazine/2015/08/31/the-terrible-teens (last accessed 5 February 2017).

Croarkin, P. E., and Ameis, S. H. 2016. "Editorial: Frontiers in Brain-Based Therapeutic Interventions and Biomarker Research in Child and Adolescent Psychiatry," *Frontiers in Psychiatry* 7: 123.

Dahl, R. E. 2004. "Adolescent Brain Development: A Period of Vulnerabilities and Opportunities," *Annals of the New York Academy of Sciences* 1021(1): 1–22.

Dasen, P. R. 2000. "Rapid Social Change and the Turmoil of Adolescence: A Cross-Cultural Perspective," *International Journal of Group Tensions* 29(1): 17–49.

Domínguez Duque, J. F., Turner, R., Lewis, E. D., and Egan, G. 2010. "Neuroanthropology: A Humanistic Science for the Study of the Culture–Brain Nexus," *Social Cognitive and Affective Neuroscience* 5(2–3): 138–147.

Downey, G., and Lende, D. H. 2012. "Neuroanthropology and the Encultured Brain," in D. H. Lende and G. Downey (eds.), *The Encultured Brain: An Introduction to Neuroanthropology*. Cambridge, MA: MIT Press, pp. 23–66.

Ferranti, N., and Rollins, C. 2017. "Is the Internet a City? Investigating Online and Offline Factors Modulating the Risk of Urban Living for Psychosis-like Symptoms in Healthy Adults," poster presented at the annual conference of the International Congress on Personal Construct Psychology, Montreal, QC.

Fine, C. 2010. *Delusions of Gender: How our Minds, Society, and Neurosexism Create Difference*. New York, NY: W.W. Norton.

Frith, U., and Frith, C. 2010. "The Social Brain: Allowing Humans to Boldly Go Where No Other Species Has Been," *Philosophical Transactions of the Royal Society* 365(1537): 165–176.

Fuhrmann, D., Knoll, L. J., and Blakemore, S. J. 2015. "Adolescence as a Sensitive Period of Brain Development," *Trends in Cognitive Sciences* 19(10): 558–566.

Galvan, A., Hare, T., Voss, H., Glover, G., and Casey, B. J. 2007. "Risk-Taking and the Adolescent Brain: Who is at Risk?," *Developmental Science* 10(2): F8–F14.

Hacking, I. 1995. "The Looping Effects of Human Kinds," in D. Sperber, D. Premack, and A. J. Premack (eds.), *Causal Cognition: A Multidisciplinary Debate*. Oxford: Clarendon Press.

Hall, G. S. 1904. *Adolescence: Its Psychology and its Relations to Physiology, Anthropology, Sociology, Sex, Crime, Religion and Education*. New York: D. Appleton.

Henrich, J., Heine, S. J., and Norenzayan, A. 2010. "The Weirdest People in the World?," *Behavioral and Brain Sciences* 33: 61–83.

Howard-Jones, P. A. 2009. "Skepticism Is Not Enough," *Cortex* 45(4): 550–551.

Huttenlocher, P. R. 1979. "Synaptic Density on Human Frontal Cortex: Developmental Changes and Effects of Aging," *Brain Research* 163(2): 195–205.

Insel, T., and Lieberman, J. 2013. "DSM-5 and RDoC: Shared Interests," *National Institute of Mental Health: Science News* 1–2. Retrieved from http://www.nimh.nih.gov/news/science-news/2013/dsm-5-and-rdoc-shared-interests.shtml (last accessed 10 February 2017).

Kendler, K. S. 2008. "Explanatory Models for Psychiatric Illness," *American Journal of Psychiatry* 165(6): 695–702.

Kirmayer, L. 2006. "Beyond the 'New Cross-Cultural Psychiatry' Cultural Biology: Discursive Psychology and the Ironies of Globalization," *Transcultural Psychiatry* 43(1): 126–144.

Kirmayer, L. J., and Gold, I. 2012. "Re-socializing Psychiatry: Critical Neuroscience and the Limits of Reductionism," in S. Choudhury and J. Slaby (eds.), *Critical Neuroscience: A Handbook of the Social and Cultural Contexts of Neuroscience*. Oxford: Blackwell.

Kuhl, P. K. 2010. "Brain Mechanisms in Early Language Acquisition," *Neuron* 67(5): 713–727.

Lederbogen, F. et al. 2011. "City Living and Urban Upbringing Affect Neural Social Stress Processing in Humans," *Nature* 474(7352): 498–501.

Lesko, N. 1996. "Denaturalizing Adolescence: The Politics of Contemporary Representations," *Youth & Society* 28(2): 139–161.

Littlefield, M. M., and Johnson, J. M. 2012. *The Neuroscientific Turn: Transdisciplinarity in the Age of the Brain*. Ann Arbor, MI: University of Michigan Press.

Ma, Y., and Han, S. 2010. "Why Respond Faster to the Self than Others? An Implicit Positive Association Theory of Self-Advantage During Implicit Face Recognition," *Journal of Experimental Psychology: Human Perception and Performance* 36(3): 619–633.

Mata, R., Josef, A. K., and Hertwig, R. 2016. "Propensity for Risk Taking Across the Life Span and Around the Globe," *Psychological Science* 27(2): 231–243.

Maxwell, B., and Racine, E. 2012. "The Ethics of Neuroeducation: Research, Practice and Policy," *Neuroethics* 1–3.

McGorry, P. D., Purcell, R., Goldstone, S., and Amminger, G. P. 2011. "Age of Onset and Timing of Treatment for Mental and Substance Use Disorders: Implications for Preventive Intervention Strategies and Models of Care," *Current Opinion in Psychiatry* 24(4): 301–306.

McGowan, P. O. 2013. "Epigenomic Mechanisms of Early Adversity and HPA Dysfunction: Considerations for PTSD Research," *Frontiers in Psychiatry* 4: 110.

Mead, M. 1928. *Coming of Age in Samoa; A Psychological Study of Primitive Youth for Western Civilisation*. New York, NY: W. Morrow & Company.

Morgan, N. 2005. Blame My Brain: The Amazing Teenage Brain Revealed. London: Walker.

Nelson, E. E., Jarcho, J. M., and Guyer, A. E. 2016. "Social Re-orientation and Brain Development: An Expanded and Updated View," *Developmental Cognitive Neuroscience* 17: 118–127.

OECD. 2002. *Understanding the Brain: Towards a New Learning Science*. Paris: OECD Publishing.

Oyserman, D., Coon, H., and Kemmelmeier, M. 2002. "Rethinking Individualism and Collectivism: Evaluation of Theoretical Assumptions and Meta-Analyses," *Psychological Bulletin* 128: 3–72.

PBS. 2002. *Inside the Teenage Brain*. Retrieved from http://www.pbs.org/wgbh/pages/frontline/shows/teenbrain (last accessed 22 February 2017).

Pfeifer, J. H., and Allen, N. B. 2016. "The Audacity of Specificity: Moving Adolescent Developmental Neuroscience Towards More Powerful Scientific Paradigms and Translatable Models," *Developmental Cognitive Neuroscience Developmental Cognitive Neuroscience* 17(6): 131–137.

Richards, J. M., Plate, R. C., and Ernst, M. 2013. "A Systematic Review of fMRI Reward Paradigms Used in Studies of Adolescents Vs. Adults: The Impact of Task Design and Implications for Understanding Neurodevelopment," *Neuroscience & Biobehavioral Reviews* 37(5): 976–991.

Rose, S. 2005. *The Future of the Brain: The Promise and Perils of Tomorrow's Neuroscience*. Oxford: Oxford University Press.

Saraswathi, T. S. 2002. "Adult-child Continuity in India: Is Adolescence a Myth or an Emerging Reality?," in T. S. Saraswathi (ed.), *Culture, Socialization and Human Development: Theory, Research, and Applications in India*. New York, NY: SAGE, pp. 213–232.

Schlegel, A., and Barry, H. 1991. *Adolescence: An Anthropological Inquiry*. New York, NY: Free Press.

Seligman, R., and Brown, R. A. 2010. "Theory and Method at the Intersection of Anthropology and Cultural Neuroscience," *Social Cognitive and Affective Neuroscience* 5(2/3): 130–137.

Singh, I. 2008. "Beyond Polemics: Science and Ethics of ADHD," *Nature Reviews Neuroscience* 9(12): 957–964.

Skolnik-Weisberg, D., Keil, F. C., Goodstein, J., Rawson, E., and Gray, J. R. 2008. "The Seductive Allure of Neuroscience Explanations," *Journal of Cognitive Neuroscience* 20(3): 470–477.

Steinberg, L. 2013. "Does Recent Research on Adolescent Brain Development Inform the Mature Minor Doctrine?," *Journal of Medicine and Philosophy* 38(3): 256–267.

Sun, L., Cao, Q., Long, X., Sui, M., Cao, X., Zhu, C., and Wang, Y. 2012. "Abnormal Functional Connectivity Between the Anterior Cingulate and the Default Mode Network in Drug-Naïve Boys with Attention Deficit Hyperactivity Disorder," *Psychiatry Research: Neuroimaging* 201(2): 120–127.

Szyf, M. 2013. "DNA Methylation, Behavior and Early Life Adversity," *Journal of Genetics and Genomics* 40(7): 331–338.

Tamnes, C. K. et al. 2013. "Brain Development and Aging: Overlapping and Unique Patterns of Change," *Neuroimage* 68: 63–74.

Vijayakumar, N. et al. 2016. "Brain Development During Adolescence: A Mixed-Longitudinal Investigation of Cortical Thickness, Surface Area, and Volume," *Human Brain Mapping* 37(6): 2027–2038.

Weber, M. J., and Thompson-Schill, S. L. 2010. "Functional Neuroimaging Can Support Causal Claims About Brain Function," *Journal of Cognitive Neuroscience* 22(11): 2415–2416.

Weisberg, D. S., Keil, F. C., Goodstein, J., Rawson, E., and Gray, J. R. 2008. "The Seductive Allure of Neuroscience Explanations," *Journal of Cognitive Neuroscience* 20(3): 470–477.

Xie, W., Richards, J. E., Lei, D., Lee, K., and Gong, Q. 2014. "Comparison of the Brain Development Trajectory Between Chinese and U.S. Children and Adolescents," *Frontiers in Systems Neuroscience* 8: 249.

Young, A. 2000. "History, Hystery and Psychiatric Styles of Reasoning," in M. Lock et al. (eds.), *Living and Working with the New Medical Technologies*. Cambridge: Cambridge University Press, pp. 135–162.

4
ART AND CREATIVITY

Jonathan Fineberg

Introduction

In 1932, the great Austrian naturalist, Konrad Lorenz, famously described the phenomenon of "imprinting," with an anecdote about incubating mallard eggs. When the eggs hatched, Lorenz explained, he began quacking "in my best Mallardese," and "the little ducks lifted their gaze confidently towards me.... As, still quacking, I drew slowly, away from them, they also set themselves obediently in motion, and scuttled after me in a tightly huddled group" (Lorenz 1952: 40–41). What parent has not observed the imitation and emulation through which children learn language, practical skills, and the norms of social interaction (see also chs. 1, 2)?

At the same time, modern research in early education has taught us not to press children to conform to adult perspectives but rather to cultivate their independence of thought and experimentation. Loris Malaguzzi, 1940s founder of the widely admired pedagogy of the schools of Reggio Emilia, wrote that

> it's necessary that we believe that the child is very intelligent, that the child is strong and beautiful and has very ambitious desires and requests.... Instead of always giving children protection, we need to give them the recognition of their rights and of their strengths.
>
> *(Malaguzzi 1995: 53)*

This polarity in the way we look at children and their art – from a pedagogical perspective or as an expression of creative thought – still frames the way we look at child art today. Yet that division vastly oversimplifies a complex subject. This essay will address the inextricably interwoven threads of thinking about child art that include pedagogy, developmental psychology, formal taxonomy, individual expression, but also the ways in which children actively use art for understanding and responding to the world.

Little ducks – pedagogy and ontogeny

On the one hand, it is the task of childhood to learn the codes of the adult world in order to survive and prosper. The continuing interest in child art from the perspectives of pedagogy and developmental psychology goes back to the sixteenth century. In *Il Cortegiano* of 1528, Conte

Baldessare Castiglione recommends teaching drawing to the young courtier. John Locke (*Some Thoughts Concerning Education*, 1693) and Benjamin Franklin (*Proposals Relating to the Education of Youth in Pensilvania*, 1749) likewise insisted on the teaching of drawing. Jean-Jacques Rousseau advocated teaching the young *Émile* (1762) how to draw in order to see nature more objectively. "Children, who are great imitators, all try to draw. I would want my child to cultivate this art, not precisely for the art itself but for making his eye exact and his hand flexible" (Rousseau 1979: 143).

Influenced by the evolutionary theories of Jean-Baptiste Lamarck (*Philosophie Zoologique*, 1809) and Charles Darwin (*The Origin of Species*, 1859), mid-nineteenth-century writers like Herbert Spencer (*Education*, 1861) began to look at children's drawings from a developmental point of view and in the 1880s the project of systematic classification and study of the motifs in children's art commenced with G. Stanley Hall's book, *The Content of Children's Minds* (1883), and Corrado Ricci's *L'arte dei Bambini* (1887).[1] This literature grew exponentially in the twentieth century in conjunction with developmental psychology.

Child art as a creative response to the world

Among a flurry of studies like Florence Goodenough's (1926) *Measurement of Intelligence by Drawings* (which attempted to do just that) in the 1920s, the work of the Swiss clinical psychologist Jean Piaget stands out for arguing that children generate knowledge and meaning from an interaction between their experiences and their ideas (Piaget 1923; Piaget and Inhelder 1948; see also ch. 1). This approach came to be known as "constructivism." Another exponent of this idea was Rudolf Arnheim, trained in Gestalt psychology while also avidly reading Freud in the 1920s. But Arnheim went further, arguing that art was a form of thinking and that artists (including child artists) articulate their experience in visual terms. He believed that perception itself is a creative process and regarded children's drawings as a means by which children organize their experience to make it comprehensible. "When a child portrays himself as a simple pattern of circles, ovals, and straight lines," Arnheim wrote, "he may do so not because this is all he sees when he looks in a mirror, and not because he is incapable of producing a more faithful picture, but because his simple drawing fulfills all the conditions he expects a picture to meet" (Arnheim 1954: 168; see also Arnheim 2006).

Child art as a cipher

It was the Romantics – poets and artists – who first looked at child art primarily from the point of view of its expressive content, insight, and aesthetic inventiveness. William Blake (*Songs of Innocence*, 1789) was perhaps the first to praise the "innocent" vision of childhood as a model for the artist. William Wordsworth famously declared, "The Child is Father of the Man" (Wordsworth 1984: 246), and he debated with his friend Samuel Taylor Coleridge, "In what sense is a child ... a philosopher? In what sense does he *read* 'the eternal deep'?" (Coleridge 2015: 138). In 1853, Charles Baudelaire admired children's "great capacity for abstraction and their highly imaginative power" (which he contrasted with "the impotent imagination of the blasé public" – Baudelaire 1964: 198).[2] But Baudelaire's romantic concept of the child had less to do with the reality of what children drew than with what the child symbolized for the poet.

Child art as a way of seeing

As early as the fourteenth century, Giovanni Boccaccio (*Decameron*, 1348–53) did look closely enough to note the unique qualities of children's drawings; describing the appearance of a certain family, he refers to "one eye bigger than the other, and there are even a few who have one lower than the other, which all gives them faces like the ones children usually make when they are first learning how to draw" (Boccaccio 1982: 395). Among painters, Hieronymous Bosch, at the end of the fifteenth century, offers an unusually early example of an artist taking inspiration from the morphology of child art, as in the figures he made consisting only of heads and limbs but no trunk (a common trope from child art, given the name "tadpole" (*têtard*) figures by Georges Rouma (1913: 31).[3]

The Swiss artist and educator Rodolphe Töpffer may have been the first to closely study the style of children's drawings, devoting three chapters of his 1848 *Reflections and Remarks of a Genevan Painter* to them (Töpffer 1858: 256–65). Töpffer was groundbreaking in extolling the expressive genius of the art of children and, by implication, he emphasized the centrality of *ideas* in art (and in child art) over technical execution. Academic skills, he thought, had less to do with the artist's mature genius than the guileless expressivity present in childhood. "There is less difference," Töpffer wrote (1858: 262), "between Michelangelo the child scribbler [*gamin griffoneur*] and Michelangelo the immortal artist than between Michelangelo after having become an immortal artist and Michelangelo while still an apprentice," thus de-emphasizing the value of academic training. As Meyer Schapiro pointed out, even such established French critics of the period as Théophile Gautier were intrigued by Töpffer's idea that children's art had the quality, in Gautier's words, of rendering a "thought in a few decisive strokes without losing any of its strength" (Gautier 1856: 130–31; cited in Schapiro 1978: 63).

Nevertheless, most artists before the twentieth century found child art merely a cipher for their own creative impulses or a symbol for innocence. Only a few looked closely at children's drawings *per se*: Pieter Jansz. Saenredam rendered the graffiti on the wall in his 1644 *Interior of the Buurkerck, Utrecht* (National Gallery, London) quite authentically; Sir David Wilkie also produced a persuasively accurate rendering of a child's style in *The Blind Fiddler* (1806, private collection), scratching a cat into the side of the wooden cupboard at the right and pinning another child's drawing on paper just above it. Courbet made a more typical representation of child art in *The Artist's Studio*, where the child stands for the supposed "innocence" of vision in his new style of "realism." He shows a child drawing a stick figure, which is an adult shorthand rather than something children actually draw. The idea of seeing like a child had a direct bearing on Camille Corot's approach to his subject too: "I always entreat the good Lord to give me my childhood back," he confessed, "that is to say, to grant that I may see nature and render it like a child, without prejudice" (Corot 1946: 96; cited in Stuckey 1984: 110). Corot is purported to have saved a body of his own childhood scribbles, which occasioned conversation among the impressionists who also had a particular interest in the issue of naive spontaneity.[4]

The ascendance of empirical observation and spontaneous discovery as values in art reaffirmed the Enlightenment concept of the child's innate objectivity of vision. This idea still lingers behind Monet's late work.[5] In *The Elements of Drawing* (1857), John Ruskin (1903: 194) had advised artists to aspire to what he called the "condition of childhood," which resembles the "state of newness" discussed by Baudelaire, and may have been what Paul Cézanne had in mind too when he told Émile Bernard in 1904, "As for me, I would like to be a child" (Cézanne, no date: 104–105).[6] As Robert Herbert pointed out, Ruskin's "condition of childhood" is what writers in the twentieth century have referred to as "primitivism" (Herbert 1964: vii).

Childhood and authenticity

"Primitivism" offered a purgative for Western culture's materialism and for the *rigor mortis* of its cultural hierarchies. In this regard, the new attraction to child art was a subspecies of primitivism. Another aspect of the primitivism of the late nineteenth century was, as Kirk Varnedoe noted,

> the notion of "the primitive," in the sense of the original, beginning condition or form, [which] preoccupied not only biologists but also social theorists, linguists, and psychologists ... all the various disciplines studied and compared the "primitif," in prehistory, in childhood, and in tribal societies, as evidence for their arguments over man's limitations, potentials, and place in the natural order.
> *(Varnedoe 1984: 181–182)*

Childhood represented the prehistory of the adult and, thus, the child became a kind of domestic Noble Savage. "In order to produce something new," Paul Gauguin (1974: 111) wrote, "one has to return to the original source, to the childhood of mankind," while in his own painting, he said, "I have gone far back, farther back than the horses of the Parthenon ... as far back as the Dada of my babyhood, the good rocking-horse" (Gauguin 1936: 41).[7]

In the 1880s and 1890s, a number of researchers connected child art with tribal art. Alfred Lichtwark (Director of the Hamburg Kunsthalle) linked them in his book, *Die Kunst in der Schule* (*Art in the School*, 1887), probably the first book to do so in a substantive way; James Sully's *Studies of Childhood* (1896) relates children's artistic development to the development of "primitive" peoples; and Carl Götze associated them with one another in his catalogue for an exhibition of free children's drawings for the Kunsthalle in Hamburg in 1898 called *Das Kind Als Künstler* (*The Child as Artist*).[8] In the 1890s, a rapidly escalating number of exhibitions of child art and studies of children's artistic development and production began appearing. In 1890 Alexander Koch, one of the founders of the Jugendstil artist's colony at Darmstadt (Germany), began publication of *Kind und Kunst*, an illustrated journal of art for and by children.

The child as artist

In the 1890s, most of the interest in child art was still anthropological, psychological, or pedagogical in character; but an influential Viennese artist and teacher named Franz Cižek became intrigued with the idea that "Child Art is an art which only the child can produce," (quoted in Viola 1944: 34) and in 1897 he decided to offer "Juvenile Art Classes" with the express purpose of providing children with creative liberty and the chance to work from imagination. Only a few of the investigators studying child art at the time shared Cižek's appreciation for the unique aesthetic of child art in itself. But there were increasing numbers of educators like Ebenezer Cooke, Konrad Lange, Georg Hirth, and Carl Götze who anticipated or confirmed Cižek's belief that art instruction, which encouraged free drawing and imagination, could awaken the creative powers of the child.

Some of the early studies of child art resulted in important collections that were either published or available to be seen in exhibitions. Ricci collected some 1,450 drawings and Georg Kerschensteiner, the superintendent of schools for Munich, gathered nearly half a million of them as a data sample for his book *Die Entwicklung der Zeichnerischen Begabung* [The Development of the Gift of Drawing] (Kerschensteiner 1905). In 1907 the first volume of the Leipzig journal, *Zeitschrift für angewandte Psychologie* [*Journal of Applied Psychology*], was devoted entirely to child art and it cites various collections and exhibitions of child art circulating at the time, including the collections of Dr. Kerschensteiner and that of the historian Karl Lamprecht in Geneva. Cižek also toured an exhibition of his collection. Indeed, there were prominent exhibitions of child art every year in important art centers from the turn of the century to the beginning of World War One.

Artists were increasingly involved in organizing the growing number of exhibitions of child art after the turn of the century while at the same time looking ever more closely at various aspects of how children drew as a stimulus to their own work. For the artists of the twentieth century, a serious interest in the art of children became as remarkably varied and complex from one artist to the next as it was pervasive. Expressionists, Cubists, Futurists, and the artists of the *avant-garde* Russian movements all hung the art of children *as art* alongside their own works in their pioneering exhibitions in the early years of the century: the first room of the 1908 Vienna "Kunstschau" (in which Oskar Kokoschka debuted) was an exhibition of children's art from the classes of Franz Cižek. Alfred Stieglitz organized four exhibitions of children's art at his "291" gallery in New York in the four years from 1912 through 1916; according to a contemporary review in the New York *Evening Sun*, the exhibition of 1912 was the first of its kind in America and it quoted Stieglitz as remarking that the work of these two through eleven-year-olds had "much of the spirit of so-called modern work" (Anonymous 1912: 9).[9] The painter and critic Roger Fry also showed child art at his Omega Workshops in London in 1917 and again in 1919, and in Cologne the 1919 Dada exhibition included child art, African art, and the art of psychotics beside those of Max Ernst and the other Dadaists (noted in MacGregor 1989: 279).

In addition, many of the greatest artists of the twentieth century avidly collected children's art and took, in some instances quite specific, motifs or stylistic ideas from them; Mikhail Larionov, Gabriele Münter, Wassily Kandinsky, Paul Klee, Pablo Picasso, Joan Miró, Jean Dubuffet, and the Cobra artists are leading examples (Fineberg 1997). But artists as far back as Anne-Louis Girodet in the early nineteenth century are reputed to have collected children's drawings (Georgel 1980: 109).[10] Matisse is rumored to have helped in organizing a *salon des enfants* in Paris before the First World War and he had enough interest in the drawings of his thirteen-year-old son Pierre to include one on the wall in the background to his paintings *Woman on a High Stool* and *Still Life with Lemons*, both of 1914 (see Barr 1951: 42, 184; Elderfield 1978: 92–94, 202–203).

On June 7th, 1914, Apollinaire reviewed an exhibition at the Galerie Malpel in Paris of "Dessins d'enfants" in which he particularly praised the work done from imagination by the children (many of whom were the children of artists, including the daughter of Van Dongen). The review concludes with two paragraphs about Matisse. "I remember when Matisse used to show off his children's drawings," Apollinaire wrote, "some of which were really astonishing. Matisse was very much interested in them. 'Nevertheless,' he used to say, 'I don't believe that we should make a lot of fuss about children's drawings, because they don't know what they are doing'" (Apollinaire 1972: 403).

Maybe not, but that did not stop Matisse from using a vocabulary of simplification that was inspired by child art as a lever "to free himself from literal renderings imposed by objects," as Jack Flam described Matisse's concerns of 1906 (Flam 1986: 174). The pivotal works were the two versions of *The Young Sailor* and *The Pink Onions* from the summer of 1906, *Portrait of Marguerite* of 1907, and the 1909 *Portrait of Pierre*. Matisse spent the summer of 1906 in Collioure and he said of himself and Derain that summer, "We were at the time like children in the face of nature and we let our temperaments speak..." (Diehl 1954: 32). Certainly, the recognition of the artistic achievement of child art was widespread in Matisse's generation and, as John Elderfield has argued, "before Fauvism, Matisse had dealt iconographically with the theme of childhood. Now, with Fauvism, he has created a form of painting made as if with the temperament of a child" (Elderfield 1992: 52).

Looking back at the end of his life, Matisse titled his retrospective glance back over his career, "Looking at Life with the Eyes of a Child," and remarked that "the artist ... has to look at everything as though he saw it for the first time: he has to look at life as he did when he was a child and if he loses that faculty, he cannot express himself in an original, that is, a personal way" (Matisse 1954). When Picasso and Matisse decided to trade paintings in 1907, it was the *Portrait of Marguerite* that Picasso selected, explaining:

> I thought it a key picture then, and still do. Critics are always talking about this and that influence on Matisse's work. Well, the influence on Matisse when he painted this work was his children, who had just started to draw. Their naïve drawings fascinated him and completely changed his style. Nobody realizes this, and yet it's one of the keys to Matisse.
> *(Ashton 1972: 164)*

Distinctions between the art of the adult and the child

By World War One, most important artists had come to see the artistic value of child art – Expressionists, Surrealists, the American Abstract Expressionists after World War Two, and most artists since have come to see child art as art (Fineberg 1997). Yet, a debate persists about whether the child's lack of intellectual development or sophistication puts child art in a different category altogether from the work of adults. By the 1950s, the vocabulary of child art and psychoanalytic introspection were so much a part of the common language that this hardly seems remarkable. All this attention to child art has increasingly emphasized the individuality of particular children's styles and the inventiveness of specific works. Yet, as Rudolf Arnheim pointed out,

> a one-sided emphasis on personality factors leads to a misinterpretation of traits that in fact arise from the stage of the child's cognitive development and the properties of the pictorial medium. Conversely, however, an equally one-sided concentration on the cognitive aspects may create the impression that the young organism is occupied with nothing but perceptual and intellectual growth.
> *(Arnheim 1974: 207)*

Finally, Arnheim concluded,

> the child meets the world mainly through the senses of touch and sight, and typically it soon responds by making images of what it perceives.... The picture, far from being a mere imitation of the model, helps to clarify the structure of what is seen. It is an efficient means of orientation in a confusingly organized world.
> *(Arnheim 2006: 20)*

Pablo Picasso speaks of the inventiveness of the young child's drawing as the "genius of childhood," and laments the loss of that "period of marvelous vision" which "disappears without a trace" in adolescence (November 17th, 1943, cited in Brassaï 1967: 86). This struggle to explore and bring coherence to experience is at the core of both children's art and the art of mature artists. In the currently fashionable emphasis on the standardized testing of "skills" we need to take care not to lose the naive freshness and freedom of a child's creative encounter with the world because that too is a survival trait, as recent research in neuroscience has shown (Fineberg 2015: ch. 4). So, is child art really art? Of course. Is it apt to demonstrate the mastery or intellectual sophistication of adult art? No. And don't expect astronomical auction prices either; the market has been flooded.

Notes

1 A detailed chronology of the literature on child art and the history of exhibitions of child art, annotated with summaries and commentary, is contained in Fineberg (2006).
2 See also Baudelaire (1961: 534): "de leur grande faculté d'abstraction et de leur haute puissance imaginative" as contrasted with "impuissante imagination ce public blasé."
3 The literature on Bosch offers no significant discussion of the sources for such images, although "surreal" combinations of human and animal or insect parts occur not only in Bosch and his followers, but earlier in the marginalia of medieval illuminated manuscripts. These too may be informed by childhood fantasy and by dreams.
4 This was reported to me by Dr. Richard Brettell, who said he saw them in the course of his research in Paris.
5 See Perry (1927: 120), cited in Stuckey (1984: 108).
6 "Quant à moi, je veux être un enfant."
7 Vincent van Gogh (1958: 20) reported in a letter to Theo that Gauguin and Bernard talked of "painting like children." Also Dr. Marc Gerstein of the Toledo Museum of Art pointed out to me that Gauguin may have taken inspiration for the geese in the background of his 1886 *Breton Women* from Caldecott's illustrations for children. See Hartrick (1939: 33) for Gauguin's remarks to Hartrick about Caldecott. Nevertheless, child art itself seems not to have influenced him particularly.
8 There is a concise history of the general idea that children resemble primitive peoples in their thought and recapitulate the evolution of the human race in Boas (1966: 60–67).
9 This review is reproduced as a plate in Norman (1960: 116).
10 In addition, Girodet's own childhood drawing of a giraffe survives today in the drawing collection of the Louvre, presumably saved by the artist who, we must conclude, found it interesting enough to save.

References

Anonymous. 1912. "Some Remarkable Work by Very Young Artists," *The Evening Sun* (New York), Saturday, April 27, 1912.
Apollinaire, G. 1972. *Apollinaire on Art: Essays and Reviews, 1902–1918*, ed. L. C. Breunig, trans. S. Suleiman. New York, NY: Viking.
Arnheim, R. 1954. *Art and Visual Perception: A Psychology of the Creative Eye*. Berkeley, CA: University of California Press.
Arnheim, R. 1974. *Art and Visual Perception: A Psychology of the Creative Eye, The New Version*. Berkeley, CA: University of California Press.
Arnheim, R. 2006. "Beginning with the Child," in J. Fineberg (ed.), *When We Were Young: New Perspectives on The Art of the Child*. Berkeley, CA: University of California Press.
Ashton, D. (ed.). 1972. *Picasso on Art*. New York, NY: Viking.
Barr, A. 1951. *Matisse, His Art and His Public*. New York, NY: The Museum of Modern Art.
Baudelaire, C. 1961. *Oeuvres Complètes*. Bruges: Gallimard.
Baudelaire, C. 1964. "A Philosophy of Toys," in *The Painter of Modern Life and Other Essays*, trans. J. Mayne. London: Phaidon.
Boas, G. 1966. *The Cult of Childhood*, vol. 29. London: Studies of the Warburg Institute.
Boccaccio, G. 1982 (1348–1353). *Decameron*, trans. M. Musa and P. Bondanella. New York, NY: New American Library.
Brassaï. 1967. *Picasso & Co*. London: Thames and Hudson.
Cézanne, P. No date. *Souvenirs sur Paul Cézanne*. Paris: Michel, pp. 104–105 (first published in *Mercure de France*, June 1921).
Coleridge, S. T. 2015 (1817). "Biographia Literaria," in J. Engell and W. J. Bate. (eds.), *Collected Works of Samuel Taylor Coleridge, Volume 2*. Princeton, NJ: Princeton University Press.
Corot, C. 1946. *Corot raconté par lui-même et par ses amis, volume I*. Vésenaz and Geneva: Pierre Cailler.
Diehl, G. 1954. *Henri Matisse*. Paris: Pierre Tisné.
Elderfield, J. 1978. *Matisse in the Collection of the Museum of Modern Art*. New York, NY: Museum of Modern Art.
Elderfield, J. 1992. *Henri Matisse: A Retrospective*. New York, NY: The Museum of Modern Art.
Fineberg, J. 1997. *The Innocent Eye: Children's Art and the Modern Artist*. Princeton, NJ: Princeton University Press.

Fineberg, J. 2006. *When We Were Young: New Perspectives on The Art of the Child*. Berkeley, CA: University of California Press.
Fineberg, J. 2015. *Modern Art at the Border of Mind and Brain*. Lincoln, NE: University of Nebraska Press.
Flam, J. 1986. *Matisse: The Man and His Art, 1869–1918*. Ithaca, NY and London: Cornell University Press.
Gauguin, P. 1936. *Intimate Journals*, trans. Van Wyck Brooks. New York, NY: Crown Publishers.
Gauguin, P. 1974 (1895). *L'Echo*; cited in D. Guérin (ed.), *Oviri, écrits d'un sauvage*. Paris: Gallimard.
Gautier, T. 1856. "Du beau dans l'art," *L'art moderne*. Paris.
Georgel, P. 1980. "L'Enfant au Bonhomme," in K. Gallwitz and K. Herding (eds.), *Malerei und Theorie: Das Courbet-Colloquium 1979*. Frankfurt am Main: Städelschen Kunstinstitut.
Goodenough, F. L. 1926. *Measurement of Intelligence by Drawings*. Yonkers-on-Hudson, NY: World Book Co.
Hartrick, A. S. 1939. *A Painter's Pilgrimage Through Fifty Years*. Cambridge: Cambridge University Press.
Herbert, R. L. 1964. "Introduction," in R. L. Herbert (ed.), *The Art Criticism of John Ruskin*. New York, NY: Doubleday.
Kerschensteiner, G. 1905. *Die Entwicklung der Zeichnerischen Begabung*. München: Verlag Carl Gerber.
Lorenz, K. 1952. *King Solomon's Ring: New Light on Animal Ways*, trans. M. K. Wilson. London: Methuen.
MacGregor, J. 1989. *The Discovery of the Art of the Insane*. Princeton, NJ: Princeton University Press.
Malaguzzi, L. 1995. "Your Image of the Child: Where Teaching Begins," *Child Care Information Exchange* 96: 53.
Matisse, H. 1954. "Looking at Life with the Eyes of a Child," *Art News and Review* (London) February 6, 1954.
Norman, D. 1960. *Alfred Stieglitz, An American Seer*. New York, NY: Random House.
Perry, L. C. 1927. "Reminiscences of Claude Monet from 1889 to 1909," *The American Magazine of Art* 18(3) – March.
Piaget, J. 1923. *Le Langage et la pensée chez l'enfant*. Neuchâtel: Delachaux et Niestlé.
Piaget, J., and Inhelder, B. 1948. *La Représentation de l'espace chez l'enfant*. Paris: Presses Universitaires de France.
Rouma, G. 1913. *Le Langage graphique de l'enfant*. Paris: Félix Alcan.
Rousseau, J.-J. 1979. *Émile or on Education*, trans. A. Bloom. New York, NY: Basic Books.
Ruskin, J. 1903 (1849). "The Seven Lamps of Architecture," in E. T. Cook and A. Wedderburn (eds.), *The Works of John Ruskin, Volume 8*. London: George Allen.
Schapiro, M. 1978. "Courbet and Popular Imagery: An Essay on Realism and Naïveté," in M. Schapiro (ed.), *Modern Art: 19th and 20th Centuries*. London: Chatto & Windus, pp. 47–85.
Stuckey, C. F. 1984. "Monet's Art and the Act of Vision," in J. Rewald and F. Weitzenhoffer (eds.), *Aspects of Monet: A Symposium on the Artist's Life and Times*. New York, NY: Harry N. Abrams.
Töpffer, R. 1858. *Réflexions et menus propos d'un peintre génevois*. Paris: L. Hachette.
Van Gogh, V. 1958. *The Complete Letters of Vincent van Gogh*. Greenwich, CT: New York Graphic Society.
Varnedoe, K. 1984. "Gauguin," in W. Rubin (ed.). *"Primitivism" in 20th Century Art*. New York, NY: Museum of Modern Art.
Viola, W. 1944. *Child Art*. Peoria: Chas. A. Bennett Co.
Wordsworth, W. 1984 (1802). "My Heart Leaps Up When I Behold," (also known as "The Rainbow"), in S. Gill (ed.), *William Wordsworth*, The Oxford Authors. New York, NY: Oxford University Press.

5
PHILOSOPHICAL THINKING IN CHILDHOOD

Jana Mohr Lone

Introduction: wondering in childhood

Wondering is a part of life for most children. Fundamentally, wonder is inspired by marvel at being alive in the world. As "a response to the novelty of experience" (Cobb 1993: 28), wonder involves a sense of the mysteries that pervade the human condition and leads to a desire to examine the deeper meaning of ordinary concepts and experiences. Indeed, an essential feature of leading a full and rich life is the ongoing development of our wondering selves, which sustains our appreciation for the partialness of our knowledge and the endless puzzles of existence.

Plato refers to wonder as the origin of philosophy (*Theaetetus*: 155d3). Although it is generally acknowledged that children engage in wondering, adults do not ordinarily consider wondering and reflection about *philosophical* issues as an important aspect of children's lives, at least not before, say, age 11 or 12. This chapter's discussion of children's philosophical thinking will focus on elementary-school-age children, between the ages of 5 and 11.

The chapter will begin by examining whether children are in fact capable of engaging in philosophical inquiry at all, and will analyze the related issue of what it means to do philosophy. We will turn to an exploration of children's philosophical thinking and a look at the epistemic openness, essential to philosophy, which is particularly prevalent in childhood. The value of philosophy for children, both instrumental and intrinsic, will be considered, including an evaluation of the ways that children's voices can enrich the larger conversations of philosophy. The chapter will conclude by discussing the ways that the failure to listen, solely on the basis of age, to children's ideas and questions constitutes a form of epistemic injustice.

Can children do philosophy?

Some philosophers and educators contend that children cannot do philosophy (Hayes 2015, 2014; White 1992; Kitchener 1990). White and Kitchener are skeptical that children are able to engage in what Kitchener describes as the skill of "thinking in a critical, reflective way," which is central to philosophy (Kitchener 1990: 419; White 1992: 74–77). Hayes argues that philosophy classes for children are nothing more than a version of therapy, that it is wrong to suggest that children can do philosophy by just expressing themselves and arguing without studying the work of professional philosophers, and that children have nothing of interest to say about philosophical issues (Hayes 2014); he further asserts that philosophy in schools is not "real" philosophy: "Childish whining is not philosophy; reading books, even difficult ones, and then having proper classroom chats about them is" (Hayes 2015). In general, critics of attempts to introduce philosophy to children point to children's lack of the necessary cognitive skills for doing so and the dissimilarities between what children do when confronted with philosophical questions, and the work of professional philosophers (that is, children talk about philosophical questions without reference to professional philosophers, while philosophers generally do so through an engagement with the work of classic and/or contemporary philosophers).

One of the central issues here is what it means to "do philosophy." There is no clear and settled definition of philosophy as a discipline. Typically, people start by noting that the word "philosophy" comes from the Greek, meaning "love of wisdom." In ancient times, philosophy was understood as the search for wisdom. Of course, what wisdom means is itself a philosophical issue. Wilson suggests that philosophy is "something like 'the investigation of concepts, categories and distinctions via the meaning of words'" and claims that philosophical inquiry must always focus on "concepts and meaning" (Wilson 1992: 18). Kitchener states that doing philosophy requires thinking in a critical, reflective way about some philosophical issue, and that learning philosophy is "a way of life." He contends:

> Philosophy as a way of life includes much more than merely being able to think critically: it means, *inter alia*, thinking about a philosophical issue (e.g., free-will vs. determinism), it means raising philosophical questions and being puzzled by things ordinarily taken for granted, it means assimilating or appropriating the historical tradition of philosophy by reading the great philosophers, it means constructing arguments in support of certain kinds of conclusions, it means engaging in various kinds of conversations about philosophy, it means being bitten by the philosophy bug so that one can not give up philosophizing, etc. When we ask whether someone outside our way of life is doing philosophy, e.g., a child, the answer is: the more closely they share these various features, the more we are inclined to say they are philosophers.
>
> *(Kitchener 1990: 425)*

White and Kitchener claim that the available evidence of children's philosophical abilities and understanding is inconclusive; 25 years later, however, there is abundant evidence that elementary-school-age children do many of the things Kitchener lists as essential to philosophy: they raise philosophical questions, are puzzled by the underlying meaning of everyday concepts and things normally taken for granted, and engage in conversations about philosophical topics (Lone 2012; McCall 2009; Haynes 2008; Matthews 1994).

Children's philosophical thinking

Children start to think about philosophical questions "because they find the grappling with basic facts fascinating in itself and because it gives order and unity to their world" (Opdal 2001: 334). Most adults, and particularly parents and teachers of young children, are aware that even very young children ask large questions (What is fairness? Are colors real? What makes something true?). Lone and Burroughs write:

> The practice of philosophy begins with persons asking and seeking answers to fundamental questions pertaining to meaning, knowledge, truth, and values that, in some

form and at some time, most of us entertain. For many children, asking these kinds of questions constitutes part of their exploration of the world around them. Children do not engage in philosophical questioning with the goal of production (of a publication, presentation, etc.) or only as they enter a designated space (the philosophy conference, university classroom, etc.).

(Lone and Burroughs 2016: 9)

During early childhood, most children are wide open to the mysteries that pervade human life, and are curious about the most basic frameworks of human experience, including such subjects as the meaning of being alive, the complexity of identity, the nature of friendship and love, how to live good lives, and whether we can know anything at all. The most unexceptional experiences give rise to the experience of discovering things about which to wonder and question in everyday life.

Aristotle noted, "All human beings by nature reach out for understanding" (*Metaphysics*: 980a21). Children's early questions about human existence and the nature of reality mark the beginning of the "philosophical self": the part of us that recognizes many of the basic facets of our own existence as deeply puzzling.[1] The philosophical self is fascinated by the perplexities at the heart of everyday life and the deeper meaning of the ordinary concepts we use, and is manifested in the propensity to ask searching questions about them. We traditionally recognize as important the development of children's physical selves, intellectual selves, moral selves, and social and emotional selves, but there is little attention paid to the cultivation of the philosophical self. Consequently, this aspect of most children's lives remains undeveloped. Children absorb the message that the concrete details of life are more important than intellectual abstractions and that there is no time for philosophical thinking, that these kinds of questions are trivial (or too difficult) and will get us nowhere, or that religion can answer them all for us. This is a loss.

Matthews writes eloquently about the ways adults frequently fail to perceive what he calls the "moments of pure reflection in children's thinking" (Matthews 1984: 52). He recounts the experience of his college student's conversation with a seven-year-old boy, Michael, about one of C. S. Lewis' *Narnia* stories. In the conversation, Michael describes his worry about the possibility that the universe is infinite. Responding to a question about why this is important, Michael replies, "It's nice to know you're *here*. It is not nice to know about nothing. I hope [the universe] doesn't go on and on forever. I don't like the idea of it going on forever because it's obvious it can't be anywhere" (Matthews 1980: 34–35). Michael demonstrates a lucid awareness of the philosophical puzzles raised by the possibility that the universe is infinite. Some adults might respond by imagining that Michael must be an unusual child. Maybe so. But the work of those engaged in the pre-college philosophy field around the world indicate that many children reflect about these kinds of questions quite spontaneously, beginning early in their lives.

White asserts, however, that having thoughts about matters such as infinity does not constitute engaging in philosophizing, which, he claims, requires "some kind of conceptual conflict" (White 1992: 80). He argues that when a child asks questions about a concept, such as whether an apple is alive, the child is "simply on the way to acquiring the concept" and is not expressing a conceptual conflict; unlike philosophers, who "have no trouble using it," and are interested in "mapping it from a higher-order perspective," children are really just expressing the need to "know how to use the concept" (White 1992: 75–76). This claim, however, is inconsistent with many philosophers' experiences doing philosophy with children – children as young as age six – who ask questions about concepts they use frequently and easily, such as the mind, thoughts, time, nothing, etc., with the goal of investigating (and not just learning how to use) these concepts (see, for example, Lone 2012: 45–57, 74–76). Lone and Burroughs write:

> None of this is to say that we should make no distinction between the activities of professional philosophers and children. Both parties practice philosophy for very different reasons, and the former—given their development, education, and training—are capable of engaging in philosophical questioning in a particularly rigorous and systematic fashion. We can draw a distinction between professional philosophers and philosophical children, but this distinction should not center on a conception of philosophy as the sole province of (adult) professional philosophers. To be sure, children do not generally write philosophical treatises or present work at conferences, but they certainly *do* engage in the practice of philosophy for the same reasons that serve as the motivation for most philosophical work. Further, they engage in this practice with a direct interest in the questions themselves, without being restricted by the traditional norms of academic philosophy. Indeed, professional philosophers would do well to emulate children's openness and playful embrace of philosophical questioning that transcends rigid disciplinary boundaries.
> *(Lone and Burroughs 2016: 10)*

Children's questioning can constitute the most primary of philosophical activities: reflecting about the meaning of the most ordinary of experiences and concepts in order to develop understanding.

Murris, in her response to White and Kitchener, maintains that what is important is that children "discuss the kinds of problems and raise the kinds of questions academic philosophers are puzzled about *when they have just started* doing philosophy," and that even if it is the case that young children just starting out in philosophy are less capable than adults just starting out in the field, this should not lead to the conclusion that children can't do philosophy or that it should not be introduced to them (Murris 2000). She notes, for example, that we don't believe that children should not be taught history because they are not able to do so as skillfully as professional historians or undergraduate history students. Likewise, with art, literature, and science. Murris points to philosopher Mary Midgley's comments:

> Of course children's arguments are not the same as the discussions of university students. But then neither is a child's eager participation when his or her parents are mending the garage just like the work which that child may do later as an engineering student. In both, what matters is to pick up the general spirit of such activities, to start seeing them as interesting and possible. And if one does not do this as a child, it is much harder to do it later. Philosophy has never been a quarantined enclave for professionals, any more than literature has, and it would die if it were to become so.
> *(Midgley 1996: 14)*

The skills essential for philosophical thinking take time and practice to cultivate, and the fact that children are beginners does not establish that they are unable to develop these skills. As Lipman notes in his 1990 response to Kitchener,

> When children play sandlot baseball, they play it as skillfully as they can and they adhere to the rules of the game. That they follow the rules is sufficient to make them baseball players: they do not have to play the game expertly. It seems to me it would

be lacking in a philosophical sense of proportion to deny that they are playing baseball simply because they are not Babe Ruths. I do not make the claim that children are "natural philosophers": that was Kohlberg's claim. I merely say that many adults are capable of doing philosophy, and so are many children, that some adults are capable of doing it well and that some children are likewise.

(Lipman 1990: 432)

Not every child (or undergraduate philosophy major, for that matter) is going to become a professional philosopher. Kitchener contends that "[t]he difference between children and adults a propos learning philosophy is that adults make philosophy an essential part of their lives: they have been taught a form of life" (Kitchener 1990: 425). However, not all adults who engage in philosophy make philosophy "an essential part of their lives" – this might be a necessary condition of becoming a professional philosopher, but it seems counterintuitive to think that it is a necessary condition of doing philosophy at all. Children's early forays into philosophical thinking generally reflect their status as novices in philosophical practice, but their newness to the enterprise also entails an openness to imagining a wide range of possibilities in thinking about philosophical problems – what Matthews characterizes as "fresh and inventive" thinking (Matthews 1994: 18).

Epistemic openness

"Philosophical inquiry is, at its best, an adventure in making life whole."

Robert Johann

For children (and ideally for adults as well), the examination of philosophical ideas is both a serious activity and a playful one, merging wonder, imagination, questioning, and reflection. In a conversation with a group of second-grade students (ages seven and eight) a couple of years ago, for example, the students, inspired by our reading of Dr. Seuss' *The Lorax*, began wondering about the main character's invention of a new tool. "It is possible," they wanted to know, "to have an entirely new idea?" This led to a conversation about imagination.

> "What is imagination?" asked a child. "Where does it come from?"
> "I think we're born with it," responded another child. "And I think that we don't have the same amount of it always. Children have more imagination than adults."
> All of the children seemed to agree.

"I think that children don't know as many things about the world," a child reflected, "and so our minds are more free to imagine things."[2]

Are children freer to imagine things? Children do seem in general to be more open than adults to the kind of playfulness with ideas that is important to philosophical inquiry – that is, they are not just more open in the sense of being less self-conscious than adults, but they are more *epistemically open* as well.[3] Epistemic openness involves two connected and essential orientations toward philosophical questions.

First, epistemic openness involves a kind of epistemological modesty – an acknowledgement that all of us are fallible and, therefore, hold views that could end up being mistaken. This entails a comfort with uncertainty, with the possibility that we might not "have all the answers," and a willingness to change our minds if persuaded to do so. Philosophical exploration involves openness to ideas that might run contrary to our ingrained thinking. Unburdened by an expansive set of assumptions about what they already know and expectations that things just *are* a particular way, children generally exemplify such openness. They tend to be much less certain than adults that they have, or should have, the answers to many of their questions, and their openness stems in large part from their comfort with questioning and with trying out ideas, without fear of seeming unintelligent or strange. Children are often prepared to look squarely and unblinkingly at what they observe and to jump candidly into exploration of difficult questions without allegiance to particular points of view.

Second, epistemic openness entails a willingness to entertain unfamiliar (and sometimes uncomfortable and perhaps seemingly strange) possibilities. Central to this is the cultivation of a flexibility of mind, in which new ideas are welcome and the potential for changing one's views is understood as part of the enterprise. We are willing to consider ideas that seem at first glance unlikely, if there are good reasons offered in support of them, and able to appreciate being introduced to perspectives very different from our own. Engaging in philosophical inquiry requires one to suspend, at least to some extent, one's beliefs, and to take seriously the idea that things might not be what they seem. This requires that we are willing to consider scenarios that seem unlikely, given our actual experiences, and are flexible in our ability to envision possible worlds very different from the way it seems to us that things are, in order to explore fully a particular question or problem in a way that makes space for what Matthews called the "free exploration of possibilities."

For example, in a fourth-grade philosophy session, students were exploring a question one of them raised: "Does everything have a right to live?" Most of the children responded initially that they thought that everything did have a right to life, and the conversation led to a discussion of whether people have a greater right to life than other living beings.

"We think that people are the most important," suggested a student, "but that's just because we're people."

"I agree," said another student. "You always see things from your own perspective. I mean, mosquitoes probably think they're the most important beings on the planet. Imagine living on a planet where we were tiny and there were these giant mosquitoes that were constantly swatting at us whenever we got near them. We wouldn't think that just because we were smaller and less powerful, that the giant mosquitoes had more of a right to life than we did."

"What you think about which creatures are the most important," responded a third student, "really depends on your attachments. We think people, and dogs and cats and other pets, are more important than mosquitoes, but that's just because we have relationships with them. If someone had a mosquito for a pet, they would probably see it differently."[4]

Children bring to philosophy a willingness to entertain a wide range of questions and possibilities, some of which most adults would rule out as farfetched and unworthy of attention. Perhaps it is in part the importance of pretending in childhood – the constant trying out of identities, whether it be superheroes, real-life adult roles such as teachers, firefighters, professional athletes, etc., or characters from books and films – that accounts for the ease with which children play with philosophical ideas. Children transform objects, play the roles of people other than themselves, act out stories in picture books, create voices for inanimate objects, and engage in various other forms of individual and shared pretend play. As Alison Gopnik notes, pretending engages children in considering possibilities, and not just actualities (Gopnik 2009: 19–31). Make-believe play involves receptiveness to the possibility that things are different than the way they seem to us, a willingness to try out things that might appear strange and unlikely (making friends with a dinosaur or fighting a battle against aliens), and to suspend one's ordinary understanding of our experiences in order to imagine unfamiliar ways of seeing. Gopnik points out that "[i]n their pretend play, young children explore the magic of human possibility in a particularly wide-ranging and creative way," as their "liberation from mundane cares lets them move into the world of the possible with particular ease" (Gopnik 2009: 240). Pretend play supports children's tendencies to question and experiment, supporting the development of epistemic openness.

Moreover, involvement in shared pretend play gives children, among other things, opportunities to communicate meaning, to negotiate control over content, and to develop relationships and trust. The trying on of identities and roles entails a vulnerability to others. Children must trust that those around them will collaborate in protecting their imaginative constructs, while allowing them to experiment with changing and, eventually, abandoning them. The creation of an imaginative world exposes a child's inner thoughts and desires, and children's fearlessness about such exposure helps set the stage for their amenability to sharing their questions and ideas relatively unreservedly in philosophical discussions. We are vulnerable when we express our ideas with the possibility of them being called into question, when we respond to another's views and risk a critical reaction, and when we share our thoughts without worrying about making a mistake or sounding silly or unsophisticated.

Philosopher John Wall suggests that vulnerability involves "an openness and relationality to the world" (Wall 2010: 39). In other words, by engaging with others, we open ourselves to being changed by them. We respond to each other's ideas and questions in a philosophy session and the encounter then shapes our thinking and perspectives. We become vulnerable, then, when we honestly express what we think and believe, and when we risk having to defend our views or acknowledge our unexamined assumptions. Children, perhaps because they are more accustomed than adults are to being in positions in which they are vulnerable, tend to be more comfortable with the vulnerability that ensues when they freely express their thoughts and questions. What an adult might describe as children's ignorance becomes, in philosophical conversations, an imaginative willingness to look with fresh eyes at difficult questions, without assuming they do or should know the answers.

The value of philosophy for children

Philosophy is both instrumentally and intrinsically valuable for children. Engaging in philosophical inquiry is instrumentally valuable in that it strengthens critical and analytic thinking skills, and also helps young people gain confidence in expressing their own views and articulating the reasons for them. Hundreds of pre-college philosophy programs have been established at universities and colleges, and many studies over the past 20 years have evaluated the effects of elementary school philosophy classes (Colom et al. 2014: 50–56).[5] In 2007, Keith Topping and Steven Trickey, in a series of studies in Scotland, found that 10- to 12-year-old students who participated in one hour of weekly philosophical discussion over 16 months improved their verbal, non-verbal, and quantitative scores on the widely respected Cognitive Abilities Test (CAT3, 2001) by an average of 7 points, compared to a control group whose scores remained steady. The researchers further found that gains made during the initial 16-month study continued in the experimental group two years after the sessions had stopped, while the scores of the control group marginally declined, and analysis of video recordings and student questionnaires administered seven months into the study revealed increased participation, better behavior, and self-reports of greater confidence, empathy, and control (Topping and Trickey 2007a: 271–88; 2007b: 787–96; Trickey and Topping 2007: 23–34).

Philosophers and educators all over the world are engaged in facilitating philosophical inquiry with children, and the field is growing rapidly. Exploring philosophical questions fosters the emergence of a critical consciousness about the way things are. The capacities cultivated by philosophy, analytic, and critical thinking are essential for contemporary life. Because philosophy focuses on the assumptions that underlie our thinking and behavior and involves questions that cannot be settled in a final way, it helps children learn to evaluate claims based on reason and analysis, rather than on fixed beliefs and prejudice. As Bertrand Russell remarks, "philosophy can give certain things that will greatly increase the student's value as a human being and as a citizen" (Russell 1950: 47). Engaging in thinking about philosophical questions with children encourages them to continue to cultivate their sense of wonder as well as an appreciation for the general tentativeness of most knowledge claims.

Philosophy with children is also of intrinsic value, in at least two distinct ways. First, because the contribution of children's voices to the questions of philosophy can broaden our understanding of these questions and the possible responses to them, children have much to contribute to philosophy, as the perspectives of children are very different from those of adults. Childhood is more than the stage of "adults in training." Every stage of life has its own point of view, and cannot just be reduced to preparation for the stages that follow. Because children are newer to the world, and the nature of childhood involves a particular set of experiences (for example, going to school, new sibling relationships, first friends, early identity formation, etc.), children often see the world differently from most adults. Gopnik points to children's unique capacities to experience awe, their appreciation for the "richness and complexity of the universe outside our own immediate concerns," and their imaginative awareness of "possible worlds beyond the world we know" (Gopnik 2009: 239), and she contends that "[t]he sense of magical possibility that is so vivid in children is also at the root of much that is real and important about our lives" (Gopnik 2009: 241). This sense of "magical possibility" and the insights of childhood are often lost when adulthood is reached. Although we were all once children, the feelings and experiences of childhood often fade with time. Listening to children can provide adults with access to children's perspectives, which can enlarge and expand our own thinking. As Matthews observes:

> Children are people, fully worthy of both the moral and intellectual respect due persons. They should be respected for what they are, as well as for what they can become. Indeed, we can learn from them and let them enrich our lives as, much more obviously, they learn from us and let us enrich their lives. The parent or teacher who is open to the perspectives of children and to their forms of sensibility is blessed with gifts that adult life otherwise lacks.
>
> *(Matthews 1994: 122–23)*

Indeed, if we take children seriously, and accord their ideas and views genuine attention, their contributions have the potential to enhance and expand our collective conversations on many subjects, including social inequalities, justice and fairness, friendship, and our moral obligations to each other, to animals (see ch. 25), and to the environment.

Second, philosophy is intrinsically valuable for children because it enhances the experience of childhood. Thinking about large philosophical issues with children involves appreciating their attempts to attain understanding and intellectual self-determination, and evaluating the ideas they suggest with the same respect accorded adult reflection. This involves taking children seriously *as children*; not pretending that children are adults, but acknowledging that children's ideas and the perspectives that emerge from childhood are worthy of attention and consideration, and not discounting what they have to say simply because they are young. Children's philosophical thinking can be appreciated in and for itself; indeed, as Matthews notes, for many people, who will not become professional philosophers, the philosophy of their childhoods is the best philosophical thinking they will ever do (Matthews 1994: 123). He speculates that:

> Perhaps it is because so much emphasis has been placed on the development of children's abilities, especially their cognitive abilities, that we automatically assume their thinking is primitive and in need of being developed toward an adult norm. What we take to be primitive, however, may actually be more openly reflective than the adult norm we set as the goal of education. By filtering the child's remarks through our developmental assumptions we avoid having to take seriously the philosophy in those remarks; in that way we also avoid taking the child and the child's point of view with either the seriousness or the playfulness they deserve.
>
> *(Matthews 1984: 52–53)*

When we dismiss children's attempts to participate in philosophical inquiry without any attempt to appreciate the meaning of and value in their remarks and questions, we undermine their nascent efforts to convey knowledge and make sense of their own experiences (see ch. 1). Children's voices often remain unheard, not because the content of what they have to say is insignificant, but simply because they are children. To take children's ideas and questions seriously involves addressing the epistemic injustice that children often experience.

Epistemic injustice

Almost all of the work in academic philosophy on epistemic injustice focuses on race and gender (Fricker 2007; Anderson 2012; Dotson 2011). Recently, though, some philosophical work has begun to focus on epistemic injustice towards children, on the ways in which children's abilities to convey knowledge to others and to make sense of their own experiences can be undermined by child-focused prejudice (Murris 2013; Lone and Burroughs 2016). Murris describes how what Fricker calls the "credibility deficit," where prejudice against some aspect of a speaker's identity leads to listeners deflating their assessment of the speaker's credibility (Fricker 2007: 17–29), operates with regard to age: the fact of being of a particular age in itself leads to the speaker being less (or more) likely to be believed.

Children are often not believed or listened to *just because* of their status as children – they are viewed as more likely not to be telling the truth, as having immature (and thus unimportant) perspectives, or as irrational and/or cute little beings who are not to be taken seriously (Murris 2013: 248–49). Moreover, of course, there are particular forms of epistemic injustice that are experienced, for example, by children of color, children from low-income backgrounds, and girls from all races and backgrounds, who face even greater obstacles than children generally when they attempt to articulate the way they see the world. Although an extensive treatment of epistemic injustice on the basis of age is outside this chapter's scope, it is important to note that epistemic injustice undermines children's abilities to see themselves as unique thinkers who are sources of valuable knowledge. Ultimately, adult refusal to see children as knowers in their own right can result in children's diminished confidence in both their abilities to make sense of their experiences and the value of their own perspectives and judgments.

All of us were once children, and children grow up; age – unlike, for the most part, gender, race, and ethnicity – is an ever-changing condition. The argument might be made, therefore, that discounting children's speech based on age does not constitute epistemic injustice, because this dynamic will dissipate and eventually disappear as children mature. There are, however, at least two objections to this argument. First, it is crucial for children to be able to express their attempts to make sense of their experiences, and for these attempts to be heard and accorded respect – at home, in schools, and in everyday interactions with adults – in order for children to develop confidence in and skill at expressing their own perspectives. Second, the credibility deficit experienced by children results in a lack of access by adults to important sources of knowledge and new perspectives. As discussed earlier in this chapter, children are generally more open to imagining new possibilities and less committed to fixed views about the world, and the perspectives that emerge from the earliest stages of life can help all of us to think about philosophical questions – about justice, ethics, friendship, etc. – in new and fresh ways.

Conclusion

Children can and do engage in philosophical inquiry. Children's epistemic openness and abilities to contribute unique insights to philosophy make the involvement of children in philosophical conversations important for children as well as for adults and the discipline in general. In a time where professional philosophy continues to grow increasingly narrow and specialized, attentiveness to and encouragement of children's inclinations toward philosophical inquiry can help to broaden the boundaries of the philosophical landscape and enlarge our conversations about philosophical topics. Paying attention to children's philosophical engagement can contribute to the ongoing effort to release philosophy from the margins of societal discourse and raise awareness about what a philosophical approach can offer to our combined thinking about ethics, social and political problems, and other important issues.

Notes

1. I do not intend, by using the phrase "the philosophical self," to posit the existence of multiple selves; I simply mean the philosophical aspect of the self, in much the same way we might refer to the "artistic self."
2. Second-grade class, John Muir Elementary School, Seattle, Washington, fall 2013.
3. I am indebted to Norvin Richards for his remarks in a 2014 American Philosophical Association "Author Meets Critics" session about my book *The Philosophical Child*, which stimulated my thinking about this point.
4. Fourth-grade class, Whittier Elementary School, Seattle, Washington, winter 2013.
5. A compilation of many of the studies that have been conducted about the impact of pre-college philosophy can be found at: https://docs.google.com/document/d/1n41h2pqe4dTb3Ek41NfZv2WAC_LUZH_buQoFYyRzyg0/edit?usp=sharing

References

Anderson, E. 2012. "Epistemic Justice as a Virtue of Social Institutions," *Social Epistemology: A Journal of Knowledge, Culture and Policy* 26(2): 163–173.
Cobb, E. 1993. *The Ecology of Imagination in Childhood*. Dallas, TX: Spring.
Colom, R., Moriyón, F. G., Magro, C., and Morilla, E. 2014. "The Long-term Impact of Philosophy for Children: A Longitudinal Study (Preliminary Results)," *Analytic Teaching and Philosophical Praxis* 35(1): 50–56.
Dotson, K. 2011. "Tracking Epistemic Violence, Tracking Practices of Silencing," *Hypatia: A Journal of Feminist Philosophy* 26(2): 236–257.
Fricker, M. 2007. *Epistemic Injustice: Power & the Ethics of Knowing*. Oxford: Oxford University Press.
Gopnik, A. 2009. *The Philosophical Baby*. New York, NY: Farrar Straus and Giroux.
Hayes, D. 2014. "Can Kids Do Kant?," *The Conversation*. Retrieved from https://theconversation.com/can-kids-do-kant-22623 (last accessed 30 June 2017).

Hayes, D. 2015. "'Philosophy for Children' Isn't Real Philosophy," *Spiked*. Retrieved from http://www.spiked-online.com/newsite/article/philosophy-for-children-isnt-real-philosophy/17193 (last accessed 30 June 2017).

Haynes, J. 2008. *Children as Philosophers*. London: Routledge.

Kitchener, R. 1990. "Do Children Think Philosophically?" *Metaphilosophy* 21(4): 416–431.

Lipman, M. 1990. "Response to Professor Kitchener," *Metaphilosophy* 21(4): 432–433.

Lone, J. M. 2012. *The Philosophical Child*. New York, NY: Rowman & Littlefield.

Lone, J. M., and Burroughs, M. (eds.). 2016. *Philosophy in Education: Questioning and Dialogue in Schools*. New York: Rowman & Littlefield.

Matthews, G. 1980. *Philosophy and the Young Child*. Cambridge, MA: Harvard University Press.

Matthews, G. 1984. *Dialogues with Children*. Cambridge, MA: Harvard University Press.

Matthews, G. 1994. *Philosophy of Childhood*. Cambridge, MA: Harvard University Press.

McCall, C. 2009. *Transforming Thinking*. London: Routledge.

Midgley, M. 1996. "Letter to Editor," *The Guardian*, 18 June, p. 14.

Murris, K. 2000. "Can Children Do Philosophy?" *Journal of Philosophy of Education* 34(2): 261–279.

Murris, K. 2013. "The Epistemic Challenge of Hearing Child's Voice," *Studies in Philosophy and Education* 32: 245–259.

Opdal, P. M. 2001. "Curiosity, Wonder and Education Seen as Perspective Development," *Studies in Philosophy and Education* 20: 331–344.

Russell, B. 1950. "Philosophy for Laymen", in his *Unpopular Essays*. London: George Allen & Unwin.

Topping, K. J., and Trickey, S. 2007a. "Collaborative Philosophical Enquiry for School Children: Cognitive Effects at 10–12 Years," *British Journal of Educational Psychology* 77: 271–288.

Topping, K. J., and Trickey, S. 2007b. "Collaborative Philosophical Inquiry for School Children: Cognitive Gains at 2-Year Follow-Up," *British Journal of Educational Psychology* 77: 787–796.

Trickey, S., and Topping, K. J. 2007. "Collaborative Philosophical Enquiry for School Children: Participant Evaluation at 11 Years," *Thinking: The Journal of Philosophy for Children* 18(3): 23–34.

Wall, J. 2010. *Ethics in Light of Childhood*. Washington, DC: Georgetown University Press.

White, J. 1992. "The Roots of Philosophy" in A. Phillips Griffiths (ed.), *The Impulse to Philosophize*. Cambridge: Cambridge University Press, pp. 73–88.

Wilson, J. 1992. "Philosophy for Children: A Note of Warning," *Thinking: The Journal of Philosophy for Children* 10(1): 17–18.

PART II

Childhood and moral status

6
THE MORAL STATUS OF CHILDREN

Agnieszka Jaworska and Julie Tannenbaum

Introduction

At the most general level, an entity is said to have moral status if and only if it or its interest matters morally for its own sake, rather than for the sake of some other entity or value. A pebble on the beach is itself of no moral concern whatsoever, while (at least some) human beings and non-human animals, or at any rate their interests, matter morally, and we regulate our actions morally for their sake. Clarity about the moral status of children is particularly important because children cannot on their own effectively secure appropriate moral recognition from others.

Broadly speaking, there are two schools of thought about the nature of moral status. On one side, Utilitarians take moral status to be a matter of whether or not one's interests are included in the utilitarian calculus (e.g., Singer 1993). Individuals matter morally to the extent that their interests must be taken into consideration in deciding which action has the overall best consequences.

On the opposing side are philosophers who think of moral status in terms of reasons to attend to the entity and its interests for the entity's own sake, even when doing so runs counter to maximizing the good and minimizing the bad. When one acts contrary to what such reasons dictate, all things considered, one wrongs the entity. We owe it to the entity to treat it in certain ways.[1]

Does moral status come in degrees? For the Utilitarians, the answer is no. For every entity that has moral status, its interests must be factored into the moral calculus in the same way – that is, proportionately to the degree to which these interests are impacted. Some non-utilitarian philosophers who think of moral status instead in terms of duties and rights owed to an entity nevertheless agree that all beings with moral status have equal status (see ch. 9). Such non-utilitarian "one status" views can have diametrically opposed accounts of the qualifications for moral status. Kant (1998), for example, holds that autonomy, a sophisticated capacity, is the necessary and sufficient qualification for moral status, while philosophers associated with the animal rights movement (e.g., Regan 2004) tend to propose rather minimal qualifications for moral status. But both Kant and Regan nonetheless emphasize equal status for all those who qualify for moral status.

However, some non-utilitarian philosophers reject the "one status" view, introducing degrees of moral status. One set of influential views focuses on separating out the highest degree of status, often called "full moral status" or FMS (e.g., Warren 1997), which roughly corresponds to the status at issue for "one status" non-utilitarians. While characterizations of FMS differ, their common key element is a claim-right not to be killed, which powerfully protects a being with FMS against, among other things, the detrimental effects of others acting on the basis of utilitarian calculations. There is a threshold for qualifying for FMS and all beings who meet this threshold (e.g., by having a certain capacity, belonging to a species, etc.) have this status equally, regardless of how robustly they instantiate the relevant feature. Moreover, there is no higher moral status than FMS; so, having additional relevant features does not enhance one's moral status. Lesser degrees of moral status are often left unelaborated.[2]

A second distinctive approach to degrees of moral status eschews that there is anything such as FMS: there is neither an upper limit to one's degree of moral status nor are the qualifications for moral status threshold in nature. Arneson (1999), for example, tightly connects one's degree of moral status to one's capacities in two ways: the degree of moral status is determined by both how advanced one's capacities are and how well one can exercise those capacities.

This chapter will focus on FMS. After giving a fuller picture of what FMS involves, we will critically review the competing accounts of what qualifies an entity for FMS. The accounts range from the demanding (cognitive sophistication), which exclude many children, to the very simple ("experiencing subject of a life"), which put children morally on a par with most animals. We end with our own account, which attempts to rectify a variety of problems with the competing accounts, especially with respect to the moral status of children.

What full moral status (FMS) involves

As we already mentioned, the common key element of various characterizations of FMS is a claim-right not to be killed.[3] An entity's claim-right not to be Φ-ed may be thought of as a powerful protection against reasons someone might otherwise have to Φ. The right altogether removes the force of some such reasons and outweighs others. For example, monetary gain, no matter how large, is altogether banned as a consideration in favor of killing an entity with FMS, while many utilitarian considerations, such as saving several equally valuable lives, are outweighed by the right not to be killed. The protection, while establishing a high justificatory bar, is nonetheless not absolute: it can be outweighed in some contexts, for example, perhaps when killing one to save the entire human race.

While some discussions of FMS focus exclusively on the claim-right not to be killed, we side with those (e.g., Warren 1997: 13) who broaden the scope of FMS to include additional claim-rights, such as a claim-right not to be forced into medical experimentation and a claim-right not to be severely harmed (physically, psychologically, etc.; this encompasses the right not to be tortured). While there are differences in the kinds of considerations that can outweigh one or another of these claim-rights, a distinctive feature of all these rights is that a utilitarian net gain of benefits over harms is insufficient to outweigh them.[4]

As we see it, the scope of FMS is yet broader, involving two elements beyond claim-rights. The first is a strengthening of reasons to provide aid to the being in question: other factors being equal, there is a stronger reason to aid beings with FMS than those who have lesser or no moral status (e.g., Jaworska 2007a and Quinn 1984,[5] in contrast to McMahan 2002: 223–224). The second is a strong reason to be treated fairly (Broome 1990–1991; Jaworska 2007a).

FMS includes neither other kinds of rights and reasons that can be generated – for example, via contract – nor protection from being treated paternalistically.[6] Hence, questions about how much latitude children should be given to decide their own affairs, etc. are not at issue here.

Qualifications for full moral status (FMS)

In the following sections, we survey the main accounts of what qualifies individuals for FMS and their implications for the moral status of children. On all accounts, some children have FMS, but there is disagreement on whether all children have FMS, and if not, when children acquire FMS in the course of development and whether some cognitively disabled children lack FMS.

We critique the accounts, partly based on their failures to accord with what we call "the commonsense view." By "commonsense view" we mean the view that, by and large, human beings have FMS and a higher moral status than that of chickens or dogs. That is, whether a human being is severely cognitively (i.e., intellectually or emotionally) impaired[7] or not, whether it is an adult or child (infant to teenager), that human has FMS. The commonsense view takes no stand on the moral status of human fetuses, humans incapable of consciousness, or sophisticated animals like great apes.

The commonsense view is currently widely accepted by non-philosophers, but providing a successful philosophical justification for it is difficult, as our survey will show. Consequently, some philosophers have questioned or even abandoned this view. However, we believe that our own account (incomplete realizations of sophisticated cognitive capacities account) makes significant progress toward vindicating the commonsense view.

Sophisticated cognitive capacities accounts

According to this type of account, an entity has FMS if and only if that entity possesses certain cognitive, very sophisticated capacities. A range of cognitive capacities, not all equally sophisticated, has been suggested as the key to FMS. Kantians single out the capacity for autonomy, often understood in terms of setting ends via practical reasoning (Kant 1998: 434, 436, Prussian Academy pagination). Others propose less demanding cognitive capacities, such as self-awareness (McMahan 2002: 45, 242), the capacity to care, understood as a sophisticated emotional capacity (Jaworska 2007a), etc.[8] Though such capacities are less sophisticated than autonomy, they are nevertheless sufficiently complex that most animals lack them. Thus, without arbitrarily privileging humans (anthropocentrism), such accounts accord with a key part of the commonsense view that elevates the moral status of you and me above that of a dog.

The age at which unimpaired children come under the protections of FMS will vary from one account to another, since the various sophisticated capacities mentioned above emerge at different stages of human development. Children might not acquire autonomy until teenage years (for a discussion, see Schapiro 1999; also ch. 10), but the less demanding capacities, such as the minimal capacity for self-awareness and the capacity to care, tend to emerge early on in childhood (around the age of 18 months; see Rochat 2003; Jaworska 2007b). Nonetheless, on all these accounts, infants and younger pre-toddlers fail to meet the necessary condition(s) for FMS since all the relevant cognitive sophistication is lacking this early in human development.

Moreover, many cognitively impaired children will fail to meet the necessary condition(s) for FMS even if they are older than the ages indicated above. In some cases, impairment delays the development of the specific capacity required by an account, and so such children would lack FMS until they are much older. For example, mild autism delays the development of self-awareness and mild Down's syndrome delays the development of the capacity for autonomy. In other cases, the impairment prevents the child from ever acquiring the relevant capacity, as illustrated by Ashley, the "pillow-angel" whose development mysteriously arrested at the level of a six-month-old baby (Gunther and Diekema 2006).

On "one status" versions of these accounts, any children who do not qualify for FMS would altogether lack moral status – starkly at odds with the commonsense view. For those who allow instead that moral status comes in degrees, it is at least possible that these children would possess a lesser moral status.[9]

The fact that not all children are granted FMS by these accounts is already a shortcoming from the commonsense perspective. But furthermore, these accounts also exclude some adults from FMS, also contrary to the commonsense view. For every proposed cognitively sophisticated capacity there are cognitively impaired adult human beings who lack it, and thus they would not fall under the protections of FMS. Granted, any of these accounts might offer only a sufficient condition for FMS, leaving open alternative routes to FMS. But until these routes are specified, the moral status of these adults and many children is left unaccounted for and possibly on a par with that of chickens and dogs.[10]

Capacity to develop sophisticated cognitive capacities accounts

Many challenges facing the previous accounts can be avoided while retaining cognitive sophistication as the ultimate ground of FMS via the following modification: sophisticated cognitive capacities *or* the capacity to develop these sophisticated capacities (without losing one's identity) are necessary and sufficient for FMS. This is usually labeled the "potential" account in the literature (e.g., Stone 1987), although some authors sidestep this terminology, and speak, for example, of the wrongness of killing due to the loss of a "future like ours" (Marquis 1989, 1995).[11]

These potentiality accounts, like the previous accounts, avoid anthropocentrism while still denying that most animals have FMS. Moreover, unlike the previous accounts, potentiality accounts come closer to capturing the commonsense view by holding that all unimpaired children, whether infants or ten-year-olds, would have FMS, as would any child (or adult) whose impairment delays but does not preclude the development of sophisticated cognitive capacities.[12]

There is a possible downside to relying on potential cognitive capacity as a sufficient qualification for FMS. Feinberg (1980: 193) argues that just as a potential US president lacks any right to command the military, potentially cognitively sophisticated beings also lack the rights associated with FMS. While this particular analogy has been contested (Wilkins 1993: 126–127; Boonin 2003: 46–49), alternative analogies make the same point. Children (potential adults) lack the rights of adults to own property (Boonin 2003: 48) or to vote (regardless of any benefit to them). Thus, potentiality for X does not generally qualify one for the same rights as actual possession of X.

A further key problem with potentiality accounts is that by treating cognitive capacity or its potential as necessary for FMS, they are still underinclusive from the commonsense perspective. Even if it could be argued (somehow) that adults with lapsed sophisticated cognitive capacities nevertheless retain FMS, the moral status of severely, permanently, cognitively impaired humans who *never* had sophisticated cognitive capacities would remain unaccounted for.

Rudimentary cognitive capacities accounts

In order to mitigate the problems of underinclusion and avoid issues of appealing to potentiality, one could make the necessary and sufficient qualifications for FMS much more cognitively basic. Some accounts, such as Regan's (2004) "experiencing subject of a life", propose cognitive capacities that appear to be so rudimentary that all unimpaired children, including infants, would qualify, as would many severely cognitively impaired children and adults. Similarly, some Kantians claim that respecting rational nature entails respecting beings that have only parts of rational nature or necessary conditions of it (Wood 1998: 197).[13]

On closer inspection though, at least for Regan's view, some problems of underinclusion remain. Regan himself defines "experiencing subjects of a life" as individuals who have

> beliefs and desires; perception, memory, and a sense of... their own future; an emotional life together with feelings of pleasure and pain; preference- and welfare-interests; the ability to initiate action in pursuit of their desires and goals; a psychophysical identity over time; and an individual welfare in the sense that their experiental [sic] life fares ill or well for them.
>
> (Regan 2004: 243)

He does not think that human infants meet these qualifications (Regan 2004: 319).

Notwithstanding this underinclusiveness of Regan's account, all rudimentary cognitive capacities accounts introduce new problems of overinclusion from the commonsense perspective. A one-year-old is an "experiencing subject of a life" in Regan's sense, but so is a cat. If we interpret Regan's phrase in a yet more rudimentary sense, then a newborn would qualify, but so would a chicken and perhaps even a snake. Whatever these rudimentary accounts gain in inclusiveness of human beings comes at the price of putting the moral status of more and more animals on a par with that of humans (see ch. 25).[14]

Regan and others happily reject the commonsense inferiority of animals' status but still wish to avoid the counterintuitiveness of, for example, the moral permission to flip a coin when choosing to throw off a hamster or an infant of an overcrowded lifeboat. They claim that even if two beings' rights are equal, when these rights conflict, differences in the interests impacted can justify differential treatment. What unimpaired humans (whether adult, child, or infant) stand to lose in being killed, due to their current or future cognitive sophistication, is much weightier than what a hamster would lose, and thus human welfare interests are weightier (Rachels 1990: 189; Regan 2004: 304, 324; DeGrazia 1996). Nonetheless, the problem remains of accounting for the differential treatment of both conscious humans with severe irreversible cognitive impairments and infants who will die due to disease before acquiring cognitive sophistication, as compared with many animals (e.g., a hamster), since here the affected welfare interests are similar.[15]

Member of cognitively sophisticated species accounts

All the aforementioned problems with the previous accounts can be avoided by positing membership in a cognitively sophisticated species as a sufficient qualification for FMS (Cohen 1986; possibly Scanlon 1998: 185–86; Finnis 1995).[16] Some authors discuss a narrower view, focused on membership in the human species (Benn 1967: 69–71), while others fail to distinguish between the narrower and broader version (Dworkin 1993, ch. 3, though Feinberg 1980 clearly distinguishes them). Because reserving FMS for the members of the human species is unacceptably anthropocentric and arbitrary, and the broader view introduces no new shortcomings, we will concentrate on the broader view.

Given that there could be cognitively sophisticated individuals, deserving moral recognition, who are outliers in their less cognitively sophisticated species (e.g., a genius parrot), this account should be disjunctive (*pace* Benn 1967): (a) having sophisticated cognitive capacities or (b) belonging to a cognitively sophisticated species is necessary and sufficient for FMS. Though disjunctive, this account is unified since both sufficient conditions ultimately appeal to the value of cognitively sophisticated capacities. In virtue of the sufficiency of (b), FMS is established for all children, including infants, regardless of their cognitive impairments. Likewise for adults. In virtue of the necessity of (a) or (b), most animals lack FMS. Thus, this account fully matches the commonsense view.

Nonetheless, such sophisticated-species-membership accounts have a serious shortcoming. Biological criteria – whom one can mate with, whom one is born of, or having the relevant DNA – determine whether one belongs to a given species. But these biological criteria cannot plausibly ground moral status. Although the human species is characterized partly by morally relevant properties such as sophisticated intellectual and emotional capacities, and not merely by biological criteria (e.g., mating abilities), the species membership criteria are purely biological. So, a token member of a species can lack all the morally relevant capacities that characterize the species. If membership in the type does not require any of the morally relevant features, how can this membership be morally relevant at all, let alone ground FMS (Feinberg 1980: 193; Sumner 1981: 97–101; McMahan 2002: 212–214, 216)?

Little (2008) suggests that being a human being is sufficient for FMS, where the membership criteria, partially following Quinn (1984), are not merely biological: one must belong to the human species *and* have the capacity to learn (Little 2008: 340). This view excludes children and adults incapable of learning and still retains the problem of arbitrariness since the morally irrelevant, merely biological feature of species membership makes a difference to moral status.

Even if the relevant criterion for FMS is membership in a cognitively sophisticated *kind*, instead of a cognitively sophisticated *biological species*, such a view faces a dilemma: either being cognitively sophisticated at some point in one's life is required for membership in the kind or not; if it is, the view excludes many severely cognitively impaired human beings; if it is not, why is this membership relevant for FMS?

Special relationship accounts

There are other accounts that invoke species membership and, thus, are easily confused with the species-membership accounts discussed in the previous section. However, these are in fact special relationship accounts that take an altogether different approach: it is *being in a relationship* with a member of one's own species that is key. On such accounts, only those moral agents who stand in this relationship to an individual owe that individual the forms of treatment associated with FMS (e.g., a duty not to kill the individual, etc.). These accounts draw on the observation that other relationships (social, etc.) generate special duties and rights. For example, the parental relationship gives the parent an especially strong reason not to kill and to aid his child. A relationship of co-membership in a species is, analogously, seen as grounding the forms of moral treatment associated with FMS (Nozick 1997; Kittay 2005: 124; and possibly Scanlon 1998: 185).

Species-based relationship accounts comprehensively cover children, since all children, regardless of their cognitive capacities, are members of the human species and are thereby in relationships with other human agents. Indeed, species-relationship accounts fully accord with the commonsense view, paralleling the species-membership accounts.[17] However, unlike the species-membership accounts, species-relationship accounts rest moral treatment on a recognizable morally relevant criterion – relationships – and not on morally irrelevant criteria (i.e., biological criteria of group membership). In fact, this is an advantage of all special relationships accounts.

Another type of special relationship account does not treat the relationship itself as a qualification for FMS, but rather as an enhancer of moral status. So, for example, one might treat sentience as necessary and sufficient for having some moral status, but this status is elevated to treatment associated with FMS from those moral agents who are in a special relationship with the being. Another variant treats having welfare, which needn't require sentience, as granting some moral status, and the special relationship that enhances this status is not species co-membership but rather "human community" co-membership, where the latter requires not only biological features but also the capacity to learn (see Quinn's discussion of the "morality of humanity" 1984: 50–54 in combination with 32–33). This variant excludes children incapable of learning, and to this extent departs from the commonsense view.

All the special relationship accounts discussed so far seem to stretch the notion of a relationship that is a meaningful ground of special forms of treatment beyond recognition. Are we really in any kind of relationship with all other humans just in virtue of our common humanity (understood at least in part biologically)? Some "enhancer" special relationship accounts avoid this problem: they appeal to more recognizable relationships. For example, in Steinbock's view, B being A's child constitutes a special relationship that enhances B's status with respect to A and anyone else who stands in a relationship with A as a fellow moral agent (Steinbock 1992: 9, 13, 69–70).

The crucial problem with all special relationships accounts, including Steinbock's, is that they do not truly deliver an account of moral status. Moral status generates impartial reasons, which are reasons for every moral agent. A being has moral status only if every moral agent, human and non-human alike, must show that being the relevant moral regard. On special relationship accounts, by contrast, only those moral agents who are in the special relationship with the being have, for example, a stringent reason not to kill the being (McMahan 2002: 222). This problem is easiest to see with species-relationship accounts. For example, all human moral agents are in a species-based special relationship with a human infant and, as a result, have a stringent reason not to kill the infant. But were there a Martian moral agent, she would not have this reason, since she and the human infant would lack this special relationship.[18]

It may seem that the special relationships approach can escape this problem by delineating the relevant interrelated community just right, such that all the moral agents would be included – for example, the community of all members of cognitively sophisticated species. This variant (or an "enhancer" version of it) might achieve the desired extension of who can claim the treatment associated with FMS from whom. But, in addition to again stretching the notion of a relationship beyond recognition, the reasons stemming from any special relationship remain partial, and hence cannot be the kind of (impartial) reasons constitutive of moral status. A father, for example, has a reason not to kill his child stemming from the parental relationship, but this mustn't be confused with his impartial reason not to kill it.

Incomplete realizations of sophisticated cognitive capacities account

While cognitively sophisticated capacities are the right kind of qualification for FMS, they leave out many beings that common sense tells us should be covered, including temporarily and permanently undeveloped children. But lowering the bar for FMS leads to overinclusion, treating children on a par with hamsters and rabbits. And other criteria are of questionable moral relevance (potentiality, membership in biologically defined species) or do not secure *impartial* moral status (special relationships).

To overcome this impasse, we have put forth a proposal that turns on the idea that cognitively sophisticated capacities can have incomplete realizations. If any of the cognitively sophisticated capacities discussed earlier justify a being's higher moral status compared to those beings lacking such sophistication, then so too the capacity to incompletely realize that same cognitive sophistication justifies a being's higher moral status. We will first address how one incompletely realizes a cognitively sophisticated *activity* before turning to incompletely realized *capacities*.

The basic thought is that even the early and clumsy steps that model a sophisticated skill – the first stages of "learning by doing" – qualify as incomplete realizations of the modeled sophisticated activities so long as they are guided by someone's end of completely realizing that skill (and certain further conditions are met). Put more precisely, we claim that a rearee (most commonly, a child) incompletely realizes a cognitively sophisticated activity in the context of a relationship with a rearer (most commonly, a parent) when:[19]

(a) The rearee's activities are guided (at least in part) by a rearer's end (end-aim or end-standard) of the rearee being able to fully master the sophisticated activity while remaining the same individual.
(b) The rearee's activities model the sophisticated activity.
(c) The rearer succeeds in making a sufficiently robust connection between the rearee's activities and the end in (a), which occurs if and only if:
(c-1) the choice of the end in (a) and of the rearee's activities as a means to this end (or the next best end-aim in the case of end-standards) is minimally reasonable;
(c-2) the rearee's activities are feasible means of achieving the end in (a) (or the next best end-aim for end-standards).

As it turns out, many activities of children who are not yet cognitively sophisticated meet these conditions, while no hamsters' or rabbits' activities do. The children's activities are directed, reasonably and feasibly, by the parents' (or other caregivers') end of transforming the child into a cognitively sophisticated being. What looks like mere peek-a-boo becomes simple rule-following as an early lesson in acting for reasons; what looks like mere cuddling becomes an emerging form of emotional attachment as an early lesson in caring for others. They are immature instances of what a mature person does. One cannot direct the activities of a rabbit in this way, however much one may try, because the end of developing the rabbit into a cognitively sophisticated being can never meet the feasibility constraint (c-2).

What about the activities of human beings who have no chance of developing sophisticated cognitive capacities? The end of turning these beings into sophisticated reasoners, carers, etc. is neither reasonable nor feasible as an aim, whether because of severe disability or a fatal disease that will cut their development short. Nonetheless, they can meet the above conditions via a different route. Caregivers of these human beings are required to adopt the end of their charges' flourishing, which (in most, if not all, cases[20]) includes their developing sophisticated cognitive capacities. This end, held as a standard, rather than an aim, that is, as a guide to determining what to aim at (Jaworska and Tannenbaum 2014: 259–262), would be reasonable for any caregiver. If, guided by this standard, the caregiver adopts a reasonable and feasible second-best aim, he can meet condition (c) above (Jaworska and Tannenbaum 2014: 264–267). This cannot be done with a rabbit because cognitive sophistication is not part of the rabbit's flourishing, so it would not be reasonable to hold cognitive sophistication as a standard in taking care of rabbits.

Notice that condition (b) imposes an important limit on which activities count as incomplete realizations of cognitively sophisticated activities. The activities must model in a primitive way the cognitively sophisticated activity in question. The age at which unimpaired children become capable of such modeling will vary depending on which kind of cognitive sophistication turns out to be relevant. We do not take a stand on this, but if the relevant sophisticated cognitive capacity is the capacity to reason practically, then a premature infant (or a severely disabled child or adult) may not be able to do anything that counts, even when subsumed under a parent's end, as an early lesson in rule-following and acting for reasons. By contrast, if the relevant sophisticated cognitive capacity is the capacity to care, then cuddling with an infant, when subsumed under the rearer's end, is as an early lesson in attachment and caring for others.

Thus far, we have focused on what an incompletely realized cognitively sophisticated *activity* is, which requires not only being in a relationship but also activity of both parties in the relationship. But it is crucial to emphasize that what matters on our account is whether the underdeveloped individual has the capacity (not merely the capacity for a capacity, that is, potentiality) to perform incompletely realized, cognitively sophisticated activities. An individual has this capacity regardless of whether the individual has exercised this capacity, and even if no adult is in a rearing relationship with that individual. It is because someone could reasonably (and feasibly for end-aims) subsume that individual's nascent activities under the end of turning her into a cognitively mature person, that she *currently* has the relevant capacity. It is the individual herself who currently has this capacity, just as it is the individual herself who currently has the capacity to play a tennis match (though this requires that someone could play with her). Hence, in spite of the relational element in our account, the account yields impartial reasons for moral regard, and even in cases with no established relationship (Jaworska and Tannenbaum 2014: 256–257). Note that ours is not a potentiality account, not only because it covers those who lack the potential for cognitive sophistication, but also because what matters is not the promise for what one will be able to do in the future, but rather what one can do now.

The strength of our account lies in its ability to escape all the main pitfalls of the existing accounts: (1) our account covers underdeveloped impaired and unimpaired humans, including children, without extending coverage to animals that seem cognitively similar; (2) it appeals to (versions of) the capacities that are widely recognized as morally relevant in grounding FMS; and (3) it grounds impartial moral reasons. Nonetheless, our account has an important limitation. We only explain why underdeveloped human beings, such as children, have higher moral status than those beings who lack the relevant cognitively sophisticated capacity or its incomplete realization. We do not establish that this higher status reaches the level of FMS and, thus, that moral agents have the full set of duties and reasons to not kill, aid, and treat these beings fairly of the strength articulated in the first section.

Conclusion

The first five accounts of FMS that we canvassed in the previous section lead to the following stalemate: cognitively sophisticated capacities seem to be qualifications of the right type for FMS, but they leave out many beings that common sense tells us should be covered, including children who currently or permanently lack the relevant cognitive sophistication. Solutions proposed to cover some or perhaps even all of these beings, including children, come with serious problems of their own. Lowering the bar for FMS to lesser cognitive sophistication lets in too many beings that should not be covered, treating children on a par with animals such as hamsters and rabbits. And the proposals for additional sufficient qualifications for FMS either turn out to appeal to criteria of questionable moral relevance (potentiality, membership in biologically defined species) or do not even secure *impartial* moral status (special relationships). Our account – the last put forward in the previous section – points to a way out of this stalemate. For any cognitively sophisticated capacities (discussed previously, under 'Sophisticated cognitive capacities accounts') that justify a being's higher moral status, so too does the capacity to incompletely realize that same cognitive sophistication.

Notes

1 The chief difference between these two approaches can also be characterized in the following way: an entity matters because its interests matter or have value (utilitarian) versus an entity's interests matter because the entity matters or has inherent value or worth (non-utilitarian).
2 Interestingly, McMahan (2002) abandons the non-utilitarian conception when it comes to lesser degrees of moral status. For alternative approaches, see Jaworska and Tannenbaum (2013).

3 For a discussion of claims-rights, see Joel Feinberg (1970). While neither Feinberg (1980) nor Thomson (1971) use the terminology of FMS, they invoke the concept in discussing the right not to be killed.
4 Some writers use "inviolability" as an umbrella term for the claim-rights associated with FMS (e.g., McMahan 2008: 98).
5 Without explicitly mentioning "moral status," Quinn clearly invokes the notion: he speaks of "rights of respect" which are "obligations owed *to* individuals and not merely obligations to act in various ways with respect to individuals" (1984: 49, italics in original).
6 Autonomy is typically held to be necessary for protection from paternalism, but not necessary for FMS on many views; hence, FMS does not entail protection from paternalism. (For paternalism, see ch. 11.)
7 As we construe it, this term excludes those incapable of consciousness.
8 Feinberg's (1980: 197) more demanding account combines the above with yet more intellectual and emotional capacities.
9 Keep in mind that, for all accounts we will discuss that are underinclusive in who they deem to have FMS, the excluded individuals might have either lesser degrees of moral status or no status.
10 One can acknowledge, nevertheless, strong reasons not to kill human beings who are cognitively underdeveloped or impaired: it would negatively impact their family members, and perhaps also the killers, etc. But these kinds of reasons have nothing to do with the underdeveloped and impaired individuals' moral status, since they are not reasons for their own sake (Feinberg 1980: 198; McMahan 2002: 232).
11 "Potentiality" refers only to a capacity to develop a capacity (e.g., one-month-olds have the potentiality to speak but not the capacity to speak, whereas we have the capacity to speak).
12 Some or all infants would be left out in the following minority views of potential: (1) unimpaired infants who will die as infants lack the relevant potential (Harman 1999: 311); (2) loss of potential is morally problematic only if the individual is sufficiently psychologically connected to the future person that would realize this potential (McInerney 1990).
13 As noted in the introduction, Utilitarians reject the notion of FMS and instead propose qualifications (often rudimentary, such as the capacity of sentience) for being included in the utilitarian calculus.
14 O'Neill (1998) offers additional critiques of the Kantian version of the approach.
15 Boonin (2003) defends having the conjunction of "a future-like-ours" (a kind of potentiality) and "actual conscious desires that can be satisfied only if [one's] personal future is preserved" as sufficient for FMS (Boonin 2003: 84). This view conjoins a potentiality account with a rudimentary cognitive capacity account, and may avoid some problems of each. But a problem shared by potentiality accounts and rudimentary cognitive capacity accounts remains: Boonin is unclear on which cognitively impaired human beings have a future-like-ours; but whether they have FMS or not, their status must be on a par with that of animals with similar prospects.
16 This approach is often implicit; for example, Korsgaard (2004) regards infants and severely cognitive impaired human beings as rational agents – presumably in the sense of being members of the kind "rational agents" – and, hence, deserving of respect.
17 Just as with species-membership accounts, the most plausible version of species-relationship accounts would be disjunctive, adding sophisticated cognitive capacities as a second sufficient qualification for FMS. These disjunctive accounts, however, lack unity because they offer two unconnected routes to FMS. Note that disjunctive versions of species-membership accounts and species-relationship accounts handle some individuals (unsophisticated members of non-human cognitively sophisticated species) quite differently.
18 Warren (1997) allows that a sophisticated cognitive capacity is sufficient for FMS, but suggests further, "That [an organism] is [1] a sentient human being and [2] a member of a human social community is also sufficient to establish that it has basic rights" (p. 176). [1] raises the problem we discussed with species-membership accounts, and adding [2] cannot secure the inclusion of those infants and severely, permanently cognitively impaired children and adults who are not currently socializing with humans. In addition, does one who meets both conditions have rights only with respect to those in the human social community (in which case, this is not an account that generates impartial reasons) or with respect to all moral agents (in which case, how can being in a human social relationship ground impartial moral status)?
19 Jaworska and Tannenbaum (2014: 254–255; see also 249, 264–266).
20 See Jaworska and Tannenbaum (2014: 262–263) and Jaworska and Tannenbaum (2015: section III).

References

Arneson, R. J. 1999. "What, If Anything, Renders All Humans Morally Equal?" in D. Jamieson (ed.), *Singer and His Critics*. Oxford: Blackwell.
Benn, S. 1967. "Egalitarianism and Equal Consideration of Interests," in J. R. Pennock and J. Chapman (eds.), *Nomos IX: Equality*. New York, NY: Atherton Press.
Boonin, D. 2003. *In Defense of Abortion*. Cambridge: Cambridge University Press.
Broome, J. 1990–1991. "Fairness," *Proceedings of the Aristotelian Society* 91: 87–101.
Cohen, C. 1986. "The Case for the Use of Animals in Biomedical Research," *New England Journal of Medicine* 315: 865–870.
DeGrazia, D. 1996. *Taking Animals Seriously: Mental Life and Moral Status*. Cambridge: Cambridge University Press.
Dworkin, R. 1993. *Life's Dominion: An Argument about Abortion, Euthanasia, and Individual Freedom*. New York, NY: Vintage Books.
Feinberg, J. 1970. "The Nature and Value of Rights," *The Journal of Value Inquiry* 4: 243–257.
Feinberg, J. 1980. "Abortion," in T. Regan (ed.), *Matters of Life and Death*. Philadelphia, PA: Temple University Press.
Finnis, J. 1995. "The Fragile Case for Euthanasia: A Reply to John Harris," in J. Keown (ed.), *Euthanasia Examined*. Cambridge: Cambridge University Press.
Gunther, D., and Diekema, D. 2006. "Attenuating Growth in Children with Profound Developmental Disability," *Archives of Pediatrics and Adolescent Medicine* 160: 1013–1017.
Harman, E. 1999. "Creation Ethics: The Moral Status of Early Fetuses and the Ethics of Abortion," *Philosophy and Public Affairs* 28: 310–324.
Jaworska, A. 2007a. "Caring and Full Moral Standing," *Ethics* 117: 460–497.
Jaworska, A. 2007b. "Caring and Internality," *Philosophy and Phenomenological Research* 74: 529–568.
Jaworska, A., and Tannenbaum, J. 2013. "The Grounds of Moral Status," in E. N. Zalta (ed.), *The Stanford Encyclopedia of Philosophy*. Retrieved from http://plato.stanford.edu/archives/sum2013/entries/grounds-moral-status/ (last accessed 16 March 2018).
Jaworska, A., and Tannenbaum, J. 2014. "Person-Rearing Relationships as a Key to Higher Moral Status," *Ethics* 124: 242–271.
Jaworska, A., and Tannenbaum, J. 2015. "Who Has the Capacity to Participate as a Rearee in a Person-Rearing Relationship?" *Ethics* 125: 1096–1113.
Kant, I. 1998 (orig. 1785). *Groundwork of the Metaphysics of Morals*, trans. M. Gregor. Cambridge: Cambridge University Press.
Kittay, E. F. 2005. "At the Margins of Moral Personhood," *Ethics* 116: 100–131.
Korsgaard, C. 2004. "Fellow Creatures: Kantian Ethics and Our Duties to Animals," in G. B. Peterson (ed.), *The Tanner Lectures on Human Values*, Volume 25/26. Salt Lake City, UT: University of Utah Press.
Little, M. 2008. "Abortion and the Margins of Personhood," *Rutgers Law Journal* 39: 331–348.
Marquis, D. 1989. "Why Abortion is Immoral," *The Journal of Philosophy* 86: 183–202.
Marquis, D. 1995. "Fetuses, Futures, and Values: A Reply to Shirley," *Southwest Philosophy Review* 6: 263–5.
McInerney, K. 1990. "Does a Fetus Already Have a Future-Like-Ours?" *Journal of Philosophy* 87: 264–268.
McMahan, J. 2002. *The Ethics of Killing: Problems at the Margins of Life*. Oxford: Oxford University Press.
McMahan, J. 2008. "Challenges to Human Equality," *The Journal of Ethics* 12: 81–104.
Nozick, R. 1997. "Do Animals Have Rights?" in his *Socratic Puzzles*. Cambridge, MA: Harvard University Press.
O'Neill, O. 1998. "Kant on Duties Regarding Nonrational Nature," *Proceedings of the Aristotelian Society* 72: 211–228.
Quinn, W. 1984. "Abortion: Identity and Loss," *Philosophy and Public Affairs* 13: 24–54.
Rachels, J. 1990. *Created from Animals: The Moral Implications of Darwinism*. Oxford: Oxford University Press.
Regan, T. 2004. *The Case for Animal Rights*. Berkeley and Los Angeles, CA: University of California Press.
Rochat, P. 2003. "Five Levels of Self-Awareness as They Unfold Early in Life," *Consciousness and Cognition* 12: 717–731.
Scanlon, T. M. 1998. *What We Owe to Each Other*. Cambridge, MA: Harvard University Press.
Schapiro, T. 1999. "What Is a Child?" *Ethics* 109: 715–738.
Singer, P. 1993. *Practical Ethics*, 2nd edn. Cambridge: Cambridge University Press.
Steinbock, B. 1992. *Life Before Birth: The Moral and Legal Status of Embryos and Fetuses*. New York, NY: Oxford University Press.

Stone, J. 1987. "Why Potentiality Matters," *Canadian Journal of Philosophy* 17: 815–829.
Sumner, L.W. 1981. *Abortion and Moral Theory*. Princeton, NJ: Princeton University Press.
Thomson, J.J. 1971. "A Defense of Abortion," *Philosophy and Public Affairs* 1: 47–66.
Warren, M.A. 1997. *Moral Status: Obligations to Persons and Other Living Things*. Oxford: Oxford University Press.
Wilkins, B.T. 1993. "Does the Fetus Have a Right to Life?" *Journal of Social Philosophy* 24: 123–137.
Wood, A. 1998. "Kant on Duties Regarding Nonrational Nature," *Proceedings of the Aristotelian Society* 72: 189–210.

7
THE VALUE OF CHILDHOOD

Patrick Tomlin

Introduction

Is childhood good? Who benefits from childhood, and how? Are there goods that children experience or bring into existence which would not exist if we were to somehow eradicate childhood? Are children's lives to be judged by the same or different standards from adults'? In this chapter I want to investigate these questions, but before I do, I wish to first separate off some questions about *the value of childhood* from some questions about *the value of new or additional people*.

When we create new children, we create new people (and, all being well, these new children will eventually become new adults). And in order to create new people, we must (in fact, if not conceptually) create new children. Some of the questions concerning whether childhood is good may simply be reducible to the question of whether it is (in general) better to exist or not, or whether it is better to have more people. For example, provided children have lives worth living, the total utilitarian – the philosopher who believes that total well-being is what matters (Parfit 1984: 387; see also ch. 8) – will count their existence as a plus: any additional child with a life worth living is a bonus. And their lives will also be good for them, in the sense that it is better for them to keep existing as children than to cease to exist. Even if children's lives are not worth living, provided the childhood is part of a life that is overall worth living, then the total utilitarian will approve of their creation. But this has nothing to do with them being *children* per se.

The present chapter concerns the value of *childhood* more specifically. There are many interesting questions we can ask about this issue, and one danger is that they can easily be confused with one another. Let us begin, then, by distinguishing some importantly different questions. According to Anca Gheaus (2015a: 35–37), three different questions are answered under the heading "the intrinsic goods of childhood":

a   Is childhood intrinsically valuable?
    Gheaus describes this issue as being one in which we investigate whether "it is worthwhile to have had a childhood" and whether it would be rational to skip childhood (2015a: 35–36).
b   Are the intrinsic goods of childhood only valuable for children?
c   What goods are owed to children?

However, these questions only form a subset of the questions we need to look at if we are interested in the value of childhood more generally. This is because they all focus on whether childhood is *intrinsically* valuable *for children*. That is why Gheaus focuses on whether it would be rational for us to skip childhood. But even that question – of the rationality of skipping childhood – is not quite the same as the question of whether childhood is intrinsically valuable for children. That is because even if childhood is bad *for children*, it may be better, overall, to have a life which includes childhood, or we may have better lives as adults if we were once children. For example, some people believe that how well our lives go overall is not simply a matter of the total amount of well-being we experience. They also think that the "shape" of a life matters. Typically, they think that a life that starts out badly and gets better is better than one which starts out well and gets worse (for example, Dorsey 2015; Temkin 2012: ch. 3; Velleman 2000: ch. 3). If we couple this view with the idea that childhood is (at least in comparison with adulthood) bad for us, then childhood is not *good for the child*, but can be *intrinsically* good for the life overall, since it can help to give it the right "shape". Daniel Weinstock, on the other hand, has recently argued that even if we view childhood as a "predicament" (that is, as a negative condition to be escaped), it has instrumental value for the adults we become – our adult lives are better as the result of having experienced childhood (Weinstock 2018).

Therefore, I think we can distinguish the following questions about the *personal value* of childhood:

1. Is childhood intrinsically valuable *for children*?
   a. Compared with not existing
   b. Compared with adulthood
2. What goods make a childhood go well?
3. Is what makes a childhood go well the same or different from what makes an adult life go well?
4. What do children need to make their lives as children go well?
5. Is childhood an intrinsically valuable part of a life overall?
6. Is having experienced a childhood an instrumentally valuable part of an adult life?

Implicit in many of these questions (or at least in the way that philosophers seek to answer them) is a comparison with adult life. For example, if we ask, "is childhood intrinsically valuable for children?" or "is childhood an intrinsically valuable part of a life overall?", and then seek to answer those questions by testing whether it would be rational for us to skip childhood, and proceed straight to adulthood, we seem to be asking, "is childhood better or worse than adulthood for someone?" But questions of intrinsic value are not necessarily comparative in this way, and even if they are (or if we want to ask a comparative question) adulthood is not the only thing we could compare childhood with. We could compare childhood with being other kinds of being, or with not existing at all. So, while I, too, will often focus on the comparison with adults and children, it should be borne in mind that this only one kind of comparison we can make.

The above questions focus on how experiencing childhood may affect our own lives, but they do not exhaust the questions of the goods of childhood. Childhood may also have two further sources of value – the ways in which childhood makes other people's lives go better, and the way in which children may have value that is not reducible to childhood being valuable *for* people. Therefore, we can also ask the following questions. Questions 7 and 8 concern the *instrumental value of childhood* for other people. Question 9 concerns the *intrinsic value of children*.

7. Is childhood valuable for those who are not experiencing childhood?
8. What goods does childhood (help to) produce in others' lives?
9. How valuable are children? How does their value compare with that of adults?

To see how 9 is a distinct question from those concerning the personal value of childhood, we need to understand the distinction between questions concerning how well one's life is going and the value one has. For example, your life may be going much better than mine, but we may nevertheless think that we are of equal value, and this judgment of equal value may play a role in us deciding that, if a third party had to choose between saving your life and saving mine, she ought to toss a coin.

It is very important to keep these issues distinct: questions of how good a childhood is *for us* are distinct from how we ought to value children. This is not to say that our *answers* to these questions must be fully distinct. For example, Jeff McMahan (1996: 9) believes that some beings have greater value than others, and that it is better *for you* to be a being of higher rather than lower value.

With these questions on the table, I can be more precise about what I will (and won't) explore in the remainder of this chapter. I will examine only some of these questions, and putative answers to them. In particular, I will examine the instrumental value that childhood and children bring to the lives of others (question 7); whether childhood is intrinsically valuable for children (question 1); and whether what makes children's lives go well is the same as, or different from, what makes adults' lives go well (question 3).

The instrumental value of children

In investigating the value of childhood, several philosophers have posed thought experiments in which we imagine giving children a pill to speed up their development, thereby shortening their childhoods (Brennan 2014; Tomlin 2018; Gheaus 2015b: 6–8). This is used to see whether we think childhood is good for us, in comparison with adulthood. But to test this, we must pose a specific question. We must not ask, "would you give the child/children this pill?"; we must ask, "would you give the child/children this pill *for their own good*?" For the issue of whether childhood is good or not *for children* is not the end of the story when we think about whether childhood is, on balance, a good thing and whether, if we could, we ought to speed up the development of children. Even if our own childhood is not valuable for us (in comparison with adulthood), we could still have reasons to keep children as children because, as adults, we value having children in our lives.

The clearest way in which adults appear to benefit from children is through parenting them. According to Harry Brighouse and Adam Swift (2014) most adults have an interest in being parents. Furthermore, they argue, this interest is not one that we can satisfy in any other kind of relationship. This is because of two features of the parent–child relationship: "The relationship as a whole, with its particular intimate character, and the responsibility to play the specific fiduciary role for the person with whom one is intimate in that way, is what adults have an interest in" (Brighouse and Swift 2014: 92). Many will agree with Brighouse and Swift that being a parent often makes people's lives go better. Many parents are fanatical advocates of parenthood, and believe their lives are greatly enriched by being parents. But the Brighouse and Swift claim is much deeper than this. We might think that being a parent makes our lives go better because it makes us happy, or because it fulfills a preference, or set of preferences, that we hold, but that is not the argument here. The argument is that the relationship is good for many of us in and of itself, aside from whatever preferences it may fulfill or happiness it may bring, and that nothing could replace it. Thus, Brighouse and Swift would most likely be unimpressed by research which shows that parents are not always as happy as we might like to think (Margolis and Myrskylä 2015). For them, we have a *direct* interest in being parents. It is a further question, however, what, if any, role this interest could play in justifying the creation of children (Hannan and Leland 2018).

Not only parents benefit from children. Other adults can form valuable relationships with children that it would be difficult to replicate or replace without the particularities of childhood. But even aside from our intimate relationships with children, children just *being around* is important to many of us. Imagine a world without children – it would be a greyer place. As Weinstock (2018) observes, "children are cute, and therefore contribute to our aesthetic enjoyment of the world." Given this, even if we think childhood worse than adulthood, we may still have reason to hold back those developmental pills. There are two ways this argument could go: existing children ought to be kept (against their own interest) as children, for the sake of existing adults. Here, we may worry that we are *using the suffering as some as a means to benefit others*. Alternatively, we might view childhood as a practice from which we all benefit – a life in which I experience the badness of childhood but get to be a parent, and live in a world with children, can be preferable to a life in which I do not experience the badness of childhood but do not get to be a parent, or interact with children.

Is childhood good for children? Thought experiments

Let us now turn our attention to the issue of whether childhood is good *for children*. I think many of us have conflicting intuitions here. These can be brought out by the following pair of cases (Tomlin 2018):

> *Left as a child:* Erin is given pills to prevent her from becoming an adult. Aged 55, she continues to be a child, both physically and mentally. She is well cared for.
>
> *Deprived of childhood:* Dane is given pills to speed up his development. Aged 6, he is physically and mentally a fully grown man.[1]

It seems like something has gone wrong in both of these cases, and, furthermore, something that is bad *for* both Dane and Erin; that is, it seems both are *harmed*. But if childhood is better than adulthood, we should be happy for Erin. And if adulthood is better than childhood, we should be happy for Dane. And if they're just as good as one another, why care? It seems, at least *prima facie*, that we cannot be right to feel bad for both Dane and Erin.

Anca Gheaus (2015b: 7–8) rightly points out that we need to be careful with these thought experiments. She proposes to tighten up *Deprived* (and, I presume, would want to do the same with *Left*) in two ways. First, she notes that, because of the variation within how well childhoods and adulthoods go, we need to pick a *particular* comparison. Otherwise, we may not be comparing fairly (if, for example, we compared a bad childhood with a good adulthood). She suggests reasonably good childhoods and reasonably good adulthoods. Second, she also notes, importantly, that "individuals do not live in a social void; rather, children and adults live in a social world structured by adults who, arguably, have a bias toward cultivating the goods of adulthood" (Gheaus 2015b: 7).

Therefore, Gheaus argues that we should compare *reasonably good childhoods* with *reasonably good adulthoods* in *a society which is structured to respect both the value of childhood and adulthood*. I agree with Gheaus that these complications need to be taken into account. But it is questionable whether this points toward the particular comparison she wants to make. For example, why should we favor the comparison within this one possible social arrangement? Here are two particular salient social arrangements we might be interested in: the current one (and nearby ones); and the best, or most just, one. But Gheaus' favored comparison society is not our own, and nor is it necessarily the best, or most just, arrangement. In stipulating that both children's and adults' interests must be served, Gheaus seems to want to test how good childhood and adulthood are "all else equal". But this seems to suggest that we can strip out the question of social arrangements, and how they affect our lives, to find the "pure comparison". Yet Gheaus' point, precisely, is that we cannot do this – we do not live in a vacuum – and we would still need to justify choosing this particular comparison.

Similarly, whilst Gheaus is right to point toward the variance *within* childhoods and adulthoods, it is not obvious that we should privilege the comparison between the *reasonably good*.[2] Imagine, for example, that very few children have reasonably good childhoods, but that lots of adults have reasonably good adulthoods – it would be misleading to then privilege this particular comparison. Or imagine, as Gheaus suggests (2015b: 7), that bad childhoods are much worse than bad adulthoods – this surely matters to our comparison.

A further reason to worry about trying to find *the* appropriate comparison is that doing so may miss something important. For it seems plausible that it is intrinsically better to be a being who can flourish in a wider variety of environments, and the approach of looking for *the* appropriate comparison misses this point completely. If your well-being is robust across a variety of social arrangements, this may be better for you than if your well-being is fragile. But if we just look at one social arrangement, this robustness cannot be taken account of.

Given all this, I propose that we should do one of the following: perform the comparisons at a variety of levels of well-being, and in a variety of social settings, or re-think the thought experiment, and make it something like this one:

> *Choosing a life*: Felix is in the original position.[3] He does not know what kind of society he will live in, nor does he know what kind of childhood or adulthood he will have. He must choose how much (if any) of his life to spend as a child, and how much (if any) as an adult.

Forcing us to contemplate childhood across a range of social arrangements brings home an important aspect of childhood – since they do not, and have never, made political decisions, they are politically vulnerable to adults (something Gheaus highlights (2015b: 7)), and within most political structures, they are left intensely vulnerable to one or two adults. As Sarah Hannan (2018) observes: "children are extremely vulnerable, especially to the adults that care for them…Even when their lives go well, the contingency of this can reasonably be regarded as bad for them."[4] On the other hand, there may be other aspects of childhood that make children's well-being less vulnerable to others. The central point here is that our comparisons are sometimes too simplistic. We should take account of a range of possible social arrangements and levels of well-being in trying to compare childhood and adulthood.

Is childhood good for children? Goods and bads of childhood

In order to see whether childhood is good or bad for children (in comparison with adulthood), we need an account of well-being against which to measure children's lives. The main question we then face is question 3 from our list: should children's lives be measured against the same standards of well-being against which we measure adults' lives? Or does an altogether different standard apply? Standardly, philosophers refer to three general approaches to well-being (Crisp 2017). The first is hedonism – the idea that happiness is what makes a life go well. The second is desire-satisfaction – the idea that what makes a life go well is getting what we (in some sense) want from life. The third is an objective list of values or interests that all human beings share. Whether these are good standards to apply to children is questionable (Skelton 2015, 2016), and is covered in greater depth elsewhere in this volume (see ch. 9).

We have, so far as I can see, three options here: 1. apply these existing theories of (adult) well-being to children; 2. develop new theories of well-being to apply to both adults and children which better take account of children's lives; or 3. develop separate accounts of well-being for adults and children. In this section, I will look at the first option, by looking at some of the features of children's lives that philosophers have argued are good and bad for children if we measure their lives against the same standards as adults'. There are some quite obvious ways in which children's lives, if they are measured against adult standards, appear to be going badly. But some philosophers have recently sought to highlight goods which children readily access but which adults either can't, or are less easily able to, access.

Whatever theory of well-being we adopt, happiness is generally thought to be, at least, an element of well-being. This initially seems to imply that children are (in general) doing well. Gheaus (2015b: 14) observes:

> children really have a remarkable ability to enjoy life. They can take more pleasure than adults in their sensations, ideas, bodies, people and places; they are more capable than adults of wholehearted fun and laughter. Also, most children seem less susceptible to some kinds of misery: They rarely, if ever, feel tired with life.

I have challenged this line of thinking (Tomlin 2018). We may like to think of children as particularly happy – and indeed, the great delight that children can take in tiny things is one of the delights of being around children – but the reality is that children are often unhappy. They experience regular lows: sobbing uncontrollably at being asked to put on their shoes; throwing themselves on the floor and pounding their fists because they couldn't do something. Young children cry. A lot. Gheaus suspects that this isn't because children are more miserable than adults, but because adults have been socialized to display pleasure but not distress. I think at most this offers a partial explanation – children are simply more emotionally volatile than most adults. Even if children are, on average, happier than adults, the fact that they swing so violently between delight and despair is itself an arguably bad feature of their lives: imagine an adult with high peaks and low troughs of happiness – wouldn't we think their life worse than an adult who is on a more even keel, and whose average happiness is only slightly lower?

Another way in which hedonism, or a concern for happiness more generally, may not suggest that children's lives are going especially well is if – with Mill (1998: ch. 2) – we adapt hedonism to take account of the *quality* of the pleasures experienced. On this view, children do not look like they are doing well. If we want to say that poetry is better than a pushpin, most of children's pleasures look distinctly pushpin-like. Children are simply incapable of appreciating many of the goods that Millian hedonists usually have in mind – they lack the mental capacity to properly engage with, and appreciate, fine art or music, for example.

Another way in which philosophers have argued that children's lives are going badly concerns interference and liberty. Many philosophers think autonomy, liberty, or freedom from domination is part of the good life for adults. As Brighouse and Swift put it:

> We think of a person as having two kinds of interest. She has an interest in anything that contributes to her well-being or flourishing; anything that makes her life go better is an interest of hers. But she also has an interest in having her dignity respected – in being treated in ways that reflect her moral status as an agent, as a being with the capacity for judgment and choice, even where that respect does *not* make her life go better [in terms of flourishing].
>
> *(Brighouse and Swift 2014: 52)*

If we apply theories of well-being that incorporate these kinds of concerns to children, their lives seem to be going badly, since they are routinely dominated (Hannan 2018; Hannan and Leland 2018; Tomlin 2018). Such interference is, of course, often justified, but it doesn't follow that it isn't *pro tanto* bad for us. A child may be overall better off being made to go to bed earlier rather than later, but *choosing* to go to bed at a reasonable time may be best for them. Many will want to argue that children don't have the same interests in autonomy that adults have – they lack the capacities which make this an interest for us (see ch. 10). But that is to posit two different theories of well-being – one for adults, and one for children.

A related, but distinct, way in which children's lives may be thought to go badly is one we have already touched upon: their vulnerability (see ch. 27). Children are dominated, and that is often justifiable. As such, we require child-rearing institutions in which adults are given control over children. This is, *ex ante*, in a child's interests (and, according to Brighouse and Swift, in adults' interests too). But this makes children particularly vulnerable to abuse and neglect, and without the resources to realize what is going on or to extract themselves from abusive relationships (Hannan 2018; Hannan and Leland forthcoming). Vulnerability is an interesting "bad" feature of children's lives. We may want to say that it isn't *itself* a bad feature; rather, children are *at risk* of having bad things happen to them. Or we may want to say that this risk is itself a bad feature of children's lives.

Put together, these kinds of concerns often lead us toward thinking about childhood as a "predicament" – something to be escaped. A group of philosophers, most notably Samantha Brennan (2014), Colin Macleod (2010), and Anca Gheaus (2015a, 2015b) have pushed back against this view. They have sought to highlight good aspects of children's lives. There are three ways this kind of argument can go: there are some fundamental goods that are unique to children in that they're only good for children (in which case we need separate accounts of well-being); there are some things that are only good for children, but they are good because they contribute to an interest or element of well-being that adults share; or there are some things that are good for both adults and children but which children are uniquely or especially good at accessing. We're looking, here, at the latter two kinds of claim.

Several aspects of children's lives have been highlighted in the literature. These include: children are better reasoners than we give them credit for; children are more empathetic than we give them credit for; children have vivid and remarkable imaginations; children have a remarkable ability to learn and change; children can ask philosophical questions; children can think like scientists; children are physically flexible; children are naturally artistic; children possess a disposition to react with wonder to new persons, objects, events; children, and their relationships, are more innocent and open, and less calculating; and children are more present-focused and able to live in the moment.

It is not clear to me that many of these "goods" should be regarded as fundamental sources of, or elements of, well-being. At best, many of them seem to be instrumental to a good life. But how much of an advantage in life is being physically flexible? And could it ever compensate for the domination children (often justifiably) suffer? Even if we accept all of these as goods, if we are judging children's lives by adult standards, it is questionable whether this list of childhood advantages is enough for us to conclude that children's lives are not inferior to adults' (Tomlin 2018; Hannan 2018).

Separate accounts of well-being?

If we judge children's lives by adult standards, we may well conclude that their lives are inferior to those of adults. Perhaps partly because this conclusion seems controversial, and perhaps partly because it doesn't seem appropriate to force adults' norms and values onto children, especially young children, several philosophers have proposed different standards of well-being for children and adults (Brighouse and Swift 2014; Skelton 2015, 2016).

There are three central problems with this. First, as everybody recognizes, "childhood" is in fact an amalgam of several quite varied life-stages: the 13-year-old has more in common with the 20-year-old than with a baby or a toddler, so if it is inappropriate to apply the same standard of well-being to the 20-year-old and the toddler, it is just as inappropriate to lump together the 13-year-old with the toddler. As I say, everyone recognizes this, but actually it creates major difficulties for any account in which "childhood well-being" is *sui generis*. One reason a simple two-group (children/adults) theory will not do is that there is clearly no precise point at which one wakes up an "adult". As Skelton (2015) observes, the account he sketches for young children won't do for older children. So, he suggests that there will be *another* account for older children. But the problem will simply repeat itself here. No matter how *many* stages of childhood we identify, and corresponding theories of well-being we come up with, any view which suggests that you go to bed measuring your life by one theory of well-being and then wake up measuring your life by another is implausible. What we require then is some view which combines the idea that the two-year-old and the 20-year-old have distinct accounts of well-being which apply to them, but without ever offering a sharp break. (Once we do this, we may also want a varying account of well-being that applies to different stages of adulthood.)

Here is my suggestion. What we require is a list-based theory of well-being (but the list can include both desire-satisfaction and happiness) under which the different elements of the list are more or less important to overall well-being at any given time. Sometimes an item may be *all* that matters to well-being, other times it may not matter at all, but its overall contribution to well-being will grow or diminish gradually. Think of it like the mixing desk of a recording studio. At the very beginning of life, we might set physical health and physical pleasure at the very highest setting, and have autonomy and sexual relationships set to zero. At the age of two, unstructured play might be set very high. By 13, that may have decreased, with autonomy playing a bigger role. The point is, any plausible view is not actually going to be a view about "the account for children and the account for adults" but rather a set of goods which continuously and gradually vary in importance (including continuing on into adulthood).

The second problem for this kind of account is that once we posit fundamentally differing accounts of childhood and adulthood goods, we potentially lose the ability to compare them. And if we lose the ability to compare them, it becomes difficult to say that either Dane or Erin is harmed in our earlier examples. As I have put it elsewhere:

> if children and adults…have fundamentally different accounts of well-being, then there is no more ultimate account of well-being to which we could appeal in assessing whether children or adults have better lives. This is why I believe that once we accept that there are childhood-specific goods, we are required to say that neither Dane nor Erin are harmed (or benefitted) by the pills they are given. That is, we are not harmed, or benefitted, just by being made to continue to be, or turned into, a certain kind of being (unless it were against our wishes, and preference-satisfaction were a kind of well-being for that kind of being), since our well-being is to be settled by reference to an account of well-being tailored to the kind of thing we are.
>
> *(Tomlin 2018: 42)*

This problem is potentially exacerbated by my previous point – that actually we require a constantly and subtly shifting account of well-being, which would properly capture our slow development from childhood to adulthood. If each subtle shift creates a new account of well-being, and we cannot compare well-being across differing accounts of well-being, then not only do we lose the ability to compare childhood and adulthood, we also lose the ability within childhood, such that we may not be able to compare well-being between a seven- and an eight-year-old.

However, I now wonder if this problem is overstated. The problem is that differing accounts of well-being are incommensurable. I assumed, in the quotation above, that this meant that we could not compare well-being across beings to whom different accounts of well-being apply. But many philosophers deny that incommensurability implies incomparability (Chang 2013).

At the very least, we can say the following: the idea of harm normally relies on a stable account of well-being, such that in order to show that I have harmed you we must show that I have made you worse off *on some particular metric*. In order to make sense of harm in terms of turning people into adults, or keeping them as children, we would need to revise this ordinary understanding, since the action either introduces a new account of well-being, or fails to introduce one. If we can live with a notion of incommensurable harm – where the harm in question is not indexed to a fixed account of well-being that applies on both sides of the comparison – then perhaps we can still make sense of Dane or Erin being harmed. But we would still be left with a puzzle: can it be true, as our intuitions suggest, that they are *both* harmed?

The third problem with this view is most forcefully stated by Hannan (2018). One reason to think childhood bad is that some aspects of old age that we think bad for us are actually quite similar to childhood. The "varying accounts of well-being view" may imply that we should also have a different account of well-being for old age, indexed to the abilities and characteristics of old age. This may then rob us of the ability to declare these aspects of old age bad for us.

Complementarity

The idea of shifting accounts of well-being is attractive in various ways, but it still seems to leave us with the idea that, at most, only one of Dane and Erin is harmed. Daniel Weinstock's (2018) view that childhood is a predicament, but, crucially, a necessary one (in principle, not just empirically) for being the kind of adult who has a flourishing life enables us to hold on to both intuitions. Dane is harmed because he misses out on forming himself and his "maxims" such that he can properly be said to endorse them or own them. His adulthood is all the worse for this. He may be able to partake in practical reasoning, but the maxims and values he uses to do so must have been imposed upon him from the outside (perhaps by the pill). They're not "his" in any real sense, because he didn't develop them in response to the predicament of childhood. Erin is harmed because she is kept in the predicament of childhood. Weinstock says,

> it is perhaps true that childhood is a "predicament".... But it is a normatively necessary predicament, one in the absence of which we could not possibly become moral agents possessed of endorsed maxims with which we engage in practical reasoning in an articulate way.
>
> *(Weinstock 2018: 56)*

To become an adult who owns and understands her own maxims and values "requires that one go through the work that the predicament of childhood represents" (Weinstock 2018).

Against this view, though, we may be concerned that Weinstock's "predicament" is one we face in virtue of being *new to the world*, not in virtue of *having the body and capabilities of a child*.[5]

Conclusion

There are many interesting questions concerning the value of childhood (and children), and we have touched upon only some of them here. It is important, however, to keep them distinct. In particular, childhood may be valuable for the life as a whole, or for the adult the child becomes, it may be valuable to others, it may have impersonal value, and it may be a valuable stage of life in itself. This last question has largely occupied us here. One crucial issue concerns whether or not the same account of well-being should apply across children and adults. If it does, despite some wonderful features of children's lives, many will think children's lives are going badly – they are emotionally volatile, dominated, and vulnerable. If it does not, then some common intuitions about accelerating or slowing progress toward adulthood may need to be let go. The idea that the stages of life are complementary – that childhood is inferior to, but necessary for, an adult life well lived is attractive, though it requires a particular, and controversial, view about what is good in adulthood.[6]

Notes

1 Some worry that the issue of manipulation may "pollute" our intuitions in these cases. I am not concerned by this. These are kids. If we can do things that benefit them, we would ordinarily think that unproblematic. For example, if they were sick, we wouldn't think it problematic to give them the pill.
2 I myself proposed this particular comparison as a "starting point" in Tomlin (2018).
3 As found in Rawls (1971).
4 A parallel argument, against the idea that disability is a "mere difference", is made in Mosquera Ramil (2017). See also ch. 23.
5 I am grateful to Sarah Hannan for this point.
6 For useful comments, I am grateful to the editors – Anca Gheaus in particular – and Sarah Hannan.

References

Brennan, S. 2014. "The Goods of Childhood and Children's Rights," in F. Baylis and C. Macleod (eds.), *Family Making: Contemporary Ethical Challenges*. Oxford: Oxford University Press.
Brighouse, H., and Swift, A. 2014. *Family Values: The Ethics of Parent-Child Relationships*. Princeton, NJ: Princeton University Press.
Chang, R. 2013. "Incommensurability (and Incomparability)," in H. LaFollette (ed.), *The International Encyclopedia of Ethics*. Oxford: Blackwell.
Crisp, R. 2017. "Well-Being," in E. N. Zalta (ed.), *The Stanford Encyclopedia of Philosophy* (Fall 2017 Edition). Retrieved from https://plato.stanford.edu/archives/fall2017/entries/well-being/ (last accessed 10 March 2018).
Dorsey, D. 2015. "The Significance of a Life's Shape," *Ethics* 125(2): 303–330.
Gheaus, A. 2015a. "The 'Intrinsic Goods of Childhood' and the Just Society," in A. Bagattini and C. Macleod (eds.), *The Nature of Children's Well-being: Theory and Practice*. Dordrecht: Springer.
Gheaus, A. 2015b. "Unfinished Adults and Defective Children: On the Nature and Value of Childhood," *Journal of Ethics and Social Philosophy* 9(1): 1–21.
Hannan, S. 2018. "Why Childhood is Bad for Children," *Journal of Applied Philosophy* 35(S1): 11–28.
Hannan, S., and Leland, R.J. 2018. "Childhood Bads, Parenting Goods, and the Right to Procreate," *Critical Review of International Social and Political Philosophy* 21(3): 366–384.
Macleod, C. 2010. "Primary Goods, Capabilities, and Children," in H. Brighouse and I. Robeyns (eds.), *Measuring Justice: Primary Goods and Capabilities*. Cambridge: Cambridge University Press.
Margolis, R., and Myrskylä, M. 2015. "Parental Well-being Surrounding First Birth as a Determinant of Further Parity Progression," *Demography* 52(4): 1147–1166.
McMahan, J. 1996. "Cognitive Disability, Misfortune, and Justice," *Philosophy & Public Affairs* 25(1): 3–35.
Mill, J. S. 1998. *Utilitarianism*, ed. R. Crisp. Oxford: Oxford University Press.
Mosquera Ramil, J. 2017. "Why Inflicting Disability is Wrong: A Reply to Elizabeth Barnes," in A. Cureton and D. Wasserman (eds.), *Oxford Handbook of Philosophy and Disability*. Oxford: Oxford University Press.

Parfit, D. 1984. *Reasons and Persons*. Oxford: Clarendon Press.
Rawls, J. 1971. *A Theory of Justice*. Cambridge, MA: Harvard University Press.
Skelton, A. 2015. "Utilitarianism, Welfare, Children," in A. Bagattini and C. Macleod (eds.), *The Nature of Children's Well-being: Theory and Practice*. Dordrecht: Springer.
Skelton, A. 2016. "Children's Well-being: A Philosophical Analysis," in G. Fletcher (ed.), *The Routledge Handbook of Well-being*. Abingdon: Routledge.
Temkin, L. 2012. *Rethinking the Good*. New York, NY: Oxford University Press.
Tomlin, P. 2018. "Saplings or Caterpillars? Trying to Understand Children's Well-Being," *Journal of Applied Philosophy* 35(S1): 29–46.
Velleman, J. D. 2000. *The Possibility of Practical Reason*. Oxford: Oxford University Press.
Weinstock, D. 2018. "On the Complementarity of the Ages of Life," *Journal of Applied Philosophy* 35(S1): 47–59.

8
CHILDREN AND WELL-BEING

Anthony Skelton

Introduction

Children are routinely treated paternalistically. There are reasons for this (see ch. 11). Children are quite vulnerable (see ch. 27). They are ill-equipped to meet their most basic needs, due, in part, to deficiencies in practical and theoretical reasoning and in executing their wishes. Children's motivations and perceptions are often not congruent with their best interests. Consequently, raising children involves facilitating their best interests synchronically and diachronically. In practice, this requires caregivers to (in some sense) manage a child's daily life. If apposite, this management will focus partly on a child's well-being. To be ably executed, an account of children's well-being will need to be articulated.

This chapter focuses on the nature of children's well-being. It has five sections. The first section clarifies the focus. The second section examines some hurdles to articulating a view of children's well-being. The third section evaluates some accounts of children's well-being. The fourth section addresses the view that children possess features essential to them that make their lives on balance prudentially bad for them. The fifth section sums things up.

Preliminaries

It is important to begin by fixing ideas. Thinking about children's well-being involves thinking about what is prudentially good for children. An account of well-being's nature in children outlines what is fundamentally, non-instrumentally good for a child, and therefore tells us how well a child's life or part of a child's life is going for her. This is distinct from thinking about the causes or goods instrumental to well-being's production.

Thinking about prudential value is distinct from thinking about whether childhood itself is non-instrumentally good (see ch. 27).[1] Thinking about the latter involves thinking about what value to place on a period in life. This usually takes the form of wondering whether, of the stages in life (e.g., adulthood and senescence), childhood has unique or special value. Thinking about children's well-being may help in thinking about the value of childhood, but thinking about the former is a distinct preoccupation. It involves thinking of the value one's life or part of one's life has from one's own perspective. It is, anyway, doubtful that childhood in itself is valuable. It is likely that the value of childhood, if it has value, is a function of the things of value possessed in it. The prudential value of a child's life is likely one such thing.

Thinking about prudential value is distinct from thinking about what makes a child's life good *tout court*. Prudential value contributes to living a good life. But other things might, too.[2] These might be the appropriate focus of those properly managing a child's life. Developing some virtues – dedication to the common weal – might contribute to the value of a child's life without making her prudentially better off. Ditto the experience of certain other, perfectionist goods, e.g., the contemplation of beauty.

Thinking about prudential value is different from thinking about the so-called "intrinsic goods of childhood", that is, "goods the value of which doesn't follow from their contribution to the goods of adult life" (Brennan 2014: 35; see also ch. 7). It is possible to establish that there are such goods without establishing that any of them are non-instrumentally *prudentially good* for a child. It seems that some things are non-instrumentally good for children, e.g., happiness, irrespective of the contribution they make to adult life. Theories of well-being seek to make sense of how and why claims such as this are true.

Hurdles

In thinking about the nature of children's well-being one has to be mindful of the fact that children develop during childhood. An infant shares little in common with a seven- or eight-year-old and has even less in common with an eleven- or twelve-year-old. The nature of consciousness, agency, expression, cognition, and the comprehension and manipulation of information changes quite radically in childhood. This is on top of profound changes in children's physical features and abilities. It is, of course, important not to overstate the point. There is some uniformity amongst children and especially younger children; they are, e.g., not fully formed agents. Nevertheless, that children typically change significantly in childhood makes developing a comprehensive and fully general view of children's well-being difficult. Perhaps the best strategy is to say what appears true generally about children's well-being, making amendments to the view as differences between the stages of childhood are noted. This will no doubt involve taking seriously that there are some differences in the nature of well-being (and certainly its causes) for infants, young children, and older children.

It is also important to note that developmental (and other) facts about children make it difficult in thinking about children's well-being to draw on accounts of well-being that are adult focused. This is true whether the focus is on fully formed rational adults or deviations from that (typical) focus. Seeing this involves considering that there are distinct accounts of well-being for children and for adults (Skelton 2015, 2016).

In developing an account of children's well-being, one is confronted by another difficulty: the individuals from whom moral philosophers often seek guidance – Aristotle, Kant, and the classical utilitarians Bentham, Mill, and Sidgwick – have little specific to say about children's well-being.

Aristotle maintains that children cannot fare well. He remarks that

> it is natural, then, that we call neither ox nor horse nor any other of the animals happy; for none of them is capable of sharing in...[virtuous] activity. For this reason also a boy is not happy; for he is not yet capable of such acts, owing to his age; and boys who are called happy are being congratulated by reason of the hopes we have for them.
>
> *(Aristotle 1999: 1099b33–1100a³)*

Aristotle's argument is as follows: well-being consists in activity in accordance with intellectual and moral excellences. Children are incapable of activity in accordance with intellectual and moral excellences. Children thus cannot fare well; in describing them as faring well we are congratulating them on having what we believe are rosy prospects.

The best reply to this argument is to reject its implicit assumption: that there is only *one* way to fare well. It is possible that at least at some point during childhood children fare well in a way that is different to adults. In this case, what follows from Aristotle's premises is that children do not fare well as adults do. It does not follow that they do not fare well.

One might also attack the conclusion of Aristotle's argument. It is false to the facts. First, it is unclear when we hope that our child fares well that we are hoping to have high hopes for our child. Second, it is not the case that when we describe a child as faring poorly that this is due entirely to the fact that we think she has poor prospects in the future. We might believe that a child's life is going poorly for her now due to an illness while believing that she has a very rosy future upon recovery.

If one desires to work out a view of children's well-being, one cannot gain much from Aristotle. Contemporary proponents of Aristotelian views have not, for the most part, it seems, improved in this regard.[3] Neera Badhwar, for example, argues that well-being consists in happiness in a worthwhile life. Her view of happiness appears not to fit children. According to her, "a happy person…[is] a person who *finds* his life both meaningful and enjoyable" (Badhwar 2014: 35; italics added). A child might find their life enjoyable. But children lack the concept of meaningfulness; therefore, they cannot find that their life falls into this category.[4] Badhwar's view of a worthwhile life comprises being reality oriented, having an understanding of oneself and general facts about the world and others, and being autonomous, thinking and living independently, and these in turn involve the possession of certain virtues or excellences of character, including fairness, open-mindedness, and honesty (Badhwar 2014: 44ff., 108). If this is what well-being consists in, children cannot fare well.

Kant is more helpful than Aristotle. At various points in his corpus he develops views of well-being applicable to children. He writes in terms of happiness; he is, however, interested in well-being. In the *Groundwork for the Metaphysics of Morals*, Kant contends that well-being consists in "the satisfaction of all inclinations as a sum" (Kant 2002: 4:399, also 4:405, 4:418). This suggests that well-being consists in the satisfaction of desire. This is an implausible view of children's well-being. Its main defect is that the depth and breadth of the desires that may legitimately be attributed to children are too few to capture all that matters to their well-being (Skelton 2015, 2016; also, Lin 2017: 9ff.)

In the *Critique of Practical Reason*, Kant suggests that well-being consists in "a rational being's consciousness of the agreeableness of life uninterruptedly accompanying his whole existence" (Kant 1997: 5:22). This appears to be a form of well-being hedonism: one is faring well when one feels on balance more pleasure than pain. This is not a view of well-being that fits the vast majority of children; they may not qualify as fully rational beings in Kant's sense (Schapiro 1999), and it is unclear that they are capable of "consciousness" of the sort called for in it.

In most cases in which he discusses well-being, Kant has rational agents in mind. However, he commits himself to a view of children's well-being in the *Metaphysics of Morals*. At least with respect to school children, he holds that well-being consists in everything always going "the way you would like it to", which he treats as equivalent to the claim that well-being consists in "enjoyment of life, complete satisfaction with one's condition" (Kant 1996: 6:480; see also Kant 2002: 4:393, 4:369, for a similar view).

This position, too, appears to be a brand of hedonism. In thinking that children's well-being consists in surplus pleasure or enjoyment or felt satisfaction, Kant is joined, of course, by the classical utilitarians who hold, on one interpretation, hedonism about well-being, the view that all and only pleasure is non-instrumentally good for one, and that all and only pain is non-instrumentally bad for one (see, e.g., Sidgwick 1907).

Might hedonism be the correct account of children's well-being? Some contemporary theorists who do not defend hedonism in general certainly seem to think so (e.g., Sumner 1996; Macleod 2010; for discussion, see Skelton 2015, 2016, forthcoming).

Before going on, it is important to report that Kant's contemporary admirers have not discussed his views on children's well-being. In the most sustained discussion of Kant on children, Tamar Schapiro does not touch on the topic in her argument that childhood is a "normative predicament" (Schapiro 1999: 730). She outlines some obligations that adults have to children, but none of them relates to children's well-being (1999: 734ff.). This might be because her focus is on the acquisition in children of a will. But it is strange nonetheless. The issue is no doubt quite complicated for Kantians: it is unclear that all children are worthy of happiness as one must be, for Kant, to legitimately possess it, since they are underdeveloped and so lack the characteristics making them worthy of happiness (Kant 2002: 4:393; cf. Kant 1996: 6:481).

Let us turn now to the question of hedonism's plausibility as a conception of children's well-being. Hedonism's popularity is rising (for defenses, see Crisp 2006; Hewitt 2010; Bramble 2016). It has a number of attractions. Pleasure seems to matter to well-being, especially when the conception of it is broad enough to capture all of the affective states mattering to it. Hedonism can explain a great deal about what seemingly matters to children's well-being, e.g., play, friendship, sport, and so on. It injects system into our thinking about prudential value; pleasure may be used to explain, justify, and reconcile conflicts between other putative prudential values (Sidgwick 1907). Hedonism applies to the broad range of subjects to whom welfare judgments are applied, e.g., animals, neonates, children, and adults. For some, this generality is an attractive feature in a theory of well-being (Sumner 1996). Finally, it captures the popular idea that only that which affects one's experience positively is capable of making one better off (i.e., an experience requirement).[5]

Hedonism has been attacked on the grounds that things other than what affects one's experience of one's life matter to well-being (Nozick 1974; Sumner 1996; Badhwar 2014). The main worry is that one might have a large surplus of pleasure because one believes that one has loving friends, esteem from one's co-workers, and a loving family when, in fact, (unbeknownst to one) one's beliefs are false and one's friends, family, and co-workers have no such attitudes. Hedonism has to claim that one's life is going quite well. But many hold that the fact that one's beliefs are false, and that one does not possess certain goods in question, makes a non-instrumental difference to how well one's life is going. The intuition is that one's life would be better were the beliefs in question true and one possessed the goods. Many infer from this that it is more than pleasure that matters to well-being. Real friendships, esteem, familial love, and so on, matter, too.

Some have tried to impugn the intuition that things other than pleasure matter to well-being (e.g., contact with reality). One line of attack is to argue that such intuitions are a result of evolutionary and/or social and/or psychological forces rather than accurate perceptions of the way things are, prudentially speaking. In this case, the intuitions have their source in mechanisms that do not preserve truth (e.g., reproductive advantage or social approval) and so are unjustified (Hewitt 2010: 345–346). Hedonists have further argued that they can explain that we have the intuitions in order to solve the paradox of happiness. The most efficient pursuit of happiness involves pursuing it indirectly by pursuing directly putative goods such as the ones above under the belief that they are, in fact, non-instrumentally good for one (Hewitt 2010: 346ff.).

Not everyone is convinced. Some wonder whether the intuitions that support hedonism are themselves subject to debunking arguments (Skelton 2015). Some take a dim view of system;

hedonism is not clearly better than its rivals, for comparing pleasures is difficult. Others might see little attraction in generality or find it attractive only if the view that is general is compelling (for discussion, see Skelton 2015). Some reject the experience requirement (Hooker 2015).

A detailed discussion of the merits of hedonism is not possible here. A plausible way to assess it is to present rivals. This is the burden of the next section. In the meantime, it is worth noting that one's departure from hedonism will likely depend on one's faith in the intuitions conflicting with it and one's tolerance for some (greater) philosophical disorder.

Children's well-being

The literature on the nature of children's well-being is in its infancy.[6] In what exists, it is agreed that children's well-being comprises an objective component.[7] How well a child's life is going for her depends on more than what resonates with her. It is hard to know exactly what accounts for this. One reason is that a child's point of view is too immature to furnish an inventory of subjective attitudes robust enough to support a fully subjective theory of children's well-being. The main contenders in the literature are objective-list views (Brennan 2014; Brighouse and Swift 2014; Wendler 2010) and hybrid views (Kraut 2007; Skelton 2015, forthcoming).

Samantha Brennan argues that children's well-being consists in the possession of the goods of unstructured imaginative play, relationships with other children and with adults, opportunities to meaningfully contribute to household and community, time spent outdoors and in the natural world, physical affection, physical activity and sport, bodily pleasure, music and art, emotional well-being, and physical well-being and health (Brennan 2014: 42).

Harry Brighouse and Adam Swift maintain there are five interests, the satisfaction of which are non-instrumentally good for children: physical interests or having one's physical needs met, e.g., "health care, nutrition, shelter", and the like (Brighouse and Swift 2014: 64); cognitive interests, comprising an interest in acquiring reflective capacities sufficient for autonomy; emotional interests, including an interest in regulating one's emotions and in connecting emotionally with others; moral interests, including an interest in understanding and adapting one's behavior to "the basic demands of morality" (Brighouse and Swift 2014: 64); and an interest in enjoying childhood, including possessing the goods of "innocence of sexuality" and "being carefree" (Brighouse and Swift 2014: 65).

David Wendler contends that there are four interests, the satisfaction of which are non-instrumentally good for children (Wendler 2010: 136): biological interests, e.g., "food and water, appropriate ambient temperature, and sufficient sleep" (Wendler 2010: 130); experiential interests, e.g., feeling contented and avoiding suffering; interests in meaningful relationships, including with people, with animals, with projects, and so on; and personal interests, including "preferences, desires, hopes, dreams, projects, and goals" (Wendler 2010: 131).

Such views face a shared difficulty.[8] Each view claims that something can be good for a child even if he or she is indifferent to or has an aversion to it. It is, for example, the case that on these views the prudential value of a child's life is improved when she has a valuable relationship with someone or something, even if it fails to make her happy or pleased or fails to resonate with her more broadly. For some, it is hard to accept that something might make one better off despite that fact that it fails to resonate with one.

Those moved by this worry (and/or some of the worries plaguing hedonism) might find hybrid theories of children's well-being more promising. Children's well-being on such views consists in the having of some subjective attitude/experience in the possession of items like those found on the above objective lists.

Richard Kraut defends what he calls developmentalism: what is non-instrumentally good for a child is to take pleasure in the development or exercise or maturation of her "cognitive, affective, sensory, and social powers (no less than physical powers)" (Kraut 2007: 137). This is a hybrid view of well-being: to fare well, a child must experience pleasure or enjoyment in the exercise or development of various powers (Kraut 2007: 130).

It is not clear that Kraut overcomes the worry targeting objective-list views. He rejects views stating that the development of a power in the absence of pleasure is good for one (Kraut 2007: 128). Presumably he has the above worry in mind. But it is not clear that by adding that one must take pleasure in the development of a power for it to be good for one he avoids the worry. This follows from the fact that it seems that pleasure, as Kraut conceives it, is a sensation to which one may be indifferent. It is possible for one to feel the sensation of pleasure and for that pleasure not to resonate with one. If it is not good for one to exercise a capacity to which one is indifferent, it is not clear that by adding a conception of pleasure to which one may be indifferent one is made prudentially better off.

If Kraut holds that when one possesses pleasure in the development or exercise of one's physical, emotional, sensory, or cognitive capacities or powers, one fares well, and one may be indifferent to both, it is possible for the pleasurable development of one's powers to be good for a child even though she is indifferent to it. In this sense, Kraut's view is similar to an objective-list view.

A hybrid view that may avoid this problem states that children's well-being consists in satisfaction or happiness in intellectual activity, valuable relationships, and play (of various sorts) (Skelton 2015). This view might be better at avoiding the worry expressed above, for, on this view, finding one's conditions satisfying involves some kind of (even if implicit) positive endorsement of the conditions of one's life or part of it. It might be implausible that very small children find the conditions of their life satisfying in this sense (Lin 2017; cf. Skelton 2015, forthcoming). If so, another attitude may be needed. The variety of pleasure in Kraut's view may be more appropriate. Perhaps this aspect of Kraut's view makes sense for very young children. The right view, then, might be that in the early stages of life pleasure in intellectual activity, play, and so on, is what well-being consists in and that once a child's perspective and judgmental capacities develop, satisfaction or happiness in intellectual activity, valuable relationships, and so on, is what well-being consists in. Such a view would not avoid the worry articulated above at the very early stages of life, but perhaps very early on in life this is less of an issue, for children may not at this point have a perspective or any judgmental capacities of any robust kind.

Hybrid views seem more plausible than objective-list views (for discussion, see Skelton 2016; Hooker 2015). They have the capacity to explain why it appears good for a child to have some of the things on the above objective lists. The version of the view defended in Skelton (2015) may be the more plausible of the two; it appears well placed to explain the value of the development of the powers Kraut mentions: developing these powers typically conduces to finding satisfaction in meaningful relationships, various forms of play, and intellectual activity. It is unclear why emotional or physical development would matter if they did not conduce to satisfaction in such items (or those like them). Moreover, Kraut is interested not just in pleasurable development, but healthy pleasurable development (Kraut 2007: 202, 135). The items on the list in Skelton (2015) provide a plausible account of healthy development (Skelton forthcoming).

A full defense of a hybrid view is not possible here (see Skelton 2015, 2016). Its proponents have to face up to an important worry: hybrid views say that to fare well a child needs to experience some subjective attitude in the possession of one of the items of the sort on the objective-list views discussed above (e.g., intellectual activity). If this is what well-being consists in, the hybrid theorist has to admit that when one experiences happiness in the absence of the items (unalloyed joy in the warmth of the sun on one's face) or when one has one of the items (play) without satisfaction, one is not made prudentially better off. For some, this is hard to believe. Surely, it is good for a child to have a very robust, stimulating relationship with her teacher even if she takes no happiness in it. It might not be as prudentially good for her as it would be were she to find happiness in it, but it is hard to think that it has no prudential value at all.

In reply, the proponent of this view might grant that the hybrid view provides an account of the highest well-being, but that the parts of the hybrid might contribute some, small amount of prudential good to one's life. The difficulty with this concession is that it then becomes harder to see the difference between this view and objective-list views. Objective-list views do not have to hold that all items on the list have the same prudential value.

It may in the end be the case that objective-list views are the most promising ones for children. All seem to agree that children's well-being has an objective component and most thinking about it think an objective-list view is the right view of children's well-being. Perhaps in the case of children, worries about resonation are not compelling. The main dispute seems to be over what belongs on the objective list. It is very hard to establish this definitively. Fortunately, this may not matter much for practice, as there is likely significant overlap in what the various views recommend as objects of pursuit. The narrowest of the lists, hedonism, tends to recommend in practice the very same things that the objective and hybrid theory lists recommend, e.g., valuable relationships, intellectual activity, play, etc.

Rather than adjudicate this dispute, the next section examines a worry for all views so far discussed. All suggest that when a child has a surplus of what they hold well-being consists in, a child is faring well – that, on balance, her life is going well for her. This is open to doubt.

Pity the children?

Sarah Hannan (2018) challenges this claim. She argues that children's lives are, on balance, bad for them. She argues as follows. First, some think there are certain prudential goods that are uniquely and/or exclusively good for children or to which they have privileged access. The possession of these makes children's lives go well. These comprise sexual innocence, an ability to enter easily into loving and trusting relationships, and carefreeness.[9] Hannan argues that these items are not good for children, for when combined with ignorance, they have very bad outcomes. Sexual innocence construed as lack of information about sexual matters can leave children vulnerable to "sexual exploitation, sexual violence, and…unrequited sexual desire" (Hannan 2018: 15). It is better for children to have information about sexual matters to avoid these things or to note the dangers of (especially) sexual interference. Carefreeness leads to bad outcomes for children in the cases where they lack awareness of the consequences of certain actions. Things are likely to go poorly for a child if she is carefree about her studies without an understanding of the costs of being so. Similarly, being able to easily enter into loving and trusting relationships might leave children vulnerable, since, unlike most adults, "children are simply predisposed to this sort of affection, irrespective of whether it's warranted or not" (Hannan 2018: 17).

Second, she argues that children's lives are characterized by four non-instrumental evils. Children lack the capacity to reason well instrumentally; it is difficult if not impossible for them to set and find the most efficient means to their ends. Children lack an established practical identity – that is, they lack a stable inventory of values determining what to do. Children's lives are almost entirely dominated by others and frequently interfered with, often without explanation or justification. Finally, children are extremely vulnerable; they cannot or find it difficult to meet their basic needs – this vulnerability is profound and asymmetric (Hannan 2018: 21ff.). Third, though certain things are non-instrumentally good for children, including play and exercises of imagination (Hannan 2018: 17–18, 25), the above evils outweigh the goods, for the evils are more severe than the goods are good (Hannan 2018: 13, 18–19, 22).

Ergo, fourth, children's lives are, on balance, not good for them; childhood is, on balance, a "bad state for children to inhabit" (Hannan 2018: 22).

A defender of the idea that there are unique or exclusive prudential goods for children has two replies. First, she might doubt that Hannan's argument establishes that these things are not non-instrumental "goods for children" at all. Even in cases where they are part of a state of affairs that is not, all things considered, good for a child, they might still possess some prudential value.[10] Happiness taken in carefreeness might be good for a child even if is part of a state of affairs that is, on balance, bad for her. The pleasure involved in a bout of heavy drinking might be good for one despite the fact that the wickedly painful hangover makes it, on balance, a bad state of affairs. Second, she might argue that although there are cases in which certain goods that Hannan discusses are (non-instrumentally) bad for a child, it does not follow that such items are (non-instrumentally) bad in every case. There may be cases in which being sexually innocent or being carefree is part of a state of affairs that is, all things considered, good and that part of the goodness lies in the sexual innocence. It might be non-instrumentally good for a child, but only when part of certain wholes.

As noted, Brighouse and Swift accept the goods of sexual innocence and of carefreeness as part of the welfare interest in having an enjoyable childhood. They note that the way in which welfare interests are to be satisfied is "sensitive to context" (2014: 64). They may argue that sexual innocence and carefreeness are non-instrumentally good only when they are part of a state of affairs that is, on balance, enjoyable and safe for a child.

This is not the best reply to Hannan. It is better to grant that the items she attacks are not non-instrumentally good for children. One might think this hard to establish in any case. One might grant Hannan's conclusion about goods she considers, but deny that this shows that children's lives are, on balance, bad for them, for there are other prudential goods.

Indeed, it is noteworthy that only one of the views of children's well-being noted above accepts that the goods Hannan attacks are non-instrumentally good for children. And on this view it seems that they might well be dispensable if they turn out not to be part of the "freedom, support, and environmental conditions [that children need] to enjoy their *childhood*" (Brighouse and Swift: 2014: 64).[11] It is possible to argue that one of the above views is right; provided that a child has a surplus of the goods it accepts, her life is going well.

This will not do as a reply to Hannan. It appears not to matter to her which inventory of prudential good one furnishes. Her view is that the prudential evils that she enumerates "outweigh whatever goods children might enjoy" (Hannan 2018: 22, cf. 25). Hannan's claim is that if one accepts her theory of children's ill fare, and her claim that the non-instrumental evils are more severe than any prudential goods children possess are good, then, even if one defends goods other than the ones she casts aside, children's lives are, on balance, bad for them.

There are replies to this version of Hannan's claim. One might argue that hers is a rather odd list of non-instrumental evils. A typical list comprises suffering, pain, loneliness, neglect, abuse (physical and emotional), dysfunctional relationships, deprivation, and things like that. The typical list does not include the evils Hannan enumerates. When one takes pity on the Syrian children whose lives have been marred by prolonged civil war, and one thinks of what makes their lives, on balance, bad (if they are), one thinks of the pain, the suffering, the unhappiness, the fact that they have no or very poor or emotionally and physically damaging relationships, that they have only trivial or no intellectual activities, that they have no or severely formed kinds of play, and so on. One does not think in addition that they are poorly off because they are rubbish instrumental reasoners or lack a practical identity or are dominated by their parents or that they are vulnerable. The presence of these do aggravate the situation, but more in the way that a poorly functioning government or lack of social programs aggravates the situation. They are impediments to well-being or causes of ill-being.

Perhaps this involves a lack of imagination about the badness of these bads.[12] I think not. Imagine the following. A child is playing a game in the warm sun with a close friend. His loving parents look on, periodically murmuring words of encouragement and support. All the while they are keenly attuned to his security needs. The child is carefree. He and his friend are playing a game they have concocted and have worked hard to finesse. They are happily immersed in it. They periodically break to express their excitement at the prospect of a visit from the Easter Bunny, punctuating it with conjectures respecting how he manages his deliveries. This child is (seemingly), on balance, faring well. Now suppose that the child's life is full of activity of this sort. He is performing well at school, diligently working each week at homework, he shares jokes and trading cards with friends, he has strong connections with the members of his family, he has solid time for play, structured and unstructured, and so on.

It is hard not to admit that his life is going well, on balance, for him. True, he cannot reason as well as a typical adult. He cannot secure and prepare his lunch or his dinner. He cannot make money. He has fewer values from which to draw (though not none). He will be told when to go to school, when to return home, what sorts of things to eat, when to bathe and how aggressively to scrub, what to read and for how long, and so on.

True, this might change our attitude, to some extent, about the prudential value of the child's life, but surely not enough to drive us to the belief that the child's life is, on balance, bad for him. Hannan's evils certainly function as obstacles to well-being (and/or causes of ill-being). But, again, they appear more like a poor functioning government or poorly provisioned social programs or discovering there is no toilet paper when you've just finished on the loo. To the extent that they are neutralized they seem unable to outweigh a robust inventory of the goods suggested above.[13]

Hannan has a reply: children who fare well "aren't robustly secure because matters could easily have gone badly for them, and there's nothing they could do to affect the outcome" (Hannan 2018: 24, also 16). Hannan's claim is that contingency of this sort is non-instrumentally bad for children. But this is hard to see. It is certainly a threat to well-being, and, thus, reason we have to be more concerned about children, but it is not obviously bad for children in itself and not bad enough to outweigh a solid inventory of non-instrumental goods. In any case, Hannan makes no attempt argue for the claim. It is open to reasonable doubt.

Hannan makes too little of the fact that children change a lot during childhood. Her view makes good sense for the beginning stages of life, especially infancy. It would not be entirely unreasonable to think that infant's lives go quite poorly. They cry a lot, get diaper rash, and seem always to be in peril; they are highly dependent and vulnerable. They cannot reason instrumentally at all and have no values of any kind. However, as children age they become more proficient and more effective at setting and meeting their goals, they adopt a more robust inventory of values, they gain freedom and independence and some discretion over what to do, and they are less and less vulnerable. It is hard to believe given this improvement that it is always the case that children's lives are bad for them, even on the assumption that the non-instrumental evils that Hannan discussed are seriously bad for children. These things might be bad, but it is hard to maintain that as children age the bads always outweigh the goods children possess or experience, even on the assumption that they are more severe than the goods are beneficial.

One of Hannan's central claims is the strong but undefended one that the evils that she presents outweigh whatever goods children are capable of. It is not clear why we ought to accept this. It is not clear why the evils that Hannan discusses are any worse than the evils listed above, including unhappiness, poor or warped relationships, and so on, and it is not clear when one has a robust inventory of prudential goods that these goods cannot outweigh the evils (especially as children age and the evils become less acute).

Suppose that Hannan's challenge can be deflected. This does not help us decide which view of children's well-being is the correct one. This will have to be determined elsewhere, by reference to a more general discussion not focused exclusively on children. Such a discussion will need to reference a view of ill fare and face up to Hannan's challenge.

Conclusion

The focus of this chapter has been children's well-being. The first section distinguished this focus from others with which it might be confused. The second section outlined some hurdles to articulating a position on children's well-being. The third section discussed and evaluated various theories of children's well-being. The fourth section investigated the claim that children possess characteristics essential to them that are non-instrumentally bad for them, and that these outweigh the goods that they might possess. A full discussion of the merits of the views of children's welfare discussed will have to wait for another occasion.[14]

Notes

1 For what looks like this suggestion, see Gheaus (2015).
2 David Wendler (2010: 136, 220–221), e.g., argues that children possess in addition to welfare interests, an interest in a good life story or good life narrative. Both active and passive contributions to valuable human achievements make a child's life better by making the life story more compelling without making a child prudentially better off.
3 Kraut (2007), which is discussed in the next section, is a notable exception.
4 This may not be true of adolescents.
5 For other putative attractions, see Bradley (2009).
6 A recent (perhaps the only) textbook on well-being (Fletcher 2016) fails even to note it.
7 This is true even if hedonism is one of the views, for it is an objective list view with one non-instrumental prudential good on the list.
8 Hedonism seems to face this worry, too.
9 For the kind of view Hannan attacks, see Brighouse and Swift (2014).
10 Hannan seems to admit this possibility in discussing her list of prudential evils (2018: 20).
11 Italics in original.
12 Though even Hannan expresses some skepticism about the claim that lacking a practical identity is non-instrumentally bad for children (2018: 20).
13 I assume that the views discussed above will in their own way endorse my conclusion about the boy's life.
14 The author wishes to thank Lisa Forsberg and Anca Gheaus for helpful comments on previous versions of this chapter and the editors of this handbook for their patience and good judgement.

References

Aristotle. 1999. *Nicomachean Ethics*, trans. Irwin, T. Indianapolis, IN: Hackett.
Badhwar, N. 2014. *Well-being: Happiness in a Worthwhile Life*. Oxford: Oxford University Press.
Bradley, B. 2009. *Well-being and Death*. Oxford: Oxford University Press.
Bramble, B. 2016. "A New Defense of Hedonism about Well-being," *Ergo* 3(4): 85–112.
Brennan, S. 2014. "The Goods of Childhood and Children's Rights," in F. Baylis and C. McLeod (eds.), *Family-making*. Oxford: Oxford University Press.
Brighouse, H., and Swift, A. 2014. *Family Values*. Princeton, NJ: Princeton University Press.
Crisp, R. 2006. *Reasons and the Good*. Oxford: Oxford University Press.
Fletcher, G. 2016. The Philosophy of Well-being: An Introduction. New York, NY: Routledge.

Gheaus, A. 2015. "The 'Intrinsic Goods of Childhood' and the Just Society," in A. Bagattini and C. Macleod (eds.), *The Nature of Children's Well-being*. New York, NY: Springer.
Hannan, S. 2018. "Why Childhood Is Bad for Children," *Journal of Applied Philosophy* 35: 11–28.
Hewitt, S. 2010. "What Do Our Intuitions About the Experience Machine Tell Us About Hedonism?," *Philosophical Studies* 151: 331–349.
Hooker, B. 2015. "The Elements of Well-being," *Journal of Practical Ethics* 3: 15–35.
Kant, I. 1996. *The Metaphysics of Morals*, trans. M. Gregor. Cambridge: Cambridge University Press.
Kant, I. 1997. *The Critique of Practical Reason*, trans. M. Gregor. Cambridge: Cambridge University Press.
Kant, I. 2002. *Groundwork for the Metaphysics of Morals*, trans. T. E. Hill and A. Zweig. Oxford: Oxford University Press.
Kraut, R. 2007. *What Is Good and Why: The Ethics of Well-being*. Cambridge, MA: Harvard University Press.
Lin, E. 2017. "Against Welfare Subjectivism," *Nous* 51: 354–377.
Macleod, C. 2010. "Primary Goods, Capabilities, and Children," in Harry Brighouse and Ingrid Robeyns (eds.), *Measuring Justice*. Cambridge: Cambridge University Press.
Nozick, R. 1974. *Anarchy, State, and Utopia*. New York, NY: Basic Books.
Schapiro, T. 1999. "What Is a Child?," *Ethics* 109: 715–738.
Sidgwick, H. 1907. *The Methods of Ethics*, 7th edn. London: Macmillan.
Skelton, A. 2015. "Utilitarianism, Welfare, Children," in A. Bagattini and C. Macleod (eds.), *The Nature of Children's Well-being*. New York, NY: Springer.
Skelton, A. 2016. "Children's Well-being: A Philosophical Analysis," in G. Fletcher (ed.), *The Routledge Handbook of Philosophy of Well-being*. New York, NY: Routledge.
Skelton, A. forthcoming. "Two Conceptions of Children's Well-being," *Journal of Practical Ethics*.
Sumner, L. W. 1996. *Welfare, Happiness, and Ethics*. Oxford: Oxford University Press.
Wendler, D. 2010. *The Ethics of Pediatric Research*. Oxford: Oxford University Press.

9
CHILDREN'S RIGHTS

Robert Noggle

Introduction

What rights—if any—do children have? Do they differ from the rights of adults, and if so, how and why?

Rights can be either moral or legal. Moral rights are thought to exist independently of any political or legal institutions. By contrast, legal rights are creations of the legal system, and they are backed by the force of law. Although one can have a moral right to something to which one does not have a legal right, and vice versa, moral rights commonly have legal counterparts. For example, the moral right to bodily integrity corresponds to a legal right against battery. Social reform movements often seek to achieve or extend legal recognition for a moral right, as when abolitionists sought to extend legal recognition of the moral rights to freedom and self-determination to all persons. This chapter will focus on moral rights, and unless otherwise specified, "rights" refers to moral rights.

Saying that Mary has a right entails that someone else has a "correlative" obligation either to do or to refrain from doing something.[1] Rights that obligate others to *refrain* from doing something are called *negative rights*. For example, my right to bodily integrity obligates others to refrain from punching, shoving, or even touching me without my permission. Negative rights often prohibit others from interfering with the right-holder's freedom to do various things, such as move about at will, express her opinions, or use her property as she wishes. By contrast, *positive rights* require someone to take some particular action or to provide resources or assistance to help the right-holder obtain that to which she has a positive right. For example, if Mary has a positive right to a basic education, then someone else must be obligated to provide it to her.

The fact that rights entail "correlative" obligations raises an important question: who has the obligation that goes with a given right? Typically, the obligations created by negative rights apply to everyone. Thus, obligations arising from my right to bodily integrity require everyone to refrain from touching me without my permission. By contrast, obligations arising from positive rights often apply only to certain people. This is because positive rights often arise from contracts or special relationships that obligate one party to provide something for the other. Thus, students have positive rights to assistance from their teachers, patients have positive rights to care from their physicians, and clients have positive rights to representation by their attorneys. A key issue in the theory of rights is this: do any positive rights—such as a right to the basic necessities of life—exist apart from contracts or special relationships, so that they create obligations for everyone (or, perhaps, for society at large)?

If children acquire positive rights from the parent–child relationship, then it would seem to follow that the obligations created by those rights fall on the parents. But do children have positive rights which are independent of the parent–child relationship, and which obligate society at large? If so, one might argue that, through the institution of the family, society delegates the obligations associated with this right to parents; in other words, society fulfills the obligations created by the child's positive rights by ensuring that each child has parents who are willing and able to participate in the parent–child relationship and fulfill the obligations created by the child's positive rights. (See Archard 1993; Blustein 1982; Macleod 2007 for versions of this view.)

Since rights entail obligations, one might wonder: why not simply speak of our obligations toward children and leave it at that?

One reason for introducing rights is that obligations arising from moral rights are often regarded as especially stringent. Moral rights—especially negative rights—are often regarded as "trumps" or "side constraints" that overrule other moral considerations and obligations (Nozick 1974). For example, your right to life prohibits anyone from killing you and using your organs to save two other people. Your property rights prohibit UNICEF from appropriating your paycheck, even if UNICEF would do more good with the money than you will. Although they are less often called trumps, positive rights are also thought to generate especially stringent obligations. My children's right to my care requires me to buy them food and clothing, even if the money that their food and clothing costs could feed and clothe many more children in less affluent countries.

Although the idea that moral rights are trumps is common, few people hold those trumps to be absolute. For example, it seems legitimate to break into a stranger's unoccupied wilderness cabin to escape a deadly storm. So, it is perhaps better to think of rights as partial trumps which cannot be violated lightly, but only when the stakes are very high (Thomson 1990; Brennan 1995). Even so, this sets rights-based obligations apart from other obligations.

A second reason for thinking in terms of rights is that attributing a right is thought to indicate that the right holder has a special, morally significant status. Consider the difference between kicking a computer and kicking *me*. Kicking the computer might be wrong—for example, if it belongs to someone else—but its wrongness does not reflect the moral status of the computer itself. By contrast, your obligation to refrain from kicking me reflects a moral status that I have as a person. The idea that I have a right not to be kicked—a right that the computer lacks—means that kicking me is wrong *because I have a certain kind of moral status* that the computer lacks.

To have a right, then, is not simply to be protected by a set of moral obligations. Rather, it is to be protected by a set of moral obligations because one is a being with an inherent moral status that gives one intrinsic moral value. Claiming that children have rights, then, is more than just claiming that we have obligations to them. If children have rights, then our obligations to them reflect the fact that they are beings with intrinsic moral value (see ch. 6).

The nature of rights

Noting that rights reflect and protect the intrinsic moral value of persons leaves open the question: which features of persons gives them the intrinsic moral value that rights reflect and protect? Rights theorists have offered two main answers to this question, and those answers have different implications for children's rights.

The "*will theory*" holds that rights protect the rights-holder's autonomy by giving her discretion over that to which she has a right. In particular, the will theory holds that having a right includes having the choice about whether to *waive* the right, or whether and how to exercise it. For example, my promise to mow your lawn gives you a right that obligates me to mow your lawn, but it also gives you the option to *waive* your right and thus release me from that obligation. Similarly, a property right allows the right-holder to decide how to use her property, and—if she chooses—to relinquish or transfer her right over some particular portion of her property to someone else. On this view, to have a right is to have a choice.

In connecting rights to choices, the will theory provides a straightforward account of why *persons* have rights. Persons possess autonomy, which is (roughly) the ability to make conscious, deliberate choices on the basis of reasons rather than simply acting on impulse or following whichever passion or appetite happens to be strongest at the moment. Since autonomy seems to be part of what gives persons their special moral status (see ch. 6), it makes sense to think that rights reflect that status by protecting autonomy and providing persons with options over which to exercise it.

However, tying rights to autonomy threatens the will theory's ability to accommodate rights for young children. The question of when children develop autonomy is difficult, but it seems clear that very young children lack autonomy (see ch. 10). Thus, the will theory seems to entail that such children lack the very thing that rights are meant to protect. If rights protect autonomous choice, and young children are incapable of autonomous choice, then it seems to follow that young children do not have rights.

One potential response to the apparent inability to accommodate rights for very young children would be to maintain that young children do have moral rights, and reject the will theory because it cannot accommodate them. Harry Brighouse (2002) and Neil MacCormick (1976) defend this position.

A second response would be to stick with the will theory, admit that it is incompatible with rights for young children, and conclude that very young children lack moral rights. This approach is defended by James Griffin (2002) and Carl Wellman (1984). However, while Griffin and Welman deny moral rights to very young children, they maintain that adults nevertheless have important non-rights-based moral obligations toward young children. While this softens the impact of denying that young children have moral rights, it is not clear that it softens it quite enough. For it detaches the obligation to take care of a young child from the special and intrinsic moral status of the child herself, and appears to make our obligations toward children more like our obligations to refrain from kicking someone's computer and less like our obligations to refrain from kicking another person.

A third potential response is to modify the will theory to enable it to accord rights to not-yet-autonomous young children. Some will theorists have suggested that adults can exercise the kind of rights the will theory posits on behalf of children, and that this enables children to have such rights. But as Andersson (2015) observes, this response makes the child's rights precarious, since they vanish if no adult is willing to exercise them for the child.

Alternatively, one might modify the will theory to include what Joel Feinberg calls "rights in trust." According to Feinberg, rights in trust:

> look like autonomy rights . . . , except that the child cannot very well exercise this free choice until later when he is more fully formed and capable. When sophisticated autonomy rights are attributed to children who are clearly not yet capable of exercising them, their names refer to rights that are to be *saved* for the child until he is an adult, but which can be violated 'in advance,' so to speak, before the child is even in a position to exercise them.
>
> (Feinberg 1980: 125–126)

Thus, the will theorist might argue that a child's rights protect choices, but that until the child achieves autonomy, they are held in in trust, during which time they lie dormant, presumably in their unwaived condition.

Some will theorists will regard this partial decoupling of rights from *actual* autonomy as an abandonment of the central idea of the will theory. Others may be willing to pay that price in order to accommodate rights for very young children. Still others may be drawn to hybrid theories—discussed below—which posit a separate kind of rights for children that do not require autonomy.

The main alternative to the will theory of rights is called the "*interest theory*," which sees rights as protecting interests rather than choices. On this view, rights protect or secure the things or conditions most vital to the right holder's well-being, such as life, bodily integrity, and the basic necessities of life. In short, this theory says that a person has a right to X because having X serves that person's vital interests. Interest theorists commonly include liberty among the vital human interests protected by rights. There are two reasons to think that liberty is a vital human interest. First, there is good reason to think that freedom is intrinsically valuable to human beings, and they cannot thrive without it. Second, since people are usually best situated to know their own best interests, allowing people to make their own decisions will tend to be the most effective way to promote their interests. Consequently, the interest theory can accommodate rights that protect, and provide a sphere for the exercise of, autonomous choice—rights to such things as self-determination, property, etc. Thus, the interest theory can accommodate most if not all of the autonomy-protecting rights posited by the will theory.

Unlike the will theory, however, the interest theory can easily accommodate rights for very young children: after all, children have interests from the get-go, long before they develop autonomy. Thus, the interest theory has no difficulty according interest-protecting rights to young children. However, this very fact also poses a problem for the interest theory, for it lacks a natural way to single out humans as having a unique morally significant status. Human infants certainly have interests, but so do cats, mice, lobsters, and trees. If having an interest is what gives a being rights, then won't all living things have rights?

Of course, many people will be willing—and indeed happy—to accept the idea of rights for non-human animals. But while the idea that all living beings have rights may appeal to some, the implications of applying the interest theory of rights to every vital interest of every living thing might be less appealing than it first seems. For if we accord every living being with a right to whatever is in its vital interests, we may have difficulty in seeing rights as reflecting and protecting something distinctively valuable about human beings. Thus, the feature that enables the interest theory to accommodate rights for very young children threatens to undermine the idea that rights mark the special moral status of persons. If rights protect vital interests of every sentient creature, then what basis could there be for thinking that the rights of my infant child are superior to those of the mouse skulking down my hallway?

Limiting rights to protecting the interests of *Homo sapiens* seems ad hoc. Limiting rights to protecting the interests of autonomous beings leaves very young children just as rights-less as the will theory threatens to do. Perhaps we could point not to autonomy but to *potential* autonomy as the basis on which to say that human infants have rights (or rights superior to those of the mouse). But we must be careful here: as a general rule, it is not the case that potentially having some characteristic entitles someone to the same status as someone who already has that characteristic. A four-year-old has the potential to drive a car, but that does not entitle her to drive now; a computer's potential owner does not already have a property right over it.

One strategy for addressing this difficulty is to argue that the capacity for developing autonomy is itself the morally significant characteristic that entitles beings with it to have their interests protected by rights (Cowden 2016, and Andersson 2015 make arguments along these lines). Alternatively, one might argue that the human infant's potential for autonomy gives her an interest in developing autonomy that the mouse lacks (Vallentyne 2002). Perhaps this interest creates rights that are sufficiently distinctive and important to set humans (and any other potentially autonomous creatures) apart from other living creatures (see ch. 6).

If this problem can be solved, the interest theory may offer a promising approach to children's rights. Since it asserts that rights protect vital human interests which include—but are not limited to—autonomy, it has the flexibility to claim that pre-autonomous children have rights that protect their interests in the necessities of life and growth, and that they gradually obtain rights that protect the liberty to exercise their gradually developing capacity for autonomous choice. Moreover, the view is compatible with Feinberg's idea of rights in trust, which protect the child's liberty to exercise her autonomy once it develops. Not surprisingly, then, several influential theorists, including Harry Brighouse (2002) and Neil MacCormick (1976), argue that those who accept children's rights should adopt the interest theory of rights.

The long-running—and so far inconclusive—debate between will and interest theories of rights has led some rights theorists to suggest hybrid theories or other alternative theories that imply the existence of both rights that protect interests and those that protect choices (see Wenar 2005; Andersson 2015). If we adopt such a view, we could hold that very young children have interest-protecting rights, but that as they mature, they gradually develop more choice-protecting rights, so that when they enter adulthood, most of their rights protect choices rather than interests. Samantha Brennan (2002) defends such an approach. Brennan's hybrid position incorporates two key observations: first, the case for thinking that children have rights that mainly protect their current well-being and future interests is especially plausible for very young children. Second, the case for thinking that children have rights that largely (if not mainly) protect their ability to make their own decisions is especially plausible for children who are close in age and maturity to adulthood. Peter Vallentyne (2002) grounds a structurally similar position within a libertarian theoretical framework.

The interest theorist might resist such hybrid approaches by claiming that the interest theory already contains sufficient theoretical resources to capture this transition between the rights of young children and the rights of teens. On the other hand, if the debate between will and interest theories has reached an impasse that can only be broken by a hybrid or other alternative, then an eclectic approach might be more natural than trying to account for both interest-protecting and liberty-protecting rights within the interest theory.

Protection or liberation?

If children have rights, what do they have rights *to*? And how, if at all, do their rights differ from the rights of adults? Attempts to answer these questions take place against the historical background of two major pro-child social movements.

Before the 20th century, children were accorded few legal rights. They had little if any say over their lives, and very little protection from the law (Mason 1994). Although parents were typically required to provide them with support and enough education to earn a living, children were expected to contribute to the family. Children were put to work at an early age, on farms, in factories, or as indentured servants or apprentices to tradesmen. Child labor was usually strenuous, and often hazardous (see ch. 25). During the Progressive Era a movement arose to ban child labor, and by the 1920s and 1930s such bans were in place. Although part of the rationale for abolishing child labor was to protect adult jobs and wages, the movement against child labor also reflected a concern for the well-being of the children themselves. The abolition of child labor was accompanied by a number of other Progressive Era programs meant to benefit children. These included free and compulsory public education, a separate juvenile justice system focused on rehabilitation rather than punishment, increased intervention by the state into families on behalf of abused or neglected children, and, ultimately, the first tentative steps toward providing financial aid to impoverished families.

On the whole, the Progressive Era children's movement focused on protecting children: protecting them from exploitation in the adult labor market; from abuse or neglect by parents; and, ultimately, from ignorance and poverty. Moreover, this movement helped create the 20th-century Western ideal of childhood as a special, protected time for "children to be children." Although the Progressive Era child protectionists appear to have conceived of their project primarily in terms of securing children's well-being, the language of rights was sometimes invoked as well. For example, the 1924 Geneva Declaration of the Rights of the Child attributes to children the right to food and medical care, "the means requisite for its normal development" and to be "put in a position to earn a livelihood, and ... protected against every form of exploitation."[2]

Ironically, a second pro-child movement, which peaked during the 1970s, sought to undo much of what the earlier Progressive Era child protection movement had achieved. This movement sought to liberate children from what it regarded as tyranny—including the tyranny of those trying to protect them. The child liberationists argued that children should have the same rights as other persons. This applied even to young children. Richard Farson's position was fairly typical:

> The achievement of children's rights must apply to children of all ages, from birth to adulthood.... [R]ights cannot be withheld from the very young solely on the basis of age any more than they can be withheld from the very old who may be similarly incapacitated. The inability to exercise one's rights at any age, old or young, should simply mean that even greater care is taken by society to guarantee the protection of these rights.
>
> *(Farson 1974: 31–32)*

Liberationists proposed making adult rights "available" to children of any age who want to claim them. This includes the right to vote, the right to work for pay (and keep their earnings), and the right to control—or even discontinue—their own education. Liberationists also argued that children should have the right to leave home and live independently or in alternative family arrangements. Although the liberationists focused mainly on negative rights to secure children's freedom from adult interference, some also argued for positive rights to financial resources, such as government-funded stipends, on the grounds that without financial independence, child liberation would not be possible.

Liberationists maintained that children are more competent than we realize, and would become even more competent if liberated. Less competent children, Howard Cohen (1980) proposed, could "borrow capacities" from adults who were willing to act as "child agents," much as an adult might borrow the expertise of an attorney, physician, or financial planner to compensate for her lack of specialized capacities. These agents would work for the child and assist her in exercising, and deciding how to exercise, her rights. Liberationists argued that recognizing the child's right to leave the family would discourage parents from adopting authoritarian parenting styles. Instead, parents would have to guide children by persuasion and by offering privileges or other incentives to children in exchange for complying with the parent's requests. Parents would still have the right to set rules for the home, and to dole out privileges and rewards for desired behavior. But they could not force children to comply, and children would retain the right of exit if they disagreed with the parents' rules.

Of course, the liberationists did not succeed in enabling children to "escape from childhood" (Holt 1974) *en masse*. But some reforms they championed did come to pass. Courts became more willing to listen to children in decisions involving custody decisions and other matters concerning them, the medical profession became more concerned to obtain their agreement before performing medical procedures on children, and the prevention of child abuse and neglect became a higher social priority.[3]

Although its policy successes were modest compared to its aspirations, the liberationist movement had a profound impact on discussions of children's rights in moral and political theory. It challenged theorists to justify the protectionist "caretaker" approach to children rather than simply assuming it. Liberationists rejected the received view that justified withholding liberty from children because they were not competent or rational by pointing out that adults are often just as irrational and ill-informed as many children, and yet we do not think it justifiable to limit their freedom. In raising these issues, the liberationists helped shape the contemporary debate about children's rights in moral and political theory. A number of theorists (e.g., Schrag 1977; Purdy 1992; Archard 1993; Brennan and Noggle 1997) have taken responding to the liberationist challenge as an important task for theories of the moral status of children.

Protection versus freedom

Proponents of relatively pure versions of liberationism can still be found (Godwin 2011), as can defenders of positions close to Progressive Era protectionism (Guggenheim 2007). However, the majority of children's rights theorists appear to defend positions somewhere between these two extremes. This "moderate view," as I shall call it, holds that young children have rights which mainly protect their interests rather than their (current) choices, but that as children mature, they gradually achieve levels of autonomy that entitle them to an ever-growing package of liberty-protecting rights.

This moderate view covers a wide swath of intellectual territory, within which there is a great deal of room for moderates to disagree about specific cases. Most moderates would agree that the interest-protecting rights are at the forefront when a first grader announces that she wants to run away and join the circus. Similarly, most moderates would likely agree that the liberty-protecting rights have significant weight when a mature, well-informed 17-year-old wants to donate bone marrow to save a distant relative. But what of a tween who wants a facial tattoo? Or a 12-year-old who wants to leave his competent and loving parents' conventional, middle-class home to live on his hippy grandparents' commune? Or a 14-year-old who wants to drop out of school and learn his uncle's welding trade? Moderates will often differ in their reactions to such cases, and it is unclear that the moderate view—or, really, family of views—can do much more than rationalize our pre-existing intuitions about such cases. On the other hand, perhaps we should concede that ethics is not an exact science, and that it is misguided to seek precision and unanimity where competing values are closely matched.

The right to an open future

The debates discussed above concern whether a parent should prioritize a child's long-term interests over the child's current preferences. Another major debate concerns the extent to which parents may legitimately shape their children according to their own values and beliefs (see ch. 20). What moral limits, if any, do children's rights place on the parent's attempts to mold the child according to the parent's vision of what is good?

This debate has been shaped by Joel Feinberg's 1980 article, "The Child's Right to an Open Future." Earlier, we mentioned Feinberg's idea of "rights in trust." He develops this idea into an overarching "right to an open future," which is a child's right not to have important decisions made for her when she cannot yet make them herself. Feinberg's compelling idea is that respect for the autonomy that the child will eventually develop requires keeping the child's options open so that she can make her own decisions once her autonomy has developed.

Feinberg's article admits of different interpretations (Lotz 2006). Some passages describe a right to "be permitted to reach maturity with *as many* open options, opportunities, and advantages *as possible*," which suggests a right to a *maximally open* future. In other passages, Feinberg seems to embrace a more moderate view, where parents "are permitted and indeed expected to make every reasonable effort to transmit by example and precept their own values to their children," which suggests that parents are allowed to engage in some attempts to shape their children's values, beliefs, etc.

Although there is some disagreement among commentators as to which interpretation to attribute to Fienberg, there is fairly wide agreement that the position expressed by the second interpretation of Feinberg's remarks is the more plausible of the two. Attributing to the child a right to a maximally open future would impose serious hardships on parents; it might prohibit parents from teaching the child their religion, and require parents to introduce the child to as many sports, performing arts, potential professions, cultures, and religions as possible.[4] Moreover, as Claudia Mills (2003) argues, a maximally open future is neither possible nor in the child's own interests. It is impossible for parents to be strictly neutral among potential options, or to avoid any slight steering of the child one way or another. Moreover, having a child hop around among different religions, sports, musical instruments, hobbies, or extra-curricular activities may not provide enough time for the child to meaningfully discover which she most prefers and which she has most talent for. It might also deprive her of the experience of sticking with one thing long enough to overcome obstacles and the temptation to give up and try something else.

Not surprisingly, many commentators (e.g., LaFollette 1989; Macleod 2003; Mills 2003; Noggle 2002; Brighouse and Swift 2014; Henley 1979) have sought a middle ground between countenancing an unlimited permission of parents to shape their children on the one hand, and a child's right to maximally open options on the other. The middle ground asserts that parents can engage in some shaping of the child's values and outlooks, so long as they fulfill certain conditions, such as not trying to "lock in" their ideas and preferences through indoctrination, brainwashing, or insulating the child from information about other ways of life; fostering (or allowing the schools to foster) critical thinking capacities that will eventually enable the child to make her own choices; and ensuring that the child develops a sufficiently diverse skill-set to give her meaningful career options.

Distinctive rights of childhood

Feinberg (1980) suggested a three-fold distinction: "A-C-rights," which both adults and children possess, such as "the right not to be punched in the nose or to be stolen from," "A-rights," which are "thought to belong only to adults," and "C-rights," which are held only by children (or adults with conditions that create vulnerabilities similar to those possessed by children). According to Feinberg, C-rights fall into two categories: rights in trust, like the right to an open future, and "dependency rights," which "derive from the child's dependence upon others for the basic instrumental goods of life—food, shelter, protection" (Feinberg 1980: 125). Assuming that there are C-rights, are there any others besides the right to an open future and dependency rights?

The logic of the interest theory of rights suggests approaching this question by asking whether there are any interests that are specific to childhood that are not directly rooted in dependency or the interest in developing and then exercising autonomy. One possibility arises from the idea that childhood is a distinctive and intrinsically valuable phase of life, with goods that are either unavailable or less available to adults (see ch. 7). Plausible candidates for such goods include free and unstructured time; play, pretend, and make-believe; a sense of wonder; and an innocence shielded from the worst aspects of the human experience. To the extent that such goods are vital to the flourishing of a child *as a child*, one might suggest that children have a right to them, regardless of whether they are necessary for her well-being once she becomes an adult.

Another possible C-right might protect goods that are specific to the child's role in the parent–child relationship. Brighouse and Swift (2014) argue that the parent–child relationship provides important "relationship goods" to children; perhaps children have a right to such goods, or at least the conditions conducive to them. Along similar lines, S. Matthew Liao has argued that a child has a right to be loved (Liao 2006; see Cowden 2016 for a critique). Even if we are skeptical that there can be an obligation to love someone, we might still claim that children have a right that their parents provide care, affection, and nurturing, and that they at least try to love them.

Critiques of children's rights

As we noted earlier, some theorists deny that young children have rights because they subscribe to the will theory of rights and deny that young children have the autonomy required to possess rights, at least as that theory conceives them.

A rather different critique of children's rights arises from skepticism about whether attributing rights to children is a helpful or appropriate way to think about family life. Onora O'Neill argues that parents have Kantian imperfect obligations to do more for their children than what children can claim as a matter of right. She worries that focusing on children's rights produces a

> narrowing of ethical vision [which] makes it hard for rights-based approaches to take full account of ways in which children's lives are particularly vulnerable to unkindness, to lack of involvement, cheerfulness or good feeling... Cold, distant or fanatical parents and teachers, even if they violate no rights ... can wither children's lives.
>
> (O'Neill 1988: 450–451)

Similarly, Ferdinand Schoeman concedes that even young children have rights, but worries that "the language of rights typically helps us sharpen our appreciation of the moral boundaries which separate people" (Schoeman 1980: 8; see also Wolgast 1987 and Schrag 1980). The worry can be illustrated by a common TV sitcom trope, where siblings or roommates react to a conflict by drawing a line down the middle of their shared space—only to find that this exacerbates the conflict and threatens the relationship. Thinking in terms of rights, so the criticism goes, is rather like drawing the line down the middle of the room: each party gets *exactly* what he or she has a right to, but the relationship suffers as a consequence.

Defenders of children's rights might concede that excessively focusing on rights can damage relationships, but still maintain that rights are important—even if things go best when they are in the background, and even if they agree with O'Neill that good parents will do much more than simply respect their children's rights. Although the roommates are ill-advised to draw the line down the room, it is still important for their relationship that each understands that the other has certain entitlements which, if pressed, would require such line-drawing. Ideally, of course, they will treat each other with warmth and kindness that makes drawing lines unappealing. As Brennan and Noggle (1997) write,

> in a good relationship, people will respect each others' rights as a matter of course, with no need to become obsessed with "legalistic" thinking. . . . [Moreover,] rights and relationships enshrine the same thing: the unique value of persons. . . For genuine relationships with others exist partly on the basis of respect for the other as a person, and so they already involve the same attitude toward persons that rights embody.
> *(Brennan and Noggle 1997: 15[5])*

In short, one need not become obsessed with the asserting of rights to think that children's rights have a role in philosophical and political theorizing about children, and in developing public policies meant to address situations where there has been a breakdown in the kinds of warm, loving relationships that O'Neill and Schoeman have in mind.

Conclusion

There is little controversy over the claim that children have at least some of the basic rights shared by all human beings—such as the right not be killed, enslaved, or made to suffer unnecessarily. Other claims about the rights of children are more contested, with important critiques being leveled against even relatively mainstream views about the nature and content of children's rights—and about the usefulness of thinking about the moral status of children in terms of rights. Thus, even proponents of widely held views about children's rights still have much work to do in providing definitive answers to critics.

Notes

1 Strictly speaking, this is only true of so-called "claimrights," which are the only kinds of rights discussed here; see Wenar 2005.
2 http://www.undocuments.net/gdrc1924.htm, last accessed 17 March 2018.
3 For a less rosy assessment of these developments, see Guggenheim 2007.
4 For an argument that parents really are morally forbidden from imparting their religions to their children, see Clayton 2011.
5 See also Beckman 2001; Archard 1993: 88–93.

References

Andersson, A.-K. M. 2015. "Rights Bearers and Rights Functions," *Philosophical Studies* 172: 1625–1646.
Archard, D. 1993. *Children: Rights and Childhood*, London: Routledge.
Beckman, L. 2001. "Rights, Rights-Talk, and Children," *Journal of Value Inquiry* 35: 509–515.
Blustein, J. 1982. *Parents and Children: The Ethics of the Family*. New York, NY: Oxford University Press.
Brennan, S. 1995. "Thresholds for Rights," *Southern Journal of Philosophy* 33: 143–168.
Brennan, S. 2002. "Children's Choices or Children's Interests: Which do their Rights Protect?," in D. Archard and C. Macleod (eds.), *The Moral and Political Status of Children*. Oxford: Oxford University Press.
Brennan, S., and Noggle, R. 1997. "The Moral Status of Children: Children's Rights, Parents' Rights, and Family Justice," *Social Theory and Practice* 23: 1–26.
Brighouse, H. 2002. "What Rights (if any) Do Children Have?," in D. Archard and C. Macleod (eds.), *The Moral and Political Status of Children*. Oxford: Oxford University Press.

Brighouse, H., and Swift, A. 2014. *Family Values: The Ethics of Parent-Child Relationships*. Princeton, NJ: Princeton University Press.
Clayton, M. 2011. "The Case against the Comprehensive Enrollment of Children," *Journal of Social Philosophy* 20: 353–364.
Cohen, H. 1980. *Equal Rights for Children*. Totowa, NJ: Littlefield, Adams, & Co.
Cowden, M. 2016. *Children's Rights: From Philosophy to Public Policy*. London: Palgrave MacMillan.
Farson, R. 1974. *Birthrights*. New York, NY: Macmillan.
Feinberg, J. 1980. "The Child's Right to an Open Future," in W. Aiken and H. LaFollette (eds.), *Whose Child?* Totowa, NJ: Littlefield, Adams, & Co.
Godwin, S. 2011. "Children's Oppression, Rights, and Liberation," *Northwestern Interdisciplinary Law Review* 1: 247–302.
Griffin, J. 2002. "Do Children Have Rights?," in D. Archard and C. Macleod (eds.), *The Moral and Political Status of Children*. Oxford: Oxford University Press.
Guggenheim, M. 2007. *What's Wrong with Children's Rights*. Boston, MA: Harvard University Press.
Henley, K. 1979. "The Authority to Educate," in O. O'Neill and W. Ruddick (eds.), *Having Children: Philosophical and Legal Reflections on Parenthood*. New York, NY: Oxford University Press.
Holt, J. 1974. *Escape from Childhood*. New York, NY: E.P. Dutton & Co.
LaFollette, H. 1989. "Freedom of Religion and Children," *Public Affairs Quarterly* 3: 75–87.
Liao, S. M. 2006. "The Right of Children to Be Loved," *Journal of Political Philosophy* 14: 420–440.
Lotz, M. 2006. "Feinberg, Mills, and the Child's Right to an Open Future," *Journal of Social Philosophy* 37: 537–551.
MacCormick, N. 1976. "Children's Rights: A Test-Case for Theories of Right," *Archiv für Rechts und Sozialphilosophie* 62: 305–317.
Macleod, C. 2003. "Shaping Children's Convictions," *Theory and Research in Education* 1: 315–330.
Macleod, C. 2007. "Raising Children: Who Is Responsible for What?," in S. Brennan and R. Noggle (eds.), *Taking Responsibility for Children*. Waterloo, Ontario: Wilfrid Laurier University Press.
Mason, M. 1994. *From Father's Property to Children's Rights*. New York, NY: Columbia University Press.
Mills, C. 2003. "The Child's Right to an Open Future?," *Journal of Social Philosophy* 34: 499–509.
Noggle, R. 2002. "Special Agents: Children's Autonomy and Parental Authority," in D. Archard and C. Macleod (eds.), *The Moral and Political Status of Children*. Oxford: Oxford University Press.
Nozick, R. 1974. *Anarchy, State, and Utopia*. New York, NY: Basic Books.
O'Neill, O. 1988. "Children's Rights and Children's Lives," *Ethics* 98: 445–463.
Purdy, L. 1992. *In Their Best Interests? The Case against Equal Rights for Children*. Ithaca, NY: Cornell University Press.
Schoeman, F. 1980. "Rights of Children, Rights of Parents, and the Moral Basis of the Family," *Ethics* 91: 6–19.
Schrag, F. 1977. "The Child in the Moral Order," *Philosophy* 52: 167–177.
Schrag, F. 1980. "Children: Their Rights and Needs," in W. Aiken and H. LaFollette (eds.), *Whose Child?* Totowa, NJ: Littlefield, Adams, & Co.
Thomson, J. 1990. *The Realm of Rights*. Cambridge, MA: Harvard University Press.
Vallentyne, P. 2002. "Equality and the Duties of Procreators," in D. Archard and C. Macleod (eds.), *The Moral and Political Status of Children*. Oxford: Oxford University Press.
Wellman, C. 1984. "The Growth of Children's Rights," *Archiv für Rechts und Sozialphilosophie* 70: 441–453.
Wenar, L. 2005. "The Nature of Rights," *Philosophy and Public Affairs* 33: 223–252.
Wolgast, E. 1987. "Wrong Rights," *Hypatia* 2: 25–43.

10
CHILDHOOD AND AUTONOMY

Sarah Hannan

Introduction

What is autonomy? Are children autonomous? Why does it matter whether children are autonomous or not? This chapter discusses why these questions are important and how they might plausibly be answered.

Autonomy is the ability to govern oneself (Buss 2013), but answering the first question in greater detail is difficult because the philosophical literature on autonomy is vast and contested. In part, this is because the concept of autonomy is central to many different debates. A non-exhaustive list includes: how our major social, political, and economic institutions should be structured, who should be permitted to participate in them, and under what terms; what we owe to ourselves and others; what we should be held legally responsible for; whether we have free will; what mental states constitute self-governance; what we can consent to, and when; and how we should be educated. In this chapter, I limit myself to examining conceptions of personal autonomy advanced within the philosophical literature on children.

"What is autonomy?" is a question about a normative concept, while the second question, "are children autonomous?", is largely empirical. The answer to the second question depends on how you settle the first. You must determine which conception of autonomy seems most apt, and then determine whether children are (or can be) autonomous. You might also work – to some extent – in the other direction. For example, if it follows from a particular conception of autonomy that children can *never* be autonomous, this might be a reason to doubt the plausibility of that conception. So, while questions about children's autonomy are important in their own right, examining this topic can also change what we think about autonomy more generally.

It matters a great deal whether children are autonomous or not. The third question asks us to explain why. Beyond satiating intellectual curiosity, discerning whether children are autonomous matters because it affects how they ought to be treated. On most views, autonomy plays a crucial role in determining our moral status, which, in turn, informs how others may interact with us. If children are as autonomous as adults, then this gives us reason to think that their moral entitlements are similar. On the other hand, if children lack autonomy or have severely circumscribed autonomy, what we owe them is likely much different than what we owe adults.

I touch on the implications of children's autonomous status, but other chapters in this collection spend more time discussing this issue. The conception of autonomy you endorse, and whether you think children are autonomous, matters for topics as diverse and important as whether children are entitled to: vote; choose who to live with; make decisions about their medical care; decide which courses to study in school, or even cease formal education entirely; take up dangerous sports or hobbies; consume alcohol; work for pay; engage in religious practices; form intimate relationships with other adults and children on their own terms; and so forth.

What is a child?

In the philosophical literature, sometimes "child" refers to humans who, in virtue of their age, have yet to develop the capacities of typical adult members of the species (Brighouse and Swift 2014: 58). This definition allows us to ask, for example, whether inhabiting the developmental states characteristic of childhood is bad for children (Hannan 2018; Tomlin 2018; see also ch. 7, ch. 8). However, it is not suitable for the present discussion, because, on this conception of childhood, children are often defined as lacking autonomy (Schapiro 1999). If "child" is taken to mean – at least in part – a heteronomous (i.e. non-autonomous) human, then it is incoherent to ask about the status of children's autonomy.

For the purposes of this chapter, "child" simply refers to a human of a certain chronological age: those under eighteen years old. This allows us to ask whether the ways that we think about and treat humans within this age range is morally justified. For instance, people under eighteen typically face legal restrictions in contemporary Western societies, which severely limit their life options. Even when the precise age range varies, age-based restrictions are a feature of almost every society, and they commonly exclude people within the specified range from exercising control over important aspects of their lives. So, while some people within this range are provided greater freedom, and others are restricted beyond the age of eighteen, the period from birth through age eighteen is suitable for our purposes. These age-based restrictions are often defended on the assumption that children lack the autonomy to decide crucial matters for themselves; this chapter asks whether this is true.

What is autonomy?

We know that autonomy refers to the ability to govern one's own life. But what does this mean exactly? What does self-governance require, and what undermines or impedes it? This section presents four views, which emphasize different aspects of personal autonomy discussed by philosophers of childhood. I focus on particular scholars who represent these distinct and broad families of thought because they are admirably explicit about what they take self-governance to require.

Tamar Schapiro offers the most developed Kantian conception of autonomy in the philosophical literature on children (Schapiro 1999; Kant 2000). On Kantian views, humans differ from non-human animals in that we can act for reasons that we give ourselves. Non-human animals must follow their natural impulses, but humans possess a capacity for critical self-reflection, stepping back from our impulses in order to decide what sorts of lives to lead (Schapiro 1999: 722). This demands reasoning skills that are only possessed by creatures with a certain level of rationality. But Schapiro illustrates that the mere ability to rationally perform this deliberative procedure is insufficient for autonomy. To see why, notice that questions about what to do confront us at every turn. We must resolve big questions like where to live, what work to pursue, and with whom to spend intimate time. But we must also make smaller choices like what to eat and how to spend an afternoon. It is possible to make rational decisions in each of these domains without exhibiting any coherence amongst our various choices. But deciding in an arbitrary manner will not suffice for self-governance. On Kantian accounts, autonomy also requires that our decisions be driven by a fairly unified self. As Schapiro puts it, the autonomous person speaks in her own voice, "the voice of one who stands in a determinate, authoritative relation to the various motivational forces within her" (Schapiro 1999: 729). Autonomous agents act on principled reasons that express who they are, what they value, and what they want to accomplish, in an integrated manner across a host of domains.

Views of autonomy that require both significant rationality and a stable sense of self have been widely criticized. Within the philosophical literature on children, Amy Mullin's work (2007, 2014) represents an alternative. She subscribes to what I will call an affective endorsement view. Mullin argues that higher cognitive processes play a diminished role, and that "personal autonomy does not always require explicit long-term planning or critical reflection" (Mullin 2014: 416). She also rejects the second component of Kantian views, the notion that autonomy requires a self that is unified and stable over time (Mullin 2007: 537).

Those in Mullin's camp are critical of what they see as an unrealistic and unnecessary focus on independence in many prominent conceptions of autonomy. Views like Schapiro's require us to distance ourselves, at least temporarily, from the internal impulses, as well as the external communities, people, and projects that move us. This distance is said to be necessary so that we can choose whether we *ought* to endorse or reject these forces. Conversely, Mullin argues that dependence on those around us, and on feelings that we cannot step back from, can be a source of autonomy.

Inspired by the later work of Harry Frankfurt (1988, 1999) and work in psychology on self-determination theory (Deci and Ryan 2008), Mullin argues that we should afford emotions a greater place in our conception of autonomy.[1] Self-governance consists in acting in accordance with what we care about, "whether these commitments are to persons, relationships, ideals, values, or even things" (Mullin 2007: 540). The thought is that we can care deeply and act on the basis of what we value – thus being autonomous – without critical reflection or fully stable selves.

A third group of views stress another component of autonomy: options. For instance, following Joseph Raz (1986), Rob Reich's work on children's autonomy contends that self-governance requires a "range of meaningful life options from which to choose, upon which to act, and around which to orient and pursue one's life projects" (Reich 2002: 92). Those endorsing an options view think it is impossible for people to be autonomous if they do not have a sufficient number of meaningful paths they can chose to walk. On this account then, autonomy requires not only the presence of internal capacities, but also external conditions.

Finally, Matthew Clayton offers a fourth view in the literature on children and autonomy. Clayton contrasts two views of autonomy: the independence account and the achievement account (Clayton 2012: 359–362).[2] These are best understood as families of views since there are different ways of filing out the details in both cases. What unites the more popular achievement views is a focus on reaching a certain state as one develops from early childhood to adulthood, namely a state in which we can autonomously endorse our lives. Getting to this state requires that others not thwart the development of our autonomy capacities or close off too many meaningful options before we can select amongst them. More demandingly, others might also be required to take positive steps to ensure that we achieve autonomy, say by providing us with information and safe environments in which to try out our capacities without bearing the full brunt of any negative consequences. Clayton agrees that it is important that we end up autonomous, and that others have duties to assist us in doing so. However, he stresses that there is another aspect of autonomy that has been largely forgotten in discussions about children. Autonomy is not merely a matter of the capacities we possess, or the life we lead, but also of *how* we got there. It is not enough that we come to have rationality, a sense of self, or strong emotional commitments. Having a set of meaningful options may be important too, but it is also insufficient. Self-governance requires that we are the author of our lives, and this means that other people cannot be.

Clayton argues that a viable conception of autonomy must reflect this fact, by giving pride of place to the notion of self-determination, or independence (Clayton 2012: 360). His understanding of independence has something in common with Schapiro's use of the term; however, Clayton draws special attention to something she does not. Views like his insist that our autonomy is violated if others decide which ends we pursue, even if we ultimately come to endorse them. Drawing on the work of Arthur Ripstein (2009), Clayton points out that being forced to serve the ends of others makes us their subjects, which is incompatible with autonomy (Clayton 2012: 360). For example, if someone takes you hostage and forces you to build their dream house, this undermines your autonomy, even if, in the end, you endorse the project you have engaged in, realize that you quite like building houses, and change careers as a result. In such cases, it is clear that autonomy requires not only that we endorse our lives, but also that we are directing them.

What about cases where we are not capable of autonomously setting our own purposes for ourselves? Clayton argues that "what is done to a person or what she is made to do by others when she is incapable of choosing for herself can affect her autonomy", even if she ends up capable of autonomous choices afterwards (Clayton 2012: 358). Demonstrating this, he turns to cases where consent is at issue. Performing an elective cosmetic surgery on someone without her consent, while she is anesthetized for another medically necessary surgery, violates her autonomy (Clayton 2012: 357). This is true even though she could not have consented to the procedure (since she was unconscious), and it remains a violation of her self-governance even if she later comes to appreciate the cosmetic surgery and is glad it was done. That this type of "independence view adds a further requirement to the ideal of autonomy, which the achievement view lacks" will be relevant to the discussion of children's autonomy below (Clayton 2012: 362).

This section highlighted some important features of rival conceptions of autonomy. It did not survey all existing views, and there is obviously more to say about the views discussed, including how they can be combined into hybrid accounts. Nevertheless, the features I have drawn attention to – rationality, a stable sense of self, affective endorsement, external options, and independence – are particularly useful to consider, since they figure importantly in philosophical discussions of children's autonomy.

Are children autonomous?

Recall that determining whether children are autonomous involves settling which normative conception of autonomy to employ and then empirically ascertaining whether children meet the requirements of that conception. This section indicates where adherents of the different conceptions of autonomy outlined above are likely to come down on whether children are autonomous, raises some issues for each view, and offers some thoughts of my own.

Asking whether humans under eighteen are autonomous is too broad, since there is considerable variation in the capacities of individuals at different ages within this range, and even between children of the same age. Here I am discussing the average capacities of individuals at a given age, supposing that they are treated justly and have developed typically. Infants do not possess the capacities required by any plausible views of autonomy. They are not sufficiently rational, and have yet to form senses of self or develop commitments and values. So, whatever your views about autonomy, it is clear that not *all* children are self-governing. The relevant question becomes whether *any* children are. What about three-year-olds, six-year-olds, twelve-year-olds, or seventeen-year-olds?

Kantian theorists have typically held that young children, and sometimes even older children, are heteronomous. For example, while some of her discussion focuses on younger children, Schapiro's view classifies children as old as eighteen as lacking the autonomy of adults (Schapiro 1999: 734). She emphasizes that "we think of adolescents as people who are characteristically 'in search of themselves'" and that their actions are "rooted in a merely provisional self" (Schapiro 1999: 733). For Schapiro, children also lack the critical rationality that autonomy requires. For this reason, she draws a distinction of kind between adults and even older children: adults are self-governing whereas children are not (Schapiro 1999: 725).

Kantian views accord with many individuals' pre-theoretic intuitions. People often respond to work on children's autonomy with, "but children aren't autonomous!" Despite their appeal, views that draw a bright line between autonomous and heteronomous people, and deem all children heteronomous, raise at least two concerns.

The first is about where to set the bar for autonomy. Given the variation in human capacities, and the extent to which our powers vary from moment to moment, what level of rationality should we require? And how unified and stable does our sense of self have to be? Adults commonly act irrationally. For instance, they are often terrible at risk assessment, and suffer from various emotional and cognitive biases, like confirmation bias and framing effects. Adults also frequently report their self-conception changing when they undergo major life changes (e.g., have children, shift careers, end major relationships, or experience religious conversions). If the bar is set such that most adults can be deemed autonomous, then it will be extremely difficult to judge all children under eighteen as heteronomous. This is because many children – especially older children – have stronger capacities for rational reflective decision-making and more established senses of self than some adults do. On the other hand, if we set the bar higher, so as to exclude everyone under eighteen, many adults, who we typically judge autonomous, will also end up heteronomous.

The second concern generated by Kantian views is that no matter where you set the bar for determining who is autonomous, it is hard to maintain that those falling on either side are different in *kind*, rather than merely in *degree*. Neither our rationality, nor our sense of who we are – or want to be – come on suddenly. Accordingly, it is hard to suggest that there is any point in an individual's life when she goes from being heteronomous to possessing full-blown autonomy. Schapiro acknowledges that children progress incrementally and are capable of self-governance in some domains before others (Schapiro 1999: 733). However, she (and other Kantian theorists) must say more about how this observation squares with thinking about people's autonomous status as a matter of kind, rather than degree.

If Kantian views appear to set the bar for autonomy too high, thereby calling into question whether any humans – let alone children – can be autonomous, views that focus on affective endorsement may set the bar too low. Emotional skills and commitments are relevant to autonomy, and anyone who spends time with children – even quite young children – knows that they can care deeply and express their commitments forcefully. In light of this, accounts that focus primarily on our capacity to care deeply return the verdict that even very young children are capable of autonomy. However, Mullin's claim that "the ability to care more about some outcomes than others in a relatively stable way is the *most important* requirement for autonomy" seems overstated and difficult to defend (Mullin 2014: 416). When she claims that a three-year-old can express autonomy by comforting a parent who is sad, I wonder if we have the same concept in mind (Mullin 2007: 543).

Mullin notes that, in order to be autonomous, people must have relatively stable goals and commitments. Depending on how you understand relatively stable, this might exclude very young children. However, she adds something that readmits them. Namely, that we need not consciously reflect on these commitments, or be able to articulate our goals, and that we should interpret commitments broadly to include things like

> the well-being of those [we] love, the ability to continue relationships with friends and loved ones, keeping prized possessions, engaging in favourite activities, feeling pleasure [...] feeling comfortable and at ease, mastering new and challenging tasks, being recognized for skills and accomplishments, and avoiding significant stress and pain.
>
> (Mullin 2014: 416)

If this is the standard, Mullin is probably right that children as young as three can be autonomous, but there is a credible case that dogs also have similar goals and commitments.

There is an important sense in which non-human animals can be autonomous, but views which focus on emotional commitment need to distinguish the self-governance that can be attributed to three-year-old humans and dogs from the self-governance typically exhibited by adult humans. Without this, the conception of autonomy cannot play the practical role we need it to in justifying the deference we show to the decisions of adults and the appropriate paternalism that we subject three-year-olds to.[3] I suspect that making such a view viable will require acknowledging that caring more about some things than others is not the most important aspect of autonomy, even if it is necessary. Importantly, the requirements that need to be added alongside Mullin's will likely increase the age at which children become autonomous.

One candidate addition is the requirement, espoused by Reich, that agents have a meaningful range of options. While I agree that we cannot *develop* or *exercise* our autonomy in the absence of live and important options, I do not think that these options are a constitutive part of autonomy itself. Individuals also need a broad range of resources in order to carry out their self-governing projects, but we do not normally think about food and wealth as constituents of autonomy. Options are similarly external.

But regardless of whether options are an element of autonomy itself, or simply needed for its exercise and development, this debate draws attention to the fact that autonomy depends, to some contested extent, on external circumstances. So, in asking whether children of various ages are capable of autonomy, we must not merely look at children as they currently are. We also need to ask whether children could be autonomous under more favourable external conditions.

Historically, children were seen as capable of self-governance at radically different ages, and there remain significant cultural differences in contemporary perceptions of children's autonomy. Some of this is likely a result of false beliefs about children's developmental capacities; no matter how we treat them, three-year-olds will not be capable of robust self-governance. But, we can affect, at least at the margins, how quickly children develop capacities for self-governance. We can help them develop their rationality, sense of self, emotional fortitude, or whatever other capacities are relevant to autonomy. We can also stifle this development.

Another complication involves the concerns raised above regarding Kantian views that attempt to draw a bright line between the autonomy capacities of adults and children. One could respond to this concern by attempting to find the most apt place to set the cut-off between adults and children. Perhaps many seventeen-year-olds are – or could be – too similar to twenty-five-year-olds to be considered heteronomous. We could redraw the line such that childhood ends earlier – at fifteen, for instance – and try to shore up the idea that there really is a difference of kind, rather than degree, at play.

I favour a different response. The question "when are children autonomous?" is misleading. Individuals are not straightforwardly either autonomous or not; they are autonomous to varying degrees in different domains of choice. Thinking of autonomy as a local property that comes in degrees can fit with different conceptions of self-governance. Regardless of whether autonomy requires rational critical reflection, a stable sense of self, strong affective endorsement, meaningful options, or more besides, these elements will vary between individuals. Even within a particular individual's life, these elements will be present in different degrees at different times and in various domains of a person's life at a given time.

Reich insists that although it is true that people can exhibit different degrees of autonomy, autonomy is best conceived as a property of whole lives, making it appropriate to regard people as, all things considered, either autonomous or heteronomous (Reich 2002: 92–93). Both Mullin and Schapiro suggest that we should reject such global judgments, though in each case this claim fits somewhat uneasily with other positions they take, and needs to be defended (Mullin 2014: 417; Schapiro 1999: 733).

Hugh LaFollette (1999) fleshes out the notion that autonomy should be conceived of as a local property, which can be exhibited fully in some domains before others.[4] For instance, someone might be able to make autonomous decisions about who to spend time with, but not about which career to pursue or whether to consent to a medical procedure. Instead of thinking of such a person as heteronomous overall, we can focus on discrete choices, acts, or areas of people's lives, which can properly be deemed autonomous.

In realizing that almost no one, adults included, exhibits autonomy in all areas of their life, we must be careful not to overstate the relevant differences between adults and children. The point is not simply that many children are capable of more than we give them credit for, but also that adults are often capable of less than we assume. We need not elevate children to the status normally attributed to adults, in part because that standard is often unrealized by many adults. LaFollette argues that even if a "15-year-old fails to largely appreciate the significance of a difficult-to-revoke transaction for her future interests over many years, that is equally true of the 40-year-old chain smoker and the 29-year-old helmetless cyclist" (LaFollette 1999: 144).

If we accept a view that conceives of autonomy as domain specific and a matter of degree, as I think we should, we can say that children's autonomy develops gradually. It begins in very limited domains to limited extents in early childhood, and slowly becomes very close to adult autonomy later in childhood. This fits well with empirical evidence on children's agential development. For instance, children's ability to assess risks of failure, or to formulate and execute complex plans, increases as they age. This trajectory is also sensitive to social conditions, like access to education, which children depend upon for developing their capacities. Other social conditions also play a role, inasmuch as they determine children's opportunities to practice or express their developing self-governance skills. Finally, children's experience of agency and the world, together with their accumulation of information, will typically enhance their ability to govern themselves. I subscribe to a gradualist view, but doing away with a distinction of kind between autonomous and heteronomous agents also has costs. Sometimes we want bright lines to be drawn between those who author their own lives and those who do not. The next section says something about why.

Why does it matter whether children are autonomous?

Children's autonomous status matters a great deal because it affects their moral entitlements, and is relevant to the justifiability of legal, social, economic, and political arrangements. Virtually all moral theories afford autonomy an important place in their accounts of what we owe people. Many philosophers value autonomy because respecting autonomy promotes well-being (see ch. 8). Insofar as we ought to promote the well-being of others, we can often do this best by deferring to their decisions about how to lead their lives. Some philosophers also take autonomy to be a constituent of well-being, holding that autonomous lives go better for agents, at least in one important respect, simply in virtue of being self-governed. Some take the stronger view that autonomy rules out paternalism of almost any form. We must defer to autonomous agents' self-regarding decisions, even when they are overall detrimental to their well-being. If children are capable of autonomy, all of these views would give them strong claims against certain forms of interference.

We often justify restricting children from guiding important aspects of their lives by asserting that they lack the autonomy of typical adults. Laws that impose age restrictions on voting, driving, marriage, property ownership, military service, leaving formal education, working outside the home, the consumption of drugs, and more besides, suppose that even teens are not as autonomous as adults. But, as we saw, it is questionable whether we can draw clean lines between the capacities of many adults and older children. For instance, if fifteen-year-olds are as capable of self-governance as many forty-year-olds, is it permissible to disenfranchise them?

I think that, with appropriate empirical guidance, we should lower the age requirements for voting, working outside the home, and medical consent, to give just a few examples. But what about the fact that different children develop their autonomous capacities at different rates? The law cannot be applied on a case-by-case basis. As a result, gradualists still have to set age cut-offs that will wrongly exclude some children from making choices that they are in a position to make autonomously. While this is regrettable, parents and other adults who interact with children can mitigate the ill effects to some degree, by giving children more discretion over their lives in accordance with their capacities. Not all exercises of autonomy are governed by laws; we can, and ought to, change the ways that we engage with children in our everyday interactions. For instance, unless their manner of dress is unsafe, children should be free to dress as they choose. Generally speaking, we should take children's views much more seriously, and grant them greater discretion over their lives.

One might reasonably resist by insisting that our primary job is to protect and promote children's well-being, and that requires overriding their choices in just the ways we currently do. But as Samantha Brennan (another gradualist) points out, this conflict between autonomy and well-being arises in the case of adults too (2002). Trade-offs and difficult decisions are an inevitable part of our moral lives, and we should not dismiss children's autonomy entitlements in favour of focusing exclusively on their well-being.

Other pieces in this collection rely – explicitly or implicitly – on views regarding children's autonomy, including those discussing: children's moral status; their rights; the extent to which paternalism of children is justified; if or when they can consent in sexual, medical, and labour settings; and what rights parents can hold over them (see ch. 9, ch. 12, ch. 15). The point here is more general: we must figure out what autonomy is, and which children have it (to what extent and in what domains), to ensure that we are treating children as they deserve. If some children are capable of greater autonomy than is currently assumed, we are wronging them by overriding their judgments about how to direct their lives. We also need to avoid mistakes in the other direction: affording children too much control over their lives before they are ready can wrong them as well.

I have suggested that children are more capable of self-governance than they are currently given credit for. Moreover, affording children more information, guidance, and experience choosing is likely to render even more children autonomous at even younger ages. If true, this has significant practical and normative implications. But some people will disagree about when children's autonomy develops. Moreover, even on my view, there are some very young children who are entirely heteronomous. What should we say about children who are not autonomous?

Joel Feinberg argues that while children are not autonomous, they nonetheless have "anticipatory autonomy rights" (Feinberg 1992: 77). Children who are heteronomous, but have the *potential* for autonomy, must not be prevented from becoming autonomous and enjoying a reasonably open future, with many life options to choose among. It is not only those who have autonomy, but also those who have the potential for autonomy, that command certain treatment.

While Feinberg's theory requires that we not prevent children from achieving autonomy as adults, Clayton's independence view holds that children's potential for autonomy forbids setting ends for them, even when this will not prevent them from being autonomous in the future. Being autonomous is a precondition for participation in a host of activities. This means that others should not enrol children into activities or ways of life, even if it will not hinder their future autonomy. For example, even if children can grow up to autonomously reject the religion their parents enrolled them in, Clayton holds that the enrolment itself is a violation of their autonomy. We violate children's autonomy – as with the unconscious patient who cannot consent to elective cosmetic surgery – by setting their purposes when they are not in a position to set them for themselves. Clayton rightly stresses that children are independent beings whose lives are not ours to author. But, in order to flourish, children require some guidance regarding what is valuable. So, independence views owe us an account of which values and purposes we can legitimately impart on children, and under what circumstances we can do so.[5]

Whichever conception of autonomy you subscribe to, and regardless of how many children you think are autonomous, you cannot escape considerations of how children's autonomy – actual or potential – bears on their entitlements. Given the various complexities and uncertainties involved, the topic of children's autonomy requires further normative and empirical attention. While questions remain unanswered, erring on the side of affording children more respect for their current and potential autonomy is often advisable, at least in cases where doing so does not put children at unreasonable risk of harm. Several plausible conceptions of autonomy indicate that many more children are, or can be, autonomous than is currently recognized, suggesting that we are committing serious moral harms and wrongs by infringing on children's autonomy as we presently do. If philosophers can show that changing how we treat children will better respect their autonomy, we should make these changes as a risk-reduction strategy for avoiding wronging and harming children, even when we remain uncertain about their autonomous status.

Conclusion

This chapter has laid out four conceptions of autonomy, which stress different requirements for self-governance. I have labelled these the Kantian, affective endorsement, options, and independence views. I have considered whether and when children are deemed autonomous on these different theories of autonomy, and raised some concerns for each view.

Kantian views will typically put the age of autonomy higher because they impose demanding conditions on autonomous agency. But these views cannot plausibly exclude all children from autonomy without excluding many adults with somewhat ordinary agential capacities as well. Affective endorsement views can rightly deem children autonomous at a younger age. But if they push the age of autonomy back too far, they threaten to lose a grip on the kind of autonomy that we think demands deference. While I do not think that meaningful options are constitutive of autonomy, options views rightly recognize that external conditions affect how children develop and exercise autonomy: children's autonomy can be hastened or slowed by the ways we raise them. Independence views point out that even fully heteronomous children normally have the potential for autonomy. This means we should not set their ends for them, even when they are not in a position to set their own purposes, and doing so will not hinder their future autonomy. Questions remain about whether such views prevent adults from giving children the values, ends, and relationships that they need to flourish (both as children and adults).

I suggested that more children are capable of autonomy than is currently recognized and that more could be autonomous if reared differently. Acknowledging that autonomy develops in domain-specific degrees makes the question of whether and when children are autonomous less dichotomous, and gains plausibility as a result. However, it introduces complications concerning where to set age cut-offs in various domains of self-governance and how to make trade-offs between children's autonomy and well-being. Adequately addressing these, and other important, issues requires further work. The last section stressed that it is important that the work be done, because whether or not children are autonomous bears significantly on their moral, legal, social, economic, and political entitlements.

For those who remain sceptical of the notion that children can be autonomous at all, I will end by noting that we have a history of being wrong in related respects. For example, women were held to be incapable of autonomy. This was used to justify the restriction of their choices and the subsumption of their rights under those of their fathers, brothers, and husbands. There are, of course, important differences between women's subjugation and the control of children. Nevertheless, it is instructive to remember that, at many times in history, people have been subjected to horrible injustices licensed by the false claim that they lacked the ability to govern themselves. We must ensure that our treatment of children is not an injustice rationalized by similarly false claims. Philosophers should continue developing conceptions of autonomy that do not unjustly exclude children who can take authority (or even partial authority) over their lives. Those in empirical fields should continue trying to establish at what age, and under what circumstance, children are capable of what our best theories tell us self-governance requires. Finally, everyone who spends time with children should ensure that they are being treated in the ways demanded by their actual or potential autonomy.[6]

Notes

1 Although Mullin's work is indebted to his, Frankfurt requires more coherence in what we care about across a wider set of domains than she does.
2 In earlier work (Clayton 2006), he called these the precondition and end-state views, respectively.
3 For an argument that we should not defer to many of the decisions adults make, see Conly (2013).
4 Also see Mills (2003). In order for children to become autonomous they need practice at choosing. Accordingly, Brighouse points out that children "must have the experience of choice before it makes sense for them to be seen as having the right to choice" (Brighouse 2002: 46). While this is true, the point made here is different. It's not simply that treating children as though they are autonomous is developmentally advantageous, but rather that children actually *are* autonomous in certain domains, and this autonomy commands respect.
5 Clayton (2006, 2012, 2014, 2015) develops his account, which holds that parents can impart values of justice (2006, 2012, 2014, 2015).
6 I am grateful to R.J. Leland, Liam Shields, and the editors of this handbook for helpful comments on earlier drafts of the chapter.

References

Brennan, S. 2002. "Children's Choices or Children's Interests: Which Do their Rights Protect?," in D. Archard and C. Macleod (eds.), *The Moral and Political Status of Children*. Oxford: Oxford University Press.

Brighouse, H. 2002. "What Rights (If Any) Do Children Have?," in D. Archard and C. Macleod (eds.), *The Moral and Political Status of Children*. Oxford: Oxford University Press.

Brighouse, H., and Swift, A. 2014. *Family Values: The Ethics of Parent-Child Relationships*. Princeton, NJ: Princeton University Press.

Buss, S. 2013. "Personal Autonomy," in E. N. Zalta (ed.), *The Stanford Encyclopedia of Philosophy*. Retrieved from https://plato.stanford.edu/entries/personal-autonomy/ (last accessed 29 July 2017).

Clayton, M. 2006. *Justice and Legitimacy in Upbringing*. Oxford: Oxford University Press.

Clayton, M. 2012. "Debate: The Case against the Comprehensive Enrolment of Children," *The Journal of Political Philosophy* 20(3): 353–364.

Clayton, M. 2014. "Anti-Perfectionist Childrearing," in A. Bagattini and C. Macleod (eds.), *The Nature of Children's Well-Being*. Dordrecht: Springer.

Clayton, M. 2015. "How Much Do We Owe to Children?," in S. Hannan, S. Brennan, and R. Vernon (eds.), *Permissible Progeny?: The Morality of Procreation and Parenting*. New York, NY: Oxford University Press.

Conly, S. 2013. *Against Autonomy: Justifying Coercive Paternalism*. Cambridge: Cambridge University Press.

Deci E. L., and Ryan R. M. 2008. "Self-Determination Theory: A Macrotheory of Human Motivation, Development and Health," *Canadian Psychology* 49(3): 182–185.

Feinberg, J. 1992. "The Child's Right to an Open Future," in his *Freedom and Fulfillment*. Princeton, NJ: Princeton University Press.

Frankfurt, H. 1988. *The Importance of What We Care About*. Cambridge: Cambridge University Press.

Frankfurt, H. 1999. *Necessity, Volition and Love*. Cambridge: Cambridge University Press.

Hannan, S. 2018. "Why Childhood Is Bad for Children," *Journal of Applied Philosophy* 35(S1): 11–28.

Kant, I. 2000. *The Cambridge Edition of the Works of Immanuel Kant*, eds. P. Guyer and A. Wood. Cambridge: Cambridge University Press.

LaFollette, H. 1999. "Circumscribed Autonomy: Children, Care, and Custody," in J. Bartkowiak and U. Narayan (eds.), *Having and Raising Children*. University Park, PA: Pennsylvania State University Press.

Mills, C. 2003. "The Child's Right to an Open Future?," *Journal of Social Philosophy* 34(4): 499–509.

Mullin, A. 2007. "Children, Autonomy, and Care," *Journal of Social Philosophy* 38(4): 536–553.

Mullin, A. 2014. "Children, Paternalism and the Development of Autonomy," *Ethical Theory and Moral Practice* 17(3): 413–426.

Raz, J. 1986. *The Morality of Freedom*. Oxford: Clarendon.

Reich, R. 2002. *Bridging Liberalism and Multiculturalism in American Education*. Chicago, IL: University of Chicago Press.

Ripstein, A. 2009. *Force and Freedom: Kant's Legal and Political Philosophy*. Cambridge, MA: Harvard University Press.

Schapiro, T. 1999. "What Is a Child?" *Ethics* 109(4): 715–738.

Tomlin, P. 2018. "Saplings or Caterpillars?: Trying to Understand Children's Wellbeing," *Journal of Applied Philosophy* 35(S1): 29–46.

11
PATERNALISM TOWARDS CHILDREN

Kalle Grill

Introduction

Discussions of paternalism in contemporary moral and political philosophy revolve around a series of related questions: to what extent may people harm themselves, risk harm to themselves, or simply fail to optimally promote their own interests? When should others interfere with potentially self-harming or sub-optimal behavior? What role should a person's will or preference, and her own view of her good, play in answering these questions? Children appear in the paternalism debate mainly as archetypical targets of justified benevolent interference. Paternalism is frequently described as treating adults as if they were children, with the assumption that children have no right to self-direction that could conflict with their being forced against their will (e.g. de Marneffe 2006; Quong 2010: 73; Tsai 2014).

At the same time, discussions of the moral and political status of children only rarely connect with the finer details of the paternalism debate (but see Aviram 1991). In this chapter, I describe the general contours of the philosophical debate on paternalism and consider how the issues raised in this debate relate to children and childhood in particular. While surveying various views, I also argue for my own view: children are like adults in some ways, importantly by having a will that warrants some measure of respect, but unlike adults in other ways, such as being less prudent and less vulnerable to the harms of paternalistic interference; there is no blanket justification for paternalism towards children, but many particular instances are justified.

Paternalism and its components

Contemporary philosophical debate on paternalism typically takes as its starting point John Stuart Mill's Liberty principle, as formulated in *On Liberty*:

> [T]he sole end for which mankind are warranted, individually or collectively, in interfering with the liberty of action of any of their number, is self-protection. [T]he only purpose for which power can be rightfully exercised over any member of a civilized community, against his will, is to prevent harm to others. His own good, either physical or moral, is not a sufficient warrant.
>
> (Mill 1859/1869: ch. 1, para. 9)

Paternalism can usefully be understood as that against which Mill's Liberty principle is directed.[1] On this reading, the debate is about what exactly should be understood by interference with someone's liberty or the exercise of power over someone, what should be understood by something being against someone's will, and what should be understood by something being warranted by someone's good. These questions can be answered either from a normative perspective, aiming to identify paternalism as something morally problematic, or from a more conceptual perspective, where the moral status of paternalism is an open question. Without settling any normative or conceptual disagreements, we may simply label the three components of paternalism the *interference component*, the *will component* and the *good component*. Paternalism involves some sort of interference, some sort of disregard for will and some sort of benevolent reason. In the rest of this chapter, I discuss these components and how they relate to children, with one section devoted to each component. After discussing the will component, I pause to consider the concept of soft paternalism, and in relation to discussing the good component, I particularly address future autonomy as a good.

Paternalistic interference with a child

Interference is what makes paternalism at least potentially morally problematic. It is quite controversial, however, what sort of things can be paternalistically interfered with. Mill's formulation "interfering with the liberty of action" sounds rather narrowly concerned with action, while his formulation "exercise of power over" sounds quite broad. Most authors nowadays accept a broader understanding such that it can be paternalism not just to prevent a person from acting, but also to, e.g., withhold information from someone or to give medical treatment to someone who is unconscious (Gert and Culver 1976).

A particular ambiguity concerns the distinction between what is self-regarding and what is other-regarding. Liberals are concerned to distinguish a sphere of each person's life that does not directly affect others, or affects others only "with their free, voluntary, and undeceived consent and participation" (Mill 1859/1869: I.12), and which, therefore, should be protected from all interference. Paternalism has been closely associated with this project, to the point of claiming that paternalism can only be interference with something self-regarding (Gray 1983: 90; Feinberg 1986: 22). This is arguably a mistake, since we can interfere with a person for her good and against her will also when she is interacting with others, or even harming them. That I harm or risk harm to others does not, or not obviously, make it less problematic to invasively promote *my* interests.

The issue of self-regarding vs. other-regarding is especially relevant for children, who, because of their dependence on others, have very small or non-existent self-regarding spheres. Almost everything a small child does will affect her parents or guardians directly and substantially. Furthermore, parents do not consent to being so affected. They may have taken on their roles voluntarily, but this does not, I propose, entail blanket consent to their children's particular behavior. Therefore, if paternalism were limited to interference with a self-regarding sphere, much interference with children would not be paternalism. As I just argued, however, we should not think that paternalism is so limited, and intuitions to the effect that children can be targets of paternalism give further support to this position.

Another controversial issue is what sorts of actions count as interfering in the context of paternalism. Traditionally, this has included only compulsion, deception, coercion, and making options more costly by, e.g., taxing them. In the conceptual debate, these action types have sometimes been operationalized in terms of diminishment of choice (Archard 1990) or substitution of judgment (Dworkin 1983). Mill is very clear that his Liberty principle does not prevent benevolent argument and persuasion, even when these are unwanted. Recently, this traditional view has been challenged by the introduction of the term "libertarian paternalism" and the ensuing debate on so-called *nudging*. In brief, nudging is influencing choice via design of the choice context rather than by any changes to the content of alternatives, and libertarian paternalism is the position that nudging should be used benevolently but that any means that significantly affect incentives should not. According to its original proponents, libertarian paternalism is paternalism because "it attempts to influence the choices of affected parties in a way that will make choosers better off" (Thaler and Sunstein 2003: 1162). Along similar lines, it has been argued specifically that even rational persuasion can be paternalistic (Tsai 2014). Some types of nudging seem manipulative because they bypass the targets of rational agency, and may, therefore, count as paternalism even on more traditional accounts (Scoccia 2013). Other nudges, however, do not seem manipulative at all, since they simply activate a person's rational agency (Hanna 2015).

With nudging, as well as with paternalism more generally, it is not easy to decide which means are interfering and which are not. Linguistic intuitions about what cases "feel" paternalistic, rather common in the conceptual debate, may not align with considered judgments about which cases are morally problematic. Leaving this demarcation problem to one side, we can note that children are often the target of compulsion, coercion, manipulation, nudging and unwanted rational persuasion, though rational persuasion of course requires that the child has at least rudimentary language skills.

Many things that are typically important to adults are not important to many children. Indeed, younger children may not even be physically able to do some things that adults value doing. Examples include marrying, running for office and hiking in the wild. It may, therefore, seem that preventing these children from doing these things cannot be coercive or cannot be paternalism. This is a mistake, because it is not generally the case that whether or not some form of prevention is interfering or paternalistic depends on whether or not the targeted person *cares* about the option that is being closed or burdened, or even whether or not she is able to utilize the option. My lack of interest in smoking does not make it innocuous to prevent me from smoking for my own good. Depending on one's theory of liberty, my (let us presume) inability to hike in the wild may or may not entail that my liberty cannot be limited by additional, redundant, preventive measures. However, such prevention would surely be obnoxious. Inability cannot *justify* prevention. What might justify prevention is if someone *is* able to do something, but is either unable to make a sufficiently competent choice to do it – paternalism's will component – or is at risk of harming herself by doing it – paternalism's good component.

Against a child's will

Benevolent interference with a person is not paternalism if she consents to it. At least this is so if the consent is sufficiently free, informed and rational (see ch. 12). I will leave to one side the intricate issue of how to categorize less clear-cut cases, when there is neither clear consent nor clear protest – some hold that there is paternalism only if the interference is actually *against* a person's will (VanDeVeer 1986; Arneson 2015), while others hold that it is sufficient that the interference is undertaken *independently* of the person's will (Gert and Culver 1976; Pope 2004). I will focus instead on what it means to will something, when we do, and to what extent children are different from adults in this regard.

Traditionally, it has been taken for granted that adults have and act on rather settled preferences, which are independent of the choice situations we face, and that this warrants respect for our will. Joel Feinberg, arguably the most important proponent of Millian anti-paternalism in the 20th century, emphasizes the many ways in which voluntary choice can be compromised by controlling influences and temporary distortions, but presumes, with Mill, that adults have settled preferences, even if we sometimes fail to act on them (1986: 115). In contrast, children are traditionally presumed to lack settled preferences. Mill lists children together with people who are "delirious" or "in some state of excitement or absorption incompatible with the full use of the reflecting faculty" as exceptions that are not protected by his Liberty principle (Mill 1859/1869:V:5). Tamar Schapiro (1999: 729) defends this traditional view in a Kantian context by pointing to a child's lack of "a unified regulative perspective which counts as the expression of her will."

These traditional assumptions can be challenged in two main ways. One is to focus on children's abilities. Amy Mullin (2014: 415–416) argues that children under ten have at least some degree of autonomy in some areas of their lives since they have sufficient volitional stability, self-control over their commitments and goals, understanding of the way their actions promote or thwart the fulfillment of those goals and confidence that they can reach those goals via those actions. Sam Frankel argues, based on interviews with children, that children aged 9–11 navigate a moral universe quite similar to that of adults, fully aware of power relations and the enforcement of moral norms, and so should be considered moral agents (Frankel 2012). David Archard argues convincingly that many children possess all three elements commonly required for autonomy: rationality, maturity and independence (Archard 2015: 88–92). Archard also cites empirical studies, including Oliva Stevens (1982), that indicate that children as young as seven are quite able to process information and use it intelligently and independently, and that by age eleven, children typically possess a political vocabulary as good as that of many adults, as well as a framework of ideas that would enable them to make informed political judgments, and so to vote in political elections (Archard 2015: 142–43). If children can deliberate about morality and politics, they can surely also deliberate about everyday matters such as whether to have or skip family dinner. While Feinberg's antipaternalism only applies to adults, he states in his explicit treatment of children that many or most "autonomy rights" (i.e. liberties) a person will have as an adult are acquired already at age "ten or twelve" (Feinberg 1980/1994: 95; 1986: 326; see also ch. 9). There are, in summary, many reasons to hold that rather young children are quite able to form and capably act on preferences.

The other way to challenge the idea that children and adults differ significantly in terms of rationality, autonomy or settled preferences is to look closer at adults (see ch. 10). Advances in behavioral psychology over the past several decades have shown that it is no easy matter to even determine what an adult person wants or prefers (Thaler and Sunstein 2008). Because we are often weak-willed and suggestible, we may not act on or express ourselves according to our own preferences. Because we are often uninformed and irrational, and because we often lack settled preferences that are independent of our immediate context, our preferences are incoherent over times and contexts. This all means that it is far from clear what it means to respect an adult person's will, and so what it means for an action to be against her will (Grill 2015). It is, therefore, far from clear that most adults have the "unified regulative perspective" that Schapiro, with Kant, presumes that we have. To the extent that we perceive ourselves to have such a perspective, this may be self-delusion.

Behavioral findings have been widely invoked to justify various involvements in people's lives designed to help them choose more rationally, i.e. more in accordance with their own long-term goals. Sarah Conly goes as far as to claim that, because respect for autonomy is based on a presumption of rationality, "our belief that autonomous actions should not be interfered with was based on a mistake" (Conly 2013: 192). In other words, Conly argues that we should treat adults more like we treat children, because adults are not much more rational.

However, an alternative reaction is to foreground Mill's invocations of the value of individuality and self-creation, which are not necessarily dependent on prudent choice. Mill argues that these values thrive when we are allowed to make our own decisions. This may be true even if our deliberative capacities are less exalted than we would like to believe, or less exalted than we had good reason to believe before behavioral psychology showed us otherwise. Instead of concluding from behavioral psychology that we have surprisingly meager reasons to respect autonomy, we might conclude that what we have good reason to respect is surprisingly meager. If we should respect the will of adults, even if it is irrational and incoherent, then it is more difficult to argue that we should not respect the will of children. Degrees are important of course, but the strong division of people into adults and children would be more plausible if adults typically reached some sort of maximal capacity for rational choice, or at least some significant threshold. With members of both groups typically scoring rather low and far from maximal capacity, the case for treating members according to what group they belong to is arguably rather weak.

Other abilities or properties have been invoked to argue that children's will is insufficiently informed and rational to warrant the sort of respect we typically give adults. Geoffrey Scarre argues that children lack the ability to make systematic plans for their own future and that this renders them as a class irrational, to the extent that it justifies a general paternalistic regime (Scarre 1980). Norvin Richards argues more recently that though children have a will that deserves some respect, they lack, at least in many cases, the self-awareness necessary for identifying as a coherent person over time, thinking of their choices in terms of self-creation (Richards 2010: 127–34). Both proposals may point to something less ambitious and so more realistic than Schapiro's unified regulative perspective, while still excluding children from consideration. However, it is not obvious that a person's lack of the ability for self-aware self-creation, or for forming systematic life plans, should undermine respect for her will. Imagine an adult person who is both inherently unsystematic in his life plans and also lacks the awareness that he is continuously creating himself via his choices. Perhaps this person is extremely unreflective and spontaneous, absorbed by one or other interest at any given time, changing between them unsystematically. Perhaps such a person would have some sort of medical condition, a personality disorder or Autism Spectrum Disorder. However, I propose that such divergence from normalcy would not justify disregarding this person's will. Therefore, similar divergences do not undermine respect for children.

I propose, in conclusion, that children have preferences and a will and that at least from the age of seven this will is not, for most children, very different from that of a normal adult in its basic functioning. However, *what* children will, or want, may often be quite myopic. Young children are often quite spontaneous, oblivious to what will be important to them in the next moment, much less the next year. Many adolescents are easily overwhelmed by strong impulses and feelings, which they may be experiencing for the first time. Adolescents also typically lack a sense of proportion and may have a strongly inflated or deflated view of themselves. This all means that children may, on average, be less prudent than adults, which means that they will more often make choices that are suboptimal or even harmful from a long-term prudential perspective. This, in turn, may give us stronger reason to interfere with them against their will and for their good. When we do so, however, we treat them paternalistically, just as we would if we did the same thing, for the same reasons, towards an adult.

Voluntariness and children: hard and soft paternalism

Paternalism is interference with a person for her good and against her will. However, Feinberg proposes that benevolent interference with a choice that is substantially nonvoluntary should count as *soft paternalism* and is morally permissible. This is, Feinberg explains, because such choices are not genuinely ours, they do not originate from our will (even when we in principle *have* one). Nonvoluntary choices are "as alien to [us] as the choices of someone else" (Feinberg 1986: 12). Therefore, Feinberg reasons, it is really only *hard paternalism*, i.e. benevolent interference with fully voluntary choices, that is proper paternalism. Feinberg's view has become standard in the philosophical paternalism debate. In more applied contexts it is often presumed without argument that soft paternalism is permissible.

It is sometimes claimed that paternalism towards children is always soft paternalism and, therefore, justified. However, while Feinberg only awards absolute protection from hard paternalism to competent adults, he never argues that all paternalism towards children is soft. Moreover, his comprehensive treatment of voluntariness does not provide much basis for such an argument. Feinberg distinguishes five families of voluntariness-reducing factors (Feinberg 1986: 115). The first is competence understood as a basic requirement for voluntary choice. Feinberg explicitly states that this excludes infants, but clearly does not mean to exclude non-infant children. The remaining four are coercion and duress, subtle manipulation, ignorance and mistake, and temporarily distorting circumstances. The first two are perhaps circumstances that befall children more often, but this is partly because paternalism towards them is widely considered unproblematic. It seems ignorance is the only factor on which children generally do worse than adults for less contingent reasons. Ignorance is also the basis on which Feinberg argues elsewhere in his book that children often cannot give valid consent (Feinberg 1986: 325–332).

It is not clear, however, that children typically make less informed choices than adults, or would do so if allowed to. Certainly, young children are typically more ignorant than adults in the sense that they have a smaller set of true beliefs (though many high school students may have an advantage over those adults whose information is outdated and fragmented). However, children also typically make choices that are more local and involve less complex information. Children in nursery choose what to play and with whom, while adults at work may choose what stock to invest in, what diagnoses to give a patient, or how to plan a new course in the philosophy of childhood and children. There are certainly some choices that young children could potentially make and for which they are not well equipped. Feinberg argues that a three-year-old is not sufficiently informed about financial matters to voluntarily invest in real estate. This sounds right. However, Feinberg goes on to argue that the same goes for a fifteen-year-old, because "he cannot yet have a full visceral appreciation of the significance of an irrevocable transaction for his future interest over the course of a lifetime" (Feinberg 1986: 325). This seems an impossibly high standard – one that no person, child or adult, could live up to.

It should be recognized that adults generally have a greater appreciation of the long-term consequences of their choices, as well as more goal-oriented behavior. This probably depends both on their greater mental capacity and on their greater life experience. Adolescents in particular seek novel experiences and take greater risk. There are neurological explanations for these behaviors, observed in many species, and presumed to aid the development of greater independence (Casey, Jones, and Hare 2008). However, it is not clear that the advantage a twenty-year-old has over a fifteen-year-old, in these regards, is any greater than what a thirty-five-year-old has over a twenty-year-old, or what a well-educated and reflective adult has over a poorly educated and unreflective adult. More importantly, it is not clear to what extent one must have a good appreciation of long-term consequences in order not to be ignorant in a way that makes one's choice non-voluntary. If the self-regarding choices of people with poor appreciation of their own future well-being is non-voluntary, then the other-regarding choices of people with poor appreciation of other's people's well-being must also be non-voluntary. But is not clear that we are any more justified in interfering with the other-regarding choices of those lacking in empathy, except to the extent to which they actually harm or risk harming others. Likewise, it is not clear that we are any more justified in interfering with those lacking in long-term prudence, except to the extent to which they actually harm or risk harming themselves. Harm and risk, however, is an aspect of the good component of paternalism, not the will component.

The last voluntariness-reducing factor is temporarily distorting circumstances. These can befall people of all ages. In fact, the kinds of circumstances that Feinberg lists arguably affect adults more than children. They include fatigue, neurosis, being under the influence of mind-numbing drugs and extreme time pressure. This indicates that it may be the choices of adults that are more often substantially nonvoluntary and, so, open to soft paternalist interference.

For both distorting circumstances and controlling influences from others (coercion and manipulation), it is important to note that the extent to which a person's will is distorted and controlled should be evaluated relative to her own non-distorted and non-controlled state. Feinberg is very clear that voluntary choices need not be reasonable by any general criteria, but may be "eccentric" and "imprudent" (Feinberg 1986: 111). Donald VanDeVeer similarly argues that paternalism towards a person is justified when she would have consented to it if *her* normal capacities for deliberation and choice were not impaired, which, he explains, should be understood in an "individualized" way, not as a general standard of rationality (VanDeVeer 1986: 75–85). This means that the fact that children are in general more spontaneous, more emotional and less rational, does not make interference with them soft rather than hard. The relevant question, for adults as well as children, is whether a person's choice is genuinely hers.

For the good of a child

Paternalism is almost universally taken to involve some sort of benefit for the person or persons interfered with, whether intended or actual or both. The benefit may be of any sort – material or moral, in terms of outcomes or opportunities. Since this is sometimes confused in the debate, it should be emphasized that the paternalist need not be imposing a foreign value on the paternalized and need not believe in any sort of perfectionist or objective values. It is paternalism if I force you to do what will maximize your preference-satisfaction or subjective well-being over time, or even if I force you to do what you think is best for yourself at the time, but that you do not do, perhaps because you seek your own detriment, or because you think other things than your own interests are more important, or simply because you do not have the willpower to do what you think best. However, that an interference is in accordance with a person's own view of her good arguably makes it a more *justified* case of paternalism.

Unlike with the interference component and the will component, there is no controversy around the fact that we can act for the good of a child. What may be controversial in the case of children is what exactly their good consists in. Childhood has sometimes been considered a mere preparation for adulthood. The more modern and, to my mind, correct view is that a child has two types of interests – the good for her now, as a child, and the good of her future adult self, as a more fully autonomous person with quite different interests (Archard 2015: ch. 3). Though it may seem obvious, the fact that a good childhood is intrinsically valuable is relatively new in mainstream political philosophy (Macleod 2010; Brennan 2014).

I will not discuss the extent to which the goods of childhood are in general distinct from the goods of adulthood (on this, see Gheaus 2015; also ch. 7). Given that there is *something* that is good for a child as a child and *something else* that is good for her as a future adult, paternalism towards her can be directed either at the former or at the latter, or both. For any individual young child, what is good for her at the moment and in her immediate future may have no correlation with what is good for her adult future self. Robert Noggle emphasizes that children typically cannot even comprehend what they will value as adults, or middle-aged persons (Noggle 2002). It may even be proposed that, morally speaking, the child and the adult are two quite different people, partly because of the differences in interests and the lack of anticipation of future interests, but also because of differences in personality, ability and social context. However, the differences between children and adults should not be exaggerated. As adults, we also develop over time and typically have quite different interests in different periods of our lives. Indeed, it could be argued that many twenty-five-year-olds cannot even comprehend what they will value in their sixties or eighties. It may even be proposed that, morally speaking, the twenty-five-year-old and her later eighty-year-old successor are different people (which is one reason for why there are statutes of limitations in the criminal law).

To the extent that a person's future values and preferences are quite different from her current ones, it may be suggested that we should to some extent respect the former and not only the latter. In the case of children, it may be suggested that we should interfere with them for their own good in order to respect their future *adult* self. David Archard notes that this idea is an instance of subsequent consent, and so potentially self-justifying: the interference may cause a child to develop into an adult of the sort that consents to the interference (Archard 2015: 72–75). This also means, Archard notes, that different treatments may create different adults, all of whom would retroactively sanction, or rather approve of, the way they were treated. However, if an interference is benign in terms of its influence on decision-making ability, it does not seem so problematic that it is only one among several that would all be subsequently approved. What seems more problematic is the very idea of deferring to a person's future preferences rather than her present one's. This idea seems to presume either that she is presently incompetent and so does not have a will, or that she is temporarily impaired and so that her choices are not genuine. Both of these possibilities were discussed above and rejected as general justifications for interfering with children.

Invoking a child's future adult self has some similarity with invoking her hypothetical, more informed and rational self. This is the sort of justification of paternalism that I attributed to Donald VanDeVeer in the previous section – hypothetical individualized consent. For someone who is normally quite competent to make choices, but who is temporarily impaired, or even just in new and unexpected circumstances, it makes sense to consider what she would have wanted if she was more informed and more rational, making inferences from her statements and choices when at full or normal capacity. For someone who has never been very competent, however, there may be no unimpaired state from which to extrapolate such hypothetical consent. This seems especially problematic for children, who are typically at their hitherto maximal capacity and competence.

Another and arguably better way to acknowledge a person's future self is to cherish and encourage her particular nature so as to further her most promising development. It might perhaps be a form of respect to treat children, or people more generally, not just in line with their will or preference or life plan, but also in line with their personality and potential, providing them with opportunities that suit them and their development (Richards 2018).

I acknowledged above that children are less prudent than adults and, so, there may often be stronger reasons to interfere with them because doing so yields greater benefits, relative to non-interference, than for adults. There is also the corresponding argument that interference is not as harmful to children as it is to adults. The proposals by Scarre and Richards that I rejected in the previous section as insufficient for undermining respect for the will of children may work in this context. For someone who is unable to make systematic plans for their own future, no such plans are jeopardized by interference. For someone who does not identify as a coherent, self-creating person, no such self-creation is disturbed by interference. Similarly, Roza Terlazzo has argued more explicitly that because settling on life projects is not as central to children's identities as it is for adults, interference with them is not as harmful to their self-respect and general well-being (Terlazzo 2015). If these authors are right, this may also mean that children do not have a view of their own good, if this means a considered judgment concerning one's interests over time. A more mundane reason for why it is less harmful to interfere with children than with adults is that children are used to being controlled by others and that it is less stigmatizing for them to be so controlled. All of these factors are more relevant for younger children and become gradually less relevant as children mature into adults. Even for young children, these plausible suggestions should not detract from the fact that many of them are oppressed and that such oppression is perpetuated by norms that normalize it by characterizing children as non-autonomous or lacking a proper will of their own.

The child's future autonomy

Autonomy is often singled out as an especially important future good for children, and so a strong justification for paternalism towards them. This aligns with a more general position that promotion and protection of autonomy provides a particularly strong justification for paternalism, since it is the very value that underpins resistance to paternalism (Mill 1859/1869; Dworkin 1972; Mitchell 2004). This general position may rest on a confusion between, on the one hand, respect for autonomy and, on the other, promotion and protection of autonomy. As Feinberg convincingly argues, to *respect* a person's autonomy includes respecting choices that diminish her own future liberty and autonomy (Feinberg 1986: 68–70). To compel a person to protect her future autonomy may be to impose a foreign value ranking on her, since she may value other things more (Arneson 1989: 435).

One could be consequentialist about this and hold that the reasons we have to respect autonomy are based entirely on the tendency of such respect to promote a person's interests, including her interests in being autonomous, now and in the future. Whether or not paternalism is justified would then depend on the costs and benefits of interference, in terms of how it affects these interests over time. Childhood is typically shorter than adult life, which means that restriction of autonomy in childhood, resulting in increased autonomy as an adult, will more likely be justified (unless an autonomous childhood is an independent and perhaps incomparable good).

There is also a more specific argument from autonomy that is sometimes invoked to justify paternalism towards children. It is based on the idea that each person should at some point in her life be fully autonomous, having the richest possible set of opportunities and the best possible ability to choose between these opportunities. This point in life is then assumed to coincide with a child's transformation into an adult, and so a (the) main purpose of childhood is to produce this optimally autonomous young adult, with, as it is often called, "an open future" (from Feinberg 1994). It is not clear why there should be such a point in one's life or why it should coincide with becoming an adult. It seems likely that we could achieve a higher degree of autonomy, and so a more open future, at a somewhat later point, perhaps at age thirty, when we are even more mature and informed, especially if our circumstances are designed to promote such development. Therefore, if we should respect the will of young adults, but not so much the will of children, this cannot be because the former have reached their full or highest autonomy.

Conclusion

I started this chapter by pointing to some difficult questions: to what extent may people harm or risk harm to themselves, or fail to promote their own interests? When should others interfere and what is the role a person's will and view of her good in this context? Throughout the chapter, I have discussed these questions in relation to the philosophical debate on paternalism and tried to draw out some lessons regarding paternalism towards children.

I have argued that children are rather like adults in many ways: they have a will, this will directs their actions, they typically act voluntarily, they can be interfered with, they have a future good that can be quite distinct from their current good, this future good includes their autonomy and they have a personality and potential that can be nurtured. I have also recognized some ways in which children are different from many adults: their future good is generally, not just potentially, very different from their current good, they have not reached the peak of their autonomy, they are typically less prudent, they have less settled and systematic life plans, they are more used to interference and interference is not as stigmatizing for them. This last difference is, of course, connected to the fact that children are widely perceived as less competent and more in need of interference.

How do these conclusions help us answer the questions stated? They do so by helping us assess what is at stake in any one instance of benevolent interference with a child, whether in a single action or in the enactment or implementation of a policy. In particular, my conclusions undermine the position that children's lesser capacity for informed and rational choice means that paternalism towards them is either conceptually impossible or generally justified. At the same time, they explain why we often have stronger reasons for interference with children than with adults, and not as strong reasons against.[2]

Notes

1 In the sentence following on from the quoted passage, Mill also rejects interference based on something being "right", which is generally taken as a rejection of *moralism* – interference motivated or justified either by the avoidance of the moral corruption of society, or by the avoidance of immoral behavior or moral fault, irrespective of its possible negative influence on the agent.
2 Thanks to Daniela Cutas, Anna Smajdor, Jurgen De Wispelaere, and especially Anca Gheaus for helpful comments.

References

Archard, D. 1990. "Paternalism defined," *Analysis* 50(1): 36–42.
Archard, D. 2015. *Children: Rights and Childhood*. London: Routledge.
Arneson, R. 1989. "Paternalism, Utility and Fairness," *Revue International de Philosophies* 43: 409–437.
Arneson, R. 2015. "Nudge and Shove," *Social Theory & Practice* 41: 668–691.
Aviram, A. 1991. "The Paternalistic Attitude Toward Children," *Educational Theory* 41: 199–211.
Brennan, S. 2014. "Goods of Childhood and Children's Rights," in F. Baylis and C. McLeod (eds.), *Family-Making: Contemporary Ethical Challenges*. Oxford: Oxford University Press.
Casey, B. J., Jones, R. M., and Hare, T. A. 2008. "The Adolescent Brain," *Annals of the New York Academy of Sciences* 1124: 111–126.
Conly, S. 2013. *Against Autonomy: Justifying Coercive Paternalism*. Cambridge: Cambridge University Press.
Dworkin, G. 1972. "Paternalism," *Monist* 56(1): 64–84.
Dworkin, G. 1983. "Paternalism: Some Second Thoughts," in R. Sartorius (ed.), *Paternalism*. Minneapolis, MN: University of Minnesota Press.
Feinberg, J. 1994. "The Child's Right to an Open Future," in his *Freedom and Fulfillment: Philosophical Essays*. Princeton, NJ: Princeton University Press.
Feinberg, J. 1986. *Harm to Self*. Oxford: Oxford University Press.
Frankel, S. 2012. *Children, Morality and Society*. Houndmills, Basingstoke: Palgrave Macmillan.
Gert, B., and C. M. Culver 1976. "Paternalistic Behavior," *Philosophy and Public Affairs* 6(1): 45–57.
Gheaus, A. 2015. "The 'Intrinsic Goods of Childhood' and the Just Society," in A. Bagattini and C. Macleod (eds.), *The Nature of Children's Well-Being*. Springer Netherlands.
Gray, J. 1983. *Mill on Liberty: A Defence*. London: Routledge & Kegan Paul.

Grill, K. 2015. "Respect for What? Choices, Actual Preferences and True Preferences," *Social Theory & Practice* 41(4): 692–715.

Hanna, J. 2015. "Libertarian Paternalism, Manipulation, and the Shaping of Preferences," *Social Theory & Practice* 41(4): 618–643.

Macleod, C. 2010. "Primary Goods, Capabilities, and Children," in H. Brighouse and I. Roybens (eds.), *Measuring Justice: Primary Goods and Capabilities*. Cambridge: Cambridge University Press.

de Marneffe, P. 2006. "Avoiding Paternalism," *Philosophy and Public Affairs* 34(1): 68–94.

Mill, J. S. 1869 (1859). *On Liberty*. London: Longman, Roberts & Green.

Mitchell, G. 2004. "Libertarian Paternalism Is an Oxymoron," *Northwestern University Law Review* 99: 1245–1278.

Mullin, A. 2014. "Children, Paternalism and the Development of Autonomy," *Ethical Theory and Moral Practice* 17(3): 413–426.

Noggle, R. 2002. "Special Agents: Children's Autonomy and Parental Authority," in D. Archard and C. Macleod (eds.), *The Moral and Political Status of Children*. Oxford: Oxford University Press.

Pope, T. 2004. "Counting the Dragon's Teeth and Claws: The Definition of Hard Paternalism," *Georgia State University Law Review* 20: 659–722.

Quong, J. 2010. *Liberalism without Perfection*. Oxford: Oxford University Press.

Richards, N. 2010. *The Ethics of Parenthood*. Oxford: Oxford University Press.

Richards, N. 2018. "Raising a Child with Respect," *Journal of Applied Philosophy* 35: 90–104.

Scarre, G. 1980. "Children and Paternalism," *Philosophy* 55: 117–124.

Schapiro, T. 1999. "What Is a Child?," *Ethics* 109: 715–738.

Scoccia, D. 2013. "The Right to Autonomy and the Justification of Hard Paternalism," in C. Coons and D. Weber (eds.), *Paternalism: Theory and Practice*. Cambridge: Cambridge University Press.

Stevens, O. 1982. *Children Talking Politics*. Oxford: Martin Robertson & Co.

Terlazzo, R. 2015. "Autonomy and Settling: Rehabilitating the Relationship between Autonomy and Paternalism," *Utilitas* 27(3): 303–325.

Thaler, R. H., and Sunstein, C. R. 2003. "Libertarian Paternalism Is Not an Oxymoron," *The University of Chicago Law Review* 70: 1159–1202.

Thaler, R. H., and Sunstein, C. R. 2008. *Nudge: Improving Decisions about Health, Wealth, and Happiness*. New Haven, CT: Yale University Press.

Tsai, G. 2014. "Rational Persuasion as Paternalism," *Philosophy & Public Affairs* 42(1): 78–112.

VanDeVeer, D. 1986. *Paternalistic Interference*. Princeton, NJ: Princeton University Press.

12
THE AGE OF CONSENT

David Archard

Introduction: the magic of consent

Consent is a normatively transformative power that is exercised through the communication of words or actions by one person to others. The normative power is principally one of waiving rights or claims, such that an individual is able to render permissible what would, in the absence of communicated consent, be impermissible. In the standard example, Smith's consent to be struck by Jones effects a change of Jones' subsequent action from an impermissible assault into a permissible physical contact. Such a power is elegantly characterized as the "magic of consent" (Hurd 1996).

In what follows I shall leave to one side the following important questions about consent: that of whether consent is an expression of will to change matters or must be given in and by a performative act (which can be verbal or non-verbal), or is a hybrid mixture of both will and performance (for defenses of each view, see, respectively, Hurd 1996; McGregor 2005; Westen 2004); that of whether consent must be communicated by word or can be transmitted by behaviors (or their absence) alone; and of what justifies the normative power of consent. Moreover, the consent I am concerned with is explicit and direct. I thus ignore, although I do not deny, the possibility of consent that is indirect or tacit.[1] Nor, finally, do I consider whether some behavior might have the same normative force as consent in giving rise to obligations, amounting to what Singer calls "quasi-consent" (Singer 1974: 47–52).

I shall assume, crucially, that consent is agreement *to* something rather than agreement *with* that thing. By which I mean that one can and often does consent to what one does not desire or wish for. I can give my consent to an outcome I would prefer is not brought about.

Inasmuch as consent is a normative *power*, it is and can be exercised only by those who have it, who are competent, and are thus able to give or to withhold consent. Moreover, it is only normatively transformative in certain circumstances or, perhaps more properly, in the absence of certain conditions. Essentially, these are ones in which the normative power, although possessed, cannot be exercised. If such conditions obtain, there is no normative transformational "magic", even if someone acts in ways that are indistinguishable from the giving of consent. These conditions are said to defeat or vitiate consent. It is common in many discussions of consent to contrast consent that is vitiated or defeated with "real", "true", or "genuine" consent. Since such a usage might, misleadingly, imply that in the relevant circumstances a weaker or *ersatz* form of consent is given, I think it better simply to say that consent is either given or not given.

The conditions that defeat consent are those in which an otherwise competent consenter is temporarily incompetent. They are those that undermine or destroy the will of the consenting party – such as ignorance of what is being agreed to, or when subject to coercion. Smith does not consent to be struck by Jones if he does not know that this is what Jones intends or if he is threatened by Brown with terrible consequences if he does not agree to Jones landing a blow.

Without begging too many important questions, it can be said in brief summary that consent is a power that a person has inasmuch as exercising it expresses her will that something normatively be the case. To be competent to make that normative transformation someone must know what it is that is to be changed and of her own free and independent volition will that it be changed.

Age and capacity

Children – or at least those below a certain age – are thought not to be capable of consent and, thus, as lacking the power to make the indicated normative transformation. Children lack the relevant capacity and this lack is both cognitive – a full understanding and appreciation of what consent means and of what might be consented to – and volitional – being possessed of and able to exercise sufficient independence of will.

When an age of consent is spoken of, it is intended to serve as a reliable marker of when an individual has developed her cognitive and volitional capacities to that point at which she has and may exercise the requisite normative power. There is of course nothing about the reaching of any age *as such* that effects the change from incompetent to competent person. To claim as much would invite a charge of arbitrariness – why should reaching some age on the stroke of a clock mark the acquisition of competence? Rather, conventionally marked chronological points serve as rough and ready signs of the progressive acquisition of abilities. On the whole, and generally, 18-year-olds are more capable in relevant respects than 17-year-olds. Age reliably correlates with capacity.

Note further that a charge, distinct from that of arbitrariness, is one that the wrong age has been fixed. It can thus be argued that the age of consent that is set is too young or too old inasmuch as the relevant capacity is in fact normally and generally acquired later or earlier than this age. Note too that it is possible to set the age of consent at different points depending upon what it is that is being consented to. There is no reason to think there is a single age of consent.

The same point about incapacity disqualifying a child from giving or withholding consent is also made when it comes to the ascription to individuals of rights (see ch. 9). Children – some or all – lack the rights – some or all – that adults have. Again, it will be said that rights-holders must have and exhibit certain properties, those that qualify them for the possession of rights. On the two standard theories of rights, this means that rights-holders must either have significant interests or be able to make choices. Children are disqualified on the latter account, and only some children qualify on the former if what it is to have an interest requires that one be, in some way, aware of oneself as having interests (Archard 2018).

There has been considerable discussion of what rights children have at what age and why (Archard and MacLeod 2002: Part I). However, the important point to be made here is that the lack of capacity that disqualifies children from having rights closely mirrors and is an analogue of that incapacity that disallows children from giving or withholding consent. Moreover, it is in both cases not age as such but age as a marker of the acquisition of the relevant capacity that marks the difference between adults and children.

There are obvious issues around how we should understand the relevant capacity for consent. This can obviously be construed in more or less robust ways, with the caveat that the more demanding the construal the less evident it would be that adults satisfy the test it sets. We should also acknowledge that competence is to be understood as relative to that in respect of which consent might be given. Thus, we can think of the content of decisions as differing in terms of their *complexity* – how many options there are to choose between; the degree of difficulty in comprehension each option presents – and in *significance* – how serious are the consequences of any decision, and how should the various possible consequences be balanced against one another. Thus, a minor, simple, risk-free medical procedure is easier to grasp than a choice between several possibilities, each difficult to make sense of and each with its own risks and potential effects on the quality of life. The cognitive capacity required for consent to the two options varies accordingly.

We should also distinguish between a *knowledge of matters* that is simply and solely factual and an *appreciation* of what certain facts entail. Thus, a 15-year-old might know that refusing treatment would mean the shortening of her life but be said not to understand what an early death means or to comprehend the utter finality of death. Or a 14-year-old might know that sex is potentially procreative but not fully grasp what pregnancy and childbirth entail.

Judgments of capacity are thus complex and by no means a simple matter of ticking relevant boxes. Equally, it will be important to determine which procedures should be in place for any determination of capacity. Where it is disputed whether a minor does in fact have the competence to consent, whom exactly should be appealed to for expert testimony in helping to make that determination of ability?

Perhaps it helps with this question to note that those below an age of consent are akin to those adults deemed to be mentally incapable of making decisions. The English *Mental Capacity Act*, for example, states that,

> a person lacks capacity in relation to a matter if at the material time he is unable to make a decision for himself in relation to the matter because of an impairment of, or a disturbance in the functioning of, the mind or brain.
>
> (Mental Capacity Act *2005: 2 [1])*

Further, in its next provision it states that,

> a person is unable to make a decision for himself if he is unable (a) to understand the information relevant to the decision, (b) to retain that information, (c) to use or weigh that information as part of the process of making the decision, or (d) to communicate his decision (whether by talking, using sign language or any other means).
>
> (Mental Capacity Act *2005: 3 [1])*

In the case of adult incapacity of this kind there is both a clear set of criteria, and an indication of what would count as appropriate evidence of incapacity.

That same Act also has as one of its key underpinning principles the following: "A person is not to be treated as unable to make a decision merely because he makes an unwise decision" (*Mental Capacity Act* 2005: 1 [4]). This principle should be endorsed. Any assessment of a person's capacity to consent should be made independently of an evaluation of the prudence of her choices. After all, adults are perfectly at liberty willingly and knowingly to consent to imprudent outcomes without it being doubted that they are generally able to give or withhold their consent. The imprudence of a child's decision may be evidence that a child is not competent. But a demonstration of her incompetence cannot rest on such imprudence alone. Rather, it should be shown that a decision is imprudent because a child is not competent to make certain kinds of choice.

The weight of consent

As we shall see, an age of consent may serve as an absolute and fixed standard as to whether a person's agreement has normative force or not – that is, that it should count as consent. By contrast, reaching a certain age may serve as a presumption of a capacity to consent but be a defeasible presumption. Thus, one could – as is the case with the *Gillick* principle discussed later – hold that all those below a certain age are presumed incompetent to consent, but allow that individuals below that age may on appropriate occasions be given the opportunity to show that they are competent.

In the case of competent adults, the giving or withholding of consent in the absence of the defeating conditions has determinative normative force. What is consented to, other things being equal, is permissible; what is not consented to is impermissible (see ch. 11). In the case of those below an age of consent, what should be allowed? There are various possibilities (Buchanan and Brock 1990). One is that others should be guided by a principle of best interests and should thus strive to do whatever is best for the child. Whilst this has obvious application in some cases such as medicine, child custody, and child protection, it is irrelevant to the case of sexual activity that will be considered. A second option is that others should be entitled to act as proxy consenters on behalf of a minor. The child's parents are the most obvious claimants to that role, although that attribution is not unproblematic. Again, this will work in some areas but not in others. It would, for instance, be bizarre to think that parents might consent, on behalf of their children, to sex, but not to believe that parents might consent to their children being subject to medical procedures.

A third possibility is that of hypothetical consent – what would the minor agree to if not incompetent to consent? However, it is hard, perhaps impossibly so, to make sense of what a child would choose if she was not childish in her grasp of matters.

Finally, we should note that even where a child's consent does not count, it does not follow that what the child prefers and expresses a wish for is without weight. Article 12 of the *United Nations Convention on the Rights of the Child* (UNCRC 1989) accords to the child "who is capable of forming his or her own views the right to express those views freely in all matters affecting the child, the views of the child being given due weight in accordance with the age and maturity of the child".

We might think that a child's views are important inasmuch as they provide "consultative" evidence of what is in a child's interests (Brighouse 2003); or hold that the child has a fundamental entitlement to have her views heard (Archard and Skivenes 2009).

It is a further interesting question as to how we might appropriately "weigh" the views of someone who is below the age of consent and confirmed as lacking the capacity to give consent. Imagine that a 15-year-old is deemed not able to consent to a medical procedure that she nevertheless expresses a clear and decisive preference not to undergo. How should that view be given "due weight"? Note that the question here is not one of determining whether she is, in fact, although below the age of consent, sufficiently capable of consenting. It is one of acknowledging that although her refusal of consent to the procedure is discounted, because her consent has no weight, her expression of a view that she should not have that procedure *should* nevertheless be counted and duly weighted according to her "maturity".

Medicine, sex, and political legitimacy

There are at least three domains in which consent's normatively transformative power is salient and significant: biomedicine, sex, and politics (see chs. 24, 33, 34, 35). In rough summary, consent is thought necessary if an individual is to undergo either biomedical research or treatment; the mutual consent of parties is essential to the moral permissibility of any sexual interaction; the exercise of coercive power by a state or government is only legitimate if those subject to it have consented.

The last – a liberal principle of legitimacy – is to be found first classically outlined and defended in the work of John Locke (1988), and subsequently expounded and endorsed by liberal political philosophers such as John Rawls and Ronald Dworkin (Simmons 1979). Interestingly, there is no talk of an "age of consent" in the domain of politics. Yet children do present a puzzle for liberal political philosophy. They are thought to be properly subject to the rule of their parents, to which rule they do not and, arguably, cannot consent. They are also subject to the power of a liberal state whose legitimacy might be vouchsafed by the consent of adults but is not by theirs.

Interestingly, Locke thought both that the authority of government was to be founded upon the freely given consent of its subjects, and that a parent's authority over his child is somehow natural and does not arise from a child's voluntary commitment. However, the obvious questions arise of why political authority should not also be construed as natural and why a child's consent should not be required for the exercise of parental authority.

There is a debate as to when children should count as citizens and how they can play their part – even if not fully the equal of adults – in the governance of their society (Schrag 1975). However, this debate is standardly construed as one about the suffrage and citizenship, and not as one about the consenting subjects of legitimate rule.

In the other two areas in which an age of consent is used – biomedicine and sex – there are both commonalities and interesting differences that will become apparent in the discussion of each respective area.

There is a final general point about capacity to be made. Children are deemed incapable of agreeing that things shall be done to them. They lack a relevant capacity. There is also a question of when and why children may be deemed capable of being held accountable for their actions. This question is broached most obviously by legal or criminal responsibility: at what age can minors be held to be responsible for their misdeeds (Scottish Law Commission 2002)? The law normally operates with a presumption of *doli incapax*. By reason of age, a child is presumed to be without exception incapable of committing a crime. There is often a distinct and higher age at which a minor is presumed incapable of criminal action, but that presumption is defeasible such that a court may determine that a minor should be held accountable for her criminal action.

Now there are two interesting questions. One is whether when it comes to consent one should similarly have two ages – one below which any child is absolutely incapable of consenting, and a second below which a minor may be shown to be capable of consent. The *Gillick* principle to be discussed later is indeed that minors at law may demonstrate maturity in respect of some matter.

The second question is whether there is an asymmetry between the manner in which ages are fixed, respectively, for consent and for responsibility, and, if so, whether that asymmetry is warranted. Thus, for example, in respect of sexual consent, one might think that below a certain age a child cannot consent to sex but is nevertheless still properly held responsible for having sex with another minor without *that* person's consent. Such a possibility is not incoherent, but it does need justification. The question of whether the *difference* in age between a young person and an adult makes a difference to the permissibility of sex between them is considered later.

Sexual consent

What might be termed the liberal orthodoxy holds that any sexual activity is morally permissible so long as it is with the consent of all parties (Archard 1998). That orthodoxy is to be contrasted with a conservative view, frequently but not necessarily associated with religious commitments, that holds sex to be impermissible unless it serves reproductive ends, or less stringently, that it is an expression of married heterosexual love. Both accounts hold that unconsented sex is wrong.

In most liberal jurisdictions, unconsented sex is regarded as a criminal offense. Indeed, rape, defined as unconsented penetrative sex, is widely characterized as one of the most serious crimes, second only to murder. It is important to emphasize the centrality of consent to the proper characterization of sexual crime. For on some traditional and historically salient views the rape of a woman was regarded as wrong only for being the improper use of a husband's or father's chattel.

In the present context we may set to one side further problems with the understanding of the crime of rape, such as, most centrally, the issue of what constitutes the *mens rea* of rape and the notorious view that a man's unreasonable but sincere belief as to a woman's consent was sufficient to acquit him of rape.

For the issue here is that of when someone's consent counts. By this I mean the age at which someone may permissibly agree to have sex with another, and at which someone's refusal to have sex is decisive in rendering it impermissible. We should note the following two points that are, to a degree, related. First, the liberal doctrine of sexual consent – comprising the two principles that sex is permissible if consented to, and impermissible if not consented to – serves two important ends. It protects each individual against that to which she does not agree, and it empowers any individual to choose when, how, and with whom she has permissible sex. Second, in the case of consent to medical research or procedures, a patient or subject agrees that something shall be done *to* her. However, by contrast, it gets consensual sex between two parties wrong to view it as that in which each agrees that something shall be done to him or her. Rather, in consensual sex I agree to have sex *with* someone, as she or he agrees to have sex with me.

The important implications for an age of sexual consent are as follows. Those below whatever is designated as the age in question are certainly protected against sex to which they have not agreed – if only because their agreement or willingness, as we shall see, does not count. Consent is absent, just as it would be if a competent person withheld her consent. However, they are also denied the opportunity to choose to have sex to which they *do* agree, again because their consent does not count. Thus, those below an age of sexual consent are disempowered from making choices in what is an extremely important area of human activity.

To say that a child's sexual consent "does not count" means that any indication she might give of agreement to or willingness to engage in sexual activity with another is not normatively transformative. It does not render what the other might do permissible. This is so even if one might reasonably judge that the minor acts willingly and in full knowledge of what she is doing. Sex with a minor – someone below the age of consent – is normally a criminal offense. The term "statutory rape" is frequently employed in this context. However, it is important to make a number of qualifying comments.

First, if two minors engage in mutually consensual sex they might both be held guilty of rape. This is so even if criminal law officers have been historically more likely to seek the prosecution of any male minor. There have also been so-called "Romeo and Juliet" statutes that attach no or a significantly reduced penalty to sex between minors who have clearly engaged in it willingly.

However, second, it may be appropriate to regard an age differential as relevant to the characterization of and severity of punishment for even willing sex between minors. Thus, the law might deem a 16-year-old having sex with a 14-year-old as morally and legally more serious than a case of two 14-year-olds having sex. It may be that in such a case of age difference we rightly regard the higher age as evidence of a superior power that is being abused. Indeed, when an adult has sex with a minor, what makes that egregiously wrongful is not just the difference in years but – and even if the minor is agreeable to sex – that the adult is abusing his authority or power as an adult (Card 1975).

Third, it is a further question as to whether "statutory rape" should be a strict liability offense; or whether a reasonable mistake as to the age of the other is a defense to the charge of rape.

Fourth, even if the consent of a minor does not count in the sense indicated, it is still possible either to have a single crime (sex with a minor irrespective of agreement), or to distinguish between a lesser offense of sex with a minor who does agree to sex (but whose consent does not count) and a more serious crime of sex with a minor whose consent does not count and who, anyway, does not agree to sex.

Turning to the specific questions that arise from setting an age of consent: the age of sexual consent – that age at which consent or its refusal "counts" – is not fixed by or as the age at which it is possible to have sex, understood as puberty – even if, historically, the age of consent has tended to coincide with that for puberty (Bullough 2005). The qualification for a capacity to consent to sex is reasonably taken as a certain psychological maturity and understanding of the nature and significance of sexual activity, where this latter encompasses the risks of heterosexual sexual activity leading to pregnancy and the risk of all sexual activity resulting in a sexually transmitted infection. By contrast, puberty characterizes a critical stage in a purely physical sexual maturation.

The average age of puberty in both males and females has dramatically reduced in the developed world in the last 150 years. That in and of itself does not mean that the age of sexual consent should progressively reduce. However, inasmuch as physical changes bring with them new dispositions and desires, it is arguable that any age of sexual consent should reflect the realities of sexual activity. Indeed, just as the age of puberty has been declining, so too has the average age of first sexual encounter.

Moreover, it is important not to ignore the fact that any understanding of what sex is and what it involves may depend upon the general cultural and social context in which minors can learn about sex. Thus, the age at which minors do acquire an appropriate understanding of sex is not fixed, as might be the case at any historical period with the milestones of biological development.

There are at least three interesting issues that arise from the setting of any age of sexual consent.

The first is whether it is permissible to distinguish between the ages that are appropriate for heterosexual and for homosexual sex. The Wolfenden Report – the UK Government's commissioned *Report of the Departmental Committee on Homosexual Offences and Prostitution* published in 1957 – is justly celebrated for its progressive liberal recommendations of the decriminalization of "private" consensual and self-regarding sexual activities, chiefly off-street prostitution and homosexuality. Nevertheless, the Report recommended an age of sexual consent for homosexual activity that was higher at 21 than the age set then for heterosexual consent, namely 18. The Committee that authored the Report reasoned that such a divergence was warranted because of the "need to protect young and vulnerable persons", especially from the attentions and pressures of older men, and because of the later "age at which the pattern of a man's (sic) sexual development can be said to be fixed" (Wolfenden 1957: para. 66, 71). The Report did not judge homosexuality to be intrinsically wrong; it did share a contemporary and prejudicial view of young men (and not women) as likely to enter into homosexual relations if pressurized to do so, and as settling upon homosexuality as a sexual preference later than would be the case for heterosexuality.

Second, the Scottish Law Commission's discussion paper on rape and other sexual offenses (Scottish Law Commission 2006) offers an interesting distinction between an age (e.g. 12) below which consent absolutely does not count because the child is considered incapable of consent, and a higher age (e.g. 16) below which consent does not count on other grounds. These might, as the paper suggests, be a worry about any exploitation of a minor who is otherwise seen as capable of consent. Moreover, one might additionally – and in terms of how the law functions – wish to convey a message that sex with minors even of that age is wrong.

Third, any age of sexual consent needs to be related to the ages at which it would be permissible or lawful for children to do certain other things. Most obviously and directly, an age of consent should be set no higher than the age at which persons are allowed to marry without parental consent. By contrast, the age at which minors might receive treatment and medical advice in respect of any sexual activity might reasonably be set at an age below that at which such activity is deemed permissible or lawful. Indeed, the *Gillick* decision – which will be further considered in the discussion of medical decision-making – arose out of a challenge to the permissibility of doctors offering confidential advice – on matters such as contraception and sexually transmitted diseases – to minors, below the age of sexual consent, who might nevertheless be engaging in or considering engaging in sexual activity. It is reasonable to believe both that minors below, for example, the age of 16 should not have sex, and that it is permissible to advise such minors who will nevertheless still have sex on the dangers of doing so and the measures that might be taken to minimize those dangers.

Medical consent

The principle of informed consent is at the heart of biomedical practice, and was made a key element of codes of biomedical practice after the Second World War (Nuremburg Code 1949). Its justification is both prophylactic, protecting individuals against the risks of harmful or exploitative medical maltreatment, and, more positively, as expressing respect for individual autonomy (Beauchamp and Childress 2013).

Inasmuch as children are below the age of consent, they cannot give or withhold consent to medical treatment. Some think that parents, as the adults responsible for the care of their children, are best placed to give their proxy consent for medical treatment (Ross 1998). It is important to note that parents may be said to derive this power to consent on behalf of their children either because the fact of parenthood generates certain rights to exclude others from decision-making about their offspring, or because they are, as parents, better placed to judge what is best for the child they care for. Needless to say, any power of proxy consent has limits such that the state, in enforcing its duty of *parens patriae*, may intervene to protect the interest of the child over and against parental wishes.

Of course, if parents have property rights or something very like such rights over their children as some are disposed to think (Narveson 1998: 272–74; Page 1984) then the state's protection of children amounts to trespass, and must be justified in ways other than simply by appeal to what is in a child's interests.

Gillick

Gillick (1985) was a celebrated English law case arising out of a parental challenge to the appropriateness of medical advice being given to minors on sexual health matters. It set out a test whereby those below the age of consent might, nevertheless, be judged competent to make their own decisions. In the famous words of the judge, Lord Scarman, "the parental right to determine whether or not their minor child below the age of sixteen will have medical treatment terminates if and when the child achieves sufficient understanding and intelligence to understand fully what is proposed".

In effect, minors – those below the age of consent – may demonstrate a capacity ("sufficient understanding and intelligence") that qualifies them to give and withhold consent. "*Gillick* competence", as it is known, is then a test of a minor's maturity.

Three immediate comments are in order. First, the original judgment set out a stringent test of maturity. It did so by insisting that a minor not only know and understand the relevant facts of any proposed treatment, but also appreciate the significance of treatment, its implications, and consequences. Second, the judgment spoke in terms of a maturity of understanding. Subsequent legal cases have additionally drawn attention to the requirement of independence. Thus, a minor may know and understand what is proposed but be unable to make an entirely free and independent decision, inasmuch as she is still unduly subject to parental influences. Third, a minor's right to make her own treatment decisions is properly distinguished from a minor's right to confidential discussion of her personal situation. The age of consent may be higher than the age at which a patient has a right to confidentiality. Indeed, some think that such a right is owed to any patient whatever her age.

English law cases made after the 1985 judgment have been characterized as a "retreat from Gillick" (Douglas 1992). The retreat was, arguably, in at least two respects. First, courts tended not to find the child competent if her decision conflicted with a view of her welfare or interests, especially if the child's decision was life-ending or life-limiting. Second, *Gillick* was interpreted as giving mature minors the capacity to consent to treatment, but not as removing parental rights of consent. Thus, a *Gillick*-competent child's decision to refuse treatment could be overruled by the consent of her parents or the court.

In respect of the first "retreat", an asymmetry has been noted between a child's capacity to consent to treatment and one to refuse treatment. No such asymmetry operates with adults; no distinction is made between the competences needed for either choice. In the case of children, it has been and has served to justify overruling an otherwise mature minor's refusal of life-saving medical treatment. It has been argued that a higher (and almost impossibly high) degree of competence is required to refuse treatment (especially life-saving) than is needed to agree to such treatment. Many find such an asymmetry utterly without warrant (Bainham 1992; Harris 2003).

Consent and assent

It was noted at the outset that consent, as agreement *to* something, is to be distinguished from agreement *with* that thing. Those below the age of consent may thus express their assent to, or dissent from, a proposed medical treatment. Clearly, a child who is happy to proceed with what is recommended will be a more cooperative patient. Thus, although her consent counts for naught, the treatment with which she agrees will work better and occasion less distress as a result of her assent.

In general, it is good medical practice to fully inform any patient, whatever their age, of their condition, possible treatment, and outcomes. Children who are in the know are more disposed to go along with what the doctors ask of them and are more responsive to treatment (Alderson 1993).

We should also note, once again, the importance of according children a voice and giving appropriate weight to their views, even whilst they may still be determined to lack the capacity and right to consent.

Consent to research

Is it permissible to conduct medical research on those below the age of consent? The benefits to other children of doing so may be considerable – both because some medical conditions only affect children, and because research obtained from consenting adults need not be applicable, even if "scaled down", to the young.

Some interpret the basic codes of medical ethics as expressly forbidding any research on children. Others argue that such an absolute prohibition is unjustifiable. What would justify research and delimit its permitted scope will involve an appeal to a number of considerations either to be balanced against one another or to serve as threshold requirements (Ross 2006). These include the following: it is imperative that the research in question can only be done on children; parents must consent; risks to the child must be acceptably minimal; and the expected benefits of any research must be acceptably great.

The use of a distinction between therapeutic (of benefit to the subject) and non-therapeutic research is also invoked in this context. However, many find such a distinction unhelpful and unclear, not least because it might distract from the basic fact that any research on someone below the age of consent is morally problematic.

Finally, an appeal to the hypothetical consent a child might give to research if competent to do so does not provide a means of justifying such research (MacCormick 1974). First, it is hard to make much sense of the idea of a competent adult in whose person a child might choose without thereby losing any grip on our sense of who the actual child is and what she wants or needs. Second, the required hypothetical consent could only be given by someone appropriately motivated by a concern for the welfare of others. And why should the consent that an adult might make if so motivated trump any actual refusal by that adult? Third, it is a familiar criticism of hypothetical consent that its justificatory work derives not from its being a particular, if weaker, form of consent but rather from the reasons that would explain its being given (Dworkin 1975).

Consent and open futures

Those below the age of consent will, hopefully and normally, grow into adults. It is a criticism of some forms of testing on children that they deny the future adults the power of consenting or not consenting to the test. This is argued especially in respect of predictive genetic testing (Malpas 2005).

In response, the following will be argued. First, there are very many interventions into the lives of children, all of which are unavoidable in some form, that remove from the subsequent adults any power of choice over some significant matter. Consider only the case of vaccination. In fact, education as such shapes an adult's life in a way that means some choices are open and others closed. However, it would seem that what really matters is not the foreclosing of later choice, but rather the number and quality of subsequent choices that are effected by early intervention.

Second, choices are made in a context of available information. Arguably, the more relevant information a person has, the better the choices are that she can make. If this is the case, then an adult cannot make fully autonomous decisions unless equipped with the personal knowledge that can only have been secured and made available through testing in childhood.

Conclusion

Although only adults get to practice the moral "magic" of giving and withholding consent, that does not mean that children lack any normative control over what is done to them and what they can do. The judgment of incapacity that disqualifies them from exercising the power of consent is properly defeasible. Indeed, *Gillick* is rightly an important and influential statement of when such a judgment is defeated. Moreover, children have a voice over their own affairs that must be appropriately weighted. Finally, it does not follow from denying children the power to consent that adults can simply choose for children as they wish. What is chosen for a child ought always to be what is in her best interests.

Note

1 Locke (1689) famously views consent to political power as being either explicit or implied.

References

Alderson, P. 1993. *Children's Consent to Surgery*. Buckingham: Open University Press.
Archard, D. 1998. *Sexual Consent*. Oxford: Westview Press.
Archard, D. 2018. "Children's Rights," *Stanford Encyclopedia of Philosophy*. Retrieved from https://plato.stanford.edu/entries/rights-children/ (last accessed 12 March 2018).
Archard, D., and MacLeod, C. M. 2002. *The Moral and Political Status of Children*. Oxford: Oxford University Press.
Archard, D., and Skivenes, M. 2009. "Balancing a Child's Best Interests and a Child's Views," *International Journal of Children's Rights* 17: 1–21.
Bainham, A. 1992. "The Judge and the Competent Minor," *Law Quarterly Review* 108: 194–200.
Beauchamp, T. L., and Childress, J. F. 2013. *Principles of Biomedical Ethics*, 7th edn. Oxford: Oxford University Press.
Brighouse, H. 2003. "How Should Children Be Heard?," *Arizona Law Review* Fall: 691–711.
Buchanan, A. E., and Brock, D. W. 1990. *Deciding for Others: The Ethics of Surrogate Decision Making*. Cambridge: Cambridge University Press.
Bullough, V. L. 2005. "Age of Consent: A Historical Overview," *Journal of Psychology & Human Sexuality* 16(2–3): 25–42.
Card, R. 1975. "Sexual Relations with Minors," *Criminal Law Review* 375–388.
Douglas, G. 1992. "The Retreat from *Gillick*," *Modern Law Review* 55(4): 569–576.
Dworkin, R. 1975. "The Original Position," in N. Daniels (ed.), *Reading Rawls*. New York, NY: Basic Books.
Gillick v. West Norfolk and Wisbech Health Authority [1985] 3 All ER (HL) 402.
Harris, J. 2003. "Consent and End of Life Decisions," *Journal of Medical Ethics* 29: 10(1): 10–15.
Hurd, H. 1996. "The Moral Magic of Consent," *Legal Theory* 2, Special Issue: Sex and Consent, Part 1: 121–146.
Locke, John 1988 (orig. 1689). *Two Treatises of Government*, ed. Peter Laslett. Revised edn. Cambridge: Cambridge University Press.
MacCormick, R. A. 1974. "Proxy Consent in Experimentation Situations," *Perspectives in Biology and Medicine* 18: 2–20.
Malpas, P. J. 2005. "Predictive Genetic Testing in Children and Respect for Autonomy," *International Journal of Children's Rights* 13: 251–263.
McGregor, J. 2005. *Is It Rape? On Acquaintance Rape and Taking Women's Consent Seriously*. Aldershot: Ashgate.
Mental Capacity Act. 2005. London: Her Majesty's Stationery Office. Retrieved from http://www.legislation.gov.uk/ukpga/2005/9/contents (last accessed 12 March 2018).
Narveson, J. 1998. *The Libertarian Idea*. Philadelphia, PA: Temple University Press.
Nuremberg Code. 1949. Retrieved from https://history.nih.gov/research/downloads/nuremberg.pdf (last accessed 12 March 2018).
Page, E. 1984. "Parental Rights," *Journal of Applied Philosophy* 1(2): 187–203.
Ross, L. F. 1998. *Children, Families, and Health Care Decision-Making*. Oxford: Clarendon Press.
Ross, L. F. 2006. *Children in Medical Research: Access versus Protection*. Oxford: Oxford University Press.
Schrag, F. 1975. "The Child's Status in the Democratic State," *Political Theory* 3(4): 441–457.
Scottish Law Commission. 2002. *Report on Age of Criminal Responsibility*. Edinburgh: The Stationery Office.
Scottish Law Commission. 2006. *Discussion Paper on Rape and Other Sexual Offences*. Edinburgh: The Stationery Office.
Simmons, A. J. 1979. *Moral Principles and Political Obligation*. Princeton, NJ: Princeton University Press.
Singer, P. 1974. *Democracy and Disobedience*. London: Oxford University Press.
UNCRC. 1989. *The United Nations Convention on the Rights of the Child*. Retrieved from http://www.unicef.org.uk/Documents/Publication/pdfs/UNCRC_PRESS200910web.pdf (last accessed 12 March 2018).
Westen, P. 2004. *The Logic of Consent, The Diversity and Deceptiveness of Consent as a Defence to Criminal Conduct*. Aldershot: Ashgate.
Wolfenden, Lord. 1957. *Report of the Departmental Committee on Homosexual Offences and Prostitution*. London: Her Majesty's Stationery Office.

PART III

Parents and children

13
REASONS TO HAVE CHILDREN – OR NOT

Christine Overall

Introduction

This chapter is an introduction to philosophical debates about whether there are objectively good reasons for choosing to procreate (or not) in order to raise the child(ren) whom one creates.[1] Although my focus is on reasons for choosing to procreate, some of the issues discussed may also apply to reasons for adopting children (see ch. 19).

After examining skepticism about the very existence of such reasons, I first discuss pronatalism and then antinatalism. Most of the commonly cited reasons for having children, including reasons for having more than one child, draw upon consequentialist or deontological assumptions, and are vulnerable to criticisms associated with such theories. I then examine a virtue ethics perspective on procreation, which values women's reproductive labor but relies on a dubious assumption about the intrinsic value of genetic connection to offspring. According to antinatalists, however, all such reasons are inadequate because they ignore the well-being of the potential child, who, they argue, will inevitably suffer. I point out some problems in the antinatalist view, and conclude by briefly suggesting that the best hope for finding good reasons to procreate lies in the relationship between parent and child.

Skepticism about the debate

The first question concerns the legitimacy of the topic. Some argue that procreation in order to parent is, by its nature, a human activity to which reasons do not or even cannot apply; it is the kind of choice about which it is not possible to be rational. Thus Elizabeth Whelan (1975) claims, "[W]e must face the fact that actual decisions about having or not having babies are not totally rational ones. *The decision to have a baby is primarily emotional*" (Whelan 1975: 13, her emphasis). The reason, according to Whelan, is that the result of a decision to have a child is highly unpredictable, since one can have no idea what one's future child will be like, and also no idea of what one will be like as a parent. Moreover, unlike marriage or friendship, the parent–child relationship is not terminable: "you cannot have an ex-child" (Whelan 1975: 13–14).

L. A. Paul (2015) offers a more structured argument purporting to show that choosing whether or not to have children is irrational, insofar as it involves attempting to reflect on what it would be like to have a child. "[H]aving one's own child is unlike any other human experience," she says; hence, one cannot know before undergoing it what having a child will be like. Having a child is, inherently, "epistemically transformative," and for many people it is also "personally transformative" (Paul 2015: 156). As a result, one cannot know ahead of time what "emotions, beliefs, desires, and dispositions will be caused" by having the child (157), and it is also impossible to know, ahead of time, what *value* to assign to having children (158). It might be objected that one can learn what having children is like by being around other people's children. But Paul claims that doing so cannot tell you "what it is like to create, carry, give birth to and raise a child *of your very own*" (Paul 2015: 159, her emphasis).[2] According to Paul, one cannot rationally use one's own preferences as a means to decide whether or not to procreate, and can only use reasons that are independent of one's preferences.

It is undeniable that the experiences of pregnancy and birth cannot be fully comprehended before they are experienced. But Paul's argument also implies – rather implausibly – that people with prior experiences of teaching, mentoring, and caring for young people (such as teachers, coaches, babysitters, camp counsellors, and those with younger siblings) are profoundly mistaken in believing that they have an understanding of what being a parent will be like. Moreover, as Meena Krishnamurthy (2015) suggests, even if certain phenomenal aspects of having children are completely unknowable ahead of time, that very fact might give one a reason to choose it – just as people may rationally choose to travel to completely different parts of the world (Krishnamurthy 2015: 174).

An alternative view of the nature of the question whether to have children is that *any* reason – or none at all – is fine; people don't have to justify their decision to procreate because it is a private, personal matter. According to Whelan, "*decisions about parenthood are uniquely personal.* In the final analysis, they are nobody's business but your own" (Whelan 1975: 37, her emphasis). But is she right?

Procreative behavior, which usually involves (hetero)sex (but may instead require technologies of insemination, or the extraction of eggs, in vitro fertilization, and insertion of an embryo) seems ineluctably private. Yet procreative behavior has consequences, first for the child who is created, second for the child's parents, siblings (if any), and grandparents, and third for members of the wider society, as well as the schools, healthcare facilities, social organizations, governments, and employers that will be affected, positively or negatively, by her existence. Consequently, the reasons for people's procreative choices are potentially of broader interest beyond the individual or the couple. The question is whether those reasons not merely are personally motivating but also objectively justify procreative choices.

Interestingly, in western societies at least, while there is a tendency not to expect or require those who have children to provide reasons for their behavior, there may be little similar cultural latitude for people who choose *not* to have children. People who are childless by choice are often regarded as peculiar or pitiable, and called upon to provide explicit justification for their decision. Corinne Maier (2008) writes, "So universal is the value accorded to family that those who have the nerve to refuse parenthood are seen as social deviants" (Maier 2008: 10). Many personal accounts (e.g., Van Luven 2006) document the extent to which heterosexual couples, in particular, are explicitly asked to justify their decision not to reproduce.

The asymmetry of the social reaction to those with children and those without is telling. First, it is unfair to place the burden of justification only on those who take the less hazardous path: not to bring a child into the world. Those who create a child take risks with the potential health and well-being of the child, as well as with the future effects of the child on her society. Second, if it is possible to give reasons for *not* having children, as interrogations of those who are childless assume, then it ought to be possible to give reasons for having children. The question of reasons to have children is inextricably linked to the issue of reasons *not* to have children. Perspectives on the justification of procreation range from antinatalism – the view that procreation is undesirable, morally unjustified, and to be discouraged – to pronatalism – the view that procreation is desirable, morally justified, perhaps even morally required, and to be encouraged.

Commonly cited reasons to have children

Some people might defend their choice to procreate by arguing that they are simply acting on a right: the right to reproduce. There are many philosophical questions about the existence and extent of such a right,[3] although they cannot be explored here (but see ch. 14). But even if there exists a right to reproduce, it cannot, by itself, constitute a reason to have a child, for one needs further reasons to *exercise* a right. For example, I have a right to drive on the highway, protest a government policy, and worship a monotheistic god, but if I do any of these things, I need further reasons for doing them.

Others might defend their choice to have a child by saying that they have a *duty* to procreate. But such a claim is also incomplete and raises a question: what is the source of or basis for the duty? It seems implausible to say the duty is owed to the potential child, for the child does not exist – and will not exist, if the supposed duty is violated. Is the duty based, for example, on God's command, cultural tradition, or recompense to one's own parents? Thus, any appeal to a right or duty inevitably must take us further into the *reasons* for exercising the supposed right or acting on the alleged duty.

Many explorations of reasons to have children or not have been written not by philosophers but by writers, journalists, and social scientists, and often take the form of advice-giving or advocacy of one particular position on having children (e.g., Silverman and Silverman 1971; Whelan 1975; Leibovich 2006; Maier 2008; Caplan 2011). In evaluating these informal discussions for and against procreation, it is important to distinguish between reasons and causes.

Two main causes are often identified as acting on individuals considering parenthood. Neither of them constitutes a good *reason* to procreate. The first is variously called an "instinct," a "drive," a "natural tendency," a "feeling," or an "urge," motivating people – women in particular – to become pregnant and have babies. While some regard it as innate – perhaps an inherent aspect of being female – its universal existence is highly improbable since so many people, both male and female, state that they do not experience it (e.g., Goldberg 2006; Tennis 2006). But even for those who do experience it, or think they do, it is not a good reason for having children. One need not always follow one's urges or conform to what feels "natural." Even if there are internal influences urging some people into parenthood, it is possible to interrogate and even resist them.

The possibility of resistance to strong influence features prominently in discussions of the second cause acting on people of procreative age, which I call social pronatalism: that is, the media messages, commercial sales promotions, and social policies that encourage reproduction and promote the role of parenthood (Peck 1972; Peck and Senderowitz 1974). Both corporations and governments play a role in pressing people to reproduce, mostly because it is in their interest to do so – whether to sell products, increase the GDP, or grow citizens who will work, pay taxes, and support the increasing numbers of inconveniently long-lived elderly persons.

Social pronatalism is not uniformly dispersed: not everyone is pressured to have children, and not at all times, not in all circumstances, and not with certain partners. Depending on the particular society or social grouping, persons of a particular age (too young or too old), a particular race (usually a minority), a particular sexual identity (not heterosexual), a particular class (poor or working class), or in a particular relationship (perhaps not married, or perhaps partnered with a person of the "wrong" race or religion) may not be expected to reproduce, and indeed may be actively discouraged from doing so.

In some societies, social pronatalism might make childrearing easier, if, for example, it contributed to a child-friendly culture in which social supports such as parental leave and early childhood education were available. (By contrast, a strongly antinatalist or anti-child culture would make childrearing more difficult.) But social pronatalism on its own is not a good reason to procreate; it is simply a cultural factor to acknowledge. One needs further justification for doing what governments, corporations, and media are pressing one to do.

Some of the cultural expectations on which social pronatalism has traditionally relied have also been cited as reasons to procreate. These include adherence to tradition, conformity to one's assigned gender role ("real women want children"; see ch. 20), validation of heterosexual identity, demonstration of personal maturity, development of a sense of self, and satisfaction of family expectations. These reasons seem related to the parents' sense of identity and their place in their community. In addition, some people say they have chosen to have children in order to save a marriage or make a good one stronger. They extol procreation as the "creation of a family," or as their connection to their community. Others advocate having children in order to obey what they take to be God's will for humankind, or to increase the numbers of members of particular racial or religious groups.

Others have argued that having children provides huge psychological rewards (Whelan 1975: 81–99). Having a child is the path to happiness and fulfillment. It is an "investment in future emotional security" (66); children provide companionship, make their parents feel needed, and give them someone to love, or to love them. Procreation provides the opportunity to experience pregnancy, birth, and perhaps breastfeeding. Children are, it is said, an opportunity to demonstrate one's parenting skills, or to relive childhood, or to live vicariously a youth one never had. Children are a source of future economic support, a comfort in one's old age. More grandly, children are said to give meaning to one's existence; they are a "major facet of human life" (Whelan 1975: 66). Children enable one to perpetuate oneself, through one's genetic link to them and to their offspring, and perhaps through passing on a name and family traditions. Children are the only sure path to immortality, or at least to some sort of survival of death.

Evaluating the commonly cited reasons to have children

Within the space of this chapter it is impossible to fully assess all of the reasons stated above. I shall confine myself to a few general comments.

All the purported reasons to have children mentioned so far fall into one of two categories: deontological and consequentialist. Deontological reasons are, roughly, those that express a supposed duty that must be undertaken for its own sake: such as preserving tradition, obeying God, honoring one's family, or conforming to one's assigned sexual, gender, marital, or religious role. Consequentialist reasons are concerned with the creation or avoidance of certain outcomes – either for others (e.g., benefiting one's parents or existing children or community) or for oneself (e.g., gaining companionship, creating future economic support, acquiring a love object).[4]

The division between deontological and consequentialist reasons is not entirely clear-cut; some reasons seem to fall into both categories. For example, building a family may be valued simply because it is thought to be the right and proper course to follow, and also because of the hoped-for happy relationships and experiences that are thereby created. One might obey God's supposed command to be fruitful and multiply both because God purportedly ordered it and also to avoid the supposed punishment that God will inflict if one fails to obey.

The biggest problem with the consequentialist reasons is simply the impossibility of knowing the future. For example, one cannot have any assurance that a child born in 2017 will be both willing and able to support her parents thirty or forty years later. And one cannot know that having a child will make one happy, contribute to one's maturity, demonstrate one's parenting skills, or save one's marriage. Children can be difficult to raise; they can divide rather than unite their parents; they can destroy many of the activities and experiences one previously enjoyed; they can compromise one's independence and personal development; they can bring out one's immature tendencies (Maier 2008; Peck 1972; Whelan 1975: 100–24; Wise 2006). There can be enormous psychological costs to having a child, as well as almost unavoidable (and unpredictably large) financial costs, which include not only the expense of caring for and educating the child, but also the foregone income incurred if a parent (usually a woman) quits work, works less, or advances less far at work in order to rear the child.

In addition, there are further questions as to whether the axiological assumptions underlying both consequentialist and deontological reasons to have children are correct. If skepticism about honoring tradition, God, one's family, or one's assigned role is justified, then one might be doubtful about their role in justifying procreation. Do we really have a duty to conform to our assigned sexual, gender, marital, or religious role? For that matter, should happiness be the main goal in life, with all human activities justified by the extent to which they facilitate it? Moreover, not everyone regards it as plausible that procreation provides a way to give one's life meaning. Maier writes, "Having a child is the best possible way to avoid asking what the meaning of life is, as everything revolves around that child, who is a marvellous [sic] substitute for the existential quest" (Maier 2008: 82).

Having more children

All the reasons so far considered apply to having one's first, second, or subsequent child, but some think there may be special reasons for having more than one child. Some people, for example, want to have a child of a different sex than that of the child or children they already have. Some are seeking a sibling for an existing child, or simply a child who will be different from the one(s) they already have. Some want a second child so the first is "less alone in the world," or even as insurance for the loss of the first.

In a recent book, economist Bryan Caplan (2011) seeks to defeat skepticism about the outcomes of procreation. A committed pronatalist, Caplan recognizes that some people reject having additional children, or reject procreation altogether, because of the hardships and problems they think it will bring. Nonetheless, he argues that "it is in the average person's enlightened self-interest to have more kids" (Caplan 2011: 2), because every additional child adds in important ways to one's benefits and enjoyment (rather than just increasing one's work, costs, and stress, as some might assume). He has several arguments in favor of this claim, but two stand out. The first is that "the benefits of children come later in life" (Caplan 2011: 3). Although Caplan admits that parents cannot expect their children to support them in their old age, he thinks it is important that, with today's longer life spans, parents will live longer to enjoy their children – and possibly their grandchildren. In choosing whether to have children, people should consider not just the short-term benefits and liabilities, but "a *lifetime's* worth of good and bad" (Caplan 2011: 117, his emphasis). Infancy does not last long; the psychological costs of children decrease as they grow older while the benefits increase. One's children are especially rewarding once they are adults (Caplan 2011: 118).

This argument is not implausible, although its applicability may vary from one parent to another. Some parents may love the stages of infancy and toddlerhood, and miss them when they're over. Others may enjoy middle childhood and adolescence more. In any case, like all aspects of parent–child relationships, there are no guarantees about how one's child will act when she is an adult. Nor are there guarantees that having multiple children will increase one's parental satisfaction; they might instead make parenting more complicated and difficult.

Caplan's second argument is that "self-interest and altruism point in the same direction. Parents who have another child make the world a better place" (Caplan 2011: 3). They do so, first, simply by creating a new person. "[A]sking yourself, 'How bad would my life have to be before I'd wish I'd never been born?' teaches a profound lesson: At least one person benefits tremendously from virtually every birth – the new baby" (Caplan 2011: 126). I'll return to this argument later.

Caplan also says that children grow up to make important contributions. People are better off today because the "main source of progress is *new ideas*" (Caplan 2011: 127, his emphasis). The more people there are, the more choices and diversity there are. Even if one's child is not a genius, he or she will be a "productive member of society whose dollars inspire smart, creative people around the world to do their thing" (Caplan 2011: 129). Moreover, in "advanced" countries, the young are legally obligated to support old-age programs; thus, one's children are a "charitable donation to future retirees" (Caplan 2011: 132).

Like the consequentialist views discussed earlier, Caplan makes unwarranted assumptions about the supposed future value of offspring. His theory implausibly assumes the existence of abundant resources, and supports, at its limit, unrestricted expansion of the human population. This view is adamantly rejected by Thomas Young (2001). Young claims that having even one child is comparable to more than doubling one's own consumption, resource depletion, and waste; they are more than doubled because the child can be expected to outlive her parents. Thus, if we do not tolerate "eco-gluttony," we should not accept procreation: "[H]aving even just one child in an affluent household usually produces environmental impacts comparable to an intuitively unacceptable level of consumption, resource depletion, and waste" (Young 2001: 183). Moreover, our children may make the situation worse by having children of their own (Young 2001: 188).[5]

One might not be persuaded by Young's argument that all procreation is immoral. Yet it is not implausible that environmental concerns should carry some weight in the decision about how many children to have. One way to take these considerations into account is by having fewer children. In *One Child: Do We Have a Right to More?* Sarah Conly (2016) claims,

> [W]e don't have a fundamental interest in having more than one child. That is, having more than one child isn't something we need to live at least a minimally decent life. It's possible that we don't really need any biological child at all to lead a minimally decent life, but if we do, we certainly don't need more than one.
>
> *(Conly 2016: 2)*

Conly argues that couples have a moral obligation to limit their procreation to one child *at most*. This obligation is justified by the environmental problems exacerbated by over-population. Indeed, so serious are they that it would be morally permissible for government legislation to try to limit the number of children couples may have – perhaps by tax penalties for those who have more than one child, or tax breaks for those who have only one (Conly 2016: 20). Conly's argument implies that while there might be good reasons, in some cases, to have one child, there cannot be good reasons, or good *enough* reasons, to have a subsequent child or children. Whatever reasons one has for a second or third child, those reasons are more than over-weighted by one's responsibility to refrain from contributing to over-population.[6]

A virtue ethics approach

An alternative to the consequentialist and deontological perspectives on reasons for having children is a philosophical approach that emphasizes moral virtue. According to Rosalind

Hursthouse, a proponent of virtue ethics, simply bearing children is "morally significant and worthwhile" (Hursthouse 1987: 299). "Most pregnancies and labours call for courage, fortitude and endurance, though most women make light of them – so why are women not praised and admired for going through them?" (Hursthouse 1987: 300). She says that "the right reason for having a child is that you *want* to have a child 'as an end in itself', not as a toy, or as heir to the estate, or because people expect it of you, or for ulterior reasons" (Hursthouse 1987: 305, her emphasis). Moreover, what is intrinsically worthwhile, according to Hursthouse, is not just having a child (e.g., in a case where a woman gestates and delivers a baby born of a donated embryo), but having a child who is one's "own," not only through parenting him but by being genetically related to him and gestating him (Hursthouse 1987: 309, 312). She likens the woman's reproductive labor to "the creation of the new and the beautiful" (Hursthouse 1987: 312), a process, she repeats, that "involves exercising courage, fortitude and endurance" (Hursthouse 1987: 315). A mother can "look upon her children as *her* achievements, her works of art, the result of her efforts and suffering" (Hursthouse 1987: 315, her emphasis).

Hursthouse's point about wanting a child as an end in herself is important, as is her emphasis on the value of women's reproductive labor. However, the supposed intrinsic value or even necessity, to parents, of creating a being who is genetically related to oneself is not self-evident (Overall 2014: 100–105). Adoptive parents rear children whom they love, and the relationship is valuable despite the absence of a genetic connection between parents and offspring.

What about the child?

As the preceding discussion indicates, proponents of procreation cite many potential benefits of having a child, some of which may be real and attainable, at least in some cases. And those who have chosen not to procreate also point out a variety of drawbacks and liabilities of procreation, at least some of which no rational potential parent can ignore or deny. But there is an important asymmetry between the persuasive effect of the reasons to have a child and the persuasive effect of the reasons not to. The asymmetry is this: if you are persuaded of the liabilities of procreation, then you have a strong justification for choosing not to procreate. By contrast, even if you are persuaded of the benefits of procreation, you do not necessarily have a strong justification for having children.

Why not? Because almost all the benefits listed so far accrue only to the prospective parents, grandparents, existing siblings (if any), and society. Almost none (other than existence itself) have anything to do with the well-being of the future child herself. Even Hursthouse, who stresses the value of the child as an end in herself, nonetheless interprets childbearing as work that is valuable because the child is the mother's own, in the sense of being something like an artistic creation. Without deliberate concern for the child who will be created, procreation can seem immature or even egotistical, especially if the future child's prospects of well-being and happiness are poor. Jim Crawford goes so far as to claim that *all* the reasons people have children are selfish ones – either "'feelings' motivated selfishness" (the sense of pleasure or achievement); "utilitarian selfishness" (seeing offspring as useful as family providers, citizens, caregivers, etc.); or "self-deluded selfishness" (the quest for immortality) (Crawford 2010: 129).

Crawford's views may be exaggerated. Nonetheless, these sorts of bad reasons to have children, self-oriented as they are, constitute good reasons *not* to have children. For example, if you want to have a child, in Hursthouse's words, merely "as a toy, or as heir to the estate, or because people expect it of you" (Crawford 2010: 305), you have only bad reasons to have a child, since you are not respecting the child herself but using her simply as a means to the furtherance of your own projects. In that case, your motivation for procreation is a good reason for you *not* to procreate, because you lack something important, even essential, to being a good parent: a concern for the child for her own sake.

Antinatalism and some criticisms of it

Most people who choose to procreate would, of course, say that they do respect the future child whom they are creating, and want to make a good life for him or her. And Caplan claims that "[a]t least one person benefits tremendously from virtually every birth – the new baby" (Caplan 2011: 126). But antinatalists such as Crawford and David Benatar (2006, 2013, 2015) argue that procreation inevitably causes harm to the individual who is created. Crawford writes, "The best intentions do not in the least mitigate the harm we do, inevitably to the children we create. We know our children will suffer and die. That makes all parents criminals"[7] (Crawford 2010: 93).

In his book, *Better Never to Have Been* (2006), Benatar gives two main arguments for his antinatalism.[8] The first is that

> [C]oming into existence is always a serious harm. ... Although the good things in one's life make it go better than it otherwise would have gone, one could not have been deprived by their absence if one had not existed. Those who never exist cannot be deprived. However, by coming into existence one does suffer quite serious harms that could not have befallen one had one not come into existence.
>
> *(Benatar 2006: 1)*

According to Benatar, there is an asymmetry between the absence of bad things and the absence of good things. The absence of bad things is good even when nobody enjoys that good, but the absence of good things is bad only when there is somebody who is deprived of these good things. "The implication of this is that the avoidance of the bad by never existing is a real advantage over existence, whereas the loss of certain goods by not existing is not a real disadvantage over never existing" (Benatar 2006: 14).

In response, Tim Bayne argues that if coming into existence is so terrible, it is hard to see why we ought to revive and continue the life of a comatose person, rather than letting him die, for in so doing, we give that person the opportunity to continue suffering harms that could be avoided by his ceasing to exist (Bayne 2010: 45). Bayne suggests that it is puzzling that Benatar does not urge people to commit suicide or to refrain from offering life-saving treatments to those who need them, because "[i]f one could have benefited by not having been born on account of the pain that one avoids, so too one can benefit from an early death on account of the pain that one avoids" (Bayne 2010: 53).

Benatar's response to this kind of argument is that "[w]e require stronger justification for ending a life than for not starting one" (Benatar 2006: 23). But Bayne insists that we properly decide whether or not to stay alive by adopting the perspective of our future self as to the quality of our future life. And that kind of perspective is also reasonable with respect to coming into existence:

> If, in adopting the perspective of the person who would be brought into existence as the result of the relevant deliberation, one decides that the expected goods outweigh the expected bads, then (*ceteris paribus*) procreation is permissible; if not, then it is not permissible.
>
> *(Bayne 2010: 54)*

Benatar's second main argument for antinatalism is a survey of what he takes to be the very bad quality of human existence, which encompasses everything from hunger, thirst, fatigue, and pain to unfulfilled desires, unrealized goals, and lack of any ultimate meaning (Benatar 2006: 70–86). Benatar documents numbing facts about war, disease, natural disasters, and violent crimes (Benatar 2006: 88–92). Indeed, "all human lives contain much more bad than is ordinarily recognized" (60) and "even the best lives are very bad" (61). He concedes that most people would likely deny that their lives are bad, and reject the idea that it would have been better never to come into existence. But their assessments of their lives are "unreliable," according to Benatar, for a number of easily identified psychological reasons (Benatar 2006: 64–69).

If Benatar is correct, then every case of procreation is or is likely to be morally wrong,[9] and good reasons for having children (if there are any) are almost always inadequate to justify procreation.[10] Thus, the antinatalist view trends, at its limit, to advocating the extinction of the human species – and indeed, Benatar accepts and endorses that implication (Benatar 2006: 194).

Most people, however, will not be convinced that life is always as bad as Benatar says. People tend to think that some lives are very bad, but others are not; some, perhaps many, are good or even very good. And the fact that so many people want to prolong their lives, and many even hope to continue their existence in an afterlife or in a future life through reincarnation, suggests that people are glad that they came into existence. Yet, if Benatar is correct, then human beings all over the planet who are happy, or even merely content, that they were born are deeply self-deceived (Bayne 2010: 42). It seems highly implausible that the majority of people could be so wrong about the value of their own existence, the value of their children's existence, and the value of raising a child they have created.

At the very least, however, Benatar's arguments remind us that, when considering reasons to have children, the well-being of the future child must be a key part of the assessment. Obviously, if a child will have a life of pain and suffering, a life not worth living, there is a strong reason not to procreate. The question, then, is whether the future child's quality of life can ever be good enough to justify procreation.

Some philosophers suggest that if people feel a need or desire to be parents, they should not procreate but instead adopt one or more of the millions of disadvantaged parentless children who already exist. Tina Rulli, for example, argues that people's reasons for wanting a genetically related child do not defeat what she regards as a duty to adopt – other than, perhaps, a one-time exception "grounded in a woman's strong desire to experience pregnancy" (Rulli 2014: 29). Other reasons that some people have for preferring genetically related children – including the desire for a child who shares one's physical traits, offers a "family resemblance," or psychological similarity – do not defeat the duty to rescue a needy child.

In addition to benefiting an existing child, adoption garners almost all of the same goods attributed to procreation. Indeed, adoption and procreation can be seen as equally worthwhile, given that "having a child" is, most importantly, the opportunity to create a valuable and distinctive *relationship* with a young human being. Harry Brighouse and Adam Swift suggest that the connection between parent and child is "a relationship that involves the adult in a quite unique combination of joys and challenge; experiencing and meeting these makes a distinctive set of demands, and produces a distinctive contribution to well-being" (2014: 14). No other connection, however intimate, can provide a substitute or replacement for the parent–child relationship. That fact may be one of the strongest reasons for choosing to procreate (Overall 2012: 209–20).

Conclusion

Many commonly cited reasons for having a child are objectively weak or flawed. They rely either on dubious deontological views about tradition, God, identity, or genetics, or upon unsubstantiated assumptions about the purported benefits of procreation. Antinatalists argue that the offspring's inevitable suffering renders procreation always unjustified. But such a conclusion relies on questionable views about the inevitable misery of human life. Instead, the justification for procreation may be located neither in the parents nor in the child, considered in isolation, but rather in the relationship between them.

Notes

1 It does not examine cases in which individuals choose to have children who will be raised by others. These cases include women who complete a pregnancy with the intention of surrendering the child for adoption, and so-called "surrogate" mothers who contract to gestate and bear a child for another individual or couple.
2 Paul's argument will presumably not apply to anyone debating whether to have a second or subsequent child.
3 See, e.g., Benatar (2010).
4 Notice that if particular consequences of procreation are thought to count in favor of having children, then other potential consequences must count *against* it. These consequences might include passing on a serious disease, being too young to parent adequately, a lack of social or economic resources, and the presence of war or endemic violence.
5 Stuart Rachels gives a parallel argument against having any children. Rearing children, he estimates, costs (at least) roughly $227,000 in today's (US) dollars. That amount of money would enable us to "immunize, feed and clothe impoverished children who already exist," or to devote the money to other, comparably effective, charitable purposes. Therefore, "it is immoral to have children" (Rachels 2014: 571).
6 Some people think there are other reasons to avoid having more than one child, reasons that have to do with individual well-being rather than global consequences. For example, it might be argued that having a large number of children, or even more than one or two, unfairly limits the amount of attention each child receives, or compromises each child's financial access to higher education.
7 Presumably he means biological parents; parents who simply foster or adopt are not guilty of the "crime."
8 Elsewhere he provides a third argument, "the misanthropic argument for anti-natalism": because human beings will *cause* "vast amounts of pain, suffering and death," we have a duty not to bring new human beings into existence (Benatar 2015: 35).
9 Rachels points out that creating a child can also be seen as "an unusual rights violation," since, by coming into existence, the child is exposed to potential harms, but cannot possibly give her permission before being created (Rachels 2014: 580).
10 The one exception Benatar recognizes is the creation of new generations with the goal of a gradual, less painful "phasing out" of people (Benatar 2006: 184).

References

Bayne, T. 2010. "In Defence of Genethical Parity," in D. Archard and D. Benatar (eds.), *Procreation and Parenthood: The Ethics of Bearing and Rearing Children*. Oxford: Oxford University Press.
Benatar, D. 2006. *Better Never to Have Been: The Harm of Coming into Existence*. Oxford: Oxford University Press.
Benatar, D. 2010. "The Limits of Reproductive Freedom," in D. Archard and D. Benatar (eds.), *Procreation and Parenthood: The Ethics of Bearing and Rearing Children*. Oxford: Oxford University Press.
Benatar, D. 2015. "The Misanthropic Argument for Anti-natalism," in S. Hannon, S. Brennan, and R. Vernon (eds.), *Permissible Progeny: The Morality of Procreation and Parenting*. New York, NY: Oxford University Press.
Brighouse, H., and A. Swift. 2014. "The Goods of Parenting," in F. Baylis and C. McLeod (eds.), *Family-Making: Contemporary Ethical Challenges*. Oxford: Oxford University Press.
Caplan, B. 2011. *Selfish Reasons to Have More Kids*. New York, NY: Basic Books.

Conly, S. 2016. *One Child: Do We Have a Right to More?* Oxford: Oxford University Press.
Crawford, J. 2010. *Confessions of an Antinatalist*. Charleston, WV: Nine-Banded Books.
Goldberg, M. 2006. "To Breed or Not to Breed," in L. Leibovich (ed.), *Maybe Baby*. New York, NY: Harper.
Hursthouse, R. 1987. *Beginning Lives*. Oxford: Basil Blackwell.
Krishnamurthy, M. 2015. "We Can Make Rational Decisions to Have a Child: On the Grounds for Rejecting L.A. Paul's Arguments," in S. Hannon, S. Brennan, and R. Vernon (eds.), *Permissible Progeny: The Morality of Procreation and Parenting*. New York, NY: Oxford University Press.
Leibovich, L. (ed.) 2006. *Maybe Baby*. New York, NY: Harper.
Maier, C. 2008. *No Kids: 40 Good Reasons Not to Have Children*, trans. P. Watson. Toronto: McClelland & Stewart.
Overall, C. 2012. *Why Have Children? The Ethical Debate*. Cambridge, MA: MIT Press.
Overall, C. 2014. "What Is the Value of Procreation?," in F. Baylis and C. McLeod (eds.), *Family-Making: Contemporary Ethical Challenges*. Oxford: Oxford University Press.
Paul, L. A. 2015. "What You Can't Expect When You're Expecting," *Res Philosophica* 92(2): 149–170.
Peck, E. 1972. *The Parent Trap*. New York, NY: Pinnacle Books.
Peck, E., and Senderowitz, J. (eds.) 1974. *Pronatalism: The Myth of Mom and Apple Pie*. New York, NY: Thomas Y. Crowell.
Rachels, S. 2014. "The Immorality of Having Children," *Ethical Theory and Moral Practice* 17: 567–582.
Rulli, T. 2014. "Preferring a Genetically-Related Child," *Journal of Moral Philosophy* 13(6): 669–698.
Silverman, A., and Silverman, A. 1971. *The Case Against Having Children*. New York, NY: David McKay.
Tennis, C. 2006. "It's Not in My Nature to Nurture," in L. Leibovich (ed.), *Maybe Baby*. New York, NY: Harper.
Van Luven, L. (ed.). 2006. *Nobody's Mother: Life without Kids*. Victoria: TouchWood Editions.
Whelan, E. M. 1975. *A Baby? ... Maybe: A Guide to Making the Most Fateful Decision of Your Life*. New York, NY: Bobbs-Merrill.
Wise, J. 2006. "Who Wants to be a Mommy?," in L. Van Luven (ed.), *Nobody's Mother: Life without Kids*. Victoria: TouchWood Editions.
Young, T. 2001. "Overconsumption and Procreation: Are They Morally Equivalent?," *Journal of Applied Philosophy* 18(2): 183–192.

14
THE RIGHT TO PARENT

Anca Gheaus

Introduction

This chapter discusses the question of how individuals acquire the right to parent, understood as a right to exercise authority in relation to a child's life as a whole rather than over particular aspects of a child's life, such as with respect to her health, her acquisition of basic literacy, and so on. The right to parent gives the right-holder a considerable degree of control over how the child's life goes, control that is denied to other individuals in relation to the same child. I assume children lack full autonomy (see ch. 10). For this reason, it is generally permissible that adults exercise some kinds of control over children's lives. The present focus is on the moral rather than on the legal right to parent. I also assume that the legal right to parent – that is, the right to be a child's custodian – should be grounded in the moral right to parent; but, as I shall explain, family law and, more generally, policy-making with respect to the family, may be unable to perfectly align individuals' legal and moral claims.

I start by laying out basic distinctions. One is between five separate questions concerning the right to parent. The second is between different kinds of theories that ground the right to parent. And the last is between the right to parent and the parental duty. I then dedicate individual sections to explaining how different theories generate particular answers to some of the questions at stake in the debates about the right to parent.

Central questions and distinctions

The first and most fundamental issue regarding the right to parent is whether such a right exists in the first place. Could it ever be legitimate for an individual to have the kind of control over a child's life that is involved in the right to parent? This is the question of whether childrearing in the family is justified or whether justice requires that children be raised in an alternative way – such as, for instance, by professional childrearers in state-run institutions or by groups of adults in larger associations of private individuals. This question may strike most readers as artificial, given that the family, in some form or another, is a universal institution – and, moreover, one regarded as closely mimicking the way in which many non-human animals raise their young. And yet, as we shall see, the family has been justified in very different, and radically incompatible, ways: sometimes as a natural extension of (self-)ownership rights; sometimes as the form of childrearing that is most likely to serve children's interest in being able to develop a sense of justice and an ability to form, revise and pursue a life plan; and sometimes as an institution that can best realise, simultaneously, children's interest in a good upbringing and prospective parents' interest in long-term intimate relationships with each other.

The second question concerns the grounds on which people acquire a right to parent *in general*. In virtue of what characteristics can it be legitimate for an individual to have the kind of control over a child's life that is involved in the right to parent? A full account of this matter would have to answer several sub-questions, including: is the right to parent fundamental – that is, is it grounded at least in part in the interest of the prospective parent – or is it derivative of the children's interests? Is the right merely negative – a right that parents are free from certain kinds of interference in the activity of childrearing? Or is there also a positive right to certain resources that are needed to parent (and, especially, to parent at a certain level of adequacy)? In particular, does the right to parent entail a qualified right to procreate? Does the right include a right to assisted reproduction and, if so, should this be subsidised? And is the right limited to a number of children?

The third question is about the grounds on which one can acquire the right to parent a *particular* child. Assuming that a person has the right to parent in general – say, in virtue of displaying certain qualities – what gives that person the right to parent a certain child? In particular, is there a right to parent one's biologically related child? If so, why? And, in doubt, which biological connection has more normative relevance – the genetic or the gestational link to the child?

Fourth is the question of what conditions one has to meet in order to *continue* to hold the right to parent a particular child. The conditions that an individual must satisfy in order to acquire a right to parent a particular child need not be the same as the conditions she must satisfy in order to continue to hold the right. The reason for this has to do with the high costs, for the child and possibly for the parent, of the interruption of an already established parent–child relationship. So, assuming, for instance, that an adult must satisfy a certain threshold N of competence in order to have the right to parent, it is plausible that, once that person is already in a parenting relationship with a child, it is in the child's best interest for the relationship to continue even if the adult falls considerably below N. A salient kind of situation in which we need to understand the grounds for continuing to hold the right is when formerly cohabiting co-parents separate and new custodial arrangements have to be made.

Fifth and finally, there is the question of the content of the right to parent.[1] Some (Brighouse and Swift 2014) call this the distinction between the right to parent and the rights of parents, which are the rights that parents can exercise in relation to their children. The limits of legitimate parental authority are themselves a very contentious matter. At the very least, parents may decide where their children live, their diets, daily routine and matters concerning their pastimes. (Certainly, the scope of parental authority varies with children's age and level of development.) More controversial parental rights concern decisions about children's education, values, medical care and high-risk activities. In general, on a view that takes children's moral personhood seriously, it is a good idea to start inquiry with this fifth question. This is because a comprehensive answer is likely to help settle the other questions at least in part: once we know what is in the child's best interest with respect to which adults should have authority over her in which respect, it seems easier to settle the issues of whether we should have families at all, and if so who should be allowed to parent in general and who should be allowed to (continue to) parent particular children.

In the rest of this chapter I will only discuss the first three questions. There is hardly any philosophical literature on the grounds of continuing to hold the right to parent (though see Shields 2016b and ch. 19). As for the question of the rights of parents, there is a large body of literature, covered systematically in other chapters in this handbook (see ch. 20, ch. 29, ch. 31 and ch. 33).

Philosophers answer one or several of the above questions by appeal to the interests of (a) would-be parents; (b) children; and (c) third parties who are affected by the existence of the family, the distribution of the right to parent and its precise content. Theories that appeal exclusively to the interests of would-be parents – as most traditional theories do – have been called "parent-centred theories." Many of them explicitly assume that children lack full moral status and, hence, rights; others do not make this assumption (at least explicitly) or even assume that children have rights. But it is difficult to see how it is possible to give parent-centred accounts answers to these questions if parenting involves the exercise of authority over vulnerable individuals who have full moral status. Liberals, at least, believe that such authority must be justified by appeal to the interests of those over whom authority is exercised, and those of third parties, rather than by appeal to the interests of those who exercise it.

Theories that appeal exclusively to the interests of children have been called "child-centred theories." Further, the interests of third parties are usually appealed to in order to generate side-constraints on various answers to the questions above: liberals, at least, believe that intimate relationships – such as the parent–child one – must primarily track the interests of those who engage in them rather than serve the interests of the larger community. At the same time, such relationships must be such that they do not put third parties at the risk of harm or rights violations. Recently, several philosophers have developed hybrid theories, answering the various questions detailed above by appealing to both the interests of the would-be parents and to those of children (Clayton 2006; Brighouse and Swift 2014). These are called "dual-interest theories."

The way in which one answers the more fundamental questions above puts theoretical pressure on answers to the subsequent questions. Thus, for instance, child-centred answers to the question concerning the justification of the family are consistent with parent-centred answers to the question of how one acquires the right to parent in general only if children's interests, on average, are served equally well by being raised in families and outside family settings. Only in such implausible case it seems coherent to allow prospective parents' interests in playing a parenting role to determine how children are reared. But this is an implausible claim. Similarly, child-centred accounts of the ground of the right to parent in general are consistent with parent-centred answers to the question of how one gets the right to parent a particular child only if that child's interests would be served equally well by allowing one or another adult to parent her. In this (also, implausible) case, it seems justified to allow prospective parents' interests to play a parenting role in relation to that child to determine who will be that child's custodian. This, too, is implausible. And so on.

Before looking closely at existing answers to various questions about the right to parent, it is important to note a final distinction: that between, on the one hand, acquiring the right to parent and, on the other hand, acquiring the duty to parent, as well as the bundle of individual duties in relation to the child that we usually ascribe to parents. In general, these are acquired together – and, indeed, the literature on the family tends to discuss them together under the concept of "parenthood." Some philosophers think that the grounds for acquiring parental rights and duties should be the same. For instance, Tim Bayne and Avery Kolers "assume that insofar as parenthood brings both rights and responsibilities it brings them *together* – that is, one does not get all the rights but none of the responsibilities, or vice versa" (Bayne and Kolers 2003: 223).

It is true that holding the right to parent a particular child entails a number of special duties towards that child. Yet, other special, childrearing duties towards that child may be attributable to different individuals; and the right to parent a particular child may have distinct normative grounds from the duty to become that child's parent. One could have certain duties towards a child in virtue of having procreated her, yet not have a right to parent her; or one could have a right to parent a particular child without having a duty to become the parent of that child. According to an influential view, procreators have extensive special duties towards their offspring in virtue of having brought them into existence (Olsaretti 2017); on this view, we collectively acquire certain duties to provide for children only in cases when their procreators fail to discharge theirs. However, some procreators, on grounds of inadequacy, may not possess the right to parent their offspring even though they remain duty-bound to provide (for example, financial) resources to the child (Austin 2007; Archard 2010). According to another view, duties owed to children are, fundamentally, collective duties which then individual parents discharge towards individual children (Vallentyne 2002), for instance because children are vulnerable to adults collectively (Goodin 2005). A version of this view says that the right to parent a particular child is held by the person who would make the best parent and who wants to play this role. It may, therefore, be possible that nobody has a duty to become a parent in general or the parent of any individual child (especially if there are fewer children than adults who can and want to rear). In this case, adults who would make exceptionally good parents could claim the right, without having any special prior duty towards the child, to become her custodian. Therefore, the rights and the duties that adults have in relation to children might have different justifications and, hence, it is possible that they are acquired independently from each other.

Can anyone have a right to parent?

Plato famously argued that children ought to be raised communally, because he thought this was the only way in which they could be socialised in accordance with a conception of justice that put the well-being of the community above individual well-being (Blustein 1982). But today we share a liberal view according to which it is unjust to instrumentalise individuals and their relationships in order to serve the common good. And virtually everybody agrees that it is best both for children and for adults if children are raised in families. Most individuals value parenting, or at least an opportunity to decide whether or not to parent – indeed, these are key components of many adults' flourishing. Children need continuous caring relationships with individuals who love them, get to know them well and are interested in their long-term well-being, and it is generally believed that they are most likely to enjoy such relationships by being raised in the family (Blustein 1982; Brighouse and Swift 2014). And some believe that the family is necessary in order to socialise children into adults who can form, reflect on and pursue their own idea of a good life; this is partly because children need parents to encourage them to develop their own individuality and make them capable of intimate relationships, and partly because the family is considered necessary in order to preserve a diversity of lifestyles and conceptions of the good in the next generation (Blustein 1982; Munoz-Dardé 1999).

In this day and age, it is easy to justify the family by pointing to the psychologists' agreement that children need parents. Yet, more traditional defences of the family did not appeal to the moral claims of children but to those of procreators, and, more specifically, to procreators' property rights. Arguments based on self-ownership explain why procreators have a right to rear their offspring, thus answering, at the same time, the first three of the five questions above. One version of this view, advanced by Jan Narveson (1989), assumes ownership in one's labour: procreators exert themselves to bring the child into existence and, the argument goes, as a result they have property rights over the child they produce. It is unclear that Narveson's argument holds. As Barbara Hall (1999) noted, in her own version of an argument grounded in self-ownership, appeal to the procreator's labour cannot do any work unless the labour in case has been exercised in relation to something that the procreator already rightfully owns.

On Hall's view, genetic procreators have the initial right to rear the child because children come from the parents' bodily parts:

> Parents are entitled to their children for the same reasons that they are entitled to anything that is a part of themselves. Thus, it is ultimately belief in the notion of self-ownership that fuels our presumption in favour of a natural parent's entitlement to her child.
>
> (Hall 1999: 76)

Hall's account, too, seems deficient: Hillel Steiner (1994: 246–48) argued that we do not own germline information and, hence, ownership over children is shared by parents and the larger society. Whether or not there are other fatal objections to any of these views, they all presuppose child ownership and therefore few, if any, philosophers will want to endorse them today.

Other parent-centred accounts seek to justify the family as a unique site where adults can pursue important projects of self-extension through the shaping of children's identities and future (Page 1984; Reshef 2013). Although these theories avoid the language of property, it is difficult to see how they can be compatible with children having full moral status: we usually think it is impermissible to use the shaping of other individuals merely in order to advance our own interest in self-extension.

One major objection to the family is that it upsets (fair) equality of opportunity: parents pass very unequal levels of economic, social and cultural capital on to their children, towards whom they are usually partial (Blustein 1982; Calder 2016). Egalitarian reforms banning forms of intergenerational transmission of inequality such as bequests or purchase of private education for one's child would alleviate, but not entirely solve, this problem (Brighouse and Swift 2014). The challenge is to understand whether and how can we justify the existence of the family to those who are at the losing end of the unequal opportunities generated by the family (Munoz-Dardé 1999). One influential answer is that a world that fully realised equality of opportunity but had no space for intimate and loving parent–child relationships is less desirable than a world that fails to live up to the principle of fair equality of opportunity, but which has ample space for these relationships (Brighouse and Swift 2014). This answer may prove unconvincing to those who failed to enjoy intimate and loving parent–child relationships in spite of being raised by families; such individuals might have been significantly better off in a world of perfect equality of opportunity, no family and adequate childrearing institutions – assuming that perfect equality of opportunity is at all compatible with any imaginable kind of childrearing. But this last assumption is implausible, assuming that childrearers will always be unequally resourceful and invested into the children in their charge (Gheaus 2018b).

The conditions for holding a right to parent in general

Assuming that the family offers a legitimate way of childrearing, what qualifies an individual for the right to play the parental role? Parent-centred views would point to either adults' property over their bodily labour and bodily parts, or to their interest to self-extend. In both cases, it is likely that holding the right to parent should be subject to certain moral constraints concerning the exercise of authority over children, given the undeniable fact that children have *some* kind of moral status.

According to the universal *status quo*, biological procreators have a negative right to (continue to) parent as long as they have not been condemned of serious child abuse or neglect. This sets a rather unambitious threshold of sufficiency as the only side-constraint on the right to parent, when it comes to biological parenting. By contrast, individuals who want to adopt can only do so subject to obtaining licences for which the threshold conditions are significantly higher than merely not to put children at risk of abuse or neglect. Many philosophers find this discrepancy objectionable (see ch. 18, ch. 19). Further, assuming that the right to parent is negative, there is no guarantee that individuals who would excel at childrearing will have an opportunity to parent if they fail to procreate naturally and lack the material means to access *in vitro* fertilisation (IVF), surrogacy (where legally available) or adoption. By contrast, biological procreators who have not been guilty of abuse or neglect may raise any number of children they want and are able to procreate.

It is difficult to see how the *status quo* could be justified on a child-centred view, according to which some people have a right to parent only because children have an interest in being parented (Hannan and Vernon 2008; Archard 2010). On one version of this view, some individuals have the right to parent because we collectively have duties towards children which, for reasons of efficiency, we discharge by entrusting different children to the care of different adults (Goodin 2005). One would expect an institutional arrangement that reflects this view to select those individuals who would be best at parenting (LaFollette 2010) – although such a selection, and more generally any form of licensing parents, raises serious difficulties (see ch. 19).

Child-centred accounts of the right to parent have been resisted because they see the right to parent as entirely derivative from the child's interest, rather than fundamental. Therefore, such accounts may deny an opportunity to parent to individuals who would make adequate – but not optimal – parents (Brighouse and Swift 2014). Many consider this implication deeply counter-intuitive, and several philosophers have defended dual-interest accounts, seeking to establish that merely adequate parents have the right to parent in virtue of both children's and their own interest in parenting (Clayton 2006; Brighouse and Swift 2014; Macleod 2015; Shields 2016b). Harry Brighouse and Adam Swift, for instance, believe that the family is justified thanks to children's interest in being parented, and that the content of the right to parent – that is, the rights of parents – is limited to what is necessary to advance children's interests. At the same time, they argued that adults who could play the parental role adequately have a fundamental interest in doing so. Specifically, the interest is in forming intimate, caring, long-lasting parent–child relationships whose particular features make them, according to Brighouse and Swift, uniquely and highly valuable. To be an adequate parent means to successfully discharge great responsibilities towards an individual who is much less powerful than you, whom you often have to coerce for her own good, whose mind you will inevitably shape as the relationship unfolds and who loves you in a spontaneous and trustful way unparalleled by other loving relationships. Brighouse and Swift believe that without a chance to parent, many – possibly most – adults would not be able to fully flourish and conclude that this makes the interest in parenting weighty enough to amount to a fundamental right.

This influential account has been the focus of much recent discussion. Given the central role the account gives to children's interests, it is difficult to see why sub-optimal parents have a right to parent as long as shortfalls from the best alternative upbringing in terms of the child's interests are more significant than the adult's interest in parenting (Shields 2016a). In other words, it matters how much better the optimal available parents are compared to the merely adequate ones. Further, it is unclear that egalitarians (like Brighouse and Swift) can endorse an interest-protecting right to full flourishing; this depends on the level of resources to be distributed (Gheaus 2015). Beyond these worries, which are partly empirical, there remains the question of whether it is possible to justify authority over another person even partly on the basis of how it advances the flourishing of the one exercising the authority. It is at least somewhat intuitive that, should babies come into the world brought by storks, we ought to allocate authority over them to the best available parents (Gheaus 2015).

Another proponent of a dual-interest account of the right to parent, Matthew Clayton (2006) starts from the fact that childhood and adulthood are stages of one and the same life. The relevant interests on which Clayton's account is based are not the interests of two different parties – children and adults – but the interests that persons have at different stages of life. He thinks that merely adequate would-be parents have a right to parent because the loss in well-being that one faces, *qua* child, if all adequate prospective parents have a right to parent is (more than) made up for by the gain one enjoys *qua* adult by having the chance to parent. This is how we can justify to children that we allow the less than best parent to control their life, as long as these children will themselves get to enjoy the goods of parenting in due course. But, of course, not all children will be parents – some will die young, or not have an interest in parenting, or will not make adequate parents (and hence, on this account, lack the right). Most importantly, it seems that letting everyone take turns in controlling another person's life for the sake of one's own interest in exercising authority is not a legitimate arrangement, even if it maximises the prospects of those individuals' lives. A worry about both these versions of the dual-interest account is that they disallow adults' interests to play any justification with respect to the content of the right to parent (and possibly of the family), yet they allow adults' interests to partly determine the justification of a right to parent in general.

Assuming some version of the dual interest account is correct, there are interesting subsequent questions concerning the nature of the right to parent. In particular, does it entail a qualified right to procreate? Since procreation is a necessary means to the end of parenting, it seems the answer is positive (Gheaus 2016a); yet, this depends on whether procreation as such is permissible and on whether childhood is a desirable state to be in (Hannan and Leland 2018). Another question is whether the right is limited to a number of children (Conly 2016; Gheaus 2016a; Meijers 2016; see also ch. 13) or is unlimited in this sense – as legislations almost universally state. And is the right purely negative, or is it positive, including an entitlement to (possibly subsidised) assisted reproduction and/or adoption? Finally, it is questionable whether the right to parent can at all be conceived as a negative; adequate parenting is resource-intensive in a unique way, because it results in future individuals requiring resources in order to satisfy their own interest in parenting (Gheaus 2016a). Thus, procreative parenting entails a demand for potentially non-limited resources, more than one individual can possibly claim as their own. The very existence of a fundamental right to parent is then dependent on the question of who ought to pay the costs of having children and on matters of justice towards future generations (see ch. 30).

The grounds of a right to parent a particular child

What gives an adult the right to parent a particular child? Currently, adults have various avenues to parenthood: people who procreate naturally may raise their offspring; those who cannot may avail themselves of IVF or, in some jurisdiction, surrogacy services; or they can adopt a child, provided the birth parents have waived their right to parent by putting the child up for adoption, or else lost it through abuse or neglect (see ch. 19). The *status quo*, therefore, privileges biological parenthood (see ch. 17) – is this justified?

Explicitly proprietarian parent-centred theories give a straightforward answer: the right to parent a child accrues to those who bring her into existence through their own labour (Narveson 1989) or by ensuring that newborns develop from their own bodily parts (Hall 1999). Note that there are two ways in which one can be a biological procreator: by being a gestational or a genetic procreator. The first version of the self-ownership account privileges the gestational procreator over the genetic one, while the second privileges the genetic procreator.

Other parent-centred theories do not appeal to self-ownership. One of them justifies the right through the performance of parental work, in which parental work is the reason for deserving the right (Millum 2010); this has the advantage of explaining the acquisition of the right *via* both procreation and adoption. A recent theory that explicitly assumes that children are right-holders explains the legitimacy of the family by appeal to children's interests, but seeks to justify procreators' right to parent their offspring by appeal to parents' interests: according to Matthew Liao (2015), biological parenting is a fundamental human right, grounded in adults' interest in creating a new right-holding individual with their own genetic material, in whose shaping they have the opportunity to significantly participate. Taking seriously the right-holding status of children seems incompatible with granting control rights over their life merely on the basis of the interests of those who have the control rights.

One child-centred account, by contrast, claims that the right to rear a child is held by the person who, of all available individuals willing to rear, would do the best job making sure that the child's rights are met (Vallentyne 2003). On this view, biological procreators have no special right to rear their offspring. Child-centred accounts need not usually deny biological procreators a right to rear their offspring. One reason is that, in most cases, biological procreators are likely to be the only individuals willing to parent the child – and, hence, also the best available parents. More generally, the genetic connection between parents and children may generate child-centred reasons for giving the right to rear to genetic procreators. David Velleman (2005) has developed an argument to this conclusion, starting from the observation that many individuals raised in closed adoptions, or whose procreation involved anonymous gamete donation, spend a significant amount of time, energy and money in search for their genetic procreators. He thinks that these individuals' desire to be reunited with their genetic procreators expresses an important interest in self-knowledge that, according to Velleman, only close acquaintance with one's genetic procreator can satisfy. On his view, knowledge of one's genetic procreators plays a crucial role in identity formation because close acquaintance with them gives one a broader context for creating meaning about one's life than one could have in the absence of such knowledge. Velleman concludes that "other things being equal, children should be raised by their biological parents" (Velleman 2005: 362). Some deny that the putative interests in identity-formation and self-knowledge can be satisfied only by acquaintance with one's genetic procreators (Archard 1995; Haslanger 2009). Moreover, it seems likely that the child's interest in self-knowledge can be satisfied by ensuring that individuals have ample opportunity to meet and spend time with genetic procreators – the latter need not have a right to rear the child (Brighouse and Swift 2014; Gheaus 2018a).

A different, consequentialist, child-centred argument seeks to show why gestational mothers have the right to rear their newborn: because gestational mothers can, during pregnancy, greatly influence the development of the foetus and, therefore, the future child's well-being, it is in the child's best interest that gestational mothers have a secure right to the custody of the children they bear (Feldman 1992). This argument, grounding the right in gestational mothers' motivational set-up, may indicate a good reason to grant them the legal right to rear, but it falls short of establishing that gestational mothers have a *moral* right to parent a child merely because, during pregnancy, it is in their power to advance or set back the child's interests (Gheaus 2018a).

Many philosophers seek to avoid both the unpalatable tension between parent-centred theories and the recognition of children's full moral status and the revisionist consequences of child-centred accounts. They do so by subscribing to some version of a dual-interest view. Brighouse and Swift's account discussed above does not provide (nor does it aim to provide) an answer to the question of who has the right to parent particular children. However, because their theory is centred on the importance of the parent–child relationship for both parties, there is a straightforward way to extend it into a theory about one kind of biological parenthood. Thus, I have argued that, because we come into the world through the bodies of other human beings, we already are, at birth, in an intimate, albeit unusual, sort of relationship with our gestational mother (Gheaus 2012). If breaking such relationships would harm the newborn and the gestational mother, this is a good reason why the latter have the right to rear the former, as long as the gestational mother satisfies a requirement of competence. Several philosophers have raised doubts about the nature of the relationship between gestational mothers and their newborn (Porter 2015; Ferracioli 2017). Another worry is that my account violates the parental parity principle, which states that "being a mother doesn't make a person more of a parent than being a father, or vice versa" (Kolers and Bayne 2001: 280).

A different group of dual-interest accounts seeks to ground a right to rear one's offspring in the duties that procreators acquire by dint of bringing a child into existence. Intentional procreators are causally and morally responsible for the existence of children, who need the care of others if they are to avoid great misfortune. Therefore, procreators have a duty to ensure that children will not come to harm. Some philosophers believe that this duty is non-transferable (Porter 2014; Porter 2015; Earl 2015) and that the right to parent one's offspring protects the procreators' interest in discharging the duty. Another version of the argument says that part of the duty is a willingness to enter oneself in the parenting relationship with the child (Olsaretti 2017) and, therefore, procreators have a right to parent their offspring. But it is difficult to see why, when a better parent is willing to rear the child, a duty to enter the relationship with the child endures and parental duties in general cannot be transferred to this person (Gheaus 2018a).

On both a child-centred and a dual-interest account, the best justification for why genetic procreators usually have the right to parent their offspring points to the higher likelihood that a genetic procreator, rather than a stranger, will bond with the child. But if gestational parents are typically already bounded with their newborns at birth, this is a reason to indicate that they should prevail in custody disputes over newborns against genetic procreators (Gheaus 2018a). As David Archard notes (1992: 102), the mere *likelihood* of bonding and love holds less weight than *actual* bonding and loving dispositions in establishing the right. This way of justifying gestational procreators' right to rear raises doubts about the legitimacy of surrogacy practices: if a pregnant mother's presumptive right to rear is based on the child's interest in having a relationship with *her*, it seems she cannot possibly transfer this right to another person (Gheaus 2016b).

Finally, it is worth considering the role third parties' interests might play in the allocation of the right to parent particular children: some have considered how allocating the right to parent by lottery could help fight racism by undermining the connection between one's race and one's parent's race (Gheaus 2012; Shields 2017; Earl 2015).

Conclusions

I have tried to disentangle the main questions at stake in understanding the nature and the grounds of a right to parent. I have outlined different kinds of justification that have been given for the institution of the family as a site for childrearing and alternative ways of understanding the right to parent as either fundamental or derived from the interests of the child. I then explained how different accounts may indicate who has the right to rear which child; in particular, it is important to consider the extent to which the universal practice of granting procreators the right to rear their children is justified.[2]

Notes

1 For the distinction between the first, the second and the fifth questions, see Brighouse and Swift (2014).

2 Work for this chapter has received funding from the European Research Council (ERC) under the European Union's Horizon 2020 Research and Innovation Programme (Grant Agreement Number: 648610; Grant Acronym: Family Justice).

References

Archard, D. 1992. "Rights, Moral Values and Natural Facts: A Reply to Mary Midgley on the Problem of Child-abuse," *Journal of Applied Philosophy* 9(1): 99–104.
Archard, D. 1995. "What's Blood Got to Do with It?," *Res Publica* 1(1): 91–106.
Archard, D. 2010. "The Obligations and Responsibilities of Parenthood," in D. Archard and D. Benatar (eds.), *Procreation and Parenthood: The Ethics of Bearing and Rearing Children*. Oxford: Oxford University Press.
Austin, M. 2007. *Conceptions of Parenthood: Ethics and the Family*. London: Ashgate.
Bayne, T., and Kolers, A. 2003. "Towards a Pluralist Account of Parenthood," *Bioethics* 17(3): 221–242.
Blustein, J. 1982. *Parents and Children: The Ethics of the Family*. Oxford: Oxford University Press.
Brighouse, H., and Swift, A. 2014. *Family Values*. Princeton, NJ: Princeton University Press.
Calder, G. 2016. *How Inequality Runs in Families. Unfair Advantage and the Limits of Social Mobility*. Bristol: Polity Press.
Clayton, M. 2006. *Justice and Legitimacy in Upbringing*. Oxford University Press.
Conly, S. 2016. *One Child. Do We Have a Right to More?* Oxford: Oxford University Press.
Earl, J. 2015. The Baby Lottery: A Challenge to the Right to Parent Our Own Children. Retrieved from https://repository.library.georgetown.edu/handle/10822/1041441 (last accessed 10 March 2018).
Feldman, S. 1992. "Multiple Biological Mothers: The Case for Gestation," *Journal of Social Philosophy* 23: 98–104.
Ferracioli, L. 2017. "Procreative-Parenting, Love's Reasons and the Demands of Morality," *Philosophical Quarterly* 68(270): 77–97.
Gheaus, A. 2012. "The Right to Parent One's Biological Baby," *Journal of Political Philosophy* 20(4): 432–455.
Gheaus, A. 2015. "Is There a Right to Parent?," *Law, Ethics and Philosophy* 3: 193–204.
Gheaus, A. 2016a. "The Right to Parent and Duties Concerning Future Generations," *Journal of Political Philosophy* 24(4): 487–508.
Gheaus, A. 2016b. "The Normative Importance of Pregnancy Challenges Surrogacy Contracts," *AnAlize* 6: 20–31.
Gheaus, A. 2018a. "Biological Parenthood: Gestational, not Genetic," *Australasian Journal of Philosophy* 96(2): 225–240.
Gheaus, A. 2018b. "What the Family Wouldn't Do," *Critical Review of Social and Political Philosophy*, doi: 10.1080/13698230.2017.1398449, 21(3): 284–300.
Goodin, E. 2005. "Responsibilities for Children's Well-being," in S. Richardson and M. Prior Carlton (eds.), *The Well-Being of Australia's Children*. Victoria: Melbourne University Press.
Hall, B. 1999. "The Origin of Parental Rights," *Public Affairs Quarterly* 13(1): 73–82.
Hannan, S., and Leland, R. J. 2018. "Childhood Bads, Parenting Goods, and the Right to Procreate," *Critical Review of Social and Political Philosophy*, doi: 10.1080/13698230.2017.1398488, 21(3): 366–384.
Hannan, S., and Vernon, R. 2008. "Parental Rights: A Role-Based Approach," *Theory and Research in Education* 6(2): 173–189.
Haslanger, S. 2009. "Family, Ancestry and Self: What Is the Moral Significance of Biological Ties?," *Adoption and Culture* 2: 91–122.
Kolers, A., and Bayne, T. 2001. "'Are You My Mommy?' On the Genetic Basis of Parenthood," *Journal of Applied Philosophy* 18(3): 273–285.
LaFollette, H. 2010. "Licensing Parents Revisited," *Journal of Applied Philosophy* 27(49): 327–343.
Liao, M. 2015. *The Right to be Loved*. Oxford: Oxford University Press.
Macleod, C. 2015. "Parental Competency and the Right to Parent," in S. Hannan, S. Brennan, and R. Vernon (eds.), *Permissible Progeny: The Morality of Procreation and Parenting*. Oxford: Oxford University Press.
Meijers, T. 2016. "Climate Change and the Right to One Child," in M. Duvell and G. Bos (eds.), *Human Rights and Sustainability: Moral Responsibility for the Future*. London: Routledge.
Millum, J. 2010. "How Do We Acquire Parental Rights?," *Social Theory and Practice* 36(1): 112–132.
Munoz-Darde, V. 1999. "Is the Family to be Abolished Then?," *Proceedings of Aristotelian Society* 99: 37–56.
Narveson, J. 1989. *The Libertarian Idea*. Philadelphia, PA: Temple University Press.
Olsaretti, S. 2017. "Liberal Equality and the Moral Status of Parent-Child Relationships," in D. Sobel, P. Vallentyne, and S. Wall (eds.), *Oxford Studies in Political Philosophy*, vol. 3. Oxford: Oxford University Press.

Page, E. 1984. "Parental Rights," *Journal of Applied Philosophy* 1(2): 187–203.
Porter, L. 2014. "Why and How to Prefer a Causal Account of Parenthood," *Journal of Social Philosophy* 45(2): 182–202.
Porter, L. 2015. "Gestation and Parental Rights: Why is Good Enough Good Enough?," *Feminist Philosophy Quarterly* 1(1): 1–27.
Reshef, Y. 2013. "Rethinking the Value of Families," *Critical Review of International Social and Political Philosophy* 16(1): 130–150.
Shields, L. 2016a. "How Bad can a Good Enough Parent Be?," *Canadian Journal of Philosophy* 46(2): 163–182.
Shields, L. 2016b. *Just Enough*. Edinburgh: Edinburgh University Press.
Shields, L. 2016c. "Parental Rights and the Importance of Being Parents," *Critical Review of International Social and Political Philosophy*, doi: 10.1080/13698230.2016.1262316, 84(1): 1–15.
Steiner, H. 1994. *An Essay on Rights*. Oxford: Oxford University Press.
Vallentyne, P. 2002. "Equality and the Duties of Procreators," in D. Archard and C. Macleod (eds.), *The Moral and Political Status of Children*. Oxford: Oxford University Press.
Vallentyne, P. 2003. "The Rights and Duties of Childrearing," *William and Mary Bill of Rights Journal* 11(3): 991–1009.
Velleman, D. 2005. "Family History," *Philosophical Papers* 34: 357–378.

15
THE GOOD PARENT

Colin M. Macleod

Introduction

This chapter will provide an overview of recent issues in moral and political philosophy concerning the nature of good parenting. First, it will consider a series of questions about the traits of good parents. Are genetic ties between parents and children relevant to good parenting? Does sexual orientation affect the capacity to parent well? How many parents should children have? Second, it will consider issues about the nature of distinctive parental duties. Is there a parental duty to love children? What duties do parents have to facilitate and respect the autonomy of children? What limits are there on paternalism? Finally, it will consider how successful at parenting a parent must be in order to be a good parent. At some point, parents who fail to attend properly to the interests of their children become bad parents, but how is that threshold to be understood? Can a good parent be merely an adequate parent, or must a good parent be the best possible parent?

It is worth observing that there is a potential ambiguity in the question: what is a good parent? Can there be a difference between a good parent and a just parent? For example, can a good parent confer unfair benefits on her children, say by sending them to an elite private school, that a just parent would not? Or is the good parent also, perhaps necessarily, the just parent? The question about the relationship between goodness and justice is an ancient one that I do not purport to resolve here. But it is worth drawing attention to the fact that this fundamental general puzzle reverberates through a number of more specific issues considered below.

The following discussion is shaped by two framing assumptions. First, children are not initially autonomous agents capable of tracking their own interests and making authoritative decisions about their own lives (see ch. 11). As a result, children, for their own good, are subject to the authority of adults. Parents, in particular, are delegated the authority for making decisions, in many domains, about how to protect and promote their children's interests. Children have (barring serious cognitive impairments) the potential to become autonomous. Children's acquisition of the capacities, knowledge and dispositions requisite to autonomy can be either facilitated or frustrated by the way in which they are parented. Yet even before they become fully autonomous, children acquire capacities to express preferences and make choices about some important facets of their lives (Mullin 2007). I assume both that children have a morally weighty interest in becoming autonomous and that good parenting requires acknowledging and suitably respecting the emerging agential capacities of children.

Second, I assume that parents stand in a special moral relationship to children both with respect to the close emotional ties that exist between parents and children and with respect to the special responsibilities parents are assigned with respect to nurturing children. Parents have special duties to their own children that they do not owe to other children and they also enjoy special prerogatives in making decisions about how to raise their own children. Although we can imagine collective schemes for rearing children in which this kind of moral relationship between specific children and specific adults does not obtain, I shall assume that collective rearing of children is neither a feasible nor attractive way of attending to the interests of children. This is, in part, because becoming a parent and raising children is, for many people, an extremely important life project that is a profound source of meaning and fulfillment.

Who can be a good parent?

Parenting is essentially a social relationship between particular adults and particular children, in which parents enjoy a significant, though not unlimited, measure of authority over children. Parents have special duties towards the children in their care to attend to their interests and help facilitate their development. In most societies, the adults who most frequently occupy this social role are also the male and female biological parents of the children that they raise. But this does not mean that biological parents are the only suitable adults to serve as social parents. Some biological parents are not fit social parents and many adults who are not biological parents strongly desire to be social parents.[1] In this context, three issues can be identified. First, is genetic relatedness an important facet of being a good parent? Second, is the gender identity of parents or their sexual orientation relevant to good parenting? Third, given that the role of social parent can be performed by one or more adults, how is the goodness of parenting affected by the number of adults who serve as social parents?

Genetic relatedness

Although no one holds that children's genetic parents are always the best adults to serve as social parents, various issues arise about whether it is, other things equal, better for children to be raised by their genetic parents than non-biological parents. Velleman, for example, has argued that children have a substantial interest in understanding and appreciating features of their family history that are grounded in shared genetic traits (Velleman 2005). Children who are raised by their genetic parents are, for Velleman, better able to construct a meaningful conception of their own identity than children raised by non-biological parents. Velleman does not claim that adopted children are completely deprived of a source of meaning grounded in a family history. But he does contend that children denied an understanding of their genetic origins are cut off from an important source of meaning. Velleman's analysis suggests that, at least along one important dimension of child rearing, genetic parents are better parents than non-biological parents. He says, "other things being equal, children should be raised by their biological parents" (Velleman 2005: 362, n3).

Velleman's position does not imply that adoptive parents or parents who have children via reproductive technologies that sever genetic ties between one or more social parents are bad parents. But it does imply that, other things equal, such parents are worse than parents with a direct genetic connection to their offspring. It is doubtful that Velleman's argument succeeds. There is no compelling empirical evidence to support the thesis, and Velleman's argument rests rather precariously on generalizations about meaning for all families that are drawn from anecdotes about what constructs his sense of identity by reflecting on traits of his own family. Moreover, although some children may construct a meaningful identity via appreciation of their genetic ancestry, there seems little reason to suppose that an essential feature of children's well-being crucially depends on acquaintance with this particular kind of family history. Haslanger (2009) directly challenges Velleman's claims. She argues that Velleman's claim about the importance, for children, of acquaintance with their genetic family ancestry is overblown and his analysis fails to adequately appreciate how various kinds of social kinship can provide sources of meaningful identity for children.

Although genetic relatedness to one's children is not an essential attribute of a good parent, different puzzles are raised by the phenomenon of transracial and cross-cultural adoption (Haslanger and Witt 2005). Against the background of racism and cultural oppression or the marginalization of minorities, good parents for adopted children are likely to be ones who have a good understanding of the ways in which racism and other forms of injustice affect the lives of children whose biological parents are from oppressed racial or cultural groups. On the assumption that members of groups who are themselves oppressed are better placed to help children from those groups negotiate discrimination and oppression, there is a reason to consider the racial or ethnic background of adoptive parents as a factor in the placement of children with foster families or adoptive parents. This does not mean that good adoptive parents are always ones who share racial or cultural traits of adopted children. It only suggests that there is a socially contingent and defeasible reason to be sensitive to cultural and racial traits in crafting adoption policies. In social circumstances in which racial and cultural oppression do not obtain, then heredity is not likely to be a significant consideration in adoption policy.

Sexual orientation and gender

The increased recognition of the rights of sexual minorities to form and openly maintain intimate relationships has generated some controversy about whether sexual orientation has a bearing on good parenting. Same-sex couples can adopt children or procreate either through the use of reproductive technology or via surrogacy arrangements. Some social conservatives and religious fundamentalists have grave misgivings about permitting children to be raised by same-sex couples. Their objections are typically grounded in little more than general homophobia and a shallow nostalgia for preservation of the traditional patriarchal family. There is no credible evidence that a person's sexual orientation is an impediment to being a good parent – to loving and nurturing one's children in a responsible and successful fashion (Farr 2017). However, the homophobia that same-sex couples still frequently encounter can itself harm the children of same-sex couples. Children of same-sex couples can be stigmatized, teased or bullied and thereby significantly harmed. But it is crucial to note that the source of the harm to children is not rooted in the sexual orientation of their parents per se, but rather in the homophobia directed towards the parents. Those who falsely claim that LBGTQ persons are, in virtue of their sexual orientation, bad parents are themselves responsible for creating a social environment that harms children.

A somewhat more sophisticated, though still fatally flawed, objection to same-sex parenting has been advanced by Sommerville who claims that children have a right to have both a male and female social parent. More specifically, she claims that children have a fundamental right to "know one's biological parents and if at all possible be reared by them within one's wider biological family" (Sommerville 2007: 198). She thinks that there are gendered differences in the parenting approaches of men and women and that exposure to parents of both genders is essential to the healthy development of children. Sommerville also shares some of Velleman's views about the importance of genetic relatedness to meaningful identity construction. But it is extremely doubtful that the gender or sexual orientation of a person is itself an impediment to meeting the needs of children. Indeed, as Woodcock (2009) points out, Sommerville adduces no evidence to show that crucial interests of children can only be reliably served by having parents of both sexes. In the absence of such evidence, there is no reason to suppose that either same-sex parents or, for that matter, single parents cannot be good parents.

How many parents?

A different issue about who can be a good parent concerns the number of adults that can successfully serve simultaneously as social parents to children. Although a traditional conception of parenting supposes that children are best raised by two parents, many children are raised by single parents, and recently legal recognition has been given to arrangements in which children have three parents. Following Brennan and Cameron (2015), we can pose the question: how many parents should children have? Since raising children frequently imposes significant demands – emotional, physical and financial – on parents, there are advantages both to children and parents of sharing the labor of raising children between adults. Other things equal, two parents are arguably better placed to meet the various needs of children than a single parent. The burdens of child rearing, providing they are equitably shared between parents, will be less onerous for a couple than for a single parent. So, adding more parents to the mix might seem advantageous and might seem to improve the quality of parenting. In a similar vein, Cutas (2011) argues that children with several parents are usually better insured against risk in the event that one of their parents leave or die or become otherwise unavailable.

However, if we assume that the formation and maintenance of close intimate ties between parents and children is integral to good parenting, it seems likely that there will be a limit to how many adults can meaningfully have close and suitably personalized parental relationships with children. "While it may be in a child's best interest to have three or four parents, it seems highly unlikely that it would be in a child's best interest to have eight or ten parents" (Brennan and Cameron 2015: 57). It is important to note that how the goodness of parenting is affected by the number of parents children have is itself influenced by the general social division of labor in a society. For instance, the capacity of single parents to be good parents will be affected by the provision of daycare and the structuring of employment in ways that are sensitive to the demands of parenting. This means we should be extremely cautious about generalizations to the effect that single parents are less good parents than dual parents. The caliber of parenting an adult can provide is influenced not only by the capacities, skills and attitudes of would-be parents themselves, but also the manner in which good parenting is facilitated and supported by the structure of social institutions and the provision of resources to parents.

Parental duties

Caring for children and ensuring that their interests are suitably promoted is a collective responsibility that does not fall exclusively to parents. Although there is debate about how the costs of rearing children should be shared between parents and non-parents, all members of a community have some duties to ensure that the justice-based entitlements of children are secured (Macleod 2007). Even though there may be other dimensions to good parenting, good parents reliably discharge their duties to children. I set aside the question of whether the goodness of parenting is affected by the character of the motive that leads parents to care for their children. It might be contended that a truly good parent is motivated by love rather than duty and that the introduction of the language of duty is corrosive to healthy relationships between parents and children (Hardwig 1984; Schoeman 1980). This is doubtful because there need be no conflict between loving one's children and recognizing and being motivated by duties to them.

In order to determine what those duties are we need to consider both what children's interests are, what claims they have to have those interests protected and advanced and who bears responsibility for attending to the variety of children's interests. As already noted, there are various ways in which the moral labor in caring for children can be shared between parents and non-parents. It is uncontroversial, for instance, that children are entitled to a healthy diet and basic education. If responsibility for meeting the educational and health care needs of children is assigned, in the first place, to parents, then a good parent will be one who supplies his or her children with proper health care and education. If, by contrast, the provision of education and health care to children falls, in the first instance, to the general public, then it need not be a condition of good parenting that parents provide their children with education and health care. (Of course, even if education and health care for children are fully provided by the state, parents will have duties to ensure that their children access those resources – e.g., by taking them to school and to health care professionals.)

Just how the division of moral labor between parents and non-parents should be effected is a complex matter that depends both on an articulation of the specific claims of children, more general principles of distributive justice and an account of the overall institutional arrangements that are most likely to ensure that the justice-based entitlements of children are met. Consider, for instance, children's claims to education. Suppose, as many egalitarians hold, that children are entitled to equally excellent education (Macleod 2012). And suppose further that public provision of education to all children is the best way to meet this entitlement and that the state provides such education. In this scenario, parents do not have a special duty to secure education for their children and whether parents have the wherewithal to secure education for their children is not relevant to assessing whether parents are good parents. By contrast, suppose that children have a right only to a basic education and education is treated as a private good (Narveson 1988: 186–188). On this conception of justice, it might be thought that in (voluntarily) deciding to have and raise children, parents incur a duty to provide their children with basic education. Against this background, our judgement about whether a parent is a good parent will be sensitive to the capacity of parents to secure decent basic education for their children. My point here is not to resolve debates about the justice-based entitlements of children (see ch. 28). It is only to illustrate that how we understand those entitlements and how we assign responsibilities to different parties for meeting these entitlements will affect assessments of what it is to be a good parent.

With that important caveat in mind, we can consider some more specific claims about the attributes of the good parent in relation to the duties of parents. However precisely the division of moral labor is effected, parents are almost always in a special position to significantly influence the character of children's lives (see ch. 16). It is clear that good parents are aware of and attentive to their children's diverse needs. They can track their children's general psychological and physical well-being and are well-placed to appreciate and respond to children's idiosyncratic personalities and preferences. In general, we expect good parents to nurture their children and help facilitate healthy physical, psychological and moral development. Bad parents harm or neglect their children. But beyond these broad platitudes, we can distinguish three facets of the influence of parents on children that give rise to issues about the goodness of parenting. First, we can be concerned about the character and quality of the emotional relationships between parents and children. Must good parents love their children or is it sufficient for them to attend to other interests without loving them? Second, there is the influence of parents on shaping values and deeply held commitments of children. What is the role of good parenting in shaping children's sense of justice and their conception of the good? Third, how should the general paternalistic duty of parents to protect their children's interests be sensitive to the evolving moral capacities of children to make their own choices?

In addressing these issues, it is important to keep in mind the distinction between the developmental interests of children and the interests that they have in having a good childhood. Although these interests are frequently related in the sense that many factors that contribute to the quality of children's lives qua children also contribute to their healthy development. For instance, providing children with opportunities for imaginative play may play an important role in the development of autonomy (Schapiro 1999). But the value of some goods of childhood can be understood independently of the contributions they make to healthy development. Many forms of play can enrich the lives of children qua children even if they do not contribute importantly to the acquisition of advanced cognitive capacities of mature agents. A narrow focus on the developmental objectives of childrearing – e.g., preparing children for success as adults – can lead to neglect of the importance of goods of childhood (Brennan 2014; Gheaus 2014; Macleod 2010). Parents, like the so-called "tiger moms" (Chua 2011), who orchestrate their children's lives exclusively towards high-level aesthetic, intellectual or athletic achievement are arguably bad parents to the extent that the focus on achievement deprives children of important childhood goods (see ch. 7).

Love

Parents typically form intense emotional bonds to their children that are motivationally powerful and highly rewarding. In their influential discussion of family values, Brighouse and Swift argue that the special intimacy that can obtain between parents and children is an enormously valuable relationship good that helps to ground the right to parent (Brighouse and Swift 2014). Parents typically love their children in special and intense ways that makes it easy for them to devote energy, care and attention to the promotion of their children's well-being. Being loved by a parent also seems very important to the well-being of children as children. In defending the claim that children have a right to be loved, Liao claims: "being loved is a fundamental condition for children to pursue a good life, because children need to be loved in order to trust others, have positive conceptions of themselves, learn how to love others, and be motivated to obey commands" (Liao 2015: 99). Since parents are best, and perhaps uniquely, placed to provide love to children, then it appears that parents have a duty to love their children. If parents are unable or unwilling to love their children, then it seems that they are not good parents. Indeed, if love is as important as Liao contends, then such parents are arguably not suitable parents at all.

Critics of this position contend both that the developmental significance of love to children is exaggerated and that love, as a special kind of emotional attitude, cannot be commanded and, hence, cannot be the subject of a duty (Cowden 2012). Whether or not love can be commanded, it is highly plausible that being loved significantly enriches the lives of children and this value can persist even if love is not a necessary precondition for the reliable development of important capacities. And this suggests that the good parent is indeed a loving parent. Those who are incapable of loving children, though perhaps not blameworthy, are not fully good parents. This does not necessarily mean that such adults should be disqualified from being parents. It is possible that the capacity of unloving parents to meet the needs of children in other respects is sufficiently good, all things considered, to qualify them as competent parents. Nonetheless, not loving one's children remains a bad trait of parents and can disqualify some adults as suitable parents. For example, extremely homophobic parents who withdraw love and affection from children they believe are gay are arguably not competent parents and can be denied the right to parent (Brennan and Macleod 2017).

Shaping children's convictions

Parents have tremendous power to influence the character and convictions of children (see ch. 29). Of course, parents are not the sole sources of influence and the kind of influence parents wield will be affected by the kind of exposure children have to other influences (e.g., schools, churches, popular culture, etc.). However, parents often hope their children will adopt beliefs, attitudes and convictions that align closely with their own. For instance, religious parents often seek to transmit their faith commitments to their children. The motivations that parents have to shape the convictions of children are various. Parents may view the possibility of rewarding and intimate relationships with their children as dependent upon sharing important beliefs, practices and traditions with their children. Parents may also view the adoption of parent commitments by children as contributing to the goodness of the parents' lives and entirely commensurate with advancing the interests of their children. Or they may view the adoption of a conception of the good by their children as crucial to the spiritual or moral well-being of children themselves. These motivations are not mutually inconsistent.

Against this background, two related issues arise. First, how strong are the prerogatives that parents have to shape the convictions of children? Second, to what kinds of reasons for shaping the convictions of children can parents legitimately appeal? With respect to the first matter, most contemporary theorists hold that parental attempts to shape the convictions of children must be compatible with facilitation of autonomy in children. So, good parents do not attempt to shape the convictions of their children by indoctrinating them. Instead, the shaping of children's convictions should occur in a way that leaves open the possibility of meaningful reflection and deliberation about the convictions in the future. Similarly, there is broad agreement that good parenting should contribute to the moral education of children. Parents should teach their children to acknowledge and respect the rights and moral claims of others. However, theorists disagree about the degree to which good parenting is compatible with shaping other convictions of children. Clayton argues that respect for children requires that parents avoid raising children in ways that systematically favor their own conceptions of the good (Clayton 2006). Brighouse and Swift, by contrast, permit parents to favor a particular conception of the good, but only insofar as doing so is a condition of realizing familial intimacy (Brighouse and Swift 2014). Macleod holds that parents may provisionally privilege a conception of the good in raising children, not only for the sake of familial intimacy, but also for the sake of encouraging children to appreciate and participate in the conception of the good held by parents (Macleod 2015). In a somewhat different vein, Richards holds that good parents display respect for children by influencing them in ways that are sensitive to the personalities and interests of children and that prepares them for living well in light of the values and commitments children are likely to have when they first become adults (Richards 2018).

Limits of paternalism

It is uncontroversial that good parents try to promote the physical, psychological and moral well-being of children. Because children cannot, in many contexts, reliably track their own interests, parents routinely make important decisions that bear upon virtually all facets of their children's lives. In exercising their paternalistic authority over children, it is often said that parents should act to promote the best interests of their children (see ch. 11). Strictly speaking, it is doubtful that parents have a literal duty to maximally promote the interests of their children. Some ways of promoting children's interests can be unreasonably demanding on parents or may be unfair to others. So, to some degree, the promotion of children's interests needs to be balanced with the interests of parents and the moral claims of others.

A different possible constraint on parental paternalism is generated by the emerging, but not fully developed, agential capacities of children. As they mature but before they are fully autonomous responsible agents, children may have strong preferences that do not fully track their interests. It is an interesting practical and theoretical question about the degree to which such expressions of juvenile agency should be respected by parents. For example, some minors wish to engage in extremely risky recreational activities (Anderson and Claasen 2012) or wish, for religious reasons, to decline life-saving medical treatment (Will 2006). How does a good parent respond to these wishes?

In some instances, respecting the poor choices of children plays an important developmental role and thus contributes, in the long run, to advancing their interests. In a related vein, Bou-Habib and Olsaretti argue that respecting the emerging autonomy of children can contribute to their well-being as children (Bou-Habib and Olsaretti 2015). However, this is not always the case and, thus, we must broach the question of whether and under what circumstances good parents should respect the poor choices of their children. Here it is important to distinguish between the importance of attending to the voices of children as a way of gaining insight into what their interests actually are (Brighouse 2003) and allowing that, in some domains, children's choices about their lives merit respect by parents (and others) even when their choices are poor (Archard 2015; Macleod 2017). The latter view leaves open the possibility that good parents sometimes permit their children to make bad choices, even when doing so serves no welfare or developmental purpose.

How good must the good parent be?

The final matter that merits brief attention is the relation between good parenting and having the right to parent at all (see ch. 14). Having children and wishing to parent are not together sufficient to generate a right to parent. Some would-be parents are not competent parents and may, on that basis, be denied the right to parent. Most obviously, parents who are grossly negligent or who subject children to abuse can be denied custody of and parental authority over their children. So, there is a threshold of parental competency that must be achieved in order to gain and maintain the right to parent. Identifying that threshold is theoretically complex for two reasons. First, how the threshold should be set will be sensitive to the division of moral labor. If responsibility for providing education for children is assigned to parents, then parents who are poor and illiterate may not be, relative to that division of moral labor, competent parents because they cannot reliably discharge an important duty to their children. Second, it is not clear whether the standard for assessing competency is an absolute one defined in relation of the capacity of parents to reliably provide a certain level of care or whether parental competency should be assessed comparatively (Shields 2016). If parents vary significantly in their parenting skills and if children have a claim on being raised by the best (available and willing) parents, then it might seem that whether a would-be parent is good enough to become a parent will depend on a comparison of the relevant parenting capacities of different potential parents.

A strongly comparative conception of parental competency is most plausibly grounded in the claim that parenting should be oriented to promoting the best interests of children. On this view, good parents for specific children are those who are most able to maximally promote the interests of the children. This position raises the specter of reassigning children from their natural, seemingly competent parents to other putatively better parents. In practice, it is quite unlikely that children's interests would be served via a general system that sought to match children with the "best" available parents, but the view could have significant practical implications for adoption policy (see ch. 19). As we have already seen, the idea that children have a literal claim to the maximal promotion of their interests is dubious, and once that premise is abandoned the strongly comparative view of parental competency looks implausible. Moreover, it arguably is insufficiently attentive to the interest that parents have in being parents.

A different approach to determining how good a good parent must be treats a standard of parental competency as a function of the justice-based entitlements of children (Macleod 2015). On this view, a good parent – or, at any rate, a parent good enough to have a right to parent – is one who can reliably fulfill the special duties that parents have to their children. The fact that some parents are better placed than others to promote the interests of children is not crucial to assessing competency. The view need not be completely insensitive to comparative judgements of competency. For example, if no available parents can fully discharge their duties to some children and if the children's claims to care will be more fully met by parents who are not fully adequate than by other arrangements (e.g., an orphanage), then it seems appropriate to compare would-be parents with respect to their relative ability to discharge child-rearing duties (Shields 2016). Rather, what matters is that parents can meet their duties, and since there is no general duty to maximize the promotion of children's interests, the capacity of parents to promote non-essential interests of children affects whether parents should be considered good parents. Whether this standard of competency is a demanding one and the degree to which it implies that some would-be parents as unsuitable depends both on how parental duties to children are characterized and the degree to which background institutional arrangements provide parents support and assistance in discharging their duties.

Conclusion

Recent work on parenting has shown that some traditional conceptions of good parenting are dubious. For example, we have seen that good parenting is not dependent on a genetic connection between parents and children, and neither is it dependent on the sexual orientation of parents. Similarly, we have seen that the traditional assumption that good parenting is best provided by two parents is open to challenge. We have also explored some distinctive duties of parents. We saw how specification of the duties of a good parent requires sensitivity to the distinctive interests of children and to the social division of moral labor in caring for children. We examined why parents may have a duty to love their children and why respect for children requires parents to help facilitate children's autonomy and to be attentive to children's preferences and choices. Respecting the emerging autonomy of children constrains the degree to which parents transmit their own conceptions of the good to their children and it imposes some limits on acceptable paternalism by parent. Finally, we broached the issue of the degree to which a person's entitlement to parent depends on the quality of care they can provide children. Having a right to parent does require meeting a reasonably high threshold of competency, but it does not require that would-be parents of a child be the best available parents for that child.

As a final remark, it is worth emphasizing that there is no single way of being a good parent. Diverse parenting styles and approaches reflecting different cultural backgrounds and family structures are compatible with fulfilling the responsibilities of good parenting. Being a good parent is multiply realizable. By the same token, not all existing approaches to parenting are good. Although the move from relatively abstract philosophical accounts of the good parent to evaluative judgements about specific parenting practices is often complex, consideration of the philosophical issues can help guide those judgements. So, consideration of the nature of the good parent is not merely intellectually interesting, it is practically important.

Note

1 A gestational parent need not have a genetic tie to the fetus. Since gestation arguably establishes a biological relation between a pregnant woman and her fetus, it is possible for children to have more than two "biological" parents. For defense of the claim that gestational parents have a special, though defeasible, claim to parent the children to which they give birth, see Gheaus (2012).

References

Anderson, J., and Claasen, R. 2012. "Sailing Alone: Teenage Autonomy and Regimes of Childhood," *Law and Philosophy* 31: 495–522.
Archard, D. 2015. "Children, Adults, Autonomy and Well-Being," in A. Bagattini and C. Macleod (eds.), *The Nature of Children's Well-being: Theory and Practice*. Dordrecht: Springer.
Bou-Habib, P., and Olsaretti, S. 2015. "Autonomy and Children's Well-Being," in A. Bagattini and C. Macleod (eds.), *The Wellbeing of Children in Theory and Practice*. Dordrecht: Springer.
Brennan, S. 2014. "The Goods of Childhood, Children's Rights, and the Role of Parents as Advocates and Interpreters," in F. Baylis and C. McLeod (eds.), *Family-Making: Contemporary Ethical Challenges*. Oxford: Oxford University Press.
Brennan, S., and Cameron, B. 2015. "How Many Parents Can a Child Have? Philosophical Reflections on the 'Three Parent Case'," *Dialogue* 54: 45–61.
Brennan, S., and Macleod, C. 2017. "Fundamentally Incompetent: Homophobia, Religion, and the Right to Parent," in J. Ahlberg and M. Chobli (eds.), *Procreation, Parenthood, and Educational Rights*. London and New York, NY: Routledge.
Brighouse, H. 2003. "How Should Children Be Heard?," *Arizona Law Review* 45(3): 691–711.
Brighouse, H., and Swift, A. 2014. *Family Values: The Ethics of Parent-Child Relationships*. Princeton, NJ: Princeton University Press.
Chua, A. 2011. *Battle Hymn of the Tiger Mother*. London: Penguin.
Clayton, M. 2006. *Justice and Legitimacy in Upbringing*. Oxford: Oxford University Press.
Cutas, D. 2011. "On Triparenting. Is Having Three Committed Parents Better than Having Only Two?," *Journal of Medical Ethics* 37: 735–738.
Cowden, M. 2012. "What's Love Got to Do with It? Why a Child Does Not Have a Right to be Loved," *Critical Review of International Social and Political Philosophy* 15(3): 325–345.
Farr, R. H. 2017. "Does Parental Sexual Orientation Matter? A Longitudinal Follow-up of Adoptive Families with School-age Children," *Developmental Psychology* 53(2): 252–264.
Gheaus, A. 2012. "The Right to Parent One's Biological Baby," *Journal of Political Philosophy* 20(4): 432–455.
Gheaus, A. 2014. "The 'Intrinsic Goods of Childhood' and the Just Society," in C. A. Bagattini and C. Macleod (eds.), *The Nature of Children's Well-being*. Dordrecht: Springer.
Hardwig, J. 1984. "Should Women Think in Terms of Rights?," *Ethics* 94(3): 441–455.
Haslanger, S. 2009. "Family, Ancestry and Self: What is the Moral Significance of Biological Ties?," *Adoption & Culture* 2(1): 91–122.
Haslanger, S., and Witt, C. 2005. *Adoption Matters: Philosophical and Feminist Essays*. Ithaca, NY: Cornell University Press.
Liao, M. 2015. *The Right to Be Loved*. Oxford: Oxford University Press.
Macleod, C. 2007. "Raising Children: Who Is Responsible for What?," in S. Brennan and R. Noggle (eds.), *Taking Responsibility for Children*. Waterloo: Wilfred Laurier Press.
Macleod, C. 2010. "Primary Goods, Capabilities, and Children," in H. Brighouse and I. Robeyns (eds.), *Measuring Justice: Primary Goods and Capabilities*. Cambridge: Cambridge University Press.
Macleod, C. 2012. "Justice, Educational Equality and Sufficiency," in C. M. Macleod (ed.), *Justice and Equality*. Calgary: University of Calgary Press.
Macleod, C. 2015. "Parental Competency and the Right to Parent," in S. Brennan, S. Hannan, and R. Vernon (eds.), *Permissible Progeny*. New York, NY: Oxford University Press.
Macleod, C. 2017. "Doctrinal Vulnerability and the Authority of Children's Voices," in C. Straehle (ed.), *Vulnerability, Autonomy and Applied Ethics*. London and New York, NY: Routledge.
Mullin, A. 2007. "Children, Autonomy and Care," *Journal of Social Philosophy* 38(4): 536–553.
Narveson, J. 1988. *The Libertarian Idea*. Philadelphia, PA: Temple University Press.
Richards, N. 2016. "Raising Children with Respect," *Journal of Applied Philosophy* 35: 90–104, doi: 10.1111/japp.12239.

Schapiro, T. 1999. "What Is a Child?," *Ethics* 109: 715–738.
Shields, L. 2016. "How Bad Can A Good Enough Parent Be?," *Canadian Journal of Philosophy* 46(2): 163–182.
Schoeman, F. 1980. "Rights of Children, Rights of Parents, and the Moral Basis of the Family," *Ethics* 91(1): 6–19.
Sommerville, M. 2007. "Children's Human Rights and Unlinking Child-Parent Biological Bonds with Adoption, Same-Sex Marriage and New Reproductive Technologies," *Journal of Family Studies* 13: 179–201.
Velleman, D. 2005. "Family History," *Philosophical Papers* 34(3): 357–378.
Will, J. F. 2006. "My God My Choice: The Mature Minor Doctrine and Adolescent Refusal of Life-Saving or Sustaining Medical Treatment Based Upon Religious Beliefs," *Journal of Contemporary Health Law and Policy* 22(3): 233–300.
Woodcock, S. 2009. "Five Reasons Why Margaret Somerville Is Wrong about Same-Sex Marriage and the Rights of Children," *Dialogue* 48: 1–21.

16
PARENTAL PARTIALITY

Jonathan Seglow

Introduction

The relationship between parents and their children is a peculiarly close, intimate, exclusive one. Parents (usually) nurture, protect, encourage and reassure their children in a context of loving care and attention. Parents' special concern is crucial for their child's flourishing, development and future well-being; while despite (though in some ways also because) of the challenges of parenthood, few parents would deny that parenting brings a unique fulfilment unavailable elsewhere. As a matter of morality, parents have very powerful duties to care for their children. Legally, parents have rights against third parties in how they raise their child and meet her interests, and thus make the loving relationship they have with her their own.[1] The parent–child relationship is thus a special, protected sphere of intimacy.

This very familiar way of thinking about the family implies that parents are and ought to be partial towards their children. They ought to give their own children, but not other people's, special care and attention. And yet, (reasonable) parents would recognise that other children are not objectively less important than their own; they have just the same basic worth and value (see ch. 6). Parents are engaged participants in an intimate relationship with their children, but they are also more detached, impartial members of the moral world they share with others. How to integrate these two basic roles – where we are partial and impartial – is a longstanding issue in moral and political philosophy. The puzzle applies also to our friends, members of our culture, perhaps also our fellow citizens (Scheffler 2001; Keller 2013; Seglow 2013; Kolodny 2010).

In the case of the family, the conflict between partiality and impartiality is not just theoretically troubling, but also of tremendous practical importance. What parents are permitted or obliged to do for their children has enormous consequences for those children's future well-being as adults, and yet parents' abilities to benefit their children are much influenced by social and other circumstances. Parents give their children love, care and attention, which shapes their characters and forges their personalities; they are guides and role models, orchestrating the introduction of the child to the larger social world. They encourage (or frustrate) their children's natural talents and abilities. When children are young, they oversee their social lives and developing interests. Parents manage a child's education, through choice of schools and the support they give learning; as well as the direction a child will take as an adult in a competitive market society (Swift 2003; see also ch. 31). Besides sometimes paying for private education, parents also make gifts and bequests to their children, and when they are older they may help pay mortgages or university fees. Thus, parents benefit their children through a variety of personal, social and economic means, and all of them are instances of partiality. They all concern what parents do for their children, but not others' children, at least not nearly to the same degree.

This partiality matters because there are huge variations in the wealth and other resources, the education and social capital, and the time, space and energy which different parents enjoy, and which affects what they can give to their children. These variations reflect the pervasive social and economic inequalities of contemporary societies. Advantaged parents in favourable circumstances can often benefit their children more than less fortunate parents. Crucially, they can defend doing so through appeal to the value of parental partiality. It seems reasonable from the perspective of advantaged parents to be especially concerned for their own children, because that is an attitude that all parents can adopt. But the consequence is that the children of advantaged parents are better equipped from the start to attend prestigious universities, enjoy successful well-remunerated careers, perhaps have better health and enjoy other interests and attachments, effects which accumulate over generations. At the same time, most of us claim to believe in *equality* of opportunity. From this impartial moral perspective, parental partiality seems grossly unfair. But parental partiality seems natural and obvious. Even if better-off parents do not *intend* for their children to do better than others in competitive, market-driven societies (though no doubt some do), the practices of partiality they engage in will achieve just that (Fishkin 2014: 50). Parental partiality sets up a cycle of inter-generational advantage very hard to break down (Calder 2016).

This intractable conflict is what I want to explore here. In doing so, I first say a little about how parents confer advantages on their children, before going on to consider the relationship of this to parental partiality and social justice. With the conflict between partiality and justice in focus, I then discuss some proposals that seek to resolve it, before briefly concluding.

Before going further, I should register that what I discuss here is *inter*-familial partiality and not *intra*-familial partiality. The latter concerns parents who direct more time, attention, care or resources to one (or more) of their children at the expense of one (or more) other(s). This may be for idiosyncratic, parochial reasons or for wider cultural ones where boys may be favoured over girls. Even where parents do not seek to favour their son's interests, the latter may be advantaged for structural reasons of which parents may not be fully aware (even as they act to maintain that structure). Susan Moller Okin drew attention to how the gendered division of responsibilities whereby men assume the principal wage-earning role while women labour at raising children and running households acts as a template in which their sons and daughters go on to adopt similarly gendered roles (Okin 1989; cf. Miller 2009; Archard 2010: 81–82; Lloyd 1994; see also ch. 20). Many other feminists have made the same complaint. Besides raising issues of freedom, socialisation and discrimination among others, this intra-familial partiality also has implications for the inter-familial partiality, which is our focus. If parents promote their sons' education over their daughters' then the former will enjoy greater opportunities than their sisters, quite apart from how affluent their parents are. In not considering intra-familial partiality further here, I do not want to signal that it is less important than the parental partiality I do discuss.

Mechanisms of advantage

It makes sense to start with the variety of concrete ways through which parents transmit advantages to their children, before going to consider, more abstractly, how far these can be defended in justice or ought to be reformed.

First, parents provide for their children "external goods"; that is, goods which have no special connection to the family (they would exist without it), are generally impersonal and are valuable in society quite generally. Money and other resources are pre-eminent external goods, as when parents make gifts and bequests to their children, fund their travelling and gap-year activities or pay their rent or mortgage as young adults. Private education is also an external good; it is an impersonal mechanism which equips children with skills, capacities and traits of character important for later study and employment (Swift 2003: 21–34). Parents who pay for a child's sporting, artistic or other activities, and thus help develop their child's talents and abilities may also do so quite impersonally, as do parents who use their social capital to secure internships and work experience for their older children. The way external goods advance children's interests in pursuing social and economic opportunities is very clear, as is the greater ability of more affluent parents to provide them (Esping-Andersen 2005).

Parenting styles are also influential for a child's future development, including her ability to accomplish her career-related aims. Until they grow older, children are intensely vulnerable to the child-raising experience managed by their parents, and the formation of traits and abilities such as self-confidence, resilience, open mindedness, assertiveness and empathy. A parent's cultural and religious attitudes no doubt also have some influence on a child's later attainment. The question is whether these styles vary in a structured way with parents' social and economic position. There is some evidence to suggest that they do. Annette Lareau's (2011) influential study of parenting styles in the US found just such a systematic difference. Middle-class parents adopted a style of "concerted cultivation": this sought to persuade rather than direct their children, taught them to assert their entitlements, engaged in conversation more often and with a wider vocabulary and took an intense interest in providing their children with opportunities to promote their future development. By contrast, working-class and poorer families facilitated their children's "accomplishment of natural growth". They ensured their basic well-being and safety while leaving them freer to fill their time; they spoke less with their children; and marked a strong boundary between parent and adult, indirectly teaching their children to regard their future institutional interactions in terms of external constraint. Though there are costs and benefits to both styles of parenting, concerted cultivation does a better job of equipping children for future economic success in an individualised, competitive, market-driven society such as the US. As Rawls reminds us, the willingness to make an effort is to some degree dependent on family circumstances (Rawls 1999: 64). Others, however, have questioned how far parental advantage is related to children's future well-being (Dermott and Pomati 2016).

Finally, parents can confer advantages to their children through the genetic inheritance which they pass on to them. A person's genetic make-up is likely to play some role in explaining her intelligence, innate talents and abilities, future health and personality traits, though exactly how much is of course hugely controversial, as is the way that our basic genetic constitution interacts with the familial and wider social environment we experience as children. Genes interact too with prenatal environmental factors such as parents' diet and, in a few cases, substance misuse – issues less likely to affect better-off parents. A child's genetic endowment seems fixed in contrast to the parenting she receives and how it provides external goods; the latter may be subject to social reform, however hard that is in practice. However, future technologies such as gene therapy on embryos may mean that we can alter the genetic constitution of children.

I cannot examine here the relative influence of these mechanisms of advantage, nor how they interact to compound each other's effects, or perhaps to mitigate them (cf. Miller 2009: 102–4). All we need to conclude is that there is good evidence that better-off parents are better-equipped to promote their children's prospects for future success.

Impartiality and egalitarian justice

We can now consider in a bit more depth the ideas of impartiality and egalitarian justice, which are in tension with better-off parents advantaging their own children (see ch. 28).

Contemporary moral philosophers often champion moral impartiality, which they see in contrast to pre-modern modes of thought where ethics began with people's rank or station. Impartiality expresses the view that each person has the same basic moral worth or standing. This need not mean that we should strive to be impartial in our everyday lives and attachments, however; to insist on impartiality as a principle we adhere to in all our social interactions – what is sometimes called first-order impartiality – would be an extremely demanding doctrine. By contrast, second-order impartiality identifies the concept instead with moral rules and principles of justice that constrain and direct individuals' behaviour in various ways but still leave us sufficient scope for enjoying our own projects and attachments at the first-order level (Barry 1995; Mendus 2002). Thus, if social justice required that we part with a certain percentage of our income to assist the worst off, we still retain the rest to spend at our discretion. The two-level view seems to offer the best of both worlds. We can discharge those obligations of justice which fairly meet everyone's interests while at the same time enjoying the space to determine our individual lives and give special weight to our personal aims and attachments.

The two-level impartial view, nonetheless, raises an issue of consistency. If we are directed to meet impartial principles of justice in our public persona as citizens – for example, principles which seek to ensure that the worst off have the same opportunities as others – then arguably we should honour the same principles in our personal lives, for instance by helping the needy in our own neighbourhoods. It might seem disrespectful not to honour those principles to which we are officially publicly committed in pursuing our aims and projects (Cohen 2008). Thus, if too many citizens were dedicated to amassing wealth for themselves and their families, we might ask how far they were genuinely personally motivated to support social justice in their own society, even as they continued to pay their taxes as the law requires.

Second-order impartiality is a fairly capacious idea; there are competing impartial theories of social justice and assessing them requires substantive moral argument. One ideal popular among philosophers, politicians and the public is equality of opportunity (Fishkin 1983; Fishkin 2014; Vallentyne and Lipson 1989; Swift 2003: 10–14; Brighouse and Swift 2014: 27–45; White 2007: 53–77; Calder 2016: ch. 4). Such equality, however, may be interpreted in a number of ways. In its least controversial form, equality of opportunity simply amounts to the idea of non-discrimination. In the competition for jobs, university places and so on, authorities have a duty not to take into account irrelevant factors such as applicants' gender, race, religion or social class, but merely to focus on their experience, qualifications, aptitude, and so on. Giving the former characteristics any weight in application decisions would reveal a partial bias towards certain sorts of people. However, factors such as a person's social class or family background can also have a substantial influence on her ability to succeed in a career or on a degree. Individuals from advantaged class and family backgrounds often have better qualifications, interview skills and social capital, leaving individuals from less privileged backgrounds with less real opportunity to attend prestigious universities or enjoy challenging, well remunerated careers – both goods in short supply.

Thinking this way takes us to the substantive view of equality of opportunity. The idea now is that it is only the effort a person expends, the choices she makes and her innate talents and abilities which should determine her success in educational and labour market competition. Extraneous factors, such as her class background and who her parents are, should not. The substantive ideal has more ambitious and far-reaching implications for policy; for example, seeking to ensure much greater parity in the schooling children receive.[2]

It is not difficult to see how parental partiality frustrates realising substantive equality of opportunity, given that such partiality involves parents directing external goods and also time, energy and attention to their children and not others who may be less advantaged, as well as the differences in the parenting styles children experience and parents' genes which they inherit.

Partiality and special duties

As we saw earlier, partiality towards one's children is bound up with the meaning of parenthood which involves acting on very basic, loving commitments. But the mere fact that parents experience their role this way does not by itself explain the *value* of parental partiality. We need to explore what that value might consist in.

One approach, in fact, denies this value. It sees parenting as no more than a convention and relocates the duties to raise children to the wider society (Goodin 1985: 79–85; Macleod 2010: 136–137). On this reductionist view, adult citizens each bear a share of the larger social duty to raise its child citizens to be competent adults, able to pursue their aims and meet their social responsibilities. Allocating this duty to parents as intermediaries is a fair and efficient way to discharge it, given children's interest in extended contact with just a handful of adults and the coordination problems in deciding who should raise which child; we want to avoid over-burdening any particular citizens. Yet, ultimately, this is a duty owed by all of us, as manifest, for example, in the financial and other support which society gives its parents. The reductionist account does not deny the intense emotional attachment between parents and children, but it does not give this social fact moral salience (it only has instrumental value insofar as it motivates parents to do a good job). The reductionist theory is amenable to egalitarian justice because if justice constrains parents from advantaging their children it will not violate any fundamental rights or duties which parents possess. Forbidding parents from spending too much money on their children, for instance, lest this gives those children an unfair advantage, could not on the reductionist view diminish the value of special parental attachment to their children because there is no such fundamental value which morally counts (Seglow 2013: 11–15; Kolodny 2010: 40–42).

The kernel of truth in the reductionist account is that much of what patents do for their children is a matter of social convention and, therefore, potentially subject to revision and change. But the account gives too much weight to impartiality. Partiality towards intimates is too basic a mode of our moral and social experience to be so easily theorised away. Egalitarian justice is a value for actual human societies. It must, therefore, make some sense of the pervasive institutions and practices through which we live our lives – including partiality towards our children – even as it criticizes them and offers proposals for reform.

How then should we theorise parental partiality's value? One possibility is to see raising children as a certain sort of long-term aim or project. Individuals certainly have special reasons to care about the success of their own projects and we attach impersonal moral importance to how far individuals realise their significant projects. Moreover, parents typically identify very strongly with their children and see their children's flourishing as part of their flourishing too. Colin MacLeod suggests a version of the projects view when he says that parents have an interest in seeing their own values and ideals carried forward in their children, an interest which he calls "creative self-extension" (Macleod 2010: 142). Yet, while children are a project in one sense, the projects-based view neglects the fact that parents are invariably committed to their children, directly as individuals, and not as vehicles for their aims (Brighouse and Swift 2014: 102). Moreover, the view implies a rather one-directional account of parental partiality which neglects what children as agents themselves bring to the evolving relationship with their parents (Richards 2010: 159).

A promising alternative sees parental partiality as arising from a special kind of value which inheres in family relationships. Several writers have suggested that intimacy is central to family life and at the core of valuable relationships between parents and children (Schoeman 1980; Brighouse and Swift 2009: 53–54; Brighouse and Swift 2014: 91; Macleod 2010: 141). Intimacy characterises an ideal of mutual authenticity and self-revelation in relationships which are direct, personal and unmediated rather than more rule-bound and institutionally structured.

As Brighouse and Swift point out, intimacy within families has a particular character not shared by other forms of intimate relationship. Young children share themselves unselfconsciously, unconditionally and spontaneously with parents who are normally committed to their interests (Brighouse and Swift 2009: 53–54). Children reveal their hopes, enthusiasms, concerns and anxieties in a protected space with parents whom they trust to raise and protect them. Intimacy between parents and children flourishes in the nexus of a child and her parents' particular interactions, reflecting their mutual investment in their relationship. It is valuable for children both developmentally and in enabling them to have a good childhood. The value of intimacy fits well with the view that childhood is an intrinsically valuable stage of life, and not merely a preparation for adulthood (Gheaus 2015; see also ch. 7).

The champion of partiality might complain that the relationships view misplaces our reasons of partiality which are owed to our children, not to the relationship with our children, and it is certainly true that the relationships view puts a wedge between the focus and the grounds of our partiality (Keller 2013: 62–64). A further question is whether the intimacy view explains all that parents do for their children. Some familial interactions are peculiarly close and their connection with intimacy seems obvious. But feeding, clothing and sheltering one's children seem more impersonal, generic goods. Is a rushed family breakfast on a school morning really an occasion for intimacy? We could conceptualise intimacy so that it really does span the whole gamut of parent–child interactions. Another option is to find some justification for parental partiality in less than intimate cases, and adopt a dual-level view where parents have different kinds of reasons to be partial in different contexts of their parenting.

This second possibility relates to the distinction between parents having special *duties* to do things with, to and for their children and parents having *reasons* of partiality to act towards their children which fall short of duties. The distinction between duties and other sorts of reasons matters because the latter are more easily over-ridable than the former by other considerations; to over-ride a reason which is not a duty does not prevent parents from doing anything which they are morally required to do. Perhaps parents have duties of partiality where family relationship goods such as intimacy are concerned, but weaker reasons in other contexts of parenting where such goods are not at issue? I will consider this in the context of advantage-conferring practices of partiality in the next section.

Tackling advantage

How might we address the tension between parental partiality and egalitarian justice? One simple way is to endorse a weaker "sufficientarian" standard of justice where the state's only duty is to ensure that no citizen falls below a certain threshold of resources or well-being, not to engineer any kind of equality (Shields 2016). Alternatively, we could insist that employers or universities no longer select on merit; that they favour candidates from worse-off backgrounds even where they are less qualified (Fishkin 1983: 55–64; Fishkin 2014: 57). The latter could support affirmative action policies, which arguably are defensible provided the less qualified are qualified *enough*. Finally, we could seek to abolish the family as it's currently constituted and replace it with more collective child-rearing arrangements which seek to give all children the same start in life.

In examining some other strategies to negotiate the conflict, it is worth distinguishing between an upstream approach which defends a revised normative view of families more amenable to egalitarian justice, and a downstream one which accepts that families will always disturb equality of opportunity to a greater or lesser degree and recommends laws and policies to counteract this. The upstream and downstream strategies are consistent, and they may sensibly be combined in a view which legitimates some permissible parental partiality, while working to mitigate the unjust inequalities which even that limited partiality will produce.

Downstream public policy measures which seek to limit the advantages which better-off families confer on their children may be more or less ambitious. Governments can increase support for state schools so that the education they provide more closely matches that available only via private education, and make high-performing state schools more genuinely accessible to all. They can tax private education, require that private schools admit at least some children from poorer families (whose fees are waived) or even outlaw them altogether. Universities can be financially incentivised to admit a greater proportion of young adults from less advantaged backgrounds. Taxes can be raised on inheritance, gifts and bequests, or they could effectively be abolished by raising tax rates to 100 per cent. Such measures would all do something to mitigate disparities in the external goods which parents confer on their children, though we need to ask how much they interfere in parents' freedoms. Parenting courses, whether universal or selective, voluntary or required, might help ensure that fewer children are relatively disadvantaged by the kind of parenting they receive. Other policy measures such as parental leave, more part-time work (for fathers too) and family centres might also help parents spend more time with their children to the advantage of both. In general, societies enjoying less severe social and economic inequalities tend to have greater rates of social mobility so that measures which reduced the gap between rich and poor more generally would give children from worse-off backgrounds a better chance of doing well later in life.

These sorts of downstream measures would mitigate to some degree the inegalitarian effects of parental partiality, but it's unlikely they would eradicate them altogether. So, it's also worth thinking more normatively about whether some moderate degree of parental partiality is defensible.

One approach is inspired by John Rawls's remarks on the moral role of the family (Rawls 1999: 405–10). Rawls suggests at one point that the family could be abolished as it is an obstacle to fair equality of opportunity (Rawls 1999: 448). Collectivised child-raising arrangements might, in principle, remove mechanisms of advantage which stem from external goods and variations in parenting styles; only innate genetic inequalities would remain. Yet Rawls argues that the family is vital as a school for the moral development of children and is necessary to instil in them a sense of justice. Though schools and other associations clearly have some role, it is the family which bears primary responsibility for the crucial task of instilling in children a commitment to justice and morality more generally so that they are able to assume their civic responsibilities as adults. On this view, parental partiality is an ineradicable feature of the family which is, in turn, necessary for justice to take root.

Is Rawls's view that some parental partiality essentially undergirds children's developing sense of justice correct? After all, children brought up in institutional care don't lack any sense of morality. Perhaps we could bring all children up in well-run orphanages, staffed by dedicated professionals who seek to instil in children a moral sense and a commitment to impartial justice (Munoz-Dardé 1999: 41), though we'd need to ensure that such professionals were genuinely impartial and equally capable of raising children, which may not be possible (Gheaus 2018). Yet, at the risk of valorising our own conventions, it's arguably true that children best learn about morality through the supervision and guidance of just a few adults, constant in their care, whom they love and rely upon. It's plausible, too, that parental love is important to instil in children a lively sense of their own worth, which, in turn, is necessary for them to affirm the worth of others. (This claim receives some support from that fact that individuals abused as children are more likely to inflict abuse on others as adults.)

Let's assume that Rawls's family hypothesis is broadly correct. As Véronique Munoz-Dardé and David Archard have separately pointed out, there is something paradoxical to Rawls's defence of the family as a school of justice (Munoz-Dardé 1999: 42; Archard 2010: 84–88; cf. Okin 1989: 89–109; Lloyd 1994). If the family is an obstacle to equality of opportunity, then it stands in the way of realising justice, but at the same time, if the moral development thesis is correct, then the family is necessary in order to bring justice about. We could just swallow this paradox and accept that the family, through its moral developmental role, is critical in creating citizens with the outlook necessary to maintain a just society, even where, because of the family, that society will fall short of all that egalitarian justice demands. But the moral development thesis is also consistent with reforming the family in an egalitarian direction. The family could in some ways support equality of opportunity, where children are taught by their parents to value flourishing relationships over external goods associated with individual, often material, success; and where parenting styles emphasise recognising others' entitlements as well as one's own. This raises the issue I mentioned in the third section of how far we can reasonably expect individuals' outlook in their personal lives to cohere with public principles of justice to which they are officially committed – a fraught issue in view of parents' quite reasonable demand for latitude in how they raise their children. Leaving that aside, it suggests how a normatively reformed family might cohere with egalitarian justice.

Harry Brighouse and Adam Swift (2014) defend a theory with some similarities to this in their influential work on the family. We have already encountered their view that a special kind of intimacy is at the core of the family's value and its members' flourishing. Brighouse and Swift argue that parents have those rights to benefit their children which are necessary to protect the particular kind of valuable familial interaction characterised by intimacy (Brighouse and Swift 2014: 129–130). This kind of parental partiality is permitted, and in part required, and involves "familial relationship goods", goods resonant of the distinctive value of the family with intimacy as its core. But, they maintain, parents do not have the right to benefit their children more generally, and thus if the state intervenes in the family to seek to mitigate the advantages it compounds, it is not doing anything which parents have a right against. In particular, the state does not set back any legitimate interest of parents or children through downstream measures such as taxing gifts, bequests and inheritance and in reforming the school system to give greater priority to worse-off children. One might object that it is valuable for children to have their parents care that their lives go better quite generally, and parental acts such as gift-giving and investing in private education are one way that parents demonstrate their love for their children (Brighouse and Swift 2014: 133–134). Yet, there would be something awry about a family where the parents mainly showed their love for their children by spending money on them, and it is intimate interactions, not these more impersonal acts, that ground the rights which parents do have over their children. In sum, by placing the value of parental partiality within certain rights-based moral constraints, Brighouse and Swift's view helps clear the way for egalitarian justice.

However, matters are not so simple, because family relationship goods also benefit children to different degrees. Brighouse and Swift use the example of bedtime stories (Brighouse and Swift 2014: 129; cf. Segall 2011). Though parents do not generally intend to advantage their children by reading them bedtime stories, if some parents have the time and motivation to read and talk about bedtime stories with their children, and others do not, this differentially benefits the children of the parents that do. Of course, banning bedtime story reading would be an unjustified intrusion into family life. Given parents' rights to act to realise familial relationship goods, Brighouse and Swift argue that the state is not justified in regulating these kinds of intimate familial interactions (Brighouse and Swift 2014: 135). Even if intimate interactions are an obstacle to fully realising equality of opportunity, the value of the family should prevail – with spontaneous, loving interactions at its heart. This view is open to the criticism that it gives *parents* a special prerogative to realise advantage-conferring familial relationship goods where analogous exemptions from egalitarian justice are not extended to childless couples, single people or groups of friends (Archard 2010: 97). Paul Bou-Habib also criticises Brighouse and Swift for assuming that parents' promotion of their children's interests is quite generally valuable (Bou-Habib 2013). On Bou-Habib's alternative moralised view, legitimate acts of parental partiality must be morally permissible in order to be genuine duties. Parental partiality, on this account, is only valuable if it is compatible with other moral requirements – and these include parents' duties to help realise other children's interests. At the very least, on Brighouse and Swift's account there is a disjunction between parental actions in the private sphere and the (second-order) impartial principles of egalitarian justice to which *ex hypothesi* parents have good moral reason to be committed.

One could interpret Brighouse and Swift's argument through the longstanding philosophical doctrine of double effect. This says that the harm a person's action causes can sometimes be excused if it was the result of an intention to do some good, and the harm was not intended itself. For example, it may be permissible to end the life of a terminally ill person in severe pain, if the aim was to alleviate their suffering rather than hasten the end of their life. Perhaps parents' actions might be excused if they intend to benefit their children through intimate interactions without setting back the interests of other children, even though that is what they do. One might think of progressive taxation as a fee more affluent families pay for the right to engage in advantage-conferring forms of interaction with their children, with the tax revenues raised used to improve the prospects of less advantaged children. More generally, parental partiality may only be justified where there are robust policies in place to remedy the effects of more affluent parents conferring benefits on their children, which those less affluent are not able to do. Matthew Clayton and David Stevens question the extent to which parental partiality is justified in unjust societies where few such policies exist (Clayton and Stevens 2004: 118–120).

Of course, parents from families who don't read to their children could be encouraged to do so, as well as reform other aspects of their parenting styles. However, we'd need to ask how effective such policies would be and whether they could be realised without invasive monitoring and intrusion. There are powerful social and economic reasons why worse-off parents engage in fewer benefit-conferring interactions to the extent that they do. These arise from culturally embedded differences in parenting styles, from economic constraints which produce disparities in the time, energy and resources parents have to realise family relationship goods with their children and from social norms besides those. If greater income, wealth, financial security, time off work, education or social connections stand in the way of worse-off parents' realising family relationship goods with their children, there is a strong case in justice for all families to assist in augmenting the social bases of these goods in society at large (Cordelli 2015; Brighouse and Swift 2014: 147–148).

Conclusion

In a world where families were not influential for children's future life prospects, parental partiality would be only a theoretical problem. But that is not our world. Parents help form their children's characters, shape their values, encourage their aptitudes, determine their education, transfer them money and pass on their genes. Children are independent people with their own interests, but they emerge from an institution where parental influence looms large. In this chapter, I have traced the variety of ways that advantaged parents are able to pass on those advantages to their children – something which, intentionally or not, comes at the expense of children from worse-off backgrounds. This undermines the widely held principle of equality of opportunity. I have argued that parental partiality cannot be theorised away merely as social convention, but on the contrary that it realises certain values, such as intimacy. In addressing how we can best respond to the injustices which parental partiality brings, I suggested that we can distinguish between a downstream approach which mitigates some of those injustices – increased inheritance taxes, for example – and an upstream approach which reflects on family structure in the first place. One upstream view defends the family as an institution necessary for children to realise an adequate sense of justice. Another justifies parental partiality because it helps realise the good of intimacy between parents and children. Both these approaches are compatible with, and indeed may support, policy measures which seek to engineer greater equality of opportunity. At the same time, though, I suggest that we cannot fully resolve the problem of parental partiality insofar as it represents two ultimately incommensurable perspectives on the question of value.[3]

Notes

1 I speak of parents throughout this chapter, but as well as "traditional" two-parent arrangements with their own biological children, what I say is meant also to encompass single-parent families, step-parenting and adoptive parenting.
2 An even more radical view of equality of opportunity – sometimes called 'luck egalitarianism' – says that individuals with a favourable genetic endowment and plentiful innate talents should not fare better in life because of their good fortune; egalitarian justice directs us to compensating the less fortunate. See White (2007: ch. 4) for a good summary of luck egalitarian justice; also Segall (2011) and ch. 28.
3 I'm grateful to the editors of this volume and to Philip Cook for helpful comments on an earlier draft of this chapter.

References

Archard, D. 2010. *The Family: A Liberal Defence*. Basingstoke: Palgrave.
Barry, B. 1995. *Justice as Impartiality*. Oxford: Oxford University Press.
Bou-Habib, P. 2013. "The Moralised View of Parental Partiality," *Journal of Political Philosophy* 22(1): 66–83.
Brighouse, H., and Swift, A. 2009. "Legitimate Parental Partiality," *Philosophy and Public Affairs* 37(1): 43–80.
Brighouse, H., and Swift, A. 2014. *Family Values: The Ethics of Parent-Child Relationships*. Princeton, NJ: Princeton University Press.
Calder, G. 2016. *How Inequality Runs in Families*. Bristol: Policy Press.
Clayton, M., and Stevens, D. 2004. "School Choice and the Burdens of Justice," *Theory and Research in Education* 2(2): 111–126.
Cohen, G. A. 2008. *Rescuing Justice and Equality*. Cambridge, MA: Harvard University Press.
Cordelli, C. 2015. "Justice as Fairness and Relational Resources," *Journal of Political Philosophy* 23(1): 86–110.
Dermott, E., and Pomati, M. 2016. "'Good' Parenting Practices: How Important are Education, Poverty and Time Pressure?" *Sociology* 50(1): 125–142.
Esping-Andersen, G. 2005. "Inequality of Incomes and Opportunities," in A. Giddens and P. Diamond (eds.), *The New Egalitarianism*. Cambridge: Polity Press.
Fishkin, J. 1983. *Justice, Equal Opportunity and the Family*. New Haven: Yale University Press.
Fishkin, J. 2014. *Bottlenecks: A New Theory of Equal Opportunity*. Oxford: Oxford University Press.
Gheaus, A. 2015. "The 'Intrinsic Goods of Childhood' and the Just Society," in A. Bagattini and C. Macleod (eds.), *The Nature of Children's Well-Being: Theory and Practice*. Dordrecht: Springer.
Gheaus, A. 2017. "What Abolishing the Family Would Not Do," *Critical Review of Social and Political Philosophy* 21(3): 284–300, doi: 10.1080/13698230.2017.1398449.
Goodin, R. 1985. *Protecting the Vulnerable*. Chicago, IL: University of Chicago Press.

Keller, S. 2013. *Partiality*. Princeton, NJ: Princeton University Press.
Kolodny, N. 2010. "Which Relationships Justify Partiality? The Case of Parents and Children," *Philosophy and Public Affairs* 38(1): 37–75.
Lareau, A. 2011. *Unequal Childhoods: Race, Class and Family Life*. Berkeley, CA: University of California Press.
Lloyd, S. A. 1994. "Family Justice and Social Justice," *Pacific Philosophical Quarterly* 75(3–4): 353–371.
Macleod, C. 2010. "Parental Responsibilities in an Unjust World," in D. Archard and D. Benatar (eds.), *Procreation and Parenthood: The Ethics of Bearing and Rearing Children*. Oxford: Oxford University Press.
Mendus, S. 2002. *Impartiality in Moral and Political Philosophy*. Oxford: Oxford University Press.
Miller, D. 2009. "Equality of Opportunity and the Family," in D. Satz and R. Reich (eds.), *Towards a Humanist Justice: The Political Philosophy of Susan Moller Okin*. Oxford: Oxford University Press.
Munoz-Dardé, V. 1999. "Is the Family to be Abolished Then?," *Proceedings of the Aristotelian Society* 99(1): 37–56.
Okin, S. M. 1989. *Justice, Gender and the Family*. New York, NY: Basic Books.
Rawls, J. 1999. *A Theory of Justice*, revised edition. Oxford: Oxford University Press.
Richards, N. 2010. *The Ethics of Parenthood*. New York, NY: Oxford University Press.
Scheffler, S. 2001. *Boundaries and Allegiances: Problems of Justice and Responsibility in Liberal Thought*. New York, NY: Oxford University Press.
Schoeman, F. 1980. "Rights of Children, Rights of Parents and the Moral Basis of the Family," *Ethics* 91(1): 6–19.
Segall, S. 2011. "If You're a Luck Egalitarian How Come You Read Bedtime Stories to Your Children?," *Critical Review of Social and Political Philosophy* 14(1): 23–40.
Seglow, J. 2013. *Defending Associative Duties*. New York, NY: Routledge.
Shields, L. 2016. *Just Enough: Sufficiency as a Demand of Justice*. Edinburgh: Edinburgh University Press.
Swift, A. 2003. *How Not to be a Hypocrite: School Choice for the Morally Perplexed Parent*. London: Routledge
Vallentyne, P., and Lipson, M. 1989. "Equal Opportunity and the Family," *Public Affairs Quarterly* 3(4): 27–45.
White, S. 2007. *Equality*. Cambridge: Polity Press.

17
THE COMPOSITION OF THE FAMILY

Daniela Cutas

Introduction

Given the task of writing a book chapter on the composition of the family, one might wish to either enumerate the properties of "family", or to dive straight into presenting various types of families and their membership. Yet either approach would face a major stumbling block: there is no agreement on what a family is and, hence, on whether it is of one or several types, or what its core characteristics are. Moreover, we can talk about "the family" or families in several senses: in a personal sense, a biological sense, a moral sense, or a legal sense, and the four (or more) dimensions do not necessarily completely overlap. One might, for example, refer to Anna, Jane's birth mother, as her *real* mother, although she is not Jane's legal mother, nor is she the person who Jane calls mother. One might refer to "Uncle Jake", a close friend, as family, although he is not related either biologically or legally. One might refer to all people sharing a home as "family" regardless of legal or biological ties. One might include non-human animals within one's family – or even favourite toys (Levin and Trost 1992). Furthermore, who is or is not a member of a family may depend on one's age and context; for example, one's parents may be considered one's family during childhood, but not once one has reached adulthood.

Beyond this richness of uses of "family" lie normative assumptions that organise the legitimacy of close personal, and notably, parent–child relationships. For example, one's legal parenthood may be overshadowed and threatened by "moral" parenthood, whether biological or of another kind. Diverse understandings of what it is that makes one a parent, or what it is that makes a family, lead to pointing in different directions when making decisions about, for example, the circumstances in which children ought to be raised. Therefore, before we can talk about the composition of the family, we need to know what is meant by "family" and address the assumptions upon which different approaches rest.

It may well be that the search for the one-fit-for-all answer to the question of what "the family" is, is futile. Perhaps we should instead be talking about families, or indeed about the family as a broad class of different kinds of families (Archard 2010: xiv, 4–17). In the Western world, the nuclear family form (mother, father, children) has been associated with the legally sanctioned (i.e. by marriage) heterosexual union, and the children born in that union – regardless of whether both partners are the children's biological progenitors: when a married woman gives birth to a child, she is by default the child's legal mother and her husband is the father, even where other people are the genetic parents (because, e.g., the woman gestated someone else's genetic offspring). This has arguably helped maintain the integrity of the family unit.[1] Therefore, the preference for biological filiation has, in practice, given way to the preference for the integrity of the apparent family form – on condition that this is of the nuclear kind. This choice of presumed parenthood has not been made in the same default way in the case of same-sex married couples (see Ravelingien and Pennings 2013 for a comparative analysis). Moreover, if a woman is single, in some states paternity testing can and has been enforced in order to ascertain fatherhood (see, e.g., Hovrätt 2015).

If people seek to avail themselves of reproductive technologies, adoption, or become a foster family for a child, they have to overcome scrutiny which may extend from the requirement to justify their choice, to eligibility criteria in terms of age, health, and relationship status, sexual orientation, or income – and demonstrate that they have undergone parenting classes. There may be good reasons for scrutiny, if not on all, at least on some of these criteria. However, this inequality of treatment between those who can and choose to procreate and those who need support or wish to provide a home for existing children has sparked criticism (see, e.g., LaFollette 1980, 2010; Cutas and Bortolotti 2010). That the more the circumstances in which children are born or raised diverge from the nuclear family model, the more they are scrutinised, has been called the *prescriptive* component of the definition of family: the nuclear family is "how the family ought to be" (Archard 2010: 2–3).

Form and function

The family has long been defined primarily in terms of its form. According to philosopher Brenda Almond, the family is "the chain of personal connections that gives meaning to our human notions of past, present and future – a mysterious genetic entity that binds us in our short span of individual existence to our ancestors and to our successors" (Almond 2006: 1). There is something compelling and inescapable about the family when defined in this way. Innovations in family-building and departures from this "chain" (including those that follow from the dislodging of traditional gender roles in the family) are, from this perspective, a threat to the privileged status of the family.

One distinct change in perceptions of the family in recent decades has been to look at *family function* rather than *family form* (Millbank 2008; Archard 2010: 9–10) to determine what a family is and who its members are. According to Archard, "the family can be minimally defined as a multigenerational group, normally stably co-habiting, whose adults take primary custodial responsibility for the dependent children" (Archard 2010: 10). Although Archard starts with characteristics in terms of family form, the second part of the definition clarifies the "multigenerational" form of the group by introducing responsibility for children: the form (multigenerational) is thus required by the function (the carrying out of responsibility for children).

This move from form to function is in line with findings in psychology according to which what seems to matter most for children's well-being is the quality of the relationships in the family rather than details of family composition such as the gender or sexual orientation of the parents, whether children have one or more parents, or whether children and parents are genetically related to each other (Golombok 2015). According to these findings, the assumption that family form is important or even essential for the well-being of children is disproved, and the correlations between family form and family outcome do not withhold scrutiny.

Family function, however, is not always defined necessarily and specifically in relation to raising children. According to Diduck and Kaganas, "in the liberal vision of the family, its social function is to provide a financially autonomous, physically and emotionally fulfilling enclave to its members" (Diduck and Kaganas 2012: 14). Unlike Archard's, this definition does not place children at the core of the family and does not require the presence of several generations for a unit to be a family. However, both capture something about what the family *does* rather than what it looks like in terms of composition.

In social work research, it has been pointed out that what tends to count as "family" can differ greatly depending on one's age and circumstances. For example, in elderly care, family tends to consist of one's spouse (*the couple family*); in the area of child welfare, of the child and her carers (*the child-centred family*); in addiction, of those who can help or hinder recovery (*the therapeutic family*) (Gŭmŭscŭ, Khoo, and Nygren 2014). Here, again, the focus is on function: who the family is for the purposes of caring for a particular person; regardless of whether caring for children or parent–child relationships are involved.

In the following, I will examine each component of the family, pertaining to its form as well as its function: whether children are a necessary ingredient for a unit to be called a family; the genetic or biological link between parents and children; the number of parents, criteria, and grounds for determining family membership; and the relationship between its members. By the end of this chapter, I hope to have highlighted that a closer analysis of the concept of family and its composition is likely to reveal its complexity as a multifaceted social phenomenon, rather than helping to clarify what *the* family is. This is important because whether a unit is perceived as a family, or an adult as a parent, determines whose close relationships are supported and who has which entitlements in relation to which children.

Are children a necessary ingredient of the family?

Children feature in many or most philosophical analyses of the family. Brighouse and Swift (2014: XI) locate the value of the family in child-rearing, for both children and adults. They acknowledge that not everyone would include child-rearing as a necessary ingredient of the family, but in their book they only discuss the goods that can be realised in parenting. Conversely, it has been pointed out that framing the discussion of children's interests in terms of "the family" colours it with expectations in terms of relationships between adults (romantic or marital) and certain kinds of links (biological) between parents and children. Abandoning the framework of "family" to discuss what types of social configurations should be accepted as child-rearing units, Munthe and Hartvigsson suggest, would get these assumptions out of the way (Munthe and Hartvigsson 2012).

Long-term coupledom is becoming less pervasive and an increasing number of adults do not marry nor live together with a romantic partner. Friends, siblings, or parents may fulfil some of the functions of the family, which may or may not include child-rearing. Brake argues that amatonormativity, or "the focus on marital and amorous love relationships as special sites of value" (Brake 2012: 5), devalues other types of care relationships. Current regulations relating to marriage and the family impose unnecessary and harmful constraints on who can be recognised as a carer or a family member. While at the same time making a case for separating parenting and marriage (Brake 2012),[2] Brake argues for extending marriage-like entitlements to recognise and sustain a wider range of caring relationships. In this understanding, then, children are not a necessary ingredient of the family, and neither are marriage or sexual intimacy between family members.

One example of a relationship whose members may consider themselves each other's family, but which is neither marital nor sexual, nor does it involve child-rearing, is that between two adults with a long history of caring for each other and sharing a home – such as in the case of Ms Sanford and Ms Inferrera, discussed by Brake (2015a, 2015b). This relationship fulfils some of the functions of marriage and family. It is, however, not sexual, reproductive, or parental. Because it is not marital, it also fails to be protected by the right to found a family (see ch. 14). It could be objected here that while caring relationships such as these may be valuable and worthy of support, they do not constitute a family. Almond, for example, claims we need to distinguish between family and household (Almond 2006: 11). However, unless one takes the family to have a certain form (i.e. parents and their biological offspring), as Almond does, it seems difficult to draw a straightforward distinction between the two in a way that does not beg the question of what the family is and why.

McCandless and Sheldon have challenged what they call the pervasiveness of the sexual family form: the family whose adult members, one man and one woman, are (presumably) in a sexual relationship which each other (McCandless and Sheldon 2010). Almost two decades earlier, Fineman had criticised the same feature, which she called "sexual affiliation" (Fineman 1995). In line with McCandless, Sheldon, and Brake, Fineman points out that the sexual family paradigm leaves unprotected and legally invisible caring relationships that are at the heart of people's lives. For Fineman, nurturing is the core family relationship, and thus it is the nurturing relationship that should be recognised as the core family unit (Fineman 1995: 200). The Mother/Child dyad is a symbol of the family, but "mother" can and should be anyone who has the capacity to take care of another, and "child" could be personified either by actual children, or by adults who are ill, elderly, disabled, etc. (Fineman 1995: 234–235).

The role of genetics

"Parent" is used to denote a genetic or biological procreator *and* someone who takes up parental responsibilities *and* someone who is legally recognised as a child's parent. As noted above, a birth mother and her husband are the prima facie legal parents of a child, regardless of genetic contributions. At the same time, in the context of gamete donation, there is a tension in representing one or the other as the *real* parent, with rearing parents in particular concerned about representing themselves and being acknowledged as the *real* parents in spite of the donation (Mac Dougall, Becker, and Nachtigall 2007). *Real* parenthood stands in moral primacy in relation to the child in a way that is not extinguished by legal conventions.

Reproductive technologies such as in vitro fertilisation have further complicated the competition between types of parenthood by allowing the division of biological motherhood into genetic and gestational. Furthermore, mitochondrial replacement allows the birth of children with nuclear DNA from a male and a female and mitochondrial DNA from a second female. This technique of avoiding the birth of children with mitochondrial disease has largely been termed in the media as "three parent reproduction". Mitochondrial DNA may amount to a very small percentage of the child's genetic make-up, and not one that is likely to be expressed in any recognisable way in the child's features. It is, however, making a significant well-being contribution by preventing the transmission of a mitochondrial disease to the child and thus allowing the child to thrive.

Furthermore, findings in epigenetics indicate that the environment in which a child is raised determines which genes are expressed and how, in ways which seem to be heritable (Kaati et al. 2007; Hens 2017). This means that, if determining a child's features amounts to biological parenthood, and insofar as the people who raise a child determine the environment around her, which has an impact on the child's gene expression, they are *also* her biological parents. Conversely, DNA from a (male) foetus can be found in their gestational mother's brain long after birth (Chan et al. 2012); thus, if genetic contribution, however small, generates biological parenthood, it means that children can be their mothers' biological parents. All these research findings and innovations in human reproduction make it increasingly difficult to point to genetic or biological connections in search of a straightforward answer to the question of who a child's parents are.

Therefore, even if we posit that biological contributors *are* a child's *real* parents, and thus a child's *real* family, the hope of keeping their number at two gendered and exclusive parents is futile. A subsequent issue here is *why* we need to answer these questions, and *what* we seek to find out. Establishing who has which responsibility in relation to children is one such motive, whether because more adults compete to being recognised as the parents of a particular child and choices need to be made between these, or because we need to be able to nominate one or several adults who *should* take responsibility for the child in question. Which family is the child a part of? Who is the person or who are the people who ought to take primary custodial responsibility for the child, and on what basis?

The question of who bears this responsibility, however, is not all we might want to know when we ask who a child's parents are. We might specifically want to know who bears legal responsibility for a child; we might want to know who her biological kin is, because she needs compatible tissue for transplant; we might want to know who has procreative responsibility in relation to that child. For example, when children are reared by their biological parents, causal as well as role responsibility coincide in the same individuals. However, with practices such as gamete donation, these types of responsibilities are split between the intended and the biological parents. Biological contributions to the creation of children generate responsibilities that are procreative, but not necessarily parental (Fahmy 2013). When asking who a child's parents are, then, we may be asking one of several questions, some of these normative, and the answers to which need not overlap.

Furthermore, the relation between biology and parenthood does not neatly correspond to the distinction between form and function. According to Velleman,

> knowing one's relatives and especially one's parents provides a kind of self-knowledge that is of irreplaceable value in the life-task of identity formation. These claims lead me to the conclusion that it is immoral to create children with the intention that they be alienated from their biological relatives for example, by donor conception.
>
> (Velleman 2005: 357)

For Velleman, then, the biological relationship is important in one's process of identity formation: it performs a valuable function for the child. In this perspective, that one *can* flourish without knowledge of one's biological origins does not mean that something of value is not lost. A relationship with one's biological kin is a personal need (Velleman 2008). Note that by "one's relatives" and "one's parents", Velleman means the biological kin and the biological parents.

Velleman is critical of the practice, associated with gamete donation, of severing the link to children's "biological past". According to him, those who uphold "the new ideology of the family" downplay the importance of biological ties, in order to prevent gamete donation from being perceived as morally problematic. Severing this link is, however, not necessarily a corollary of gamete donation; some legislatures, such as Sweden and the UK, do not allow anonymous gamete donation. Awareness of the circumstances of one's conception can be difficult to avoid – such as in the case of same-sex parents, who clearly could not both be their children's genetic parents, and in the case of which disclosure is much more common (Scheib and Hastings 2012). Research suggests that "the combination of early and honest disclosure, having information about the donor, and being open to children's questions about their family's origins may lead to the best outcomes yet observed for DI [donor insemination] families" (Scheib and Hastings 2012: 76).

Velleman's conclusion is that becoming parents via gamete donation is immoral: children should be raised by their biological parents (Velleman 2005: 362). However, that there is value in knowing one's ancestry does not mean that one needs to be raised by one's biological kin. Although Velleman makes a compelling case for the value of this knowledge – in a way that is supported by empirical findings such as those reviewed by Scheib and Hastings – more is needed to show that children should not only know their genetic origin but also be parented by their biological (and specifically genetic) parents.

In some countries, children conceived via gamete donation do not know the identity of the gamete donors. Furthermore, when they want to have more children, some parents go to great lengths to use gametes from the same (anonymous) donor so that the children are full genetic siblings (Somers et al. 2015). This example highlights the ambivalence of attitudes towards the value of the genetic link – and this corresponds to what Velleman calls "moral incoherence" (Velleman 2005: 374). To prevent children from knowing one side of their ancestry while having gone to great lengths as a prospective parent to secure a genetic link (to at least one of the parents), and to have "full siblings", suggests a double standard on the valuing of genetic ties. If genetic ties are unimportant and, thus, preventing children from being aware of them and relating to their biological kin is unproblematic, then such an effort is excessive; embryo donation should be just as desirable as gamete donation, and there is no need to have gametes from the same donor for multiple children. If, however, genetic ties *are* important, then children may have a legitimate claim to know their biological kin.

Another important aspect here is whether legal parents harm their children by preventing them from developing a relationship with their biological kin – and on what grounds they are permitted to do so. Furthermore, *because* people value genetic connections, whether children and their genetic kin know about each other and are allowed to interact affects many more individuals than the child and her parents or gamete donors. For example, a donor's own parents may perceive their child's genetic offspring as their grandchildren – sometimes the only grandchildren that they will ever have.[3] In most legislatures, a child's legal parents may, however, exclude others from the child's life, regardless of biological or other connections[4] (Bartlett 1984; Gheaus 2012, 2018). If, as Velleman claims, knowledge of and acquaintance with one's biological kin is important in the process of identity formation, then children have an interest in not being denied this knowledge and acquaintance.

The importance of biological ties for personal identity has, however, been questioned by other authors. Sociologists Nordqvist and Smart (2014) claimed that rather than resting on knowledge of biological connections, identity is relational in nature. Nordqvist and Smart endorse the view that identity

> ebbs and flows and changes (imperceptibly perhaps) in relation to the people one relates to in different contexts over time (…) a more sociological understanding of identity recognises that it can only be formed through relationships with others, at first mostly family members. (…) These insights into the meaning of belonging and identity add in important ways to our understanding of family life as a complex web of emotions, proximities, relationships, memories, biographies and various forms of connectedness.
> *(Nordqvist and Smart 2014: 25–26)*

From this perspective, it is family practices, rather than genetic connections, that create relatedness. The fact that genetic connections and family relations have so often coincided has contributed to the expectation that they are dependent upon each other – but they are not.

If this is the case, then Velleman's claim that knowledge of one's biological relatives is "of irreplaceable value" in identity formation (Velleman 2005: 357), in such a way as to make gamete donation "immoral", is too strong.

Haslanger supports a position similar to Nordqvist and Smart's, from a philosophical (and adoptive parent's) perspective: just because most children have formed their identities in relation to their biological parents, does not mean that they should, or that it would necessarily be "very difficult" (Velleman 2005: 366) for them to form a family-resemblance concept of themselves without this relation. Drawing on literature on the development of personal identity in transracial families, Haslanger argues that while it would be harmful for children that their parents damage their identity formation, there does not seem to be an obligation to offer them particular ingredients which are not essential in this process (Haslanger 2009: 10). According to Haslanger, for there to be such an obligation, it would need to be the case that acquaintance with one's biological relatives is a basic good, a good that is necessary for a minimally good life – which it is not.

Others have pointed towards birth mothers as the holders of *prima facie* claims to be recognised as children's legal parents, whether or not they are genetically related to each other (Gheaus 2012). Because birth mothers have gestated the child, they are the first to have developed a relationship with that child, and it is relationships rather than genetics or contracts that generate a parent–child bond. In virtue of their intimacy with the birth mother, her partner may similarly have already formed a relationship with the child. This perspective offers a different type of justification for recognising children's birth family as the default family. The severing of this relationship is a harm for both the birth mother and the child (van Zyl 2002). Regardless of who is eventually recognised as the child's legal parent, there may be reasons why the current exclusive understanding of parenthood fails to capture the complexities that ensue from the many ways in which children are conceived and raised (Shanley and Jesudason 2012).

Parenthood is not only often seen as exclusive, it is also presumed to be preferably shared by no less (Cutas and Smajdor 2017) and no more (Cutas 2011) than two adults. In most legislatures, children can only have up to two legal parents – even when in practice more than two adults contribute whichever properties we see as determinative of parenthood, such as long-term caring or biological ingredients. That a child has more than two biological parents (e.g. genetic mother, birth mother, and genetic father) or social parents (e.g. legal mother, legal father, and the step-parent, who may have contributed significantly to raising the child) is invisible in the eyes of the law. At the same time, it is taken as axiomatic that children need more than one parent and that, therefore, elective solo parenthood is problematic. For example, in some European countries fertility treatments are only available to couples. The expectation that solo parenthood is harmful for children has not been confirmed in practice: when people have become solo parents by choice, children seem to do at least as well as children in two-parent families. It is socio-economic conditions or the loss of a parent that cause negative outcomes from solo parenting, rather than the fact that the child has only one parent (Murray and Golombok 2005; Graham 2012). This expectation in terms of parental numerosity matches the model of biological parenthood – at least in principle, because as we have seen above even biological parenthood is no longer confined to no more than two.

The relationship between parents

Shared parenting is seen as generating duties between co-parents that derive from children's interests as well as from the sharing itself (Cook 2012). In the words of Cook, the duties of shared parenting are not exhausted by the interests of the child. Those who engage in shared parenting have duties to each other derived from the child's interests, but they also have additional duties to each other as sharers in parenting. These additional duties are constituted by a combination of the general features of forming a shared intention, and by the special features of sharing an intention to parent a child.

(Cook 2012: 169)

Although, Cook continues, parenting should be voluntary, once parental duties have been taken up, they cannot be extinguished through a unilateral decision (Cook 2012: 169). A similar point is made by Giordano who argues that, in addition to the risks for the children, the retreat of one parent from their parental responsibilities puts the other parent as well as others around them at risk of stress and hardship (Giordano 2007).

As Fineman pointed out, framing the family in terms of mother, father, and their children, leaves families that do not conform to these standards outside of the many protections conferred to families, and in a strict reading outside of the concept of family altogether. A post-separation parent's access to her children may be restricted to visitation and the provision of financial support to the child. In common parlance, a family in which parents are divorced is often referred to as a "broken" family. If, however, the focus is on responsibility for children, then a divorce or other change in relationships between the parents is a reorganisation rather than a dissolution of the family.

The association between romantic relationships between adults and co-parenting has been pervasive and has had a number of consequences for parents, such as determining them to stay married for the sake of the children. According to recent research in public health in the US, state authorities, including mental health services, judges, law enforcement officials, and child custody systems, go to great lengths to preserve the two-parent family. This is done even in severe cases of domestic violence, prioritising the family unit over the safety of women and children (Shoener 2014, 2016). Once partners have separated, states can and often do allow or enforce contact, even when this is clearly not in the interests of family members – and of children in particular (Bruno 2016).

These effects have been aggravated by circumstances such as the difficulty in practice to co-parent after divorce. It has been a common assumption that divorce harms children and that parents should, thus, for the sake of their children, not divorce. Empirical research, however, indicates that rather than parental divorce per se, it is associated factors such as the deterioration of the relationships in the family, inter-parental conflict, or socio-economic hardship which are harmful for children (Golombok 2015: 145–146).

Finally, even within the *nuclear* family model, family roles are being reconfigured, from gendered and hierarchical, to more equal and with increasing expectations of sharing in the rights and responsibilities (Fineman 2004), which includes those related to parenting. The responsibilities of co-parenting create a lasting relationship between the co-parents, which displaces the romantic relationship between them from centre stage in relation to the child. If marriage used to be seen as the lifelong commitment within which reproduction and parenting ideally unfolded, it is increasingly co-parenting that creates a lasting relationship between parents, whether or not they are married to each other.

Conclusion

In this chapter, I have briefly reviewed some of the hurdles of trying to specify what a family is, what determines whether a unit is or is not a family, and who should be recognised as whose family member and on what grounds: are dependent children a necessary ingredient of any family? Who are a child's parents? What are the implications of co-parenting on the relationship between co-parents?

Family has been defined in terms of its form (e.g. mother, father, and their children), as well as its function (e.g. child-rearing). Most often it has been assumed to necessarily include dependent children. Conceptions of the family have been structured in terms of biological connections, or social ones, or both. Perceptions of *real* parenthood (either, most often, biological, or social) may be seen as a threat to the parent–child relationship, even where legal claims are not raised. For some commentators, being raised by one's biological parents is of utmost importance for the process of identity formation in children. Relationships between parents determine the recognition of parenthood and, conversely, co-parenthood generates duties between parents as co-parents. The increasing diversity of family-building and family-living strategies puts pressure on any hope to keep the definition of family simple. Progress in genetics and epigenetics contributes further to this landscape, as do changing expectations from parents.

Assumptions and expectations about what the family is, or should be, have a bearing on which relationships are supported and legally recognised. Biological connections are clearly still seen by many as very important in determining family relationships. The preference for the so-called sexual or nuclear family trumps the importance of these connections, at least from a legal perspective. The determination of parenthood outside the nuclear family is, however, much more vulnerable, not only to the importance awarded to biological connections, but also to norms about appropriate sexuality and parenthood (Cutas and Chan 2012); ideas about the importance of marriage and of biological connections for children continue to shape these expectations, regardless of findings from social science.[5]

Notes

1 This is further confirmed by recent discussions in, for example, Germany, where a legislative proposal has been advanced which would make it a requirement for women to reveal the identity of the biological father during disputes over child support. According to this legislative proposal, once the marriage is over, the association between biological fatherhood and fatherhood *tout court* is restored – even in such cases in which presumably the husband has been legally recognised as, and acted as, the child's father (Associated Press 2016).
2 This has also been suggested by Cutas (2011) and Brennan and Cameron (2016).
3 For an exploration of these kinds of real-life complications, see, e.g., Nordqvist and Smart (2014).
4 This *status quo* has started to be successfully challenged in courts by grandparents (Henderson 2005).
5 Work towards this chapter has been supported by the Swedish Research Council (grant number 421-2013-1306).

References

Almond, B. 2006. *The Fragmenting Family*. Oxford: Oxford University Press.
Archard, D. 2010. *The Family. A Liberal Defence*. London: Palgrave Macmillan.
Associated Press. 2016. *German Plan Would Make Mothers Reveal Child's Biological Dad*. Retrieved from bigstory.ap.org/article/66dce37e5ad74949a441bd403cfae6f9/german-plan-would-make-mothers-reveal-childs-biological-dad (last accessed 24 March 2018).
Bartlett, K. 1984. "Rethinking Parenthood as an Exclusive Status: The Need for Legal Alternatives When the Premise of the Nuclear Family Has Failed," *Virginia Law Review* 70: 879–963.
Brake, E. 2012. *Minimizing Marriage. Marriage, Morality, and the Law*. Oxford: Oxford University Press.
Brake, E. 2015a. "Recognizing Care: The Case for Friendship and Polyamory," *Syracuse Law and Civic Engagement Journal*. Retrieved from slace.syr.edu/issue-1-2013-14-on-equality/recognizing-care-the-case-for-friendship-and-polyamory/ (last accessed 24 March 2018).
Brake, E. 2015b. "Why Can't We Be (Legally-Recognized) Friends?," *theForum* (LSE). Retrieved from

blogs.lse.ac.uk/theforum/why-cant-we-be-legally-recognized-friends/ (last accessed 25 March 2018).
Brennan, S., and Cameron, B. 2016. "Is Marriage Bad for Children? Rethinking Personal Relationships in a Marriage-Free State", in E. Brake (ed.), *After Marriage. Rethinking Marital Relationships*. Oxford: Oxford University Press.
Brighouse, H., and Swift, A. 2014. *Family Values. The Ethics of Parent-Child Relationships*. Princeton, NJ: Princeton University Press.
Bruno, L. 2016. *Ofridstid. Fäders våld, staten och den separerade familjen*. Uppsala: Uppsala Universitet.
Chan, W. F., Gunrot, C., Montine, T. J., Sonnen, J. A., and Nelson, J. L. 2012. "Male Microchimerism in the Human Female Brain," *PLoS One* 7(9): e45592.
Cook, P. 2012. "On the Duties of Shared Parenting," *Ethics and Social Welfare* 6(2): 168–181.
Cutas, D. 2011. "On Triparenting. Is Having Three Committed Parents Better than Having Only Two?," *Journal of Medical Ethics* 37: 735–738.
Cutas, D., and Bortolotti, L. 2010. "Natural versus Assisted Reproduction: In Search of Fairness," *Studies in Ethics, Law, and Technology* 4(1): 1–18.
Cutas, D., and Chan, S. (eds.). 2012. *Families – Beyond the Nuclear Ideal*. London: Bloomsbury Academic.
Cutas, D., and Smajdor, A. 2017. "'I am Your Mother and Your Father!' In Vitro Derived Gametes and the Ethics of Solo Reproduction," *Health Care Analysis*, 25(4): 354–369.
Diduck, A., and Kaganas, F. 2012. *Family Law, Gender and the State. Text, Cases and Materials*. Oxford: Hart Publishing.
Fahmy, M. 2013. "On Procreative Responsibility in Assisted and Collaborative Reproduction," *Ethical Theory and Moral Practice* 16: 55–70.
Fineman, M. A. 1995. *The Neutered Mother, the Sexual Family, and other Twentieth Century Tragedies*. London: Routledge.
Fineman, M. A. 2004. *The Autonomy Myth. A Theory of Dependency*. New York, NY: The New Press.
Gheaus, A. 2012. "The Right to Parent One's Biological Baby," *Journal of Political Philosophy* 20(4): 432–455.
Gheaus, A. 2018. "Children's Vulnerability and Legitimate Authority over Children," *Journal of Applied Philosophy* 35: S1: 60–75.
Giordano, S. 2007. "Crimes and Misdemeanours: The Case of Child Abandonment," *Journal of Medical Ethics* 33(1): 28–37.
Golombok, S. 2015. *Modern Families. Parents and Children in New Family Forms*. Cambridge: Cambridge University Press.
Graham, S. 2012. "Choosing Single Motherhood? Single Women Negotiating the Nuclear Family Ideal," in D. Cutas and S. Chan (eds.), *Families: Beyond the Nuclear Ideal*. London: Bloomsbury Academic.
Gŭmŭscŭ, A., Khoo, E., and Nygren, L. 2014. "Family as Raw Material – The Deconstructed Family in the Swedish Social Services," *Journal of Comparative Social Work* 2: 1–27.
Haslanger, S. 2009. "Family, Ancestry and Self: What Is the Moral Significance of Biological Ties?," *Adoption & Culture* 2(1): 91–122.
Henderson, T. 2005. "Grandparent Visitation Rights: Successful Acquisition of Court-Ordered Visitation," *Journal of Family Issues* 26(1): 107–137.
Hens, K. 2017. "The Ethics of Postponed Fatherhood," *International Journal of Feminist Approaches to Bioethics* 10(1): 103–118.
Hovrätt 2015-T 7895 [Decision of the Swedish Court of Appeals].
Kaati, G., Bygren, L.O., Pembrey, M., and Sjöström, M. 2007. "Transgenerational Response to Nutrition, Early Life Circumstances and Longevity," *European Journal of Human Genetics* 15(7): 784–790.
LaFollette, H. 1980. "Licensing Parents," *Philosophy and Public Affairs* 9: 182–197.
LaFollette, H. 2010. "Licensing Parents Revisited," *Journal of Applied Philosophy* 27(4): 327–343.
Levin, I., and Trost, J. 1992. "Understanding the Concept of Family," *Family Relations* 41(3): 348–351.
Mac Dougall, K., Becker, G., and Nachtigall, R. D. 2007. "Strategies for Disclosure: How Parents Approach Telling their Children that they are Conceived with Donor Gametes," *Fertility and Sterility* 87(3): 524–533.
McCandless, J., and Sheldon, S. 2010. "The Human Fertilisation and Embryology Act (2008) and the Tenacity of the Sexual Family Form," *Modern Law Review* 73: 175–207.
Millbank, J. 2008. "The Role of the 'Functional Family' in Same-Sex Family Recognition Trends," *Child and Family Law Quarterly* 20(2): 155–182.
Munthe, C., and Hartvigsson, T. 2012. "The Best Interest of Children and the Basis of Family Policy: The issue of reproductive caring units," in D. Cutas and S. Chan (eds.), *Families: Beyond the Nuclear Ideal*. London: Bloomsbury Academic.

Murray, C., and Golombok, S. 2005. "Going it Alone: Solo Mothers and their Infants Conceived by Donor Insemination," *American Journal of Orthopsychiatry* 75(2): 242–253.

Nordqvist, P., and Smart, C. 2014. *Relative Strangers. Family Life, Genes and Donor Conception.* New York, NY: Palgrave.

Ravelingien, A., and Pennings, G. 2013. "The Right to Know Your Genetic Parents: From Open-Identity Gamete Donation to Routine Paternity Testing," *The American Journal of Bioethics* 13(5): 33–41.

Scheib, J., and Hastings, P. 2012. "Donor-conceived Children Raised by Lesbian Couples", in D. Cutas and S. Chan (eds.), *Families: Beyond the Nuclear Ideal.* London: Bloomsbury Academic.

Shanley, M. L., and Jesudason, S. 2012. "Surrogacy: Reinscribing or Pluralising Understandings of Family?," in D. Cutas and S. Chan (eds.), *Families: Beyond the Nuclear Ideal.* London: Bloomsbury Academic.

Shoener, S. 2014. Two-Parent Household Can Be Lethal. Domestic Violence and Two-Parent Households, *New York Times*, 21 June. Retrieved from nytimes.com/2014/06/22/opinion/sunday/domestic-violence-and-two-parent-households.html (last accessed September 2016).

Shoener, S. 2016. *The Price of Safety. Hidden Costs and Unintended Consequences in the Domestic Violence Service System.* Nashville, TN: Vanderbilt University Press.

Somers, S. et al. 2015. Couples Needing Sperm Donation Favour the Same Donor for all Conceptions. Retrieved from eurekalert.org/pub_releases/2015-06/esoh-cns061015.php (last accessed September 2016).

Velleman, D. 2005. "Family History," *Philosophical Papers* 34(3): 357–378.

Velleman, D. 2008. "The Gift of Life," *Philosophy and Public Affairs* 36(3): 245–266.

Zyl, Lezl van. 2002. "Intentional Parenthood and the Nuclear Family," *Journal of Medical Humanities* 23(2): 107–118.

18
PARENTAL LICENSING AND DISCRIMINATION

Carolyn McLeod and Andrew Botterell

Introduction

In order to protect children from risks associated with bad parenting, some philosophers have recommended that all parents be licensed, in much the same way in which drivers of motor vehicles and many professionals, such as physicians, are licensed (see, e.g., LaFollette 1980, 2010). In this chapter, we clarify what parental licensing is, describe philosophical theories about it, and assess these theories in terms of how well they deal with problems of discrimination in parental licensing.

Our discussion revolves around the following fact: that while some parents—namely adoptive and foster parents—are licensed, people who become parents through (unassisted or assisted) reproduction generally are not (see ch. 19 and ch. 32). This situation represents, in general terms, the *status quo on parental licensing* in most Western jurisdictions. Our argument in this chapter proceeds against this backdrop, although it should be noted that most philosophers do not approach the problem of parental licensing in this way. To the contrary, they begin by asking whether there should be parental licensing at all, thereby ignoring or downplaying the fact that parental licensing already occurs in the context of adoptive and foster parenting. This is a problem with most philosophical theories about parental licensing.

A further problem with these theories is that they tend to pay insufficient attention to forms of discrimination that may be inherent in, or result from, a system of parental licensing. For example, by situating these theories in relation to the *status quo*, we aim to show how many of them reinforce what philosophers have called "biologism" or "bionormativity": the privileging of families formed through biological reproduction over families formed in other ways (Haslanger 2009; Baylis and McLeod 2014). While much of our discussion focuses on biologism, we also touch on other forms of discrimination that parental licensing can cause or exacerbate, such as classism, sexism, homophobia, racism, and ableism. Our view is that any adequate proposal in favor of parental licensing must take worries about discrimination seriously. Unfortunately, most philosophical proposals fail to do so.

The chapter proceeds as follows. In the second section we explain what parental licensing is before describing, in the third section, the current *status quo* on parental licensing. Then, in the fourth section, we turn to philosophical arguments for and against different parental licensing schemes. Our main goal throughout is, again, to highlight ways in which these schemes could be discriminatory or could promote discrimination that targets adoptive and foster families in particular.

The nature of parental licensing

Parental licensing involves restrictions on the freedom to parent a child that are imposed by the state on individuals who may never have mistreated children. In requiring that individuals be licensed, the state demands that they show some competency in being a parent before they actually become one in a social sense. Since, typically, the relevant restrictions are prospective in nature—they occur before someone has had the opportunity to parent a child—what lies at the core of parental licensing is "prior restraint": people are restrained in the activity of parenting prior to showing any incompetence in doing so (i.e., by harming a child; LaFollette 1980: 188).

Any process of licensing is meant to test whether someone is competent to perform an activity at some appropriately specified level, both now as well as in the future. The standards of competence could be set very high, thereby excluding a relatively large number of applicants, namely those who are predicted not to perform the activity very well. Alternatively, the standards could be set quite low, thereby excluding only a small number of applicants, namely those who are predicted to perform the activity poorly. As Hugh LaFollette explains (1981), licensing therefore involves a standard of behavior together with a prediction about future performance. Since its purpose is to "decrease potential [future] harm," it must focus on whether someone *will* meet the required standard of performance, not simply whether they do so now (LaFollette 1981: 181; for disagreement, see Frisch 1981). The purpose of *parental* licensing is, therefore, to determine whether someone *will* treat their children well or, more weakly, *will not* mistreat them.

What is interesting about parental licensing, however—and what differentiates it from many other types of licensing—is that predictions about future competence are typically *not* based on assessments of present performance.[1] Instead, these predictions are based on two assessments: first, on whether, by possessing certain capabilities, such as emotional or financial capabilities, individuals are likely to exhibit competence in parenting at the desired level in the future; and second, on whether a given individual indeed possesses these capabilities. By contrast, with many other forms of licensing, applicants must actually perform the relevant activity at the desired level before they are granted a license. For example, one has to drive a car competently for an assessor before the state will issue one a driver's license, or one must have given competent patient care during a medical residency before being licensed to practice a particular form of medicine. The fact that parental licensing typically involves only an assessment of capabilities deemed to be relevant to the performance of the licensed activity (namely parenting) may not make this form of licensing unique compared to *all* other forms of licensing. All the same, this aspect is important and helps to explain some of our misgivings about certain schemes of parental licensing proposed by philosophers.

The *status quo* on parental licensing

As we have noted, many philosophers have ignored or downplayed the fact that parental licensing actually occurs. In many jurisdictions, some individuals—namely, adoptive and foster parents— must be licensed before they are legally allowed to parent a child. Although these people do not receive an actual *license* to parent, similar to a driver's license, what they undergo is still properly called parental licensing. They are prevented from becoming a parent unless they complete a home study, which itself involves criminal background checks together with assessments of one's financial situation, physical and mental health, place of residence (i.e., whether it is child friendly), and family history including relationships with one's parents and any current or previous spouse(s).[2] Additional requirements may include follow-up visits from social workers and, less commonly, attendance at government-mandated parenting classes.

To be sure, the state sometimes interferes with the ability of other parents to care for children, although not in a way that involves licensing. Rather, child welfare investigations occur when there are serious concerns that parents of any kind are abusing or neglecting their children. Here, the state intervenes to determine whether there *is* abuse or neglect, not whether there *will be* such harm.[3] It is, therefore, not licensing parents through these interventions. In general, non-adoptive and non-foster parents do not require a license to parent.

To be sure, the *status quo* on parental licensing is somewhat more complex than what we have just described. This is because not *all* adoptive parents have to fulfill licensing requirements such as a home study. Indeed, it is common for people who do "family-member" or "relative" adoptions, such as step-parent adoptions, not to be subject to such screening (McLeod and Botterell 2014: 154). The *status quo*, therefore, requires licensing mainly for *non-family member adoptions*. It also usually involves no licensing for people who become parents via assisted or unassisted reproduction, although in some cases of assisted reproduction, a subsequent adoption—one that may involve licensing—is required for the same-sex partner of a woman who gives birth to a child who is biologically related to her, but not her partner. Also, there are jurisdictions (e.g., the UK) where licensing must occur before certain forms of assisted reproduction can proceed, namely with contract pregnancies (i.e., surrogacy) and/or pregnancies conceived through the use of donor embryos.[4]

Although the *status quo* is descriptive of a certain social and institutional reality—some prospective parents are licensed, and others are not—it also has important normative implications. The reason is that this system privileges biological connections to the child who will be parented. If one is the biological parent of a child, or the spouse of someone who is the biological parent of a child (unless one is a same-sex spouse and lives in a jurisdiction where same-sex spouses do not count as family members for the purposes of adoption), then one will be spared the intrusion of a home study, the need to attend parenting classes, and so on. One will be able to become a parent without having to show that one is competent to do so.

Philosophical positions on licensing and discrimination

While most philosophers do not focus their discussion of parental licensing on the *status quo*, many acknowledge that some parents are already licensed and question whether this situation is morally consistent or fair. According to some, the absence of licensing for biological parents is problematic because it exposes large numbers of children to significant risks of serious harm (e.g., LaFollette 1980, 2010; Vopat 2007; Overall 2015). These philosophers believe that the *status quo* is insufficiently general, and that there should be greater licensing of parents than what presently occurs. Others are opposed to greater licensing, either because they think the *status quo* is justified, or because they question the appropriateness of licensing parents in the first place (Archard 1990, 2004; Engster 2010; De Wispelaere and Weinstock 2012). Still, others argue—without specifying whether there should be more or less licensing of parents—that we need a new *status quo*, since the current one is simply unjustified (McLeod and Botterell 2014; Botterell and McLeod 2015, 2016). This section summarizes these different positions and discusses whether, in defending them, philosophers deal appropriately with the problem of discrimination in parental licensing.

Arguments in favor *of greater licensing*

In his classic paper, "Licensing Parents," Hugh LaFollette (1980) argues that all parents should be licensed. His motivation is child-centric: licensing parents is required in order to prevent child abuse or neglect. Some philosophers have followed LaFollette in recommending universal parental licensing (though not always for child-centric reasons; see, for example, Taylor 2009).[5] By contrast, others have suggested that parental licensing should expand, yet only into the realm of assisted reproduction. Our discussion of arguments in favor of greater licensing than what now occurs with the *status quo* will center mainly on LaFollette's pioneering work, including his later paper, "Licensing Parents Revisited" (LaFollette 2010). Yet, along the way, we will also mention arguments made by other philosophers.

LaFollette (1980) makes the following case for universal parental licensing. We are justified in licensing individuals who engage in an activity A if (i) A can harm others, (ii) the "safe performance" of A requires a certain competence, and (iii) we have a "moderately reliable procedure" for determining the presence or absence of such competence in relation to A (LaFollette 1980: 183).[6] This argument applies to activities such as driving a car and engaging in many professions—for example, medicine, law, or being an airline pilot—that now require individuals to be licensed before pursuing the activity. But interestingly, according to LaFollette, the argument also applies to parents, because parenting meets conditions (i)–(iii).

To see why parenting satisfies the above criteria, consider the following. Parenting, when done badly, can cause serious physical and psychological harm to children (LaFollette 1980: 184–85; 2010: 331–32). What is more, to avoid such outcomes, parents need to have certain dispositions, a certain amount of knowledge (i.e., about children, and perhaps about themselves), and certain abilities (e.g., to feed, care for, and nurture children) (LaFollette 2010: 332–33). They need, in other words, to be competent at parenting. LaFollette believes that moderately reliable procedures exist to test for this competency (see Mangel 1988; for criticism see Sandmire and Wald 1990)—although he claims that if that is not the case, then we could "undoubtedly" develop such tests in the future (LaFollette 1980: 192). The benefits of parental licensing also outweigh its costs, according to LaFollette, particularly if it aims—as he thinks it should—at eliminating very bad parenting, rather than marginally bad or simply not very good parenting.

LaFollette's main argument in favor of parental licensing is, therefore, not concerned with the unfairness of licensing only some parents, although he does recognize that some, and only some, parents are now licensed. (He mentions only adoptive parents in this context.) Rather, his concern is with the interests of children. He explains in this context that adoptive parents are much less likely than biological parents to abuse or neglect their children, a fact that he and others attribute to the licensing of these parents (LaFollette 1981: 183; see also Vopat 2007). He also sets the standard of parental competency that he wants all parents to meet lower than the standard currently expected of adoptive (and foster) parents. In light of these points—along with the fact that "none of us would seriously entertain abandoning" adoption licensing—LaFollette concludes that we are "rationally compelled" to accept his proposal for greater parental licensing (LaFollette 1981: 183).

Still, LaFollette recognizes that many people will have serious objections to universal parental licensing. He considers a number of objections, including, among others, the claim that people "have a right to have children" (by which he means a right to have biological children), that the potential for the "unintentional misuse" or "intentional abuse" of tests of parental competency by administrators is too great, and that a universal licensing scheme would be too difficult to enforce. Concerning the right to have children, LaFollette states that it is not unconditional, but rather exists only insofar as "one is not going to abuse or neglect" one's children (LaFollette 1980: 188;

for a similar argument in support of a conditional right to parent, see Brighouse and Swift 2006). He also dismisses concerns about the misuse and abuse of competence tests by saying that "there is no reason to believe that the licensing of parents is more likely to be abused [or misused] than driver's license tests or other regulatory procedures" (LaFollette 1980: 192). (He is less dismissive about these concerns, however, in his 2010 paper.) Lastly, concerning enforceability, LaFollette insists that we could deal with "violators"—that is, people who have children without first obtaining a parental license—in a fair and reasonable way. For example, we "might not punish parents at all—we might just remove the children and put them up for adoption" (LaFollette 1980: 193).[7]

In a significant departure from his 1980 paper, LaFollette argues in his 2010 paper that we should not punish people at all for failing to obtain a parental license before having children, but rather should reward people for doing so, with tax breaks for example. He calls this scheme one of "limited licensing." Although limited licensing is not without its problems—LaFollette worries that it "favours the rich," who do not need tax breaks, and may hurt the poor, who, if they are unlicensed, will pay more money in taxes and have less money to care for their children relative to others—he again believes that the benefits outweigh the costs (LaFollette 2010: 339). Other philosophers would disagree, however, in particular Mark Vopat, who argues against a proposal that is very much like LaFollette's later one (namely, Westman's 1994 proposal). Such voluntary licensing would, according to Vopat, "result in discrimination against those of lower economic classes," and is objectionable for this reason (Vopat 2007: 82).

Like LaFollette, Vopat argues in favor of greater licensing than what exists with the status quo. He defends a form of universal licensing that he calls "minimal licensing," and that is designed specifically to minimize the ways in which parental licensing can be discriminatory (Vopat 2007: 83–86). He, more than most philosophers, is concerned with the problem of discrimination in parental licensing, although as we shall see, Vopat's licensing scheme does not reduce the discriminatory effects of parental licensing as much as we believe it could or should.

Yet another philosopher who has argued in favor of greater parental licensing is Christine Overall (2015). Unlike LaFollette and Vopat, however, Overall contends not that *all* parents should be subject to (or, in the case of the later LaFollette, rewarded for) licensing, but rather that a greater subset of parents than just adoptive and foster parents should be licensed. For her, this subset is composed of individuals who become parents via contract pregnancy. She believes that it is appropriate to require parental licensing whenever there is a transfer of responsibility for the care of a child from one person (or institution, if the child is a ward of the state) to another. In her view, such transfers are what justify parental licensing in the case of adoption and foster care, yet they occur as well in contract pregnancies: responsibility for the care of a child is transferred from the contract pregnant woman to the commissioning individual or couple. Thus, according to Overall, the reason for requiring licensing for adoptive and foster parents exists as well in the case of contract pregnancies and speaks in favor of licensing the individuals who commission these pregnancies.

To summarize this discussion, some philosophers have argued that current parental licensing should be expanded to include all parents or just some parents who engage in assisted reproduction. Also, the later LaFollette believes that any expansion of licensing should be voluntary, so that only parents who want to be rewarded (e.g., with tax breaks) will be licensed. Let us reflect on how well these philosophers handle the concern that parental licensing can be discriminatory, before moving on to describe the views of those who disagree with greater licensing. And let us start with discrimination against non-biological families. On the assumption that the *status quo* on parental licensing reinforces biologism, the philosophers who argue for greater licensing oppose this outcome to some extent, though not overtly. For example, both LaFollette and Vopat think that there are no reasons why biological parents should not be licensed, if adoptive or foster parents are licensed. Also, in arguing that current licensing should be expanded to include the intended parents in contract pregnancies, including parents who may be genetically related to the resulting child(ren), Overall rejects—again, not overtly, and also clearly not to the same degree as LaFollette and Vopat—the privileging of biological relations within the *status quo*.

Still, none of these philosophers completely rejects the *status quo* and the biologism that may underlie it. For notice that the views of the early LaFollette and of Vopat are consistent with there being more intrusive licensing for adoptive and foster parents than for biological parents. The early LaFollette argues for a scheme of licensing for biological parents that, by his own admission, would be less onerous than the sort of licensing that occurs in adoptions. Vopat's minimalist licensing scheme is similar in this regard. Whether adoptive (and foster) parents would be subject to the less rigorous licensing they propose for biological parents is left unclear in their papers, although given how valuable they believe the licensing of adoptive parents is in preventing child abuse and neglect, it is doubtful that they would want to change it.

Another issue has to do with whether the administrators of parental licensing schemes will rely, either explicitly or implicitly, on their own prejudices in deciding who gets a license. Recall that the early LaFollette responds to this problem by saying that "there is no reason to believe" that the "intentional abuse" or "unintentional misuse" of licensing would occur more frequently with parental licensing than with forms of licensing that we already accept (LaFollette 1980: 192). Yet we doubt that is actually true. Three considerations are relevant here. First, consider how *many* stereotypical images of minority groups target, directly or indirectly, their ability to be a good or decent parent (and how relatively few stereotypical images concern their ability to be a decent driver, for instance). Examples include images of Black women as matriarchs or welfare moms (Hill Collins 2000), of gay men as pedophiles, of indigenous people as lazy or violent, and of people with disabilities as helpless and vulnerable.[8]

Second, with parental licensing, there is arguably more opportunity for discriminatory biases to enter into assessments of people's competence. Recall that with such licensing, there is usually no test of present performance. Evaluators do not get to see whether the person can parent at the desired level, but rather have to make a judgment based on whether this person possesses capabilities that are thought to be relevant to good or decent parenting (see ch. 15). Discriminatory biases can enter in at various stages: deciding which capabilities are relevant to parenting, at what level the applicant needs to possess them, and whether the applicant does indeed possess them at this level.

The result is that discriminatory bias *is* more of a worry with parental licensing than it is with many other forms of licensing. Although the testing with other types of licenses can certainly be biased, we suspect that there is less chance of bias with them than with parental licensing. Consider as well that the effects of such bias—in particular, when licenses are denied to those who are discriminated against—can be much more damaging in the case of parental licensing, compared to other licensing. That is true based on the value of opportunity lost (parenting vs. driving, for example) and what the denial of the license expresses about the individual (that she would be a bad parent vs. a bad driver).

As this all-too-brief discussion reveals, the concern about discriminatory bias in parental licensing is somewhat complex, but should be central to debates about parental licensing. Yet most philosophers pay little attention to this issue. Vopat and Overall mention the problem, but do not go into depth about it.[9] Moreover, while Vopat is particularly concerned about discrimination in parental licensing, his minimalist scheme demands that licensed parents have a high school diploma (Vopat 2007: 84), a requirement that does not exist with licensing for adoption or foster care, and which arguably discriminates against people who have little formal education. To be fair, Vopat insists on this criterion only because, when conjoined with a mandatory high school parenting class, it would "allow us to assume a certain minimal level of parental knowledge" (Vopat 2007: 85). But if that is the justification for the requirement of a diploma, then why not simply require stand-alone parenting classes instead, as some governments do now for adoption and foster care?

Arguments against *greater licensing*

Unlike the philosophers we have just discussed, others oppose the imposition of greater licensing on parents, and object, in particular, to universal parental licensing (with most of their work targeting LaFollette's 1980 paper). Although these philosophers do not set out to defend the *status quo*, they are generally content with it—with the exception of Jurgen De Wispelaere and Daniel Weinstock (2012), who believe the *status quo* should be reevaluated from the ground up (more on their view below). Moreover, those who are satisfied with the *status quo* (i.e., on parental licensing) are not necessarily satisfied with the *status quo* on the extent to which the state monitors or supports parents. On the contrary, most of these philosophers contend that the state ought to invest more in parenting through greater monitoring of, or social assistance for, parents.

Among the reasons philosophers have given for objecting to LaFollette's (1980) proposal, and proposals like it, are that licensing will not effectively weed out people who would be very bad parents; that, overall, greater monitoring of parents by the state is a better solution to the problems of child abuse and neglect than licensing parents; and that the problems of enforcing licensing schemes are too great. Let us comment briefly on each of these objections.

First, some—such as Lawrence Frisch (1981) and David Archard (1990, 2004)—argue that it would be a mistake to license more parents because parental licensing would not, in fact, succeed in reducing child abuse and neglect. The reason is that it could not reliably predict which individuals will mistreat their children. For example, Frisch suspects that most child abuse and neglect occur in response to extraordinary social or economic stress, and that since licensing cannot duplicate these conditions and test how people react under them, it cannot prevent child abuse and neglect (Frisch 1981: 176). By contrast, Archard claims that child abuse is the result, in part, of individual psychopathology, but that research on child abuse has so far failed to "produce a clear and distinct psychological picture of the abusing parent" (Archard 2004: 188). Hence, we cannot predict with sufficient accuracy which people will abuse their children and should therefore be denied a parental license.

Second, various authors have suggested that, over time, licensed parents would have to be re-evaluated to ensure that they are still fit to care for their children. But if that is the case, then wouldn't it be simpler, as these philosophers ask, simply to monitor parents' treatment of their children in a more comprehensive way than we do now? Archard insists that such a solution would be less "cumbersome" than a system of repeat licensing (Archard 1990: 191). It also would not involve many of the difficulties of licensing, including the need to make predictions about people's future performance in parenting, predictions that would have to "cover all eventualities" (Archard 1990: 191).

Third, there is the question of whether parental licensing could be enforced in a fair or reasonable way. This problem—variously described in terms of the "viability" (Engster 2010) or "feasibility" (McLeod and Botterell 2014) of licensing—receives its best treatment from Daniel Engster (2010). Engster explains that it would be difficult to enforce parental licensing without causing women great hardship, and thus without furthering gender inequality. For example, women without a license to parent a child who experience an unplanned pregnancy would be forced to consider having an abortion or having a child with whom they were in a close physical relationship for nine months taken away from them (Engster 2010: 247–48). To be sure, they could try to hide their pregnancy, which would involve foregoing assistance from health care professionals during pregnancy and birth; but, of course, this option would pose serious risks to their health and the health of their child (Engster 2010: 247–48). Men, on the other hand, would not generally face choices as distressing as these as a result of parental licensing. Even after the birth of their child, their situation would not be the same as that of women who give birth. For instance, given the unequal economic status between women and men, the choice between staying with a partner who is denied a parental license and keeping one's child would not be as difficult, on average, for heterosexual men compared to heterosexual women (Engster 2010: 248). For Engster (2010), the disproportionate burden that widespread parental licensing would have on women is too great.

These objections to a system of universal parental licensing are certainly compelling. Yet, notice that the first two apply equally well to our current system of parental licensing. If we have no good way of predicting who will abuse or neglect children, then we should not be licensing *any* parents, assuming that our purpose in doing so is to ensure that people will not mistreat their children. Moreover, if we could achieve this aim through the greater monitoring of parents rather than the licensing of them, then there is a strong case to be made for doing that instead. Philosophers who have expressed these concerns about universal parental licensing generally fail to extend them to the licensing of adoptive and foster parents. For example, Frisch does not even mention this form of licensing, while Archard tries to justify it by pointing to the fact that "natural parents," as he calls them, have a claim to "rear their own children" that *seems*, he says, to be stronger (he does not *argue* that it is stronger) than any claim an adoptive parent has to raise a child (Archard 2004: 189).[10]

Archard also says that

> if adoptive or foster parents are assessed it is not simply or solely to gauge whether they are fit parents as such. It is to evaluate whether or not they are well suited and situated to cope with children who, because they are being adopted or fostered, may present particular and possibly serious difficulties—those, for instance, arising from the fact that they have been rejected or abused by their natural parents. Adopted and fostered children differ from others in that they may be much harder to rear.
>
> *(Archard 2004: 191)*

Before evaluating this argument, we want to be clear that insofar as Archard is suggesting that *all* adopted or foster children are "rejected or abused by their natural parents," then he is mistaken (since, of course, some of these children are relinquished by their parents in a morally responsible way, while others are not rejected at all, but find themselves without parents due to an unexpected death). He is correct, however, that these children can present some difficulties, at least early on in their placement.[11] Still, the statement we have reproduced above is question-begging. For Archard assumes without argument that we can devise a test to determine whether someone may be a fit parent for children who "may present particular or possibly serious difficulties," even as he denies that we can devise a test to determine whether an individual is a fit parent "as such." He insists that there must be evidence of our ability to predict who will be a minimally decent parent before we can license so-called "natural parents," but seems not to apply the same standard to the licensing of adoptive or foster parents.

Moving on, there are philosophers who object to greater licensing but make no attempts to defend the *status quo,* namely Jurgen De Wispelaere and Daniel Weinstock (2012). Like others, they target (the early) LaFollette and object to licensing schemes like his for two reasons. First, such schemes will inevitably and systematically generate false positives, meaning that they will overestimate the number of individuals who ought not to be granted a right to parent (De Wispelaere and Weinstock 2012: 200–1). Second, authors such as LaFollette radically underestimate the costs to people who are denied licenses, costs that De Wispelaere and Weinstock explain largely in terms of a right to parent. Following Harry Brighouse and Adam Swift (2006), they contend that people have a right to parent that is grounded in an interest in experiencing the special sort of intimacy that is characteristic of parent–child relationships. This intimacy makes parenting a unique good—that is, non-substitutable. As De Wispelaere and Weinstock write, "[t]he next best thing to raising a child might be taking care of a cat, but surely no one would insist that cats, lovely companions though they are, are in any way reasonable substitutes for children" (De Wispelaere and Weinstock 2012: 199). In De Wispelaere and Weinstock's view, given that there is no plausible proxy for the parent–child relationship and people generally have a strong interest in being a parent, denying someone the opportunity to do so on the basis of a licensing scheme that over-generates false positives is seriously problematic. Notice in their work on parental licensing a shift away from arguments that are purely child-centric towards arguments that are parent-centric.

Notice too that De Wispelaere and Weinstock would reject Archard's claim that "natural parents" have more of a claim to parent their "own" children than adoptive parents do to parent any child. This is because, in their view, the fundamental interest in parenting a child is as much an interest of prospective adoptive parents as it is of biological parents. Since the goods of parenting (as described in Brighouse and Swift) do not depend on the existence of a biological connection to a child, De Wispelaere and Weinstock conclude at the end of their paper that we should reevaluate licensing for adoption and foster care as well, rather than simply reject licensing for biological parents.

Arguments for a new status quo

Finally, some philosophers have argued that the *status quo* is morally unjustified without making any claims about what system of parental licensing, if any, ought to replace it. This has been our approach in the series of papers we have published together about parental licensing (McLeod and Botterell 2014; Botterell and McLeod 2015, 2016). We have considered the best arguments we could think of in support of the *status quo* and argued that none of them is any good. For example, like Overall, we contend that if the justification for licensing adoptive parents is that with adoptions there is a transfer of responsibility, then that justification applies equally well to some forms of assisted reproduction. On the other hand, if the justification for the *status quo* is that universal parental licensing is not feasible since many pregnancies are unplanned, then we need only point to the fact that there are no unplanned pregnancies among individuals who seek to form families via assisted reproduction. Perhaps the most interesting argument in support of the *status quo*, however, is the following: that what exempts biological parents from parental licensing is that such individuals exercise a right to reproduce when they have children, which is not something that adoptive parents do. We have criticized this argument (Botterell and McLeod 2015) on two general grounds: first, that it is doubtful that there is a right to reproduce; and second, that to the extent that such a right exists, it is most plausibly understood as a right to parent, a right that adoptive parents have to the same degree as biological parents. In short, there is no morally salient difference, in our view, between parents who are currently licensed and those who are not that could morally justify the *status quo* on parental licensing.

In terms of what we think should replace the *status quo*, we lean towards greater frequency of licensing, although we do not support universal licensing for reasons having to do with the feasibility of licensing people who become parents through unassisted reproduction. Instead, we are inclined to endorse some licensing in the case of fostering and adoption (including family-member adoption), as well as in assisted reproduction, especially when it is government-funded (see ch. 19).[12]

At the same time, we think greater attention needs to be paid to the effects of discrimination in the operation of parental licensing systems. In an effort to correct for this problem, we would recommend licensing that is minimal and employs objective measures, such as criminal background checks. We would also require extensive education of adoption practitioners and social workers about the role that implicit biases can play in assessments of people's capacity to be a good or decent parent.[13] It is clear that discrimination exists in the current licensing of adoptive and foster parents: single people, LGBTQ people, and people with disabilities—to cite a few examples—can have a much harder time becoming licensed due to stereotypes about their ability to parent. Philosophers who argue in favor of parental licensing need to take this reality seriously, as we would aim to do in devising our own scheme of parental licensing.

Conclusion

We have framed our discussion of parental licensing using the backdrop of the *status quo*, rather than by asking the familiar question of whether there should be parental licensing at all. This choice was deliberate, and was motivated by two things. First, we wanted to emphasize that parental licensing *exists*; any discussion of parental licensing must acknowledge this fact and say something about whether, and if so how, the *status quo* can be justified. Second, and more importantly, we wanted to show, by situating philosophical arguments about parental licensing in relation to the *status quo*, that most of them reinforce biologism. They promote, in other words, a form of discrimination that targets adoptive and foster families, or more generally, non-biological families. We have also exposed in some of these arguments a lack of attention to other ways in which parental licensing can be discriminatory. These are flaws that seriously undermine the cogency of these arguments, in our view. That said, we acknowledge how difficult it is to devise a scheme of parental licensing that does not simply (and unnecessarily) reinforce inequalities in society. This task is challenging to be sure; nonetheless, it must be met before any form of parental licensing will be fully justified.[14]

Notes

1 LaFollette makes a similar point (1981: 182), explaining that the "grounds for the prediction" with parental licensing differ from other forms of licensing, such as the licensing of drivers.
2 See McLeod and Botterell (2014) and Vopat (2007) for descriptions of what home studies are like, specifically in Canada.
3 Such investigations are *reactive* when it comes to child abuse and neglect (or heightened concern about it), while parental licensing is *proactive* (Vopat 2007: 73). Moreover, they may result not in the removal of the children from the parents' care, but rather in supervision of the family by social workers.
4 In the UK, licensing is required for the intended parents of children created through contract pregnancy *and* embryo donation (see http://www.hfea.gov.uk/1424.html#5).
5 Taylor (2009) favors universal licensing as a means of restricting parenthood to people who can parent without public support.
6 In "Licensing Parents Revisited," LaFollette adds the criterion that the benefits of licensing should outweigh its costs (LaFollette 2010: 328, 336). This point significantly amends his 1980 position and raises the question of which "costs" should be considered in this balancing act. For discussion, see De Wispelaere and Weinstock (2012).
7 As if there was no punishment in that!
8 To be clear, in our view, these stereotypes are as likely to corrupt current licensing schemes as they are to corrupt the schemes that LaFollette proposes. We are concerned here simply with how well LaFollette deals with concerns about discrimination with any sort of parental licensing.
9 Although to her credit, Overall recognizes that such concerns are significant and that "to explore them thoroughly would require another paper" (Overall 2015: 360).

10 Engster mentions licensing for adoption (but not foster care) and tries to justify it, in part, by citing Archard's statement below, though mainly by pointing to the "greater viability" of such licensing compared to licensing for biological reproduction. For criticism, see McLeod and Botterell (2014). We argue that licensing in the context of *assisted* reproduction is no less viable than it is in the context of adoption.
11 For discussion, see Blake, Richards, and Golombok (2014: 75–76).
12 Our thinking here is this: if the state is using taxpayer dollars or other means (such as tax credits) to defray the costs of assisted reproduction, then the state should make very sure that the individuals it is giving those financial benefits to are capable of being good parents to the children they—and the state—are helping to create. The best way to do this is through parental licensing.
13 On implicit biases and how to take responsibility for them, see, for example, Kelly and Roedder (2008) and Holroyd (2012).
14 Thanks to Veromi Arsiradam for her masterful research assistance.

References

Archard, D. 1990. "Child Abuse: Parental Rights and the Interests of the Child," *Journal of Applied Philosophy* 7(2): 183–194.
Archard, D. 2004. *Children: Rights and Childhood*, 2nd edn. New York, NY: Routledge.
Baylis, F., and McLeod, C. (eds.) 2014. *Family-Making: Contemporary Ethical Challenges*. Oxford: Oxford University Press.
Blake, L., Richards, M., and Golombok, S. 2014. "The Families of Assisted Reproduction and Adoption," in F. Baylis and C. McLeod (eds.), *Family-Making: Contemporary Ethical Challenges*. Oxford: Oxford University Press, pp. 64–85.
Botterell, A., and McLeod, C. 2015. "Can a Right to Reproduce Justify the Status Quo on Parental Licensing?," in R. Vernon, S. Hannan, and S. Brennan (eds.), *Permissible Progeny*. New York, NY: Oxford University Press, pp. 184–207.
Botterell, A., and McLeod, C. 2016. "Licensing Parents in International Contract Pregnancies," *Journal of Applied Philosophy* 33(2): 178–196.
Brighouse, H., and Swift, A. 2006. "Parents' Rights and the Value of the Family," *Ethics* 117: 80–108.
De Wispelaere, J., and Weinstock, D. 2012. "Licensing Parents to Protect our Children?," *Ethics and Social Welfare* 6(2): 195–205.
Engster, D. 2010. "The Place of Parenting within a Liberal Theory of Justice: The Private Parenting Model, Parental Licenses, or Public Parenting Support?," *Social Theory and Practice* 36(2): 233–262.
Frisch, L. 1981. "On Licentious Licensing: A Reply to Hugh LaFollette," *Philosophy and Public Affairs* 11(2): 173–180.
Haslanger, S. 2009. "Family, Ancestry, and Self: What Is the Moral Significance of Biological Ties?," *Adoption and Culture* 2(1): 91–122.
Hill Collins, P. 2000. "Mammies, Matriarchs, and Other Controlling Images," in P. Hill Collins, *Black Feminist Thought: Knowledge, Consciousness, and the Politics of Empowerment*. New York, NY: Routledge, pp. 69–96.
Holroyd, J. 2012. "Responsibility for Implicit Bias," *Journal of Social Philosophy* 43(3): 274–306.
Kelly, D., and Roedder, E. 2008. "Racial Cognition and the Ethics of Implicit Bias," *Philosophy Compass* 3(3): 522–540.
LaFollette, H. 1980. "Licensing Parents," *Philosophy and Public Affairs* 9(2): 182–197.
LaFollette, H. 1981. "A Reply to Frisch," *Philosophy and Public Affairs* 11(2): 181–183.
LaFollette, H. 2010. "Licensing Parents Revisited," *Journal of Applied Philosophy* 27(4): 327–343.
Mangel, C. P. 1988. "Licensing Parents: How Feasible?," *Family Law Quarterly* 22(1): 17–39.
McLeod, C., and Botterell, A. 2014. "'Not for the Faint of Heart': Assessing the Status Quo on Adoption and Parental Licensing," in F. Baylis and C. McLeod (eds.), *Family-Making: Contemporary Ethical Challenges*. Oxford: Oxford University Press, pp. 151–167.
Overall, C. 2015. "Reproductive 'Surrogacy' and Parental Licensing," *Bioethics* 29(5): 353–361.
Sandmire, M. J., and Wald, M. S. 1990. "Licensing Parents—A Response to Claudia Mangel's Proposal," *Family Law Quarterly* 24(1): 53–76.
Taylor, R. S. 2009. "Children as Prospects and Persons: A Liberal Antinomy," *Social Theory and Practice* 35(4): 555–576.
Vopat, M. 2007. "Parent Licensing and Child Protection," in S. Brennan and R. Noggle (eds.), *Taking Responsibility for Children*. Waterloo, ON: Laurier University Press, pp. 73–96.
Westman, J. C. 1994. *Licensing Parents: Can We Prevent Child Abuse and Neglect?* Cambridge, MA: Perseus Publishing.

19
ETHICAL CHALLENGES FOR ADOPTION REGIMES

Jurgen De Wispelaere and Daniel Weinstock

Introduction

As the philosophy of children and parenting has come into its own in recent years, philosophers are also starting to get interested in the ethical issues surrounding adoption – both in its own right, and in relation to natural or assisted procreation.[1] Much of the current philosophical debate concerns the ethics of adoption as it pertains to the level of personal choice, such as prospective parents deciding to adopt instead of procreate. Very little philosophical analysis is devoted to evaluating the background policies informing people's choices to adopt rather than procreate, and many related ethical issues. The purpose of this chapter is to remedy this lack of ethical analysis of *adoption regimes* – understood as the different ways in which the state simultaneously regulates the demand and supply side of the adoption process, and its normative justification for doing so.

The next two sections briefly characterise the key ethical features of adoption and discuss the "claim from adoption", which holds that we ought to prioritise adoption over procreation. In the remainder of the chapter we then examine whether the claim from adoption requires that we amend the *status quo* which insists upon strict screening and monitoring of prospective adopting parents. While we find that legitimate expectations go some way towards justifying the differential treatment of procreative and adoptive parents, we suggest the current adoptions regulations aimed at protecting children from neglect or abuse nevertheless may cause harm to some children who fail to find an adoptive family.

Adoption – a concise characterisation

Adoption is the legal process through which the state establishes a parental relationship, with all its attendant rights and duties, between a child and a (set of) parent(s) where there exists no previous procreative relationship. Historically and across cultures, the meaning of adoption, attitudes towards adoption and the adoption process itself has been subject to considerable variation (United Nations 2009; Conn 2013). This variation carries over into the philosophical and ethical questions that surround the adoption process and into the different *adoption regimes* instituted around the world.

Two central features of adoption set it apart from the two alternative modes of establishing parental relations, natural and assisted procreation. Where natural and assisted reproduction involve the creation of a new person, adoption concerns the current and future well-being of an already existing child. This distinctive feature of adoption is widely accepted, but its ethical implications remain a matter of considerable dispute (e.g., Petersen 2002). In addition, adoption necessarily involves the authoritative power of the state to establish a legal parental relation between prospective adoptee and adopter (Woodhouse 2005). In the cases of natural and assisted reproduction, the state also codifies the legal relation between parent and child, but the level of state involvement in the adoption process takes matters to an altogether different level. Compared to natural and assisted reproduction, the state not only affects a broader range of "stakeholders" in the adoption process, but it also takes on a more involved role in determining which child ends up being parented by which (set of) parent(s). This feature is specific to adoption, with neither natural nor assisted reproduction facing questions about matching specific children to a suitable parental unit.[2]

It is, at present, very difficult in most jurisdictions to adopt a child in cases where one is not already connected to the potential adoptee by ties of blood or marriage. Putting aside the financial burden that the process customarily involves, governments and adoption agencies typically impose strenuous requirements on prospective adoptive parents (McLeod and Botterell 2014). To meet these requirements, such prospective parents must not only fit a set of descriptive parameters – candidates are often excluded from the outset on the basis of "demographic" characteristics such as age or income status – but also have to demonstrate competence and good intention through various tests, interviews and home visits. The process of determining potential adopters' suitability can be very demanding and intrusive, with adoption agencies delving in considerable detail into deeply private matters such as the prospective adopter's past experience with parenting or being parented, the nature of her relationship with past and current partners, and even her sexuality (McLeod and Botterell 2014).

This demanding process of becoming a parent through adoption contrasts markedly with alternative routes to parenting through either natural or assisted procreation (De Wispelaere and Weinstock 2015). Most obviously, it is comparatively very easy for people to become parents through sexual reproduction. The ability to bear children is widely considered a sufficient condition, both factually and morally, for becoming a parent. In fact, the "biological bias" surrounding parenting is so manifest, that little thought is given to the idea that the act of reproduction (giving birth) can be separated – philosophically as well as practically – from the act of parenting (raising a child). Perhaps more surprisingly, even where parents require assistance through assisted reproductive technologies (ART) – medically, emotionally and, in many cases, financially a very demanding process – there is little or no consideration of the potential parent's parenting competence or intention. Instead, assessment of suitability for the procedure typically takes the form of strict medical criteria (Widdows and MacCallum 2002). Current practice views parenthood grounded in natural and assisted procreation as roughly similar, while the "socially assisted" basis of parenthood is taken to be an entirely different matter.

Given the importance of the state and its authority in the adoption process, it is surprising that much of the ethical debate on adoption ignores the policy level and instead focuses on discussing the rights of prospective adoptees and the corresponding duties of prospective parents as a matter of personal choice. The basis upon which the state claims justified interference in the adoption process, including the unequal treatment of adoptive parents and children compared to those engaged in natural or assisted procreation, remains largely unchallenged. This discrepancy is surprising because it would appear the state has legitimate grounds for taking an interest in the adoption process. For instance, economic research suggests that adoption represents a significant cost-saving compared to long-term fostering or institutional care (Hansen 2008). More broadly, we might think that the state's interest in the production of well-functioning future citizens justifies some form of regulation of the family-making process writ large, and this includes adoption (Reed 2012). In this chapter, we want to rebalance the debate by ascertaining whether different adoption regimes, and the extent to which they treat adoption different from procreation, can be affirmed philosophically.

The claim from adoption

A sizeable part of the recent philosophical literature aims to advance the *claim from adoption*, which in one variant reads as follows: "resources used to create and care for new children in developed countries ought instead to be devoted to the adoption and care of existing, and often destitute, children" (Petersen 2002: 353–54). Narrowly conceived, the claim from adoption only applies to those prospective parents with sub-par infertility considering ART to produce a biological child, while a wide (and philosophically more interesting) version applies to every prospective parent interested in procreating a child.[3]

The literature offers both positive and negative justifications for the claim from adoption. Negative justifications include the anti-natalist view that procreating is not permitted when bringing a child into the world constitutes harming that child. Most prominently, David Benatar (2006) argues that the pain associated with existence always outweighs the absence of pleasure of non-existence, and that procreation should, therefore, be resisted. A different negative justification for the claim from adoption holds that procreation implies additional strain on scarce environmental resources, whereas adoption appears neutral in this regard (Young 2001). In both cases, the negative justification focuses on the bad of procreation and the capacity of adoption to offer a solution when pitching anti-natalism against the strong desire of many people to become parents. However, upon reflection, the negative justification for the claim from adoption appears too weak, especially when broadened beyond those who are reliant on ART to procreate (Rivera-López 2006). On the one hand, the numbers don't quite add up: robust anti-natalists such as Benatar would rapidly run out of prospective adoptees to satisfy the very widespread desire to be or become a parent – there are simply not enough prospective adoptees to satisfy the demand. On the other hand, the environmental argument also runs into trouble in trying to accommodate the fact that relocating a prospective adoptee from a low-income country to a high-income country would entail precisely the sort of additional pressure on our scarce environmental resources the argument sets out to avoid.

The claim from adoption may be better served by an argument that emphasises the positive ethical value of prioritising adoption over procreation. Recent advocates have started to explore the analogy between adoption and standard rescue cases (Friedrich 2013; Rulli 2014a, 2016). In a nutshell, prospective adoptees have a strong interest in growing up in a stable family as opposed to a care institution or a series of foster families.[4] It is commonly accepted (although certainly not true in all cases) that stable family units are comparatively better suited at providing children with physical security and well-being, emotional care and love, and the sort of long-term commitment to the child's developmental and well-being needs that comes with being its parent. Cue the prospective parent who is able to provide the child with a stable home and parental environment.

Tina Rulli (2014a) and Daniel Friedrich (2013) are adamant that adoption allows for the rescuing of "children in waiting" at minimal cost to the adopting parent(s), commonly taken as a critical condition in rescue cases. Adoption is often misunderstood by those unfamiliar with the process and many of the negative views associated with adoptive parental relationships – e.g., that adoptive children are less emotionally attached and more difficult to parent – are not borne out by the evidence (e.g., Fisher 2003). Leaving aside personal and financial costs associated with the adoption procedure, there is no reason to think adoption will not result in a stable and satisfying parental relationship or a well-adjusted child, provided adequate preparation and post-adoption support is in place (Wind, Brooks and Barth 2008; Younes and Klein 2014).[5] Conversely, adoptive parents' commitment to their children is found to be equal *or even higher* to that of procreative parents (Hamilton, Cheng, and Powell 2007). Parenting itself is costly in terms of time, effort and money spent on raising a child, but by-and-large those costs are similar for adoptive and biological parents – and, importantly, so too are the benefits and value of parenthood.[6] Children currently awaiting adoption while residing in a care institution or a foster home are in need of rescue, and prospective parents are well-placed to engage in the rescue effort by prioritising adoption over procreation.

Those advocating the positive justification go so far as to couch the claim from adoption as a *duty to adopt* (Friedrich 2013; Rulli 2014a, 2014b). This move has been resisted on general philosophical grounds: we may want to accept that the decision to adopt instead of procreate is particularly praiseworthy (and its opposite blameworthy), while nevertheless resisting the idea that it could constitute a moral duty (Rieder 2014). More commonly, many object to a duty to adopt on the grounds that parents should be at liberty to engage in the biological procreation of a child of their own, should they prefer to do so. The difficulty is deciding what sort of moral weight to give the widespread desire for a biological child in light of its impact on prospective adoptees.[7] On one end of the spectrum, reproductive autonomy insists that procreative – and indeed adoptive – decisions are primarily the purview of the prospective parents (for a critical discussion, see Conly 2005). On the other end, we find the view that few (if any) of the reasons typically put forward to justify one's preference for a biological child are valid: upon reflection, most beliefs about adoption turn out to be inaccurate, incomplete, irrelevant or simply insufficiently weighty to do the justificatory work (Friedrich 2013; Rulli 2014a). In between these two positions we find some prospective parents trying (and often failing) to separate out good and bad reasons for favouring procreation over adoption. However, in practice, most parents travel the procreative route without having deeply considered the adoption alternative; despite the intimate nature of parenthood, as social creatures we are prone to respond to social conventions rooted in "biologism" (Bartholet 1995) or "bio-normativity" (Haslanger 2009).

The precise implications of a widespread norm in favour of procreation for a duty to adopt remain unclear. So are its implications for adoption *policy*. Those advocating a duty remain entirely focused on the level of personal reasons and decisions without enquiring how state regulation of the adoption process might affect those reasons and decisions. Yet, a renewed focus on policy rather than personal choice is warranted, because both domains raise different sets of ethical concerns. Whereas the ethics of a personal choice to adopt rather than procreate is made against a backdrop of policy realities, the ethics of adoption *policy* is precisely about whether we ought to change those realities. For instance, the availability of adoptable children – a key parameter in the claim from adoption – is a fixture for the personal decision of prospective parents, but a variable in the policy domain where government rules and regulations determine which or how many children enter the adoption process. Or consider the role of ART for deciding whether to adopt. Parents unable to procreate naturally are given a choice whether to adopt or procreate (or remain childless) in cases where ART is both available and accessible (i.e., subsidised), but it is the government that decides how easy it is to access artificial reproduction, thus indirectly affecting the balance of reasons for many prospective parents (De Wispelaere and Weinstock 2014). Moving the debate around adoption to the policy process implies finding answers to ethical questions about ends as well as means, responding to concerns about how to balance the interests of the many stakeholders involved in the policy process, as well as the appropriateness of state intervention in the private, even intimate, domain of parenthood.

Adoption regimes: regulating the adoption triad

In the case of adoption, state interference affects each of the "stakeholders" in the so-called "adoption triad": birth parents, adopted children and adopting parents (Fisher 2003). In the first place, the state regulates how and when birth parents are allowed or forced to relinquish their parental rights, which is one factor affecting the supply of children in need of a family.[8] In some cases, the state may allow for birth parents to retain contact with the adopted child through so-called open adoptions, which some argue offers important benefits for the adopted child (e.g., Velleman 2005).

The state also determines which children are deemed adoptable, as not all children in need of a family are made available for adoption. The downward trend in international adoptions that led global numbers from 2004 onwards to decline to pre-1998 numbers was largely driven by policy decisions by sender countries (Bartholet 2010). A 2009 UNICEF report estimates 145 million children worldwide have lost one or both parents (Carlson 2011), while the same year recorded merely 30,000 international adoptions (Selman 2012). Paradoxically, the decline in international adoptions means older children, those with a long history of institutionalisation and children with special needs – until recently deemed "less eligible" for adoption – are suddenly facing improved chances at finding a family.[9] The policy decisions taken by adoption regimes have a major impact on the *supply* of children available for adoption, but they have an equally critical influence on the *demand* for adoption.

One key parameter affecting the demand for adoption is the ease by which those who cannot avail themselves of natural procreation have access to ART (De Wispelaere and Weinstock 2014). Sociological research shows parents are willing to incur many personal and financial costs to procreate with the assistance of new reproductive technologies before turning to adoption, if at all (Fisher 2003; Jennings et al. 2014). But equally important is the extent to which prospective parents are supported or hindered in their attempts to adopt. The difficult, frustrating, costly and ultimately uncertain path towards adoption is well documented (McLeod and Botterell 2014), and much of this is due to the state either directly making the adoption process more difficult or refusing support that could make it easier. Chief among the hurdles imposed by the state is the intrusive screening process that prospective parents need to submit to before granted permission to adopt, as well as extensive monitoring post-adoption.

The rationale for the extensive screening of adoptive parents is exemplified in a classic argument in favour of parental licensing put forward by Hugh LaFollette (1980, 2010). Famously, LaFollette argued that there is an inconsistency in the fact that whereas we impose licensing requirements on people before we allow them to drive an automobile or to practice certain professions, we make no such requirement of parents, despite the fact that the risks involved in bad parenting are just as great as are those involved in bad driving or bad lawyering. At first glance, a parental licensing scheme would seem to be a relatively straightforward instrument to prevent harm to children while allowing parents who pass the screening to get on with the business of rearing their children – perhaps even without any intrusive monitoring by the state.

The licensing argument has generated numerous objections (e.g., Archard 1990; Engster 2010; De Wispelaere and Weinstock 2012; Botterell and McLeod 2015) and is discussed elsewhere in this volume in more detail (ch. 18). One particular worry we want to briefly address is that screening and monitoring parents would involve a state overtaxing its epistemic capacity. When the state decides to regulate the parenting of children – whether *ex ante* through screening for aptitude, or *ex post* through monitoring conduct – it must judge an activity that exemplifies complexity: the sheer multiplicity of factors that interact in complex ways to bring about a nurturing and stimulating parenting environment rapidly exceeds the state's capacity to comprehensively and indiscriminately evaluate parental performance. To return to LaFollette's example, parenting is a far more complex activity than are automobile driving or lawyering, and so the formulation of criteria of good parenting would be an accordingly complex task, one that surely defies the epistemic carrying capacity of even the most well-intentioned state officials. The risk is that they would fall back on their own culturally indexed views about what good parenting involves.

These risks can only be avoided if licensing and monitoring requirements are construed in a *minimalist* fashion. By minimalist, we mean they should focus on selecting against catastrophic parenting rather than selecting for excellent parents (Shields 2016; see also ch. 15). When the right to parent is denied on the basis of a concern with the avoidance of catastrophe, rather than on the basis of a standard of "excellent" or even of "good" parenting, then the imposition of risks to the good of prospective parents is more readily justified. Relatedly, it is easier for the state to define *operational* minimalist criteria of harm and neglect, and to apply them without overtaxing its epistemic capacity, than it is to define and apply more ambitious criteria. Minimalist requirements to do with the avoidance of catastrophic parenting thus does not involve the kind of overtaxing of the state's epistemic competence in the way that more ambitious requirements do.

Minimalism is the guiding principle of how the state interacts with procreative parents: states do monitor parents in various non-intrusive ways, but they only take the extreme step of removing children from the care of their parents in cases in which children are subjected to catastrophic harm within the family (for an endorsement of this approach, see Archard 1990; see also ch. 32). But the state takes a contrasting position when it regulates adoptive parents: the default position here is that prospective adoptive parents face extensive screening and monitoring in order to ensure the best interest of the child is safeguarded at all times. One implication of the denial of minimalism in the case of adoption is that it necessarily results in less children being adopted, which in turn seems to go against the claim from adoption outlined before.

Legitimate expectations in adoptive and procreative parenthood

The minimalist account sketched in the previous section implies there are limits to the extent of state intervention into the procreative decisions parents make, notably in terms of screening for how suitable parents are to raise their biological child. The claim from adoption suggests the state should favour adoption over procreation, but when it comes to adoption we find precisely that the state adopts a position of insisting on stringent screening and monitoring requirements for prospective adoptive parents. This poses both a puzzle in terms of squaring current practice with the claim from adoption and a serious concern about the *prima facie* unfairness of treating adoption and procreation differently.

We want to argue that the mere fact that different sets of criteria apply to biological and adoptive parents does not in and of itself signal injustice. In other words, while natural and adoptive parents are indeed treated unequally in a relevant sense – one faces strict licensing requirements, the other does not – this does not *necessarily* amount to injustice. The basis for justified differential treatment of natural and adoptive parents lies in the fact that there is a morally relevant difference between the types of criteria that need to be invoked in order to remove a child from the custody of the people who have brought it into the world, and the criteria that justify delivering a child to prospective parents where no prior "biological" (genetic or gestational) relation exist between the parents and child.[10]

We do not want to argue that there is any kind of a natural right for people to parent the children that exist because of their procreative activity (for discussion, see Archard 1994; Conly

2005). The range of familial and parenting arrangements that have existed through history and across cultures, both in reality and in the imaginings of writers and philosophers, suggest that the kinds of arrangements that have become dominant in a culture such as ours – to the point where many of us may come to think of them as "natural" – are, in fact, social decisions. Parenting and family life as we practice them in our culture are *institutions* that confer rights and obligations upon certain persons rather than others, on the basis of calculations of overall balance of costs and benefits, rather than on the basis of pre-existing natural rights. On this institutional view, no one has a right to parenting and family life being organised in one way rather than another.

But familial institutional schemes do create rights, obligations and patterns of *legitimate expectations* on the basis of which people can make claims to having been treated unfairly. Legitimate expectations have the following intriguing feature:

> they are not baseless but instead *justifiable*, meaning that the agent has epistemic justification or warrant for expecting, […] that some other agent, such as a governmental administrative agent or agency, will and should do or not do something in the future.
> (Brown 2017: 436)

The literature discerns a number of accounts of what makes an expectation legitimate in the relevant, epistemic sense: expectations can have a firm basis in existing law or legal entitlements, a grounding in substantive or procedural justice, or rooted in the authority of governing agents. Alexander Brown (2017) proposes a novel account whereby the legitimacy of expectations depends on governmental agents bringing about certain beliefs while being placed in a position of competence and discretion for making decisions in a field to which those beliefs pertain. In short, when a government agency has the discretion to produce certain expectations in individuals – for instance, by promulgating a rule about who can and cannot adopt under what conditions – those individuals are subsequently entitled to treat these expectations as legitimate. This holds even where the agent was not fully authorised in doing so, or even where the expectation does not fully accord with substantial justice. Brown's account is an epistemic account in that it tells us under what conditions a person is warranted in believing a certain expectation is legitimate.

Brown's account of legitimate expectations seems readily applicable to the cases of procreation and adoption. When an institutional scheme supports the default that children will be parented by the people that have "naturally" conceived them, individuals who bring children into the world have a legitimate expectation to parent their biological children unless they explicitly act in a way that disqualifies them as parents. Why? Both the general assumption that parents are allowed to parent the biological children they brought into the world, and the stipulation that this right is forfeited in cases of abject neglect or abuse, are considered legitimate expectations by virtue of it being actively promulgated by government agents across several legal and policy domains – primarily family law, but also medical law and health policy, education policy, and so on. On this view, parents engaged in procreation are fully warranted to expect to rear the child they brought into the world; the expectation to raise one's biological child is legitimate in the required epistemic sense. The expectation is only defeasible when the prospective parent fails to meet the most basic requirements of parenting, which is an integral part of the legitimate expectation.

But no such legitimate expectation exists in the case of prospective adoptive parents. The difficulty is as follows: in the case of the adoption process there exist no children of whom we can truly say that the defeasible expectation is that they will be raised by *this* set of adopting parents rather than by other parents or by state institutions. Whereas, in the case of procreation there is a genetic or gestational tie between a specific child and specific (set of) parent(s), such a tie is absent in the case of adoption. It is true that at some point in the adoption process such a tie may materialise, notably when a prospective adopter has been "allocated" a prospective adoptee, at which point the relevant agency has effectively created a legitimate expectation that, all things going well, they are soon to become a family. But, until that point, no legitimate expectation exists. And even when the legitimate expectation has been created, specific obligations to accept continued monitoring (especially in the early phases of the adoption) or to avail oneself of support instruments may be part-and-parcel of the arrangement if fully explicated by the relevant agent. Interestingly, our legitimate expectations view is supported by the practice of allowing intra-family adoptions – adoptions by blood relatives of step-parents in cases of second families – to take place without the restrictive conditions placed on stranger adoptions. Unlike in the general adoption case, intra-family adoption entails a legitimate expectation that the child should be raised in *this* specific family.

The role of legitimate expectations explains why the state may be justified in treating prospective parents differently depending on whether they take the procreative or adoption route. In the case of biological parents, a normative presumption exists such that it would be inappropriate only to license parents who would be the "very best" parents imaginable for this particular child or to take away a child in the absence of clear neglect or abuse on the grounds that a better set of parents could be found. No such presumption exists in the case of adoptive parents. This is not to deny that prospective parents who are prevented from adopting suffer a considerable setback to a quite fundamental interest in parenting (Brighouse and Swift 2006). However, in the absence of a claim grounded in a legitimate expectation that prospective adoptive parents might have over a *specific* child, the state is not necessarily treating parents denied adoption *unjustly* in virtue of being excluded by well-established and reasonable (i.e., non-arbitrary and non-discriminatory) criteria. Nor do adoptive parents have a valid complaint against the state or adoption agencies about the unequal treatment they suffer through a strict licensing system, causing much frustration and resulting in many prospective parents being prevented from adopting a child.

Protecting *all* children in the adoption process

Legitimate expectations may go a long way towards explaining and even justifying the *status quo* by which adoption regimes allow for considerably more screening and monitoring of adoptive parents than would be acceptable for families established through natural or assisted reproduction. An acceptable adoption regime must nevertheless operate within important restrictions, the violation of which gives rise to legitimate complaints on the part of parents and children who are adversely affected.

Prospective adoptive parents may have valid reasons for objecting not to the fact that they are licensed whereas biological parents are not, but rather to the specific requirements that are deployed in adoption licensing schemes. Specifically, it seems to us that constant vigilance against the use of unduly intrusive procedures and arbitrary selection criteria lies at the heart of a reasonable adoption system. (e.g., Reed 2012 on the arbitrariness of sexual orientation). Adoptive parents have a legitimate expectation that their privacy will be respected as much as possible, which requires that methods to ascertain their competence or intention must satisfy the *principle of least intrusion* (Dworkin 1972). In other words, the complaints of adoptive parents are not exhausted by considerations of comparative justice; non-comparative justice may demand considerable reform of the adoption process.

More interesting for present purposes, prospective adoptive children too may have cause for complaint where large-scale licensing of adoptive parents may impact on their chances to find a stable home. Paradoxically, the system that is installed with the best interests of children in mind may end up in practice delivering suboptimal outcomes, with too few children ending up in decent homes, even when the stringent requirements may end up saving some other children from neglect and abuse. If the balance between these two considerations is too skewed, we believe children have a legitimate cause for complaint and reform is mandated.

Strict adoption regulation is typically regarded as pitching the interests of prospective parents in becoming a parent against the greater interests of protecting children against potential neglect and abuse. Viewed as a *parent–child trade-off*, different perspectives on the obligations of the state converge on prioritising the well-being of the child and affirm the imposition of robust screening, licensing and monitoring requirements.[11] For some, this priority is warranted because the state must act *in locus parentis* and finds itself under a legal obligation to further the interests of the child; others would refer to more general moral principles, such as protecting the most vulnerable party in the relationship (e.g., Goodin 1985; see also ch. 27).

However, this point of view is incomplete, as it ignores how strict regulation of the adoption process implies what we elsewhere have termed *child–child trade-offs* (De Wispelaere and Weinstock 2012). Child–child trade-offs arise when attempts to protect one set of prospective adopted children ends up putting another set of children at risk. The vast majority of children who are presently available for adoption are living in sub-optimal conditions – especially when we include international adoption (Bartholet 2007). By focusing only on the potential harm of neglect or abuse by prospective adoptive parents, a regime may end up providing some children with excellent prospective parents but at the cost of leaving other prospective adoptees in these sub-optimal conditions. Generally speaking, the stricter the screening of prospective adoptees, the less children will be adopted and the more will end up in institutional or foster care (or worse); conversely, the more relaxed the screening, the more children will be adopted but the risk of neglect and abuse within adoption families could potentially increase. The judgements involved in balancing the different sides of the child–child trade-off are unsavoury, but impossible to avoid. A narrow perspective on the state's role as the child's advocate *in loco parentis* is of little help here because the state is presumed to have a responsibility to *all* prospective adoptees – those adopted and those remaining in care while awaiting adoption, both of whom potentially are at risk of neglect and abuse. There is no genuine moral reason why, to put it in stark terms, the interests in avoiding neglect or abuse within adoptive families ought to outweigh the interest in avoiding neglect or abuse within care institutions.[12]

What is the appropriate baseline for assessing when the adoption regime requires reform? Our argument suggests at least two routes that might mitigate the concerns mentioned. First, we might set up adoption criteria in such a way that they preclude not sub-optimal parents, but only catastrophic ones (see ch. 15). In other words, children's interests might be best served by embracing a screening system that uses more relaxed criteria of acceptable adoptive parenthood. This can then be combined with our second route: introducing increased monitoring and related support programs that take up the slack caused by relaxing the licensing criteria as such (De Wispelaere and Weinstock 2012). We are thinking about parental education classes that could be made mandatory for adoptive parents – and, indeed, parents in general – as one important support mechanism (Engster 2010).

Conclusion

Adoption raises a host of philosophical issues, both issues of personal ethics and of normative political philosophy. While much of the philosophical literature analyses the ethics of adoption at the personal level, our aim in this chapter was to examine the principles underlying adoption policy. The main focus of our chapter concerns the ethical concerns associated with the unequal treatment of adoptive and procreative parents in current adoption policy and practice. Where the regulation of parenting is guided by "minimalist principles" in the case of procreative parenthood, adoption involves extensive screening and monitoring of prospective parents. A first ethical question is whether this unequal treatment amounts to a comparative injustice that requires remedy. Our response is to deny the injustice of the current arrangements on the grounds that procreation establishes a legitimate expectation for parents to rear the child they brought into the world, while such a legitimate expectation does not exist in the case of adoption. But current adoption policy raises a second ethical worry: the selective institution of rigid and invasive screening and monitoring of prospective adopters contravenes the "claim from adoption", which holds that we ought to prioritise adoption over procreation. Once we appreciate that too much regulation simultaneously protects and harms children – what we refer to as the child–child trade-off – we argue that adoption regimes need to rebalance their guiding principles and policies to make it easier for parents to pursue the adoptive route towards parenthood.

Notes

1 Two recent collections discussing adoption in relation to assisted and natural procreation are Baylis and McLeod (2014) and Hannan, Brennan and Vernon (2015).
2 While the question of whether to reallocate children to a new set of parents upon birth – perhaps in the form of a baby lottery – is discussed widely in the philosophical literature (e.g., Shields 2017), it does not feature in practical policy debates.
3 The philosophical debate on the value of procreation – either on its own or in relation with adoption – is complex. For a critical overview, see Overall (2012) and ch. 13.
4 We think this is true even where there might be reasons for appreciating the value of institutional care (Gheaus 2011).
5 In addition to adequate preparation and post-adoption, the age of the prospective adoptee (which often serves as a proxy of the time spent in institutional care) is an important factor in explaining variation in successful adoption.
6 Tina Rulli (2014b) argues that adoption entails a unique value by virtue of being solely grounded in love and care. For a contrasting perspective, see Ferracioli (2017).
7 Some philosophers have suggested child-centred reasons why biological parenthood might be preferable over adoptive parenthood (e.g., Velleman 2005; Liao 2015). But none of these arguments speak to the claim from adoption where children in need of families already exist and the choice for procreation reduces their chances of becoming part of a family.
8 History offers too many occasions where birth parents of a particular religion, socio-economic class or ethnicity were unjustly forced to relinquish their children in order for them to live better lives with new families. Today, similar concerns of unfair coercion in relinquishing children are at play in relation to international adoption, in particular in countries that have experienced natural or social tragedies such as civil war, droughts or earthquakes or health pandemics (Carlson 2011; Selman 2012).
9 This notwithstanding, debates about the appropriateness of employing screening instruments such as pre-adoption genetic screening aimed at providing prospective parents with better-suited candidate adoptees are ongoing (Freundlich 1998; Leighton 2014).
10 On the nature of biological parenthood, see Gheaus 2017.
11 The question remains whether licensing actually succeeds in this task. For a critical perspective on this aspect of licensing, see De Wispelaere and Weinstock (2012) and McLeod and Botterell (ch. 18) for a general assessment.
12 Here, we side-step the complication implicit in international adoption where a state may be said to be responsible for the children it places because they are deemed to be under its jurisdiction compared to children living in subpar conditions abroad.

References

Archard, D. 1990. "Child Abuse: Parental Rights and the Interests of the Child," *Journal of Applied Philosophy* 7(2): 183–194.

Archard, D. 1994. *Children: Rights and Childhood*, 2nd edn. Abingdon: Routledge.
Bartholet, E. 1995. "Beyond Biology: The Politics of Adoption and Reproduction," *Duke Journal of Gender Law & Policy* 2(1): 5–14.
Bartholet, E. 2007. "International Adoption: The Child's Story," *Georgia State University Law Review* 24: 333–379.
Bartholet, E. 2010. "International Adoption: The Human Rights Position," *Global Policy* 1(1): 91–100.
Baylis, F., and McLeod, C. (eds.). 2014. *Family Making: Contemporary Ethical Challenges*. Oxford: Oxford University Press.
Benatar, D. 2006. *Better Never to Have Been: The Harm of Coming into Existence*. Oxford: Oxford University Press.
Botterell, A., and McLeod, C. 2015. "Can a Right to Reproduce Justify the Status Quo on Parental Licensing?," in R. Vernon, S. Hannan, and S. Brennan (eds.), *Permissible Progeny*. New York, NY: Oxford University Press.
Brighouse, H., and Swift, A. 2006. "Parents' Rights and the Value of the Family," *Ethics* 117: 80–108.
Brown, A. 2017. "A Theory of Legitimate Expectations," *Journal of Political Philosophy* 25(4): 435–460.
Carlson, R. R. 2011. "Seeking the Better Interests of Children with a New International Law of Adoption," *New York Law School Law Review* 55(1): 733–779.
Conly, S. 2005. "The Right to Procreation: Merits and Limits," *American Philosophical Quarterly* 42(2): 105–115.
Conn, P. 2013. *Adoption: A Brief Social and Cultural History*. Basingstoke: Palgrave Macmillan.
De Wispelaere, J., and Weinstock, D. 2012. "Licensing Parents to Protect Our Children?," *Ethics and Social Welfare* 6(2): 195–205.
De Wispelaere, J., and Weinstock, D. 2014. "State Regulation and Assisted Reproduction: Balancing the Interests of Parents and Children," in F. Baylis and C. McLeod (eds.), *Family Making: Contemporary Ethical Challenges*. Oxford: Oxford University Press.
De Wispelaere, J., and Weinstock, D. 2015. "Privileging Adoption Over Sexual Reproduction? a State-Centered Perspective," in S. Hannan, S. Brennan, and R. Vernon (eds.), *The Morality of Procreation and Parenting*. Oxford: Oxford University Press.
Dworkin, G. 1972. "Paternalism," *The Monist* 56(1): 64–84.
Engster, D. 2010. "The Place of Parenting Within a Liberal Theory of Justice: The Private Parenting Model, Parental Licenses, or Public Parenting Support?," *Social Theory and Practice* 36(2): 233–262.
Ferracioli, L. 2017. "Procreative-Parenting, Love's Reasons and the Demands of Morality," *Philosophical Quarterly*: 1–21. OnlineFirst: doi: 10.1093/pq/pqx022.
Fisher, A. 2003. "Still 'Not Quite as Good as Having Your Own'? Toward a Sociology of Adoption," *Annual Review of Sociology* 29: 335–361.
Freundlich, M. D. 1998. "The Case Against Preadoption Genetic Testing," *Child Welfare* 77(6): 663–679.
Friedrich, D. 2013. "A Duty to Adopt?," *Journal of Applied Philosophy* 30(1): 25–39.
Gheaus, A. 2011. "Arguments for Nonparental Care for Children," *Social Theory and Practice* 37(3): 483–509.
Gheaus, A. 2017. "Biological Parenthood: Gestational, Not Genetic," *Australasian Journal of Philosophy* 9: 1–17.
Goodin, R. E. 1985. *Protecting the Vulnerable: A Reanalysis of Our Social Responsibilities*. Chicago, IL: University of Chicago Press.
Hamilton, L., Cheng, S., and Powell, B. 2007. "Adoptive Parents, Adaptive Parents: Evaluating the Importance of Biological Ties for Parental Investment," *American Sociological Review* 72(1): 95–116.
Hannan, S., Brennan, S., and Vernon, R. (eds.). 2015. *The Morality of Procreation and Parenting*. Oxford University Press.
Hansen, M. E. 2008. "The Value of Adoption," *Adoption Quarterly* 10(2): 65–87.
Haslanger, S. 2009. "Family, Ancestry and Self: What Is the Moral Significance of Biological Ties," *Adoption & Culture* 2(1): 91–122.
Jennings, S., Mellish, L., Tasker, F., Lamb, M., and Golombok, S. 2014. "Why Adoption? Gay, Lesbian, and Heterosexual Adoptive Parents' Reproductive Experiences and Reasons for Adoption," *Adoption Quarterly* 17(3): 205–226.
LaFollette, H. 1980. "Licensing Parents," *Philosophy and Public Affairs* 9(2): 182–197.
LaFollette, H. 2010. "Licensing Parents Revisited," *Journal of Applied Philosophy* 27(4): 327–343.
Leighton, K. J. 2014. "Accepting Adoption's Uncertainty: The Limited Ethics of Pre-Adoption Genetic Testing," *Journal of Bioethical Inquiry* 11(2): 245–260.
Liao, M. S. 2015. *The Right to Be Loved*. Oxford: Oxford University Press.
McLeod, C., and Botterell, A. 2014. "'Not for the Faint of Heart': Assessing the Status Quo on Adoption and Parental Licensing," in F. Baylis and C. McLeod (eds.), *Family-Making: Contemporary Ethical Challenges*. Oxford: Oxford University Press.

Overall, C. 2012. *Why Have Children? The Ethical Debate*. Cambridge, MA: MIT Press.
Petersen, T. S. 2002. "The Claim from Adoption," *Bioethics* 16(4): 353–375.
Reed, R. 2012. "Are the Kids Alright? Rawls, Adoption, and Gay Parents," *Ethical Theory and Moral Practice* 16(5): 969–982.
Rieder, T. N. 2014. "Procreation, Adoption and the Contours of Obligation," *Journal of Applied Philosophy* 32(3): 293–309.
Rivera-López, E. 2006. "The Claim from Adoption Revisited," *Bioethics* 20(6): 319–325.
Rulli, T. 2014a. "Preferring a Genetically-Related Child," *Journal of Moral Philosophy* 13(6): 669–698.
Rulli, T. 2014b. "The Unique Value of Adoption," in F. Baylis and C. McLeod (eds.), *Family Making: Contemporary Ethical Challenges*. Oxford: Oxford University Press.
Rulli, T. 2016. "The Ethics of Procreation and Adoption," *Philosophy Compass* 11(6): 305–315.
Selman, P. 2012. "The Global Decline of Intercountry Adoption: What Lies Ahead?," *Social Policy and Society* 11(03): 381–397.
Shields, L. 2016. "How Bad Can a Good Enough Parent Be?," *Canadian Journal of Philosophy* 46(2): 163–182.
Shields, L. 2017. "Parental Rights and the Importance of Being Parents," *Critical Review of International Social and Political Philosophy* 84(1): 1–15.
United Nations. 2009. *Child Adoption: Trends and Policies*. New York, NY: UN Department of Economic and Social Affairs.
Velleman, D. 2005. "Family History," *Philosophical Papers* 34(3): 357–378.
Widdows, H., and MacCallum, F. 2002. "Disparities in Parenting Criteria: An Exploration of the Issues, Focusing on Adoption and Embryo Donation," *Journal of Medical Ethics* 28(3): 139–142.
Wind, L. H., Brooks, D., and Barth, R. P. 2008. "Adoption Preparation," *Adoption Quarterly* 8(4): 45–74.
Woodhouse, B. B. 2005. "Waiting for *Loving*: The Child's Fundamental Right to Adoption," *Capital University Law Review* 34: 297–329.
Younes, M. N., and Klein, S. A. 2014. "The International Adoption Experience: Do They Live Happily Ever After?," *Adoption Quarterly* 17(1): 65–83.
Young, T. 2001. "Overconsumption and Procreation: Are They Morally Equivalent?," *Journal of Applied Philosophy* 18(2): 183–192.

20
GENDER AND THE FAMILY

Amy Mullin

Introduction

In this chapter I explore how gender and parenting interact, why some of the interactions are ethically and politically problematic, and the ethical issues they raise for parents of young children and adult children in their interactions with their parents. I set aside ethical dilemmas about sex or gender and fetuses (such as sex-selective abortion) and limit myself to topics concerning interactions of parents and children once the latter are born. Although I speak generally about gender and the family, this chapter concentrates on issues that arise in OECD countries, particularly those in which a considerable proportion of mothers of young dependent children work outside the home.[1]

"Gender" can be used in a variety of ways. Sometimes it is used as a synonym for biological sex. Sometimes it refers to gender roles, with masculine roles assigned to men, and feminine roles assigned to women. Gender identity is a subjective sense of being masculine, feminine, on a spectrum between them, or neither. Gender expression may be an outward expression of subjective gender identity or conflict with it, especially to conform to social expectations. Cisgender (or gender normative or genderstraight) people are those whose gender identity and expression conform to gender roles assigned to people of their biological sex (although being assigned to a biological sex may itself be a contested matter for people deemed intersex). People who are intersex may be born with genitalia which problematize being assigned either male or female, or those whose secondary sex characteristics as they emerge at puberty are of indeterminate sex, or those whose primary and secondary sex characteristics combine features of both sexes. Those who are not cisgender include people who are transgender (who might identify with and/or express a gender identity, wholly or in part, associated with a sex other than the one to which they were assigned) and those who are gender variant (who may not identify with either socially defined gender, or be fluid with respect to gender identity and expression). Gender-variant people may prefer to use and be referred to using third-person plural pronouns "they/their" or new third-person singular pronouns such as "ze/hir/hirs". Terminology in this area, it must be observed, is fluid and politically both sensitive and contested.

Gender can interact with the family in a number of different ways, with impacts on both children and parents. One of the most topical concerns the responses that parents make to children whose preferences and identities vary from social expectations connected to gender.

Parents whose children are transgender or gender variant must balance concerns for the social acceptability and safety of their children against the children's need to be loved and accepted as they are, all the while potentially struggling to parent children who do not conform to their own expectations. While many parents need to balance desires that their children be safe and socially acceptable against the desire that they learn to take pride in who they are, parents of transgender children face additional challenges, and some find a variety of gender essentialism an unlikely resource. Gender essentialism holds that there are innate differences between men and women, including differences with respect to behaviour. Parents of transgender children born female may assert that those children are innately boys, while those born male are innately girls, in order to encourage acceptance of their children, although this will only be a feasible strategy for children who identify strongly with the gender not typically associated with their bodies. Popular discourse about parenting transgender and gender-variant children speaks of the need for unconditional love to rise to the challenges they present, but I argue that this way of speaking can underplay the potential rewards involved in parenting these children, and the challenges involved in parenting all children.

Children who are cisgender, and conform to social expectations that their gender expression match their biological sex, also raise issues for social policy and parents, because female children, including those who are cisgender, often face limited opportunities for social equality when compared to cisgender men. Moreover, parents' gender roles and their beliefs and attitudes about gender roles influence those of their children, and affect children's aspirations and opportunities. Parents' gendered behaviours and attitudes can, therefore, perpetuate gender disparities that reduce women's opportunity for social equality as well as men's opportunities to engage fully with their children, and call for both public policy responses and individual ethical decision-making to minimize these impacts.

After discussing issues raised by children's gender, with a focus primarily on children who are transgender, gender variant or intersex, I turn next to the impact of gendered parenting on parents and families. Unequal unpaid domestic labour, typically exacerbated by parenting, affects parents in their home and work lives. Women often do more parenting, with negative consequences for mothers' work lives and fathers' relationships with their children. I then examine the impact of rigidly gendered parenting roles on the family. Here I observe that social science research is frequently misused to suggest that children cannot flourish unless raised by a mother and a father, and that this has negative consequences when parents are not part of a heterosexual couple. In addition, gendered roles for children affect parents of adult children. Attitudes about the proper roles of sons and daughters can shape children's willingness to contribute to the care of their parents when their parents are elderly or in need of assistance.

Children's gender: transgender, gender variant, intersex, and cisgender children

For many decades some parents, influenced by feminism, have aimed to raise their children in ways that are gender neutral to some degree, such that both girls and boys are encouraged to play with toys or undertake activities that are more traditionally associated with the other gender. For instance, girls may be encouraged to dress as firefighters and play with vehicles and construction toys, and boys encouraged to play with kitchen toys and engage in arts activities, in ways that depart from earlier generations' expectations of rigid gender roles. The notion that gender is at least in part a product of socialization is widely embraced by popular books on child-rearing (Martin 2005). Daughters' departures from rigid gender roles are often initiated by parents, celebrated, and associated with expectations of future career success, although parents typically expect their daughters to add an interest in activities gendered male to those gendered female rather than to replace them (Kane 2006). However, as both Kane and Martin note, acceptance of childhood gender variance in sons tends to be limited to occasionally accepted departures from gendered expectations (boys can use glitter in their art), and generates worry and concern in many parents when boys depart in more than trivial ways from what is expected (for instance, when boys wear tutus, or prefer playing with Barbies to action figures).

Boys' acquisitions of domestic skills and demonstrations of empathy are often well accepted, but desires to dress in ways deemed feminine, and expressions of fear and weakness are not. Considerable gender variance, especially on the part of boys, often leads to parental fears that those boys will be rejected by adults, their peers or both (Kane 2006) and is associated with homosexuality, which continues to be stigmatized (Kane 2006; Martin 2005), Moreover, parents' concerns about their sons' departures from traditional masculinity are found regardless of the ethnicity, social class, and sexual orientation of their parents, and are typically greater on the part of fathers than mothers (Kane 2006).

Given the limited extent to which parents are comfortable with even fairly mild gender variance in their sons, it is perhaps unsurprising that considerable gender variance in their children can be bewildering and worrying to parents. Immediately below, I discuss how social exclusion faced by transgender and gender-variant children leads parents to dilemmas both like and unlike those posed by other situations in which children face prejudice and discrimination.

Sara Ruddick's (1995) work on maternal thinking (which may be carried out by men or women, and refers to the characteristic skills and virtues required to care well for young children) stresses that one of parents' aims is to ensure, as children grow and develop, that they become socially acceptable members of society. Ruddick is careful to point out that this may conflict with other aims of parents, including the desire that a child be viewed compassionately and realistically (Ruddick 1995: 98). Parents' desires to see their children develop and flourish can also be at odds with the desire that their children be socially acceptable when the larger society is characterized by various forms of prejudice, such as racism, sexism, and classism (Ruddick 1995: 22). When children belong to oppressed groups, parents' desires that their children conform sufficiently to social norms to avoid social isolation and violence can conflict with development of self-esteem and agency.

Any parent raising a child who belongs to a group facing prejudice and discrimination needs to balance demands for social acceptability (which may include children's diminished expectations for social respect, or acceptance of unequal treatment) with the desire to foster children's self-respect and evolving ability to self-direct. However, very often the parents will themselves be members of the targeted group or groups, and can draw upon their own experience and those of other group members as they seek to find the right balance between challenging injustice and keeping their children safe. Even when parents do not belong to the maligned group (for instance, fathers in a sexist society), they will often have a history of close relationships with members of that group (as fathers will typically have had many interactions with women, including those in their own families of origin).

Parents of transgender, gender-variant, and intersex children, by contrast, will often have had no personal experience of discrimination against people who do not conform to gender binaries, and no close contact with others who have experienced it. This is particularly likely as many transgender people in the past sought to keep their variance from gender norms hidden (whether by presenting as a cisgender person, or by keeping their gender identity hidden by expressing the gender they were expected to present). Transgender and gender-variant children have become more visible in the last two decades. Rahilly notes that raising gender-variant children would have been culturally unintelligible until recently (Rahilly 2015: 338), and transgender people are increasingly given positive representations in the popular media. However, violence against transgender people is not abating and may be increasing (Michaels 2015). Therefore, parents of transgender and gender-variant children are often parenting in a context in which they have little experience to guide them, and yet the stakes are high, as they have legitimate fear that their children may face not only social exclusion and damaged self-respect, but also violence. In another difference from the parenting challenges faced by racialized people and other members of oppressed groups, parents of transgender and gender-variant children (who may also, of course, be members of other disadvantaged groups) are often blamed by other parents, teachers, doctors, and family members for dealing inappropriately with their gender-variant children (Rahilly 2015: 342).

In addition, parents' expectations about their relationships with their children are often highly gendered, leading them to experience a sense of loss in coming to terms with how their children, and the relationship they have with them, are different from what they expected. Instead of having a cisgender son, parents may need to come to terms with a child whose preference for toys, clothes, playmates, and sense of self are more aligned with what they would have expected in a daughter. Love for their children, and concern for their well-being, can lead parents whose children are not cisgender in their identity or gender expression to embrace not only children's variance from expected activities, toys, clothes, and preferred playmates, but also variance in gender identity (Rahilly 2015: 340). Furthermore, some of these parents may find a kind of gender essentialism (in which their male children are understood as really their daughters, or female children as really their sons) a resource in resisting social expectations that they correct and control their children's gender identities and expressions (Rahilly 2015: 356). However, strategies like these would be less productive and potentially harmful when children are gender variant, and do not identify with one or only one gender.

Parents who affirm their children's transgender or gender-variant identities may now be able to find social work, mental health, and other medical professionals who will support them, although this would have been very unlikely in decades past. In these professions, supportive responses to children's gender variance are increasingly seen as promoting children's resilience (Riley et al. 2013: 644), although this approach remains controversial. Now, if requested by parents, some doctors will give children medication to delay the onset of puberty, in order to allow them to mature further before deciding whether to take medications or choose surgical interventions to support their transgender identities (Vanderburgh 2009). Mental health and social support is sometimes accessible with both or either of the challenges of raising transgender or gender variant children, or being such a child, in a society that can isolate, condemn, and harm people who are not cisgender.

Riley et al. describe parents of transgender and gender variant children as needing access to supportive peers, professional interventions, and information, including ideally contact with transgender people, and the children as needing a safe place to discuss their feelings, proper use of pronouns, and unconditional love (Riley et al. 2013: 645). This reference to transgender and gender-variant children's need for unconditional love is also found in self-descriptions of the parents of these children and in transgender adults' accounts of what they needed, when young, from their parents. For instance, Nutt's recent book about a family's experience with a transgender daughter includes a pamphlet written by the father arguing that transgendered children deserve unconditional love (Nutt 2015: ch. 34). Similarly, in Yuan and Wong (2015)'s story about Tracy Norman, a trans female model in the 1970s, Norman credits her mother's acceptance of her to unconditional love.

I have argued elsewhere that claims that only parents whose love is unconditional can love disabled children are confused or problematic (Mullin 2006). If all that is meant is that children should be recognized and appreciated for their individuality, and that no child should have to be perfect, or conform to all of a parents' expectations and ideals, in order to be loved, then this is clearly true of all children, whether or not they are disabled, transgender, or gender variant. Children, like adults, are imperfect and evolving, and parental care should never be denied to them because of their flaws or because of mismatches between parental expectations and children's realities. However, the claim that some children, such as those who are not cisgender, can only be loved if their parents' love is unconditional presents being other than cisgender as such an outstanding "defect" that only a love that can accept all defects could accommodate gender-variant or transgender children. Transgender and gender-variant children are diverse and will have strengths and virtues that can be appreciated, as well as weaknesses and vulnerabilities that can be supported, by parental love that does not need to be unconditional in the sense of accepting absolutely any "defect" or mismatch between expectations and reality. All children, cisgender, gender variant, and transgender, need love that is responsive to their particular features, accepting of limitation and difference, and open to finding and appreciating children's strengths, virtues, and talents, as well as their own love for their parents.

Expectations that children will conform to strict gender binaries can also have seriously negative impacts on children who are intersex and their parents. As with the language that describes children who do not conform to gender norms, language here is contested, with many in the medical profession preferring in recent years to refer to "disorders of sex development" rather than "intersex" (or the older term "hermaphroditism") (Feder and Karkazis 2008). Whatever the terminology chosen, Feder and Karkazis persuasively argue that mere sex atypicality should not be seen as a problem requiring a medical solution (such as cosmetic genital surgery or hormonal treatment). At the same time, real medical needs should not be neglected out of commitment to intersex as a political identity (Feder and Karkazis 2008: 35). Health and functioning should be what matters when it comes to medical intervention rather than passing as unambiguously male or female. However, when children cannot be straightforwardly slotted into the categories of male and female, it can confound parents in societies where the first question they are often asked is if their child is a boy or a girl. Parents of an intersex child, like those children themselves, will need support to accept sex atypical bodies as not themselves disorders requiring correction, even while some with atypical bodies might benefit from medical treatment for specific needs. Larger social changes that demote the importance of sex typicality to identity will no doubt be required to fully remove psychological pressures associated with sex atypicality.

While I have focused to this point on the impact of expectations about gender on transgender, gender-variant, and intersex children, cisgender children are also impacted significantly by gender. Parents' gendered roles, and their implicit attitudes and explicit beliefs about gender roles, very often involve them interacting with and shaping cisgender children whose gender roles match their biological sex. Parents whose behaviour and attitudes towards gender roles are cisgender can limit daughters' career aspirations. Parents' beliefs shape not only their children's beliefs about gender roles in domestic labour, but also their views about what they are likely to do and be in the future. Girls are more likely to see themselves as working outside the home, for example, if their fathers report gender-egalitarian attitudes and behave in gender-egalitarian ways when it comes to domestic labour, and if their mothers see themselves as work-oriented (Croft et al. 2014: 1426).

Boys' career aspirations do not appear to be similarly affected by their parents' attitudes towards gender and domestic labour, or gender and occupations (Croft et al. 2014: 1426), although one suspects that their attitudes towards gender roles are affected. It is precisely for this reason that feminist parents aim for the gender-egalitarian child-rearing discussed above. It is not enough for parents to focus only on how they treat their children (with respect to toys, types of play, and behaviours considered acceptable for sons and daughters). It is also important for parents to focus on how they interact with one another, and whether or not they interact with their children in ways that model gendered roles for parents. Otherwise the evidence discussed above suggests their own gendered roles may perpetuate traditional gender roles and limit girls' ambitions.

What measures should be taken to combat parenting practices that perpetuate gender roles that limit social equality, in part, by limiting girls' aspirations? Public educational institutions can aim to counteract gender stereotypes about appropriate forms of higher education and careers for girls and women by campaigns aimed at encouraging more girls to study STEM (science, technology, engineering, and mathematics) disciplines, and by encouraging girls to job shadow men as well as women, and boys to job shadow women as well as men. Efforts at workplaces aimed at encouraging work–family balance should make explicit efforts to engage with men as well as women, and to ensure that neither men nor women who take parental leave or limit work hours are disadvantaged when it comes to opportunities for career advancement. In addition, as I will discuss below, public policies that aim at gender-egalitarian parenting can have positive impacts on children by making children's understanding of their own gendered roles less rigid. Moreover, individual parents can seek to interrogate their own practices and decisions, out of concern for their daughters' social equality, and those who interact with parents can be supportive of parental efforts to rethink the gendered expectations parents (and other members of society) often have for sons and daughters.

Gender roles and their impact on parents

Gender roles affect not only children but also parents. Feminists have long argued that unequal, unpaid domestic labour disadvantages women in both their domestic lives and in the paid labour market. They further argue that parenting frequently exacerbates the unequal division of domestic labour, limiting women's, and especially mothers', fair equality of opportunity and political liberty, and making them more vulnerable to abuse of power at the hands of their male partners (Okin 1989). Mothers who leave paid work for some time, or those who choose part-time or flex work in order to accommodate parenting, often lose out on income, pension entitlements, and opportunities for professional advancement. Those who continue in paid work often work a "second shift" at home, doing more to maintain the home and raise children than male partners (Bond et al. 2002). Scholars are divided, however, as to whether to seek merely to remove barriers to equality of opportunity such that unequally gendered domestic division of labour reflects individuals' uncoerced choices, or to support public policies, such as a period of parental leave reserved solely for fathers, that aim explicitly at equality of outcomes with respect to domestic labour (Gheaus and Robeyns 2011). Much here depends upon the variety of egalitarianism to which the scholar in question is committed. For instance, is the commitment primarily to equality of opportunity, equality of resources, equality of welfare or opportunity for welfare, or social equality (the ability to be free from oppression and domination, and to interact as an equal both as a citizen and as a member of civil society; Anderson 1999)?

So long as women's gendered parenting results in negative socio-economic and personal consequences for them, public policies should seek to minimize the negative impacts of gendered parenting, rather than merely removing discriminatory barriers to individuals' choices. Moreover, individuals making decisions about which parent's career should be prioritized, and who should take on various tasks connected to raising children, should consider the impact of gendered norms connected to parenting on their choices and actions and the gendered consequences that can flow from their private decisions. Furthermore, it is clear that the gendered division of labour harms mothers. In OECD countries, women do fewer hours of paid work, are more likely to leave work to care for children, and earn less than their male partners, with their contribution to the couple's income ranging from 18% to 38% (Gornick and Meyers 2008: 318). Gendered parenting roles encourage employers to expect women to be less committed to their careers and limit women's opportunities for career advancement. As a result, even heterosexual parenting couples committed to gender equality often prioritize the father's career.

Mothers, even those employed full-time outside the home, perform considerably more housework and childcare (approximately twice as much childcare) than their male partners, at the cost of their own leisure, sleep, and personal care (Gornick and Meyers 2008: 318). Although fathers' time spent on childcare has increased over the past several decades, they spend less time than mothers, and the tasks they undertake often leave primary responsibility to mothers (Rehel 2014: 113). Moreover, mothers, particularly those who choose to work and are successful in their careers, can experience negative social consequences (Okimoto and Heilman 2012: 704). Mothers who work full-time in occupations gendered masculine typically face doubt about their competence in their professions and as mothers (Okimoto and Heilman 2012). They are judged less likeable than either working fathers or mothers who do not work outside the home (Okimoto and Heilman 2012: 704).

A gendered division of labour in parenting can also negatively affect men. Fathers often increase their involvement in paid work after the birth of a child (Rehel 2014: 111), perhaps because of expectations that fathers should provide income for their families. Rehel's research shows that fathers who take paternity leave become more active parents, and become more confident about their parenting than fathers who do not (Rehel 2014: 111). Brighouse and Swift (2014) argue that intimate relationships are important for human flourishing and that different types of intimate relationships meet different needs (Brighouse and Swift 2014: 87). They further argue that for many adults, male as well as female, loving relationships with children are required for full flourishing. The kind of parental love that Brighouse and Swift have in mind requires close attention to the needs of a child, and considerable emotional intimacy, as well as significant responsibility for meeting the child's current and developmental needs and authority to do so (Brighouse and Swift 2014: 88–92). Gender stereotypes around the proper roles of fathers and mothers can discourage fathers from spending as much time with their children as mothers do, attending as closely to children's needs, and helping children develop physically, intellectually, and emotionally. Fathers who fail to develop emotionally intimate relationships with their children because of unequally gendered parenting will lose out on important relationship goods, ones that are key in Brighouse and Swift's estimation, to full flourishing. Furthermore, one need not share Brighouse and Swift's strong views about the connection between flourishing and parental love to recognize that parental love is a very important source of relationship goods in the lives of many adults and, hence, to fail to fully experience it is a burden for those fathers whose relationships with their children are emotionally distant.

Measures responding to unequally gendered parenting

Although feminists are typically united in lamenting the negative impacts on both women and men of unequally gendered parental division of labour, they are divided when it comes to whether or not the state should take action to mitigate the negative impacts and either enable or promote making parenting more gender egalitarian. Political liberals are committed to the principle that justifications for the exercise of political power should appeal to fair terms of social cooperation rather than conceptions of the good that all citizens do not share (Schouten 2015: 5). Elgarte makes a useful distinction between public policy measures that might enable greater gender equality and those that promote it (Elgarte 2008: 6). Liberals are, therefore, more comfortable with the former, which are compatible with the state respecting all its citizens' decisions, than the latter, which seem incompatible with state neutrality with respect to individuals' varying conceptions of the good life.

Public policy approaches that enable gender-egalitarian parenting or mitigate the impact of inequality include limitations on the number of hours worked weekly and restructuring of school hours (to make paid work more compatible with childcare), paid leaves, affordable high-quality childcare, and provision of a basic income (Elgarte 2008: 6). If the state were to provide a basic income, giving funds sufficient to meet basic needs, either to all adult citizens or to those below a certain income floor, women engaging in unpaid domestic labour would be offered greater independence as they would not depend upon partners doing paid work for the income needed to meet basic needs. Elgarte suggests that state provision of a basic income might also reduce gender-based violence associated with women's lower status and reduced options to exit from relationships (Elgarte 2008: 2–4). However, provision of a basic income in a society where reproductive labour is gendered as women's work may reinforce or even exacerbate a gendered division of labour, even while it removes some of its most negative repercussions (Elgarte 2008: 5).

Public policy measures that most would consider to actively promote gender-egalitarian parenting include public education aimed directly at encouraging such parenting, regulating the content of media aimed at children to encourage depictions of gender-egalitarian norms, and creating incentives for men and women to become more equally involved in parenting (Elgarte 2008: 6). The latter, more specifically reserving a portion of parental leave for men, is the most discussed public policy measure to encourage gender-egalitarian parenting, and has been promoted in a variety of OECD countries (see Brighouse and Wright 2008; Gornick and Meyers 2008; Gheaus and Robeyns 2011). Schouten argues that reserving a period of paid parental leave for fathers should not be read as promoting gender-egalitarian parenting (which would conflict with liberal neutrality towards conceptions of the good), but instead as merely making it more feasible for parents to make such a choice (Schouten 2015: 13–18). She further argues that pervasive gender norms around parenting (what she refers to as the male breadwinner, female homemaker dichotomy) and social institutions, such as workplaces and childcare options, built around these gender norms, make it difficult for people to choose gender-egalitarian parenting. Finally, she argues that the option to parent in this way is key to the political autonomy and equality of citizens, and social stability based on faith in those institutions, and, hence, liberal states are not only permitted but also required to take action to make gender-egalitarian parenting genuinely feasible for people in all walks of life (Schouten 2015: 7–8). Whether or not one agrees that it is politically legitimate for governments to actively promote gender-egalitarian parenting or merely to remove barriers to people opting for it, it is important to ensure that measures chosen, such as reserving a period of parental leave for men, do not have negative repercussions on single parents and same-sex couples (see ch. 17). Single parents should be able to access a full parental leave, and co-parents, regardless of their gender, should each be eligible for a period of leave.

In addition to public policies aimed at making parenting more gender egalitarian – or making it more feasible for parents to choose a gender-egalitarian approach – intellectual work to combat gender stereotypes (such as those that suggest that women who are successful in male-dominated fields cannot also be good parents) needs to be ongoing and can be embraced by liberals, as it does not seek to promote some life choices over others, but instead to ensure that a wide range of life choices are available to all. Anyone who evaluates another person's parenting has reason to be cautious about gender stereotypes, as does anyone who employs parents. Employers with human resources professionals should ensure that they educate managers about the power of gender stereotypes to affect performance evaluation and hiring decisions. Finally, individuals making choices connected to their parenting have good reason to reflect on the personal and social consequences of a gendered division of parenting labour. Those who become parents need to be aware that they may be vulnerable to expectations about gendered division of labour in parenting and the greater importance of fathers' careers, even if they are explicitly committed to gender equality. It is also important for parents to recall that gendered parenting roles can diminish women's opportunities for social equality. To the extent that men are encouraged to prioritize their careers, increase their hours of work when they become parents, and deem their female partners to be more competent parents than they are themselves, this may also harm men's relationships with their children.

Rigid gender norms and the family

Rigid gender norms around men and women's parenting impact on the family in ways distinct from the diminished social equality for women and lesser involvement in parenting for men discussed above. For instance, since children are frequently said to need both a mother and a father, parents who do not form a male–female dyad are encouraged to think that their parenting decisions (or unchosen circumstances) will negatively affect their children. Those parents may also face social condemnation. While there is evidence that dual-parent families (so long as the parents' relationship is low in conflict) can provide more emotional and material resources to their children (Biblarz and Stacey 2010: 5) than single-parent families, there is little evidence that parenting success is tied to gender, or that children need both a male and a female parent to flourish. Despite this, academic arguments suggesting children do not need to be raised by both a mother and a father are highly controversial, and tend to be dismissed in the popular media, the courts, and by social scientists who compare children in dual-parent families with those in lone-parent families, and make conclusions about the role of parental gender (Biblarz and Stacey 2010: 3–4). However, when studies about parental gender compare only dual-parent families (whether with two mothers, two fathers, or a mother and a father) with one another, and single-parent families (whether with a mother or a father) with one another, it emerges that parental gender has little impact on children's psychological adjustment and social success (Biblarz and Stacey 2010: 3).

Erroneous assumptions about children's need for both a male and a female parent can also negatively affect people who would like to adopt but do not plan to parent in a male–female dyad. These assumptions can lead to unjust judicial determinations of best interests of children, undue social pressure for parents to co-parent with someone who is not fit to do so, and negative social consequences for those who do not parent with someone of the other sex. They may also lead some parents to unjustifiably worry about whether their children's futures will be negatively affected by not having both a father and a mother. It is, therefore, important for nuanced social science research about what children need from their parents to be presented carefully in the popular media, and for courts and politicians to be open to this research, rather than expecting social science to confirm their prejudices. Individuals who interact with parents who care for children outside a male–female dyad should be open to appreciating their strengths, and to recognizing that behaviour associated with mothers can be found in fathers who have primary responsibility for children's care (Rehel 2014).

Parents are also impacted by the manner in which sons and daughters conform to gender roles when those children are grown and the parents need assistance. Pushkar et al. (2014) show that parents of daughters report more satisfaction with their relationship with their children than parents of sons (Pushkar et al. 2014: 297). This is perhaps unsurprising given that Schmid, Brandt, and Haberkern show that throughout Europe daughters provide higher levels of sporadic help to their elderly parents than do sons, and considerably more intensive support (Schmid, Brandt, and Haberkern 2012: 39). Moreover, this is true regardless of whether children are legally obligated in a given country to provide care to their parents, and whether or not cash-for-care schemes (that pay caregivers directly or allocate funds to those who need care) are in place. The only public policy that makes children's care to parents more gender egalitarian is social provision of good quality eldercare (Schmid, Brandt, and Haberkern 2012: 39). Since intensive provision of care for one's parents is associated with increased depression and anxiety, poorer physical health, and reduced paid employment (Schmid, Brandt, and Haberkern 2012: 40), this unequally gendered provision of parental care is associated with a variety of disadvantages for women, and should be targeted by public policies (whether those that seek to minimize negative effects on women or those that directly promote gender-egalitarian provision of care to elderly parents) and taken seriously by individuals seeking to make ethical decisions about whether, when, and how to care for elderly parents. In addition to providing reasons, beyond concern for the elders themselves, to support state provision of high-quality elder care, the unjustly gendered provision of elder care gives reasons for individuals making decisions about how to support their parents' needs to seek to avoid and compensate for women's greater provision of care.

Conclusion

In conclusion, both parents and children experience negative consequences associated with gendered expectations for sons and daughters, and mothers and fathers. Even parents who express a commitment to gender-neutral child-rearing rarely follow through, particularly when it comes to interacting with sons. Expectations that children will be cisgender can cause tremendous suffering for some children and place their parents in difficult situations where they need professional support because of social opposition to transgender, gender-variant, and intersex people. Cisgender children also raise issues for parents because of a lack of social equality for women. Parenting is rarely gender egalitarian, with negative consequences for mothers when it comes to economic opportunities, demands on their time, and social attitudes towards both their parenting and their work, and potentially negative consequences for fathers' relationships with their children. Those who parent outside a male–female dyad face inappropriate social censure and may unjustifiably worry about their children's well-being. Finally, adult daughters, and elderly parents of sons, may both suffer negative consequences from the way sons and daughters are differently gendered such that daughters provide more parental care. Therefore, we have ample reasons to work towards more gender-egalitarian parenting and a considerable weakening of expectations that children conform to gendered expectations and gender roles, both when we contemplate public policies, and when we make individual decisions about our own parenting, and interact with people who are parents.

Note

1 Information about the OECD may be accessed here: http://www.oecd.org/

References

Anderson, E. 1999. "What Is the Point of Equality?," *Ethics* 109(2): 287–337.
Biblarz, T. J., and Stacey, J. 2010. "How Does the Gender of Parents Matter?," *Journal of Marriage and Family* 72: 3–22.
Bond, J. T., Thompson, C., Gallinsky, E., and Prottas, D. 2002. *Highlights of the National Study of the Changing Workforce No. 3*. New York, NY: Families and Work Institute.
Brighouse, H., and Swift, A. 2014. *Family Values: The Ethics of Parent-Child Relationships*. Princeton, NJ: Princeton University Press.
Brighouse, H., and Wright, E. O. 2008. "Strong Gender Egalitarianism," *Politics & Society* 36(3): 360–372.
Croft, A., Schmader, T., Block, K., and Bader, A. S. 2014. "The Second Shift Reflected in the Second Generation: Do Parents' Gender Roles at Home Predict Children's Aspirations?," *Psychological Science* 25(7): 1418–1428.
Elgarte, J. 2008. "Basic Income and the Gendered Division of Labour," *Basic Income Studies: An International Journal of Basic Income Research* 3(3): 1–7.

Feder, E. K., and Karkazis, K. 2008. "What's in a Name? The Controversy over 'Disorders of Sex Development,'" *The Hastings Center Report* 38(5): 33–36.
Gheaus, A., and Robeyns, I. 2011. "Equality-Promoting Parental Leave," *Journal of Social Philosophy* 42(2): 173–191.
Gornick, J. C., and Meyers, M. K. 2008. "Creating Gender Egalitarian Societies: An Agenda for Reform," *Politics & Society* 36(3): 313–349.
Kane, E. 2006. "No Way My Boys are Going to be Like That!," *Gender & Society* 20(2): 149–176.
Martin, K. 2005. "William Wants a Doll. Can He Have One?," *Gender & Society* 19(4): 456–479.
Michaels, S. 2015. "More Transgender People Have Been Killed in 2015 Than in Any Other Year on Record," *Mother Jones*. Retrieved from http://www.motherjones.com/mojo/2015/11/more-transgender-people-have-been-murdered-2015-any-other-year-record (last accessed 2 February 2016).
Mullin, A. 2006. "Parents and Children: An Alternative to Unconditional and Selfless Love," *Hypatia* 21(1): 181–200.
Nutt, A. E. 2015. *Becoming Nicole: The Transformation of an American Family*. New York, NY: Random House.
Okimoto, T. G., and Heilman, M. E. 2012. "The 'Bad Parent' Assumption: How Gender Stereotypes Affect Reactions to Working Mothers," *Journal of Social Issues* 68(4): 704–724.
Okin, S. M. 1989. *Justice, Gender, and the Family*. New York, NY: Basic Books.
Pushkar, D., Bye, D., Conway, M., Wrosch, C., Chaikelson, J., Etezadi, J. Giannopoulos, C., Li, K., and Tabri, N. 2014. "Does Child Gender Predict Older Parents' Well Being?," *Social Indicators Research* 118(1): 285–303.
Rahilly, E. P. 2015. "The Gender Binary Meets the Gender Variant Child: Parents' Negotiations with Childhood Gender Variance," *Gender & Society* 29(3): 338–361.
Rehel, E. M. 2014. "When Dad Stays Home Too: Paternity Leave, Gender and Parenting," *Gender & Society* 28(1): 110–132.
Riley, E. A., Sitharthana, G., Clemsona, L., and Diamond, M. 2013. "Recognizing the Needs of Gender-Variant Children and their Parents," *Sex Education* 13(6): 644–659.
Ruddick, S. 1995/1989. *Maternal Thinking: Towards a Politics of Peace*. Boston, MA: Beacon Press.
Schmid, T., Brandt, M., and Haberkern, K. 2012. "Gendered Support to Older Parents: Do Welfare States Matter?," *European Journal of Aging* 9: 39–50.
Schouten, G. 2015. "Citizenship, Reciprocity, and the Gendered Division of Labor: A Stability Argument for Gender Egalitarian Interventions," *Politics, Philosophy & Economics* 16(2): 174–209.
Vanderburgh, R. 2009. "Appropriate Therapeutic Care for Families with Pre-Pubescent Transgender/Gender Dissonant Children," *Child and Adolescent Social Work Journal* 26(2): 135–154.
Yuan, J., and Wong, A. 2015. "The First Black Trans Model Had Her Face on a Box of Clairol." Retrieved from http://nymag.com/thecut/2015/12/tracey-africa-transgender-model-c-v-r.html# (last accessed 2 February 2016).

21
FILIAL DUTIES

Diane Jeske

Introduction

Most people have a deeply felt sense that adult children have unique and particularly strong moral obligations to their parents. We reserve some of our strongest moral disapprobation for children who disrespect or ignore the needs of their parents. Recently, a 20-year-old follower of ISIS publicly executed his own mother because she had tried to convince him to flee with her to a safer place. While we certainly condemn ISIS executions in general, our moral outrage at a son killing his own mother exceeds that which we direct toward other brutal ISIS killings. In a more familiar sort of example, many people take their elderly parents into their homes in order to care for them. Taking someone into your home is often a great burden, but we tend to think that parents have legitimate expectations that their adult children do this for them, while they would have no such legitimate expectations of any other persons.

Accounts of filial duties aim to justify such judgments by explaining why we have duties to our parents that (at least usually) we do not have to any other persons. In the second section, I will explain what one needs to do in order to offer an adequate account of filial duties, and distinguish between two types of such accounts: the deflationary and the non-deflationary. In the third to fifth sections I will present three of the most prominent and plausible accounts of filial duties: the gratitude account, the friendship account, and the special goods account. In the sixth section, I will apply these theories to an example from the film *Music Box* that illustrates in a very stark and dramatic manner the moral complexities raised by the peculiar nature of our relationships to our parents.

Definitions and distinctions

Filial duties are standardly understood to be a type of special obligation as opposed to a type of natural duty.[1] My natural duties are those that I owe to all moral patients merely in virtue of their status as the kind of being to whom moral duties can be owed. My special obligations are owed only to some subset of moral beings, and the grounds of the obligation are not merely the status of the obligee as a moral being, but also some fact about the nature of my relationship to the obligee (other than the fact that I am causally placed so as to aid the obligee). The dispute between different accounts of filial duties is a dispute about *which feature* of the parent–child relationship *grounds* the special obligations that children have to their parents.

The first task of any theory of filial duties is an account of the parent–child relationship, i.e. of what makes it the case that C is P's child. There are roughly two sorts of accounts of the parent–child relationship, one appealing to the biological connection between parents and children and the other appealing to the care-giving that parents provide (or, are supposed to provide) for their children. According to the biological account, P is C's parent if and only if P has provided genetic materials such as a sperm or egg which are biologically necessary for creating the human being C. According to the custodial account, P is C's parent if and only if P is charged by the relevant social or legal authorities to be, more than temporarily, a primary care-giver, where care involves raising the child to some agreed upon conception of maturity.

It is important to see that I have explained custodial parenthood by appealing not to who actually cares for the child but to who has the social or legal responsibility to raise the child. I think that it is important not to understand B as C's parent merely because B happens to be the one primarily engaged in the task of raising the child. We can imagine a wealthy couple, Martin and Maria, who have a biological child, Bertie, whom they leave entirely in the care of a nanny, Jeeves. Even so, Martin and Maria remain Bertie's parents, although Bertie and Jeeves will likely have the sort of relationship that children usually have with their custodial parents. Jeeves *acts as* Bertie's parent, but that is not sufficient to render him Bertie's parent.

As we will see, however, many of the duties that adult children owe to their parents are grounded by the fact of the latter having actually fulfilled their custodial responsibilities. Given this, it will turn out to be the case that Bertie will have the same sorts of obligations to Jeeves that most of us have to our custodial parents. But I think that it is still important to see that as a matter of conceptual analysis, Jeeves is not Bertie's parent, even though Bertie will be in a position of owing to Jeeves, not to Martin and Maria, what most of us owe to our parents.[2]

Once we have an account of parenthood in hand, we will be able to classify any given account of filial duties as either deflationary or non-deflationary. Non-deflationary accounts of filial duties ground the duties on some feature of the parent–child relationship that is essential to that relationship, i.e. on that feature(s) of the relationship that makes it a parent–child relationship. Thus, a non-deflationary account of filial duties will ground such duties on the fact of biological creation, on the fact of the occupation of the custodial role, or on some combination of biological and custodial facts. If a non-deflationary account is correct, then filial duties are types of duties that we cannot have to anyone other than our parents, and we *necessarily* have such duties to our parents.

Few advocates of special filial duties offer non-deflationary accounts.[3] Such accounts would have to defend either the claim that the mere fact that P contributed genetic material to C grounds a duty on the part of C to P, or the claim that the mere fact that P occupies the custodial role vis-à-vis C grounds C's duty to P. If the former, then a child would have filial duties to the man who raped her mother or to a sperm donor. If the latter, then Bertie would have filial duties to Martin and Maria regardless of their failure to fulfill their custodial responsibilities. Such claims seem, to say the least, highly implausible, and so I will focus on deflationary accounts of special filial duties.

Deflationary accounts of filial duties ground them on features of the parent–child relationship that may not be present in all parent–child relationships and is at least sometimes present in relationships other than parent–child relationships. According to deflationary accounts, filial duties are a particular instance of a more general type of special obligation. The three accounts that I will present understand filial duties as instances of duties of gratitude, duties of friendship, or duties arising from the receipt and conferral of "special goods."

It is important to point out that we may have more than one type of duty to our parents. In other words, the three accounts that I will be discussing need not be seen as incompatible: we may owe our parents duties of gratitude, duties of friendship, *and* duties to provide special goods. So we can understand our inquiry as asking whether one or more of the following accounts is plausible as an account of at least some of the duties that we have to our parents. After all, once we have put aside non-deflationary accounts of filial duties, we have thereby admitted that there are no *sui generis* filial duties, i.e. no duties that occur always and only in parent–child relationships, and thus have no reason to look for *the* account of filial duties.[4]

The gratitude account

If filial duties are duties of gratitude, then they meet the condition of being special obligations: C owes P a duty of gratitude if and only if P has benefitted C under certain conditions. Thus, duties of gratitude are not owed to all moral beings, but are owed to that subset of moral beings to whom one stands as beneficiary to benefactor. Further, on a gratitude account, filial duties are not *sui generis* – they are only an instance of a more general type of special obligation, obligations of gratitude, where such obligations can certainly be owed to people who are not our parents. So the gratitude account of filial duties is a deflationary account.

As I said, C owes P a duty of gratitude if and only if P has benefitted C *under certain conditions*, so we need to lay out those conditions to see whether they are satisfied in any particular case of a parent P and a child C.[5] First, it seems that I owe a debt of gratitude to someone only if that person has benefitted me freely, intentionally, and by choice. Nozick (1974) offers the case of someone whose best form of exercise is throwing books which land in my yard. Even if these books are ones that I read and enjoy, it does not seem that I owe the weird exerciser any gratitude, because she had no intention of benefitting me (or anyone else).

Do parents intend to benefit their children when they bring them into existence? One might think that the answer to this question is obviously "no," given that at the time of the "gift" of an egg or a sperm, there is not yet a child to receive the gift. However, we can compare the biological gift to the endowment of a scholarship by a wealthy person, who designates that recipients be chosen via certain criteria. If I get a scholarship, it is true that the wealthy endower did not aim at benefitting me in particular, but she did aim at benefitting the sort of student that I am, and it does seem that I ought to be grateful to the endower. So the fact that there was not yet any particular person whom the benefactor was aiming to benefit does not seem sufficient to undermine the possibility of the beneficiary owing a debt of gratitude to the benefactor.

Nonetheless, it doesn't seem to be true that parents, when they have children, are aiming at benefitting some future person. People usually have children because they want to have a family, and, in most cases, what they have to do to get a family is to have sex, usually not an onerous endeavor.[6] Consider an analogous case: does a colleague who has benefitted from my presence in his department owe me a debt of gratitude for taking a job in his department? He might say, "I am so grateful that I have Diane as a colleague!" but this claim seems to express how happy he is with the resultant situation, not that he is grateful *to me*. A child might say, "I am so grateful that my parents had me!" without its being the case that she is grateful *to her parents*. So parents seem too much like Nozick's strange exerciser when it comes to biological gifting.[7]

A more plausible basis for a duty of gratitude to parents is the fulfilling of custodial responsibilities. Clearly, the mere occupation of the custodial role is not sufficient to generate duties of gratitude, as the case of Bertie makes clear. So we need to consider a case in which those who occupy the custodial role do their best to fulfill their custodial responsibilities. In my own case, I am well aware of all that my mother has done for me, and her intentions were clearly aimed at providing me with benefits such as safety, health, and education. I am sure that such is true of many parents, and so custodial care seems to be a benefit given by parents with the intention of benefitting the child.

But the generation of duties of gratitude requires more than merely freely and intentionally being benefitted. But if, for example, Lucy regularly brings Charlie coffee in the morning, but does so only because Charlie is her boss and she is trying to curry his favor, it does not seem that Charlie ought to be grateful to Lucy. While Lucy intended to benefit Charlie and did so freely, she did so only as a means to getting something for herself. So duties of gratitude seem to be generated by intentional acts of benefitting only if the benefactor is acting, at least in part, from the motive of doing good for the beneficiary for the latter's own sake. And I think that most parents, in fulfilling their custodial duties, satisfy this condition: they act primarily out of concern for their child's good in and of itself. Thus, parents benefit their children freely and intentionally, and do so for the right sorts of reasons.

It also seems that not just any benefit is sufficient to generate a duty of gratitude, no matter what the motives and intentions of the benefactor are. In providing someone with a benefit, I am often doing no more than what I am already obligated to do for them. However, we do not want to conclude, as some do, that we *never* owe debts of gratitude to those who benefit us in the ways that they are obligated to benefit us. Some duties are onerous to fulfill, either because of the nature of what is required or because of the nature of the person who has the duty. A senior colleague has a duty to mentor junior colleagues, but if the former performs this mentoring in an excellent manner and exerts great effort in doing so, it seems that the junior colleagues have a duty of gratitude to her.

For some parents, doing what they are morally required to do demands great effort and self-sacrifice, but for others it does not. Thus, the debt of gratitude that children owe to their parents is not directly proportional to the quantity of the benefits that their parents have bestowed upon them, but to the effort needed to provide those benefits. We can imagine wealthy parents who are able to provide the best of everything that money can buy for their children, but the cost is a mere drop in the bucket to them and requires little effort on their part to provide. Some poor parents, on the other hand, have to put in long hours just to pay medical bills and to put food on the table. Thus, children of poor parents may owe more to their parents than do children of wealthy parents, even before we weigh in the non-material benefits – love, care, a moral sense – that parents may provide to their children.

Thus, if we accept that we have duties of gratitude, it seems very plausible to suppose that we have such duties to custodial parents who make a serious attempt to carry out their responsibilities. Of course, as the case of Bertie and Jeeves shows, it is the not the fact of parenthood itself which grounds the obligations, but the provision/receipt of benefits. Thus, what is owed to custodial parents who take their responsibilities seriously is no different from what would be owed to someone who is not one's parent but does everything that is usually and ought to be done by custodial parents. Nonetheless, as a matter of fact, most of us, it seems, will have duties of gratitude to our custodial parents.

The friendship account

Most people understand themselves as owing obligations to their friends, and they understand those obligations as special obligations: they think that they have duties to those who are their friends *because* they are their friends.[8] The important question for any account of duties of friendship is, what makes it the case that two people stand in a relationship of friendship with each other? It is beyond the scope of this paper to present and defend a particular account of friendship, so my aim here will be far more modest. I am going to consider some features of a relationship that many take to be at least partly constitutive of friendship, and I will then show that relationships between parents and adult children often exhibit these features. Hopefully, establishing this much will be sufficient to justify exploring the claim that filial duties are duties of friendship.[9]

First, it seems that friends care about each other for their own sake, not merely as means to some other end. So if Lucy cares about Charlie and about her relationship with him only as a possible route to a promotion, then Lucy and Charlie are not friends. This is true even if Charlie cares about Lucy for her own sake, because it seems right to suppose that friendship requires *mutual* caring of the right sort. In such a case, Charlie might regard Lucy as a friend, but will likely cease to regard her as such when he discovers her attitudes toward him.

This first condition is clearly often met in the case of adult children and their parents. Parents care deeply about their children, and that deep affection is often reciprocated. The interactions between parents and their adult children provide abundant evidence of this mutual deep concern: parents continue to provide financial and emotional support to their children to whatever extent they are able, while adult children make great sacrifices in caring for aging parents as the latter become both physically and mentally frail.

Second, friends know each other. This does not mean that they know everything about one another and that they have no false beliefs about each other. Rather, friends know each other in ways that no mere stranger does or could, although each of my friends may know me in different ways. For example, one old friend may have shared the trials and tribulations of graduate school with me, and thereby understand how I have grown and developed both personally and professionally over the last 20 years. Another friend might be someone whom I have more recently met, with whom I regularly get together to share complaints about a shared workplace and to gossip about shared acquaintances. We often find ourselves sharing or revealing different aspects of ourselves to different friends. One important aspect of the knowledge that friends have of one another is what we might think of as experiential in character: we know what it is like to share jokes, to be comforted by each other, etc.

Parents and adult children know each other in ways that no one else possibly can. Parents have watched their children grow and develop over the entire course of their lifetime, while children have known their parents as guardians, protectors, and confidantes. Of course, children don't know their parents in the way that they know, for example, spouses or friends made during college or at work. But, similarly, they do not know the latter in the way that they know their parents. As I said above, we know different friends in different ways and to differing degrees.

Third, friends like and want to spend time with each other. It is our friends with whom we want to go to movies, take vacations, have dinner, spend the holidays, etc. Of course, how much time we want to spend with a friend and how we want to spend that time varies. There are people about whom we care deeply, and yet we are content to see them every few years or to keep in touch only via e-mail or Facebook. Other friends are such that we need to see them much more frequently in order to sort through life events. Some friends are wonderful people with whom to share good times, while others are the ones we seek out when we need comfort. The important point is that we want to be with different friends in different ways and in differing amounts.

Adult children and parents may not want to engage with each other in the activities in which they engage with friends who are their own age, but they want to see each other to, for example, share holiday traditions, participate in family celebrations, and to support each other through difficult times such as illness. For some adult children, any protracted time spent with parents can be difficult, as it is easy for both children and parents to slip back into old dynamics: parents will persist in admonishing or providing unwanted advice, while adult children become petulant and immature. But we have limits with all of our friends, even or maybe particularly with those with whom we choose to spend our lives, such as spouses.

Keeping in mind the variety of friendships that people have is important to assessing the friendship account of filial duties. Some have argued that parents and adult children can never be friends because there will always remain a certain inequality in their relationship.[10] But there are various types of inequality in many of our friendships. Colleagues often become friends, even if one of them began as a senior colleague and mentor to the other. Professors become friends with their graduate students after the dissertation is complete and defended. As long as inequality doesn't prevent mutual concern, knowledge, and desire to be together, it need not undermine friendship. So, just as many, but not necessarily all of us, have duties of gratitude to our parents, similarly we have duties of friendship to our parents.

The special goods account

Simon Keller (2007), who defends the special goods account, admits that it is a deflationary view, saying that "your duties to someone who is not your parent may be just like the duties that you would have to him if he were."[11] He also insists that the parent–child relationship "is a singular kind of relationship giving rise to a singular set of duties, and … it needs to be understood on its own terms" (Keller 2007: 121). In other words, custodial parents have relationships with their children that are unique in important ways, and when one has relevantly similar duties to someone who is not a parent, it is because the relationship looks much like that standardly had between children and their custodial parents.

The singular nature of the parent–child relationship can be understood by examining the special goods that are unique to that relationship (or to any relevantly similar relationship).[12] Keller defines special goods as those "which the parent can receive from no one (or almost no one) but the child, or the child can receive from no one (or almost no one) but the parent" (Keller 2007: 124). Some examples of the special goods that parents often receive from their child result from the fact that parents both watch and shape their children's development from birth to adulthood and beyond: "a sense of continuity and transcendence" and the "joy and wisdom" derived from watching this complete, life-long development.[13]

Keller claims that these facts about special goods ground special obligations or duties: adult children can provide special goods to their parents that no one else can, and they thus have special obligations to provide those goods to their parents. One worry about this view is that it limits our duties to our parents to the provision of special goods, and so it seems that I would be justified in not aiding my mother if there are others who could also help her. A more fundamental challenge for the special goods account of filial duties, as Keller himself admits (Keller 2007: 274), is to defend the claim that the mutual provision of special goods grounds special obligations. Why not suppose that we have duties to provide special goods, like any other goods, whenever we are positioned to do so? It just happens that I am the only one positioned to provide these goods to my parents. I am also the only person who can provide you with a copy of this article signed by its author, but that fact does not seem to ground a special obligation on my part. However, even if the special goods account fails to offer an account of filial duties as special obligations, it is nonetheless worth seeing how it applies to a problematic case.

"What do we know about our parents?"

The film *Music Box* presents a case in which a daughter faces horrific revelations about her beloved father. Ann Talbot is the daughter of Hungarian immigrant parents. Her mother died when she was young, and she and her brother were raised by their father, Michael. Michael had told them that he was a farmer in Hungary, before he and their mother came to the US. It is clear that Ann and Michael have a very close, very loving relationship.

Then Michael is charged with lying on his application for US citizenship. The Department of Justice is asserting that Michael Laszlo was a member of a special police squad in Hungary that engaged in war crimes, and they are seeking to revoke his citizenship and then meet the Hungarian government's demand for extradition. Michael insists that he is not the man that they are looking for, although he admits to Ann that he was a policeman, but only a clerk who never harmed anyone.

Ann immediately agrees to represent Michael as his lawyer. She has no doubt that her father is innocent, saying "I'm his daughter. I know him better than anyone." But she is wrong – her father performed terribly sadistic acts during 1944 and 1945, and Ann gets proof of this in the form of photographs. When she confronts Michael, he refuses to admit that he is guilty. Ann tells her father that she never wants to see him again, that he is dead to her. After her confrontation with her father, she sends the photographic proof of his crimes to the Justice Department prosecutor in charge of her father's case.

How should we judge Ann's obligations in this case? Near the beginning of the film, Ann's brother says of Michael that he "busted his guts thirty years in that mill. And he did that all for us." Michael clearly put forth great effort in raising his children as a widowed father with a full-time job in a steel mill. Ann went on to become a very successful lawyer. So it seems that a gratitude account of filial duties would tell us that Ann owes her father a debt of gratitude. While he was certainly morally obligated to raise his children well, he did so under less than optimal conditions, giving Ann what she needed to be a strong, confident professional woman and an excellent mother to her own young son. It does not seem that the fact that her father has a far worse moral character than she believed changes the facts about what he did for her as her parent.

The friendship account comes to a somewhat different conclusion. Before the revelations, we would certainly describe Ann and her father as friends. We see them spending time together and generally being involved in each other's life. Ann and Michael care deeply about each other, and we have reason to think that that concern is not merely instrumental. Further, Ann claims special knowledge about her father, saying "He is not a monster. I'm his daughter. I know him better than anyone," and "I know him. He raised me."

But, of course, it turns out that Ann does not know some very important facts about Michael's past, which are revelatory of his vicious moral character. At the end of the film, she makes it clear to him, particularly in light of his unwillingness to tell the truth, that whatever was true of their relationship in the past, she cannot be friends with him anymore. She cannot even bear to look at him, so it is quite clear that she does not want to spend time and share activities with him: she does not want him to be part of her life anymore.

However, even if Ann and her father cease to be friends, she may still have duties of friendship to him if they were friends prior to the revelations. Here it seems that everything depends on whether we can say that Ann genuinely cared about her father. At one point, her ex-husband says to her, "What if he did it? You'd still love him. He'd still be your dad. Blood's thicker than spilled blood." But can Ann love or care about a man about whom she has mistaken beliefs with respect to important aspects of his character and personality? I think that it is possible, if the features of her father in virtue of which she loved him and that he actually had would have been sufficient for her to love him even if he was a sadistic war criminal. In Ann's case, no fact can make up for the heinous acts that he performed and the lies that he has told. If she cannot be said to have ever loved him, then Ann and her father never were friends, and Ann never had special filial duties to her father according to the friendship account.

The special goods account is much closer to the friendship account than to the gratitude account in what it says about this case. According to the special goods account, we have special filial duties to our parents because they have provided us with special goods and we are capable of giving them special goods that nobody else can. But the mutual provision of special goods depends on the character of the relationship not undergoing certain kinds of dramatic changes. Ann might no longer be able to trust her father to give her a wider account of her life because she no longer trusts him or his judgment. Perhaps more importantly, her emotional repugnance at his past and at his lies about his past will impair her ability to provide him with special goods. If he knows how she views him, then his participation in her life will be significantly diminished and degraded. He can no longer take the same joy at watching her growth and development when he knows that she views him with contempt. The special goods account yields the result that filial duties cease to exist if dramatic shifts in the parent–child relationship render the reciprocal provision of special goods extremely difficult or even impossible.

Although it presents a highly unusual case, *Music Box* highlights some of the most unique and most problematic aspects of the parent–child relationship. Our parents provide us with the most basic goods of life at a time when we are unable to provide them for ourselves. So we must accept the benefits provided by our parents, even if our parents prove to be the kinds of people to whom, later in our lives, we would refuse to become indebted. The vulnerability and dependence of children makes it the case that, if the gratitude account is correct, we all come to have duties to our custodial parents before we can even really understand who our parents are, and our adult attitudes and values are largely irrelevant.

The friendship account puts us more in control of whether we come to have duties to our parents, because the development of friendship between adult children and their parents requires some degree of choice: we must choose to interact in caring ways, we must be able to respond with the right sort of concern for the other person, and we must have a certain knowledge of the other. Interactions in childhood will not be sufficient, then, to generate filial duties. The adult Ann, for example, was a person with values and judgments of her own, and she was capable of understanding what her father did and of abhorring it. The revelations of her father's war crimes could then factor into her judgments about whether to sustain a friendship with him and even her judgments about whether she ever had the requisite attitudes to him for them to have been friends in the past.

The special goods account falls somewhere between these two accounts, but, like the friendship account, it allows that the character and values of the adult child may undermine the grounds of filial duties, in so far as revelations about a parent could threaten our ability to provide special goods. Interactions between children as children and their parents may be necessary for special goods but are certainly not sufficient, particularly if the adult child comes to view her parent as morally reprehensible.

Of course, in assessing what we ought to do for our parents, we need to always keep in mind that, whatever the grounds or strength of our filial duties, they are not the only duties that we have. Ann, for example, had the duties of a parent to her son, and not condemning her father may have been a violation of her duty to shape her son's moral character. It is certainly not the case that nothing can come before family – blood must be weighed against spilled blood, and which wins will vary between situations.

Conclusion

Most people assume that adult children have special obligations to their parents. While it does not seem plausible to suppose that we have such obligations to our parents *merely in virtue of their being our parents*, it nonetheless does seem plausible to suppose that many of us often have some such obligations. This raises questions as to what duties these might be – obvious candidates are duties of gratitude, duties of friendship, and duties to provide special goods – and the circumstances in which they apply. There are good reasons to suppose that in cases where biological or custodial parents make genuine efforts to raise their children well, that those children will have duties of each of those types to their parents. However, it will also be the case that most people who do what custodial parents ought to do, i.e. who nurture and care for a child, will be owed the same duties by the adult child. Which duties and how strong they are will always depend on the nuances and details of the particular parent–child relationship in question. Thus, there is a strong case for concluding that not all adult children will have special obligations to their parents, and even in cases where they do have such obligations, those obligations can vary in strength and content. Adult children must reflect on the nature of their unique relationships to their parents in order to discern what they owe the latter and how to weigh those obligations against their other moral requirements.

Notes

1 For more on my definition of "special obligation," see Jeske (2014).
2 For more on the nature of being a parent, see Baynes and Kolers (2003) and Hill (1991).
3 Exceptions are Belliotti (1986), Hoff Sommers (1986), and Hardimon (1994). For criticism of these views, see Jeske (1998).
4 See Schinkel (2012).
5 I do not intend to fully canvass all of the conditions that would need to be incorporated into any adequate account of when a debt of gratitude is owed, but only some that seem plausible and are relevant to asking whether and when children have a duty of gratitude to their parents.
6 Some ways of becoming a parent are more onerous, involving contending with costly and time-consuming fertility treatments or with the adoption system. If biological gifting could provide grounds for a duty of gratitude, children gotten by other than standard biological means would seem to owe stronger duties to their parents.
7 I have been proceeding under the assumption that a parent benefits a child in giving birth to the latter. Given that, even with this assumption, biological gifting cannot seem to ground duties of gratitude, I have not questioned that assumption. For challenges to this assumption, see Gardner (2016) and Benatar (2006).
8 For the first statement of the friendship account, see English (1979).
9 My approach here diverges sharply from that famously taken by Aristotle (1985), whose account of friendship takes the virtuous character of the parties involved as essential. See Jeske (2008) for more on the approach taken in this section.
10 See Kupfer (1990).
11 Would Keller's view be non-deflationary if (i) certain special goods were only realizable between children and those who act as their custodians, i.e. those who raise them, and (ii) parents were identified with all and only those who raise children? At the most general level, the answer remains "no": we have duties to provide special goods to many people (friends, spouses, lovers, etc.), and so our filial duties remain only one instance of a more general type. However, it will be true that we will have duties to provide certain special goods to all and only those who are our parents. Thus, with respect to the duty to provide the special goods of the parent–child relationship, Keller's account would be non-deflationary.
12 Brighouse and Swift (2009) base their account of the justification of parental partiality toward children on an appeal to the relationship goods inherent in the parent–child relationship (11–12).
13 Children also receive special goods from their parents, but, because we are here concerned with filial duties, not parental duties, I will not discuss these parent-to-child special goods.

References

Aristotle. 1985. *Nicomachean Ethics*, trans. T Irwin. Indianapolis, IN: Hackett.
Baynes, T., and Kolers, A. 2003. "Toward a Pluralist Account of Parenthood," *Bioethics* 17: 221–242.
Belliotti, R. A. 1986. "Honor Thy Father and Thy Mother and to Thine Own Self Be True," *The Southern Journal of Philosophy* 24: 149–162.

Benatar, D. 2006. *Better Never to Have Been Born: The Harm of Coming into Existence*. New York, NY: Oxford University Press.
Brighouse, H., and Swift, A. 2009. "Legitimate Parental Partiality," *Philosophy and Public Affairs* 37: 43–80.
English, J. 1979. "What Do Grown Children Owe Their Parents?," in O. O'Neill and W Ruddick (eds.), *Having Children*. Oxford: Oxford University Press, pp. 351–356.
Gardner, M. 2016. "Beneficence and Procreation," *Philosophical Studies* 173: 321–336.
Hardimon, M. 1994. "Role Obligations," *The Journal of Philosophy* 91: 333–363.
Hill, J. L. 1991. "What Does It Mean to Be a 'Parent'? The Claims of Biology as the Basis for Parental Rights," *New York University Law Review* 66: 353–420.
Hoff Sommers, C. 1986. "Filial Morality," *The Journal of Philosophy* 83: 439–456.
Jeske, D. 1998. "Families, Friends, and Special Obligations," *Canadian Journal of Philosophy* 28: 527–556.
Jeske, D. 2008. *Rationality and Moral Theory: How Intimacy Generates Reasons*. New York, NY: Routledge.
Jeske, D. 2014. "Special Obligations," *Stanford Encyclopedia of Philosophy*. Retrieved from http://plato.stanford.edu/entries/special-obligations/ (last accessed 20 January 2016).
Keller, S. 2007. *The Limits of Loyalty*. Cambridge: Cambridge University Press.
Kupfer, J. 1990. "Can Parents and Children Be Friends?," *American Philosophical Quarterly* 27: 15–26.
Nozick, R. 1974. *Anarchy, State, and Utopia*. New York, NY: Basic Books.
Schinkel, A. 2012. "Filial Obligations: A Contextual, Pluralist Model," *Journal of Ethics* 16: 395–420.

PART IV

Children in society

22
CHILDHOOD AND RACE

Albert Atkin

Introduction

Amongst the many social factors that impact upon children, race is arguably one of the largest. Race is an ever-present social category that governs many elements of a child's interaction with others, and especially for racial minority children it exerts a deep influence on their understanding of themselves. In this chapter, we shall begin by examining what the concept of race really amounts to, emphasizing its status as a socially constructed concept, before examining in the following section how children first come to recognize the existence of race, and to understand their own racial identity. We will then look at two important areas that illustrate the profound impact that the social presence of race and the child's developing understanding of racial identity have upon the social conditions of many children. First, we will examine how race and childhood intersect in matters of educational opportunity and achievement, before moving on to examine the issue of transracial adoption in the final section. One final point is also worth making here, at the outset – although there is a complex interplay between race, lower socio-economic status, and its impact upon children of racialized groups, we shall not address such connections in this paper. There are two reasons for this: first, the interplay between race and poverty is complex and needs separate treatment, not least because the prejudices that create conditions of poverty for racial minorities are the same prejudices that generate many of the negative outcomes faced by racial minorities. Poor social outcomes for racial minorities aren't simply explained away by poverty when the conditions that create that poverty are themselves a consequence of deep racial prejudice. Second, much contemporary social and political research on race and childhood recognizes that even if we do treat poverty as though it were an easily separable term of analysis from race, it still does not explain the many differences in outcome that accrue to children of difference races (for a good recent example, see Quinn 2015).

The ontology of race

Understanding the ontology of race helps us to understand the interaction between childhood and race. In particular, it is helpful to see that in scientific terms race is a myth, and insofar as the concept of race has any reality at all, it is constructed from and constituted by our social and political practices. In short, race is not biological; it is social and political.

The biological emptiness of race is best illustrated by noting that our ordinary "folk" concept of race is not reducible to any viable nearby concept in the biological sciences. Our ordinary talk and practice with racial concepts seems to suggest that races are demarcated as groups of people with particular bodily markers, such as shared skin color, that are inherited from parents, and which are ultimately tied to ancestral origins – in particular, geographic regions. For example, we describe a race of people as "black" because they ordinarily exhibit such physical characteristics as dark skin, broad noses, coarse hair, etc., which are taken to be inherited from their parents, and assumed to be manifest in virtue of a recent ancestral origin in Africa. Such considerations are often taken to give us five racial groups – black, white, Amerindian, Asian, and Oceanic/Melanesian – although we might be inclined to identify one or two more distinct racial groups amongst this. However, this "folk" division of human populations into races is simply not underpinned by any corresponding scientific concept.

Consider, for example, the notion of sub-species; arguably the best scientific candidate for explaining races. In so far as the biological sciences treat the concept of sub-species as a legitimate category, the standard threshold for dividing two populations of the same species into different sub-special groups is that at least 25% of the genetic difference between two members of this larger species-group be due to their membership of different population sub-groups. However, any two human beings are 99.8% genetically similar and of the 0.2% genetic difference that exists between them, only 4–7% is due to their membership of different population sub-groups – significantly short of the threshold for sub-special difference. Whatever human races may purport to be, they simply cannot be sub-species. Indeed, from the point of view of scientists, there is no viable biological category that they could be (see Atkin 2017).

Despite its biological emptiness, race is still real in a very crucial sense. The social outcomes and lived experiences for individuals can vary quite starkly depending on their race. For example, Indigenous Australian children are three times more likely to die before the age of five than their white counterparts, and the biological emptiness of race does nothing to defang such stark racial differences as these. Which raises an important question: if the division of humans into racial groups is not supported by scientific evidence, what is it that makes race real? The short answer is that races and racial categories are socially constructed.

Describing race as socially constructed is simply to make the claim that our social practices are constitutive or, in some sense, reality-conferring for that concept: it is we who make race real. Socially constructed concepts are common, and despite debate about how far social facts confer reality upon a concept, there are straightforward examples. Consider, for instance, *money*. Money is not a natural feature of the world and depends upon the social practice of representing economic value and managing the exchange of this value for goods and services. Of course, the physical tokens we use to denote monetary value have physical properties, but none of these things are crucial to the concept – we might choose to use cowry shells instead of metal coins and polymer notes, for instance. Race is similar in so far as it is not a natural feature of the world even if we make use of certain natural features in its construction – we often pin race to such bodily markers as skin color, which we can explain in naturalistic terms, but importantly, we need not pin racial concepts to those particular bodily markers. Instead, what matters are the series of practices and behaviors that designate races, and which we use and abide by in many of our social endeavors. Reliance on social facts does not make race any less real, and the impact of race is clearly felt and certainly measurable. Indeed, the interaction of race and childhood is one area of the social world where the impact of race is most keenly felt and frequently measured.

Children's understanding of race

Children, like anyone else, are assigned racial identities and so develop an understanding of the racial contexts in which they are raised. The importance of this interaction emerges in two different aspects of the child's understanding of race. First, how do children develop an understanding that race exists? This is simply to examine how the social and psychological developmental of racial concepts in childhood leads children to understand their social world. And second, how do children come to understand the significance of their own racial identities? This question tends to raise issues about how children come to understand and recognize racial prejudice. We shall examine these two questions separately.

Children's conception of race

A common belief is that children lack the concept of race, and only become attuned to its existence later in childhood when adults begin to impose the social construction of racial difference upon them. Evidence from developmental psychology, however, suggests that children develop a concept of race startlingly early. By analyzing the time spent looking at pictures of adult faces, researchers found that children from three months old show a preference for faces of their own race (Kelly et al. 2005). This race-aware behavior in infants ordinarily develops rapidly, and by ages three and beyond, most children have an increasingly sophisticated understanding of racial concepts.

Young children, regardless of their own race, are able to identify themselves in racial terms. For instance, a landmark study using black and white dolls with black children aged three to seven (Clark and Clark 1947), showed the majority had the ability to self-identify with the dolls by racial category. Later studies on white children of the same age showed parallel results (Goodman 1952). Despite these similarities though, there were differences between the ratios of black and white children identifying with dolls of their own race: around two-thirds of the black children identified themselves with dolls that matched their own race compared to around 95% of the white children. Indeed, black three-year-olds were much more likely to identify with the white doll, and only tended to show high accuracy rates when they reached seven years old.

Overall then, race awareness develops in early infancy, and by ages three to five children show a clear understanding of racial categories. Indeed, evidence suggests that those children are also beginning to use their understanding of race to explain differences in the behaviors of others (Aboud 1988). In short, children understand that their social world contains racial categories from much earlier than many people suspect. Whilst there is some speculation about the role that social exposure plays in the acquisition of race concepts, there are related issues of how parents might best navigate the topic of race with their children. Recent research suggests that white parents are especially reluctant to address questions of race with their preschool children (Pahlke, Bigler, and Suizzo 2012) and that attempts to preserve "racial innocence" are misguided – pre-school children not only display racial attitudes, but parental attitudes have little bearing on the racial attitudes of their child. Indeed, if the developmental literature is correct about the ages at which children become aware of race and begin to express racial preferences, the commonly expressed hope of preventing racial problems by "color-blind" parenting is naive and largely ineffectual.

Race, prejudice, and identity

As children develop an awareness of race they become increasingly aware of how that leads to differential treatment. It is clear that people of different races experience differential treatment, and, in particular, that minority racial groups are often treated poorly. Moreover, children from racial minorities are not exempted from poor treatment or negative perceptions in virtue of being children. We know, for instance, that the time taken to administer pain relief to black children reporting to emergency departments is greater than for their white counterparts; it seems that black children are perceived to be less susceptible to pain (Zempsky, Corsey, and Mckay 2011). Similarly, black children from as young as five are perceived to be more like adults than their white counterparts, and are more likely to receive inappropriate treatment from adults in authority as a result (Goff et al. 2014). The usual assumptions of childhood innocence, or need for adult protection, fall way much more readily for black children and lead to harsher treatment in schools, in health care, in law enforcement, and even contributes to earlier sexualized treatment. Unsurprisingly, young children show awareness of racial discrimination, and by the age of ten are aware that racial stereotypes often inform negative racial interactions (McKown and Weinstein 2003). Further research suggests that the more children become aware of racial stereotypes, the more likely they are to view negative interactions as racial discrimination (Brown and Bigler 2005). A white teacher's negative judgment about a black child's behavior, for example, is much more likely to be perceived as discriminatory by those children who are aware that others rely on racial stereotypes to form beliefs.

Children's awareness of race and racial discrimination, then, poses interesting questions about how race impacts upon the child's developing sense of identity. As we noted, black and white doll studies suggest that by school-age children do use racial categories to self-identify (Clark and Clark 1947). However, a corresponding awareness of discrimination can be seen as having negative impacts upon black children and their sense of identity. For example, when asked to explain their preference for particular dolls, those black children who expressed a preference for white dolls gave such reasons for not selecting the black doll as "because it looks like a negro" and "it looks bad all over," and such reasons for selecting the white doll as, "because its white, its pretty" (Clark 1963). These findings were generally taken to mean that young black children would prefer to be white and had internalized much of the racism prevalent in wider society. Interestingly though, there is now clear evidence that as children enter adolescence, this awareness of discrimination may have no real impact on self-esteem (Cross 1991), and that strong racial identity may boost self-esteem in the face of racial discrimination (Buckley and Carter 2005). In fact, awareness of racial stereotypes and discrimination may be a crucial tool for black children in learning to cope with racial inequalities and racist treatment – adolescents who do not anticipate racial discrimination tend to have higher rates of depression and stress, and respond more frequently with acts of violence when they do encounter racism (Caldwell et al. 2004).

The picture that emerges, then, is that race forms an early and important part of a child's sense of identity, but especially significant for children from racialized minorities is the awareness that society expresses a preference for, and privileges, whiteness. Awareness of discrimination plays an important part in helping children of race to navigate a world that is often hostile to them as a result of their racial identity.

Race and education

One of the main arenas where race and childhood interact is in education, and it is here that many of the most troubling aspects of racism and racial inequality emerge for children of race. The focus in this section will be what is commonly called "the racial achievement gap" – that is, the fact that in mainstream education white children outperform their minority counterparts by significant margins in many standardized tests. In the USA, for instance, where most studies of the racial achievement gap are focused, long-term trends, as measured by the National Assessment of Educational Progress (NAEP), show that the average black student will score lower on standardized tests than 75% of his or her white counterparts (Lee 2002). Similarly, Gypsy Roma and Traveler (GRT) children in the UK have significantly lower rates of educational attainment and in many cases are unlikely to complete more than two or three years of post-primary education (Derrington 2007).

The educational achievement gap has long been a matter of interest and concern, and arguments about its underlying cause are significant because they often influence policy proposals for closing the gap. Arguments that racial achievement gaps are due to genetic differences in intelligence between races (Rushton and Jensen 2005) are often used to suggest that closing the gap through increased investment in educational resources for minority children is restricted by the natural limitations on the intelligence of those racial groups. In short, if the gap is due to genetics, funding social programs to close that gap is wasted money. Even setting aside any discussion of the problems with studies that suggest intelligence is genetic (Nisbett et al. 2012), we've already seen from our brief overview of the ontology of race that no biological explanations of race will be forthcoming. If we then factor in the difficulty of simply equating IQ and general intelligence to educational attainment, we can then see that getting genetics, race, intelligence, and educational attainment to lineup for an orderly biological explanation is a hopeless endeavor. Importantly though, such crass biological fatalism simply cannot be used to influence educational policy.

Another putative explanation for the achievement gap is that there is an oppositional culture to education amongst racialized groups. A common explanation for why GRT children have poor educational outcomes in the UK, for instance, is that GRT culture sees no value in mainstream education (O'Hanlon and Holmes 2004). Problematically, though, this explanation tends to lead to policy that intervenes directly in the culture of the groups themselves, or to claims that it is incumbent upon minority groups to solve the problems facing their children for themselves. Such explanations are particularly unsatisfactory in light of clear evidence that the attitude of minority racial groups towards education is often favorable and positive rather than negative (Reynolds, McCartan, and Knipe 2003). Just as with attempts to explain the gap through genetics, the explanation in terms of oppositional culture is inaccurate and unhelpful – there is little evidence that minority groups do not place a value on education.

Better explanations of the achievement gap come from examining the complex social and structural factors that influence the educational performance of children from racial minorities. There are many such factors, but the following three illustrate how social conditions influence the academic performance of minority children in schools.

First, as already noted, the more that children become aware that others are influenced by racial stereotypes, the more likely they are to see differential treatment as the result of racial discrimination. Studies show that teachers tend to have different responses to racialized children: they often have lower expectations of black students compared to white students of similar ability (McKown and Weinstein 2008). And as we have already noted, adults are likely to respond to black children's behavior as though it were more adult and less "innocent" (Goff et al. 2014). Even setting aside the racism inherent in such differential treatment, it is unsurprising that racialized children respond negatively to institutional environments which they are readily able to interpret as discriminatory, and which feel unwelcoming or even openly hostile to their educational needs.

Second, the coping strategies required of racialized children remaining within education often challenge their racial identities. A common experience of minority children, for example, is that their race is incompatible with educational attainment. A perceived schism between the "whiteness" of educational attainment and black American identity leads many young black boys to reject education in order to preserve racial identity and authenticity (Fordham and Ogbu 1986). Chris Derrington (2007) notes a similar pattern amongst GRT children in British secondary schools, along with the additional coping strategy of concealing racial identity. The strategy of concealment in order to reconcile educational attainment with racial identity is, as Derrington notes, a "maladaptive coping strategy as it roots are in denial and repression, which may have negative psychological consequences" (Derrington 2007: 365). For many children, then, their racial identity has been constructed in such a way that any interface with mainstream education must lead to either an abandonment of racial identity, a rejection of education, or a strategy of concealment and lying. Importantly, we have to be clear that although these coping strategies suggest the rejection of education, they are not evidence of an oppositional culture. Children and families who are prepared to hide or even abandon their racial identities in order to retain access to the same education that white children have aren't displaying an oppositional culture. Moreover, children and families who abandon education to preserve their racial identities aren't rejecting the value of education so much as responding to the message that they are not welcome in the educational space. The pressures and conflicts that come from reconciling racial identity with the demands of educations are such that few white children will ever face them during their years in school.

Third, and finally, minority children must perform in an educational setting that couples constant assessment and benchmarking of attainment with a broader set of social signals that indicate to racialized children that their educational abilities are diminished by their racial identity. Now-famous research on stereotype threat by Steele and Aronson (1995) shows that when individuals are made aware of stereotypes about some aspect of their group identity (gender, race, or age for instance) they are then more likely to perform on tests in accord with those stereotypes. For example, black Americans outperform white Americans on a golf task when the task is framed as a test of "natural sporting ability," but white Americans outperform their black counterparts when that same test is framed as a test of "sporting intelligence." Interestingly, children are also susceptible to stereotype threat, especially as they become more aware of stereotypical beliefs about their group identities (McKown and Weinstein 2003). Problematically, then, in an environment where minority children are subject to lower teacher expectations, and are sensitive to seeing differential treatment as discrimination, stereotype threat looms large. Children from minority groups are typically in an educational environment that contains all the conditions needed for them to conform to stereotype, fail, and compound the racial gap in educational attainment.

Having noted the role that social factors play in the racial achievement gap, it is worth concluding this section with some observation on how these factors might be ameliorated. First, it is important for educators to talk openly about race. Just as with parenting, there is a common assumption that young children are unaware of race, and that color-blind teaching represents best practice. We know, however, that teaching children about race in early childhood is a useful tool for teaching all children to recognize and challenge racial inequality (Husband 2012). Second, it is important that we pay close attention to the experience and quality of teachers that engage with minority children. Research by Robert Dreeben (1987) finds that given equally challenging and well-supported instruction, black children attain comparable reading levels to white children. However, in his study of over 300 Chicago first-grade students, he found that black students were generally less well supported and were taught by more inexperienced teachers. Third and finally, we must look at the impact of testing in schools itself. As we have noted, minority children are susceptible to stereotype threat, and the greatest impact of this will play out through testing and benchmarking. It may be that testing children doesn't merely measure the attainment gap, but helps to create and preserve it (Knoester and Au 2017). If this is the case, then testing is itself part of the problem for children from racial minorities.

Transracial adoption

An area where race and childhood intersect in challenging ways is in matters of transracial adoption – that is, where children are adopted by parents of a different race (see also ch. 19). Most ethical and legal questions about transracial adoption are raised in the American context where the adoption of black children into white families has been a common source of controversy. Similar concerns have been raised about the adoption of Asian, Latinx, and Native American children into white families, although most commentary concerns black child/white parent cases. In what follows we shall use the black child/white parent context in the USA as our primary source for discussion, but many of the concerns raised apply to other transracial adoptions, and in other contexts. So, what are the chief concerns about transracial adoption?

Arguably, transracial adoption highlights a tension in our thoughts about the kind of society we want our children to be raised in, and the practical realities they must deal with in terms of their racial identities. On the one hand, there exists both a common assumption that children are naive to the realities of race, and a common aspiration that we raise children in a color-blind manner. This suggests that when placing a child with adopted parents, racial matching should be a marginal consideration at most and shouldn't trump other benefits that come from being part of family. On the other hand, our concern for the future well-being of adopted children means that we must acknowledge the benefit of learning about one's racial identity from those with whom we share such identities – we may aspire to safeguard the racial innocence of children, but we know that they do not remain children forever, and part of their flourishing will be a well-supported exploration of their racial identity. This suggests that when placing a child with adopted parents, race ought to be a leading factor in considering what the child has to benefit from adoption. This simple tension leads to arguments both for and against transracial adoption.

Focusing on the needs of the child, the main argument against transracial adoption concerns how we are to secure the proper conditions for supporting the child's developing sense of racial identity. In general terms, the argument is that racial identity is a major component in a child's sense of self, but that this cannot be developed without the support of a larger same-race communal group – for instance, our family. An Asian child is best placed to understand their Asian racial identity when raised in an Asian family, just as a black child needs a black family, and so on. Furthermore, children of minority races need to understand how to respond to racial prejudice and, again, are best placed to do this if they understand where it fits into their social identity as a raced individual (Caldwell et al. 2004). They are best taught this aspect of racial identity by individuals who share their racial identity. To deny a black child this kind of support by failing to consider race during adoption is, arguably, to impose a harm upon that child.

In contrast to this, arguments in favor of transracial adoption tend to contrast the practical constraints of obtaining race-matched adoptions with the more pressing need to secure the welfare of the child in a safe family environment. Racialized children in adoption systems, for instance, tend to remain in institutional care far longer than white children. Some reports suggest that in the American adoption system, as many as half of all children in foster care and institutional homes are black (Fogg-Davis 2002: 398). This is due, in part, to the fact that the majority of parents looking to adopt are white, and the practicalities of placing black children in black families are too restrictive. Even if we accept that race-matched adoption is preferable for supporting a child's developing racial identity, it is hard to argue against claims that the benefit of a secure family setting is to be preferred over the potential damage of long-term institutional care. If we compare the benefit to a child of transracial adoption over no adoption at all, with the benefits a child gains from understanding their racial identity in a same-race family context rather than a mixed-race context, then insisting on race-matched adoptions for minority children looks detrimental.

A further element to the arguments for transracial adoption comes from studies that seem to suggest that transracial adoptions are beneficial for adopted children. Between 1972 and 1982 Rita Simon and Howard Alstein tracked the outcomes for over 200 transracial adoptions (Simon and Alstein 1987) and suggested that the children in their study bonded well with their adopted parents, and in the long term had no problems identifying positively with their black racial identities. Black children adopted into white families also appear to score higher on IQ tests than black children in race-matched adoptions (Moore 1986), and in some studies there seems to be no educational achievement gap for black transracially adopted children (Raleigh and Kao 2013). This might, at first pass, seem to suggest that there is much less need to be concerned about the impact on the child's developing racial identity as many have assumed. However, there are reasons to approach research that suggests unequivocal support for transracial adoption with caution. Here we will mention just two.

First, we need to be clear that in many cases, the markers by which an adoption is deemed to be successful are set using "whiteness" as a normative ideal (Park and Greene 2000). For instance, good educational outcomes in transracial adoption tend to be judged by IQ results, and the outcome of test scores tend to be benchmarked by equivalence with white counterparts – is the transracially adopted child more like a white child with its biological family, or like a black child with its biological family? Similarly, research that suggests black transracial adoptees have a well-adjusted attitude to their own racial identity tend to rely on teacher and parent assessment, and simple "yes/no" or tick-box responses to questions about comfort with one's racial category (Simon and Alstein 1987: 68). In many ways, this mirrors the common treatment of whiteness as value-neutral – whiteness is seen less as a race and more of a neutral or "normal" standpoint from which to judge racialized others. In terms of transracial adoption, the worry is that many of these measures of apparent success and adjustment are white and assimilationist.

A second related concern is that the markers of whiteness that are used to benchmark successful adoptions are the same markers used to identify acceptable adoptive parents. It is true of the current system in the US that there are far more white parents in the system than there are black parents; however, it also seems that there has been a long history of exclusion of black families from the system by social workers who privilege whiteness when judging the suitability of potential parents (McRoy 1989). So, whilst arguments for transracial adoption look to be supported by social research in the area, it is worth noting that adoption systems and how we judge them privilege white markers of success and suitability. This makes the case for transracial adoption look far less clear-cut that some would have it.

To conclude this section, we will note two important things about the debate over transracial adoption. First, as framed here, the acceptability of transracial adoption is framed by the question of how a child's racial identity and development of self is supported or affected. There are, though, alternative ways to frame this debate. Sally Haslanger (2005) and Hawley Fogg-Davis (2002) both note that exactly how we think racial identity is formed might impact upon how we think transracial adoption supports the child's racial sense of self. Haslanger, for instance, points out that we can view racial identities as "aggregate" in transracial adoptions (a kind of "mixed" identity) – alongside his own white experiences, the white parent of a black child will experience the racial features of his child's life in ways that a white parent of a white child will not. As Haslanger, herself a white parent of adopted black children, notes: "I have, in an important sense, been re-socialized by my kids, and although I do not share their 'blood,' I have 'inherited' some aspects of their race" (Haslanger 2005: 285). This introduction of different racial experiences and, by extension, the aggregating or mixing of racial identities is something that black children in transracial adoptions experience too – a black child with white middle-class parents will, in certain contexts, experience some of the social realities that come from white privilege. This suggests that identity formation and the developmental impact of transracial adoption is a complex matter, and these aggregated racial identities (for both parents and children) are best judged not in terms of older divisive and fixed racial binaries, but in terms of a forward-looking and ameliorative role in, as Haslanger puts it, "disrupting the embodiment of racial hierarchy and the hegemony of current racial categories" (Haslanger 2005: 287). We may not accept Haslanger's view here, but it demonstrates the complexity of racial identity in the case of transracial adoption.

Second, it is important to acknowledge that adoption is itself part of the institutional tools of racial oppression, and that this makes weighing the benefits of adoption for racialized children a difficult matter. To take a simple example, amongst GRT groups in Europe, and Indigenous groups in North America and Australia, adoption has long been a state tool used to confiscate children from their same-race families. For many of these groups, forced adoption alongside forced sterilization has been used to manage the eradication of racial minorities. Similarly, for black Americans, the historical and structural conditions of slavery and white supremacy in America mean that the State has and continues to impose itself upon black families and black parenthood in ways that are destabilizing and demeaning (Pinderhughes 2002). It is unsurprising that many racialized parents and families are either actively excluded, or in the interests of their own safety self-exclude from interaction with a system that has been used to control, demean, and eradicate them. Simple questions about the relative benefits and deficits of transracial adoption for children of racial minorities can, when contrasted against the role that adoption has played in structural oppression, seem misdirected. Put simply, since adoption is one of the many systematic tools used to the de-stabilize the racial family, to devalue broader racial kinship groups, and by extension leads to the disproportionate placing of racialized children into institutional care, it is not enough to reduce arguments about transracial adoption to simple questions about whether black children do better with white parents than they do in care homes.

Conclusion

As we have seen, the social interaction of race and childhood raises important issues. Race may not be a scientifically robust concept, but its social construction means that children learn to recognize its existence very quickly. Indeed, they become adept at recognizing the role race plays in human interactions much earlier on in their childhood than many parents and teachers assume. What is more, understanding their own racial identity is crucial for the child's own developed sense of self. This is especially so for racialized children, who experience racial prejudice and discrimination as a common part of their social lives and need a robust sense of social identity to navigate these conditions. Something else that also seems clear is that, in many respects, we are not sufficiently sensitive to matters of race when it comes to childhood. Race is a social reality, and we need to talk to and teach our children about race and racial prejudice much more purposefully and much more directly. We also need to pay closer attention to how race intersects with the lives of racialized children when we develop policies and social practices that impact upon children. Do our general practices of testing and benchmarking take account of influence that racial inequality has on testing outcomes? Is our teacher training sensitive to the impact of bias and teacher expectations on racialized children? Do our adoption systems show proper awareness of the role that state intervention into the family plays as a longstanding tool of racial oppression? These are all important considerations and need much greater attention in our philosophical reflections on race and childhood.

References

Aboud, F. E. 1988. *Children and Prejudice*. New York, NY: Blackwell.
Atkin, A. 2017. "Race Science and Definition," in N. Zack (ed.), *The Oxford Handbook of Philosophy and Race*. Oxford: Oxford University Press, pp. 139–150.
Brown, C. S., and Bigler, R. S. 2005. "Children's Perceptions of Discrimination: A Developmental Model," *Child Development* 76: 533–553.
Buckley, T., and Carter, R. 2005. "Black Adolescent Girls: Do Gender Role and Racial Identity Impact their Self-esteem?," *Sex Roles* 53(9–10): 647–661.
Caldwell, C. H., Kohn-Wood, L. P., Schmeelk-Cone, K. H., Chavous, T. M., and Zimmerman, M. A. 2004. "Racial Discrimination and Racial Identity as Risk Factors for Violent Behaviors in African American Young Adults," *American Journal of Community Psychology* 33(1/2): 91–105.
Clark, K. B. 1963. *Prejudice and Your Child*, 2nd edn. Boston, MA: Beacon Press.
Clark, K. B., and Clark, M. P. 1947. "Racial Identification and Preference in Negro Children," in H. Proshansky and B. Seidenberg (eds.), *Basic Studies in Social Psychology*. New York, NY: Holt Rinehart and Winston, pp. 308–317.
Cross, W. E. 1991. *Shades of Black: Diversity in African American Identity*. Philadelphia, PA: Temple University Press.
Derrington, C. 2007. "Fight, Flight and Playing White: An Examination of Coping Strategies Adopted by Gypsy Traveller Adolescents in English Secondary Schools," *International Journal of Education Research* 46(6): 357–367.
Dreeben, Robert. 1987. "Closing the Divide: What Teachers and Administrators Can Do to Help Black Students Reach Their Reading Potential," *American Educator: The Professional Journal of the American Federation of Teachers* 11(4): 28–35.
Fogg-Davis, H. G. 2002. *The Ethics of Transracial Adoption*. Ithaca, NY: Cornell University Press.
Fordham, S., and Ogbu, J. U. 1986. "Black Students' School Success: Coping with the 'Burden of Acting White'," *Urban Review* 18(3): 176–206.
Goff, P. A., Jackson, M. C., Di Leone, B. A. L., Culotta, C. M., and DiTomasso, N. A. 2014. "The Essence of Innocence: Consequences of Dehumanizing Black Children," *Journal of Personality and Social Psychology* 106(4): 526–545.
Goodman, M. E. 1952. *Race Awareness in Young Children*. New York, NY: Collier Macmillan.
Haslanger, S. 2005. "You Mixed? Racial Identity without Racial Biology," in S. Haslanger and C. Witt (eds.), *Adoption Matters: Philosophical And Feminist Essays*. Ithaca, NY: Cornell University Press, pp. 265–289.
Husband, T. 2012. "'I Don't See Color': Challenging Assumptions about Discussing Race with Young Children," *Early Childhood Education Journal* 39(6): 365–371.
Kelly, D. J. et al. 2005. "Three-Month Olds, but Not Newborns, Prefer Own-race Faces," *Developmental Science* 8(6): 31–6.
Knoester, M., and Au, W. 2017. "Standardized Testing and School Segregation: Like Tinder for Fire?," *Race, Ethnicity and Education* 20(1): 1–14.
Lee, J. 2002. "Racial and Ethnic Achievement Gap Trends: Reversing the Progress Toward Equity?," *Educational Researcher* 31(1): 3–12.
McKown, C., and Weinstein, R. S. 2003. "The Development and Consequences of Stereotype-Consciousness in Middle Childhood," *Child Development* 74(2): 498–515.
McKown, C., and Weinstein, R. S. 2008. "Teacher Expectations, Classroom Context, and the Achievement Gap," *Journal of School Psychology* 46(3): 235–261.
McRoy, R. 1989. "An Organizational Dilemma: The Case of Transracial Adoptions," *The Journal of Applied Behavioral Science* 25(2): 145–160.
Moore, E. G. J. 1986. "Family Socialization and the IQ Test Performance of Traditionally and Transracially Adopted Black Children," *Developmental Psychology* 22(3): 317–326.
Nisbett, R. E., Aronson, J., Blair, C., Dickens, W., Flynn, J., Halpern, D. F., and Turkheimer, E. 2012. "Intelligence: New Findings and Theoretical Developments," *American Psychologist* 67(2): 130–159.
O'Hanlon, C., and Holmes, P. 2004. *The Education of Gypsy Traveller Children*. Stoke on Trent: Trentham Books.

Pahlke, E. Bigler, R. S., and Suizzo, M.-A. 2012. "Relations Between Colorblind Socialization and Children's Racial Bias: Evidence from European American Mothers and their Preschool Children," *Child Development* 83(4): 1164–1179.

Park, S., and Greene, C. 2000. "Is Transracial Adoption in the Best Interests of Ethnic Minority Children?: Questions Concerning Legal and Scientific Interpretations of a Child's Best Interests," *Adoption Quarterly* 3(4): 5–34.

Pinderhughes, E. 2002. "African American Marriage in the 20th Century," *Family Process*. 41(2): 269–282.

Quinn, D. M. 2015. "Kindergarten Black-White Test Score Gaps: Re-examining the Roles of Socioeconomic Status and School Quality with New Data," *Sociology of Education* 88(2): 120–139.

Raleigh, E., and Kao, G. 2013. "Is there a (Transracial) Adoption Achievement Gap?: A National Longitudinal Analysis of Adopted Children's Educational Performance," *Child and Youth Services Review* 35(1): 142–148.

Reynolds, M., McCartan, D., and Knipe, D. 2003. "Traveller Culture and Lifestyle as Factors Influencing Children's Integration into Mainstream Secondary Schools in West Belfast," *International Journal of Inclusive Education* 7(3): 403–414.

Rushton, J. P., and Jensen, A. R. 2005. "Thirty Years of Research on Race Differences in Cognitive Ability," *Psychology, Public Policy, and Law* 11(2): 235–294.

Simon, R., and Alstein, H. 1987. *Transracial Adoptees and Their Families: A Study of Identity and Commitment*. New York, NY: Praeger.

Steele, C. M., and Aronson, J. 1995. "Stereotype Threat and the Intellectual Test Performance of African Americans," *Journal of Personality and Social Psychology* 69(5): 797–811.

Zempsky, W., Corsey, J., and Mckay, K. 2011. "Pain Scores: Are they Used in Sickle Cell Pain?," *Paediatric Emergency Care* 27(1): 27–28.

23
CHILDHOOD AND DISABILITY

Gideon Calder and Amy Mullin

Introduction

Some children are disabled; all disabled people either are or have been children. Both childhood and disability are areas long neglected in philosophy, or regarded as "niche" concerns, but which have recently attracted fuller attention, and are at least somewhere closer to philosophy's mainstream. We now find fertile debates around the nature, significance and normative implications of each. In applied ethics, disability arises in two main contexts: choices about children yet to be born, and determinations of the status, rights or quality of life of disabled people compared to people more generally. Thus, for example, under the first heading, now come fine-grained bioethical analyses of whether it might be wrong to bring children with this or that disability into the world, or whether or when the identification of an impairment via prenatal screening should be grounds for abortion. Under the latter heading come discussions about whether or how severe disability affects the moral status of a disabled child once born (see ch. 6), how disabilities may relate to the development of personhood and the dynamics of disabled children's development in relation to their parents, to other children and to the responsibilities of relevant professionals.

This chapter leaves aside the first of those contexts. Prenatal choices about potential quality of life are generally concerned with future *people*, rather than with future children per se. Our own focus is on how disability connects specifically with the lived experience of childhood and parenthood. These connections warrant close attention in their own right. Philosophical treatments of childhood tend not to linger on questions of blindness or deafness, limitations to mobility or to cognitive capacity. They will not usually mention these at all. Our focus is on what happens when we place them in the foreground. The chapter takes a series of steps. First, we look at broad definitions of disability. We then consider whether disabled children constitute a distinct group, with features in common, before identifying some key ethical themes with which treatments of disability and childhood will grapple. Next, we address disability as an aspect of parent–child relationships, whether the disabled person in question be child or parent. Finally, we address questions concerning the relations of non-parents to disabled children, in the educational setting. These focal points serve as examples, rather than as building a comprehensive survey of philosophical questions concerning childhood and disability. Yet they help convey the range of those questions, and their intricacy.

Defining disability

Disability has commonly been regarded as a feature of an individual – a lack of physical or mental capacity, whether present from birth or acquired. This "lack" may be assumed to be inherently disadvantageous, in ways which may worsen the longer it is not tackled. Thus, viewed this way, the identification of a disability is a call to manage or compensate for the dysfunction, or, where possible, to repair it through medical intervention. Historically, this conception of disability arrived first, and gained real traction amid the general 19th-century zeal for the (often hierarchical) categorization of human "types", and their segregation via social institutions. At an everyday level, it may inform the assumption of a responsibility to correct for impairments in children when possible – for example, the use of cochlear implants in cases of deafness. An alternative, the social model of disability, increasingly influential since the 1970s, accounts for disability in terms of social forces. Crucial here is the distinction between an *impairment* – a feature of an individual – and *disability*, which is the process by which such individuals are disadvantaged by environmental circumstances, dominant attitudes and other social barriers. On these terms, impairments are not *inherently* disadvantageous: disability is contingent upon circumstances. Disability is thus better understood as a form of oppression – arising not from the individual's body or capacities, but from their exclusion from full participation in society (Cole 2007; Oliver 1990, 1996; UPIAS 1976). Viewed this way, the use of cochlear implants may be regarded as a way of stigmatizing deafness: treating it as an individualized, medical deficit, rather than (for example) seeking to tackle "disabling" attitudes among the non-deaf who know little about the condition, or assume that it is inherently negative.

The contrast between the medical and social models of disability is illuminating, but can also be conceptually frustrating. Both approaches may be depicted as reductive, and to neglect crucial features of the experience of disability. Thus, the assumption that an impairment such as deafness, restricted growth or Down's syndrome is a kind of personal tragedy, an *inherent* disadvantage, residing in the individual, which there may be some moral responsibility to "fix", can be put into question simply by due consideration of the ways in which people with such conditions may regard them as a blessing, a crucial part of their identity or – in any case – as features of their lives which they would prefer not to give up (Scully 2008; Smith 2005; Overall 2013; we return to the deafness example below). Likewise, the notion that disability is (as one geneticist has put it) an "inherently degrading state", such that "seeing the bright side of being handicapped is like praising the virtues of extreme poverty" (Watson 2000: 207), fails to take into account that degradation itself is a relational condition, rather than a biological given. Whether a child's impaired mobility feels degrading to them clearly depends substantially on the quality of day-to-day facilities available (wheelchairs, ramps, lifts), and on wider awareness of what it's like to be her.

Meanwhile, though, depicting disability as entirely socially constructed may seem similarly lopsided as an ontological stance. Some aspects of our social interaction are unavoidably constrained or defined by our biological constitution. That the limitations connected to an impairment necessarily vary according to one's social environment does not mean that social forces are sufficient to explain those limitations. While degradation depends on relations with others, extreme pain does not. Many strong adherents to the political cause of equality for disabled people have pointed out that impairments are complex and multidimensional, rather than simply inert features of a human life which social circumstances then render "problematic" or not. The matrix of factors contributing to anyone's sense of their own well-being is too complex to parse out each factor and attribute it either to social or biological sources. And to claim that some impairments might be better prevented, or their impacts reduced, need not be to denigrate those who have them. It may be to acknowledge that just as an impairment should not be regarded as a personal tragedy, neither should it be defined in terms which have nothing to do with hardship (Morris 1991; French 1993; Shakespeare 2006; Terzi 2004, 2009).

In response to this, some have recommended dropping "models" of disability altogether (e.g. Beaudry 2016). Others have recommended a non-reductive, "interactivist" account of disability, in which it is seen as a complex interplay between physiological, social, economic and cultural factors (e.g. Danermark and Gellerstedt 2004; Shakespeare 2006; Williams 1999; Calder 2011). For such perspectives, addressing the complex ontology of disability will form a crucial role in how normative questions are themselves negotiated. Approaches in political philosophy seeking to bring disability into the apparatus with which questions of social justice are addressed tend, in practice, to rely on a non-reductionist and multi-layered view (Kittay 1999; Nussbaum 2006; Wolff 2009).

Who are disabled children?

Answers to this question may be more or less inclusive. Some start from a characterization of human lives as universally shaped by vulnerability, limitation, physical imperfection and interdependence (see, e.g., Fineman 2008). Thus, for Alasdair MacIntyre, "disability and dependence on others are something that all of us experience at certain times in our lives and this to unpredictable degrees" (MacIntyre 1999: 130). On this basis, some may deem disabled children not to be a separate group at all, but located on (as it were) a continuum with all other children – their impairments more severe, or more permanent, but not fundamentally different in kind from the physiological and cognitive limitations which define the early stages of all human lives (as well as the latter stages of most). This makes disability a collective rather than a specialized concern. At the other end of the scale sit radically separatist understandings of disability, in which, in virtue of their situation and their interests, the disabled constitute a distinct minority group. From this point of view, the inclusive view, however generously intended, may obscure these lines of difference and so reinforce disadvantages which disabled people face.

Both alternatives face versions of a hurdle concerning the relationship between sharedness and difference. For the separatist view, the challenge is to identify what might count as the defining feature(s) which unite all disabled people – whether their impairments are cognitive or physical, and across intersections of gender, class, ethnicity, geographical location and other differentiating categories – and draw a line between their shared situation or experiences, and those of others. What do hearing-impaired, visually impaired, paraplegic and dyslexic childhoods hold in common? What do children with two or more of these impairments share with those with only one? In the absence of any other homogenizing link, it may seem that they are united at most by being atypical – by their minority status – and by their association with disadvantage. The terms "disabled" and "impaired" do not "track a single phenomenological experience" (Wasserman et al. 2016); nor are they subject to a single set of social attitudes or barriers. Meanwhile the maximally inclusive view risks eliminating the category of "disabled children" altogether, replacing it with a non-differentiated version of "childhood" in which no distinguishing features are deemed salient. This seems normatively unsatisfactory. It will overlook the propensity for a disabled childhood to be distinctly disadvantageous – or distinctly valuable – and reinforce the discriminatory tendencies tied up with a lack of recognition of the particular situation of disabled children (Ikäheimo 2009; Calder 2011).

One response to this – and to the ontological complexities raised in the previous section – is to classify disability as a "difference-making" feature of a life, but one which is not necessarily negative, and may itself be experienced in different ways. Elizabeth Barnes has offered such a view. On her view, disability is not necessarily sub-optimal – it does not automatically make a person worse off – even though it is in a looser sense "the sort of thing which makes life harder" (Barnes 2009: 352). Disabled people share non-standard status, but the marker of their difference – their disability – need not by definition have a net negative impact on their quality of life. Whether it does so depends on how the hardships associated with disability weigh against its possible concomitant benefits, and fit into the wider shape of a life. Although not especially developed by Barnes in this direction, this view may be particularly helpful in the case of children. It affords a way of appreciating the particularity of disabled children's circumstances, without presuming in advance that disability is of itself a disadvantage in terms of their overall prospects for flourishing.

Questions of dependency, vulnerability and agency

We have seen that at one level, debates about disability focus on whether it represents a distinct kind of disadvantage. Here, there is a clear mirroring of debates about childhood. Both are often viewed as sub-optimal or incomplete states of being, by comparison with some putatively full, self-sufficient version of human functioning. Childhood might be associated with greater dependency on others, greater vulnerability, or diminished agency (see ch. 7, ch. 10, ch. 27; also Hannan 2018). Yet, alongside these echoes, there are important differences between childhood and disability in these respects. Even if assumed to be a diminished form of being in comparison with adulthood – with children regarded as having less capacity to grant consent, make decisions or direct their own lives – childhood is not customarily regarded as the occasion for *pity*, or assumed hardship. There are two main reasons for this. One is that childhood is regarded as a transitional phase, or series of phases – directed towards the ultimate destination of adulthood. Even if deemed inferior to (rational, independent) adulthood, childhood is not treated as an undesirable state – precisely insofar as it is the necessary vehicle by which adulthood is reached. It has instrumental value, even for those to whom it is merely a ladder to be discarded once climbed. But secondly, there is no "stock" presumption that childhood is indeed inferior. As a stage in the life course, it is as likely to be envied as pitied (see Gheaus 2015). Worse-off children may be regarded as being disadvantaged in comparison to their more privileged peers. But nostalgia for the simplicity or freedoms of childhood is hardly scarce. If these points are true of everyday discourse on the life course, they come through just as strongly in the philosophical literature on childhood.

It might be assumed that where childhood is identified as a stage – compared to adulthood – of particular vulnerability, greater dependence and diminished agency, then disability will necessarily accentuate these features. There are strong reasons to unsettle that assumption. One is that, as we have seen, disability itself covers such a range of features and experiences that there is neither a single sense in which it diminishes a child's life, nor any guarantee that it is not also an enhancer of childhood. Those blind from birth often speak of lacking a sense of absence about their impairment – and often, of having had to *learn*, during childhood, to regard it as an impairment at all (see, e.g., Magee and Milligan 1998). There is well-established phenomenological evidence that the absence of one of the senses deepens and sharpens the work of the others. Another reason is that the assumption of lack of capacity can itself reduce an individual's agency, particularly where there is an inference from a specific disability to the presumption of a wider lack of competence – for example, where dyslexia has been mistaken in school for lack of academic ability, or wheelchair users are presumed to have diminished cognitive capacities. Scully has argued that "the conceptual segregation of disabled people into a category marked specially vulnerable, significantly increases the risk that they will be seen as radically other to normative citizens: more dependent, more of a burden" (Scully 2014: 219). Professional or familial concern for the "vulnerability" of disabled children may render them more passive, less resilient, less likely to develop their own coping mechanisms (Clough 2017). Like degradation, vulnerability and dependency are relational in character, and so will be affected by, and indeed arguably (as the social model will stress) produced by, social dynamics. The presumption that a disabled childhood is diminished in comparison to adulthood, or to other versions of childhood, is much too hasty. Much will vary, from case to case.

Children's disabilities and parental love and care

Precisely because all young children are to an extent dependent and vulnerable, whether or not they have disabilities, they need care, ideally care delivered in the context of an ongoing loving relationship. When children have disabilities, their needs may bring additional challenges. Jim Sinclair, an important advocate for neurodiversity, acknowledges that parenting a child with a disability, when the parents do not share it, can require parents to mourn the loss of the child and relationship they expected. He writes:

> What it comes down to is that you expected something that was tremendously important to you, and you looked forward to it with great joy and excitement, and maybe for a while you thought you actually had it – and then, perhaps gradually, perhaps abruptly, you had to recognize that the thing you looked forward to hasn't happened. It isn't going to happen.
>
> *(Sinclair 2012: 3)*

He urges that any grief needs to be put aside to focus "the parents' perceptions of the child they do have: the autistic child who needs the support of adult caretakers and who can form very meaningful relationships with those caretakers if given the opportunity" (Sinclair 2012: 1).

At a more general level, Andrew Solomon studies parents who do not share an important aspect of their child's identity and argues they face a challenge similar to that identified by Sinclair above: a challenge of overcoming expectations and learning to love and care for the child they have (Solomon 2012). This challenge is not unique to the experience of parents of children with disabilities and would be faced, for instance, by cisgender parents of transgender children. In addition, it would not characterize relationships in which children and parents share a disability and helps to explain why some parents hope to have a child who shares their disability, even if they regard their physical or mental difference as a disability, and not simply a cultural identity (see, for example, O'Toole and Doe 2002). This contrasts sharply with theorists who see parents as having a responsibility to choose a child whose genetic endowment gives it the best chance to enjoy the most well-being (Savulescu and Kahane 2009).

The challenge of responding to the unexpected and learning to love a child different from oneself is one all parents share, but parents whose children's difference manifests sharply, and may make life more difficult, can experience it to a far greater degree. Indeed, some argue that loving a child with a disability can require the parents to love unconditionally (discussed and critiqued in Mullin 2006). What precisely this involves is rarely spelled out clearly, but if it means that the love must rise above the particular nature of the child, rather than respond to it, that downplays both the contributions children with disabilities make to mutually loving relationships, and the qualities they have that make them lovable.

Uncertainty around how to care for a child whose needs one does not fully understand, along with the grief Sinclair discusses, and a desire to make life easier for a child whose physical or mental differences may not be well accommodated, can lead parents to seek to remedy a child's differences. One very controversial instance of this approach to "fixing" a child involves cochlear implant surgery to provide deaf children with some ability to hear. Given that many deaf adults view Deafness as a cultural identity (typically capitalized) rather than a defect, cochlear implants can appear to destroy a cultural identity and remove pressures from mainstream society to accommodate the Deaf identity (Sparrow 2005). Other instances, however, when parents seek to enable capacities (like the ability to communicate) through language therapy, or seek to enhance a child's balance or strength to enable mobility, are less controversial. They typically do not involve overcoming/removing a child's disability so much as finding ways to ensure that a child's potential is fully developed.

Questions about caring for a child with disabilities are distinct from questions about loving children with disabilities. One can take care of someone (meeting their needs, including their needs for emotional intimacy) without loving them (in the sense of having one's life shaped by their personal value and importance, and being attached to them). Similarly, one can love someone without that relationship being primarily focused on the provision of care to meet needs. Caring for a child with disabilities, in a world that is not designed to accommodate their gifts and their needs, can be very demanding of time and finances, and require carers to learn to navigate complicated bureaucracies and relationships with people considered experts in meeting the needs of children with the disabilities in question. Solomon (2012) documents the toll this can take on some parents, as well as the ability of many to rise to the occasion, particularly when they get support from social services or other parents with similar experiences.

To the extent that a culture privatizes the responsibility for a child's care and expects parents to be the primary or sole persons who meet children's needs, children with disabilities that require potentially expensive accommodations can have unmet needs, unless their parents have considerable personal resources. Thus, children with impaired mobility, or those who need additional assistance to develop their ability to communicate, or need considerable support in personal care longer than others, may fail to develop their potential. This means they will not be able to enjoy the exercise of capacities they might have developed with supports their parents cannot afford. It also means, as Eva Kittay argues, that parents of children with disabilities may face barriers to achieving both personal goals and political ones (such as civic participation) not faced by other parents. This is because these parents often receive insufficient support to meet the needs of the children they care for. Those parents may also need support in meeting their own needs so as to be able to care for their children, in addition to support in caring for the children themselves (Kittay 2001).

Children and parents' disabilities

Just as privatizing responsibility for caring for children can serve children with disabilities and their parents poorly, so too can it negatively affect the parenting of parents with disabilities. Parents are frequently thought responsible to meet all or the overwhelming majority of their children's needs on their own (with the frequent exceptions of formal education and medical care, which parents might be expected to oversee and perhaps fund rather than provide). As a result, parents who cannot do so without assistance, perhaps because of their disabilities, will be considered inadequate, and may lose the right to raise their children (see ch. 14, ch. 30). By contrast, parents with cognitive disabilities argue that they need supportive others to work with them, and when they receive the supports necessary (to understand what their children need at different developmental stages, and to interact positively with their children in times of stress, for instance) they can do the work well (Ehlers-Flint 2002; Strike and McConnell 2002).

While all parents arguably need considerable social support to meet the needs of their children, parents with disabilities may need supports tailored to their disabilities, such as provision of the information mentioned above for parents with cognitive disabilities, or a paid assistant or adaptive equipment to help with the physical demands of caring for babies for parents with physical disabilities. What they may face, if they request support, is suspicious oversight of their parenting, rather than a more cooperative and facilitative approach. Greater understanding that members of a society share responsibility to support the development and care of children with children's parents, can instead encourage that more cooperative approach. As Ora Prilleltensky argues, measures to support the caregiving of parents with disabilities should be seen as equivalent to a "ramp for parenting" – enabling access rather than disqualifying one from it (Prilleltensky 2003: 39).

In addition to arguing that the need for support in parenting does not mean a parent with disabilities is unfit, Prilleltensky argues that it should not be routinely seen as problematic when young children of parents with disabilities help their parents meet some of the parents' or familial needs (Prilleltensky 2004). Yet this has been seen as problematic, with the situation of "young carers" assumed to be worrying (Calder 2018). When it is learned that children provide some care for parents, particularly when those parents have disabilities, this can lead to judgments of the parents as primarily care receivers who are not also providers of care, and of the children as primarily care providers, rather than also people who receive care. Olsen (1996) and Keith and Morris (1996) both criticize debates around "young carers" for associating needing physical care, in particular, with being a child, and providing physical care or assistance with being a parent. Obviously, children should not be expected to carry physical and emotional burdens too great for them, but it can be positive for children to learn that they can make valuable contributions to the well-being of their parents and that they can help meet family goals.

Education of children with disabilities

All those charged with the care of children have a responsibility to develop their potential. This does not change when those children have mental and/or physical disabilities, but the specific educational goals and methods may change. There are two main models for those goals and methods. The first is one of special education, in which children receive education tailored to their specific needs alongside other children with similar needs. The dangers of this model are (1) lowering expectations, not to provide achievable goals for these children, but to conform to prejudices about the children's potential, and (2) fear that educating children solely alongside children with similar disabilities may inhibit their social inclusion both while children and later as adults. The second model is one of inclusive education, whereby children are matched with their peers on the basis of their age rather than their specific needs, so as to avoid the two dangers specified above. However, the dangers of this model are (1) educating children in proximity to one another may substitute for true social inclusiveness if the proximity is not supplemented by genuine efforts to enable cooperative social interactions, and (2) the presence of children with wildly varying abilities and needs may make it difficult to properly develop any of the children's potential.

Although the models are quite different, they can be combined as children may be educated in age-matched groups for some subjects, with some of those children provided with assistance when appropriate, and educated alongside peers based on shared needs and goals rather than shared age for other aspects of the curriculum. The more that schools and individual educators design their courses from the outset to benefit a broad variety of learners, including those with disabilities (sometimes known as Universal Design for Instruction or Universal Design for Learning), the more likely inclusive education – at least for certain subjects – is likely to succeed, particularly if the built environment in the school is similarly so designed, and there are well-trained support professionals available to assist teachers.

However, even when the built environment and course design are intended to be inclusive of a wide spectrum of learners, inclusion can be quite complicated when some of those learners are young people with social and emotional behavioral difficulties (SEBD). Shearman discusses the very significant challenges associated with attempting to educate all such children alongside their age-matched peers. Some can feel disrespected and rejected and act in a manner that is disruptive to their own and other children's ability to learn, and the stress and pressure experienced by teachers and support personnel can be enormous (Shearman 2005). However, there are some promising interventions, such as providing children with SEBD with support groups that encourage them to reflect upon their values and aspirations, and help them when they experience challenges and rejection (Mowat 2010). While such interventions withdraw children from the classroom for part of the instructional day, they enable re-integration on better terms.

It is also an open question as to whether all children with physical or mental differences and their families will value inclusive education if it makes it more difficult for those children to connect with others who are similarly situated. For instance, sending deaf children to schools where they interact with hearing children, even if only part of the time, may detract from developing their skills with sign language and knowledge of Deaf culture (Lane 2005). If the deaf children are expected to interact in part by lip reading, and the hearing children are not expected to learn sign language, this sends messages about inclusion by means of suppressing difference, rather than truly interacting with one another in ways that see diversity as a potential source of strength.

Garry Hornby (2015) advocates a synthesis of the methods and goals of special education and inclusive education in what he terms "inclusive special education". He argues that primacy should always be placed upon the child's right to learn, rather than the particular environment in which that learning takes place, and that the goal of inclusion should focus on the social inclusion of children when they are adults (something he argues will be enabled by developing their communication skills, skills that can allow them to live independently and to make economic contributions). However, there are reasons to be concerned about the failure of children to be regularly exposed to other children with diverse needs and abilities while they are still children, especially given that public schools are one of the few places where children may regularly encounter others significantly different from them. It may also be problematic to focus upon skills required for independence rather than interdependence. Both children with disabilities and those without can benefit from interacting with others who differ from them, in order to learn about one another, be challenged by new perspectives and learn how to work together effectively.

The moral status of children with cognitive disabilities

While adults and children alike can be uncomfortable around children with any type of disability, children whose disabilities are solely physical are unlikely to have their moral status questioned, except qua children, insofar as a philosopher argues that no child has moral status before developing adult capacities for rationality and morality. However, some theorists question the moral status of children whose disabilities are both cognitive and significant, arguing that only children with the potential to develop into paradigmatically rational, autonomous adults who can interact with others on an equal basis, have full moral status (discussed and critiqued in Mullin 2011). Yet others recognize all humans as morally considerable, not because of their own capacities but as members of the human species, and still others critique this approach as speciesist, and unfairly favoring human beings over non-human animals that may have capacities that exceed those of individuals with cognitive disabilities (Singer 2009; McMahan 2005).

Some give moral weight to the interests of children with significant cognitive impairments that prevent them from becoming paradigmatic adults only insofar as they have a capacity for welfare, and can feel pleasure and pain (Singer 1990). Others argue these children are morally considerable only because of the interests more paradigmatic people take in them either due to relationships with them or fellow feeling for members of one's species (Sapontzis 1987). Kittay's view that children with disabilities are all some mother's child is a more advanced version of this approach, in that she observes that people with disabilities contribute to, rather than solely being the beneficiaries of, relationships (Kittay 2005). A more recently articulated perspective that builds upon Kittay's work is that children who have the capacity to be in morally valuable relationships, in which each member reacts to the other as having intrinsic value, have moral consideration for this reason (Mullin 2011). If children with disabilities have the potential to be in morally valuable relationships, then adults have the responsibility to develop this potential. Jaworska and Tannenbaum (2014) similarly argue that both infants without disabilities and children and adults with significant cognitive disabilities can have their moral status enhanced by their capacity to be in a relationship with someone who aims to help them develop the capacities most standardly associated with moral status, such as the capacities to make evaluative judgments and care for others.

Conclusion

This chapter has moved from broad questions and themes pertaining to childhood and disability, to particular areas bearing out the conceptual and ethical challenges at stake. In so doing, we find that a critical understanding of each – childhood and disability – sheds light on the other. There are senses in which a disabled childhood raises questions with much wider purchase, about the nature and value of human development, of agency, of independence and interdependency. There are also senses in which the questions we encounter here are very specific – and where how they unpack varies substantially between different forms of impairment, and different childhood circumstances. Cognitive and physiological disabilities, for example, may not necessarily sit in the same place in the ethical landscape, and the playing out of how disability affects children's relationships with their parents will vary widely according to age and family set-up. There are strong grounds for addressing each case in its particularity, and adopting a "posture of genuine humility" (Salter 2017: 196) when considering the position of the disabled child. This is a young field, in philosophical terms. Entering it, we should not presume that our well-tuned conceptual apparatuses anticipate all of the questions it raises.

References

Barnes, E. 2009. "Disability, Minority and Difference," *Journal of Applied Philosophy* 26(4): 337–355.
Beaudry, J.-S. 2016. "Beyond (Models of) Disability?," *Journal of Medicine and Philosophy* 41(2): 210–228.
Calder, G. 2011. "Disability and Misrecognition," in S. Thompson and M. Yar (eds.), *The Politics of Misrecognition*. Aldershot: Ashgate.
Calder, G. 2018. "Young Carers," in M. Verkerk, H. Lindemann, and J. McLaughlin (eds.), *Where Families and Health Care Meet*. Oxford: Oxford University Press.
Clough, B. 2017. "Disability and Vulnerability: Challenging the Capacity/Incapacity Binary," *Social Policy and Society* 16(3): 469–482.
Cole, P. 2007. "The Body Politic: Theorising Disability and Impairment," *Journal of Applied Philosophy* 24(2): 169–176.
Danermark, B., and Gellerstedt, L. C. 2004. "Social Justice: Redistribution and Recognition – A Non-Reductionist Perspective on Disability," *Disability and Society* 19(4): 339–353.

Ehlers-Flint, M. L. 2002. "Parenting Perceptions and Social Supports of Mothers with Cognitive Disabilities," *Sexuality and Disability* 20(1): 29–51.
Fineman, M. 2008. "The Vulnerable Subject: Anchoring Equality in the Human Condition," *Yale Journal of Law and Feminism* 20(1): 1–23.
French, S. 1993. "Impairment or Something in Between," in J. Swain, S. French, C. Barnes and C. Thomas (eds.), *Disabling Barriers, Enabling Environments*. London: SAGE.
Gheaus, A. 2015. "Unfinished Adults and Defective Children: On the Nature and Value of Childhood," *Journal of Ethics and Social Philosophy* 9(1): 1–22.
Hannan, S. 2018. "Why Childhood is Bad for Children," *Journal of Applied Philosophy* 35(1): 11–28.
Hornby, G. 2015. "Inclusive Special Education: Development of a New Theory for the Education of Children with Special Educational Needs and Disabilities," *British Journal of Special Education* 42(3): 234–256.
Ikäheimo, H. 2009. "Personhood and the Social Inclusion of People with Disabilities,' in K. Kristiansen, S. Vehmas, and T. Shakespeare (eds.), *Arguing About Disability: Philosophical Perspectives*. London: Routledge.
Jaworska, A., and Tannenbaum, J. 2014. "Person Rearing Relationships as a Key to Higher Moral Status," *Ethics* 124: 242–271.
Keith, L., and Morris, J. 1996. "Easy Targets: A Disability Rights Perspective on the 'Children As Carers' Debate," in J. Morris (ed.), *Encounters With Strangers: Feminism And Disability*. London: The Women's Press.
Kittay, E. F. 1999. *Love's Labor: Essays on Women, Equality, and Dependency*. New York, NY: Routledge.
Kittay, E. F. 2001. "A Feminist Public Ethic of Care Meets the New Communitarian Family Policy," *Ethics* 111(3): 523–547.
Kittay, E. F. 2005. "At the Margins of Moral Personhood," *Ethics* 116: 100–131.
Lane, H. 2005. "Ethnicity, Ethics and The Deaf-World," *Journal of Deaf Studies and Deaf Education* 10(3): 291–310.
MacIntyre, A. 1999. *Dependent Rational Animals: Why Human Beings Need The Virtues*. Chicago, IL: Open Court.
Magee, B., and Milligan, M. 1998. *Sight Unseen*. London: Phoenix.
McMahan, J. 2005. "Our Fellow Creatures," *The Journal of Ethics* 9: 353–380.
Morris, J. 1991. *Pride Against Prejudice*. London: Women's Press.
Mowat, J. 2010. "Inclusion of Pupils Perceived As Experiencing Social And Emotional Behavioral Difficulties (SEBD): Affordances And Constraints," *International Journal of Inclusive Education* 14(6): 631–648.
Mullin, A. 2006. "Parents and Children: An Alternative to Unconditional and Selfless Love," *Hypatia* 21(1): 181–200.
Mullin, A. 2011. "Children and the 'Argument from Marginal Cases'," *Ethical Theory And Moral Practice* 14: 291–305.
Nussbaum, M. 2006. *Frontiers of Justice*. Cambridge, MA: Harvard University Press.
Oliver, M. 1990. *The Politics of Disablement*. London: Macmillan.
Oliver, M. 1996. "Defining Impairment And Disability: Issues at Stake," in C. Barnes and G. Mercer (eds.), *Exploring the Divide: Illness and Disability*. Leeds: The Disability Press.
Olsen, R. 1996. "Young Carers: Challenging the Facts and Politics of Research Into Children and Caring," *Disability And Society* 11(1): 41–54.
O'Toole, C. J., and Doe, T. 2002. "Sexuality and Disabled Parents with Disabled Children," *Sexuality And Disability* 20(1): 89–101.
Overall, C. 2013. *Why Have Children? The Ethical Debate*. Cambridge, MA: MIT Press.
Prilleltensky, O. 2003. "A Ramp to Motherhood: The Experiences of Mothers with Physical Disabilities," *Sexuality And Disability* 21(1): 21–47.
Prilleltensky, O. 2004. "My Child is Not My Carer: Mothers with Physical Disabilities and the Well-Being of Children," *Disability And Society* 19(3): 209–223.
Salter, E. 2017. "Introduction: Childhood and Disability," special thematic issue on "Childhood and Disability," *HEC Forum* 29: 191–196.
Sapontzis, S. 1987. *Morals, Reason And Animals*. Philadelphia, PA: Temple University Press.
Savulescu, J., and Kahane, G. 2009. "The Moral Obligation to Create Children with the Best Chance of the Best Life," *Bioethics* 23(5): 274–290.
Scully, J. L. 2008. *Disability Bioethics*. Lanham, MD: Rowman And Littlefield.
Scully, J. L. 2014. "Disability and Vulnerability: On Bodies, Dependence, and Power," in C. Mackenzie, W. Rogers, and S. Dodds (eds.), *Vulnerability: New Essays in Ethics and Feminist Philosophy*. Oxford: Oxford University Press.

Shakespeare, T. 2006. *Disability Rights and Wrongs*. London: Routledge.
Shearman, S. 2005. "What Is the Reality of 'Inclusion' for Children with Emotional and Behavioral Difficulties in the Primary Classroom?," *Emotional And Behavioral Difficulties* 8(1): 53–76.
Sinclair, J. 2012. "Don't Mourn For Us," *Autonomy, The Critical Journal of Interdisciplinary Autism Studies* 1(1): 1–5.
Singer, P. 1990. *Animal Liberation*. New York, NY: Avon.
Singer, P. 2009. "Speciesism and Moral Status," *Metaphilosophy* 40(3–4): 567–581.
Smith, S. R. 2005. "Keeping a Distance in Compassion-Based Social Relations," *Journal of Moral Philosophy* 2(1): 69–87.
Solomon, A. 2012. Far from the Tree: Parents, Children, and the Search for Identity. New York, NY: Scribner.
Sparrow, R. 2005. "Defending Deaf Culture: The Case of Cochlear Implants," *The Journal of Political Philosophy* 13(2): 135–152.
Strike, R., and McConnell, D. 2002. "Look at Me, Listen to Me, I have Something Important to Say," *Sexuality And Disability* 20(1): 53–63.
Terzi, L. 2004. "The Social Model of Disability: A Philosophical Critique," *Journal of Applied Philosophy* 21(2): 141–158.
Terzi, L. 2009. "Vagaries of the Natural Lottery? Human Diversity, Disability, and Justice: A Capability Perspective," in K. Brownlee and A. Cureton (eds.), *Disability and Disadvantage*. Oxford: Oxford University Press.
UPIAS. 1976. *Fundamental Principles of Disability*. London: Union of the Physically Impaired Against Segregation.
Wasserman, D., Asch, A., Blustein, J., and Putnam, D. 2016. "Disability: Definitions, Models, Experience," *Stanford Encyclopedia of Philosophy*. Retrieved from https://Plato.Stanford.Edu/Entries/Disability/
Watson, J. D. 2000. *A Passion for DNA: Genes, Genomes, and Society*. Oxford: Oxford University Press.
Williams, S. 1999. "Is Anybody There? Critical Realism, Chronic Illness and The Disability Debate," *Sociology of Health and Illness* 21(6): 797–819.
Wolff, J. 2009. "Disability Among Equals," in K. Brownlee and A. Cureton (eds.), *Disability and Disadvantage*. Oxford: Oxford University Press.

24
CHILDHOOD AND SEXUALITY

Jennifer Epp and Samantha Brennan

Introduction

Childhood sexuality is both contested and underexplored in academic philosophy. Historically, philosophers have not paid much attention to children, and those philosophers who have done so say little about children and sexuality. Where the subject of childhood and sex is discussed within philosophy, typically what is at issue is the protection of children from adult sexuality or the best route for children to become happy, competent adult sexual beings. There is almost no attention paid to childhood sexuality in its own right, let alone how to nourish children's sexuality, beyond protecting them from adult harm.

If one looks, instead, for contemporary encyclopaedia entries on philosophy and sexuality, most only mention "children" or "childhood" in the context of deviant adult desire. If children are mentioned as sexual agents at all, it is at the outer limits of childhood and the main question is the age of sexual consent (see ch. 12). Likewise, encyclopaedia entries on philosophy and childhood do not mention sex or sexuality except in discussions of sexual innocence and childhood sexual abuse. Sexual rights, the relation between sexuality and childhood well-being, and sexual citizenship are, however, emerging topics of concern. We think that philosophers should continue to investigate the nature of childhood, especially as it relates to innocence, childhood autonomy, and the ability or inability of children to consent to sexual activity, sex education, access to sexual health services, parental rights, and the goods of childhood. We will review discussions in these areas and suggest directions for future research.

These discussions focus on children in North America and Britain. They take place in a wider context of moral panic over hook-up culture, sexting, the content of sex education, LGBTQ identities, and attempts to control female sexuality in relation to reproduction. They also take place in a context where people both problematize rape culture and deny that it exists. Conflicts over the need to teach children about consent to sexual activity are part of that larger battle. Some theorists critique discussions about consent by thinking about racism and colonialism (Smith 2005). For the most part, however, philosophers interested in childhood sexuality ignore intersectionality altogether.[1]

Philosophers tend to talk about sexuality in fairly naive terms, with the focus being on sexual acts, particularly intercourse. If that is what is meant by "sexuality" then it makes sense that the focus of discussions about childhood and sex are on the age of consent and on rape.

But sexuality is much broader than merely sexual acts. One's sense of oneself as a sexual being occurs long before sexual acts (one hopes) and needn't involve another person at all. The harm/danger focus explains why we think about children and sex in terms of abuse and rape, as well as the harmful effects of sexual activity, i.e. pregnancy and STIs. But this is not all that sexuality encompasses.

Think about discussions of the age of first sexual activity. What makes an activity "sexual"? That's a puzzling question even for adults (Christina 2006). It is even more difficult with children precisely because of their developing nature. When very young children play with certain body parts because it is pleasurable, for example, it is not clear how to characterize such actions. Such play is not yet masturbation and not yet an explicitly sexual act, but it's clearly a kind of bodily exploration that over time will *become* sexual. It's part of a child's sexual development even if it's not overtly sexual behaviour yet.

Early work in political philosophy viewed childhood sexuality in the context of parental rights and the state. What limits, if any, are there in relation to what parents may teach (or protect children from learning) about sex and sexuality? More recent scholarship includes children as agents in their own right and we mean this chapter as a contribution to that approach. While we will try to present relevant debates fairly, we do take a stand by insisting that children matter morally independently of adults. In the debate on whether parents or the state should control sex education, for example, children's well-being is a factor that matters in addition to the interests of parents and the interests of the state.

Conceptions of children and childhood sexuality

Conceptions of childhood and children have changed over time. Changes have to do with who counts as a child, the value of childhood, what children are capable of, need, have a right to, and how they ought to be raised. Very broadly, in the ancient world children were not thought to matter in and of themselves, but instead as future adults (Cunningham 2003; Vopat 2015). Plato, for example, treats education for youth as a process intended to create virtuous citizens capable of flourishing (Plato 2006: Book IV 424e, 429d–e). He writes of childhood as a stage one must properly pass through in order to reach one's adult telos.

Regarding sexuality, Plato named temperance, which excludes lust (Plato 2006: 402e), as one of four chief virtues of the Republic. He understood it to mean "good order and mastery of certain pleasures and desires." He claims that "multifarious desires and pleasures and pains are especially found in children" (Plato 2006: 431c) and suggests that there is no greater pleasure than sex (Plato 2006: 403a–b). Platonic education was meant to enable youth to resist the temptations of pleasure and desire (Plato 2006: 389e, 429d–e, 430e). It is likely, therefore, that Plato would recommend education aimed at creating sexually virtuous adults.

According to Plato, young children are highly impressionable, poor in judgment, and they imitate that to which they are exposed. Therefore, they must be sheltered from stories involving excess, whether emotional, hedonistic, or acquisitive (Plato 2006: 387d). With this advice and the idea that children are morally malleable, Plato initiated a demand that is ubiquitous in the West in the Twenty-First Century: children must not be exposed to certain images and ideas. In so doing, he forged links between protection and virtue, including about sexuality, which continue to be influential.[2]

During the medieval period in the West, children were understood as bearers of original sin in need of immediate salvation. Then, during the Enlightenment and the Romantic period, children came to be seen as naturally unsullied innocents in need of moral protection (Cunningham 2003; Piper 2000; Vopat 2015). These frameworks influenced understandings of children's sexuality. If children were understood as bearers of original sin, then they were at risk from sexual sin. If children were sexually innocent, then they were at risk of losing that innocence by gaining knowledge of adult desires and activities (Piper 2000).

The notion of childhood innocence resonates with Locke's understanding of the mind as, initially, a blank slate. He recommends instilling virtuous habits in children as soon as possible by teaching them to be guided by reason. To do so, "children should be us'd to submit their desires, and go without their longings, even from their very cradles" (Locke 1998: section 38). He adds that infants are initially incapable of vice. They are, however, highly impressionable, "beset on every side, not only with the temptations, but instructors to vice" (Locke 1998: section 37). Thus, he warns that parents who do not begin moral education immediately may "corrupt the principles of nature in their children" (Locke 1998: sections 34–35). Locke's alarming warnings about corrupting influences reinforced Victorian thinking about innocence, risk, and protection from sexual knowledge.

Transitioning from the Enlightenment to the Romantic period, Rousseau also conceives of childhood as a time of natural innocence. "There is no original sin in the human heart, the how and why of the entrance of every vice can be traced," he writes, implying later on that "a happy ignorance may prolong the innocence of children" (Rousseau 1921: Book II). Both boys and girls, he thought, were without sexual desire until puberty, which could "be extended until the age of twenty" if they were "kept in ignorance" (Ice 2009: 3).

Rousseau holds that sexual desire is the beginning of *amour propre* – roughly, the desire to be socially successful in comparison with others. *Amore propre* arises when, at puberty, young men begin to compete for the attention of women. The sentiment is dangerous; young men must be educated to control it, young women to be enticing yet modest. Uncontrolled, *amore propre* results in the fall of humanity from natural innocence into social corruption as people resent their social positions and try to dominate others to secure respect (Rousseau 1921: Book II; Bertram 2012). Once again, themes of innocence, risk, and protection from corruption arise in relation to children and sexuality. Further, while Rousseau values childhood, his goal is to produce certain kinds of adults – women who will submit to their husbands, and men able to live together without being overcome by their desire for esteem.

Four themes weave through this historical overview. First, children, whether sexual or not, are of concern primarily as future adults. Second, children are pictured as innocent and impressionable. Third, children must either be habituated into virtue or shielded from corruption, and their innocence, always at risk, must be protected. Finally, very little room appears for children to be legitimately sexual, if sexual at all. These themes appear repeatedly in contemporary North American and British debates about children and sexuality (Brennan and Epp 2015; Campaign Life Coalition 2016; Ferguson, Benzie, and Rushowy 2010; Fields 2005; Harden 2014; Jones 2015; Meeker 2004; Millstein 2015; The Associated Press 2016).

Freud is an influential exception to the tendency to asexualize children. His theory of psychosexual development posits that people are influenced by sexual drives (libido) that begin at birth and develop in five stages during childhood into puberty. On his view, even infants experience sexual pleasure. Such drives, he thought, played an important role in identity formation. They were also sources of risk, as adults could develop neuroses if they did not move through each stage properly (Freud 2011). Freud's work made it possible to treat children as sexual. Risk remains an important theme, however, and childhood sexuality is still of interest largely in relation to adulthood.

Philosophers writing on children and sexuality tend to discuss adolescents and not younger children. This may be because of ideas about what counts as "sex" or "sexual." Intercourse, oral sex, "petting," and masturbation come to mind. But these are either activities that young children rarely engage in or, as with masturbation and preadolescent sex play, they are things that people avoid acknowledging that younger children do. It is reasonable, however, to suggest both that sexuality encompasses much more and that younger children do sometimes engage in sexual activity.

What else might sexuality encompass? Feelings and emotions including love, jealousy, and desire (both romantic and sexual); activities like flirting, dating, hand-holding, and cuddling; curiosity about bodies and sexual activities; gender, especially as it affects one's sense of self as a sexual being or one's behaviours in relationships; sexual and romantic orientation; and more. Acknowledging that sexuality encompasses more than sex makes it easier to recognize and investigate sexuality as expressed and experienced by younger as well as older children.

Children change radically between two and eighteen years of age. Nevertheless, people often treat childhood either only as adolescence or as a longer homogenous period of time. Given the radical changes that children undergo, answers to theoretical questions about children and sexuality may differ by age group. If so, it will be more accurate and useful to ask about sexuality throughout all stages of childhood. How to identify those stages will depend both on facts about patterns of change as children become older and on the kinds of questions one investigates.

Children's sexual rights

Children's rights are controversial.[3] Sexual rights are also controversial. The combination, children's sexual rights, are even more so. While we won't wade into debates about the status of children as the bearers of moral rights, there are some legal rights for older children – for example, the right to consent to sexual activity and the right to access information – that seem pretty straightforward.

What seems clear is that a child's right to consent to sexual activity, understood narrowly, depends on whether they possess a certain skill set that makes up competence. David Archard writes that in order to be competent one needs "a certain level of cognitive development—that is, an ability to understand the relevant facts, a certain degree of acquired knowledge." One must be mature enough to appreciate those facts and to act based on that appreciation (Archard 1998: 124). Archard also thinks that we need to pay attention to the ages at which most kids actually choose to engage in a particular behaviour when considering where to set the age of majority for such acts (Archard 1998: 126).

In our paper "Children's Rights, Well-Being, and Sexual Agency," we note that sexual consent relates to a wide range of behaviours (Brennan and Epp 2015). It seems reasonable to posit that a child's level of competence does not need to be as high to consent to lower-risk activity, such as kissing or genital touching with a peer, as it does for higher-risk activity, such as intercourse. People define higher- and lower-risk activity differently. Some argue, based on homophobic premises, that the age of consent for same-sex sexual activity ought to be higher than for the same behaviours with members of the opposite sex. Currently the Bahamas, Bermuda, Chile, and Paraguay have a higher age of consent for same-sex sexual activity. The United States used to have twenty-one as the age for same-sex sexual consent between men, sixteen as the age of consent between men and women, and no mention of an age of consent to sex between two women. Other jurisdictions, such as Queensland in Australia, make no mention of the sex of the participants but instead set a higher age for different kinds of sexual acts. The age of consent to anal sex is higher than the age of consent to vaginal intercourse.

We leave Archard and others to argue against age of consent proposals based on sexual orientation, though we believe them to be discriminatory and flawed. Notice though, that such proposals appear to contradict themselves by telling bisexual young people that they both are and are not legally ready to have sex.

Another flaw in age of consent laws concerns gender. Some states have historically mandated higher ages of consent for girls than for boys. The best argument for such differences points to power imbalances between male and female citizens, yet such laws both serve to protect young women and re-entrench the attitude that girls are less competent than boys and less legitimately sexual. Arguments stating that girls incur higher risks from sexual activity than boys do not warrant unequal legal status by gender. Rather, girls and boys should receive sex education that includes information on contraception and they should have access to adequate sexual health services. Age of consent discrimination by gender is especially flawed given the developmental gap between boys and girls which favours an earlier age of consent for girls, rather than the other way around. In the end, we advocate a single age of consent to sexual activity for all persons.

One common argument against children's rights is that children may make mistakes. It is important to note that adults too can make mistakes about decisions that are protected by rights. Further, adolescent sexuality is a period marked by experimentation and learning, including from mistakes. So, unless this objection is really a concern about competency, the worry is off base.

Children's rights in the area of sexuality go beyond the age of consent question. In the following two sections, we discuss some of the ways this might go.

Sexual citizenship for children

If one argument for reasonable sex education comes from the well-being of children, another set of arguments can be found in the concept of child as sexual citizen, with rights to access sexual information. What is sexual citizenship? Recent work in citizenship theory, addressing primarily adults as citizens, rejects the notion of the ideal citizen as neutral, disembodied, gender neutral, and asexual. Instead, work by such theorists as Shane Phelan (2001), and David Bell and Jon Binnie (2000) posits the citizen as sexual being, complete with gender and sexual identity.

The social theorist Jeffrey Weeks, who coined the term "sexual citizen," puts it this way:

> The "sexual citizen" is a new phenomenon in the erotic world, and a new player in the political and cultural arena, a product of the new primacy of sexual subjectivity in contemporary societies. Living at the fateful juncture of private claims to space, self-determination and pleasure, and public claims to rights, justice and recognition, the sexual citizen is a hybrid being, who tells us a great deal about the pace and scale of cultural transformation and new possibilities of the self and identity.
>
> *(Weeks 1998: 35)*

We might think of the term "sexual citizen" as a contradiction in terms insofar as sexuality as a private matter and citizenship is a public matter. But this way of thinking misunderstands all that is involved in citizenship. Only a member of the mainstream group whose sexuality is the assumed norm can conceive of sex as strictly a private matter. There are two aspects to citizenship, generally speaking. The first is having equal rights under the law and the second is having one's status as citizen and rights-bearer recognized. If the concept of "citizen" necessarily includes sexuality and gender orientation, then recognition of minority sexual and gender orientations needs to begin early and it is a public matter.

What kinds of rights follow from the notion of sexual citizenship? Here are some: same-sex marriage, military participation, housing, education, parental rights, health care, labour market participation, taxation, pensions and insurance, partner benefits, political representation, and immigration laws. According to Gert Hekma, it is notable that no country has accorded equality to all its citizens in all these areas. Many countries routinely deny GLBTQ citizens most of these rights. Hekma writes that the denial of institutional equality in these fields is a clear example that gay men and lesbians and other erotic groups are not fully recognized as citizens (Hekma 2004).

The situation gets worse, not better, when we turn to children. Most of these rights apply to adults, but if citizenship rights extended to children, then the list of rights would include access to sexual information as well as sex education that goes beyond just the provision of information. One clear example is the right of children to determine their own gender identity and to have access to medical resources required to delay puberty, which makes gender transitioning easier. As well, the recognition of sexual-minority youth is necessary for social respect. This is especially the case for youth who face intersectional oppression. Since such youth face the risk of family rejection, appreciation of oneself as a full citizen with legitimate access to state protection and services is all the more important.

Sex education

The version of sex education that follows from picturing children as both innocent and at risk, including from information and premature exposure to sexuality, is heavily protection focused. It often recommends abstinence. There is, to use Christine Piper's formulation, little room here for the idea that "children + sex = okay." Instead, "children + sex" is thought to equal "adult" or "abuse" (Piper 2000: 28–29). Such sex education is guided by the aim of maintaining purity and innocence. It is based on fear, primarily of corrupting children with knowledge. Another fear is that children will be harmed by premature sexuality where any expression of childhood sexuality is deemed premature. How might things be different if we saw children as legitimate (and developing) sexual agents?

A sex education program that focuses on good sex and how to get it is far more likely to influence teenagers than one which points only to dangers and counsels sexual abstinence. Abstinence-only education may even lead to, rather than prevent, risky behaviour and bad decision-making. A teen who believes that choosing to have sex is terribly wrong may not acquire or use condoms, for example, because doing so would indicate the premeditated choice to have sex – an action perceived as morally worse than being "swept away." Since abstinence-only education condones sex within marriage, it may also push some young people to marry earlier, perhaps before they have the skills to partner well (see Regnerus 2007).

Further, young people's sexual behaviour is influenced by peer pressure often in ways that press young women, but not young men, to provide but not to expect pleasure (Armstrong, England, and Fogarty 2012; Backstrom, Armstrong, and Puentes 2012). Abstinence-focused sex education does nothing to teach teens to value male and female sexuality equally. Instead, it is likely to harm young women by reinforcing discourses that represent sexually active women, but not men, as sluts. Sex education that includes a component on good sex and how to get it, aimed at all genders and focused on consent, could mitigate these problems. This is especially so if it emphasizes that *everyone* is entitled to seek consensual pleasure without being pressured to act as anyone else's pleasure dispenser.

Innocence- and protection-focused sex education gets things wrong in at least two more ways. First, it focuses on the adult the child will become not the person the child is now. "Innocent" and "at risk" as overriding descriptions of childhood erase the complexity, needs, desires, and activities of actual children. Sex education based on these idealizations cannot respond to children as people rather than as place-holders for ideas about natural purity. Further, innocence- and protection-focused education aims to produce sexually pure adults (those with no prior sexual experience and no inclination to pursue non-normative sex) at the expense of allowing children to explore themselves and their bodies at their own pace.

Recent work on childhood in ethics and political philosophy argues that we need to pay attention to both the child's future adult self and to what is good for the child as child. Childhood well-being matters for its own sake (Gheaus 2015; MacLeod 2010; Tomlin 2018; Brennan 2014; Skelton 2014, 2015). The right approach to including children in moral and political philosophy cannot be one that ignores or devalues childhood itself. Children aren't merely "saplings," to use Tomlin's term, not yet what they are meant to be. And good parenting pays attention to childhood well-being and the goods of childhood (see ch. 7, ch. 15). For older children especially, sex and sexuality may be a good of childhood.

Second, innocence- and protection-focused sex education ignores the child as a sexual citizen. That is, it does not treat children as people who are entitled to self-determination (in accordance with their capacities) and pleasure, or to various rights, just treatment, and recognition related to sexuality.

Recall that there are two aspects to citizenship. The first is having equal rights under the law, the second is having one's status as citizen and rights-bearer recognized. Much sex education is entirely forward looking. It seeks to protect children from risks and to produce adults capable of making good sexual choices while ignoring citizenship considerations altogether. What might sex education look like it if recognized children as citizens and as presently sexual beings? Before examining a particular case – that of sex education for disabled teens – consider these general points:

As sexual citizens and participants in government-provided sex education, children are owed, at the least, accurate and useful information, respect for their agency as learners and sexual beings, recognition of their diversity, and equal representation in curriculum. And if sex education admitted that children are sexual in various ways, then it might aim to support a healthy experience of sexuality. This would be a child-focused sex-positive sex education.

For all age groups, curriculum could address the following topics: biology, diversity, pleasure, consent, and self-care/relationships. Discussion of biology could cover anatomy, reproduction, puberty, and sexual health.

Attention to diversity allows discussion of sex, gender, and orientation as non-binary and sometimes fluid. As a result, the curriculum could cover agender, transgender, and bi-gender possibilities as well as masculine and feminine genders. It could separate out romantic and sexual orientations and discuss asexuality, demisexuality, bisexuality, heterosexuality, homosexuality, monogamy and polyamory, as well as transsexuality and intersexuality. The curriculum could also emphasize differences in libido, types of desire, and variation in bodily appearance.

A sex ed curriculum that acknowledges diversity would need to discuss intersectional oppression, including sexism, racism, ableism, classism, homophobia, and power. Research suggests that teaching methods focused on building critical thinking skills work best when teaching this material (Haberland 2015). This part of the curriculum may help to disrupt oppression. In addition, teaching about gender and power has been found to reduce rates of STIs and unwanted pregnancy (Haberland 2015). Covering these topics within a framework that treats each person as an equally valuable citizen teaches children to respect themselves and each other, all of which supports children's present and future well-being.

Next, sex education that takes children as legitimately sexual would discuss pleasure and desire; it would talk about what good sex is like, how to identify what you do and don't want, and how to get it (with attention to mechanics, social interaction, and emotions). It would reveal that people can want different things at different times, that you can stop wanting something that you wanted before, that something may feel good with one person and not another, that you may only like something under some conditions, and so on. Admitting that sex is pleasurable makes sex education more credible. Knowing, accepting, and valuing your own desires, pleasures, and physical and emotional needs is protective and healthy. This is as true for children as it is for adults.

Education about pleasure is related to children's sexual well-being in complex ways. For example, people who know about their own pleasures and desires are in a better position to learn to give and ask for consent. Justin Hancock, a sex educator, writes,

> If I were to ask them whether sex they had was consensual, their immediate response would be: "Yeah, it wasn't rape." But if I ask them about whether they enjoyed it, how they communicated, what kind of sex they actually want and whether they actually want sex – then it can reveal a very different picture about just how consensual the sex was and how healthy the relationship really is.
>
> *(Hancock 2015)*

Hancock's observations suggest that the consent portion of a sex education curriculum should be practical. It should address not just what consent is – an enthusiastic and voluntary response to another's actions or offers – but what consent "looks, feels, and sounds like" (Hancock 2015). Practice with seeking consent and recognizing when it is present and absent is important, as is the knowledge that consent must be ongoing and revocable. Learning how to respectfully express romantic and sexual interest is also important.

Next, sex education will better support well-being for children if it includes a component on self-care and relationships. Communication skills, body image, how to form and maintain boundaries, signs of abuse and where to get help, healthy ways to build self-worth, self-care skills related to sleep, food, social connection, and exercise, how to identify and express emotions, what trust feels like, and what love looks and feels like in practice are all potential topics. This section would discuss how to treat others ethically, especially in romantic and sexual situations. And it would help students to understand the value of non-sexual relationships.

Finally, good sex education is not simply about content. How the education is delivered matters a great deal. Is it condescending, or does it acknowledge what students already know, desire, value, and believe? Does it allow students to ask questions and choose discussion topics? Are teachers prepared for the possibility that students have experienced sexuality-related bullying or abuse? Does it allow students to respond to what they are learning and to gather information privately? Approach as well as content is directly related to whether or not sex education respects children as sexual citizens in ways that support their present well-being.

Consider the following example of how these considerations come together. Sexual citizens can claim legitimate access to state protection and services. But state protection services have often been used to segregate disabled individuals in ways that radically limit sexual expression and deny full participation in society (Clare 1999; Desjardin 2012). Disabled teens are less likely to be given sex education than their non-disabled peers, and they may be explicitly taught not to expect sexual and romantic relationships with others. They are also likely to encounter norms that demand permanent abstinence from disabled people and representations of themselves as either asexual or over-sexed (Shakespeare, Gillespie-Sells, and Davies 1996).

Sex education that respects sexual citizenship and values both childhood and pleasure would acknowledge that disabled youths are, and have a right to be, sexual agents in line with their present capacities, just like everyone else. Among other things, it would represent disabled sexuality positively, while being sensitive to different manifestations of both disability and sexuality. Such education would explicitly criticize ableist stereotypes. It would teach practical skills with disability-specific content, when needed, about how to have good sex. One might learn, for example, about non-genital orgasm, adaptable sex toys or positioning equipment, or about how to navigate caregiver assistance during dates or for the purpose of facilitating sex. The component on self-care and relationships could discuss differences between caregiver, friend, and romantic relationships, and it would discuss abuse and how to lessen vulnerability without overstating risk. This information would be taught as a regular part of the curriculum so as to publicly recognize and respect disabled youth as citizens, benefit everyone, and interrupt ableist assumptions from peers. Teachers would respect student agency by inviting all students to ask their own questions, while helping to find the answers. The goal would not be to "fix" disabled kids, and the program would recognize sexuality as a present and not only future good.

Conclusion

Historically, childhood sexuality has been a neglected philosophical topic. When it is discussed, the focus is usually on protecting childhood innocence in the face of adult danger. Positive accounts of childhood sexuality are largely absent, and most often children are treated as future adults in development. We have suggested that childhood matters in its own right and that sex and pleasure can be goods of childhood. We have also discussed sexual rights and citizenship for children, taking sex education as a case in point. It is our view that accounts of children's well-being and rights need to pay attention to child sexuality. This field is a rich area for philosophical exploration with implications for education, politics, well-being, health, and family ethics. We have pointed to some of these implications and raised many more questions that have yet to be answered.

Notes

1 Intersectionality refers to the ways that multiple, socially meaningful aspects of a person's identity combine and operate together to position them in social systems, in particular in relation to oppression and privilege. Areas of intersection may include age, ability, race, class, gender, sexual orientation, religion, and so on. As a result, one might be affected in particular ways by homophobia, ageism, sexism, and racism, not separately as queer, a child, a female, or as Black, but as a queer Black girl. See Collins (2015).
2 Aristotle took a similar view of pleasure, temperance, and moral education. He too treated childhood as a preparatory stage for what was really important: virtuous adult citizenship. See *Nichomachean Ethics*, Book II, part II and *Politics*, Book I, part VII and XIII.
3 For a strong argument against, see, for example, Purdy 1992; see also ch. 9.

References

Archard, D. 1998. *Sexual Consent*. Boulder, CO: Westview Press.
Aristotle. 350 BCE. *Nichomachean Ethics*, trans. W. D. Ross. *The Internet Classics Archive*. Retrieved from http://classics.mit.edu/Aristotle/nicomachaen.2.ii.html (last accessed 2 April 2018).
Aristotle. 350 BCE. *Politics*. Trans. B. Jowett. *The Internet Classics Archive*. Retrieved from http://classics.mit.edu/Aristotle/politics.1.one.html (last accessed 2 April 2018).
Armstrong, E. A., England, P., and Fogarty, A. C. K. 2012. "Accounting for Women's Orgasm and Sexual Enjoyment in College Hookups and Relationships," *American Sociological Review* 77(3): 435–462.
Backstrom, L., Armstrong, E. A., and Puentes, J. 2012. "Women's Negotiation of Cunnilingus in College Hookups and Relationships," *Journal of Sex Research* 49(1): 1–12.
Bell, D., and Binnie, J. 2000. *The Sexual Citizen: Queer Politics and Beyond*. Cambridge: Polity Press.
Bertram, C. 2012. "Jean Jacques Rousseau," *Stanford Encyclopedia of Philosophy*. Retrieved from http://plato.stanford.edu/archives/win2012/entries/rousseau/ (last accessed 2 April 2018).
Brennan, S. 2014. "The Goods of Childhood, Children's Rights, and the Role of Parents as Advocates and Interpreters," in F. Baylis and C. McLeod (eds.), *Family-Making: Contemporary Ethical Challenges*. Oxford: Oxford University Press.
Brennan, S., and Epp, J. 2015. "Children's Rights, Well-Being, and Sexual Agency," in A. Bagattini and C. Macleod (eds.), *The Nature of Children's Well-Being: Theory and Practice*. Dordrecht: Springer.

Campaign Life Coalition. 2016. "Ontario's Radical Sex Ed Curriculum." Retrieved from http://www.campaignlifecoalition.com/index.php?p=Sex_Ed_Curriculum (last accessed 18 March 2018).
Christina, G. 2006. "Are We Having Sex Now or What?" Retrieved from http://gretachristina.typepad.com/greta_christinas_weblog/2006/09/are_we_having_s_1.html (last accessed 18 March 2018).
Clare, E. 1999. *Exile and Pride*. Cambridge, MA: South End Press.
Collins, P. H. 2015. "Intersectionality's Definitional Dilemmas," *Annual Review of Sociology* 41: 1–20.
Cunningham, H. 2003. *The Invention of Childhood*. London: BBC Books.
Desjardin, M. 2012. "The Sexualized Body of the Child," in R. Mcruer and A. Mollow (eds.), *Sex and Disability*. Durham, NC: Duke University Press.
Ferguson, R., Benzie, R., and Rushowy, K. 2010. "McGuinty Backs Down on Sex Ed Changes." *The Toronto Star*, April 22. Retrieved from https://www.thestar.com/life/parent/2010/04/22/mcguinty_backs_down_on_sex_ed_changes.html (last accessed 26 March 2018).
Fields, J. 2005. "Children Having Children: Race, Innocence, and Sexuality Education," *Social Problems* 52(4): 549–571.
Freud, S. 2011 (orig. 1905). *Three Essays on the Theory of Sexuality*, trans. J. Strachey. Mansfield Center, CT: Martino Publishing.
Gheaus, A. 2015. "Unfinished Adults and Defective Children," *Journal of Ethics and Social Philosophy* 9(1): 1–21.
Haberland, N. 2015. "The Case for Addressing Gender and Power in HIV and Sexuality Education: A Comprehensive View of Evaluation Studies," *International Perspectives on Sexual and Reproductive Health* 4(1): 31–42.
Hancock, J. 2015. "This is What Sex Education Should Look Like," *The Guardian*, 9 March. Retrieved from https://www.theguardian.com/commentisfree/2015/mar/09/young-people-lessons-consent-sex-relationships-education (last accessed 29 March 2018).
Harden, P. K. 2014. "A Sex Positive Framework for Research on Adolescent Sexuality," *Perspectives on Psychological Science* 9(5): 455–469.
Hekma, G. 2004. "Sexual Citizenship," GLBTQ: An Encyclopedia of Gay, Lesbian, Bisexual, Transgender and Queer Culture. Retrieved from http://www.glbtqarchive.com/ssh/sexual_citizenship_S.pdf (last accessed 21 February 2018).
Ice, T. 2009. *Resolving the Paradox of Jean-Jacques Rousseau's Sexual Politics*. Lanham, MD: University Press of America.
Jones, A. 2015. "Ontario Education Minister says Parents Upset with Sex Ed can Pull Kids from Class. Many have Already Done So," *The National Post*, 8 September. Retrieved from http://news.nationalpost.com/news/canada/ontarios-education-minister-says-parents-upset-with-sex-ed-can-pull-kids-from-class-many-have-already-done-so (last accessed 26 March 2018).
Locke, J. 1998 (orig. 1692). "Some Thoughts Concerning Education," in P. Hassal (ed.), *Internet Modern History Sourcebook*. Retrieved from http://sourcebooks.fordham.edu/mod/1692locke-education.asp (last accessed 2 April 2018).
MacLeod, C. 2010. "Primary Goods, Capabilities and Children," in H. Brighouse and I. Robeyns (eds.), *Measuring Justice: Primary Goods and Capabilities*. Cambridge: Cambridge University Press.
Meeker, M. 2004. *Epidemic: How Teen Sex is Killing Our Kids*. Washington, DC: LifeLine Press.
Millstein, S. 2015. "Sex Education in the United States 1835 Through Today," *Digg*. Retrieved from http://digg.com/2015/sex-education-history (last accessed 10 January 2018).
Phelan, S. 2001. *Sexual Strangers: Gays, Lesbians, and Dilemmas of Citizenship*. Philadelphia, PA: Temple University Press.
Piper, C. 2000. "Historical Constructions of Childhood Innocence: Removing Sexuality," in E. Heinze (ed.), *Of Innocence and Autonomy*. London: Ashgate Publishing, pp. 26–46.
Plato. 2006 (orig. 380 BCE). *The Republic*, trans. R. E. Allen. New Haven and London: Yale University Press.
Purdy, L. 1992. *In Their Best Interest?: The Case Against Equal Rights for Children*. Ithaca, NY: Cornell University Press.
Regnerus, M. D. 2007. *Forbidden Fruit: Sex and Marriage in the Lives of American Teenagers*. Oxford: Oxford University Press.
Rousseau, J. J. 1921 (orig. 1762). *Emile, Or Education*, trans. B. Foxley. London and Toronto: Dent. Retrieved from http://oll.libertyfund.org/titles/rousseau-emile-or-education (last accessed 26 March 2018).
Shakespeare, T., Gillespie-Sells, K., and Davies, D. 1996. *The Sexual Politics of Disability: Untold Desires*. London: Cassell.

Skelton, A. 2014. "Utilitarianism, Welfare, Children", in A. Bagattini and C. Macleod (eds.), *The Nature of Children's Well-being: Theory and Practice*. New York, NY: Springer.

Skelton, A. 2015. "Children's Well-being: A Philosophical Analysis," in G. Fletcher (ed.), *The Routledge Handbook of Philosophy of Well-being*. London: Routledge, 2015.

Smith, A. 2005. *Conquest: Sexual Violence and American Indian Genocide*. Cambridge, MA: South End Press.

The Associated Press. 2016. "Parents, Schools Divided as Sex Ed Controversy Erupts," *CBS News*, 19 January. Retrieved from http://www.cbsnews.com/news/sex-education-controversy-erupts-in-omaha/ (last accessed 10 January 2018).

Tomlin, P. 2018. "Saplings or Caterpillars? Trying to Understand Children's Wellbeing," *Journal of Applied Philosophy* 35(1): 29–46.

Vopat, M. 2015. *Children's Rights and Moral Parenting*. Lanham, MD: Lexington Books.

Weeks, J. 1998. "The Sexual Citizen," *Culture & Society* 15(3): 35–52.

25
CHILDREN AND ANIMALS

Sue Donaldson and Will Kymlicka

Introduction

Throughout the history of Western philosophy, children and animals have been linked as paradigmatic examples of groups deemed unable to exercise the rights and responsibilities of citizenship, and who are therefore naturally governed by others. Thus, for example, Hobbes says:

> Over natural fools, children, or madmen there is no law, no more than over brute beasts; nor are they capable of the title of just or unjust, because they had never power to make any covenant or to understand the consequences thereof.
> *(Hobbes Leviathan II.xxvi.12)*

As Clifford notes, this "capacity contract" – creating a hierarchy between the self-governing and the "naturally governed" – runs very deep in the Western philosophical tradition (Clifford 2014).

Indeed, the exclusion of children under the capacity contract is arguably a constitutive feature of modern citizenship. As Rollo notes, "concepts related to childhood and democratic politics emerged as conceptually coeval and mutually exclusive", so that democratic politics has been conceptualized precisely as the outcome of a progression of "the feral child" out of childhood and animality into full human agency (Rollo 2018). To claim democratic citizenship, individuals, groups (e.g. women), or indeed entire societies (e.g. colonized peoples) have needed to demonstrate their progress from "the feral child's non-linguistic deficiency of humanity" to a fully human state which "venerates logos, language, and reason as the definitively human form of relating to the world and to others" (Rollo 2018: 64).[1]

Although children and animals have both been excluded by the capacity contract, there are two crucial differences in their respective statuses.[2] Children, though lacking many rights enjoyed by so-called competent adults, are nevertheless deemed to possess certain fundamental human rights by virtue of their species membership, providing a backstop to the potential costs of political exclusion (Archard 2014). Animals, by contrast, have almost no legal protection from violence, deprivation, and exploitation. Moreover, as future adults, children have certain entitlements ("rights-in-trust", or anticipatory autonomy and welfare rights) because they are anticipated to *become* full citizens or rights-bearers, as animals are not (Archard 2014; see also ch. 9).

While the capacity contract runs very deep, it is increasingly being challenged by advocates of children's citizenship. In recent years, and especially since the adoption of the 1989 United Nations Convention of the Rights of the Child (UNCRC), many people have argued that children should be citizens in their own right and not just as prospective future citizens – as "beings" not just "becomings" (Arneil 2002). In place of the capacity contract, they have argued for a more inclusive citizenship which starts from the facts of social membership and a commitment to include and empower all members of society, across the spectrum of cognitive and other forms of diversity. On this view, insofar as children are members of society, then this fact of membership is sufficient to ground rights to have a say in collective decisions. As Roche puts it: "the demand that children be included in citizenship is simply a request that children be seen as members of society too, with a legitimate and valuable voice and perspective" (Roche 1999: 479). Similarly, Lister says that "at one level, children's claim to citizenship lies in their membership of the citizenship community": children themselves understand and claim citizenship as a status "enjoyed by virtue of membership of the community or nation" (Lister 2008: 10). As members of society involved in dense webs of trust, communication, and cooperation with others, children have both rights of participation to help shape social norms as well as responsibilities to comply with those social norms. These rights and responsibilities may be differentially enacted, but rest on a foundation of full and equal citizenship.

This challenge to the capacity contract is not surprising. After all, while the capacity contract runs deep in the Western tradition, it contradicts other core political values. Virtually all contemporary democratic theories appeal to some version of the "all-affected" principle. All those affected by political decisions (or all subjected to the law, or all stakeholders) should have a say in shaping those decisions. This is the cornerstone of political legitimacy today. Traditional assumptions that some members of society (such as women, racial castes, people lacking property or literacy) are "naturally" governed by those deemed more independent, mature, and responsible (such as white, propertied men) are now discredited. Historically subordinated groups have rejected the idea that difference can be used to justify political hierarchy, or to diminish the moral imperative for voice and representation. It was inevitable that the exclusion of children would similarly come under scrutiny.

These new models of inclusive citizenship represent some of the most exciting and innovative work being done in children's studies. To date, however, theorists of children's citizenship have not explored the implications of these models for animals, and have typically assumed that animals can and should continue to be excluded. We believe that this is a missed opportunity, and that reflecting on the parallels between children and animals can help deepen and enrich our understanding of both social membership and political citizenship. Indeed, we will suggest that failure to consider these parallels renders recent theories of children's citizenship unstable. As Rollo's reference to the "feral child" makes clear, attitudes to childhood are linked to attitudes to animality, and a sustainable model of inclusive citizenship requires rethinking both.

It is an interesting question why this parallel has not been explored. Part of the reason is the general invisibility of animals in the social sciences. But it may also reflect persistent efforts to present children's rights and animal rights as zero sum (Flegel 2009). Burning-house scenarios – "Would you save your child or the dog?" – abound. Medical researchers accuse animal advocates of sacrificing children's health in the name of rights for rats and mice (Paul 2001). Proposals for off-leash dog parks are challenged on the grounds that parks should be for children and families (Urbanik and Morgan 2013: 292). Animal lovers without children are accused of using animals as child substitutes, devoting to animals the love and care which should instead be devoted to humans (Amiot and Bastian 2015). On this zero-sum view, the mark of society's respect for children is the steepness of the moral hierarchy between children and animals: sacralizing the human child and sacrificing the animal.

We will suggest, on the contrary, that the fate of children and animals is deeply interconnected. The political ideologies and legal mechanisms used to subordinate animals also operate to diminish children's political standing. Children and animals share powerful interests in relation to adult/human society, interests which have been obscured and suppressed both under the traditional capacity contract and under recent theories of children's citizenship.

We explore these issues in two steps. In the first part of this chapter, we explore the ways in which children's social world is an interspecies social world. This fundamental fact, obvious to most children, becomes invisible to most of us by the time we achieve adulthood, having been taught to relegate animals to the natural, not social, world (while making exceptions for a few companion animals here and there). This exclusion of animals from our sense of society is the result of intense social and ideological conditioning, camouflaged as "growing up", "facing the facts of life", and learning that the use and consumption of animals is "normal, natural and necessary" (Joy 2011; Piazza et al. 2015; Gibert and Desaulniers 2014). Recently, however, sociologists, anthropologists, human geographers, and developmental psychologists have begun to rethink basic ideas of sociability, empathy, friendship, and work in light of the fact that we belong to "more than human" societies.

In the second part of the chapter, we move from the social to the political, and explore emerging membership-based models of children's citizenship, according to which all members of society, regardless of age or ability, have the right to participate in shaping the norms that govern our shared social world, in ways that are meaningful to them. We suggest that the logic of this position extends to animals as well: an interspecies society requires an interspecies politics. We then discuss some recent experiments in inclusive democracy which illustrate this idea, offering possible answers to critics who challenge its feasibility, and providing a tantalizing glimpse of how including children and animals could renew democracy.

Before proceeding, however, two terminological notes. First, we use the term "children" to refer to human children, and "animals" to refer to non-human domesticated animals. This is potentially misleading, since children are animals, and domesticated animals have their own stage of childhood before developing into experienced and competent adults. One of the many injustices we impose on animals is precisely denying childhood to them – for example, by forcibly separating calves from their mothers on dairy farms, or capturing infant animals to stock zoos or labs (Bryant 2010). Second, our discussion is restricted to domesticated animals because, as we have argued elsewhere, there is a compelling moral case for recognizing them as members of an interspecies society and demos (Donaldson and Kymlicka 2011). Domesticated animals include animal companions, laboring animals, farmed animals, and others who have been selectively bred in order to perform certain functions in human society, and are as a result dependent (to varying degrees) on human care. Domesticated animals are capable of physically proximate, communicative, trusting, and cooperative relations with humans (and *vice versa*). These animals have been incorporated into our society over millennia, contributing to and shaping our schemes of cooperation, but as a subjugated caste. At least in the short term, they have no alternative society to "exit" to, and, in any case, we have no right to expel them. As we will see, these facts about domestication help to explain why parallels between children and animals in relation to social membership and political citizenship can be so revealing.[3]

A shared social world

Gail Melson's landmark 2001 book, *Why the Wild Things Are*, was the first major work of developmental psychology devoted to the exploration of children's relationships with animals. As she notes, the field of developmental psychology, from its origins, has been profoundly humanocentric, "assuming that only human relationships – with parents, siblings, relatives, friends, teachers, other children – are consequential for development", without ever bothering to consider interspecies relationships (Melson 2001: 8).[4] The results of Melson's research are astounding. Children live, breathe, and dream animals. Their earliest dreams are of animals, and the first words learned by infants, apart from mama and daddy, are names of animals (Melson 2001: 84). For children aged 2–10, 50% of inkblot interpretations involve animals (Melson 2001: 137). Children between seven and ten years of age use the same vocabulary to describe both pets and siblings as playmates (Melson 2001: 39). When asked to identify their most important relationships (after parents), half of Scottish 9–12-year-olds said a pet, higher than the number who said grandfather, friend, aunt, teacher, or neighbor. And elementary school children say that relations with their pets are more likely to last "no matter what" than relations with friends and family (Melson 2011: 17). Subsequent research has confirmed not only the vital role companion animals play as attachment figures for humans, but also the vital role humans play as attachment figures for companion animals. These bi-directional attachment bonds can be documented using the same standard measures (proximity seeking, safe haven, secure base, separation distress) (Amiot and Bastian 2015). In short, "the emotions and personalities of animals, real and symbolic, are immediate to children in the same way that the emotions and personalities of people are". It is only later that the "categorically human self" emerges, with its "strict division between human attributes and often negatively valued animal characteristics" (Melson 2001: 20).

In parallel with Melson's work, sociologists, social workers, health practitioners, and anthropologists have opened their eyes to the more-than-human nature of families and neighborhoods, societies, and cultures. Criminologists have long recognized that animal abuse predicts and co-occurs with abuse of humans, and social workers know how attachments to animals make them pawns and victims in situations of family breakdown and domestic violence (Lockwood and Arkow 2016; Febres et al. 2014; Girard and Pozzulo 2012; Ascione et al. 2007). A vast industry of animal therapy is now dedicated to the healing power of relationships with animals for children with attention deficit disorder (ADD) and autistic spectrum disorder (ASD), as well as people suffering from depression, post-traumatic stress disorder (PTSD), loneliness, anxiety, and other health issues (Benvenuti 2016; Weisberg 2016).[5] Evolutionary psychologists claim that we co-evolved with other animals, specifically dogs (Schleidt and Shalter 2003). Sociologists now recognize that animals are responsive agents in interspecies social relationships – at home, on the street, at the park, at school, at work (Peggs 2012). And anthropologists have begun to explore how animals are not just cultural objects, but agents in cultural creation with humans. No human society is known to have existed without close human–animal relationships of companionship and cooperation (Serpell 1996).

Given this overwhelming evidence for the reality that children inhabit, mentally and physically, an interspecies social world, the puzzle becomes how this interspecies fellowship becomes broken. In Melson's words, how can we "pinpoint the process by which children shift from engaging animals as coequal other beings to straddling the barrier of a radical species divide" (Melson 2001: 190)?

The severance of children from their more-than-human companions is accomplished through multiple processes. Louv (2005) examines how urbanization and technology separate children from the natural world, and the relationships to be formed there. Stewart and Cole (2014) analyze the vast ideological enterprise operating in homes, schools, and the media for transforming animals from the equal fellow beings of childhood into objects to be used instrumentally. They explore how the violence of the animal industry is hidden away; how children's sociality with non-humans is transferred onto fuzzy sentimental toys and images (and pets); how children are habituated into eating (and developing pleasure from) meat before they understand what it is; and how children are gradually indoctrinated with ideologies of human exceptionalism and the rightfulness of human instrumentalization of animals (see also Pedersen 2010).[6]

Stewart and Cole's analysis of a gradual ideological shift describes the situation for many urban children in Western societies. The process for rural and farm children is often much more brutal, as captured in Matt Stensland's photo of Tyler Boyer (a 4-H member, aged 11) sobbing into the neck of his steer, Leonard, whom Tyler has raised since infancy and is now sending off to slaughter.[7] The Internet is full of YouTube videos of children being "socialized", "cajoled", or "shamed" into killing animals.[8] Such practices are on a continuum with the more familiar case of parents tricking, prodding, coercing, and confusing their children into the belief that consuming animals is "normal", "natural", and "necessary", or the role of schools in re-educating children to see animals as tools of inquiry, rather than fellow subjects (Oakley 2013). Humans have killed and consumed animals in most times and places, and for most traditional societies killing animals was indeed necessary for survival. But this was usually seen as a regrettable necessity, and so cultural practices of apology, gratitude, and expiation were elaborated to deal with the psychological trauma of killing (Serpell 1996). In modern societies, the practice is largely hidden, and cultural imaginaries of regret and gratitude have given way to ideologies of self-righteous entitlement – ideologies that require rupturing, whether gradually or brutally, the interspecies lived experience and worldview of children.

This process is so normalized that as a society we have barely yet asked – let alone attempted to measure – what might be the costs to children of this assault. Social psychologists have long studied the harmful effects on children of participating in, or being exposed to, "abnormal" acts of animal cruelty – that is, acts of cruelty that flow from deviant individual personality – but have only recently begun to investigate the harmful effects on children of being indoctrinated into "normal" acts of animal exploitation.

We do, however, have growing evidence that this ideological indoctrination has negative spillover effects on issues of human rights and human equality. Defenders of a steep species hierarchy often argue that, by sacralizing "the human" and instrumentalizing "the animal", we provide a clear and secure foundation for protecting the rights of all humans, including vulnerable racial groups. Species hierarchy may render animals more vulnerable, but at least it helps provide secure recognition for the rights of vulnerable human outgroups, who share in the sacredness of the human. In reality, however, the evidence shows that inculcating attitudes of human superiority over other animals worsens, rather than alleviates, negative attitudes towards minorities, immigrants, and other "out" groups. This finding – known in the literature as the "interspecies model of prejudice" – has now been widely replicated, including amongst children. The more children are taught to place the human above the animal, the more they are likely to display racial prejudice (Costello and Hodson 2014). As Hodson, MacInnis, and Costello put it,

> overvaluing humans, relative to nonhumans, lies at the heart of problems not only for animals but also for humans.... We may collectively need to face an inconvenient truth: The premium placed on humans over animals – overvaluing humans as an unchallenged truism – fuels some forms of human dehumanization.
> *(Hodson, MacInnis, and Costello 2014: 104, 106)*[9]

Conversely, humane education regarding animals – emphasizing interspecies affinities and solidarities – is known to encourage greater empathy and pro-social attitudes towards other humans (Thompson and Gullone 2003).

In short, the rupturing of children's sense of interspecies sociability and solidarity, and their inculcation into ideologies of human supremacism, is one of the most consequential – and, we would argue, damaging – features of contemporary practices of childhood socialization and education. It is traumatic for many children, it exacerbates inter-group prejudice, and it is catastrophic for animals. What this reveals is that, counter to claims that children's rights and animal rights are in zero-sum conflict, members of both groups are harmed by an ideology and practice whose actual purpose is to serve the animal-exploiting interests of certain sectors of adult human society. And the ideological reinforcement of this purported right of animal exploitation requires a direct assault on the interspecies attachments of children. If children or animals had a say on the matter, it is unlikely that this is what they would vote for.

Towards political inclusion

But, of course, children and animals do not have a vote on the matter. Just as animals and children share a social world, which adult society ignores and ruptures, so too they share a state of exclusion from a political world which adult humans jealously guard for themselves. Through invocation of the capacity contract, neither children nor animals are recognized as full democratic citizens, with equal rights to political voice, participation, and co-authorship of laws and social norms.

There are formidable difficulties in imagining how exactly to enable a voice for young children or animals, and opponents of their inclusion invoke these difficulties as grounds for maintaining the capacity contract. But while we should not underestimate the challenges of inclusive citizenship, nor should we underestimate the problems of democratic illegitimacy that result from continued exclusions, or the pernicious impact on members of these groups of being denied meaningful political input and influence. It is striking how rarely defenders of the capacity contract offer any solution to these problems.[10]

To move beyond this impasse requires leaving behind the abstract theoretical terrain of "the ideal citizen" and going beyond inherited ideas of how citizenship must be enacted (e.g. through voting, petition, protest). It requires that we explore the actual performance of citizenship by different groups, and the creation of new practices which allow them to enact their citizenship in ways that are meaningful to them.

If children are to be enabled "to form and express a view" on "all matters affecting" them – as required by the UNCRC – we will need "child-sized" spaces for citizenship (Jans 2004). This means going to the places where children (and domesticated animals) are situated, and then observing them, listening to them, empowering them to choose and reject representatives, and requiring that their input actually shape decision-making. Children and animals may not have the capacity to engage in Rawlsian public reason or Habermasian deliberative democracy, but they have capacities for communication (including embodied language and utterances), trust, and engagement, and these make possible new modes of participation through interdependent agency and supported decision-making.

Many commentators have wondered how these new practices of citizenship will work. How can children and animals be consulted and meaningfully involved in democratic decision-making? How can manipulation and the inappropriate imposition of burdens be avoided? These are serious challenges, but solutions to them are being developed through actual practice, for example, in the mobilization of child workers (Liebel 2012), or proposals for empowering children to sanction adults for failure to protect common goods (Zakaras 2016). The movement for people with cognitive disabilities has also advanced novel practices to enable participation by individuals with limited or atypical linguistic and cognitive repertoires (Sonnicksen 2016).

In our own work we have explored how some farmed animal sanctuaries represent experiments in interspecies citizenship, observing and responding to animals in ways that allow them to co-author the norms of a shared society. Every animal has an individual, subjective good, and, moreover, has privileged insight into that good. This doesn't mean that there are no situations in which animals (like children) can't understand important dimensions of what is at stake, and in which paternalistic decisions are appropriate. It just means that there are also many situations in which they understand things about their good which we can only learn from paying attention and being responsive to them on an ongoing basis. For example, for the last 50 years the "Five Freedoms" have represented the gold standard of animal welfare for domesticated animals, adopted by welfare organizations around the world. In addition to basic provision and protection, they include "the freedom to behave normally – by making sure animals have enough space, proper facilities and the company of other animals of their own kind". In other words, animal advocates have assumed that animals' social world is limited to their own species. This bias has been continuously reinforced by practices of segregating animals by species on farms, a practice retained on many sanctuaries. A few sanctuaries, however, operating on the assumption that individual animals might have their own ideas about the kinds of community they want to form, have discovered that many animals prefer to form interspecies communities, engaging in activities, friendships, and social structures that cross species lines. Being responsive to this agency of animals has led to dramatic change in the design of these communities, and the kinds of lives individuals lead there (Donaldson and Kymlicka 2015).

In short, experiments in inclusive citizenship are emerging on the ground, in relation to children, people with cognitive disability, and domesticated animals. We have already left far behind the narrow vision of democracy entailed by the capacity contract, and are moving towards an inclusive membership-based model. Needless to say, many people are nervous about this trend, particularly in relation to domesticated animals, and so seek to define citizenship as exclusively human, applicable only to human members of society. On our view, however, so long as citizenship is defined in opposition to feral animality, feral children's claim to citizenship will always be insecure. Extending inclusive citizenship to domesticated animals would represent the fullest confirmation and expression of society's commitment to a membership model of citizenship, and would secure children's claim to full citizenship on the basis of their full animal being. And as we noted earlier, we suspect that many children would quite happily accept this extension.

Reimagining the future

What would happen if society empowered children and domesticated animals to act upon their interests, many of them shared? We believe it could have a transformative effect on politics, from how we think about the natural environment to how we organize social space, foster social relationships, define social contribution, and provide social services.

Protecting the environment: It is widely noted that adults and children may have diverging interests regarding the environment. Adults benefit from existing growth-based extractive economies, whereas young children are likely to bear the costs down the road (Zakaras 2016). In fact, children and domesticated animals are already paying the environmental costs. Children and animals like to spend time outdoors, playing in parks and fields, swimming in lakes and rivers, exploring woods, tidal pools, vacant lots, back streets and alleys, rail and dockyards, abandoned industrial sites, and ground-level mud, detritus, and cubby holes. They share powerful interests in these places being safe and uncontaminated. Human adults spend less time in the muck, and can tolerate much higher levels of environmental pollutants (lead, mercury, pesticides, tobacco smoke, dioxins, and polychlorinated biphenyls (PCBs)) than either young children or domesticated animals. In what is described as the "new pediatric morbidity", the five major illnesses affecting children in industrialized societies are all environmentally related (Trasande et al. 2006). And small animals like the mice who share our homes are increasingly looked to by scientists as "canaries in the coal mine" for environmental pollutants such as endocrine disruptors. Their small bodies are affected much more quickly and seriously. Animal companions, like young children, are increasingly affected by neurodevelopmental disorders, cancers, and poisoning. Sadly, and ironically, both groups are also facing increased obesity and diabetes as they are increasingly kept indoors, away from an outdoors that has become unsafe and inaccessible. Children and domesticated animals share a profound interest in restoring the outdoor environment to ecological health rather than treating it as a dumping ground for the externalized costs of adult wealth creation.

For the same reason, children and animals have an interest in shifting from treatment-centered to prevention-centered health care. An adult who has developed a particular morbidity has a strong interest in investments into disease treatment and cures. Animals and young children have a much greater interest in not developing chronic disease in the first place. It is indicative of existing power relations that the environmentally triggered illnesses of childhood are poorly understood by doctors, and woefully under-researched (Trasande et al. 2006), and that, more generally, health dollars are invested more heavily in treatment than in prevention.

Accessing public space: Children and animals are not just being restricted from accessing the natural environment, but are also increasingly restricted in their social spaces. Public spaces are overwhelmingly designed by and for human adults – spaces to conduct business, to enjoy a quiet drink or meal, to relax and read, to consume culture, shop, park, drive, get efficiently from A to B. Children and animals are often perceived as not belonging in such public spaces, except for the occasional park. This restricted access is sometimes justified on paternalistic grounds, to protect children from dangers. The amount of unsupervised free time that children spend outside, and their range of movement, has plummeted in the past 50 years – due in large part to parental perceptions of increased risks (real and illusory). Fifty years ago, breaking a bone was a childhood rite of passage. Now it is a rarity. In this way, children are moving closer to the situation of domesticated animals whose movement is highly restricted and scheduled by adults.

If we ask children themselves, however, they are quite clear that they do not want to be restricted and monitored in these ways (Alderson 2008). If cars are dangerous, they say, restrict the cars, not us. If the outdoors is polluted, clean it up – don't restrict our right to explore. If you're worried that crowds of urban youth will vandalize adult-oriented public spaces, then invest in spaces which respond to, and respect, our interests – don't impose curfews. A common political agenda for children and domesticated animals would not just halt the century-long ascendancy of car culture and its impact on urban design. It would re-prioritize the design of public space around creatures who like to walk, run, bike, skateboard, hop on and off public transportation, play, hang out, disrupt, and explore. It would reimagine public space, and the outdoors, as places where "feral children" feel at home and can take ownership – rather than feeling like barely tolerated interlopers.

Social integration: Even with healthy natural environments and redesigned public spaces, children and domesticated animals, especially in their younger years, will still be highly dependent on adult humans to protect and provide for them. This, naturally, sets limits on their independence and free movement. However, it is not inevitable that they be dependent on just one or two adults – their parents or guardians. Currently, children and domesticated animals are assigned to specific spaces (homes, schools, farms, recreational sites), within which a few designated adults (parents, teachers, farmers) exercise enormous power over them, often in spaces that are hidden from public view, and from which these vulnerable beings cannot escape. Even adults with the best intentions have only so much energy that they can devote to attending and responding to children and animals in their care. Children and animals are structurally vulnerable to caregivers, and caregiving is subject to inevitable failures (Gheaus 2011), and we therefore owe it to children and animals to distribute care and interaction across multiple relationships and sites.

Imagine a more socially distributed approach to caring and interdependent relationships in which the social and geographic segregation of adults from children, seniors, people with sicknesses and disabilities, and domesticated animals would be replaced with a more integrated social life. Crèches and schools would be integrated with workplaces, seniors' residences, therapeutic settings, sanctuaries for farmed animals, daycares for companion animals, green spaces, and community gardens and kitchens. Large, linked, car-free spaces would be created for safe movement within multi-purpose, socially integrated mini-communities. By multiplying the number of adults with eyes on, and taking an interest in, individual children and animals there is less likelihood of abuse, neglect, or isolation. Dogs wouldn't pine alone at home all day, lonely and dependent on one or two humans for all of their social interaction, but would have an enlarged sphere of social contacts – senior volunteers, school visitors, and other dogs and domesticated animals. Children wouldn't be completely dependent on parents, teachers, or peers for attention, support, and stimulation, but would be able to build complex social networks with a variety of people with whom they cooperate in various forms of activities. Mutual interaction, care, and support could emerge across diverse social groupings. In such circumstances, rather than greater freedom and mobility for children and animals posing risks to them, it would increase their safety by reducing social isolation and their vulnerability to the vagaries of any one individual's will.

Work and contribution: Finally, consider how such a society might think about work and contribution. Work is widely seen as the most important source of self-respect and social recognition (Shklar 1991). Yet, at the moment, the rhetoric of Western societies is that we don't want or expect children to work. Childhood is defined as a time for play and education, insulated from adult responsibilities to work or contribute. This perspective obscures the fact that children do in fact work, in all societies, sharing in the burdens as well as the benefits of social cooperation. And while it is crucial to ensure adequate time for play and education, children are adamant that these goods should not preclude opportunities for appropriate and safe employment. They do not want to be banned from work, which they, too, see as a source of self-esteem, personal development, and social recognition. They want to have access to safe and properly compensated jobs that are compatible with their interests in education and other activities, and they want their contributions to be valued and recognized (Gasson and Linsell 2011; Liebel 2012). However, because our prevailing ideology privileges paid adult work, children's work tends to be unrecognized, inadequately compensated, and out of children's control. For example, education is typically framed as a privilege or benefit, rather than a compulsory job. Similarly, children's work in the domestic sphere (caring for younger siblings, for sick family members, for domesticated animals, doing household tasks) is often unrecognized or undervalued – they are said to "help out" rather than "to work" – and is unprotected by labor legislation (see ch. 26). Emerging research suggest that 12–20% of youth are involved in extensive care work for ill or disabled family members, aging grandparents, or siblings (Lu 2015). Interviews with youth caregivers indicate that they don't want to be shielded from these roles, but they do want more support and recognition. In short, even as society in fact depends heavily on the cooperation and contribution of children, it denies them social recognition, compensation, or labor rights.

Domesticated animals face an even more extreme version of this hypocrisy. Millions of domesticated animals fulfil contributing roles in society (transportation, haulage, plowing, vegetation control, therapy, assistance, rescue, detection, protection, companionship, etc.). Yet, like children, their forms of contribution are not recognized as "work", and so they are accorded no rights or recognition as workers. It is in the interests of adult society to define work in ways that render invisible the work of children and domesticated animals, and to paint them instead as recipients of adult care or protection. A common agenda for children and domesticated animals would recognize the diverse forms of work that social members engage in, and ensure that they are safe, non-exploitative, and fairly compensated.

Conclusion

Advocates for children's citizenship have challenged the capacity contract, and argued instead for a membership-based conception of citizenship. All members of society, whatever their capacities for independent rational reflection, have a right to a say in how shared social practices are governed. This development has led to a richer understanding of children's current roles as social members, and their potential roles as political citizens. We have suggested, however, that further insights can be gained if we consider how children's membership and citizenship is interconnected with that of domesticated animals. Both have been excluded by the capacity contract, and both have suffered social misrecognition and political marginalization as a result. Moreover, they share important interests in relation to the natural environment, the built environment, the structure of social relationships, and the nature of work, all of which are neglected in adult-dominated political processes. We don't know what kind of world children and domesticated animals would create if they had power in shaping society. But what is clear is that philosophical theories that position children and animals as adversaries are a reflection of adult ideologies and interests, not of the hopes, dreams, or identities of children or animals themselves.[11]

Notes

1 Rollo argues that the subjection of children and of colonial peoples rested on homologous processes of rationalizing coercive rule by the "fully human" over the "immature".
2 People with intellectual disabilities, dementia, and other cognitive disabilities are also excluded by the capacity contract (Sonnicksen 2016).
3 Parts of our discussion may have relevance for non-domesticated animals – whether "liminal" urban wildlife or wilderness animals – but they are not our primary focus here.
4 According to Melson, the child–animal relationship has been ignored by all the major theories of child development, including theorists of cognitive development (Piaget); attachment theorists (Bowlby); ecological theorists (Bronfenbrenner); network theorists; and self psychologists (Kohut): "in short, children's ties to animals seem to have slipped below the radar screens of almost all scholars of child development" (Melson 2001: 12). As Serpell notes, this is true of the social sciences more generally: "the sad truth is that psychologists and social scientists have shown a baffling lack of scholarly interest in the child-animal relationship, considering its extraordinary prominence in our culture. Not one of the major textbooks on psychology or child development offers more than a passing reference to the topic, a good illustration of this selective blindness" (Serpell 1999: 92). Serpell and Myers attribute this blindness to the "tendency to view children as essentially unformed and animal-like while regarding human development as a process of shedding these animal-like attributes in favour of the actualization of adult qualities defined as uniquely human" (Serpell 1999: 92; Myers 1999).
5 Louv's work (2005) has stimulated important research in this area, as well as various initiatives to repair children's fractured relationship with the more-than-human world. See summaries at: http://www.childrenandnature.org/learn/research-resources/summaries/
6 Zoos and marine parks also play a crucial role in "educating" children about their separation from other animals. Consider the impact it must have on children to see veterinarians and zookeepers – who are held up as animal lovers and animal experts – engage in routine killing of animals for trivial purposes, while making children complicit in the practice (as in the recent case of the Copenhagen zoo's killing, and public dissection, of Marius the giraffe). On the role of zoos in constructing the species divide, see Acampora (2010) and Gruen (2014).
7 See Inglis (2011). See Ellis and Irvine (2010) for a study of the socialization process by which children in 4-H programs go from seeing farm animals as friends and family to "market animals" or livestock.

8 Or at least it was, e.g. this video of a young girl being bullied into shooting a pig, which was recently taken down from YouTube: https://www.youtube.com/watch?feature=player_embedded&v=FVBv-PhorUQ (last accessed 13 February 2016).
9 See also Veser, Taylor, and Singer (2015).
10 See Wall (2011) for a discussion of this problem in relation to children. For examples of theorists who invoke the capacity contract to exclude animals, without offering any proposals about how to be responsive to their interests, see Hinchcliffe (2015) and Planinc (2014).
11 We are grateful to Anca Gheaus, Gideon Calder, and Christiane Bailey for commenting on an earlier draft.

References

Acampora, R. (ed.). 2010. *Metamorphoses of the Zoo*. Lanham, MD: Rowman & Littlefield.
Alderson, P. 2008. *Young Children's Rights*. London: Jessica Kingsley.
Amiot, C., and Bastian, B. 2015. "Toward a Psychology of Human–Animal Relations," *Psychological Bulletin* 141(1): 22–23.
Archard, D. 2014. "Children's Rights," *Stanford Encyclopedia of Philosophy*. Retrieved from http://plato.stanford.edu/archives/sum2016/entries/rights-children/ (last accessed 19 March 2018).
Arneil, B. 2002. "Becoming Versus Being: A Critical Analysis of the Child in Liberal Theory," in D. Archard and C. Macleod (eds.), *The Moral and Political Status of Children*. Oxford: Oxford University Press.
Ascione, F. et al. 2007. "Battered pets and Domestic Violence," *Violence Against Women* 13(4): 354–373.
Benvenuti, A. 2016. "Evolutionary Continuity and Personhood: Legal and Therapeutic Implications of Animal Consciousness and Human Unconsciousness," *International Journal of Law and Psychiatry* 48: 43–49.
Bryant, T. 2010. "Denying Childhood and its Implications for Animal-Protective Law Reform," *Law, Culture and the Humanities* 6: 56–74.
Clifford, S. 2014. "The Capacity Contract: Locke, Disability, and the Political Exclusion of 'Idiots'," *Politics, Groups and Identities* 2(1): 90–103.
Costello, K., and Hodson, G. 2014. "Explaining Dehumanization Among Children: The Interspecies Model of Prejudice," *British Journal of Social Psychology* 53: 175–197.
Donaldson, S., and Kymlicka, W. 2011. *Zoopolis: A Political Theory of Minority Rights*. Oxford: Oxford University Press.
Donaldson, S., and Kymlicka, W. 2015. "Farmed Animal Sanctuaries: The Heart of the Movement?," *Politics and Animals* 1: 50–74.
Ellis, C., and Irvine, L. 2010. "Reproducing Dominion: Emotional Apprenticeship in the 4-H Youth Livestock Program," *Society and Animals* 18: 21–39.
Febres, J. et al. 2014. "Adulthood Animal Abuse Among Men Arrested for Domestic Violence," *Violence Against Women* 20(19): 1059–1077.
Flegel, M. 2009. "'Bend or Break': Unraveling the Construction of Children and Animals as Competitors in Nineteenth-Century English Anti-Cruelty Movements," *Journal of Critical Animal Studies* 7(1): 53–73.
Gasson, R., and Linsell, C. 2011. "Young Workers: A New Zealand Perspective," *International Journal of Children's Rights* 19: 641–659.
Gheaus, A. 2011. "Arguments for Nonparental Care for Children," *Social Theory and Practice* 37(3): 483–509.
Gibert, M., and Desaulniers, E. 2014. "Carnism," in P. Thompson and D. Kaplan (eds.), *Encyclopedia of Food and Agricultural Ethics*. Berlin: Springer, pp. 292–298.
Girard, A., and Pozzulo, J. 2012. "The Significance of Animal Cruelty in Child Protection Investigations," *Social Work Research* 36(1): 53–60.
Gruen, L. (ed.). 2014. *The Ethics of Captivity*. Oxford: Oxford University Press.
Hinchcliffe, C. 2015. "Animals and the Limits of Citizenship," *Journal of Political Philosophy* 23(3): 302–320.
Hodson, G., MacInnis, C., and Costello, K. 2014. "(Over)Valuing 'Humanness' as an Aggravator of Intergroup Prejudices and Discrimination," in Paul Bain et al. (eds.), *Humanness and Dehumanization*. London: Routledge.
Inglis, N. 2011. "Routt County 4-H members raise animals with hard work youngsters show off talents at Routt County Fair," *Steamboat Pilot & Today*. Retrieved from https://www.steamboattoday.com/explore-steamboat/routt-county-4-h-members-raise-animals-with-hard-work/ (last accessed 13 February 2016).
Jans, M. 2004. "Children as Citizens: Towards a Contemporary Notion of Child Participation," *Childhood* 11(1): 27–44.
Joy, M. 2011. *Why We Love Dogs, Wear Cows and Eat Pigs*. Newbury Port: Conari Press.

Liebel, M. 2012. "Do Children Have a Right to Work? Working Children's Movements in the Struggle," in K. Hanson and O. Nieuwenhuys (eds.), *Reconceptualizing Children's Rights in International Development*. Cambridge: Cambridge University Press.

Lister, Ruth. 2008. "Unpacking Children's Citizenship," in Antonella Invernizzi and Jane Williams (ed.), *Children and Citizenship*. London: SAGE.

Lockwood, R., and Arkow, P. 2016. "Animal Abuse and Interpersonal Violence," *Veterinary Pathology*. 53(5): 910–918.

Louv, R. 2005. *Last Child in the Woods: Saving Our Children from Nature-Deficit Disorder*. Chapel Hill, NC: Algonquin.

Lu, S. 2015. "Invisible Caregivers," *American Psychological Association Newsletter* 46(8): 36–38.

Melson, G. 2001. *Why the Wild Things Are: Animals in the Lives of Children*. Cambridge, MA: Harvard University Press.

Melson, G. 2011. "Principles for Human-Animal Interaction Research," in P. McCardle et al. (eds.), *How Animals Affect Us*. Washington, DC: American Psychological Association.

Myers, E. 1999. "Human Development as Transcendence of the Animal Body and the Child-Animal Association in Psychological Thought," *Society and Animals* 7(2): 121–140.

Oakley, J. 2013. "'I Didn't Feel Right About Animal Dissection': Dissection Objectors Share Their Science Class Experiences," *Society and Animals* 21(4) 360–378.

Paul, E. F. 2001. "Introduction," in E. Paul and J. Paul (eds.), *Why Animal Experimentation Matters: The Use of Animals in Medical Research*. New Brunswick: Transaction.

Pedersen, H. 2010. *Animals in Schools: Process and Strategies in Human-Animal Education*. West Lafayette, IN: Purdue University Press.

Peggs, K. 2012. *Animals and Sociology*. Houndmills: Palgrave.

Piazza, J. et al. 2015. "Rationalizing Meat Consumption: The 4Ns," *Appetite* 91: 114–128.

Planinc, E. 2014. "Democracy, Despots and Wolves: On the Dangers of Zoopolis's Animal Citizen," *Canadian Journal of Political Science* 47(1): 1–21.

Roche, J. 1999. "Children: Rights, Participation and Citizenship," *Childhood* 6(4): 475–493.

Rollo, T. 2018. "Feral Children: Settler Colonialism, Progress, and the Figure of the Child," *Settler Colonial Studies* 8(1): 60–79.

Schleidt, W., and Shalter, M. 2003. "Co-evolution of Humans and Canids," *Evolution and Cognition* 9(1): 57–72.

Shklar, J. 1991. *American Citizenship: The Quest for Inclusion*. Cambridge, MA: Harvard University Press.

Serpell, J. 1996. *In the Company of Animals*. Cambridge: Cambridge University Press.

Serpell, J. 1999. "Guest Editor's Introduction: Animals in Children's Lives," *Society and Animals* 7(2): 87–94.

Sonnicksen, J. 2016. "Dementia and Representative Democracy: Exploring Challenges and Implications for Democratic Citizenship," *Dementia* 15(3): 330–42.

Stewart, K., and Cole, M. 2014. *Our Children and Other Animals*. Aldershot: Ashgate.

Thompson, K., and Gullone, E. 2003. "Promotion of Empathy and Prosocial Behaviour in Children through Humane Education," *Australian Psychologist* 38: 175–82.

Trasande, L. et al. 2006. "The Environment in Pediatric Practice," *Journal of Urban Health* 83(4): 760–72.

Urbanik, J., and Morgan, M. 2013. "A Tale of Tails: The Place of Dog Parks in the Urban Imaginary," *Geoforum* 44: 292–302.

Veser, P., Taylor, K., and Singer, S. 2015. "Diet, Authoritarianism, Social Dominance Orientation, and Predisposition to Prejudice," *British Food Journal* 117(7): 1949–1960.

Wall, J. 2011. "Can Democracy Represent Children? Towards a Politics of Difference," *Childhood* 19(1): 86–100.

Weisberg, Z. 2016. "Reimagining Animal Assisted Intervention via Interspecies Citizenship Theory," in C. Overall (ed.), *Pets and People: The Ethics of Our Relationships with Companion Animals*. Oxford: Oxford University Press.

Zakaras, A. 2016. "Democracy, Children, and the Environment: A Case for Common Trusts," *Critical Review of International Social and Political Philosophy* 19(2): 141–162.

26
WHAT'S WRONG WITH CHILD LABOR?

Philip Cook

Introduction

Is child labor morally wrong? Your initial response might be: "Yes, of course." Perhaps you take the view that child labor is wrong because it is harmful. However, this clear moral intuition may be quickly qualified when we consider the practical problems of abolishing child labor. On the one hand, we know that simply abolishing child labor may, at least in the short-term, make many children worse off. Much child labor is motivated by necessities of poverty. Simply eliminating it would make many poor children poorer. On the other hand, we would probably admit that some work might be good for children. Work that is safe and fulfilling may benefit children in lots of different ways. So, on reflection, if asked "is child labor wrong?" a more considered response might be: "Yes, when it is harmful. We should only permit work that benefits children."[1]

If these thoughts capture your moral intuitions about child labor, you are in good company. Most international organizations and moral philosophers working on child labor take a similar view. I do not disagree with this moral outlook on child labor, but I will explain why I think it is incomplete. In particular, I will explain why harm-based objections to child labor are more problematic than they appear at first sight: they have problems establishing baselines for comparison, and they quickly run into Non-Identity problems. The dominant focus on harm-based objections has meant that other important moral considerations regarding child labor are neglected. Although many objections to child labor appear to be harm-based, I will suggest they are in fact concerned with duties to benefit children by replacing child labor with something better, usually schooling. Failing to provide a benefit is a different kind of wrong from committing a harm, and it is worth getting this straight in our thinking about child labor. Most crucially, neither considerations of harm nor failing to provide a benefit exhaust the moral objections to child labor. Many children perform work that is not harmful, and from which they derive some benefit, but we still find it morally troubling. This is because it is exploitative. Objections to exploitative child labor need to be distinguished clearly from harm and failing-to-benefit objections. If I am right that there are (at least) three different kinds of objections to child labor (harm, failing-to-benefit, and exploitation), we find a surprise: we have a duty to promote child labor.

What's the harm of child labor?

The dominant view of harm regards a person as harmed if they are worse off because something happened compared to if it had not happened. This is usually called the comparative counterfactual view of harm.[2] Harm is a matter of comparing one state of the world in which something happened against another in which it did not. Is a child worse off if they grow up in a society in which they need to work instead of growing up in a society in which they do not?

Some kinds of work are almost always harmful: work that injures or makes children unwell, perhaps due to hazardous conditions or toxic materials, or work that is debasing or criminal, such as sex work, drug trafficking, or bonded labor (where children are unfree to leave until a debt is repaid through work).[3] There is broad international agreement that these "worst forms" of child labor should be abolished with greatest urgency.[4] Happily, this is the minority of work done by children, and it seems to be declining.[5]

Harm-based arguments give us a clear basis on which to object morally to the "worst forms" of child labor. But there are many more children working in conditions where the harm is unclear. Consider a child who works in agriculture or textile manufacturing, or in a service job such as shining shoes or in a laundry. The work may be basically safe, but might involve long hours and be low paid. The child may depend on the income to support themselves and their family, and this work might be better than any available alternative. Many such children may be worse off if prevented from working. Does this mean that any child labor that is better than not working is not harmful and, thus, not wrong? Not necessarily.

We can imagine a world in which a child is compensated for the income lost through giving up work. Now we are faced with a comparison between the child growing up in a world where they work long hours for low pay, and growing up in a world where they do not work but they enjoy the same income. There are, in fact, many such programs that compensate families for income lost through preventing their children from working.[6] These schemes are an example of a counterfactual to a world in which children work for income due to poverty. If we make this comparison, the comparative counterfactual view of harm seems to explain what is wrong with the great majority of work done by children: even children who do not do the "worst forms" of child labor are harmed by work, as they would be better off with no work and no loss of income. Even with no other change in their circumstances they would likely have more time, more energy, and so would be better off. But the comparative counterfactual account of harm stumbles in explaining properly *that* this kind of child labor is harmful, and it struggles to identify *who* is harmed by this kind of child labor. The first problem involves comparative baselines; the second problem involves Non-Identity. I will look at each in turn.

In order to illuminate the problem of baselines in comparative counterfactual views of harmful child labor, it is useful to introduce a distinction between ideal and non-ideal theory. The difference and relationship between ideal and non-ideal theory in political philosophy is quite vexed, but at least part of the difference seems to consist in recognizing different purposes of theorizing.[7] Are we trying to *explain* what is right or wrong, or good or bad, about some political arrangement? It can be useful to make certain assumptions if this is our goal, such as "let's assume everyone follows the rules, and let's assume people know enough to understand the options before them properly, etc." This helps makes the moral evaluation of complicated political arrangements easier if we simplify and hold constant important complexities. We may have a different purpose though, which is to understand what we should *do* to make the world a better place (more just, equal, democratic, or whatever). If we are interested in this problem, we need to know the degree to which people are likely to follow different rules, or how likely people are to make a rational decision given the complexity of the information, amongst many other things. How does the comparative counterfactual view of the harm of child labor fare in either of these roles?

Let's take the explanatory, more ideal-theory, role of the comparative counterfactual view of harm: a world in which children work is worse than a world in which they do not, and they lose no income from not working. What is the appropriate baseline for comparison? Is it the income received by the child? If so, then on this comparative counterfactual view a child may not be harmed by not working if they receive compensation. This explains the wrong-because-harmful nature of arrangements that allow children to work versus those that compensate children directly for not working. But most children's income is not kept to themselves; it is included in a combined family income. So, this suggests we should change the baseline to family income, and not an individual child's income. But family income is not a suitable baseline either. Income is only one dimension that affects the relationship between family well-being and work. Much work done by children is done alongside their family, often at home, where work and care are often intermingled. This suggests our baseline should include the effect on caring relationships. If a child is absent from work, and so unable to give or receive care, this may incur greater costs on parents who provide care to children while working. This may create additional caring "costs" for other members of the family. Will other family members, perhaps older, non-working relatives, have to provide care? Will some form of paid care be required? It is unclear what the balance of harms to wider family life is in these comparative counterfactuals. This is partly because of the problems of defining a baseline involving income and care for both individuals and families.[8] These are examples of the problems of comparative counterfactuals in explaining the harm of child labor in ideal theory due to the obscurity of the relevant baselines of comparison. If we understand harm from a comparative counterfactual point of view, and if we cannot establish an appropriate baseline for comparing counterfactuals regarding child labor, then we cannot explain the harmfulness of child labor.

Perhaps the comparative counterfactual view of harm fares better in guiding our comparison of different practical arrangements regarding child labor; that is, from a more non-ideal point of view. Let's begin again with the original baseline that seemed to work well in explaining the harm of child labor: a world in which children work compared to a world in which they do not work and lose no income. If around 165 million children are currently working around the globe, it will take an unprecedented effort to ensure no child is harmed through loss of earnings in abstaining from child labor. We are not likely to make the world less harmful if we try to abolish child labor according to this baseline, and no-one seriously suggests so. What should we take as our more practical baseline?

The most practical approach might involve tackling the root of the problem: poverty. The structural elimination of poverty likely involves long-term reforms such as improving education to increase the value of production and consumption. Higher-value production and consumption tends to lead to a rise in prices and wages through growth. Such structural reforms may include requiring children to attend school rather than work. As children are eliminated from the labor market, adult wages should rise, thus also helping reduce poverty. So, the practical comparisons should be between worlds in which there is a progressive shift towards children spending more time at school and less time at work. But school is often more harmful than work, whether we consider baselines of individual child or family well-being.

Schooling in countries with substantial poverty and child labor is normally costly. If we choose the income received by an individual child as our comparative baseline, a child is likely to incur additional costs through substituting schooling for working. These include the opportunity costs of failing to learn practical skills through work that may have positive labor market value at the expense of gaining school credentials for which there may be little market value (Krafft 2017). Even if the quality of schooling is good, this does not imply that the value of the credentials earned is high. This depends on numerous factors including the demand for the credential, and the ability of families and employers to access credit to invest in education and higher-value production. Increasing schooling alone is often insufficient to shift an economy away from poverty to high-value growth (Baland and Robinson 2000). Replacing child labor with compulsory schooling may be more harmful to individual children.

We might assume that adult wages would rise if they performed the same labor as the now-schooled children, as there would be less supply for a constant demand for labor. So, if we take family well-being as our baseline, increased adult wages may mitigate costs of compulsory schooling. But there is no necessary connection between adult wages and the supply of child labor into non-related work. This only applies in conditions where adults' and children's work is "substitutable" and not complementary. Schooling can simply reduce the supply of children's labor for the type of work done by children, leaving adult wages unaffected.[9] Consequently, even if we take family well-being as our baseline, increased schooling often results in greater harms. The comparative counterfactual account of the harm of child labor struggles to guide our choices between more or less harmful practical arrangements regarding child labor.

The comparative counterfactual view of harm struggles to explain *that* child labor is harmful due to its trouble with baselines. It also struggles to explain *who* is harmed by child labor. This is particularly clear if we concentrate on the non-ideal role of the comparative counterfactual view of harm: its role in helping us choose practical arrangements to govern child labor. Let's imagine a world in which the big problems with baselines have been solved, and we have found a way to reduce harmful child labor through increased schooling. In this world, over several generations, children leave the labor market and mostly attend school (as happened, for instance, in the UK during the nineteenth century where child labor was replaced by compulsory schooling). This world is progressively very different compared to a world in which this policy has not been followed. Family life is different; indeed, families are likely to be different as patterns of fertility are affected by the changed economic circumstances of children being less economically active.

These two worlds are populated by different people. We are comparing two worlds over time. In one, child labor is progressively replaced by schooling, and child Alice grows up to have a child Beth, who has a child Clara, who has a child Dawn. In the other world, where child labor persists, child Alice grows up to have a child Ben, who has a child Charlie, who has a child Danny. If we compare these two worlds, can we say that Danny is harmed compared to Dawn because he works, whereas Dawn does not? Not easily, because though Danny exists in a world with child labor and no schooling, at least Danny exists (and let's assume his existence is perfectly good enough for him to get value from life). If the world was one of schooling and no work, Danny would not exist. We cannot say that Danny is harmed in a world with child labor, because without child labor, Danny would not exist. This is of course a version of the Non-Identity problem, associated famously with Parfit (1984: pt. IV). The Non-Identity problem affects the comparative counterfactual view of harmful child labor as soon as we recognize that reducing child labor will take several generations. Those who argue we should gradually replace child labor with schooling owe us an explanation of how child labor can be harmful to someone who would not exist without it.

It is clear that the widely held comparative counterfactual view of harm explains that the worst forms of child labor are harmful and should be abolished. However, the comparative counterfactual view provides less clarity regarding the harmfulness of the most common form of child labor: safe work done by most children to increase their income in conditions of poverty. The comparative counterfactual view struggles to explain *that* this kind of labor is harmful due to problems comparing it with both ideal or non-ideal baselines. It also encounters the perplexity of Non-Identity problems when taken as a basis for long-term policies to reduce child labor in favor of alternatives such as schooling. The comparative counterfactual view struggles to explain *who* is harmed by failing to abolish child labor across several generations. Harm-based objections to child labor seem more limited than we might have first thought.

Must children benefit?

If you have a headache, and I play loud music, I harm you. If you have a headache, and I decide not to give you some of my painkillers, I fail to benefit you. You are no worse off after my failing to give you the benefit of my painkillers, so I have not harmed you. But I have failed to benefit you. Harming and failing to benefit are different (see, e.g., Shiffrin 1999). We normally take wrongs done through harm as more serious than wrongs done through failing to benefit. Many of our moral concerns with child labor become muddled between preventing harm and failing to benefit. It is important for us to be clear about the difference.

Let's remember that most child labor is not of the "worst forms," which are clearly harmful and which we should try to eliminate. Most child labor might be arduous, but it is often less harmful than not working, for the reasons set out above. We may not have a duty to eliminate most of the child labor that occurs around the world today if we are concerned solely with reducing harm. This is because harm-based arguments may only lead to duties to eliminate child labor in a rather narrow range of cases: cases where the harm is unequivocal (worst forms of child labor), or where we are able to overcome obscurities about comparative baselines or conundrums about Non-Identity. However, we may have other duties towards children who work: duties to provide a benefit. The difference between duties against harming and duties to provide a benefit is important. The difference is especially important if duties based on harm do limited work in either explaining the wrongness of child labor or in guiding our decisions about how we should address the issue of child labor practically.

Many campaigners around child labor proclaim slogans such as: "stop child labor, school is the best place to work!"[10] Such slogans might be good for campaigning, but they are not so good for thinking carefully about the morality of child labor. This is because they easily confuse duties we might have to end child labor because it is bad for children in some way with duties we might have to promote benefits for children, such as schooling. However, they do express what seems to be a common-sense intuition: children benefit from schooling, and schooling should replace work. Even if work is not harmful to children, we might wrong children by failing to provide them with the benefit of schooling. However, there are two problems with the view that we have a duty to promote children's development through replacing work with schooling. First, it is unclear that development is a benefit and, second, it is unclear that schooling is a benefit. Let's look in turn at the problems with viewing development and schooling as benefits.

Many take it as given that children benefit from development. Childhood is seen as a stage of life defined by the gradual acquisition of the capacities that characterize adulthood (see Pierik and Houwerzijl 2006: 198; Satz 2010: 157). Though commonplace, this view is controversial. Critics of the "developmental" or "deficit" view of childhood disagree that childhood is a stage of life that is characterized by a lack of qualities we associate with adulthood (Farson 1978; Holt 1974). Such critics may accept that children are significantly dependent on and vulnerable to others in today's Western societies (see ch. 27). But they argue that this is a product of our wrongful treatment of children. Preventing children from working may be a significant cause of children's dependence and immaturity. Children's need for development may be a symptom of treating children wrongly. There are, no doubt, various responses to this objection available to those who wish to argue in favor of the benefit of development. But few make them. Pointing out this problem at least invites those who assume that development is a benefit to set out and defend the argument more fully than is currently typical.

The claim that schooling is a benefit faces at least two compelling challenges. First, we should clarify whether we are claiming that schooling or education is beneficial to children, because they are quite different. If we simply take education to mean growth in understanding and ability, there is little doubt that this is beneficial for everyone, not simply children. But schooling is not education. If we understand "schooling" as the experience of being at school, we quickly notice that the experience of being at school involves a lot more than education (see ch. 31). It often involves, amongst many other things, promoting democratic values, cultivating civic virtue, or providing the "goods of childhood," etc. (see, e.g., Callan 1997; Gutmann 1999; Macleod 2018). We may choose to define all these as "education" in the broadest sense. But if we do take a broad view of education, then we must also accept that education takes place beyond the school: at home; in extra-schooling lessons, perhaps involving sport, arts, or languages; or even, for many children, at work. So, the first problem faced by the argument that we have a duty to benefit students by promoting their development through schooling, is to make clear whether it is schooling, or education, that is the benefit we owe children.

The second problem faced by the argument that we have a duty to benefit students by promoting development through schooling is that schooling may provide no benefit. As we saw earlier, schooling is often costly and subsequently harmful to children. It may not provide beneficial education, perhaps because the quality is poor (Guarcello and Rosati 2007; Rammohan 2000; Rossi and Rosati 2007). But even if we can ensure that no child is harmed by going to school, it is not clear that it is beneficial. School may be less useful at providing the benefits of education, and more useful at reproducing existing social inequalities (Bowles and Gintis 2013; Willis 2000). We may have a duty to provide the benefit of education to children, but this may lead us to promote education beyond schooling. It may in fact lead us to a duty to abolish schooling, and to promoting the benefit of education elsewhere (Illich 1983). If we have a duty to benefit children, it is not clear that this duty means we should replace work with schooling.

I have argued that it is important to distinguish harm-based from failure-to-benefit objections to child labor. As we look at each of these different kinds of objections more carefully we find numerous difficulties. Many of these difficulties may be remedied, but this work is yet to be done by those concerned with the morality of child labor. Even if these problems are resolved so that we can use harm-based and failing-to-benefit objections to child labor more confidently, a further problem remains. There are many cases where child workers are not harmed and where they derive some benefit from their work. Is this work morally acceptable? Not necessarily, but to show this we need to be clear about a third and different objection to child labor. Once we understand this third kind of objection to child labor, we also find we may have a duty to promote child labor.

Is child labor necessarily exploitative?

Children often work alongside adults doing the same jobs – for example, working in "chop shops" (restaurant/bars) in Ghana. Children and adults wash dishes, clean the premises, serve food, and help to prepare and cook the meals. The work is safe, and both children and adults benefit from the wages. But children are paid less for this work than adults, though there is no evidence adults are more productive (IPEC 2007). If this work is not harmful, and if it provides the benefit of income for children, what could be wrong with it? It is wrong because it is exploitative.

A person may be exploited without being harmed; indeed, exploitation may even provide some benefit to a person.[11] In the case of the Ghanaian children working in "chop-shops," the children are benefiting from their income, but the employers are taking unfair advantage of children by paying them less than a fair market price for their labor. This kind of exploitation seems a common feature of child labor: infamously, it led thousands of child workers in Bolivia to organize into a trade union (UNATSBO) to campaign for an end to unequal pay for the same work, no less than a minimum wage for any work, and for lowering the minimum legal age for work (Fontana and Grugel 2015; Liebel, Meade, and Saadi 2017). These child activists argued that their work was the least harmful and most beneficial option before them, but that it was exploitative. How should we respond to cases such as this? It is crucial to distinguish the wrong of exploitative child labor from the wrongs of harmful child labor and the wrongs of failing to benefit children. Without this distinction we are unable to understand that even if work does not harm children, and in fact benefits them, it may still be wrong.

The concern with exploitation seems to motivate Satz's argument that child labor is an intrinsically noxious market because children have weak agency and are in asymmetric relations of knowledge and power with adults (Satz 2010: 155–70).[12] Non-exploitative child labor seems impossible as children are always likely to be treated worse than adults in the labor market due to their vulnerability. This might be the strongest objection to child labor, with the widest implications. Even if much child labor is not harmful, and even it provides some benefit, it is always likely to be exploitative given children's vulnerability. It should, therefore, be eliminated. An interesting response to this problem emerged from the children involved with UNATSBO. They were aware that lowering the legal age for child labor may increase exploitation as greater numbers of younger, more vulnerable, children would enter the labor market. But they also claimed that even young, vulnerable children had an important interest in non-exploitative work. They proposed that although many children might be incapable of preventing their own exploitation, children's interests could be protected by official representatives.

This model of representatives protecting children's interests complements developments internationally to protect children's independent interests given the difficulties they often have in protecting their interests themselves. Children's Commissioners, or Ombudsmen, are now widely established (Flekkøy 2002). They represent children's interests, often with statutory power.[13] If children are likely to be in a vulnerable position in labor markets, and, therefore, open to exploitation, we may have duties to protect vulnerable children from such exploitation (Goodin 1985; see also ch. 27). So, even if we agree with Satz that children are intrinsically at risk of exploitation due to their weak agency and asymmetries of knowledge and power, this does not mean we necessarily have a duty to eliminate markets in child labor. We may be able to protect vulnerable children from exploitation through institutions such as Commissioners. These may offer ways to fulfil the ambitions of child unionists in UNATSBO, and clarify that we have duties to end exploitative child labor, but not child labor itself.

We are now left with an interesting question that has a surprising answer. How should we regard child labor that is not harmful, that provides benefits, and is not exploitative? We might be surprised to find that we have no moral objection to this kind of child labor. Indeed, from the moral points of view we have considered here, we might be surprised to find that we have a duty to promote this kind of child labor. If we do not promote it, are we failing to benefit children? The qualification that child labor is wrong unless it benefits children is usually noted in philosophical discussions of child labor, but it is not explored in detail (Pierik and Houwerzijl 2006: 195–204; Satz 2010: 168). The idea that child labor is permissible if it is beneficial might appear as a minor qualification given the scale of the moral problem of child labor. But this qualification is important for our moral duties regarding child labor. We may have duties to promote the benefit of non-harmful, non-exploitative child labor. If we do not promote this child labor, we are wronging children by failing to benefit them. At the very least, this suggests that we need to look more closely at the range of moral duties we have regarding child labor.

Perhaps we should pay more attention to the possible moral value of work for children, and our duties to promote rightful child labor. More practically, this might also mean that we have to look more carefully at our practical choices regarding consumption and international development. Ethical consumption might mean both avoiding consuming goods produced through wrongful child labor, and choosing to consume goods made through rightful child labor. Ethical development might mean investing in child labor unions so that they are empowered to improve working conditions and resist exploitation, or providing "child labor commissioners" to prevent exploitative child labor. These conclusions suggest we might need to ask a different question about child labor: rather than asking "is child labor morally wrong?" we should ask "what are the rights and wrongs of child labor?"

Conclusion

There is long-standing and widespread moral concern about child labor, but very limited philosophical analysis of the problem. I have tried to set out systematically the nature of the dominant moral arguments regarding child labor, and have argued that we should distinguish more clearly between comparative counterfactual harm-based objections, failing-to-benefit objections, and exploitation-based objections. Each of these types of objections to child labor may offer valuable moral insights. But they need further development. The harm-based objections need to address problems with comparative baselines and puzzles about Non-Identity; failing-to-benefit objections need to establish that development through schooling is beneficial for children; exploitation-based objections need to explain if exploitation is a necessary part of child labor markets due to children's weaker position compared to adults, or if non-exploitative child labor is possible. There are many more outstanding questions regarding the morality of child labor than I have addressed here. These include important questions regarding the effects of gender, race, and age differences on the rights and wrongs of child labor. Much more philosophical attention is needed for us to be able to answer: "what's wrong with child labor?"[14]

Notes

1 A distinction is often made between child labor (which is regarded as morally problematic) and child work (which is regarded as permissible) (e.g. Pierik and Houwerzijl 2006: 195). However, this distinction is rejected by others (Bourdillon, Levison, Myers, and White, 2010). I agree with those that find it unhelpful, so use child labor to refer to all forms of work done by children.
2 For a helpful introduction to different views of harm, see Hanser (2013). I leave aside competing versions such at the temporal comparative and the non-comparative versions; these versions raise important issues for understanding the harm of child labor, but need more detailed consideration than is possible here. For an interesting discussion of different accounts of harm, and childhood specifically, see Jonas (2016).
3 It is, of course, possible that some children doing this work would be even worse off without it, but for most children caught in this kind of work almost any alternative would make them better-off.
4 This motivates wide adoption of the international convention ILO 182 which focuses on abolishing the "worst forms" of child labor: http://www.ilo.org/dyn/normlex/en/f?p=NORMLEXPUB:12100: 0::NO:12100:P12100_INSTRUMENT_ID:312327:NO
5 In 2012 (the latest international data available) 85 million children were estimated to be involved in this "worst forms" of child labor – a decrease from 115 million in 2008, and 170 million in 2000. Child labor, more broadly, is also said to be in decline from around 245 million in 2000 to around 168 million in 2012 (Diallo, Etienne, and Mehran 2013).

6 These schemes are an example of a counterfactual to a world in which children work for income due to poverty. These schemes normally compensate families for a child's loss of earnings *if* a child attends school, so they are usually called "conditional cash transfers." In these cases, the cash the family receives acts as both compensation for loss of earnings and incentive to provide the potential benefit of schooling. The functions of compensating for a loss and incentivizing for a benefit are separable though. To help us understand how a child may be harmed through work, I will concentrate on the (artificial) comparison of a child working for income in conditions of poverty with a child not working and being compensated for loss of income with no additional benefit beyond not working, such as schooling.
7 For an introduction to some of the main issues in this broad-ranging debate, see Valentini (2012).
8 For an investigation of the complexity of costing care in family life, see Folbre (2010).
9 The question of whether children and adults' labor is substitutable or complimentary is debated by economists (for sense of the issues, see Basu and Van 1998; Bhukuth and Ballet 2006).
10 This slogan is used by the prominent campaign organization *Stop Child Labor*. http://www.stopchildlabor.eu. The sentiment is shared widely by anti-child-labor campaign groups.
11 The nature of exploitation is contested: for useful overviews, see Sample (2003); Wertheimer and Zwolinski (2015). I cannot consider the various positions here, so adopt a broad notion that is hopefully intuitive, which involves one party, A, taking unfair advantage of another, B, due to some kind of vulnerability of A.
12 A similar argument is made by Pierik and Houwerzijl (2006: 202).
13 For a justification of the representation of children's interests, see Goodin (2003: 218).
14 Thanks to the editors and Elizabeth Cripps and Kieran Oberman for valuable written comments on previous drafts.

References

Baland, J.-M., and Robinson, J. 2000. "Is Child Labor Inefficient?," *Journal of Political Economy* 108(4): 663–679.

Basu, K., and Van, P. H. 1998. "The Economics of Child Labor," *The American Economic Review* 88(3): 412–427.

Bhukuth, A., and Ballet, J. 2006. "Is Child Labor a Substitute for Adult Labor?: A Case Study of Brick Kiln Workers in Tamil Nadu, India," *International Journal of Social Economics* 33(8): 594–600.

Bourdillon, M., Levison, D., Myers, W., and White, B. 2010. *Rights and Wrongs of Children's Work*. New Brunswick, NJ: Rutgers University Press.

Bowles, S., and Gintis, H. 2013. *Schooling in Capitalist America: Educational Reform and the Contradictions of Economic Life*. Chicago, IL: Haymarket Books.

Callan, E. 1997. *Creating Citizens*. Oxford: Oxford University Press.

Diallo, Y., Etienne, A., and Mehran, F. 2013. *Global Child Labor Trends 2008 to 2012* (International Programme on the Elimination of Child Labor). Geneva: International Labor Organization. Retrieved from www.ilo.org/ipec (last accessed 10 July 2017).

Farson, R. 1978. *Birthrights*. New York, NY: Penguin.

Flekkøy, M. G. 2002. "The Ombudsman for Children: Conception and Developments," in B. Franklin (ed.), *The New Handbook of Children's Rights: Comparative Policy and Practice*. London: Routledge.

Folbre, N. 2010. *Valuing Children: Rethinking the Economics of the Family*. Cambridge, MA: Harvard University Press.

Fontana, L. B., and Grugel, J. 2015. "To Eradicate or to Legalize? Child Labor Debates and ILO Convention 182 in Bolivia," *Global Governance: A Review of Multilateralism and International Organizations* 21(1): 61–78.

Goodin, R. E. 1985. *Protecting the Vulnerable: A Reanalysis of our Social Responsibilities*. Chicago, IL: University of Chicago Press.

Goodin, R. E. 2003. *Reflective Democracy*. Oxford: Oxford University Press.

Guarcello, L., and Rosati, F. C. 2007. *Does School Quality Matter for Working Children?* (Understanding Children's Work). Rome: Understanding Children's Work Project, University of Rome 'Tor Vergata'. Retrieved from http://www.ucw-project.org/research-papers-details.aspx?id=11949&Pag=8&Year=-1&Country=-1&Author=-1 (last accessed 28 August 2017).

Gutmann, A. 1999. *Democratic Education*, rev. edn. Princeton, NJ: Princeton University Press.

Hanser, M. 2013. "Harm," in H. LaFollette (ed.), *International Encyclopedia of Ethics*. Oxford: Blackwell Publishing, pp. 2299–2307.

Holt, J. C. 1974. *Escape from Childhood*. Harmondsworth: Penguin.
Illich, I. 1983. *Deschooling Society*. London: Harper Colophon Books.
IPEC. 2007. *Child Labor Wages and Productivity: Results from demand-side surveys*. Geneva, Switzerland: International Programme on the Elimination of Child Labor (IPEC), International Labor Organisation. Retrieved from http://www.ilo.org/global/publications/ilo-bookstore/order-online/books/WCMS_091334/lang--en/index.htm (last accessed 27 August 2017).
Jonas, M. 2016. "Assessing Baselines for Identifying Harm: Tricky Cases and Childhood," *Res Publica* 22(4): 387–404.
Krafft, C. 2017. "Is School the Best Route to Skills? Returns to Vocational School and Vocational Skills in Egypt," *The Journal of Development Studies* 54(7): 1100–1120, doi: 10.1080/00220388.2017.1329524.
Liebel, M., Meade, P., and Saadi, I. 2017. "Working Children as Subjects of Rights," in M. Ruck, M. Peterson-Badali, and M. Freeman (eds.), *Handbook of Children's Rights: Global and Multidisciplinary Perspectives*. London: Routledge.
Macleod, C. M. 2018. "Just Schools and Good Childhoods: Non-preparatory Dimensions of Educational Justice," *Journal of Applied Philosophy* 35(S1): 76–89.
Parfit, D. 1984. *Reasons and Persons*. Oxford: Oxford University Press.
Pierik, R., and Houwerzijl, M. 2006. "Western Policies on Child Labor Abroad," *Ethics & International Affairs* 20(2): 193–218.
Rammohan, A. 2000. "The Interaction of Child labor and Schooling in Developing Countries: A Theoretical Perspective," *Journal of Economic Development* 25(2): 85–99.
Rossi, M., and Rosati, F. 2007. *Impact of School Quality on Child Labor and School Attendance: The Case of CONAFE Compensatory Education Program in Mexico* (UCW Working Paper Series). Rome: Understanding Children's Work Project.
Sample, R. J. 2003. *Exploitation: What It Is and Why It's Wrong*. Lanham, MD: Rowman & Littlefield.
Satz, D. 2010. *Why Some Things Should Not Be for Sale: The Moral Limits of Markets*. Oxford: Oxford University Press.
Shiffrin, S. 1999. "Wrongful Life, Procreative Responsibility, and the Significance of Harm," *Legal Theory* 5: 117–148.
Valentini, L. 2012. "Ideal vs. Non-ideal Theory: A Conceptual Map," *Philosophy Compass* 7(9): 654–664.
Wertheimer, A., and Zwolinski, M. 2015. "Exploitation," in E. N. Zalta (ed.), *The Stanford Encyclopedia of Philosophy* (Summer 2015). Retrieved from http://plato.stanford.edu/archives/sum2015/entries/exploitation/ (last accessed 28 August 2017).
Willis, P. 2000. *Learning to Labor: How Working Class Kids Get Working Class Jobs*. Aldershot: Ashgate.

27
THE VULNERABLE CHILD

Mianna Lotz

Introduction

It has been suggested by Sigal Benporath (2003: 127) that "the single most relevant trait of childhood is…the vulnerability of children's lives and well-being." While positioned within a Kantian analysis, Benporath's insight is reflective of a growing philosophical emphasis on vulnerability as an especially salient and normatively potent feature of human life. This chapter examines the specific contribution of vulnerability theory to our understanding of the nature of children's lives and experience, bringing to the fore the distinctive philosophical questions posed and addressed within such an analysis.

I begin with a brief overview of general vulnerability theory and of the specific nature of the child's vulnerability, before focusing more closely on the distinct vulnerability of children within the parent–child relationship, analyzed within the conceptual framework of *relational* vulnerability.[1] Rather than seeking to exhaustively detail the forms and manifestations of childhood vulnerability, the discussion will focus on four philosophically important questions that arise in relation to the child's vulnerability. These include the key forms of vulnerability distinctive of the child's life; how the child's vulnerability should be morally assessed; whether realization of the significant goods of both childhood and parenting *requires* the substantial vulnerability of the child; and how we should understand the nature and scope of the obligations generated by an analysis of the child's vulnerability.

The nature of vulnerability and of the specific vulnerability of children

Philosophical vulnerability theory was first systematically developed by Robert Goodin (1985), but conceptions of vulnerability have subsequently been expanded and refined in important ways.[2] Goodin proposed that a focus on vulnerability will provide the most comprehensive foundation for the generation of all moral obligations, not just those towards persons with whom we are in a relationship with or for whom we voluntarily assume responsibility. For Goodin it is the vulnerability of dependent others to our actions and choices that is most fundamental and the "true source of all the standard special responsibilities that we so readily acknowledge" (Goodin 1985: 11).

At the most basic conceptual level, to be vulnerable is to be susceptible to harm.[3] Beyond this basic conceptualization, vulnerability has been philosophically theorized in two distinct yet ultimately compatible ways: first, as a universal, inherent and ontological feature of human beings and lives, such as we find in the accounts of Eva Kittay (1995, 1997, 1999) and Martha Albertson Fineman (2008, 2010); and, contrastingly, as a contingent, special susceptibility to harm of some kind, of specific persons and groups in specific kinds of conditions, as first conceptualized by Goodin.

So-called *ontological* accounts construe vulnerability as a fragility and susceptibility to both physical and psychological harm and suffering, but emphasize that this is "a universal, inevitable, enduring aspect of the human condition" (Fineman 2008: 8). Contrasting with ontological accounts, Goodin's and other accounts (such as Mackenzie, Rogers and Dodds 2014; Straehle 2016) focus on vulnerability as a function of *contingent, situational* and *circumstantial* features and conditions of a person's life. Where such conditions significantly impede agency and welfare interests, they present serious impediments to moral agency and generate weighty moral responsibilities on others. We are situationally and circumstantially vulnerable – and differentially so – to a wide range of threats and harms, including illness, loneliness, neglect, abuse, violence, grief, unemployment, homelessness and exploitation, to name just a few. Furthermore, situational vulnerability may be either dispositional (i.e. potential) or occurrent (i.e. actual). Identifying the distinct forms, sources, degrees and manifestations of vulnerability provides an important basis for specifying the kinds of actions required for appropriate response to the vulnerability in question.

What might be said, however, of the specific vulnerability of the child? Children share the ontological and inherent vulnerabilities of all human beings – to sickness, disability, poverty, homelessness, abuse, etc. – but as I have noted elsewhere (Lotz 2014) they also have a special vulnerability *qua* children. This distinctive vulnerability of the child derives both from their particular dependency on the actions and choices of those charged with their care, and from their temporary lack of the full suite of agential skills and competencies that marks mature adulthood and helps mitigate the risks of dependency on others, as well as freeing them from restrictive socio-structural and systemic conditions and roles that create or sustain their vulnerability. As the child grows older, becomes more independent and develops increasing skills and capacities, their distinctive vulnerability as children is hopefully gradually reduced, though their ontological vulnerability persists throughout their lives. Eva Kittay (1999) refers to the child's vulnerability as "inevitable dependency," and there is an obvious sense in which the vulnerability arising from the child's dependency is inherent in childhood; yet, its (ideally) transitional nature means that it is not appropriately regarded simply as an aspect of general ontological vulnerability. As indicated, the distinct vulnerability of the child is reduced and hopefully eliminated over time, as a result of both the child's internal, self-directed, natural development and of the autonomy-promoting support of her carers.

Hence, while not fully coextensive with general adult ontological vulnerability, the child's specific vulnerability is a non-contingent and necessary aspect of her life: there is no childhood without vulnerability. More specifically, there is no childhood without the dependency-based risks of neglect, abuse (physical and emotional), mistreatment, disrespect, lack of access to primary social goods and adequate educational opportunity, autonomy-inhibition, disenfranchisement and unjustified forms of paternalistic intervention and restriction. Such risks incurred as a result of childhood vulnerability are connected to a child's development in such a way that they can have impact well beyond childhood and, indeed, can potentially culminate in the causing of harm to the future adult. Vulnerability to lack of an adequate education is a key case in point: if a child is not provided with quality education, the negative impact of that deficit will be manifested well into and indeed throughout the person's adulthood.

It is particularly important here to highlight the child's special vulnerability to domination, subjugation and exploitation by adults, a result both of their dependency on others and of the fact that they are not regarded as fully autonomous agents with individual voices and wills entitled to full acknowledgement and respect. Macleod (2017: 173) refers to this as the child's comparative lack of "presumptive decisional authority." The assumption that children "lack relevant cognitive, emotional and moral capacities that permit them to understand, appreciate and act upon a wide set of important reasons for action" (MacLeod 2017: 174) means that the decisional authority attributed to them is "weak and qualified" at best, at least until they become mature minors.

We should distinguish two claims here. The first is about the child's *lack of cognitive, emotional and moral capacities* – what Sarah Hannan (2018: 8–9) has referred to as the child's "impaired practical reasoning"; the second is the child's lack of *attributed authority* in relation to her desires, judgments and will. As Tamar Schapiro (1999: 717, 729) has elucidated, in general we do not feel bound by children's expressions of their wills because "the condition of childhood is one in which the agent is not yet in a position to speak her own voice because there is no voice which counts as hers." Hannan refers to this as the lack of an established and stable practical identity, and notes how this manifests in greater flux in relation to their plans and commitments and, therefore, in greater challenges with leading the relatively coherent, organized and self-aware kind of life that contributes to flourishing and well-being, and helps agents fulfill their desires and goals and access valuable opportunities. Claims of the extent to which a child is autonomous or pre-autonomous, and of the extent to which their emergent autonomy should be respected, are of course contestable (see ch. 10). But our current society significantly and systematically denies children substantial authority in respect of their own wills, preferences, desires and goals, rendering them vulnerable to a degree of paternalistic treatment that must always be justified, and will not always be justifiable (see ch. 11).

For Schapiro, children's incapacities of executive control mean that they are, in Kantian terms, in a temporary non-ideal state – a *normative predicament* – escape from which requires assistance from others and thus imposes obligations on the adults around them. These obligations include refraining from inhibiting children's efforts to develop their own perspectives and commitments, and from in any way obstructing or delaying their development as agents and deliberators. This latter obligation rules out forcing children to rely on adult authority in relation to matters they are capable of deciding for themselves. Thus, Schapiro (1999: 736) says: "Where they have achieved sovereignty over some domain of discretion, we are not to subject them to our control"; we must instead "make children's dependency our enemy" by contributing directly to the development of their autonomy.

The lack of a voice and will entirely of their own, combined with their interest in and need for adult assistance to enable them to develop autonomous wills, also means that children are especially vulnerable to domination by those on whom they depend, particularly in relation to the inculcation of values. As Colin Macleod observes,

> a social environment in which various beliefs, convictions, and commitments are inculcated in the young through the conscious or unconscious employment of subtle and not so subtle techniques of indoctrination can profoundly influence the sort of person a child may become and the sort of life she can lead.
> *(Macleod 1997: 118–119)*

I have discussed elsewhere (Lotz 2014: 377–378) that attention to the distinct vulnerability of children brings into needed focus the significant power inequality that exists between them and their parents, and have argued that there are ways of attempting to influence a child's values that constitute exploitation of the dependency relation and, therefore, unacceptable parental domination.[4]

Specifically, I have argued that the child's distinct vulnerability to parental values inculcation arises as a result of at least four respects in which parents enjoy a privileged position relative to their children. First, parents have a "priority privilege" in virtue of the fact that they are typically the child's first source of values. They also have a "proximity privilege" in being able to communicate their values more readily, frequently and continuously to their children than can any other adult. Furthermore, parents have an "authority privilege" that means that their communication of values to their children will be infused with their authority in relation to other information they are relied upon to provide, and as such will carry special epistemic force. Finally, parents enjoy what I have called an "affect privilege," in that "the values endorsed by parents are, from the perspective of a child, entirely bound up not only with general informational exchanges but also, importantly, with the emotional exchanges occurring within the parent-child relationship." This, too, will imbue the parents' communication of values with a special appeal and force that may be difficult, if not impossible, for the child to disentangle from their communication of affect.[5] Where a parent's sense of entitlement to inculcate values is accompanied by overt coercion and a threat of rejection should those values not be accepted by the child, they exploit their parental privilege and subject the child to a morally serious form of domination. Such domination can severely impede the child's capacity to develop into an independent chooser and endorser of her own values, and will thereby significantly undermine her autonomy development and what Joel Feinberg famously termed her *right to an open future* (Feinberg 1980). It is clear, then, that a child's very attachment and dependency to her caregiver(s) renders her vulnerable not only to abuse, neglect, and more benign kinds of care failures, but also to potentially significant inhibition of her autonomy.

The dependency that lies at the heart of a child's distinctive vulnerability establishes that the child is a paradigmatic case of what Goodin claims is actually true of all vulnerability – namely, that it is *relational*. Before exploring Goodin's analysis of relational vulnerability I want to consider a question pertaining to the implications of taking seriously the nature and extent of the child's vulnerability. This is the question of whether children's vulnerability ought to be regarded as univocally unfortunate and regrettable.

How should children's vulncrability be morally assessed?

Importantly, to suggest that the child's vulnerability might be unfortunate, bad or wrong is not to claim that it is unjust. As Christine Straehle (2016: 35) suggests, the "background conditions of vulnerability" – those which make a person susceptible to not having significant interests met and to being reliant on others for welfare and protection – are "a fact of human life, but they are not immediately justice relevant." This is because they do not necessarily give rise to harm. Moreover, they are ineliminable and may even be essential for a child's appropriately gradual development. Hence, questions of justice properly arise only where children are deliberately kept in conditions of vulnerability beyond what is appropriate and necessary for their level of autonomy and capacity development, and where they are subjected to harm, neglect and abuse.

Some go beyond denial of its inherent injustice to claim that the vulnerable condition of the child may actually, in certain key respects, be morally *valuable*. The claim here is that the child's vulnerability occasions significant moral goods, the realization of which is only possible as a function of that vulnerability. For example, noting both the distinctive fragility and the potential resilience of the child, Colin Macleod (2015: 58–63) explains that while the lack of mature agency is usually regarded as exclusively a deficit condition for children, and its acquisition an unqualified benefit, it should instead be appreciated both that "the acquisition of mature agency does not uniformly diminish vulnerability" and that there are "good components of a human life to which children as juvenile agents have privileged and perhaps unique access." Accordingly, he says, "the very features of juvenile agency that render children vulnerable also give them access to important human goods" that comprise key elements of flourishing – namely, for Macleod, "innocence" and "imagination." Proper recognition of this means that we ought not regard ourselves to have reason to pre-emptively circumscribe childhood (where we could do so) in an effort to expedite the acquisition of mature agency and its vulnerability-reducing capacities, attributes and protections.

Macleod thus urges against the adoption of an overly "protectionist" view of childhood vulnerability according to which it is a uniformly detrimental aspect that we are obligated to eradicate wherever possible; for example, via pre-emptive and precocious inculcation of capacities for mature agency. Hence, his analysis is not fundamentally at odds with that of most other vulnerability theorists; he merely seeks to balance accounts of the risks of vulnerability with recognition of its potentially valuable dimensions.

The importance of these goods, and the moral seriousness of potential lack of access to them, leads Gheaus (2014, 2018) to argue for a moral obligation to ensure the robust access of all children, from a young age, to forms of non-parental childcare that can provide them with sufficient opportunities for enduring caring relationships with adults outside of the immediate family – a critical and necessary means, according to Gheaus, by which to mitigate and minimize the bads and vulnerabilities of childhood. Without such non-parental care children's vulnerability rightly becomes a matter of serious moral concern.

The suggestion that potential intrinsic goods are afforded by childhood despite (and even because of) the vulnerability that conditions it, certainly does not entail that the vulnerabilities and disadvantages of childhood are, on balance, a good thing. Sarah Hannan (2018: 5), for example, is highly critical of claims of the intrinsic goods of childhood. She points out the ways in which the alleged goods – such as sexual innocence, for example – themselves expose children to risk and vulnerability. Hannan ultimately rejects the suggestion that any genuine benefits of the ignorance, unreserved trustfulness and "incautious emotions" typical of children can override or adequately offset the significant risks and vulnerabilities that accompany such traits and states. Whether or not the proposed goods are realized depends entirely upon the highly contingent and unreliable factor of whether proximate adults are suitably protective, competent, sensitive, nurturing and worthy of children's trust and love.

The absence of such assured protections makes it difficult to be persuaded of the overriding value of the traits, states and dispositions referred to as intrinsic goods of childhood. There is something troublingly precarious about the goods in question – their realization overly contingent and other-dependent – a feature noted also by Hannan (2018: 6):

> the fact that children are extremely vulnerable, especially to the adults that care for them, means that there's a serious risk that their lives will go very badly, and there's almost nothing they can do to avoid this. Even when their lives go well, the contingency of this can reasonably be regarded as bad for them.[6]

Any recognition of the goods of childhood thus fails to undermine the claim that vulnerability is a significant and persistent feature of children's lives that warrants serious moral attention. One need not argue that childhood is, on balance, bad or an all-things-considered harm for children in order to give due acknowledgment and weight to the facts of a child's vulnerability, and to the obligations that the vulnerability imposes on the adults around them.

Let us turn now to a closer examination of the specific nature of the child's *relational* vulnerability within the parent–child relationship.

The child's relational vulnerability

Analysis of a child's inevitable dependency on others highlights what is most central to Goodin's account of vulnerability – namely, the essentially *relational* character of all vulnerability. The child's relational vulnerability is especially significant for understanding the distinctive vulnerabilities of childhood. Importantly, Goodin argues that we should not object to dependency or vulnerability as such, but rather to the implicit power involved in dependency relations, and the attendant risks of that power being abused. Thus, he proposes that what is really wrong with dependency relationships is that they necessarily create opportunities for exploitation of the weaknesses of those who are most vulnerable and dependent in the relationship.

Goodin holds that due to the inherent risk of exploitation there is something potentially "morally objectionable" about dependency relationships, including the parent–child relationship. This is a claim that warrants closer consideration. Before we consider that question, however, I want to note at this point that for some philosophers the child's relational vulnerability to her parents is *intrinsically* tied *to* the realization of parenting goods for adults. Hannan and Leland (2018: 11) have argued that there is a necessary link between the significant interest of adults in having parental relationships with children, and children's subjection to the bad features of childhood, including to what they refer to as their inescapable "profound and asymmetric vulnerability." In other words, the claim is that the realization of the adults' parental interests is not simply correlated with but *dependent upon* the child being subjected to those bad features: the subjection – we might even call it *subjugation* – of children to parents is not a mere side effect of the parenting relation.

The starting point for Hannan and Leland's argument is the connection Brighouse and Swift (2014: 88–91) draw between the goods of parenting and four special features of the parent–child relationship: unequal standing; children's dependency for care, which entails a degree of paternalistic parental coercion and manipulation; the child's lack of conception of their own good; and the child's disposition to love and trust their parents spontaneously and unconditionally. For Brighouse and Swift, these features jointly explain why parents derive both special responsibilities and special and unique satisfactions from being in the parenting role – namely, opportunities for personal development, as well as special forms of intimacy and affection that contribute in unique and significant ways to their flourishing. Accepting this claim of a necessary connection between parental goods and childhood vulnerability, Hannan and Leland (2018: 7) claim to strongly suspect that "any attempt to explain the special value of the parent-child relationship will fail to account for its uniqueness or profound importance to adults if it doesn't essentially involve children's asymmetric dependence, vulnerability, and need for parental care and control." They argue that most people who want to parent have an interest in parenting someone who is a poor practical reasoner, lacks an established practical identity, needs extensive control and is significantly and asymmetrically vulnerable to them. They believe that in the absence of those features "many [parents] would no longer have an interest in parenting, because they could not derive the same special goods from raising such children" (Hannan and Leland 2018: 21).

If correct, such a *child vulnerability–parental goods* nexus seems a deeply troubling feature of the parent–child relationship, and of the child's vulnerability. But I am not persuaded that it is correct. The claim conflates an important distinction between *being interested* in something, and something being *in one's interests*. Moreover, while existing norms, conceptions and expectations of the goods of parenthood support the current perceived connection between parental goods and children's vulnerability, what is unclear is whether, in different conditions and contexts, it would be impossible to realize significant parental goods *in the absence of* those forms of vulnerability. That is, there is a significant question as to whether the alleged existing connection between parental goods and childhood bads, and the expectations arising from it, are indeed strictly necessary or rather, merely contingent and artefactual, even if robustly so. Such expectations concern parental entitlement to decisional authority over children; the extent to which children in some sense belong to their parents; the value and perhaps "naturalness" of the private, nuclear family within contemporary capitalist society; and so on. These expectations are shaped and conditioned by the material, structural and socio-political conditions in which parenting is carried out, typically within dyadic nuclear families in which parents are vested with substantial responsibility and authority over children's care, education and lives in general. Where such conditions are socially accepted as necessary and normative – as in present so-called western societies – it is no surprise that parents regard them as central to their interests in the parenting role and to its goods and satisfactions. Yet, no matter how powerful and entrenched they may be, social norms do not establish the necessity of such conditions nor, therefore, of the connection between parental interests and childhood vulnerability. The claim that substantial influence and authority over children is essential for realization of the goods and satisfactions of parenting therefore needs a lot more defending.

Is the child's relational vulnerability morally objectionable?

Let us return to the question of whether the dependency relation between children and parents, as construed by Goodin, is morally objectionable in virtue of the child's vulnerability. Perhaps counterintuitively, Goodin (1985: 195–196) seems to suggest that it is. Acknowledging that some dependency relationships pose greater threats than others, he characterizes a risk of exploitation, and derivatively the moral objectionability of the dependency relation, as increasing with the extent to which the relationship is based upon the following key features: an asymmetrical balance of power in which one (subordinate) party has *vital need* for resources that the other (dominant) party has *discretional* and *exclusive* control over. Notably, the child's dependency on her parent(s) or primary caregiver(s) appears to fulfill Goodin's three conditions for morally objectionable vulnerability, suggesting that he would indeed view the parent–child relationship as inherently morally problematic.

To understand this, consider that what a child has *vital need for* – specifically, love, food, shelter, security and guidance – is intimately connected to her flourishing and, indeed, necessary for it. Moreover, it does, indeed, lie within a parent's *discretional* capacity to meet the child's fundamental needs. Matters are slightly more complicated in relation to the third condition, the *exclusivity* condition. Is it the case that parents are the *unique* sources of a child's vital needs? The answer here may initially appear to be negative, since it might be thought at least possible for another carer or carers to, in all significant respects, fulfill the child's fundamental needs. If that is accepted, then the child is not, after all, genuinely exploitable by her parents, and the dependency-based vulnerability that characterizes her relationship to her parent(s) is not of the morally salient or objectionable kind.

I suggest, however, that such a conclusion would be unwarranted. Whatever might be the case in relation to a child's needs for certain material goods, a child cannot simply transfer their equally vital emotional and other nurturance needs away from an existing parent with whom they are in an established, dependency-based relationship, to other care-providers.[7] Recognition of this fact underscores what is surely already widely appreciated: that an established relationship between a child and parent is in important and distinctly emotional respects *non-fungible*. Understood correctly, then, a current parent *is* in an exclusive discretionary position to meet (at least many of) the child's vital needs, and the child *is*, therefore, relationally vulnerable to her parent

The vulnerable child

in just the way that Goodin was concerned about. As such, the parent–child relationship is one of morally objectionable inequality and monopolization.

Must we accept this conclusion? Goodin points out a potential way in which we might seek to avoid it. He notes that the dependency relationships that we are likely to find intuitively unproblematic are those embodying not merely dependency but *inter*dependency. In these there is a *mutuality* of vulnerability: each party depends on the other for something significant, has the capacity to negotiate terms and conditions and, as a result, there is a much lower risk of exploitability. Thus, he says, "[o]nly asymmetrical power relations, only *unilateral* dependencies, create opportunities for one side (the stronger) to exploit the other (the weaker)" (Goodin 1985: 196). Mutuality, therefore, serves to block the moral objectionability of dependency relations.

It might be thought that Goodin is suggesting here that only dependency relationships in which there is *complete and equal* mutuality, reciprocity and dependency, can be morally acceptable. But, as he himself makes clear, that is not his view. Almost no relationships are perfectly dependency-symmetrical; hence, an equal mutuality requirement would render the vast majority of our relationships morally objectionable. Instead, Goodin proposes the "minimum conditions" of an acceptable dependency or vulnerability relationship to include that each party stands to gain something from the relationship (or lose something if the relationship is terminated). Hence, while we must allow for some asymmetry of need and, therefore, vulnerability within dependency relationships, the power asymmetry must not be *too great*. In addition, Goodin says, there needs to be a *capacity of exit* for the most vulnerable person: they need to be able to withdraw from the relationship without incurring too severe a cost. Nevertheless, the ideal is to prevent exploitability by forestalling the threat of exploitation within the relationship, and this should be achieved wherever possible by ensuring that no party has exclusive discretionary control over access to significant and basic resources needed by the other.

Accepting, then, that the parent–child relationship cannot be one of perfect mutuality, is the child's relational vulnerability ameliorated by sufficient mutuality of the required kind, or is it characterized by precisely the extent of asymmetry of need and vulnerability that establishes moral objectionability? It is surely difficult to see that Goodin's minimum conditions of mutuality obtain in parent–child relationships to an extent sufficient to mitigate moral concern. While each party may stand to gain something from the relationship or lose something if it is terminated, not only is there parental discretionary control over essential resources needed by the child, there is also no genuine exit capacity for the child. As highlighted by Anne Alstott (2006) and others (e.g. Brighouse and Swift 2006: 93), for the child the relationship is both involuntarily entered into and preclusive of voluntary exit (at least while she is young). A further potential moderator mentioned later by Goodin (1985: 199) is the capacity of the subordinate party to reduce their want or need of the relevant goods from the superordinate. This, too, fails to apply in the child's case. As such, the basis for moral concern persists regarding the child's potential exploitability within the unequal and asymmetrical relationship that is the parent–child relation.

To this it may be objected that the extent of the exit asymmetry is overstated in ways that fail to accurately capture features of the parent's relationship to their child. A parent's capacity of relationship exit is seriously constrained, after all, in legal and material but also important psycho-emotional respects. Parents are by no means fully free and unencumbered to relinquish the parental role and relationship at will. Yet, while it is important not to exaggerate the exit asymmetry, it is undeniable that a young child, at least, effectively has *no capacity* for voluntary exit, whereas the parent has at least *constrained capacity*. This exit asymmetry may not be as extreme as the entry asymmetry (in intentional parenthood at least); and it may sometimes be exaggerated in ways that grossly overestimate the parent's freedom – legal and otherwise – to exit the relationship. But there is no denying that the exit asymmetry is significant, and that whatever mutuality does inhere in the parent–child relationship, it is insufficient to render the relationship morally unproblematic according to Goodin's criteria.

Implications and obligations

We have arrived at what many may find a counterintuitive conclusion: that, considered in light of a relational vulnerability analysis, the parent–child relationship embodies an asymmetry and inequality that is to be regarded as morally objectionable. We have the option to reject that account on grounds that it fails the intuition test. But, to my mind, there is too much that is important and fruitful in it, in terms of identifying the general nature and source of the kinds of vulnerability that we ought to be most morally concerned about. Moreover, it alerts us to fundamental features of the parent–child relationship that make the child's position of potential exploitability within these relationships a matter warranting careful moral attention and diligent moral protection. An alternative resolution is needed.

It is neither possible nor in many respects desirable to seek to eliminate the child's vulnerability within these relationships, since to attempt to do so would either fundamentally alter the nature of the relationship and/or undermine core aspects of its significant moral value. The necessary connection between vulnerability and intimacy and the fact, highlighted by Brighouse and Swift (2014), that the distinctive intimacy afforded by parent–child relationships is one of the central moral goods for children as well as parents, establishes that efforts directed at vulnerability elimination would be wrongheaded. Instead, I suggest we accept Goodin's analysis on the grounds that doing so alerts us to the fact that children's vulnerability to their parents is morally hazardous, exposes them to some very serious risks of harm and imposes moral obligations to take appropriate protective and ameliorative measures in response to at least some of those risks. Such obligations fall on parents in the first instance; but they extend far beyond the parent–child relation to the extended family, non-parental carers, schools and the State. The child's vulnerability within the parent–child relationship makes imperative the need for strong protections to be available outside that relationship, since we cannot entrust to the very person(s) to whom a child is most vulnerable the discharge of the protective responsibilities arising from her vulnerability.

As such, my analysis supports Anca Gheaus's arguments (2011, 2018) for a justice-based moral obligation to ensure that all children have access to good quality, non-parental, institutional care, as a means to overcoming parents' morally objectionable monopoly of care over their children. Making such care available as a matter of entitlement and right will ensure, as Gheaus suggests, that all children have a number of caring adults in their lives who are independent from each other and can provide care as well as support for each other, and with whom the child can have enduring relationships – a mechanism that will reduce the care monopoly and thereby the child's morally hazardous vulnerability to abuse, neglect and domination, while at the same time preserving sufficient access to the parental goods and satisfactions that constitute the value of parenting for so many adults. Moreover, it will also open up access for an increased number of adults to the goods and satisfactions of close care-based relationships with children, even if those are more limited than the goods afforded to the parents themselves.

Importantly, however, adults' vulnerability-related responsibilities for children extend beyond *protective* obligations, to a wider set of what we might call *facilitative* and *ameliorative* responsibilities. These include responsibilities to promote the development of the child's autonomy, but also, in recognition of the proposed intrinsic goods of childhood, to provide and support opportunities for adequate enjoyment of those goods by the children in their care. And as I have argued elsewhere (Lotz 2016), these also include obligations of resilience promotion in children. The development of autonomy is central to the child's progression from childhood to adulthood. But co-existing with autonomy-promotion duties are obligations to help children develop the skills and capacities that will enable them to respond in healthy and constructive ways to adversity and challenge, and to be able to recover psychologically from harms and setbacks. This is a core obligation arising from recognition of the child's vulnerability, since risk of harm and hardship cannot be extinguished from any child's or person's life. As we have noted, defenders of the goods of childhood urge that we should not be so focused on autonomy development as to rush children's development into fully fledged autonomous adults, since to do so is to forego opportunities for enjoyment of childhood's distinctive goods. I suggest that the developmental space between full vulnerability and full autonomy can be very effectively bridged with the fostering of resilience capacity, especially since this capacity will provide significant benefits to people, even in situations and conditions in which autonomy is underdeveloped, denied or seriously inhibited.

Conclusion

Understanding the child's distinctive vulnerability lies at the crux of understanding the child and the stage of life that is childhood, as well as the particular nature of the child–parent relationship. While at the most fundamental level vulnerability is a susceptibility to harm, I have suggested here that protectionist duties do not exhaust the nature and scope of adults' vulnerability-related obligations towards children in their care. The child's vulnerability is distinctive and multifaceted and should by no means be thought of as an unequivocally negative aspect of her life. Relatedly, parents' obligations towards children are not merely protective but, as I have indicated, also facilitative and ameliorative. And, as also argued here, these obligations distribute more widely than to parents alone. Significant societal changes may ultimately be required if we are to manifest in practice a wider distribution of vulnerability-related obligations within our communities. But those will be changes that are well supported by vulnerability analyses, as well as by a full understanding of the genuine goods and interests of both children and adults.

Notes

1 The child is not only relationally vulnerable to its parents but to all persons on whom it is in some sense dependent, including extended family, other carers and teachers.
2 Most importantly by Kittay (1995, 1997, 1999), Fineman (2008, 2010), Butler (2004, 2009) and Mackenzie, Rogers and Dodds (2014).
3 Harm is understood here in Feinberg's (1980) sense of the setting back of a person's welfare or significant interests.
4 Macleod (2017) has more recently referred to this as "doctrinal vulnerability."
5 This is a point also made by Clayton (2006).
6 Hannan also questions the idea that the other goods mentioned as intrinsic goods of childhood are uniquely available to children, or at least necessarily so. I am only interested here in the vulnerability of children, so I leave aside those childhood goods that are not directly connected to vulnerability, including perhaps imaginative play, capacity for fun and openness to the future. I am inclined to agree with Hannan that any apparent adult incapacity here is predominantly socially contingent.
7 Indeed, such transferability does not even reliably hold in relation to two existing parents: in some cases, attachment bonds with one parent are not replicated with the other.

References

Alstott, A. L. 2006. *No Exit: What Parents Owe Their Children and What Society Owes Parents*. Oxford: Oxford University Press.
Benporath, S. R. 2003. "Autonomy and Vulnerability: On Just Relations Between Adults and Children," *Journal of Philosophy of Education* 7(1): 127–145.

Brighouse, H., and Swift, A. 2006. "Parents' Rights and the Value of the Family," *Ethics* 117(1): 80–108.
Brighouse, H., and Swift, A. 2014. *Family Values: The Ethics of Parent-Child Relationships*. Princeton, NJ: Princeton University Press.
Butler, J. 2004. *Precarious Life: The Powers of Mourning and Violence*. London: Verso.
Butler, J. 2009. Frames of War: When Is Life Grievable? London: Verso.
Clayton, M. 2006. *Justice and Legitimacy in Upbringing*. Oxford: Oxford University Press.
Feinberg, J. 1980. "A Child's Right to an Open Future," in W. Aiken and H. LaFollette (eds.), *Whose Child? Children's Rights, Paternal Authority, and State Power*. Totowa, NJ: Littlefield, Adams & Co.
Fineman, M. A. 2008. "The Vulnerable Subject: Anchoring Equality in the Human Condition," *Yale Journal of Law and Feminism* 1(20): 1–23.
Fineman, M. A. 2010. "The Vulnerable Subject and the Responsive State," *Emory Law Journal* 60: 251–275.
Gheaus, A. 2011. "Arguments for Nonparental Care for Children," *Social Theory and Practice* 37(1): 483–509.
Gheaus, A. 2014. "The 'Intrinsic Goods of Childhood' and the Just Society," in A. Bagattini and C. Macleod (eds.), *The Nature of Children's Well-Being*. Dordrecht: Springer.
Gheaus, A. 2018. "Children's Vulnerability and Legitimate Authority over Children," *Journal of Applied Philosophy* 35(S1): 60–75.
Goodin, R. 1985. *Protecting the Vulnerable: A Reanalysis of Our Social Responsibilities*. Chicago, IL: University of Chicago Press.
Hannan, S. 2018. "Why Childhood Is Bad for Children," *Journal of Applied Philosophy* 35: 11–28.
Hannan, S., and Leland, R. J. 2017. "Childhood Bads, Parenting Goods, and the Right to Procreate," *Critical Review of Social and Political Philosophy* 21(3): 366–384.
Kittay, E. F. 1995. "Taking Dependency Seriously: The Family Medical Leave Act Considered in Light of the Social Organization of Dependency Work and Gender Equality," *Hypatia* 10(1): 8–29.
Kittay, E. F. 1997. "Human Dependency and Rawlsian Equality," in D. T. Meyers (ed.), *Feminists Rethink the Self*. Boulder, CO: Westview Press.
Kittay, E. F. 1999. *Love's Labour: Essays on Women, Equality and Dependency*. New York, NY: Routledge.
Lotz, M. 2014. "Parental Values and Children's Vulnerability," in C. Mackenzie, W. Rogers, and S. Dodds (eds.), *Vulnerability: New Essays in Ethics and Feminist Philosophy*. New York, NY: Oxford University Press.
Lotz, M. 2016. "Vulnerability and Resilience: A Critical Nexus," *Theoretical Medicine and Bioethics* 37(1): 45–59.
Mackenzie, C., Rogers, W., and Dodds. S. 2014. "Introduction," in C. Mackenzie, W. Rogers, and S. Dodds (eds.), *Vulnerability: New Essays in Ethics and Feminist Philosophy*. New York, NY: Oxford University Press.
Macleod, C. 1997. "Conceptions of Parental Autonomy," *Politics and Society* 25(1): 117–140.
Macleod, C. 2015. "Agency, Authority and the Vulnerability of Children," in A. Bagattini and C. Macleod (eds.), *The Nature of Children's Well-Being*. Dordrecht: Springer.
Macleod, C. 2017. "Doctrinal Vulnerability and the Authority of Children's Voices," in C. Straehle (ed.), *Vulnerability, Autonomy and Applied Ethics*. New York, NY: Routledge.
Schapiro, T. 1999. "What Is a Child?," *Ethics* 109: 715–738.
Straehle, C. 2016. "Vulnerability, Health Agency and Capability to Health," *Bioethics* 30(1): 34–40.

PART V

Children and the state

28
CHILDHOOD AND THE METRIC OF JUSTICE

Lars Lindblom

Introduction

Any theory of justice must do two things. It must present a criterion and a metric of justice. The criterion explains what structure a distribution must have in order to count as just – for example, strictly equal, prioritarian or sufficientarian. The metric explains what should be distributed according to the chosen criterion, for instance welfare, resources or capabilities. The debate on the appropriate metric of justice has standardly been conducted with the characteristics and capacities of adults in mind. Recently, this approach has been challenged. This contribution aims to explain this development and to identify the philosophical issues at stake.

The chapter starts with an exposition of the standard theories of the metric of justice that identifies responsibility and neutrality as core issues in this debate. This sets the stage for presenting the two major areas of debate regarding childhood and the metric of justice. The first of these is the Agency Assumption; standard theories of the metric assume an ideal of responsible agency that makes them inappropriate as a metric for children. This raises questions about the structure of the metric. A monistic approach aims for a metric that works for both children and adults, whereas on a pluralistic view there are different metrics for different kinds of individuals. The second area of debate revolves around the issue of the intrinsic goods of childhood (see ch. 7). The starting point is that there are some human goods that are only, or especially, valuable in childhood. Since standard theories have been devised with adults in mind, it must be asked if the metric should be revised in order to incorporate them. This raises questions regarding the characteristics of intrinsic goods of childhood, their relationship to the ideal of state neutrality and the content of the metric of justice.

Standard theories of the metric of justice

Historically, the usual candidate for the metric of justice has been welfare, or utility. The core meaning of welfare is concerned with people's lives going well for them, but this thought can be interpreted in several ways. On the hedonistic account welfare is understood as pleasurable feeling, whereas on the desire, or preference, account it is interpreted as getting what one wants. A third option is the objective list view: a life goes well when it contains the values that are part of this objective list (Griffin 1986; cf. Sumner 1996). The contemporary debate on the metric of justice, however, started with John Rawls (1971) and his rejection of the idea that welfare should be the metric of justice. He argued that the correct metric of justice is primary social goods. These goods are such that they are rational to want more of, regardless of what more specific goals one has in life. They are:

> (i) the basic rights and liberties, (ii) freedom of movement and free choice of occupation against a background of diverse opportunities, (iii) the power and prerogatives of offices and positions of authority and responsibility, (iv) the all-purpose means of income and wealth, and (v) the social bases of self-respect.
> (Rawls 2001: 58–59)

One reason to prefer primary goods to welfare is that this allows one to get around the notoriously difficult problem of how to measure welfare. But a second set of reasons is more important for the ensuing debate:

> Justice as fairness ... does not look behind the use which persons make of the rights and opportunities available to them in order to measure, much less maximize, the satisfaction they achieve. Nor does it try to evaluate the relative merits of different conceptions of the good. Instead, it is assumed that the members of society are rational persons able to adjust their conceptions of the good to their situation. There is no necessity to compare the worth of the conceptions of different persons once it is supposed they are compatible with the principles of justice. Everyone is assured an equal liberty to pursue whatever plan of life he pleases as long as it does not violate what justice demands.
> (Rawls 1971: 94)

Two important things happen here. First, people are assumed to be able to adjust their goals and plans on the basis of the goods they have access to. They are responsible for their own well-being. In this sense, primary goods take account of personal *responsibility*. Second, the argument takes an ideal of *neutrality* as its starting point (see ch. 29). The theory of justice should avoid evaluating peoples' conceptions of the good. This focus initially only concerned the metric of justice, but in later writings, Rawls reworked his entire theory from the starting point of neutrality. Since the only way that people in a free society would come to an agreement on a conception of the good would be through unacceptable coercion, the theory of justice should start from a normative ideal that could be acceptable to all, regardless of conception of the good. This ideal, Rawls claimed, was the ideal of free and equal citizens. Primary goods were then derived from considerations about what such citizens needed in order to choose to develop their two moral powers: the rational (the ability to have a conception of the good, and thereby being able to decide for oneself what kind of life to live) and the reasonable (the capacity to act from justice, and therefore being able to cooperate with others on fair terms) (Rawls 2001). These two aspects of the metric – responsibility and neutrality – have come to characterize the following debate on the metric of justice.

This debate often goes under the heading "equality of what?", which comes from the title of a paper by Amartya Sen (1980), who argues against both welfarism and Rawls's account. He notes that Rawls's theory "seems to take little note of the diversity of human beings" (Sen 1980: 215). Sen presents a case where a person, later to be identified as Tiny Tim by G. A. Cohen (1989), is disabled, but blessed by a sunny disposition. Since Tim has an unusual ability to feel happiness, he would not, on the one hand, be compensated for being disabled by a welfarist theory of justice. He is doing very well in that metric. On the other hand, Rawls's resourcist metric may fail to recognize that Tim needs extra resources to have similar options to others. If each person should be given an equal share of the resources that are listed as primary goods, then there is no room for giving Tim more than this equal share.

These problems lead Sen to present an alternative view, the capability approach, which starts from the distinction between functionings and capabilities. A functioning is a state of being or doing something. In Tim's case the relevant functioning could be being able to move around without being restricted by a disability. Capabilities are abilities to achieve functionings. A common example is the difference between a fasting and a starving person. The former has the capability to achieve the functioning of being nourished, whereas the latter lacks this capability. The capability approach, like Rawls's theory, takes account of responsibility by giving choice an essential role. Achieving a functioning is the responsibility of the individual; in order to have a functioning one must choose it.

It may seem that the route to neutrality is straightforward. Since it is up to each person what functionings to choose, the state will not interfere people's conceptions of the good. However, there are numerous possible capabilities, and some index of which ones are most important is needed. Martha Nussbaum (2000) responded to this challenge, with a list of ten fundamentally important capabilities to be used as the metric of justice.

(1) Life
(2) Bodily health
(3) Bodily integrity
(4) Senses, imagination and thought
(5) Emotions
(6) Practical reason
(7) Affiliation
(8) Other species
(9) Play
(10) Control over one's environment

(Nussbaum 2000: 33–35)

This version of the capability approach has Aristotelian roots, which can be useful for comprising a list, but might also cause problems with regards to neutrality. If one's conception of the good contains other goods than those on the list – for example, mindless fun – then this metric seems to support a more cerebral conception of the good to the detriment of one's own. Capability theorists might have to choose between solving the index problem and running afoul of neutrality. However, Nussbaum argues for her list from the value of dignity, not Aristotelian flourishing. Dignity is commonly thought to be compatible with neutrality, but this still raises the question of why these identified capabilities, and not others, are those necessary for dignity.

Sen (1980) also uses the problem of expensive tastes as an argument against welfarism. An expensive taste is a taste that costs more than average tastes to satisfy. For instance, one has an expensive taste if one needs champagne to achieve the level of welfare that other people get from drinking beer. Ronald Dworkin (2000) has developed this problem into an argument that the metric of justice should be resources, both external, like money, and internal, such as talents. He asks us to imagine a society where equality is achieved. Louis finds that he is missing something in his life, and sets out to develop a taste for pre-phylloxera claret and plovers' eggs. These goods are so expensive that Louis will not be able to afford much of them. Consequently, his level of welfare will be lower than other people's. If welfare were the metric, the implication would be that Louis should now be given an extra amount of resources so he can achieve the same level of welfare as others. But why would justice demand that Louis' expensive taste be subsidized? On a resourcist account of the metric, Louis will be responsible for his choice to develop this expensive taste, and not afforded extra resources. It is not clear that the capability approach can handle expensive tastes (Robeyns 2003). If enjoyment of what one drinks and eats is a functioning, then the theory could imply that Louis should be compensated so that he too has the capability to achieve it. Similar problems can be devised for Nussbaum's list; Louis could have an expensive taste for play, for example. Therefore, Dworkin's argues that we should prefer resources to welfarism for both responsibility and neutrality reasons.

Richard Arneson (1989) argues that Dworkin moves too fast when he rejects welfare for responsibility reasons. Responsibility can be integrated in a welfarist metric by opting for equal opportunity for welfare. This is the view that justice is achieved when each person faces equal sets of alternatives in terms of expected welfare. Differences in achieved welfare will then be explained by the choices people make. Thereby, responsibility is incorporated. This seems to bring the argument between Arneson and Dworkin to a draw. Can there be some reason to prefer one account of the metric over the other? Both philosophers agree that Louis should be free to choose his conception of the good, but not in a way that cuts into the fair share of others. Dworkin claims that in order to make sense of this intuition, welfarism needs to appeal to a conception of a just share of resources, which would make welfarism parasitic on resourcism, and that the latter, therefore, gives the fundamental account of the metric.

G. A. Cohen (1989) claims that we do not have to choose between welfare and resources, since the metric should comprise both. Justice should be understood as equal access to advantage, where both welfare deficiencies and resource deficiencies count as distinct forms of unjust disadvantage. He uses the example of Tiny Tim to make his case. The fact that it is difficult for Tim to move around without a wheelchair shows that he suffers from a lack of resources. However, Tim also faces the following difficulty. He has full movement of his arms, but using them hurts. This is a problem of welfare, and not of resources. Cohen claims that an egalitarian would compensate for both deficiencies, and that, therefore, the metric should include both resources and welfare. Moreover, Cohen uses the concept of access to combine two other important ideas in the debate on distributive justice: having the *opportunity* to achieve a good and actual *outcomes*. The concept of access includes not only opportunity, but also "anything which a person actually has as something to which he has access" (Cohen 1989: 917). This addition is motivated, for Cohen, by a case where Tim has opportunity to use his arms, but where the pain makes him unable to take advantage of this opportunity. This kind of inability can also be a kind of injustice. In this way, access combines both opportunities and outcomes. Summing up, the debate on the metric of justice has, for reasons of responsibility and neutrality, been focused on finding alternatives to welfare. In the next two sections, we will investigate, first, responsibility arguments and, then, neutrality arguments from the perspective of children.

The Agency Assumption

Colin Macleod argues that standard theories of the metric are based on what he calls the Agency Assumption, and that this is problematic, since it does not apply to children (Macleod 2010). Macleod explains the assumption in terms borrowed from the later Rawls:

> First, in thinking about what constitutes justice-salient advantages we assume that persons have and can exercise the two moral powers. Second, in virtue of their possession of the moral powers agents must assume responsibility for their ends. Third, persons

are able and expected to interact with others in ways that respect the agency of fellow participants in social cooperation.

(Macleod 2010: 179)

Primary goods, in both early and late Rawls, matter to those who have the ability to use them for autonomous agency, but since children are not yet autonomous agents, they look irrelevant to the interests of children. Children have yet to develop the characteristics needed for responsible agency, and holding them responsible seems mistaken. Childhood is, of course, a matter of development, so there will be differences with regards to responsibility characteristics between children at different stages of development. But even so, the responsibility arguments in the debate on the metric of justice seem out of place. Moreover, the later Rawls argues that primary goods are motivated by their connection to the development of the two moral powers, but if childhood is not "a mere preparatory phase of life" (Macleod 2010: 182), one could ask if there are other goods in childhood that do not have to do with the future development of these two powers. Macleod asks us to compare two schools, one that has an abundant program for fun extra-curricular activities, and another that does not. Both are equally effective in providing the pupils with primary goods; the development of the two moral powers of the children in each school is equally well provided for. Does this difference between the two schools amount to an injustice? Intuitively, one would tend to say yes, but this injustice cannot be explained in terms of primary goods. "Yet surely the difference is one that is salient from the point of view of justice since it is unreasonable to hold the children responsible for the significant differences in the quality of their childhoods" (Macleod 2010: 182–183). We need an account of the metric for children that does not rest on the Agency Assumption.

A generalized Agency Assumption says that for the purposes of the theory of justice we assume that persons have the ability to exercise responsibility, and that they must assume this responsibility and act responsibly towards others. Macleod shows that this also causes problems for the capability approach. The argument for why capabilities are more appropriate than functionings as the metric of justice is that people are responsible for their own ends, but if children have not yet developed to the stage when they can be responsible for their choices, then the capability approach will hold them responsible for things that they cannot be held responsible for. This suggests that the metric for children should consist of outcomes, such as functionings, rather than the opportunities provided by capabilities.

Similar problems beset the theories of Dworkin and Arneson (Lindblom 2016). Dworkin argues against welfare on the basis of people being responsible for their ambitions, but if this is so only for adults, there would be little reason to prefer resources over welfare for children. In the case of Louis, the problem is that he makes a choice, for which he is responsible, to develop an expensive taste. A child that develops an expensive taste for, say, Belgian chocolate over Swedish Fish, has yet to develop the characteristics necessary for holding him or her responsible for the taste. For children, the problem of expensive tastes does not seem to support resourcism over welfarism. Arneson argues for his position with an example where two autonomous people have equal opportunity for welfare and gamble voluntarily. One of them wins and ends up rich; the other loses and becomes impoverished. Since both parties are responsible for their decisions, this outcome is just. However, it seems too strict to hold children responsible in a similar situation. We might want to teach a child about the dangers of gambling by making it somewhat costly, but this would be for instrumental reasons and not for fundamental reasons of responsibility. The step from welfare to opportunity for welfare does not seem motivated for children.

For Cohen's view the difficulties for resourcism and opportunity for welfare might combine, but by including both outcomes and opportunities, access might also allow a way around the problem caused by the agency assumption. Children could have goods directly as an outcome, and not through choices as is the case with other metrics that we have investigated, whereas the appropriate metric for adults could be thought of in terms of opportunities. If different arguments regarding responsibility succeed and fail for children and for adults, what should the structure of the metric be? One possibility would be a pluralistic metric with different content of the metric for children and adults. One such position could be to have welfare for children and resources for adults. This would raise questions about what accounts of resources and welfare are adequate, and the theory may seem unpleasingly messy by combining different kinds of metrics. Another approach would be to develop a general account of the metric that makes sense of the results for children and adults by generalizing them to some higher level. One could think of a capability approach with functionings for children and capabilities for adults, or a welfarist theory with opportunity for adults and welfare, as an outcome, for children along such monistic lines. It is also possible that continued work on this issue will lead us to genuinely new approaches to the metric.

There might be ways to avoid these theoretical choices. One could deny that the agency assumption is problematic by claiming either that children are responsible for their choices or that neither adults nor children are. This latter approach may not be very attractive, but there are arguments to the effect that children are competent decision makers in more respects than they are traditionally taken to be (Gheaus 2015a), which could serve as a starting point for the first strategy. However, even if children can be held responsible, there may be independent reasons for not holding them responsible. Schweiger and Graf (2015) argue that childhood is characterized by vulnerability (cf. Lotz 2014). The process of turning into an autonomous adult can be derailed by physical, social and mental causes. Since there is high value in developing into an adult, there is good moral reason to shield children from things that, due to vulnerability, could undermine this process, such as too much responsibility too soon. Another approach for avoiding these theoretical choices would be to deny that the theory of justice should take children into account. One could argue that distributive justice is a value that only comes into play between autonomous and responsible agents. Children's interests could then be understood as being instrumentally valuable, since children will develop into adults.

We cannot hope to settle the question of the structure of the metric, however, without discussing its content. In the next section, we will investigate two questions that might both help us decide on the appropriate metric and complicate the search for it: intrinsic goods of childhood and the ideal of neutrality.

Intrinsic goods of childhood and the metric of justice

Samantha Brennan has investigated "whether there are goods the value of which doesn't follow from their contribution to the goods of adult life" (Brennan 2014: 11), and Macleod has suggested that such *intrinsic goods of childhood* may be needed to make sense of our intuitions in the school thought experiment. Childhood goods raise many questions. First, is childhood intrinsically valuable? If we could skip childhood and go directly to adulthood, would anything of value be lost? Second, if there are goods of childhood, are they good only for children, or is, for example, play a good for adults as well? *Special goods of childhood* would, then, be goods that are only good for children. Third, there is the question of what we owe children. Here we ask what the right metric of justice is for children (Gheaus 2015b). There could be overlap between these issues, but the focus of this section is the last question. However, intrinsic goods of childhood raise further questions, which are relevant for the content of the metric of justice. First, what are they? Second, what kind of value do they have? Regarding the latter question, Brennan notes that it could be the case that there are intrinsic goods of childhood, but that they do not matter very much, since adulthood goods would always take precedence. However, she claims that childhood goods, in fact, are not overridden in importance, and that this explains our intuition that it would be a mistake to skip childhood and go directly to adulthood. We would miss out on childhood goods. To evaluate this claim, we need to look closer at what these goods are. Brennan suggests the following list of intrinsic goods of childhood (but does not take a position on whether they are also special goods of childhood):

(1) Unstructured, imaginative play
(2) Relationships with other children and with adults
(3) Opportunities to meaningfully contribute to household and community
(4) Time spent outdoors and in the natural world
(5) Physical affection
(6) Physical activity and sport
(7) Bodily pleasure
(8) Music and art
(9) Emotional well-being
(10) Physical well-being and health

(Brennan 2014: 21)

Any such list will raise the question of whether it contains the right and only the right goods. In this, Brennan's list is similar to Nussbaum's list. The two lists are also interestingly similar in content, which could be taken to indicate that even if these goods are intrinsic goods of childhood, they are not special goods of childhood, since they would be goods not only for children but also for adults. There are also other, partially overlapping, suggestions in the literature. Macleod (2015, 2018) argues that play, imagination and innocence are intrinsic goods of childhood. Gheaus (2015b) suggests learning, play, discovery of the world at one's own pace, carefreeness, unstructured time and developing capacities not related to work could be important childhood goods. Brighouse and Swift (2014) propose a way that one could think both about interests of adults and children, which seems straightforwardly translatable to a metric. They propose that Nussbaum's list is a useful starting point for thinking about adult flourishing. Children have two interests that distinguish them from adults, one in developing their agency, and a second in enjoying childhood, the latter meaning that they have an interest in enjoying the intrinsic goods of childhood. They do not present a full list of childhood goods but suggest that innocence, including sexual innocence, and imagination are two values that should be on the list.

From these considerations, it seems that we could get to a pluralistic metric of justice. This pluralism would, it seems, rest on the assumption that the intrinsic goods of childhood are also special goods of childhood. Gheaus (2015b) is skeptical of this assumption and argues that what is good for children is also good for adults, even if it might be the case that these goods are more accessible to the former. For instance, play is valuable regardless of when in a human life it takes place, and even innocence about sexuality can sometimes be valuable for adults. But if childhood goods are also good for adults, we could ask if the suggested intrinsic goods of childhood reduce to other metrics of the kind that have been thoroughly investigated on the adult level. One salient alternative for the project of reduction is welfare. Brennan's list could be read as a recipe for a happy childhood. In Macleod's school example, one salient difference between the schools is that one seems much more fun than the other, something that could be interpreted as hedonistic welfare. This might indicate that welfare is a kind of childhood good. It is also noticeable that happiness is not a part of any of the accounts of intrinsic goods of childhood, even where such goods are brought forward to complement resourcist metrics for adults.

Anthony Skelton (2015) has investigated the nature of welfare for children and is doubtful that hedonism is the right account of welfare for children (see ch. 8). He uses a thought experiment developed by Robert Nozick (1974) to show why. Imagine that scientists have invented a machine that stimulates the brain in a way that gives one the experience of what makes one the most happy, without this actually happening. By entering the machine, you could guarantee that your life will contain the maximum possible amount of hedonistic welfare. If one thinks that hedonism is the correct theory of value, then one should choose to hook up to the machine. Moreover, if hedonism is correct for children, parents have a *pro tanto* reason to connect their children to the machine, since this would ensure a happy childhood. This, however, is counterintuitive and, therefore, hedonism for children should be rejected. Skelton also notes that if childhood goods on an objective list did not make children happy, then we would hesitate to say that they are, in fact, good for children. Skelton supports a version of the desire theory of welfare, which overlaps to some extent with objective list theory. Welfare for children, on this account, "consists in being happy in what is worthy of happiness" (Skelton 2015: 98). Happy, here, should be read as taking satisfaction in something. This opens the question of what things are worthy of happiness for children, and Skelton suggests intellectual activity, loving and valuable relationships and play. The first of these include the kind of development gotten through education, and one might wonder if education is not valuable for children's welfare regardless of whether they take satisfaction in it or not, but perhaps this is an aspect that could be handled by including instrumental preparatory goods as a distinct category in the metric. Skelton's account of welfare is perfectionistic. He explicitly denies that neutrality is an appropriate condition on theories of welfare for children, since the theory must be able to make room for the notion that paternalism can be welfare-enhancing for children.

We have now returned to the second core issue in the standard debate on the metric of justice: the question of neutrality (see ch. 30). Starting from broadly Rawlsian premises and the ideal of independence for all, children included, Matthew Clayton (2006, 2015) argues that neutrality does indeed apply to children. Independence means that the rules that govern a person's life should be endorsed by that person. However, children would not be able to endorse rules with any normative force until rather late in their development. The solution for Clayton is retrospective endorsement. When the child becomes adult she or he can decide whether or not to endorse the rules that regulated her or his childhood. Since independence is the fundamental value, the lack of retrospective endorsement presents a serious moral problem. Clayton supports a resourcist metric. Children are owed the assistance they need, first, to develop a conception of the good in a timely manner with regards to their development, and, second, to develop the sense of justice and morality necessary for securing that all can live together in independence. This rules out a moral right of the state, or of parents, to enroll children in specific conceptions of the good. However, it is permissible to bring other values into children's lives, such as intrinsic goods of childhood, as long as this does not imply enrolment into a conception of the good. Parents may encourage, for example, play, even if the adult child would, for puritanical reasons, not give retrospective endorsement, as long as it is done within the constraints of non-enrolment. For Clayton, neutrality implies that the metric of justice cannot be perfectionistic for either adults or for children. If intrinsic, or special, goods of childhood are perfectionistic, then Clayton's theory implies that they should be rejected as a part of the theory of justice for children.

Timothy Fowler (2014) argues for restricted perfectionism – that is, perfectionism for children and neutrality for adults. Fowler's responses to both Clayton's arguments for neutrality and Rawls's position that the state must be neutral in order to achieve stability and be acceptable to all regardless of conception of the good, start from the same point: children do not yet have conceptions of the good. Arguments for neutrality that start from the notion that conceptions of the good should be respected do not apply to persons who have not developed to the degree that they can have or choose a conception of the good. This leads to a position with neutrality for persons who can have a conception of the good and perfectionism for those who have yet to develop this capacity, which allows for perfectionist intrinsic goods of childhood in the metric for children. Restricted paternalism raises questions about the relation between childhood and adulthood. Fowler approvingly quotes the old saying "give me the child for his first seven years and I will give you the man" (Fowler 2014: 5). However, if one is allowed to raise a child in such a manner that it guarantees that he or she will have a particular conception of the good as an adult, then the ideal that autonomous agents should be free to choose their own conception of the good would be severely undermined. If adulthood neutrality has very high value, as its proponents tend to hold, it could be the case that perfectionist goods of childhood do not satisfy the condition that they should not be over-ridden in importance by adulthood goods.

The discussion on the intrinsic goods of childhood has proceeded mostly on the basis of philosophical intuition, but it also raises empirical questions that could be answered by turning to social and behavioral science. Schweiger and Graf (2015), who support such an approach to research on the metric of justice and endorse the project undertaken by Biggeri and Mehrotra (2011), drawing on both the practical knowledge of experts on children – including researchers, UN representatives and NGO practitioners – and theoretical considerations, have developed a list of capabilities for children:

(1) Life and physical health
(2) Love and care
(3) Mental well-being
(4) Bodily integrity and safety
(5) Social relations
(6) Participation
(7) Education
(8) Freedom from economic and noneconomic exploitation
(9) Shelter and environment
(10) Leisure activities
(11) Respect
(12) Religion and identity
(13) Time autonomy
(14) Mobility

(Biggeri and Mehrotra 2011: 51)

This list includes most of the candidates for being intrinsic goods of childhood, but many of them are also goods for adults, and therefore raise questions about to what degree they are intrinsic or special goods of childhood. Furthermore, this approach seems to bring us full circle; this is a list of capabilities and the discussion about the agency assumption showed that functionings would be preferable for children from a capability approach perspective. Schweiger and Graf make an important point about the metric that has some potential to get us out of this circle. The metric for children should be thought of in dynamic terms, rather than in the static terms of adulthood and childhood. Children change throughout childhood. This development should be reflected in the metric, and develop from a focus on welfare interests to agency interests, and from functionings towards capabilities. However, even if this solved the problem of responsibility, the issue of neutrality will remain and has yet to be figured out. The philosophical debate on childhood and neutrality will have to continue.

Conclusions

We have investigated two areas of debate regarding children and the metric of justice. The first of these concerned the Agency Assumption. The discussion here indicated that questions regarding responsibility that have been taken for granted in standard theories of the metric must be revisited. If children are not the kind of agents that can or should be held responsible, then the metric of justice for them should not incorporate responsibility into the good that is to be distributed. The second area of debate revolved around intrinsic goods of childhood, with the upshot that even if neutrality is an appropriate condition of the metric of justice for adults, it may not be so when it comes to children. Some form of perfectionism with regards to the metric may be suitable for children.

These issues of responsibility and neutrality have implications for both the structure and the content of the theory of the metric of justice. We seem to stand before a choice of conceiving of the metric as either monistic or pluralistic, where a monistic theory would imply that the same goods should be in the metric for both children and adults and the pluralism would say that different goods are appropriate for adults and for children. There are, of course, many different monistic approaches one could take, but one surprising upshot of the debate on childhood and the metric of justice is that when children are brought in, welfare might make a comeback. Moreover, the overlap between accounts of welfare, the intrinsic goods of childhood and different versions of the capability approach is striking. Similar or the same goods appear in all the theories. This might also indicate that the capability approach would be a candidate for a monastic metric of justice. However, any such monistic theory must give an account of the roles of neutrality and responsibility for children as well as adults. Responsibility could be taken account of by choosing outcomes, in terms of welfare or functionings, for children and capabilities or opportunities for welfare for adults, but this would leave the neutrality issue to be resolved. Perfectionism could be suitable for children, but not for adults, and restricted perfectionism may be unstable in the sense that perfectionism for children could undermine neutrality for adults. This may, then, force a split in the metric with different kinds of welfare, or functionings and capabilities, for children and for adults.

This suggests that the metric of justice should be pluralistic. One approach would be to go for a metric consisting of welfare and resources for adults. This would, of course, raise the question of which account of resources for adults to prefer, Dworkin's, Rawls's or something else? Perhaps some structured version of Cohen's access of advantage could be used, but until the issues of responsibility and neutrality have been resolved, such a multidimensional approach may also, perhaps, complicate issues further. Maybe starting with a metric appropriate for adults and trying to revise it to make room for children is leading us down the wrong path. It may be better to look for a new account of the metric altogether. There are surely more possible positions to be explored. The conclusion must be that the discussion on childhood and the metric of justice has just begun.

References

Arneson, R. 1989. "Equality and Equal Opportunity for Welfare," *Philosophical Studies* 56: 77–93.
Biggeri, M., and Mehrotra, S. 2011. "Child Poverty as Capability Deprivation: How to Choose Domains of Child Well-being and Poverty," in M. Biggeri, J. Ballet, and F. Comim (eds.), *Children and the Capability Approach*. Houndsmills: Palgrave Macmillan.
Brennan, S. 2014. "The Goods of Childhood, Children's Rights, and the Role of Parents as Advocates and Interpreters," in F. Baylis and C. McLeod (eds.), *Family-making: Contemporary Ethical Challenges*. Oxford: Oxford University Press.
Brighouse, H., and Swift, A. 2014. *Family Values: The Ethics of Parent-Child Relationships*. Princeton, NJ: Princeton University Press.

Clayton, M. 2006. *Justice and Legitimacy in Upbringing*. Oxford: Oxford University Press.
Clayton, M. 2015. "Anti-Perfectionist Childrearing," in A. Bagattini and C. Macleod (eds.), *The Nature of Children's Well-Being*. Dordrecht: Springer.
Cohen, G. A. 1989. "On the Currency of Egalitarian Justice," *Ethics* 99: 906–944.
Dworkin, R. 2000. *Sovereign Virtue*. Cambridge, MA: Harvard University Press.
Fowler, T. 2014. "Perfectionism for Children, Anti-Perfectionism for Adults," *Canadian Journal of Philosophy* 44: 305–323.
Gheaus, A. 2015a. "Unfinished Adults and Defective Children," *Journal of Ethics & Social Philosophy* 9: 1–22.
Gheaus, A. 2015b "'The Intrinsic Goods of Childhood' and the Just Society," in A. Bagattini and C. Macleod (eds.), *The Nature of Children's Well-Being*. Dordrecht: Springer.
Griffin, J. 1986. *Well-Being: Its Meaning, Measurement, and Moral Importance*. Oxford: Oxford University Press.
Lindblom, L. 2016. "Equality of What for Children," in J. Drerup, G. Schweiger, G. Graf, and C. Schickhardt (eds.), *Justice, Education and the Politics of Childhood*. Dordrecht: Springer.
Lotz, M. 2014. "Parental Values and Children's Vulnerability," in C. Mackenzie, W. Rogers, and S. Dodds, (eds.), *Vulnerability: New Essays in Ethics and Feminist Philosophy*. Oxford: Oxford University Press.
Macleod, C. 2010. "Primary Goods, Capabilities, and Children," in I. Robeyns and H. Brighouse (eds.), *Measuring Justice. Primary Goods and Capabilities*. Cambridge: Cambridge University Press.
Macleod, C. 2015. "Agency, Authority and the Vulnerability of Children," in A. Bagattini and C. Macleod (eds.), *The Nature of Children's Well-Being*. Dordrecht: Springer.
Macleod, C. 2018. "Just Schools and Good Childhoods: Non-preparatory Dimensions of Educational Justice," *Journal of Applied Philosophy* 35: 76–89.
Nozick, R. 1974. *Anarchy, State, and Utopia*. New York, NY: Basic Books.
Nussbaum, M. 2000. *Women and Human Development: The Capabilities Approach*. Cambridge: Cambridge University Press.
Rawls, J. 1971. *A Theory of Justice*. Cambridge, MA: Harvard University Press.
Rawls, J. 2001. *Justice as Fairness: A Restatement*. Cambridge, MA: Harvard University Press.
Robeyns, I. 2003. "The Capabilities Approach: An Interdisciplinary Introduction," Department of Political Science and Amsterdam School of Social Sciences Research Working Paper. Amsterdam: University of Amsterdam.
Schweiger, G., and Graf, G. 2015. *A Philosophical Examination of Social Justice and Child Poverty*. Houndsmills: Palgrave Macmillan.
Sen, A. 1980. "Equality of What?," in S. McMurrin (ed.), *The Tanner Lectures on Human Values*. Cambridge: Cambridge University Press.
Skelton, A. 2015. "Utilitarianism, Welfare, Children," in A. Bagattini and C. MacLeod (eds.), *The Nature of Children's Well-Being*. Dordrecht: Springer.
Sumner, L. W. 1996. *Welfare, Happiness, and Ethics*. Oxford: Clarendon Press.

29
CHILDREN AND POLITICAL NEUTRALITY

Matthew Clayton

Introduction

Most children are raised in particular religious or ethical traditions. They are brought up as Christians, Muslims, Hindus, or humanists, for example. Their parents and teachers require them to observe the rules and practises of a particular religion or conception of what a good life consists in, and they encourage them to develop an appreciation of and commitment to its values and norms. In certain societies, the direction of children towards approved religious and ethical views is the policy of the political community: the state aligns itself with a specific religion and its schools are required to direct pupils towards it. In other societies, such as the USA or France, which observe a separation between religion and the state, publicly funded schools are required to remain neutral on questions concerning religion. Still, even in those societies children are schooled within, and made to pursue, particular religious views by their parents or private institutions to which their parents choose to send them—private schools that have a distinctive religious or ethical character or after-school institutions like churches or Sunday schools for Christians, or mosques or evening madrasahs for Muslims.

Children could be raised differently—that is, neutrally or non-directively—with respect to ethics and religion. We could educate children about the nature of different religious and humanist traditions that capture people's attention without aiming to get them to subscribe to a particular view. In our roles as parents or teachers, we could teach certain issues as controversial—as topics on which people, in good faith, disagree—but remain neutral between the different sides of the debate.

Is the direction of children towards particular religious or ethical standards morally acceptable, or are children entitled to an upbringing in which teachers remain neutral on controversial questions concerning religion? Does the answer to that question depend on whether the agents making educational decisions are parents or state-employed teachers? For example, does the *government* have the moral right to require schools to direct pupils towards a particular religion? Do *parents* have the moral right to direct their children towards particular religious standards?

In this chapter, we consider these questions by exploring the moral ideal of political neutrality—the view that it is not the proper business of the state to get involved in identifying and promoting a particular view of religion or the good life. First, we review the idea of political neutrality and its justification. Thereafter, we assess its implications for how states ought to raise and educate its citizens as children, and ask whether the idea of neutrality should be extended to constrain parents.

What is political neutrality?

Several prominent recent political philosophers propose that the state should remain neutral between conceptions of the good (see the selection in Klosko and Wall 2003). Before asking why they make that proposal it is important to understand how they interpret the idea of political neutrality. We can do this by considering the *reach*, *meaning*, and *site* of neutrality.

Reach: Ethics, religion, and morality deal with several evaluative, normative, and metaphysical questions. Is there a god and, if there is, must we obey its commands? How ought we treat others? What are the properties that make one's life successful or good? People disagree profoundly about what are the right answers to these questions. Given that fact, may the political community adopt particular answers to these questions that do not command universal assent and use its powers to promote the conception it adopts? It has plenty of powers at its disposal: it could enact laws that criminalise and punish those who follow religious views that it takes to be mistaken; it could use its power to tax and spend to penalise the pursuit of certain activities and subsidise others; or it could promote approved conceptions in educational campaigns run through schools or other media. But should it use these powers to promote particular conceptions of morality, religion, and ethics?

Advocates of political neutrality argue that the state has a duty to enforce certain controversial *moral* ideals, but that it must remain neutral with respect to other disputes, those concerning *ethics* or *religion*. So, it must uphold the rule of law and criminalise certain wrongs such as murder, various kinds of bodily harm, theft, fraud, and so on; it must also force citizens to pay taxes to fund a legal system that protects our important civil rights and socioeconomic arrangements that fairly distribute various goods such as education, health, and welfare. The government is morally permitted to adopt and pursue these policies even when some citizens believe that the ends it pursues are misguided or wrong. With respect to certain questions about what we owe to each other, then, the government's task is to identify certain truths about justice and enforce them.

However, with respect to questions about religion, sexuality, and occupation, neutralists argue that the state must remain neutral. It should not have a view of which religion, if any, is true and it may not use its powers to promote a particular conception of the good life. Although there are further questions about how precisely to draw the distinction between ideas of justice, on the one hand, and religion and views of human flourishing on the other, it is one that tracks the reasonably familiar distinction between two questions: (1) 'what do we owe to each other?' (questions concerning morality and justice); and (2) 'what makes for a flourishing human life?' (questions concerning religion, sexuality, occupation, and so on). Those who advocate political neutrality claim that the state must remain neutral with respect to conceptions of (2), but may enforce at least certain truths about (1) (Rawls 1996: 173–95; Dworkin 1985, 2011: 364–78).

Meaning: In some ways, the language of 'neutrality' is unhelpful because there are different understandings of what it means to remain neutral. In the field of international relations, for example, the term 'neutrality' is often used to describe the position of a country that does not favour a particular side in an international dispute or war—Switzerland is the classic case. The idea is that the neutral country must not act in ways that benefits one of the warring parties more than another: if the neutral country sells arms to one warring country then neutrality demands that it sells to other countries involved in the war. According to this conception of justice, the neutral country must not act in ways that help or hinder one side more than another.

But the ideal of political neutrality proposed by political philosophers is rather different. It does not say that the consequence of state action must not set back or advance the interests of one religious group, say, compared to others. Rather, the proposal is that the state's laws and policies must not be *justified* by reference to the intrinsic merits of any particular conception of the good. So, for example, when deciding what laws to enact or policies to pursue, the government must not take a stand on whether Christianity is true or false. Even supposing that it could correctly identify that a particular conception of religion is false, it may not act on that fact by taking steps to discourage citizens from believing or pursuing it. For this reason, it is common to distinguish between *consequential* neutrality (the kind of neutrality discussed in international relations) and *justificatory* neutrality (sometimes called 'neutrality of *reasons*'), which is how political philosophers who defend neutrality understand the idea (see Rawls 1996; Dworkin 1985; Kymlicka 1989). The idea of political neutrality, then, involves political agents excluding from consideration certain values that animate them in other parts of their lives: a committed Muslim who steadfastly pursues her religion in her non-political life must, neutralists claim, set those convictions aside if she is a politician deciding whether a particular piece of legislation should be passed.

Site: Because political neutrality requires agents to set aside their convictions about religion and the good when acting *politically*, it is important to clarify what counts as a political decision. There is agreement among neutralists that the principle applies to the decisions of judges, government officials, and legislators. Beyond that there is some disagreement. For example, some claim that what Rawls calls 'constitution essentials and matters of basic justice' (Rawls 1996) are the only institutions that count as political. But what about citizens? Are they morally permitted to vote for politicians or laws according to the dictates of their religious beliefs? Although some neutralists allow this kind of appeal (De Marneffe 1990), others argue that the neutrality principle applies whenever an agent is participating in the process of deciding what the law ought to be (Quong 2004). On this view, citizens must disregard their religious convictions and beliefs about what makes for a good life when they vote for their political representatives. As we shall see, addressing the issue of what is the appropriate site of principle of neutrality is important for understanding the implications of neutrality for children's upbringing.

To summarise, the ideal of political neutrality requires political actors to set aside their convictions about human flourishing and religion. Political decisions ought to enforce important moral requirements so that individuals' rights and claims to resources are satisfied. But it is not the business of the state to try to identify and use the levers available to it to promote the correct religion or view about what makes a life a success. In a sense, the idea of political neutrality is an extension of the idea of the separation of church and state. As it was initially conceived, the idea of separation was the thought that political institutions should stand above disagreements between different religious groups. Political neutrality extends that requirement to other controversies, such as those concerning occupational choice, sexuality, and other goals people adopt in their personal lives.

Why political neutrality?

Different justifications of political neutrality have been developed (Ackerman 1980; Dworkin 2011; Nagel 1991; Klosko and Wall 2003). Perhaps the most influential defence is offered by John Rawls (1996), whose argument goes roughly as follows. Suppose citizens live in a political community that protects various important rights, such as the right to practice and express one's religion, the right to freely associate with others and to participate as equals in the political process. Rawls notes that the inevitable consequence of legal institutions that protect such rights is that citizens will disagree about various evaluative and normative matters, including questions concerning what we owe to each other and questions about which religion, if any, is sound.

Now, a political community that protects various freedoms and socioeconomic opportunities that enable citizens to make effective use of those freedoms is already committed to a certain way of living together; it has already taken a stand on and enforces a particular answer to the question of justice. But the issue arises whether it ought to take a stand on other matters, such as those concerning religion and how individuals ought to use their freedoms.

Rawls argues that it should not, because if it did so it would jeopardise individuals' political autonomy. It is important for free and equal citizens to be able to understand and affirm the institutions and laws that profoundly affect their life chances and shape how they understand themselves, and to endorse the justifications the political community offers in defence of those institutions and laws. If the state were to recognise as true a controversial conception of religion or ethical success then, given the inevitable presence of disagreement about those questions, it would jeopardise that important interest in political autonomy, because those who dissent from the officially recognised view would be incapable of fully affirming the institutions that govern them. Suppose, for example, that in addition to protecting important civil and political liberties, the government sought to advance Christianity by using tax revenues to subsidise activities that encourage people to adopt that religion. That would violate political autonomy, because citizens who follow a different, or no, religion would not agree with the aims for which taxes are coercively levied. Of course, the same result would obtain if the government promoted atheism or a different religious doctrine. Thus, for the sake of political autonomy the government must not take a stand on the truth of different religious views and promote them in society.

The political autonomy argument for neutrality obtains even when the government merely recognises, but does not promote, a particular religion. Suppose that the government does not use its powers to promote a specific religious or ethical conception by trying to get citizens to adopt and practice it. Suppose it merely recognises a certain religion as true by, for example, conducting its official ceremonies by reference to the religion in question—by reading from its central text in the investiture of a government or by requiring witnesses in court to promise not to lie by touching a particular book. Although these recognitional practises do not aim to promote a particular religion, they nevertheless fall foul of the ideal of political autonomy because citizens who reject the officially recognised religion cannot fully accept the legal and political system that rules over them. For that reason, the deeper ideals to which a political community appeals to justify its institutions and laws must be ones that do not take a stand on questions about the good life or religion that divide citizens.

Of course, political neutrality is a controversial political ideal; it is rejected by political *perfectionists* who argue that the state has a role in perfecting the lives of its citizens. They typically argue that advocates of neutrality overstate the importance of political autonomy or personal authenticity, or they argue that there is space for the state to successfully promote citizens' well-being by identifying the religious or ethical views that are sound and using some of its legal powers to encourage individuals to embrace them (see Raz 1986; Wall 1998).

Should parents or teachers be neutral?

It might be thought that although it is possible for the *state* to remain neutral between different conceptions of the good, neutrality is not a possibility for teachers or parents who have hands-on responsibilities to raise and educate children, because how they act in their roles inevitably affects children in their charge one way or another. But as suggested above, this impossibility objection rests on a *consequentialist* interpretation of neutrality that is rejected by those who endorse the *justificatory* interpretation of neutrality. The relevant question, then, is whether parents and teachers can perform their roles without taking a stand on religious or ethical questions, and it seems that they can. It is possible for them to raise a child to develop a sense of justice and morality and to reflect on different views about religion, sexuality, occupation, and so on, without aiming to steer her towards endorsing particular views: they can, in short, proceed non-directively.

Thus, the issue becomes whether parents or teachers *should* take a neutral stance in the justificatory sense: when parenting or teaching, should they put to one side their own religious and ethical convictions and educate without trying to steer the child in any particular direction? Consider teachers first. One defence of teacher neutrality rests on the observation that most teachers in many countries work in state-regulated schools financed by general taxation. If the argument for political neutrality is sound, then it appears to be unjust for the government to tax citizens in order to fund schools that serve controversial religious or ethical views. If it took taxes to fund religious schools, for example, that would violate the political autonomy of atheists. On this view, a state-financed school should not endorse a particular view of the good or religion in its curriculum or ethos. Instead, it should develop its pupils' capacities to think for themselves and to deliberate about the different ethical and religious views that people find attractive. Of course, it should also develop their sense of justice so that they can show appropriate concern and respect for others. But that kind of moral direction is compatible with a neutral education with respect to religion and what makes for a good life. True, there might be certain aspects of ethical or religious views that are in tension with children developing a sense of justice and toleration—parts of religious texts, for example, that recommend inferior civic status for women or violence towards heretics. Plainly, in those cases, schools have a duty to challenge the religious views in question. However, doing so is compatible with remaining neutral with respect to the rest of the religious doctrine in question.

Some reject the view that political neutrality requires educational neutrality (MacMullen 2007). It is not a violation of neutrality, they say, if the state allows and funds parents to send their children to a school with a distinctive religious character; the state is not, thereby, endorsing any particular religion. Under that educational policy, the kinds of schools that are available would reflect the choices that parents make on behalf of their children. There would be schools that practice and promote Christianity, Judaism, Islam, Hinduism, Buddhism; there would also be schools that are animated by atheism and different humanist viewpoints. A regime of parental choice, then, permits the existence of a plethora of different types of schools without the state aligning itself with any particular conception of the good.

The compatibility of political neutrality with an educational policy that allows parents to use public money to pay for their child to be educated in a religious school might be questioned on the grounds that the regime forces some (atheists) to pay taxes to fund schooling that promotes (religious) doctrines that they reject as mistaken or, perhaps, ethically dangerous. To be neutral, the basis for forcibly taxing citizens must be one that cannot be rejected by reasonable citizens (i.e., those who are committed to honouring their duties of justice to others). To rebut that concern, the argument for parental choice needs to explain why parents should have the legal right to use public money to give their child a schooling that favours a particular religious viewpoint.

No doubt different arguments for that policy might be suggested. One popular argument is that parents have an interest in pursuing their own conception of the good, which might require them to give their child an upbringing that encourages her to appreciate, endorse, and live by the values of their religion (Galston 2002; Macleod 2002; MacMullen 2007). But that argument is inadequate, it seems, because it is open to those who disagree with the religious view to claim that people have no general interest in practicing their conception of the good. For example, some atheists believe that people's lives go better when they are free of religion. It is difficult to see why atheists who hold such beliefs cannot reasonably reject the state taxing them to fund religious parents' pursuit of their conceptions of the good; after all, from their point of view, they are being taxed to enable others to make a mess of their own lives as well as their children's. If the appeal to parents' interests in pursuing their own religion violates the principle of neutrality, then advocates of parental choice must offer other neutrality-respecting arguments to defend their view.

All of this suggests that if the state ought to be neutral, and the case for neutrality is that it is important that reasonable citizens accept the justification for the rules that govern them, then it is difficult to see how the public funding of schools that prioritise distinctive ethical or religious values can be justified. But that does not imply that distinctive religious schools should be legally prohibited. Political neutrality is compatible with the state allowing the existence of *privately* funded religious schools, even if it cannot legitimately support them by coercing citizens to fund them. On the basis of the discussion so far, then, in a neutral state one would expect to see a mixed educational regime. First, there would be a state sector in which schools and teachers teach in a neutral way, not taking a stand on the merits of different conceptions of religion, occupation, sexuality, or leisure pursuits and, instead, concentrating on enhancing pupils' capacities to develop and exercise a sense of justice and their own independent judgement about these further matters. Second, it is likely that there would be a range of private schools that cater for parents who want their children to be educated towards distinctive conceptions of the good.

There is, however, another dimension to the issue of political neutrality and children, which might challenge the mixed regime described above. Recall the 'site' issue we reviewed earlier, which addresses the question of what counts as 'political' such that the principle of neutrality applies. Some have suggested that the relationship between parents and children is similar to the state–citizen relationship in morally relevant ways and, because that is the case, parents are duty-bound to remain neutral when raising their children (Clayton 2006). If the extension of neutrality to regulate parental conduct is sound, then the justice of private religious schools is also called into question.

What is it about the state relationship with its citizens that supports political neutrality? Rawls's argument rests on the observation that the relationship is non-voluntary, coercive, and profoundly affects the life chances and values of citizens (Rawls 1996: 67–68). First, it is non-voluntary because, putting aside the complicating case of immigrants, most citizens have no choice with respect to the political arrangements that govern their lives: they are born into them and escaping from them is often very difficult or costly. Second, the state exercises considerable power and coercion over the lives of citizens by enacting and enforcing laws. Finally, the laws of a society profoundly affect the life chances of different citizens and the values they come to hold. As reviewed in the previous section, Rawls's ideal of political autonomy demands that the state–citizen relationship should be regulated by neutral principles of justice that can be endorsed by every reasonable citizen, regardless of the distinctive conception of the good or religion she practices.

The argument for *parental* neutrality begins by noting that the three features Rawls believes justify the need for political autonomy and, therefore, neutrality, are also present in the relationship between parents and children. First, a child's membership of the family in which she is raised is non-voluntary—she is either born into it or allocated to it by prevailing adoption arrangements and there is little opportunity to leave it in childhood. Second, parents exercise force and, sometimes, coercion over the child they raise. Although she often takes more control over her life as she develops into youth, as a young child the environment she encounters— including the activities she engages in, the children she plays with, the books she reads, and so on—is chosen for her by her parents. Furthermore, the choices her parents make on her behalf can significantly affect her life chances and her values. If Rawls is right that these features support the need for regulatory principles that can be endorsed by those they affect, then it seems that the principles that apply to parenting must similarly be ones that are acceptable to the children over whom parental power is exercised.

This argument faces the challenge that political autonomy is important to realise only for those who are capable of enjoying it. Because many children, particularly young children, lack well-formed beliefs and values, they are incapable of enjoying political autonomy in the sense of endorsing the coercive rules that constrain their lives. For that reason, parents need not worry about constraining their conduct out of respect for the political autonomy of their children (Bou-Habib and Olsaretti 2014).

This objection proceeds too quickly. Even though a young child is incapable of endorsing the principles that guide her parents' conduct, in the course of a normal human life she will be able later to review and endorse or reject the principles that governed her upbringing. Since that is the case, according to the ideal of political autonomy it is important for her parents to regulate their conduct as parents by principles that can be endorsed retrospectively by their child. This seems to support an extension of the principle of neutrality to parenting. Parents cannot know the particular religious doctrine or view of the good life around which their child will organise her life as an adult. It appears, then, that they are duty-bound to parent according to values and principles their child can retrospectively endorse, regardless of the specific conception of the good she adopts later in life (Clayton 2006, 2012a, 2014). In short, they must observe the principle of parental neutrality.

What does parental neutrality demand? In the first instance, it is important to note how revolutionary the ideal is compared to current practise. The majority of parents throughout the world regard themselves as morally permitted to raise and educate their children so that they come to know the truth about religion and how to make a success of their lives. Parental neutrality denies such a permission. It claims that parents should disregard certain kinds of knowledge when it comes to raising their child. For the sake of her political autonomy, they must set aside even sound convictions about religion and raise their child according to reasons that she can later share, regardless of the religious or ethical ideals that guide her life. So, parents must not baptise their children or educate them directively—that is, school them with the aim that they endorse and practice a particular faith. Similarly, atheists may not design an upbringing for their children that encourages them to reject theism or religion.

Notice, however, that parental neutrality is not the same as its political counterpart. *Political* neutrality is part of a larger ideal in which citizens are treated with equal concern and respect, and legal and political institutions operate with scrupulous impartiality between different citizens. In the family context, children have an interest in developing an intimate relationship with their parents. For that reason, even though they do not aim to recruit their children to a particular view of religion, the role of parents is to care for children, to develop their sense of justice, and to attend to their specific needs and interests. For the sake of a flourishing, intimate relationship between parent and child, which aids the development of the child into an independent and morally motivated individual, neutral parents should not display the same kind of impartiality and foresight as neutral judges or politicians do (see ch. 16). Accordingly, if the ideal of neutrality ought to regulate parental conduct, the ideal needs to be elaborated in a way that is tailored to the specific roles parents play in society.

In addition, those who advocate parental neutrality are also liberals who support arrangements that develop the child's sense of justice, her ability rationally to deliberate about the merits of competing conceptions of the good, and the wherewithal to make choices and pursue a particular conception. For that reason, parental neutralists would join with those who advocate that every child receives an upbringing that preserves for her an 'open future' with respect to religious affiliation (Feinberg 1992); and they would also insist on the cultivation of a sense of morality and justice—the disposition to treat others with concern and respect.

Objections to neutral childrearing

Those who reject educational neutrality do so for three kinds of reason. Some argue that it is bad for the child to be raised neutrally; some claim that neutrality places too many burdens on parents; others defend the view that neutrality would threaten the maintenance of valuable relationships between parents and their children.

(a) *Bad for children?* The view that political or parental neutrality is bad for children is a natural one. Are not states and parents under a duty to ensure that children enjoy the opportunity to live flourishing lives? If so, then neutrality for children is mistaken. On this account both governments and parents ought to raise and educate children in a way that enhances the prospects of them pursuing better rather than worse lives. Children ought to be directed towards religions or lifestyles that are worth pursuing or that would enhance their ability to pursue valuable goals. By contrast, a neutral upbringing in which states and parents disregard the truth about what makes one's life go well would be one that leaves more open the prospect of the child coming to endorse lifestyle activities that are not worth pursuing. How can that be in the best interests of children?

One variant of this position argues that governments ought to take a perfectionist stance towards children, even if they remain neutral towards adult citizens (Fowler 2014). The government might frame its social work and education policy by reference to the best assessment of what would improve the flourishing of children's lives, even if it refrained from trying to encourage adults to adopt religions and lifestyles that are most worth pursuing. However, that kind of asymmetric stance—perfectionism for children but neutrality for adults—is difficult to sustain. If neutrality is premised on the claim that reasonable citizens can justly be constrained to support only laws and policies that are acceptable to them, it is difficult to see how it would be legitimate to coerce everyone through the tax system to support an education policy that directs children towards or against particular conceptions of religion. Given the inevitable disagreement that exists in a society of reasonable people on the question of religion, any positive or negative stance that the government took towards religion in its education policy would make some serve a conception of the good that they reject.

Even if an asymmetric view that restricts political perfectionism to children cannot be sustained, that does not rule out a thoroughgoing perfectionist view in which the state constrains both adults and children to pursue policies that promote valuable conceptions of the good (Raz 1986; Wall 1998). However, the argument for that position would need to respond to the powerful moral ideals that motivate neutralists, such as the ideal of political autonomy, which asserts that individuals who treat others justly should not be constrained to follow laws justified by religious or ethical ideals they reject.

A more promising defence of perfectionism for children holds that, although states cannot be perfectionist towards children without violating the legitimate claims of adults, parents can and should promote their child's flourishing. Parents who enrol their child into, let us assume, a set of *valuable* religious practises do not, thereby, make other adults fund or support those religious ideals. True, they make their child practice and develop a specific, controversial religious doctrine. However, many reject the view, outlined in the previous section, that it is always wrong for parents to enrol their child into controversial religious practises (Macleod 2002; MacMullen 2007; Brighouse and Swift 2014). For example, some reject the view that even if it is likely that an individual will later retrospectively reject the religious ideal that she was made to practice as a child, that fact does not make her religious enrolment by her parents morally problematic. According to this view, endorsement of the rules that constrain one is morally important only for those who presently possess the capacity to form informed and rational views about religion and ethics, which young children lack (Bou-Habib and Olsaretti 2014). The dispute between parental neutralists and parental perfectionists, then, turns on what is the right view of the conditions under which a reasonable individual's rejection of a conception of the good counts as a reason against forcing her to serve that conception and, in particular, whether *retrospective* rejection is morally troubling.

(b) *Too burdensome to parents?* One objection to the view that states may compel children to attend religiously neutral schools is that it would place considerable burdens on parents with respect to their opportunity to pursue their own conception of the good (Galston 2002). In the previous section, I discussed the claim that parents have a qualified right to access public funds to school their child in their own religious doctrine and suggested that neutralists would reject such a right. Here it is worth raising the more basic question of whether a neutral schooling would interfere with parents' pursuit of their own conception of the good and whether, if it does, there is a reason to allow parents to raise their child non-neutrally to avoid such a burden.

Some argue that educational neutrality demands too much of parents. Everyone has an interest in successfully pursuing her conception of the good. Social policy, including the choice of educational regime, should be sensitive to this interest. Now, some people's conception of the good includes passing on a specific religion or view of how one ought to live one's own life to one's children; for other parents, having their child practice their religion makes it easier for them to pursue their faith. Accordingly, educational policy should allow parents to spend their own resources to ensure that they succeed in passing on their conception of the good to their child (Galston 2002; MacMullen 2007).

In reply, neutralists might note that if an individual's retrospective rejection of the ideals that governed her childhood supports the principle of parental neutrality, it is difficult to see how the parents' interests in pursuing their own conception of the good can override that principle. Consider the political analogue. Political neutralists object to citizens voting for legislation that compel others to support or practice a specific religion; they do not treat the fact that neutrally justified laws make it harder for certain religious groups to flourish as a reason to allow those groups to campaign for such laws. If that is the right approach to political neutrality, it is difficult to see why parents are morally permitted to force another (the child in their custody) to support or practice a specific religion on the grounds that it makes it easier for them (the parents) to pursue what matters to them.

(c) *Jeopardises family values?* Finally, it might be argued that educational neutrality practiced by either the state or parents would jeopardise the maintenance of intimate relationships between parents and their children. Such relationships, characterised by children receiving day-to-day spontaneous loving attention from specific adults, have considerable value for both child and parent, for both instrumental and non-instrumental reasons. Some argue that one of the key elements of an intimate child–parent relationship is the pursuit of 'shared enthusiasms': the relationship is characterised by the child and parent pursuing particular activities together (Macleod 2002; Brighouse and Swift 2014). The worry about neutrality is that if children are educated in religiously neutral schools then the relationship will suffer because the degree to which parents and children share a life will be diminished.

Parental neutralists might reply to these concerns in several ways. First, they might question whether government policy should be premised on the value of intimate family relationships at least to the extent that family values are a contested conception of the good life (Clayton 2012b). Second, even if they accept the need for some kind of intimate relationship between parent and child to be protected, they might challenge the claim that it follows that education policy or parents' choices should facilitate parents and children sharing of a religion or a conception of the good. Instead, they might suggest that sharing enthusiasms is not necessary for intimate familial relationships or that, if it is, the shared enthusiasm might be the pursuit of a just society or the child's interests, both of which are consistent with neutrality, rather than making the child adopt her parents' religious convictions (Clayton 2006).

Conclusion

The ideal of political neutrality is a controversial conception of how adults ought to live together in political community. It is even more controversial as a moral ideal that ought to shape how the government and parents ought to approach the upbringing and education of children. Particularly controversial is the view that parents should be neutral, where that requires them to put to one side their own convictions about religion and what makes for a good life when making decisions about the character of their child's life and education: controversial because it is a view that challenges most people's assumptions about the morality of parenting. Still, as I have suggested, there are powerful reasons to adopt parental neutrality, and it is incumbent on those who defend the *status quo* to offer more forceful arguments against the view that children are entitled to a neutral upbringing than have been developed to date.[1]

Note

1 For helpful comments and conversation about this chapter I am grateful to the editors, Viktor Ivanković, Andrew Mason, Tom Parr, David Stevens, Adam Swift, Ruth Wareham, and Andrew Williams. I also thank The Spencer Foundation (grant #201500102) for supporting this work.

References

Ackerman, B. 1980. *Social Justice and the Liberal State*. New Haven, CT: Yale University Press.
Bou-Habib, P., and Olsaretti, S. 2014. "Autonomy and Children's Well-Being," in A. Bagattini and C. Macleod (eds.), *The Nature of Children's Well-Being*. Dordrecht: Springer.
Brighouse, H., and Swift, A. 2014. *Family Values: The Ethics of Parent-Child Relationships*. Princeton, NJ: Princeton University Press.
Clayton, M. 2006. *Justice and Legitimacy in Upbringing*. Oxford: Oxford University Press.
Clayton, M. 2012a. "Debate: Against the Comprehensive Enrolment of Children," *Journal of Political Philosophy* 20: 353–364.
Clayton, M. 2012b. "Equal Inheritance: An Anti-Perfectionist View," in J. Cunliffe and G. Erreygers (eds.), *Inherited Wealth, Justice and Equality*. London: Routledge.
Clayton, M. 2014. "Anti-perfectionist Childrearing," in A. Bagattini and C. Macleod (eds.), *The Nature of Children's Well-Being*. Dordrecht: Springer.
De Marneffe, P. 1990. "Liberalism, Liberty, and Neutrality," *Philosophy and Public Affairs* 19: 253–274.
Dworkin, R. 1985. "Liberalism," in R. Dworkin (eds.), *A Matter of Principle*. Oxford: Oxford University Press.
Dworkin, R. 2011. *Justice for Hedgehogs*. Cambridge, MA: Harvard University Press.
Feinberg, J. 1992. "The Child's Right to and Open Future," in J. Feinberg (eds.), *Freedom and Fulfillment*. Princeton, NJ: Princeton University Press.
Fowler, T. 2014. "Perfectionism for Children, Anti-Perfectionism for Adults," *Canadian Journal of Philosophy* 44: 305–323.
Galston, W. 2002. *Liberal Pluralism: The Implications of Value Pluralism for Political Theory and Practice*. Cambridge: Cambridge University Press.
Klosko, G., and Wall, S. (eds.). 2003. *Perfectionism and Neutrality: Essays in Liberal Theory*. Lanham, MD: Rowman & Littlefield.
Kymlicka, W. 1989. "Liberal Individualism and Liberal Neutrality," *Ethics* 99: 883–905.

Macleod, C. 2002. "Liberal Equality and the Affective Family," in D. Archard and C. Macleod (eds.), *The Moral and Political Status of Children*. Oxford: Oxford University Press.

MacMullen, I. 2007. *Faith in Schools? Autonomy, Citizenship, and Religious Education in the Liberal State*. Princeton, NJ: Princeton University Press.

Nagel, T. 1991. *Equality and Partiality*. New York, NY: Oxford University Press.

Quong, J. 2004. "The Scope of Public Reason," *Political Studies* 52: 233–250.

Rawls, J. 1996. *Political Liberalism*, paperback edition. New York, NY: Columbia University Press.

Raz, J. 1986. *The Morality of Freedom*. Oxford: Clarendon Press.

Wall, S. 1998. *Liberalism, Perfectionism and Restraint*. Cambridge: Cambridge University Press.

30
THE COSTS OF CHILDREN

Serena Olsaretti

Introduction

"Children", economist Nancy Folbre notes, are "an expensive crop" (Folbre 2008: 65). Raising an average child in the UK to the age of 21 is estimated to cost parents £231,843, more than the average house[1]; in the US the average cost of raising a child born in 2015 to 17 years of age has been calculated to amount to $233,610.[2] How expensive children are has changed substantially across time and still varies greatly from one society to another. What has also changed and varies is how the costs of children are distributed between parents and other family members on the one hand and public institutions on the other, and across socially salient groups such as women and men. On account of this last fact – specifically, because almost everywhere women have borne a disproportionate part of the costs of raising children – feminist scholars have been pioneers in putting the question "Who pays for the kids?" center stage in various academic disciplines. Undoubtedly, the question continues to have significance, in part, because of its connection to persisting concerns about gender justice. But, as this chapter highlights, the question of who should pay for the costs of children plays a more central role in our understanding of the demands of social justice generally than has been appreciated thus far. Political philosophers and theorists of justice in particular have reasons to pay close attention to it.

After clarifying the question and explaining its relevance in the first section, this chapter identifies and examines, in the second and third sections, the main arguments for the view that justice for parents requires that the costs of children should be shared between parents and society at large. These arguments appeal to the equality claims of parents and to the fairness obligations of non-parents, respectively. In so doing, the chapter considers a number of challenges these arguments face.

An important cautionary note that must be mentioned at the outset is this: although the discussion that follows mostly focuses on the costs of children, it does not ignore the fact that having and rearing children involves creating benefits as well. These, too, can be distributed differently under different arrangements – a fact that, as the third section makes clear, raises important questions of justice.

Which costs, and whose interests, are relevant?

The question, "Who should pay for the costs of children?", can be understood in different ways, and invites different answers, depending, first, on what the costs of children are taken to include and, second, on whose interests are deemed to be salient for settling this question.

Consider, first, the issue of what the costs of children include. A familiar understanding of the costs of children – the one assumed by the calculations mentioned above – refers to the *financial* costs which *parents* incur in *raising* children to the point at which they are of age or are (likely to be) financially self-sufficient. Under scrutiny, this understanding of the costs of children may be at once too narrow and too wide, if our focus is on gauging what a just distribution of the costs of children is among citizens, and, in particular, between parents and the rest of society (I explain shortly why this will be the focus in this chapter). To see this, it is helpful to bear in mind three distinctions concerning the costs of children.

The first is between the costs of care on the one hand (these include the time, energy, and material resources required to *raise* children from infants into autonomous adults) and the costs of added adult members on the other (these are the costs new people create as adults, such as, for example, the facts that they contribute to overcrowding and pollution and that they make claims on publicly funded services). The second distinction, which cuts across the first one, is between costs that are morally required (centrally, the costs of meeting the justice-based claims of children, both while they are children and as adults) on the one hand, and those that are not (for example, the costs of ensuring that one's child goes to elite schools). Finally, it is helpful to also note that when we talk about the costs of children, we could be talking about either "net" or "gross" costs, i.e. either about the costs of children once we have taken into account, and duly deducted, the benefits of children (which, like the costs of children, can be of the various different types); or about the costs independently of the benefits which may accrue.

Once we keep these distinctions in mind, it becomes clear why the understanding of the costs of children deployed in standard calculations may be at once too narrow and too wide.

It may be too narrow because, as feminists have been keen to emphasize, the costs of raising children include more financial and non-financial costs than just *the income spent* on children. They include, crucially, the opportunity costs of forgone paid labor of those, typically women, who care for children while they are infants, and, consequently, lower pensions prospects, loss of autonomy, and greater economic dependence (Folbre 1994a, 2008; Gornick and Meyers 2004). That understanding may, furthermore, be too narrow because raising children involves costs beyond those currently borne *by parents* alone, and also because the costs of children go beyond the costs involved *in raising* them: when people have children, they add persons to the ranks of fellow citizens, or our fellow human beings, who will have claims on us throughout their lives. This last point, especially with regard to the environmental costs of having children, is salient for those who voice worries about overpopulation (Kates 2004; Conly 2015).

But the understanding of the costs of children reflected in the standard measurements mentioned earlier may also be in important respects over-inclusive, both because they may include some non-morally required costs (some of the costs of sending children to private higher education institutions, included in the UK calculations, amounting to £17,815 a year between the ages of 18 and 21, may be a case in point), and because they represent only gross costs where, arguably, we should also take into account some of the benefits that having and rearing children produces, which can and do accrue to parents and society at large in varying amounts. If our concern is with the just distribution of the costs of children among parents and citizens at large – as opposed to, say, the intra-family distribution of costs between parents of different genders – it seems justified to presume that the non-morally required costs of children are ones which reflect parents' particular values and which society does not have an obligation to share with them.

Moreover, in order to know where the morally required costs of children should justly fall, it may be relevant that parents do or could gain some non-monetary benefits, in terms of life-fulfillment or welfare-satisfaction or support in old age, and/or that fellow citizens benefit by the constant renewal of the workforce and tax-paying population that relies on people's having and rearing children. Whether or not these judgments are ultimately defensible (this will depend, as will be discussed in the second and third sections, on the principles of justice we defend and deploy), bearing in mind that "the costs of children" include importantly different types of costs is essential for formulating clear questions and answers concerning their distribution.

The question, "Who should pay for the costs of children?", can also be understood – and answered – differently, secondly, depending on *whose interests* are taken as relevant for settling it. Having and rearing children creates costs and benefits for *those who have and rear them* (standardly, the children's procreators, who are also, standardly, their parents), for *the children themselves* (we could think that their coming into existence is a benefit or a harm to them; and certainly we think that once children exist, how they are reared crucially affects their interests), *and for third parties* (there are various salient categories of third parties, which include: other contemporary parents, contemporary non-parents, future fellow-citizens; contemporary and future non-citizens). The question of how the costs of children should be distributed can take a different focus, and have a narrower or wider scope, depending on whose interests are taken as salient.

For example, as mentioned earlier, many existing discussions of the costs of children, such as those that have been moved by a concern with gender justice, have focused on the distribution of the costs of children between those children's parents, i.e. the father and mother of children in heterosexual families (Folbre 1994a; Okin 1989). Other treatments of who should bear the costs of children take the interests of children themselves as decisive for settling that question: we could think, for example, that considerations of justice to children tell in favor of socializing the costs of children, ensuring that non-parents as well as parents share those costs, because we have reasons to believe that this is necessary to meet all children's basic needs and entitlements to fair equality of opportunity (Esping-Andersen 2009; Putnam 2015).

Once we acknowledge that, besides parents and the children themselves, third parties are also substantially affected by people's having and rearing children, the question of how the costs of children should be distributed acquires a wider scope. In particular, considerations of intergenerational and of global justice, as well as of gender and childhood justice, become important for settling the question of how the costs of children should be distributed. For example, given that the number of children people have affects the size of the next generation and, indirectly, of more distant generations, and given that the size of each generation is a very important determinant of the claims of justice that members of that generation will be able to make on each other and on members of earlier and later generations, the procreative choices of the earlier generation should arguably be constrained by principles of justice (Ackerman 1980; Rakowski 1991; Steiner and Vallentyne 2009). Moreover, given that any plausible theory of justice accords some weight to the interests of those beyond the borders of our domestic societies, and since non-citizens, too, can and do incur some of the costs of our having and rearing children, we must determine what global justice – including, importantly, climate justice in a global context – demands vis-à-vis our having and rearing children. It may be argued, for example, that given the very elevated carbon footprint of each new child born in an advanced industrial society and the background context of unjust global inequalities, citizens of globally rich countries are unjustified in supporting fellow citizens who are parents by socializing the costs of children, perhaps especially when they do so while excluding immigrants (Casal 1999; Meijers 2016), and that they should bear a very large proportion of the burden of having to reduce global population size by having fewer children (Overall 2012; Conly 2015).

The question of how the costs of children should be distributed, then, can refer to different things. Tackling the widest version of it, such that the interests of all the parties who are affected by people's having and rearing children, and so that all the relevant costs of children are duly paid attention to, requires us to take into account considerations of gender justice, justice for children, intergenerational and global justice. However, the rest of this chapter will focus on examining a narrower version of the question at hand, the question of "parental justice" (Olsaretti 2013), which focuses on the distribution of the morally required costs of children (both of care and of added members) between parents and a subset of third parties – namely, non-parents.[3] Specifically, the question of parental justice asks what justice has to say with regard to whether parents, by dint of choosing to have and rear children,[4] should or may bear some or all of the costs of children themselves, or whether non-parents should or may be required to share these costs with parents. Addressing the question of parental justice is necessary for formulating a complete theory of justice (see Olsaretti 2017) as well as of importance when tackling the question of gender justice (Olsaretti 2013).

Arguments for the claim that all members of society, both non-parents as well as parents, should share the costs of children (henceforth, *pro-sharing arguments*) can be grouped into two main families, in line with whether they appeal to, first, parents' claims to distributive equality and, second, non-parents' obligations of fair play, incurred as a result of their benefiting from parents' having and rearing children. The next two sections examine these two families of arguments in turn.

The case for sharing the costs of children (i): equality

Consider, first, the possibility that the demands of equality for parents ground the pro-sharing case. Philosophical discussions over the last 50 years have revealed that the demands of egalitarian justice can be interpreted very differently, depending, among other things, and crucially for our purposes here, on which aspect of people's situation is argued to be relevant for assessing their relative claims – or, in other words, on what is the so-called "currency of egalitarian justice" (Cohen 1989; see also ch. 28). Accordingly, different versions of the egalitarian pro-sharing case can be formulated, appealing to equality of welfare, equality of basic capabilities, and equal autonomy.

Equality of welfare at first seems like an obvious candidate for grounding a case for sharing the costs of children. As an *outcome* view – requiring, that is, that people be equally well-off in terms of the extent to which their preferences are satisfied, or in terms of how happy they are – it would recommend that the costs of children be shared if doing so were needed to ensure that the welfare of adults who do or would like to have and raise children is on a par with that of others with different preferences. This argument would only offer support for parents contingently, depending on whether it is, in fact, true that, overall, their welfare would be worse than the welfare of others if the costs of children were not socialized. This point may not worry defenders of the pro-sharing view, in that it seems likely that an overworked, stretched parent is an unhappy person. Indeed, existing empirical studies on parents' self-reported welfare levels suggest that parents are generally less happy than non-parents, and also that this happiness gap decreases when good childcare provision and parental leave policies are in place (Pullman-Shult 2014; Glass, Simon, and Anderson 2016). So, compensation for them may seem warranted.

There are, however, two key problems for the welfarist argument. First, there are competing ways of understanding what welfare is, and different people care differently about welfare on any given understanding of it. Someone may value hedonic contentment, while someone else judges that his life goes well to the extent that her preferences are satisfied, even if their being satisfied leaves her feeling depressed. Selecting any one of these understandings of welfare as the measure of people's claims seems to unjustifiably privilege some people's view of what makes life go best over those of others (Dworkin 2000). To see this, note that some empirical studies can be read as reporting parents as being less hedonically happy than non-parents, but as having a greater sense of fulfillment or purpose than non-parents (for a survey of these studies, see Nelson, Kushlev, and Lyubomirsky 2014). If parents were to assert that non-parents must share the costs of children so as to offset parents' hedonic welfare deficit – by giving them opportunities to be less overworked and tired, say – non-parents could complain that parents fare *better than* non-parents in terms of how fulfilled they feel. If we take the latter aspect of welfare as relevant, parents no longer seem to have a valid claim.

Secondly, the outcome welfarist view fails to take due account of the role of personal responsibility in determining our justice claims, and requires us to equalize how well-off people are, regardless of whether they experience a welfare loss as a result of factors beyond their control or as a result of their own choices. But it seems unfair, according to this *responsibility challenge*, to ask us to compensate other people's welfare deficits which result from their deliberate choices (Dworkin 2000). At best, if welfare matters, only unchosen welfare inequalities should be compensated for in the name of justice (Cohen 1989). Since we assume that many or most parents in a just society freely choose to have children in the sense appropriate for holding them responsible for some outcomes of their choices, the welfarist case for sharing the costs of children seems implausible.

The equality of basic capabilities view might ground parents' claims, even in the face of this challenge, in that it holds that there are certain aspects of individual well-being which everyone should have the real freedom to do well by, regardless of whether faring well or badly by them reflects ambitions we have or choices we have made. For example, everyone should have the real opportunity to be well nourished and that of being able to engage in recreational activities, independently of whether engaging in recreational activities is something that one chooses to do, and regardless of whether one is in danger of being poorly nourished because one has squandered one's salary. There has been considerable debate on the capabilities approach since Amartya Sen and Martha Nussbaum first proposed it as a standard for interpersonal comparison that allegedly avoids the pitfalls of both welfarist standards and of resourcist measures, especially those focusing on people's possession of easily measurable economic resources like income and wealth (Sen 1992; Nussbaum and Sen 1993). This is not the place to offer a general overview of the capabilities approach and its merits, but two brief remarks about it are helpful in order to see how a pro-sharing argument that adopted capabilities as the currency of egalitarian justice could proceed.

First, on the view in question, an objective standard of well-being is used to identify the relevant *functionings*, i.e. the valuable states of doing and being, such as being healthy or being well nourished, which are relevant for an assessment of people's claims. Second, people are thought to have claims to the real or effective freedom (or the *capability*) to achieve only a subset of the valuable functionings, those which are of central importance to a good life, or without which a life of dignity is compromised (Nussbaum 2006). Starting from these premises, a capabilities-based pro-sharing argument could proceed in one or both of two ways: it could offer a defense of the claim that having and raising children is one of the central capabilities, or it could show that being able to have and raise children helps realize, or is involved in realizing, many of the (other) central human capabilities. Existing accounts of capabilities, for example Nussbaum's, lend themselves to the latter strategy: reproductive freedom is seen as part of the capability of "bodily integrity" (Nussbaum 2000: 78), which then protects the choice of *having* (as well as not having) children.

Raising children, together with caring for dependents generally, could be seen as captured by the capability of "affiliation", which refers to, among other things, "[b]eing able to live with and toward others, to recognize and show concern for other human beings, to engage in various forms of social interaction" (Nussbaum 2000: 79; see 168–69 on her reason to not conceive of "care" as an extra capability).

Alternatively, or additionally, a pro-sharing view could draw on recent arguments for the distinctive value of the parent–child relationship (Macleod 2002; Austin 2004; Brighouse and Swift 2014) in order to show that *raising* (and, on some versions of this view, *having* as well as raising) children is a capability in its own right. This line of argument would draw on the claims that the parent–child relationship is a unique and irreplaceable source of well-being, being a relationship in which an adult and a dependent child enjoy the good of familial intimacy (Brighouse and Swift 2014) and in which parents can obtain creative self-extension by parenting (Macleod 2002).

The capability-based answer to the question of parental justice warrants more attention than it has received thus far. However, like all capabilities-based claims, it faces a challenge from *neutrality*. In a nutshell, this holds that in matters of political morality – that is, when settling questions about what coercive social, political, and economic institutions may and should do in the name of justice – we are barred from appealing to controversial comprehensive convictions, i.e. convictions about the good which reasonable persons could disagree with (see Rawls 1993). Claims about objective well-being of the kind invoked by the capability argument, such as the claim that the parent–child relationship is uniquely valuable, and the apparently less controversial claim that being able to live with other human beings and caring for them is essential to a good life, seem to be ones which some reasonable people could reject and which we should, therefore, abstain from invoking in the context of formulating principles for regulating our shared institutions. If we accept the constraints of neutrality (see ch. 29), it looks as though we have to find some other way of grounding the egalitarian pro-sharing case (Casal and Williams 2008; Taylor 2009).

In view of the neutrality challenge, defenders of the pro-sharing view can appeal to the autonomy, rather than well-being, of parents, where autonomy is understood, thinly, as the capacity to form, act on and revise one's own view of the good. A version of this argument begins with the observation that the parenting role is extremely demanding in terms of autonomy: adults who take it up are expected to provide continuity of care for nearly two decades, without the option of revising their commitment, in order to bring up their children to become well-functioning adults. Moreover, the argument continues, these expectations are enforced by coercive institutions, since the state only grants parental rights to those adults who comply with these expectations (Alstott 2004; see ch. 19, ch. 32).

These observations, however, are not enough to ground a case on parents' behalf: what also needs showing is either that the expectations which parents are held to are not morally necessary, or that the costs that attach to fulfilling them are unfair. Consider, first, the possibility that the expectation to which parents are held – namely, that of providing continuity of care – is not morally necessary; that is, it does not reflect moral obligations which parents owe their children. Perhaps all of a child's interests could be (sufficiently or comparably) satisfied in the context of more flexible child-rearing arrangements in which parents do not commit to care for the child for 18 or more years. If society were to structure the parenting role so that it places great demands on the parents' autonomy without this being actually owed to children, parents might be able to complain that they are being expected to put up with an unjustified loss in their autonomy. Alternatively, or additionally, parents may claim that non-parents should share the costs of their children because, while they do owe their children the long continuity of care they are expected to give them, the costs of providing that care are unjustifiably high, in terms of the impact it has on their capacity to pursue other valuable and valued projects (Bou-Habib and Olsaretti 2013).

The latter line of argument seems more promising than the former, since continuity of care does seem to be owed to children, and, in the context in which adults can choose freely whether to have children and have adequate opportunity to avoid incurring parental obligations, it is not clear that their autonomy is hindered in any way by being held to those obligations. By contrast, it is undeniable that a system in which the costs of children for parents are shared by non-parents – a system in which having a child does not mean forgoing as much of one's income, say, because there are publicly funded institutions that cater well for all of one's children's educational and health needs – is one in which parents enjoy greater autonomy than otherwise (Casal and Williams 2008). Showing this, however, does not suffice to ground the pro-sharing conclusion. For that conclusion to be warranted, what needs to be true is not only that socializing the costs of children allows parents more autonomy than *they*, i.e. the parents, could otherwise have; it must also be shown that socializing the costs of children redresses what would be an unfair inequality in autonomy between parents and non-parents. So, the question arises: would equal respect for people's autonomy require securing the option of "subsidized" parenting?

A recent argument for this conclusion appeals to the fact that, under fair background conditions, people would purchase an "insurance plan" to ensure that they are able to parent adequately if at some point they choose to become parents and their income-earning capacity is too low for them to parent adequately (Bou-Habib 2012). This hypothetical insurance argument draws on Ronald Dworkin's theory of equality of resources, which is grounded in a commitment to respect "the responsibility and right of each person to decide for himself how to make something valuable of his life" (Dworkin 2011: 2), and can be interpreted as identifying what respect of equal autonomy requires (Bou-Habib and Olsaretti 2016). The main idea is that people who face an equal risk of lacking the income-earning capacity they need to raise children adequately would agree to an insurance plan that gave them support in case they lack that capacity, and that requires them to pay tax in order to support others in case they turn out to have more than sufficient income-earning capacity. This is because many people either would like to have children, or are open to the possibility of having them at some point if circumstances are right, and because they know that being able to pursue this life plan, should they come to have it, would be of great importance to them. The kind of insurance plan people would choose to buy under fair background conditions, on this view, sets the parental subsidies that people would be entitled to receive, and the tax they would be required to pay to fund those subsidies.

The hypothetical insurance case for sharing the costs of children has the advantage of meeting the neutrality challenge (it gives people the package of entitlements they would choose for themselves) and the responsibility challenge (people would only have the subsidies they would be prepared to pay for, as a way of offsetting inequalities that are due to unequal brute luck, i.e. the brute luck of having greater or lesser income earning potential). However, as several commentators on Dworkin's view have remarked (see, for example, Macleod 1998; Cohen 2004), the fact that this view makes people's entitlements depend on people's choices of what kind of insurance they would be prepared to buy means that those entitlements will reflect factors that seem morally irrelevant. In the case at hand, if a society were composed of a majority of adults who chose to stay childless, preferring to spend their income on consumption goods, it is likely that the hypothetical insurance model would offer no support for parents. Yet, it may seem unfair that those who do have children in this society would have to internalize all the costs of children themselves, especially once we take into account that

> [p]arents who raise happy, healthy, and successful children create an especially important public good.... Employers profit from access to productive workers. The elderly benefit from Social Security taxes paid by the younger generation.... Fellow citizens gain from having productive and law-abiding neighbors.
>
> *(Folbre 2001: 50)*

According to the pro-sharing arguments we now turn to, everyone, non-parents included, has obligations of fairness to contribute to the costs of children if they benefit as a result of parents' having and raising them.

The case for sharing the costs of children (ii): fairness

The fairness-based case for sharing the costs of children has, as its first, normative, premise, a commonly shared intuition – namely, that free riding on others is unfair. More precisely, the intuition is expressed by the so-called principle of fair play, which holds that when some people engage in a cost-incurring, benefits-producing cooperative scheme, those who benefit have an obligation to do their fair share in bearing the costs needed to produce the benefits (Hart 1955; Rawls 1971). The second, factual, premise of the fairness-based argument, which feminist scholars have done much to buttress, is that reproductive work is socially valuable – indeed, socially necessary – work (Folbre 2008; Bubeck 1995). Together, it seems, these two premises support the conclusion that the fact that the work done by parents is unpaid, is unfair to parents. The latter are owed support for the costs of children by all fellow citizens, given that we all benefit from our society's regenerating itself and continuing across time. Without new children being raised into well-functioning adults, it would not be possible to maintain a healthy economy, shared social and political institutions, and publicly provided services. Children are, thus, *positive externalities* (i.e. benefits which flow from, but are external to, people's decision to have and rear kids) or *public goods* (i.e. non-excludable, non-avoidable, non-rival benefits), which everyone has an obligation to help support.

The fairness-based pro-sharing case is often invoked in public debates on sharing the costs of children and has often been adopted by social scientists (Folbre 1994b, 2001; George 1987, 1993; Esping-Andersen 2009). It has also received some endorsement in philosophical debates about who should pay for children (Alstott 2004; Anderson 1999), although in this context it has also been heavily criticized (Rakowski 1991; Casal and Williams 1995, 2004; Casal 1999). Like the equal autonomy argument, the fairness-based argument seems well-equipped to meet both the responsibility and the neutrality challenges. When children are net positive externalities, as the fairness-based argument's factual premise affirms, the grounds for holding parents responsible seem lacking (Casal and Williams 1995, 2004; Olsaretti 2017). The fairness-based case also seems to meet the neutrality challenge, since the argument need not rely on controversial claims about the good. Instead, it can rest on the claim that parents' work is necessary for creating some central benefits everyone has reason to want.

Nonetheless, some philosophers have raised further challenges to the fairness-based argument. In particular, they have put pressure on both its normative and factual premises, arguing that, on a plausible version of the former, the pro-sharing case flounders since the requisite empirical premise will not hold true. The thrust of this argument is that an unqualified principle of fairness, which holds people who benefit from others' cost-incurring activities under an obligation to contribute, regardless of *why* those others incurred those costs, is indefensible (Casal 1999; Casal and Williams 2004). For one thing, it would justify holding us hostage to too wide a range of obligations; for another, it mistakenly seems to conceive of obligations of fairness as analogous to obligations to respect people's producer entitlements (i.e. entitlements to gain rewards from productive activity). A duly qualified principle of fairness holds that obligations of fairness are incurred if one receives benefits as a result of others' intentional partaking in a cooperative, benefits-creating activity, not if one receives benefits which are a "pleasant surprise" of the activities which others carry out without regard for the benefits they are producing for others (Casal 1999). Since parents have and rear children in order to realize their own life plans and so as to do what is good for their children, not in order to benefit others, to internalize those benefits (as a non-parent whose pension is paid by others' children does) without sharing the costs of children is not to unfairly free ride on parents. So, on a defensible version of the normative premise of the fairness-based argument, the pro-sharing conclusion does not follow, because the requisite empirical premise (that parents' having and rearing children constitutes *intentional* partaking in a cooperative, benefits-producing scheme) is false (Casal 1999; Casal and Williams 2004).

There are two possible ways of defending the fairness-based case in response to this challenge.

The first accepts the stated version of the principle of fairness just mentioned, but claims that, once some morally salient facts are taken into account about the institutional context in which parents typically act, parents' activities do, in fact, constitute intentional partaking in a cooperative, benefits-producing scheme. The overlooked facts are that any shared social and economic institutions that provide publicly funded services deliberately aim at socializing the benefits which people's having and rearing children create; these institutions thus constitute the relevant cooperative, benefits-producing scheme in which parents intentionally partake when they have and rear children whose future tax contributions will be shared among everyone, not just among parents. Children are, in this sense, best seen as deliberately socialized goods, rather than public goods, and seeing this helps ground the fairness-based case (see Olsaretti 2013).

A second way of defending the fairness-based case proceeds by arguing that an alternative interpretation of the principle of fairness supports the pro-sharing conclusion. On that interpretation, we incur obligations of fairness when we benefit from other people's incurring costs in producing a good there is a moral duty to produce, or at least an unconditional good (Casal 1999), i.e. a good whose goodness does not depend on people's valuing it. By having and rearing children, people may be producing a good of one or both of these kinds, if it is true, for example, that there is a duty to be "fruitful and multiply" (Arneson 2014), to contribute to non-extinction for the sake of avoiding suffering to the last generation(s) (Gheaus 2016), or that the continuation of society and humanity is essential to the very possibility of having valuable projects (Scheffler 2014).

As can be expected, some of the objections these two alternative versions of the fairness-based pro-sharing case face are different. The socialized goods argument may be thought deficient in that it only focuses on some of the goods that parents produce by having and rearing children (i.e. the economic benefits which are deliberately redistributed to everyone by our public institutions), and, relatedly, it only provides a conditional case for sharing the costs of children (only if and to the extent that the benefits of children are socialized do those who receive those benefits have an obligation to share the costs of children). The moral duty/unconditional goods argument, by contrast, meets with the objection that its normative premise is controversial, and may be in tension with the neutrality constraint mentioned earlier. Whether or not these objections can be answered, the fairness-based case for sharing the costs of children merits further attention.

Conclusion

There are several questions about the just distribution of the costs of children which this chapter has not tackled, and, by way of conclusion, one in particular is worth mentioning, due to its pressing practical urgency and philosophical complexity. This is how concerns about overpopulation at the global level affect the applicability and force of arguments for the claims of parental justice in the context of liberal democratic societies with a very high life expectancy, a declining birth rate, and an ageing population. How we answer this question will depend, among other things, on our theory of global justice, including our view on how responsibilities for offsetting climate change should be distributed; on our account of the state's right to exclude; and our view about the nature and weight of people's procreative and parenting rights (see ch. 14).

Currently, some scholars advance arguments in favor of sharing the costs of children in the context of developed economies with a declining birth rate that can be criticized for not looking beyond that context (Longman 2004). At the same time, others arguably make the opposite mistake of moving all too quickly from concerns about overpopulation and climate change to the conclusion that having children is a harmful activity (Young 2001; Broome 2012; MacIver 2015; Conly 2015).

Discussions of the just distribution of the costs of children should steer away from both these tendencies when addressing the thorny questions that arise from acknowledging, on the one hand, concerns about population pressure, as well as, on the other, that parents contribute socially necessary labor whose costs need to be distributed fairly.[5]

Notes

1 This figure is given by the insurer LV=, which uses data compiled by the Centre of Economic and Business Research (CEBR). Source: https://www.lv.com/about-us/press/article/cost-of-a-child-2016 (last accessed 16 July 2017).
2 US Department of Agriculture's "Expenditures on Children by Families, 2015", https://www.cnpp.usda.gov/sites/default/files/expenditures_on_children_by_families/crc2015.pdf (last accessed 16 July 2017).
3 For the question of whether *children* should share the costs of their upbringing with their parents, see Tomlin (2015).
4 Throughout, I assume that parents' having *and* rearing children, versus merely procreating or merely parenting, is at issue.
5 I am grateful to Paul Bou-Habib and the editors of this volume for their comments. Work for this article has received funding from the European Research Council (ERC) under the European Union's Horizon 2020 Research and Innovation Programme (Grant Agreement Number: 648610; Grant Acronym: Family Justice).

References

Ackerman, B. 1980. *Social Justice in the Liberal State*. New Haven, CT: Yale University Press.
Alstott, A. 2004. *No Exit. What Parents Owe Their Children and What Society Owes Parents*. Oxford: Oxford University Press.
Anderson, E. 1999 "What Is the Point of Equality?," *Ethics* 109: 287–337.
Arneson, R. 2014. "What Do We Owe Poor Families?," *Law, Ethics and Philosophy* 2: 7–31.
Austin, M. 2004. "The Failure of Biological Accounts of Parenthood," *Journal of Value Enquiry* 38: 499–510.
Bou-Habib, P. 2012. "Parental Subsidies: The Argument from Insurance," *Politics, Philosophy and Economics* 12: 197–216.
Bou-Habib, P., and Olsaretti, S. 2013. "Equality, Autonomy and the Price of Parenting," *Journal of Social Philosophy* 44: 420–438.
Bou-Habib, P., and Olsaretti, S. 2016. "Equality of Resources and the Demands of Authenticity," *Critical Review of International Social and Political Philosophy* 19(4): 434–455.

Brighouse, H., and Swift, A. 2014. *Family Values: The Ethics of Parent-Child Relationships*. Princeton, NJ: Princeton University Press.
Broome, J. 2012. *Climate Matters. Ethics in a Warming World*. New York, NY: W. W. Norton & Company.
Bubeck, D. E. 1995. *Care, Gender and Justice*. Oxford: Oxford University Press.
Casal, P. 1999. "Environmentalism, Procreation, and the Principle of Fairness," *Public Affairs Quarterly* 13: 363–376.
Casal, P., and Williams, A. 1995. "Rights, Equality and Procreation," *Analyse & Kritik* 17: 93–108.
Casal, P., and Williams, A. 2004. "Equality of Resources and Procreative Justice," in J. Burley (ed.), *Dworkin and His Critics*. Malden, MA: Blackwell.
Casal, P., and Williams, A. 2008. "Equality," in C. MacKinnon (ed.), *Issues in Political Theory*. Oxford: Oxford University Press.
Cohen, G. A. 1989. "On the Currency of Egalitarian Justice," *Ethics* 99: 906–944.
Cohen, G. A. 2004. "Expensive Taste Rides Again," in J. Burley (ed.), *Dworkin and His Critics*. Oxford: Blackwell.
Conly, S. 2015. *One Child. Do We have a Right to More?* Oxford: Oxford University Press.
Dworkin, R. 2000. *Sovereign Virtue. The Theory and Practice of Equality*. Cambridge, MA: Harvard University Press.
Dworkin, R. 2011. *Justice for Hedgehogs*. Cambridge, MA: Belknap Press.
Esping-Andersen, G. 2009. *The Incomplete Revolution*. Cambridge: Polity Press.
Folbre, N. 1994a. *Who Pays for the Kids? Gender and the Structures of Constraint*. New York, NY: Routledge.
Folbre, N. 1994b. "Children as Public Goods," *The American Economic Review* 84(2): 86–90.
Folbre, N. 2001. *The Invisible Heart*. New York, NY: The New Press.
Folbre, N. 2008. *Valuing Children. Rethinking the Economics of the Family*. Cambridge, MA: Harvard University Press.
George, R. 1987. "Who Should Bear the Costs of Children?," *Public Affairs Quarterly* 1: 1–42.
George, R. 1993. "On the External Benefits of Children," in D. T. Mejers et al. (eds.), *Kindred Matters: Rethinking the Philosophy of the Family*. Ithaca, NY: Cornell University Press.
Gheaus, A. 2016. "The Right to Parent and Duties Concerning Future Generations," *The Journal of Political Philosophy* 24(4): 487–508.
Glass, J., Simon, R. W., and Anderson, M. A. 2016. "Parenthood and Happiness: Effects of Work-Family Reconciliation Policies in 22 OECD Countries," *American Journal of Sociology* 122(3): 886–929.
Gornick, J. C., and Meyers M. K. 2004. "Supporting a Dual-Earner/Dual-Carer Society: Lessons from Abroad," in J. Heymann and C. Beem (eds.), *A Democracy that Works: The Public Dimensions of the Work and Family Debate*. New York, NY: The New Press.
Hart, H. L. A. 1955. "Are There Any Natural Rights?," *Philosophical Review* 64: 175–191.
Kates, C. 2004. "Reproductive Liberty and Overpopulation," *Environmental Values* 31: 51–79.
Longman, P. 2004. *The Empty Cradle: How Falling Birthrates Threaten World Prosperity (and What to Do About It)*. New York, NY: Basic Books.
MacIver, C. 2015. "Procreation or Appropriation?," in S. Hannan, S. Brennan, and R. Vernon (eds.), *Permissible Progeny? The Morality of Procreation and Parenting*. Oxford: Oxford University Press.
Macleod, C. 1998. *Liberalism, Equality, and Markets: A Critique of Liberal Equality*. Oxford: Oxford University Press.
Macleod, C. 2002. "Liberal Equality and the Affective Family," in D. Archard and C. Macleod (eds.), *The Moral and Political Status of Children*. Oxford: Oxford University Press.
Meijers, T. 2016. *Justice in Procreation. Five Essays on Population Size, Parenthood and New Arrivals*. PhD manuscript, Université Catholique de Louvain.
Nelson, S. K., Kushlev, K., and Lyubomirsky, S. 2014. "The Pains and Pleasures of Parenting: When, Why, and How Is Parenthood Associated with More or Less Well-Being?," *Psychological Bulletin* 140: 846–895.
Nussbaum, M. 2000. *Women and Human Development. The Capabilities Approach*. Cambridge: Cambridge University Press.
Nussbaum, M. 2006. *Frontiers of Justice. Disability, Nationality, Species Membership*. Cambridge, MA: Harvard University Press.
Nussbaum, M., and Sen, A. eds. 1993. *The Quality of Life*. Oxford: Clarendon Press. Okin, S. M. 1989. *Justice, Gender, and the Family*. Basic Books.
Olsaretti, S. 2013. "Children as Public Goods?," *Philosophy & Public Affairs* 41: 226–258.
Olsaretti, S. 2017. "Children as Negative Externalities?," *Politics, Philosophy and Economics* 16(2): 152–163.
Overall, C. 2012. *Why Have Children? The Ethical Debate*. Cambridge, MA: MIT Press.

Pullman-Shult, M. 2014. "Parenthood and Life Satisfaction: Why Don't Children Make People Happy?," *Journal of Marriage and Family* 76(2): 319–336.
Putnam, R. 2015. *Our Kids. The American Dream in Crisis*. New York, NY: Simon & Schuster.
Rakowski, R. 1991. *Equal Justice*. Oxford: Clarendon Press.
Rawls, J. 1971. *A Theory of Justice*. Oxford: Oxford University Press.
Rawls, J. 1993. *Political Liberalism*. New York, NY: Columbia University Press.
Scheffler, S. 2014. *Death and the Afterlife*. Oxford: Oxford University Press.
Sen, A. 1992. *Inequality Reexamined*. Oxford: Clarendon Press.
Steiner, H., and Vallentyne, P. 2009. "Libertarian Theories of Intergenerational Justice," in A. Gosseries and L. Meyer (eds.), *Intergenerational Justice*. Oxford: Oxford University Press.
Taylor, R. 2009. "Children as Projects and Persons: A Liberal Antinomy," *Social Theory and Practice* 35: 555–576.
Tomlin, P. 2015. "Should Kids Pay Their Own Way?," *Political Studies* 63: 663–678.
Young, T. 2001. "Overconsumption and Procreation: Are They Morally Equivalent?," *Journal of Applied Philosophy* 18: 183–191.

31
SCHOOLING

Gina Schouten

Introduction

Not all schooling is educational. Attempts to educate can misfire (for example, when ineffective or ill-supported teaching fails to generate student learning), and schools may intentionally serve non-educational ends (for example, when they provide nutrition through subsidized meal programs). Nor is all education schooling. Important learning occurs in the home and in public spaces like libraries and museums. One of the philosophically most important distinctions between education and schooling is that schooling as we know it is pervasively coercive. This does not mean that it is unjustified or harmful.[1] Rawls regarded all exercises of political power as coercive (Rawls 2001: 40). Assuming that many enactments of political power are justified, justified coercion abounds.

"Coercion" is a highly contested term, but some elements are widely regarded as essential: the coercer undertakes to affect the behavior of the coercee by altering the costs and benefits of the various actions available (Anderson 2008). Few regard these elements as *sufficient* for coercion to occur, but I take it that compulsory schooling as a large-scale public enterprise meets intuitive criteria for coercion; certainly politically enforced compulsory schooling meets Rawls's notion of coercion. The working hypothesis of this chapter is that many debates over contemporary schooling can fruitfully be understood as debates about the coercion it involves.

Like all publicly funded social projects, schooling coerces taxpayers. Through the appropriation of funds, the state compels citizens to finance a program of schooling that complies with politically determined and enforced specifications. And, assuming parents have some prerogative to direct the lives of their young children, schooling might be regarded as coercive to parents as well: they are required to accept schooling for their children that meets certain externally imposed curricular requirements, whether they endorse those requirements or not. But this is a book about children, and this chapter focuses largely on the ways in which compulsory schooling coerces the children it aims to educate. These children are compelled to attend school and to participate in transformational educative experiences while there. Ideally, these experiences develop students' knowledge, skills, and dispositions in beneficial ways. But much of the educational experience is not chosen by students for themselves. We generally regard coercing children as more easily justified than coercing adults, and so much of the debate over schooling's coercion of children centers not on whether it is justified but rather on what forms it should take—on what forms of schooling best serve children's interests.

Schooling is *coercive* education, and this chapter explores it as such. I begin by showing how common controversies about schooling can be regarded as disagreements over the coercion it imposes. I then consider the goods that schooling is commonly thought to provide. By getting clearer on just what schooling should aim to accomplish, I suggest, we can begin to develop principled answers to questions about the extent to which—and the ways in which—it may justifiably coerce children, parents, and taxpayers.

Challenges for schooling

Schooling coerces children into learning certain things and becoming certain sorts of people. It occupies hundreds of hours of children's lives, whether they want it to or not. Few reject educational coercion altogether. Instead, debates over schooling's coercion center on the *nature* of the coercion that schooling embodies. Philosophers have long worried that schooling can coerce children in the wrong ways—perverting their natural dispositions (Rousseau 1762), inhibiting individuality (Mill 1859), or failing to prepare them to live well (Dewey 1916).

Childhood matters not only as preparation for adulthood, and several contemporary philosophers argue powerfully that the "goods of childhood" matter in their own right (Macleod 2010; Brennan 2014). We might worry that schooling coerces children in ways that inhibit their realization of those goods, or that it fails positively to promote them when it should.

Some examples will illustrate. In the US, "charter schools" receive public funds but are exempt from many of the regulations that typically apply to public schools. Some charter schools locate in high-poverty areas and make it their mission to educate socially disadvantaged students. Many of these schools embrace severe, zero-tolerance disciplinary regimes that appear responsible for much of their success in preparing students for college (Thernstrom and Thernstrom 2003; Mathews 2009). But severe discipline might inhibit students' attainment of intrinsic goods of childhood, for example by causing high levels of stress or anxiety.[2] These short-term costs *may* be justified by the long-term payoff of college readiness, and the calculation of how to balance these concerns should inform our judgment about whether this constitutes justified coercion. Trade-offs between the preparatory aims of education and the intrinsic goods of childhood are not unique to charter schools; nor does the need to balance preparatory educational goods with intrinsic goods of childhood arise only with respect to school discipline. But the use of severe discipline to educate children and maintain order exemplifies complications about which forms of educational coercion best promote students' interests.

Other worries concern the increased exposure of students to the influence of corporations and consumerism (Molnar 2005). Consider "Channel One" programming in the US: Channel One provides schools with television and video equipment in return for which they have a guaranteed captive audience during their twelve-minute daily newscast—and, thus, premium commercial time to sell to advertisers (Brighouse 2005). Exposure of children to consumerist influences in schools is not a distinctly American phenomenon; marketing to children in schools has also gotten attention recently in Canada (Norris 2007), France (Zwarthoed 2015), and elsewhere. We might object to this practice because the class time could be spent on more educationally valuable activities, because exposure to commercial programming in schools undermines students' rational capacities to evaluate their own consumerist desires, or because it affirms and perpetuates mainstream consumerism generally (Brighouse 2005). All of these are objections to the ways in which *status quo* schooling coerces children.

Other disputes over schooling concern the ways in which it coerces *parents*. Compulsory schooling constrains parents' ability to dictate the terms of their children's education, and disputes about the division of authority over children's education abound. For example, proponents of school choice want to give parents more control over their children's education through initiatives like school vouchers, which allocate educational funding directly to students to be used to attend any eligible school (Friedman 1962; Brighouse 2000). School choice initiatives are not true consumer-choice mechanisms: students are the *consumers* of schooling, but the *choice* is generally made by parents, who may choose based on schools' spiritual commitments, student composition, disciplinary environment, curriculum focus, or pedagogical style. As such, initiatives like vouchers expand parents' options for educating their children, thus limiting political constraints on parental prerogatives. In the US, homeschooling limits political constraints on parents as well. States vary in the requirements they set for homeschooling, but even within the confines of the most restrictive among them, parents enjoy considerable latitude to dictate the terms of their children's education (Vopat 2009).

It might seem odd to think of schooling as coercive to parents. After all, restricting parental prerogatives simply limits parents' capacity to coerce their children. But whether or not claims on behalf of parents are valid, they are coherent. Sharing one's values with one's child is a fundamental aspect of parenting (Brighouse and Swift 2014), and few dispute its moral permissibility wholesale (but see Clayton 2006; see also ch. 29). As long as parents enjoy *some* prerogative in this regard, political measures to constrain that prerogative can coherently be thought of as coercive to parents.

Finally, consider objections to schooling's coercion of third-party taxpayers. I am aware of no theorists who argue against *all* coercively appropriated public support of education, but plenty oppose the *extent* of the appropriation and the ways in which it is spent. For example, Milton Friedman argues that public expenditures should be limited to the aspects of schooling that generate clear "neighborhood effects," or benefits that return to the public: "a minimum degree of literacy and knowledge" that citizens need, the provision of which contributes to general welfare "by promoting a stable and democratic society" (Friedman 1962: 86). Friedman's objection to *status quo* schooling targets its coercion of taxpayers through the appropriation of funds.

How are we to assess the legitimacy of schooling's coercion of children, parents, and taxpayers? In the next section, I examine the aims of schooling. Only by carefully identifying those aims and weighing their importance can we think well about how to settle these disputes.

Aims of schooling

A general presumption favors allowing individuals to make their own choices, free from external coercion. Clarifying the goods coercion can secure is crucial for determining when this presumption is overridden. To some degree, plausibly, children fall outside the purview of this presumption. But by determining the ends that schooling justifiably aims to serve, the relative importance of those ends, and the extent to which coercion is essential to realizing them, we can better answer questions about *how* children are to be coerced and *who* has the authority to decide. The putative aims of schooling include student-centered aims, collective-goods aims, and justice aims. These categories need not be exclusive or exhaustive; schooling might justifiably aim to achieve multiple goods in multiple categories, and it might serve certain ends beyond those I consider. Still, these three types of aims are central to justifying schooling's coercion.

First, consider student-centered aims. Much philosophical discussion of the educational goods schooling generates for students concerns autonomy. Schooling can help students develop the intellectual capacities to evaluate the life courses available to them and to judge well among them. It can expose students to values beyond those espoused by their families and beyond those of the prevailing mainstream culture in which they are raised, and it can provide training and opportunities for students to scrutinize those values. In short, it can develop students' capacity to live a life of their own choosing, based on their own judgements and on values they can authentically endorse (Gutmann 1995; Brighouse 2006; Callan 1997; Macedo 1995).

But the value of autonomy is highly controversial, and autonomy education has plenty of critics. Philosophical criticisms tend to emphasize the rights of parents to determine whether their children should be equipped with skills for autonomy (Burtt 1994; Lomasky 1987; Galston 1995). Parents who celebrate spiritual heteronomy and believe that the best life is one lived in obedience to God might worry that autonomy leads to spiritual alienation. Even those who don't regard autonomy as harmful in itself might worry that equipping children for autonomous choice means risking that they will not choose well. If I am convinced I know what kind of life is best for my child, I might sensibly think she is better off non-autonomously living it than autonomously choosing something worse. We might also worry that autonomy development can threaten traditional and communal ways of life, thereby—assuming those are *good* ways of life—harming the children who are a part of them.

Even if autonomy is not always valuable for all children, we might think that it is a necessary means for *some* children to secure *other* goods that schooling should provide. Harry Brighouse argues that schooling should promote students' prospects for leading flourishing lives (2000). Plausibly, many students must develop the capacity for autonomy in order to flourish, because some will be born into ways of life that do not fit them well. To equip these students to flourish, schooling must enable them to find a way of life that they can endorse authentically and live well (Brighouse 2000: 69). If autonomy is valuable only insofar as it is a good tool to help some students live flourishing lives, then its value must be weighed carefully against other contributors to flourishing, such as connectedness to community. Schooling that enables students to lead flourishing lives will plausibly equip them with the skills associated with autonomy; but it will also, for example, foster skills for maintaining personal relationships. Educational time and resources are scarce, and some educational goods come at a cost to others. Often, a balance will need to be struck. A balance must be struck, too, between equipping students with the skills for adulthood and enabling them to attain intrinsic goods of childhood (Macleod 2016).

Even without getting very precise about what flourishing is or what schools should do to promote it, we can draw an important conclusion: the student-centered aims of schooling can justify many *non-educational* projects of schooling. Students need adequate nutrition and health care, protections against threats to their safety and security, and caring relationships with adults. These needs have historically been met by other social institutions, like families, churches, or social welfare regimes. But increasingly, students show up at school without having these non-educational needs met, and schools have tried to meet them. In part, this effort is justifiable on the basis of schools' *educational* remit: hungry, ill, or fearful students do not learn well. But schooling that aims to promote students' prospects for flourishing can more directly justify efforts that go beyond basic educational provision: even if students could be *educated* without adequate nutrition or health care, they cannot *flourish* without these. Perhaps other institutions could provide these conditions for flourishing more efficiently than schools. But as long as other institutions fail to do so, schools aiming to promote student flourishing will find non-educational tasks falling within their remit. Insofar as the promotion of flourishing justifies coercive schooling, it apparently justifies non-educational aspects as well as educational aspects.

Apart from serving important interests of students themselves, schooling provides certain positive externalities or "neighborhood effects" (Friedman 1962).[3] I'll refer to the relevant externalities as "collective goods." The most widely discussed collective goods of schooling are the preparation students receive for economic participation and for good citizenship.

We have already seen that economic preparation is valuable for students: to prepare them to live flourishing lives, schooling must impart the skills necessary for economic independence. But economic participation also generates collective goods. Equipping students with the skills to develop into independent adults prepares them to contribute to a modern society. Insofar as schooling does this *well*, we all benefit. For example, collective goods are generated when we educate students to excel at and pursue socially valuable careers and projects, like caregiving.

Economic participation is not *always* a collective good, all things considered. Students might subsequently participate in socially dis-valuable ways; and even if their participation is not socially dis-valuable, it might not be socially *beneficial*. A great deal of political rhetoric emphasizes schools' role in preparing students to fuel economic *growth* and *competition* (see Allen 2015 for discussion). But growth may not be a collective good. In already wealthy societies, there is good reason to doubt that further growth, and the increased material wealth that it brings, actually translate into better lives. In his summary of the evidence regarding the effects of economic growth on subjective well-being, Robert Frank notes that "once income levels surpass a minimal absolute threshold, average satisfaction levels within a given country tend to be highly stable over time, even in the face of significant economic growth" (Frank 1999: 72). We certainly owe it to students to equip them to participate meaningfully in a modern economy, and collective goods are generated if we orient them toward particular kinds of participation. But in wealthy societies, educational expenditures aimed at driving economic growth aren't necessarily justified by collective-goods considerations.

Now consider the collective good of citizenship. We all stand to benefit if schools develop children into good citizens disposed to be careful, deliberative decision-makers. According to Amy Gutmann, "the aim of democratic education is to create democratic citizens, people who are willing and able to govern their own lives and share in governing their society" (Gutmann 1993: 1). Harry Brighouse argues that, among other things, "schools should educate children so that they can be effective, and reasonable, participants in public decisionmaking and execution" (Brighouse 2006: 2). But precisely what constitutes good citizenship? Does it require a capacity for autonomy (Galston 1995; Gutmann 1995; Brighouse 2006; Callan 1997; Macedo 1995)? Does it involve the cultivation of certain dispositions, such as a disposition to be mutually respectful toward those who are different than us (Gutmann 1995)? Or will mere tolerance suffice (Galston 1995)? Does citizenship involve a disposition to live sustainably (Zwarthoed 2015)? Though many agree that students educated for citizenship are a public good, disagreement abounds as to just what citizenship education should look like.

Justice aims constitute a third type of educational aim that justifies coercive schooling. Liberal democracies generally aspire to be places of equal opportunity and social mobility. Disagreement as to just what the ideal of equal opportunity requires is in no short supply, but on any reasonable understanding, education has a clear role to play. Universal provision of education has long been regarded as crucial to ensuring that all have a fair shot to compete for unequally distributed social and economic rewards (Curren 1994). These rewards include income and wealth, further educational opportunities, secure jobs, status, etc. Because of its position as a gateway to these rewards, a fair distribution of educational goods for students is one that promotes equal opportunity in the competition for the rewards that accrue *outside* of schooling.

What must education provide if it is to help us in discharging this obligation of justice? A tempting answer is that we should invest equal educational resources, or *inputs*, into each child's schooling. But in very unequal societies like the US, equalizing educational inputs across students will not help realize equal opportunity. Students arrive at school unequally ready to make good use of educational inputs. This unequal preparation is due in large part to differences in social class (Rothstein 2004). For any set amount of per-student resources, some students will flourish, and others will flounder. Providing equal resources, then, will do little more than reinforce unequal opportunities that already exist.

In a foundational paper on educational justice, Christopher Jencks (1988) assesses candidate principles for the distribution of educational resources. A commitment to equal opportunity suggests that it is unfair for students to have less favorable prospects due to social contingencies beyond their control. If this is right, Jencks reasons, then perhaps we should expend educational resources to compensate for social disadvantage. We could calibrate educational inputs (e.g., resources like good teachers) in order to achieve more equal educational *outputs* (e.g., college readiness)—to break the link between students' social class background and their subsequent educational achievement. This would require unequal per-student funding, with socially disadvantaged students receiving more resources to enhance their prospects to attain the goods to which education serves as a gateway. But notice, Jencks continues, that if we care about mitigating disadvantage due to circumstances beyond one's control, we seem to have as much reason to mitigate *naturally caused* disadvantage as *socially caused* disadvantage. This suggests that we should invest extra resources in disadvantaged students, whether their disadvantage is due to their social class backgrounds *or* natural characteristics like innate intelligence. Jencks refers to this principle of unequal investment to equalize outcomes as "strong humane justice" (SHJ). SHJ calls for schools to favor disadvantaged students with disproportionally large shares of educational resources in order to break the link between students' social and natural circumstances and their subsequent educational achievement.

Jencks rejects SHJ on the grounds that it constitutes a principle of equal educational *outcomes* rather than equal educational *opportunities*. But if educational justice consists in equalizing opportunities in *subsequent competitions* for social and economic advantage, then the fact that SHJ calls for equal educational outcomes constitutes no grounds for its rejection. Equal educational outcomes may be required to ensure equal *opportunities* in competitions subsequent to education. A worry remains, however: in a highly unequal society, it is impossible for schools to fully sever the link between students' unchosen social and natural circumstances and their educational achievement. So long as students arrive at school vastly unequally prepared to learn, schools cannot equalize their prospects for attaining success upon leaving. SHJ thus seems impossible to realize. This may be no problem in itself; it is no mark against a principle of educational justice that it is not fully realizable so long as other social institutions remain deeply unjust. The problem is that the steps SHJ appears to license in pursuit of educational equality seem morally repugnant: even recognizing that SHJ is impossible fully to realize, it calls for radically favoring disadvantaged students in the allocation of educational resources, and thereby appears to license neglect and deprivation of more advantaged students. Apart from harming these students, this educational deprivation risks diminishing the pool of human capital from which we all benefit (Anderson 2007; Satz 2007).[4]

I think this challenge can be met. The justice aims of schooling are only one part of the good that schooling should provide, and thus only one among many considerations that should inform schooling policy (Brighouse and Swift 2009). Schooling should promote equal opportunity, but it must also promote student-centered aims and collective-goods aims. To some extent, these aims can be pursued concurrently. But at some point, pursuing one will mean accepting costs in terms of the others. Considered within this context, SHJ avoids its apparent counterintuitive implications (Brighouse and Swift 2009). The need to arrange schooling to provide educational goods for all students and to generate public goods constrains what we may do to pursue equal opportunity. SHJ would require depriving advantaged students if we cared *only* about arranging schooling to promote justice. But we also care about goods for students, and thus about promoting *all* students' prospects for flourishing. And we care about *collective* goods, and thus about preparing all students for citizenship and for publicly valuable economic participation.

I suggest that schooling should aim to accomplish some version of each educational aim considered above. It should provide goods for students themselves by enhancing their prospects for all-things-considered flourishing. It should provide the collective goods of preparation for citizenship and economic participation. And it should promote equal opportunity by investing in students disproportionately to help offset the effects of social and natural disadvantage. In particular, schooling should pursue *prioritarian* educational justice (Schouten 2012). Prioritarianism is a version of SHJ because it directs us to calibrate unequal inputs to offset the effects of social and natural disadvantage on students' life prospects subsequent to schooling. It is prioritarian in directing us to prioritize benefits in proportion to students' disadvantage: we should allocate educational resources as a weighted function of students' disadvantage, where disadvantage is understood in terms of students' prospects for living good lives.

Not all goods of schooling will fall neatly into one of the three categories. Economic preparation is valuable for both students and for the public. Promoting students' prospects for flourishing is an obligation of justice as well as being valuable for each student's own sake. Still, the categorization is illuminating. Competing schooling regimes will provide different benefits to different stakeholders. Categorizing the aims of education enables us to think carefully about the trade-offs we confront. To take just one example, consider a new policy that would benefit disadvantaged students by diverting resources from enrichment programs that, under the *status quo*, primarily benefit already advantaged students. A possible reason *against* this reallocation is that, by lessening promising students' opportunities for enrichment, we risk reducing the stock of developed human capital that the schooling system produces. But we must ask: for what are we trying to produce developed human capital? If for the sake of collective goods, then we must further ask whether at some level of provision, the requirement to generate collective goods gives way to the interests of students themselves. If for the sake of justice, then we must ask whether the advantaged students' enlarged stock of human capital is likely subsequently to enhance the prospects of the disadvantaged. If for the sake of the advantaged students themselves, then we must ask how the aim of enhancing *all* students' prospects is to be weighed against the goal of *equalizing* prospects, given the scarcity of educational resources. These questions are relevant both for determining which educational policies will best serve the appropriately weighted aims of schooling and for determining whether and in what ways schooling may justifiably coerce children, parents, and taxpayers.

The challenges reconsidered

In this section, I return to the disputes over schooling with which we began, re-examining those disputes in light of schooling's aims. This discussion is conjectural and all too brief, and will examine only a few of the many interesting issues we could discuss. But it illustrates how the aims of schooling bear upon the justifiability of coercion. It illustrates, too, the work still to be done in clarifying the relative weight of the different aims—not only for determining the proper allocation of scarce resources, but for determining what types of coercive schooling are justified, all things considered.

First, consider the coercive appropriation of funds to pay for education. Public funding of some amount of education is justified on the grounds that education provides collective goods: because we benefit by living in a society in which children are educated, we should contribute to the system that educates them. But the case for public funding goes beyond this. Plausibly, we are required to pull our weight in ensuring that the society we live in is fair (Hart 1955). Assuming that a fair society is characterized by equal opportunity and fair competition for unequally distributed social and economic rewards, schooling has an indispensable role to play in promoting justice. If we all share responsibility for building and maintaining a just society, then we incur some obligation to support the institutions that prepare citizens to compete on equal footing for good jobs, security, status, and other social and economic rewards. This requires ensuring that all students receive a share of educational goods, since those goods are necessary to have a fair shot in life; and it requires allocating the resources of schooling so as to mitigate the effects of students' unchosen social and natural endowments on their life prospects.

These considerations reveal a schematic picture of justified taxpayer coercion to fund schooling: the collective goods of education justify coercive appropriation to an extent—up to some threshold, it is in the public's interest to prepare students to contribute economically and to be good citizens.[5] Beyond that threshold, collective goods don't justify further expenditures. But so long as schools remain the best-equipped institutions in society to ensure that all children develop opportunities to lead flourishing lives, and to ensure that those opportunities be distributed fairly, the justice- and student-centered aims of schooling justify far more expansive educational expenditures. And the fact that justice- and student-centered aims do the justifying above the collective-goods threshold has implications for how the funds should be spent.

Now consider how the aims of schooling bear on questions about rigorous disciplinary regimes and consumerism in schools. Both consumerism in schools and severe disciplinary regimes have been accused of jeopardizing one of the collective-goods aims of schooling: citizenship. Alex Molnar and others have argued that consumerism in schools undermines students' development of citizenship skills and constitutes "a profound threat to democratic civic institutions" (Molnar 2005: 16). Sigal Ben-Porath (2013) has argued that severe disciplinary regimes are incompatible with students' development of civic virtues.

The student-centered aims of childhood flourishing also appear to tell against both manners of coercion. Consider the question of discipline first: plausibly, being subject to the anxiety associated with severe discipline makes many children flourish less as children.[6] Still, several points must be borne in mind. First, while childhood flourishing matters, childhood flourishing does not *replace* the preparatory aspects of schooling (Macleod 2010). In some circumstances, severe disciplinary regimes might benefit students by better preparing them to compete for social and economic advantage as adults (Thernstrom and Thernstrom 2003). If so, then calculations of how well or badly such regimes promote student-centered aims of schooling must incorporate a metric for weighting the preparatory elements of education against childhood flourishing. Childhood flourishing matters, but short-term losses can, in principle, be outweighed by long-term gains. Even in the short-term, the judgment that discipline imposes a flourishing cost must be made with alternatives clearly in mind: perhaps the schools that students would otherwise attend are even worse—not just anxiety-inducing, but positively dangerous. For all these reasons, it might be *other-things-equal* bad for students to go to schools with severe discipline, but nonetheless good for them, *all things considered*. Similar remarks apply to the question of discipline in light of the *justice* aims of schooling: perhaps schools that rely on rigorous disciplinary regimes have the overall effect of promoting justice, given the non-ideal world in which we live (Brighouse and Schouten 2014).

At a glance, consumerism in schools seems an easier case: it seems clearly to frustrate the student-centered aims of education. Plausibly, most students would experience more childhood flourishing if they could be insulated from the influences of consumerism in schools—from the fear of judgment for not wearing brand-name clothing, for example. Apart from the anxiety consumerism might generate, exposure to consumerism seems inimical to students' development of capacities for autonomous reflection and judgment (Brighouse 2005; Zwarthoed 2015). Limiting consumerism in schools thus appears critically important for enabling students to be autonomous and, thus, to flourish. But here, too, we must be careful. Increasingly, schools turn to corporate partnerships to generate much-needed revenue (Norris 2007). If corporate contracts generate revenues for schools to provide important educational experiences, then allowing some access to students might promote student-centered aims, all things considered. And if gains from corporate partnerships can be directed toward disadvantaged students, such partnerships might promote justice aims, all things considered. Given the likely effects of consumerist influences on children, it is *unfortunate* that budget constraints would render such partnerships schools' all-things-considered best option for promoting student- and justice-centered aims and this gives us reason to object to those constraints. But it may nonetheless be *true* that such partnerships represent the best course for some schools, all things considered.

This illustrates an important point: the all-things-considered judgments are ultimately the important ones. We need to know what action is right, under the relevant circumstances, given the feasibility constraints we face. But other-things-equal questions remain critically important. For one thing, we will want to know when we have reason to *expand* our feasibility set. Suppose we decide that, in a particular school, severe discipline is best for students, all things considered, because it enhances their long-term job marketability enough to outweigh short-term childhood flourishing costs. Still, we want to know what those flourishing costs are. Only then do we know whether we have reason—and how urgent the reason is—to rearrange the alternatives so that severe discipline is no longer the best of bad options. Other-things-equal judgments are also important to determining whether there are ways of easing the bad that the all-things-considered best option inflicts. With regard to discipline, this might mean teaching students to "code-switch" so that highly regimented school cultures don't undermine students' sense of belonging in their home cultures (Morton 2014). With regard to consumerism in schools, we might look for ways to mitigate the negative effects of consumerism on students' autonomy. School curricula might be designed to incorporate discussion of the commercial partnership itself, as exemplified by a Canadian civics textbook that invited students to scrutinize a bid by Pepsi for exclusive sales rights in Toronto District Schools (Norris 2007). In a very unjust world, all-things-considered judgments can strike us as depressingly concessive. But we must act within the world as it is. By continuing to make other-things-equal judgments at the same time, we can more clearly track and better manage the trade-offs that our circumstances necessitate.

Conclusion

This chapter has examined some contemporary disputes over schooling as debates about the justifiability of the coercion that schooling involves. Some of these disputes are disagreements over how schooling can justifiably coerce the students themselves—about where their best interests lie, and about when their interests may permissibly yield to concerns of social justice and public goods. Others are disputes over who has the authority to make decisions concerning educational coercion: when should parents' prerogative to direct the upbringing of their children prevail, and when may the state impose requirements based on shared, democratic notions of what best serves children's interests (see ch. 19, ch. 32)? When does the public's interest justify restricting parental prerogatives and requiring that children be educated for citizenship or economic participation? And, finally, who should finance these goods that schooling provides, and what justifies their being made to do so?

By clarifying just what schooling should aim to accomplish, we can begin to develop principled answers to these questions about the extent to which—and the ways in which—it may justifiably coerce children, parents, and taxpayers. I have proposed that schooling should promote students' prospects for flourishing, *equalize* those prospects, and prepare students for citizenship in a pluralistic, democratic society. If this is right, then verdicts on the controversies considered here must ultimately be informed by judgments about what kind of coercion is necessary if schooling is to achieve these ends. In the meantime, identifying the aims of schooling helps us sort out the relevant considerations: it helps us make precise the values at stake, clarify the conflicts among those values that will need to be resolved, and identify what missing information we will need in order to make all-things-considered judgments.

Schooling is coercive education. Questions of the justifiability of coercion are always, in large part, questions about the aims it serves. Compulsory schooling is justified on the basis of the crucially important social goods that schooling can provide. But establishing *that* schooling is justified coercion is only the first task. Much work remains in clarifying the aims and their relative importance before we can determine with precision what form schooling should take, how it should be funded, how compulsory it should be, and how its goods should be distributed.

Notes

1 See Anderson (2008). For a well-known account of coercion according to which it *is* moralized, see Wertheimer (1987). For an account according to which it isn't, see Zimmerman (2002).
2 See Brighouse and Schouten (2014) for a discussion.
3 See Olsaretti (2013) for a discussion of children as public goods.
4 Some theorists respond to these perceived problems by embracing *adequacy* principles of educational justice. Defenders of adequacy principles deny that justice requires *equalizing* students' prospects; all that is required is that we educate all students so that their prospects are *good enough* (Anderson 2007; Satz 2007; Curren 1994). Space limitations preclude a full consideration of adequacy principles in this chapter, but I join critics in finding them to be implausible as stand-alone principles of educational justice (Brighouse and Swift 2009).
5 Although I do not find adequacy principles to be plausible stand-alone principles of educational *justice*, I *do* think they can be helpful for thinking about public expenditures to produce *collective* educational goods.
6 Although some accounts do not depict it as anxiety-provoking. See Mathews (2009).

References

Allen, D. 2015. "What Is Education for?," *Boston Review*. Retrieved from http://bostonreview.net/forum/danielle-allen-what-education (last accessed 19 March 2018).
Anderson, E. 2007. "Fair Opportunity in Education: A Democratic Equality Perspective," *Ethics* 117(4): 595–622.
Anderson, S. 2008. "Of Theories of Coercion, Two Axes, and the Importance of the Coercer," *The Journal of Moral Philosophy* 5: 394–422.
Ben-Porath, S. 2013. "Deferring Virtue: The New Management of Students and the Civic Role of Schools," *Theory and Research in Education* 11(2): 111–128.
Brennan, S. 2014. "The Goods of Childhood and Children's Rights," in F. Baylis and C. Mcleod (eds.), *Family-Making: Contemporary Ethical Challenges*. Oxford: Oxford University Press.
Brighouse, H. 2000. *School Choice and Social Justice*. Oxford: Oxford University Press.
Brighouse, H. 2005. "Channel One, the Anti-Commercial Principle, and the Discontinuous Ethos," *Educational Policy* 19(3): 528–549.
Brighouse, H. 2006. *On Education*. New York, NY: Routledge.
Brighouse, H., and Schouten, G. 2014. "To Charter or Not to Charter: What Questions Should We Ask, and What Will the Answers Tell Us?," *Harvard Educational Review* 84: 341–364.
Brighouse, H., and Swift, A. 2009. "Educational Adequacy versus Educational Equality," *Journal of Applied Philosophy* 26(2): 117–128.
Brighouse, H., and Swift, A. 2014. *Family Values: The Ethics of Parent-Child Relationships*. Princeton, NJ: Princeton University Press.

Burtt, S. 1994. "Religious Parents, Secular Schools: A Liberal Defence of an Illiberal Education," *Review of Politics* 56: 51–70.
Callan, E. 1997. *Creating Citizens: Political Education and Liberal Democracy*. Oxford: Oxford University Press.
Clayton, M. 2006. *Justice and Legitimacy in Upbringing*. Oxford: Oxford University Press.
Curren, R. 1994 "Justice and the Threshold of Educational Equality," in Michael Katz (ed.), *Philosophy of Education*. Urbana, IL: Philosophy of Education Society.
Dewey, J. 1916. *Democracy and Education: An Introduction to the Philosophy of Education*. New York, NY: Macmillan.
Frank, R. 1999. *Luxury Fever*. Princeton, NJ: Princeton University Press.
Friedman, M. 1962. *Capitalism and Freedom*. Chicago, IL: University of Chicago Press.
Galston, W. 1995. "Two Concepts of Liberalism," *Ethics* 105: 516–534.
Gutmann, A. 1993. "Democracy and Democratic Education," *Studies in Philosophy and Education* 12: 1–9.
Gutmann, A. 1995. "Civic Education and Social Diversity," *Ethics* 105: 557–579.
Hart, H. L. A. 1955. "Are There Any Natural Rights?," *Philosophical Review* 64: 175–191.
Jencks, C. 1988. "Whom Must We Treat Equally for Educational Opportunity to be Equal?," *Ethics* 98: 518–533
Lomasky, L. 1987. *Persons, Rights, and the Moral Community*. Oxford: Oxford University Press.
Macedo, S. 1995. "Liberal Civic Education and Religious Fundamentalism: The Case of God v. John Rawls," *Ethics* 105: 468–496.
Macleod, C. 2010. "Primary Goods, Capabilities and Children," in H. Brighouse and I. Robeyns (eds.), *Measuring Justice: Primary Goods and Capabilities*. Cambridge: Cambridge University Press.
Macleod, C. 2016. "Just Schools and Good Childhoods: Non-preparatory Dimensions of Educational Justice," *Journal of Applied Philosophy* 35: 76–89.
Mathews, J. 2009. *Work Hard. Be Nice: How Two Inspired Teachers Created the Most PROMISING Schools in America*. Chapel Hill, NC: Algonquin.
Mill, J. S. 1978 (orig. 1859). *On Liberty*. Indianapolis, IN: Hackett.
Molnar, A. 2005. *School Commercialism: From Democratic Ideal to Market Commodity*. New York, NY: Routledge.
Morton, J. 2014. "Cultural Code-Switching: Straddling the Achievement Gap," *Journal of Political Philosophy* 22(3): 259–281.
Norris, T. 2007. "Consuming Schooling: Education as Simulation," *Philosophy of Education Yearbook*: 162–171.
Olsaretti, S. 2013. "Children as Public Goods?," *Philosophy and Public Affairs* 41(3): 226–258.
Rawls, J. 2001. *Justice as Fairness: A Restatement*. Cambridge, MA: Harvard University Press.
Rothstein, R. 2004. *Class and Schools*. Washington, DC: Economic Policy Institute.
Rousseau, J. J. 1955 (1762). *Emile*, trans. B. Foxley. London: Dent.
Satz, D. 2007. "Equality, Adequacy, and Education for Citizenship," *Ethics* 117(4): 623–648.
Schouten, G. 2012. "Fair Educational Opportunity and the Distribution of Natural Ability: Toward a Prioritarian Principle of Educational Justice," *Journal of Philosophy of Education* 46(3): 472–491.
Thernstrom, A., and Thernstrom, S. 2003. *No Excuses*. New York, NY: Simon and Schuster.
Vopat, M. 2009. "Justice, Religion, and the Education of Children," *Public Affairs Quarterly* 23(3): 203–225.
Wertheimer, A. 1987. *Coercion*. Princeton, NJ: Princeton University Press.
Zimmerman, D. 2002. "Taking Liberties: The Perils of 'Moralizing' Freedom and Coercion in Social Theory and Practice," *Social Theory and Practice* 28: 577–609.
Zwarthoed, D. 2015. "Creating Frugal Citizens: The Liberal Egalitarian Case for Teaching Frugality," *Theory and Research in Education* 13(3): 286–307.

32
CHILDREN AND THE CARE SYSTEM

Gideon Calder

Introduction

The focus of this chapter is on "looked-after children", to use a now-common term: children whose care is the direct responsibility of the state. Such children may be placed – for example – in residential institutions of different kinds, with foster parents, or in the legal guardianship of a member of the extended family.[1] They will be taken into care because their current parents or carers are not in a position to look after them adequately. In most cases, they will have experienced neglect or abuse.

Only a small minority of children will be in the care system at any time: typically, less than one in a hundred.[2] Yet their situation sheds distinct light on questions recurring throughout this handbook, about children's well-being, the value of family relationships, and the rightful role of the state with respect to each of these. Meanwhile, the place of looked-after children is also worthy of attention for its own sake: for what it tells us about *their* childhoods, as well as childhood in general. Any full treatment of this life stage must critically address versions of it that diverge from dominant social norms and expectations. For all these reasons, while applied philosophy lacks a clearly distinct, developed body of work on children and the care system, it is important to stake out how looked-after children fit into better-established fields of debate. We will approach it in terms of four questions, covered in turn in the following sections. First, what moral and social significance does "taking" children into the care of the state hold? Second, on what grounds should children be "taken into care"? Third, what entitles *the state*, in particular, to do this, and how far does that entitlement go? And fourth, what wider questions of social justice are raised as we compare the situation of children in care with that of other children?

The moral and social significance of "taking children into care"

The "care system" for children typically kicks in selectively, as a back-up – a stand-in for when the family, with its presumptive rights to fulfil the child-rearing role, does not function in the expected way. This points us towards three salient aspects of the moral and social significance of taking children "into care".

The first aspect concerns the relative roles and status of social and medical care in contemporary liberal democracies. Customarily, jurisdictions impose regulations on the birth process and operate a mandatory system for monitoring the health of all babies in early infancy – regarding, for example, adequate birth weight, inoculation, nutrition, and physical and intellectual development. These interventions will be professionalised and standardised. Meanwhile child-rearing is typically treated as a matter of discretion, with a wide range of forms of practice tolerated and the case for professional intervention to be made only by exception, when problems emerge. (Not all interventions happen *ex post*, after problems have occurred: they may be *ex ante*, where harms are predicted and deemed preventable. But still, *ex ante* interventions are based on clear evidence of an exceptional problem.) This signals a split between medical and social delineations of parenting adequacy, and also an order of precedence: medical considerations are treated as primary (despite the *prima facie* case for treating rearing as similarly fundamental to the child's present and future well-being – see ch. 7, ch. 8, ch. 18).

This split, in turn, may be founded on various assumptions: that "hard", scientifically grounded attention to the objective conditions of child health rightly take priority over looser, more values-based questions about how we should live; that the medical conditions of well-being remain universal and uniform, even while diverse lifestyles proliferate; or that parental care is something which "comes naturally" to lay understanding, whereas medical knowledge belongs to a specialised, professional realm. However well ensconced, such suppositions can certainly be challenged. Many will point out the limitations of medical models of well-being, or their contestability, or their value-laden underpinnings (see ch. 33). There are well-rehearsed defences of the right of parents to depart from "expert" medical decisions about the well-being of their children (see, e.g., Goldstein 1977; Ross 1998; Austin 2007). And we can certainly question the extent to which adequate standards for the care and rearing of children somehow "look after themselves", as if self-evident or somehow naturally occurring (see ch. 14, ch. 17, ch. 18).

The second aspect reflects the moral and social significance of the family, in a contemporary liberal society. The care system does not cater proactively for all children. Certain children are, in the familiar phrase, *taken* into it. The very phrasing reflects background assumptions about the relationship between family and state – namely, that the accepted place of children is either with their birth parents or an organic successor to that set-up,[3] and that intervening in this set-up, and *a fortiori* removing children from it, requires justification. So, children are taken into care by exception, in response to an identified risk of harm: it is an operation that overrides and supplants the parental autonomy otherwise taken to apply. The burden of justification lies on the side of the intervening authority. To be sure, any conception of parental rights will allow for such exceptions: however strong the presumption in favour of the familial *status quo*, any society will need to make provisions for when those circumstances are untenable. But under liberal assumptions (as indeed in many other forms of jurisdiction, though sometimes for different reasons) such interventions occur only in the last instance.

The third aspect points us towards the connection of care – and specific caring relationships – to justice. Arguments for a care system as a requirement of social justice may take various forms. But before getting down to details, such arguments face a prior question: is care a matter of justice at all? There are three main routes to a sceptical response here. One is to suggest that, *a priori*, care and justice are fundamentally different kinds of currency, so that one cannot be converted into or allocated according to the other (Gilligan 1982, 1986). On these terms, care, while crucial to human well-being and normatively central, is by its nature not amenable to (for example) rules, systems of rights, or abstract principles such as "fairness" or "equality". The second arises from the position that because all matters of justice are matters of duty, care – as a "relationship good", which like friendship and love depends on the complex dynamics of human interaction, context, and sentiment – cannot be a matter of justice.[4] And a third is to argue that whether or not there is a justice-based case for doing so, these relational qualities of care make it prohibitively difficult to redistribute. Thus, no fine-tuning of systems or structures within a society can allocate or choreograph caring relationships with anything like the reliability that justice would require. Separately, these stances suggest that the care of looked-after children, however much a priority in other respects, is not a matter of social *justice*. We return to this later.

In this contested terrain, there are points of consensus. So, the social care of children is accepted to be a key factor in their well-being as current children and future adults, however it should best be situated with regard to medical considerations. There are clear reasons to intervene in the operations of the family as the main site of caregiving to children, regardless of what normative weight is placed on the family as an institution. And the case for including the care of children as a key moral and social priority stands independently of whether this runs alongside, or is part of, questions of justice.

Grounds for "taking children into care"

Who should be taken into care, when, and on what basis? We can assume that in any society, a certain number of children will be especially vulnerable due to current or potential inadequacies of parental care. And at least in the era of the welfare state, we have assumed that the state has a responsibility to identify and to make suitable provisions for those children – however minimal, and however qualified by allowances for parental autonomy. Those who have lost their parents are one obvious such group. The other is those children deemed not to be receiving parenting sufficient to cater for their well-being and interests. Inadequate parenting may take the form of neglect: being insufficiently attentive to a child's basic developmental needs for nutrition, interaction, stimulation, and security. Or it may take the form of abuse – whether physical, sexual, or emotional. The line between abuse and neglect is often blurred. It might be assumed, for instance, that abuse is active and intentional, whereas neglect is characterised by inaction and lack of direct intent. But that contrast is too simple. Emotional abuse, for example, may often be inflicted on a child indirectly – for example, in the course of their living in a household where violence against others is taking place. And rather than treating it as separate, many definitions of abuse include neglect as a core subcategory. See Mullin (2014) for a full and detailed discussion of different forms of emotional harm which may be experienced by children. The effects of neglect or abuse may be more or less overt, with different kinds of symptoms, from the physiological (e.g. weight loss or bruising) to the behavioural (e.g. withdrawal, anxiety, loss of confidence).

Identifying neglect or abuse requires a clear baseline, picking out an acceptable standard of care falling beneath which signals the need for intervention. Such a threshold is more elusive than it may first appear, not least because there are various possible comparators against which this standard might be measured, ranging from what children need to survive or develop *at all*, to the best possible upbringing with which they might realistically be provided (Archard 1999).

There are further levels of complexity. On the one hand, notions of "normality" or "sufficiency" in parent–child relations clearly shift through history. The notion of "child abuse" is itself a late 19th- and 20th-century development (Hayden et al. 1999; cf. Pfohl 1977). The category has since expanded, in terms of what counts as abuse or neglect of children – with regard to child labour, sexual relations, adequate nutrition, corporal punishment, and so on. Which is to say, once-normal practices are now regarded as unacceptable, and we can expect future adaptations to any established category of abuse. Meanwhile, there will be clear cultural discrepancies on these issues *within* any historical period. What is unremarkable or indeed correct in one culture, by way of the treatment of children, may be flatly impermissible in another. This will affect not simply how abuse is defined in a formal sense, but how it is experienced – and perhaps indeed *whether* this or that putatively abusive practice is even experienced as a harm. Practices viewable both as promoting children's welfare and as abuse include cliterodectomy, corporal punishment, and sending one's children to boarding school. In each case, whether it is harmful at all is in dispute, rather than (or perhaps sometimes as well as) whether any harms caused may be morally justified. There is clear evidence that relevant professionals experience, on the one hand, a tension between respecting different groups' varying cultural practices and, on the other hand, applying consistent standards of child protection to every child.[5]

And while there is a tendency to see abuse in individuated, domesticated terms, there are compelling reasons to address how – on any robust definition of maltreatment – forms of it may be perpetrated or at least facilitated by policies or social arrangements. This may happen either directly (for example, via policies which increase child poverty rates, or by insufficient social security provisions – see Parton 1991) or by reinforcing the circumstances in which abuse thrives – for example, through poor processes of detection, lack of attention to the voice of children, or to the implications of gender inequalities (Featherstone 2006). Attention to these more collective, or macro-level, causes of abuse is crucial, if nothing else, because of sheer reasons of scale. More children will be harmed by adverse socio-economic circumstances than are victims of severe parental maltreatment.

Contemporaneously with the recognition of child abuse as a phenomenon has come a steady consolidation of the principle that the interests of the child are primary, in the evaluation of their relations with parents and other carers. This goes for recent theoretical treatments of the relationship between child, family, and state (see, e.g., Archard 1993, 2003; Brighouse and Swift 2014). It is reflected too in the 1989 United Nations Convention on the Rights of the Child, which specifies that "the best interests of the child shall be a primary consideration" in their treatment by all relevant agencies (Article 3.1), and requires that state parties undertake "to ensure the child such protection and care as is necessary for his or her well-being" (Article 3.2), and "to protect the child from all forms of physical or mental violence, injury or abuse, neglect or negligent treatment, maltreatment or exploitation, including sexual abuse" (Article 19.1) (United Nations 1989). Though pitched at the most general level possible and designed to be global in their application, these commitments are non-neutral, in the sense that they include notions – "well-being", "adequacy of treatment" – which may only be unpacked in ways involving commitments to this or that understanding of human flourishing.

Partly for this reason, a convergence on the primacy of the child's interests and well-being does not itself resolve the question of what counts as grounds for taking a child into care. Alongside the different forms of harm itself, there are different ways of weighing their implications – which are rarely simple in themselves, and often complicated by the intricate nature of parent–child relations, and by the passing of time. For example, the interests of the child as they currently are may be set against the interests of the child as a future adult. A familiar pattern in the justification of inflicting short-term hardship or sacrifice on children – at school, via punishment, or through deprivation – is that it is vindicated instrumentally, by longer-term benefits to be reaped in adulthood. How we navigate this balance will depend, in part, on how we view the goods of childhood in relation to the goods of adult life – and, in particular, whether we assume that adulthood is a completion of, or is otherwise superior to, childhood (Brennan 2014; Gheaus 2015; Hannan 2018; Tomlin 2016).

So what counts as unacceptable harm resulting from abuse or neglect needs to be set against this putative distinction between harm to the child of now, and harm to the child as a future adult. In many cases this will not demand much critical attention, just because the current harms in question are likely to have long-term ill effects – or clearly count as unacceptable regardless. Sexual abuse would fall straightforwardly into this category. But in other cases, assessing harms over time may be more problematic. For example, take a parent who contributes to a rich and joyful childhood on the part of his children by providing them with hugely enjoyed food-based treats, based around family rituals, themselves a source of meaning and warmth and the girding of strong relationships. Evidence shows that the regular consumption of those items shortens the lifespan and is linked to painful chronic medical conditions in later life.[6] Have those children been subjected to abuse? In effect, this is the reverse of the "I benefited from being beaten as a child" claim familiar from endorsers of corporal punishment, where the point is not (we can take it) that this individual benefited at the time of being beaten, but in the longer term. Matters are complicated further by the fact that even the clearest-cut cases of child abuse may not be experienced as abuse at all, if normalised through regular occurrence or simply the acceptance of parental authority. At any rate, the experience of abuse may distort the agency of the victim (Graf and Schweiger 2017: ch. 5). Preferences may be adapted so that hardship becomes normal, expectations are lowered, and the feeling of being violated or neglected fades as circumstances become habituated.

Some of these examples may seem marginal or point-missing next to the real world of abuse, where clean "before" and "after" contrasts are relatively hard to find, and most abuse seems unambiguously harmful. There is abundant evidence that abused and neglected children experience difficulties across the spheres of their lives as they unfold, from behavioural problems to holding down relationships to academic attainment (on which, more later). There is a well-recognised pattern of intergenerational transmission of abuse: a significant proportion of those abused or neglected as children go on to maltreat children as adults in ways which mirror their own maltreatment (see, e.g., Kim 2009). But still, we need non-circular standards of what counts as maltreatment in order for these harms to be addressed as such – and will want to interrogate any given set of standards according to their internal coherence, and their fit with other principles and priorities. The very urgency of child maltreatment makes it urgent to pin down, but also requires an openness to revision, in light (for example) of fresh scientific findings.

One means by which to gauge the implications of abuse – and to determine when intervention is required – is to deploy a familiar distinction between our interests in well-being (or welfare, or flourishing) on the one hand, and in agency (or liberty, or dignity) on the other.[7] If we take the former interests to be objective – in that things can be good or bad for us without our knowing it – then the point of the latter is that we have reason to have our agential choices respected, regardless of whether they contribute to our well-being in that first sense. Child protection tends to focus on well-being interests: following what is best for the child from an external assessment of what is best for them, rather than their own preferences. This assessment is complicated by attachments, and adaptive preferences, both of which may serve to widen the gap between an objective assessment of a child's well-being, and the choices they themselves would make about their circumstances. Thus, all things being equal, the separation between the two kinds of interests is cleaner the younger the child is. But one question this poses is who is in the best position to make that assessment of their interests.

The role and reach of the state

Why should the *state* fulfil this role of ultimate arbiter of the child's best interests, in putative cases of child abuse or neglect? Here are four distinct possible reasons.

> *Knowledge.* The state is in the best position to identify when abuse is taking place, and to gauge its severity.
>
> *Legitimate efficacy.* Only the state is in a position legitimately to compel relevant agencies to take the necessary steps, and to coordinate and regulate practice in this area.

Consistency. Only the state is in a position to ensure that children in need of care-based interventions receive these in a consistent and systematic way. Only the state is in a position to ensure that there is a care *system*.

Resources. The state has the deepest pockets, so must bear "back-up responsibilities" in cases where those with primary responsibility for children are not providing adequate care.[8]

Three immediate points are worth noting. First, these reasons are mutually non-exclusive: it may be that the strongest case for state involvement lies in an aggregation of all four, and/or others as well. Second, they do not tell us what the state should actually do in *prima facie* cases of maltreatment, or what form alternative child-rearing arrangements should take. Whether foster families or residential homes work best – for example – is a question set apart from that of who must bear back-up responsibilities to ensure that children are adequately looked after (see ch. 19). Third, each reason needs scrutiny. Thus, when it comes to knowledge, the state is limited and fallible. It is not in a position to detect all cases of abuse, or to assess each case accurately, or always to trace the interests of children case by case – and will, in practice, be reliant on non-state organisations and individuals (charities, members of the public) for what knowledge it has. It will need reliable systems of advocacy on behalf of at-risk and looked-after children. And while it alone has the wherewithal and authority to coordinate, access, and regulate provision, and to enforce compliance, it is not self-evidently best placed among all relevant agencies to ensure that individuals have the right kinds of caring relationships (see ch. 19). In practice, the state's role will be in delegating responsibilities to those best positioned to act on behalf of children in need of care.

This role of stand-in is reinforced by the "last instance" model of state intervention in family autonomy – in the presumed responsibility of parents for their children's welfare, and their entitlement to bring up those children as they see fit. Under liberal models, family autonomy is supplemented by a commitment to privacy – so that the realm of family life is treated as insulated from state intrusion.[9] This presumption may be overridden in the case of confirmed maltreatment. At this stage, as David Archard puts it,

> the guardianship of a child then passes from its parents to the State which, guided by the best interests of the child, determines an appropriate course of action – eventual return to the parents or the reallocation of the child to new caretakers, such as a residential institution or foster parents.
>
> *(Archard 1993: 111)*

Precisely because it is so well-established, it is important to pick out the premises on which this rests, and how they, in turn, inform the scope and role of the care system.

The entwinement of family autonomy, family privacy, and the care of children amounts to a distinct and challengeable normative package. For it places children's rights under the effective jurisdiction of the family, right up to the "last instance". This suggests that alternative modes of care to those provided by the nuclear family are *definitively* sub-optimal.[10] This package might be compared with two alternative approaches to the care of children. One is longer-standing: that children start out as a collective responsibility, with families being delegated a caring role, in so far as they have it, because this is the most effective way of realising a society's shared stake in there being well-reared children. Here, "well-reared" means "well-reared to suit the collective good". Another is far more recent, and crystallised in the United Nations Convention: that children have rights independently of their family circumstances. Rearing here is geared towards the good of the child as an individual. Though clearly quite distinct, both models shift the balance of the child–family–state relation in a similar way. They start from the presumption that children are, in the first instance, the responsibility of wider society rather than the family itself, and that it is on that basis that upbringing within a family is commended as a good (perhaps the best) vehicle by which to realise the well-being of children as the distinct individuals they are (in the case of the rights-based approach) or the well-being of society at large (in the collectivist approach). Parents – or other carers – are *granted* primary responsibility for the care of children, rather than this being assumed "naturally" or as a matter of course.

Considering such alternatives to the "last instance" model of the care system puts into question assumptions that tend to accompany it. Many of these pivot on the treatment of children's care and entitlements as primarily a private family responsibility. There may be a presumption that children's vulnerability is a matter for private concern until taken into public hands through state intervention (Hartas 2014: 135–140). We may discern a neglect of the senses in which children are a public good (see ch. 30; also Olsaretti 2013) and of the extent to which the basic rights of all children – not only those in the care system – simply cannot be upheld by parents themselves. The notion that being in the care system is inherently disadvantageous is partly a self-reinforcing one: it both presupposes and promotes the idea that departure from conventional family models is a last resort, and that the family itself is generally capable of upholding the rights of children in a self-sufficient way. If dominant, such ideas may reinforce the experience of stigma and marginalisation on the part of those not brought up in conventional circumstances. In this sense, treating children in the care system as emblematic of *all* children rather than as already definitively exceptional or in a necessarily sub-optimal position may be helpful in overcoming part of their disadvantage. It may also assist in configuring what Daniel Engster has called an "alternative, collaborative model of state-family cooperation" (Engster 2015: 49), and what Selma Sevenhuijsen (1998, 2002) calls a democratisation and de-privatisation of care – and a rethinking of the division of responsibility between public and private life. But whatever the outcome of an overall assessment of the "last instance" model, consideration of the care system is – perhaps unexpectedly – inseparable from these wider-ranging questions in political philosophy.

Social justice and looked-after children

Looked-after children are subject to disadvantage, often in quite drastic ways. This disadvantage may derive, in part, from experiences of the care system, but will also, almost always, reflect the prior circumstances of the child. Establishing the relative influence of either factor is difficult. But in terms of outcomes, the message is stark. Some examples from recent UK studies will help convey how this goes. Children from the poorest localities are ten times more likely to be looked after than those from the richest (Bywaters and Sparks 2017). Formerly looked-after children make up 37% of young people in prison (HMIP 2016). Almost half of looked-after children meet the criteria for a psychiatric disorder (Luke et al. 2014: 2). Severely abused and neglected children currently or formerly in care are almost nine times more likely to attempt suicide and almost five times more likely to self-harm compared to those who have not been severely maltreated (NSPCC 2011). In Wales, only 2.4% of looked-after children attend university (Mannay et al. 2016). Attention to such examples highlights basic questions about justice, of which there is space here to broach only selectively and in brief. We can see them as a series of different priorities, all of which are interconnected, and many which are likely to be in tension with each other. Each will also intersect with wider patterns of inequality – concerning, most prominently, class and gender.

Fair life chances. Let's say as a simple gauge, adapting Fishkin (2014: 27), that fair life chances obtain insofar as, on entering a hospital ward full of newborn babies, we cannot make predictions on how well their lives will go based on their races, genders, parents' income, the neighbourhoods where they will grow up, or whether they will spend time in the care system. As Fishkin frames it, the concern here is with the overall shape of a life, rather than the goods of childhood per se. The example of the UK figures mentioned above shows how especially far we are from fair life chances for looked-after children. Again, poorer life chances do not result simply from being in the care system itself: most looked-after children are disadvantaged before they enter it. UK studies have found that a child's chances of being taken into care increase with deprivation (Bywaters et al. 2015). Some have argued that models of "good parenting" carry a class inflection, so that they reward typically middle-class attitudes and orientations – and that structural causes of children's vulnerability are obscured in an assessment of parents' individual character traits and their identification as inadequate (Hartas 2014). Meanwhile, the figures confirm that the system does not compensate. This may be, in part, because of how it works in itself. But also key here are the general effects of the prioritising of family autonomy, which allows for privileged parents to reinforce their children's positions of advantage in ways which inevitably disrupt fair life chances and bolster inequalities between children from different backgrounds (see, e.g., Fishkin 1982; Calder 2016). Children in residential homes, or moving between foster families, are not in a position to benefit from such leverage, or any obvious kind of approximation to it.

Access to "familial relationship goods". Brighouse and Swift (2014) offer an account of "familial relationship goods" as making a distinctive contribution to well-being, and as proper distribuenda in a complete theory of justice. On these terms, some of the goods of childhood (in itself, rather than as a stage on the development into adulthood) are linked to some of the goods of parenthood. For example, by any measure, access to such goods on the part of looked-after children is patchy at best. Foster parenting and residential care may provide versions of them, the longer those relationships last. But the mere prospect of discontinuity is disruptive of the kinds of stability under which such relations stand to flourish. And discontinuity is the norm. Neither fostering nor residential care can be provided on a continuous basis as a matter of course, up to adulthood – among other reasons, because this would require undue restrictions on employees' freedom of occupational choice. In the UK, the average placement in a foster family or care home is four months (Layard and Dunn 2009: 144). There are strong grounds for arguing that a care system geared towards justice would prioritise continuity of care.

The relationship between looked-after child and birth parents. The birth mother whose child is taken into care – particularly, when this is against her will – is uniquely deprived. Statistically, she herself is disproportionately likely to have experienced social disadvantage, including abuse – often at the hands of the perpetrator of abuse against her children. The experience of giving up children tends to reinforce the mother's vulnerability, and the instability of circumstances and lifestyle which, typically, place children under state protection in the first place (Memarnia et al. 2015). Women whose babies are taken into care will frequently keep having babies to replace those they have lost (Broadhurst et al. 2017). Although it is by no means always the case that they do, both a person taken into care and their birth parents will have clear reasons to feel a strong sense of severance and loss that is not obviously compensable or fungible.

Agency and participation. Children in the care system are more likely to experience social exclusion – understood in terms of barriers to full participation in activities enhancing autonomy and status. This may predate children being taken into care, as well as then being reinforced by it (Axford 2008) – but the patterns of outcomes for looked-after children mentioned above suggest that at any rate, the services provided do not serve to break those barriers. It may be that in some respects, the workings of care systems risk themselves undermining children's agency interests, considered separately from their well-being interests. "Care" itself has often been conceived and implemented in ways which position the recipient as passive, rather than as an engaged participant – a carer, for example, as well as cared for (Lynch et al. 2009; Holland 2010; Calder 2018). The extent to which secure, long-term family attachments are uniquely placed to address the child's interest in developing agency is – naturally – contested.[11]

Conclusion

While the care system itself gets limited philosophical coverage, we have seen in this chapter how it connects with a range of well-trodden lines of debate, albeit in quite specific ways. The state of being "looked after", as a child, is synonymous with disadvantage. Most of the reasons for why this is so are socially changeable. There is a mistake in assuming that the priorities of a care system will hold implications only for looked-after children, either in practice or in principle. Even in jurisdictions placing the highest premium on family autonomy, the state will regulate the care of all children in more or less direct ways. Yet there are also clear, pressing questions about the extent to which children in the care system should or can be treated consistently with others. Precisely because of this, there is also a risk, because of their position in non-ideal and radically unequal societies, in assuming that such children do not represent a special case. In turn, that case illuminates enduring philosophical questions about the nature and scope of care, about the conditions under which human beings flourish, and about the collective responsibilities of a society towards the vulnerable.

Notes

1 Note that the category of "looked-after children" does not include adopted children, who, once the relevant legal procedures have been undergone, are "parented" in the conventional sense. Such children will, though, have standardly spent time in the care system prior to being formally adopted. See chapter 19 in this volume for a discussion of specific questions concerning the relationship between childhood and adoption.
2 This is consistently the case in the UK (Department for Education 2017). The figures cited apply to England, but the proportions are broadly similar in the other UK countries. While criteria by which children are taken into care, and provisions then made for them, will vary from country to country, the numbers are below 1% in the USA (Children's Bureau 2017), and across Europe and Central Asia (Petrowski, Cappa, and Gross 2017). Numbers in formal alternative care are highest in the industrialised countries.
3 By "organic", I mean evolving through the dynamics of the relationships between those concerned – so the contrast is with family arrangements, such as fostering, which are the result of outside intervention.
4 For a related discussion, see Gheaus (2017).
5 The recent uncovering of large-scale, long-term, organised child sex abuse in Rotherham in the UK – among other similar cases – has involved accounts of child protection workers being more wary to intervene where possible perpetrators are members of ethnic minorities, for fear of perceived victimisation.
6 This example embellishes another provided in conversation by Matteo Bonotti.
7 For discussions of this contrast, see Archard (2003: 28–31) and Brighouse and Swift (2014: 52, 61).
8 The phrase "back-up responsibilities" is Goodin's, who labels this the "deepest pockets" argument (1985: 151–53).
9 It should be stressed here that the term "liberal models" is being used as loose shorthand for a kind of paradigm of thinking emerging through policy and wider kinds of "common sense". Liberal thinking has itself been aware of the problems with such models, and on its own terms has had good reason to unpick them. Mill, in *On Liberty*, for example, is biting about the proprietorial, patriarchal model of the family which assumes complete autonomy and privacy to be some kind of natural right: "One would almost think that a man's children were supposed to be literally… a part of himself, so jealous is opinion of the smallest interference of law with his absolute and exclusive control over them" (Mill 1991: 116).

10 It is worth noting that in some respects, these positions may be mirrored in other traditions in political philosophy besides mainstream liberalism – for example, in libertarian positions for whom the state's role should be minimal (see, e.g., Mount 1982, and the stances discussed in Harding 1997: ch. 2), or for those explicitly conservative positions placing strong priority on the family as the key organ of moral order and social welfare (see, e.g., Almond 2006).

11 See Brighouse and Swift 2014 for one version of a case in favour.

References

Almond, B. 2006. *The Fragmenting Family*. Oxford: Oxford University Press.
Archard, D. 1993. *Children: Rights and Childhood*. London: Routledge.
Archard, D. 1999. "Can Child Abuse be Defined?," in M. King (ed.), *Moral Agendas for Children's Welfare*. London: Routledge.
Archard, D. 2003. *Children, Family and the State*. Aldershot: Ashgate.
Austin, M. 2007. *Conceptions of Parenthood: Ethics and the Family*. Aldershot: Ashgate.
Axford, N. 2008. "Are Looked After Children Socially Excluded?," *Adoption and Fostering* 32(4): 5–18.
Brennan, S. 2014 "Goods of Childhood and Children's Rights," in F. Baylis and C. McLeod (eds.), *Family-Making: Contemporary Ethical Challenges*. Oxford: Oxford University Press.
Brighouse, H. S., and Swift, A. 2014. *Family Values: The Ethics of Parent-Child Relationships*. Princeton, NJ: Princeton University Press.
Broadhurst, K. et al. 2017. *Vulnerable Birth Mothers and Recurrent Care Proceedings: Final Report*. London: Nuffield Foundation.
Bywaters, P., and Sparks, T. 2017. "Child Protection in England: An Emerging Inequalities Perspective," *Journal of Children's Services* 12(2–3): 107–112.
Bywaters, P. et al. 2015. "Exploring Inequities in Child Welfare and Child Protection Services: Explaining the Inverse Intervention Law," *Children and Youth Services Review* 57: 98–105.
Calder, G. 2016. *How Inequality Runs in Families: Unfair Advantage and the Limits of Social Mobility*. Bristol: Policy Press.
Calder, G. 2018. "Young Carers," in M. Verkerk, H. Lindemann and J. McLaughlin (eds.), *Where Families and Health Care Meet*. Oxford: Oxford University Press.
Children's Bureau. 2017. "Trends in Foster Care and Adoption," Retrieved from https://www.acf.hhs.gov/cb/resource/trends-in-foster-care-and-adoption (last accessed 20 October 2017).
Department for Education. 2017. *Statistics: Looked After Children*. Retrieved from https://www.gov.uk/government/statistics/children-looked-after-in-england-including-adoption-2016-to-2017 (last accessed 28 September 2017).
Engster, D. 2015. *Justice, Care, and the Welfare State*. Oxford: Oxford University Press.
Featherstone, B. 2006. "Why Gender Matters in Child Welfare and Protection," *Critical Social Policy* 26(2): 294–314.
Fishkin, J. L. 1982. *Justice, Equal Opportunity and the Family*. New Haven, CT: Yale University Press.
Fishkin, J. 2014. *Bottlenecks: A New Theory of Equal Opportunity*. Oxford: Oxford University Press.
Gheaus, A. 2015. 'Unfinished Adults and Defective Children: On the Nature and Value of Childhood,' *Journal of Ethics and Social Philosophy* 9(1): 1–22.
Gheaus, A. 2017. "Love and Justice: A Paradox?," *Canadian Journal of Philosophy* 47(6): 739–759.
Gilligan, C. 1982. *In A Different Voice: Psychological Theory and Women's Development*. Cambridge, MA: Harvard University Press.
Gilligan, C. 1986. "Remapping the Moral Domain," in T. Heller, M. Sosna, and D. Wellbury (eds.), *Reconstructing Individualism: Autonomy, Individuality and the Self in Western Thought*. Stanford, CA: Stanford University Press.
Goldstein, J. 1977. "Medical Care for the Child at Risk: On State Supervention of Parental Autonomy," *Yale Law Journal* 86: 645–670.
Goodin, R. 1985. *Protecting the Vulnerable: A Reanalysis of Our Social Responsibilities*. Chicago, IL: University of Chicago Press.
Graf, G., and Schweiger, G. 2017. *Ethics and the Endangerment of Children's Bodies*. Houndmills: Palgrave Macmillan.
Hannan, S. 2017. "Why Childhood is Bad for Children," *Journal of Applied Philosophy* 35: 11–28, doi: 10.1111/japp.12256.
Harding, L. F. 1997. *Perspectives in Child Care Policy*, 2nd edn. Harlow: Longman.

Hartas, D. 2014. *Parenting, Family Policy and Children's Well-Being in an Unequal Society*. Houndmills: Palgrave Macmillan.
Hayden, C., Goddard, J., Gorin, S., and Van Der Spek, N. 1999. *State Child Care: Looking After Children?* London: Jessica Kingsley.
HMIP (Her Majesty's Inspectorate of Prisons). 2016. *Children in Custody 2015–16*. London: Her Majesty's Inspectorate of Prisons.
Holland, S. 2010. "Looked After Children and the Ethic of Care," *British Journal of Social Work* 40: 1664–1680.
Kim, J. 2009. "Type-specific Intergenerational Transmission of Neglectful and Physically Abusive Parenting Behaviors among Young Parents," *Children and Youth Services Review* 31(7): 761–767.
Layard, R., and Dunn, J. 2009. *A Good Childhood*. London: Penguin.
Luke, N., Sinclair, I., Woolgar, M., and Sebba, J. 2014. *What Works in Preventing and Treating Poor Mental Health in Looked After Children? Executive Summary*. London: NSPCC.
Lynch, K. Baker, J., Cantillon, S., and Walsh, J. 2009. "Which Equalities Matter? The Place of Affective Equality in Egalitarian Thinking," in K. Lynch, J. Baker, and M. Lyons (eds.), *Affective Equality: Love, Care and Injustice*. Houndmills: Palgrave Macmillan.
Mannay, D., Staples, E., Hallett, S., and Andrews, D. 2016. *Understanding the Educational Experiences and Opinions, Attainment, Achievement and Aspirations of Looked After Children in Wales*. Cardiff: Welsh Government.
Memarnia, N., Nolte, L., Norris, C., and Harborne, A. 2015. "'It Felt Like it Was Night All the Time': Listening to the Experiences of Birth Mothers whose Children have been Taken Into Care or Adopted," *Adoption & Fostering* 39(4): 303–317.
Mill, J. S. 1991 (1859). "On Liberty," in J. Gray (ed.), *On Liberty and Other Essays*. Oxford: Oxford University Press.
Mount, F. 1982. *The Subversive Family*. London: Jonathan Cape.
Mullin, A. 2014. "Children, Vulnerability, and Emotional Harm," in C. Mackenzie, W. Rogers, and S. Dodds (eds.), *Vulnerability: New Essays in Ethics and Feminist Philosophy*. New York, NY: Oxford University Press.
NSPCC (National Society for the Prevention of Cruelty to Children). 2011. *Child Cruelty in the UK 2011: An NSPCC Study into Childhood Abuse and Neglect over the Past 30 Years*. London: NSPCC.
Olsaretti, S. 2013. "Children as Public Goods?," *Philosophy and Public Affairs* 41(3): 226–258.
Parton, N. 1991. *Governing the Family: Child Care, Child Protection and the State*. Houndmills: Macmillan.
Petrowski, N., Cappa, C., and Gross, P. 2017. "Estimating the Numbers of Children in Formal Alternative Care: Challenges and Results," *Child Abuse and Neglect* 70: 388–398.
Pfohl, S. 1977. "The 'Discovery' of Child Abuse," *Social Problems* 24(3): 310–323.
Ross, L. F. 1998. *Children, Families and Health Care Decision-Making*. Oxford: Oxford University Press.
Sevenhuijsen, S. 1998. *Citizenship and the Ethics of Care*. London: Routledge.
Sevenhuijsen, S. 2002. "A Third Way? Moralities, Ethics and Families," in A. Carling, S. Duncan, and R. Edwards (eds.), *Analysing Families: Morality and Rationality in Policy and Practice*. London: Routledge.
Tomlin, P. 2016. "Saplings and Caterpillars: Trying to Understand Children's Well-Being," *Journal of Applied Philosophy* 35(1): 29–46.
United Nations. 1989. *The United Nations Convention on the Rights of the Child*. Retrieved from https://www.unicef.org.uk/what-we-do/un-convention-child-rights/ (last accessed 23 April 2017).

33
CHILDREN AND HEALTH

Havi Carel, Gene Feder and Gita Gyorffy

Introduction

Despite their vitality and energy, children are also vulnerable. They are physically vulnerable to many diseases adults contract, as well as childhood illnesses. They are emotionally vulnerable and depend on adults for guidance, support and care. They are epistemically vulnerable, because they have less knowledge, experience and confidence, and can be gullible and naïve. Especially as infants and toddlers, but also later on, children share much vulnerability and dependence with the elderly, the sick and the disabled.

Singling out these groups is not intended to deny the vulnerability that is the lot of humanity in general (MacIntyre 1999), but to point our attention to the accentuated vulnerability and need that characterises children and the infirm. In other work we discuss in detail the specific vulnerabilities of these groups (Carel 2016; Carel and Gyorffy 2014). Our claim here is that this vulnerability, although partially and temporarily masked in healthy adulthood, is always present. Thus, what children further reveal is that we are all vulnerable to differing degrees; their dependence on us is a more naked version of our own dependence, vulnerability and fragility.

When children are themselves ill, a new group emerges. One that requires more protection and demands more specialised care than either group on its own. Children who are also patients raise unique and demanding challenges for health professionals, carers and society. The task of this chapter is to examine the intersection of the two groups – children and those who are ill – and put forward a general characterisation of children as uniquely embodied, and, hence, uniquely vulnerable to illness and disability.

In order to understand the role health and illness play for children and how children encounter health problems and the healthcare system, we propose using a phenomenological stance that is empathic to their worldview, and eschews paternalism, chauvinism and reductive physicalism. Epistemically, the phenomenological stance cultivates attentiveness for the child's perspective. Thus, it calls on us to listen to children's testimonies, reject the presumed epistemic superiority of adults and open ourselves to non-adult-focused narratives. Ontologically, this approach views the patient as a whole person, and eschews a view of illness (disruption of lived experience) as reducible to disease (physiological dysfunction) (Carel 2013, 2016; Toombs 1987). By working on these two levels in this chapter we hope to deepen our understanding of children as patients, as well as to point to more helpful, egalitarian and just healthcare practices.

Our phenomenological approach takes it as a fundamental premise that children exist as embodied, enacted and situated. Children's bodies delimit their possibilities and actions, but they also change dramatically in a short space of time. Children's agency and possibility for action is limited (legally and practically), but children have unique abilities to influence adults in a variety of ways. Finally, children are situated in a family, culture, language and environment which shape their development. These interrelated theoretical considerations inform this chapter.

A final point before we start: we use the term 'children' here as an umbrella term that is useful shorthand but requires some refinement. There are significant differences between infants, toddlers, primary school age children and adolescents. The term 'children' is coarse-grained and may be a misleading category, in particular in medico-legal areas such as consent and confidentiality. Throughout the chapter we, therefore, make references to these more specific and developmentally distinct groups, paying particular attention in our examples to adolescents as a precarious and under-recognised entity. We use the term 'children', but only as shorthand for these disparate groups and with due attention to these differences.

In what follows, we suggest that children who are ill (and are, therefore, often also patients) are uniquely:

1. *Embodied*: children have bodies that constantly change. Their embodied schema differs dramatically from that of the fully mature adult. The developing child's experience of change is radically different to the experience of growing old (ageing) and to bodily changes caused by illness. What happens when this embodied entity, which is also on a developmental trajectory, becomes ill?
2. *Enacted*: we make decisions for children and limit their ability to make choices and act on them, often in the name of their best interests and safety. How are these limits enacted when it comes to health and, in particular, in the healthcare arena? Can children who are ill make choices that enact their agency and identity in more potent ways than we currently allow?
3. *Situated*: children largely live in families and these families are treated as a basic unit with which health professionals collaborate and communicate. Working with families requires interacting with several people who are interlinked, and this is different to working with an individual adult who may or may not have a family. This impacts on children (i) when they are ill and (ii) when they experience illness in the family.

The structure of the chapter will follow these headings, elaborating on each and using a leading clinical example to illustrate these main themes. In the chapter we oscillate between the multiple perspectives relevant to each situation: the child, her parents or carers, health professionals and society at large. We thematise each situation by viewing it from these multiple perspectives, aiming to reveal the complexity of such situations. There are multiple actors with differing views and goals, so that the healthcare encounter can only be judged successful if these differing views are made intelligible to one another. Therefore, we articulate the differing views in order to explore sources and possible solutions to conflict around the child's illness.

Embodiment and health

Children have bodies that continuously change. Their bodies and brains grow and develop, allowing for new behavioural and bodily repertoires, as well as increased independence and growing sophistication in all domains, in particular language, cognition and autonomy (Gopnik 2009). This sets the backdrop to a challenging encounter with healthcare professionals, and this for several reasons.

First, the ill child changes during the course of treatment. This may make it difficult to discern a reaction to treatment (e.g. change to sleep patterns) from developmental change (e.g. needing less sleep as the child matures). It may also make long-term relationships between the child and the healthcare professional more complex, as in the several months that may elapse between appointments the child may change in significant ways, and the health professional will need to constantly adapt to the child's development. This is not particularly a problem in acute illness, but manifests in the care of children with chronic conditions, such as diabetes. The transition into adolescence of children with Type I diabetes is often associated with poorer adherence to treatment, deteriorating control of blood sugar and increased risk of psychological disorders (Jaser 2010).

For example, one of us had a 15-year-old patient who stopped attending the paediatric diabetes clinic, and became erratic in testing his blood sugar levels and adjusting his insulin dose. He also started smoking and drinking alcohol. A supportive school and family and a psychologically astute diabetes specialist nurse with adolescent diabetes expertise helped him regain control of his diabetes. A key feature of the parental and professional response was its empathic and non-judgmental character.

Second, the child may not be able to recognise the significance of symptoms, either because they are too young, do not have the language, awareness or concepts, or because they may think that a particular change is part of normal growth. For example, some young teenage girls may become pregnant, but not be aware of this. We have encountered the case of a 13-year-old girl who denied being pregnant despite putting on weight, her breasts growing and not having periods. The girl said she had no idea she was pregnant, and her pregnancy was discovered because a teacher referred her to a GP. The girl gave birth two weeks later to a full term, healthy baby.

Third, in the case of chronic illness, the child patient will grow and develop with the illness, and thus their understanding of it will change, mature or become more troubled as they grow. Children who are cystic fibrosis patients are known to become more difficult to engage and less compliant as they enter adolescence, with compliance rates below 50% (Modi and Quittner 2006). One of us observed a cystic fibrosis clinic in which a teenage patient worried about his IV antibiotic treatment clashing with Glastonbury music festival. The consultant and patient discussed this at length and in the end reached a compromise: the young person would agree to be hospitalised for IV antibiotic treatment, leave for Glastonbury for a few days and then come back to continue his treatment. The consultant later revealed how worried he was about the young person camping at the festival, but was realistic about talking him out of going to the festival altogether.

We propose that children's embodied schema differs dramatically from that of the mature adult. Adults live for some time with a fairly stable bodily schema and this leads them to develop a cumulative sense of bodily stability and trust (Carel 2013). Children's experience of their own bodies contains more fluidity and change. They constantly grow, and enjoy having their height measured and recorded on a doorway, for example. They experience themselves as getting older, bigger, stronger and more mature, and compare themselves to other children. It may be that being used to experiencing themselves as continuously changing entities, children might also adapt to some medical procedures more quickly, or that they are more open to further changes caused by the disease.

The experience of change in the context of growth and development typical of children is different to other kinds of changes, for example ageing or illness. The changes associated with growth are usually perceived as positive and entail increasing abilities, in contrast to the changes of illness and ageing, characterised by diminishing abilities and decline, measured against one's youthful abilities also compared with peers. Indeed, one may say that the two types of bodily change are diametrically opposed, as can be seen from this account of respiratory illness:

> During that time (of respiratory decline), it seemed that every week my world was shrinking more and more. Every week I discovered, in a grotesque reversal of childhood development, yet another thing I could no longer do. I cancelled my gym subscription. I took the bus. I no longer tried to scale a hill.
>
> *(Carel 2013: 7)*

Finally, it may be that very young children are not able to fully grasp or verbalise the nature of their illness or disorder, but it is still experienced in a bodily manner, as well as inferred from social interactions with both children and adults, which may convey pity or fear of the child's disorder. This has important repercussions for the way the child develops their own embodied sense of themselves as disordered.

An adult may perceive their disorder as an alien intrusion, threatening their previously intact bodily integrity (Carel 2013, 2016). A child, on the other hand, can have a very different relationship to their illness. For example, if they are born with a congenital condition they may simply experience themselves thus. Even if they fall ill or have a poor prognosis, they may accept the change more easily either because they cannot understand the full ramifications of a condition or because they have not yet developed the associated stereotypes and stigmas which adults attach to certain conditions (cf. Goffman 1963; Crichton, Carel, and Kidd 2017).

One of us recalls a young woman whose arm was missing from the elbow down. She recounted how, as a child, her parents used to take her to see health professionals who suggested various prosthetic fittings, which she found confusing. Why did she need these artificial attachments when she experienced her body as whole? She recalls the sense of confusion and then shame that was inculcated in her after contact with health professionals, who saw her as having a medical problem requiring amelioration. She lives happily today with no prosthetic limb, and manages cycling, driving and rock climbing with no apparent difficulties.

The normal bodily changes of puberty are challenging enough for children to understand and deal with when they occur in the expected way; significant delay or early changes can cause additional distress. Simply talking about this and being examined can be a major difficulty for some children, and requires delicacy in the paediatric setting. For example, manually measuring the volume of someone's testicles (using a string of different sized beads) can be quite intimidating; one of us encountered a child with autistic traits who reported he thought he had been sexually abused because he did not fully understand what had taken place.

A child may be bewildered by early pubertal changes, though often it is the parents who are most concerned. Children may be concerned because they feel left behind and may be suffering social embarrassment or exclusion, for example, if they are being dropped from a sports team. This problem is compounded by the fact that early and late bloomers are often treated according to their apparent physical age, rather than their chronological age.

One case that illustrates the level of concern is of a 14-year-old boy who presented with delayed pubertal development. It was not immediately clear whether he needed or wanted treatment; however, he eventually agreed that he would like the testosterone injections to kick-start puberty (a fairly common procedure). He clearly found it difficult to express how much this problem was bothering him, and this became apparent when it was discovered that he was agreeing to the treatment despite (mistakenly) thinking he would have to suffer intra-testicular injections! (This is not something we would subject a conscious child to. The injections are intramuscular injections like a vaccination.)

Where growth is concerned, the child can be equally dismayed at their stature if it is out of range for the family, even if it is within the normal range for the population. However, just as often, if the child is not suffering social disadvantage they may not be distressed by it. It is the parents who are projecting their concerns onto the child, who medicalise and problematise their child's stature. One child in question was made to feel her 'shortness' as her parents complained about the lack of medical intervention to 'make her grow', when in fact she was simply at the bottom end of the normal range and had the same predicted height as the doctor treating her. The paediatrician must take the family's expectations into account as this is the setting in which the child will be dealing with their problem whilst making sure they do not collude by agreeing to unnecessary treatment.

In summary, the embodiment of the ill child is unique for several reasons: their bodies and capacities continuously change; they may conflate disease symptoms with other changes; in cases of long-term illness, the child will develop and change with her condition; and finally, some children may not be able to understand their illness, but will still experience it in an embodied fashion. These characteristics of the embodied ill child give rise to unique considerations and require a distinctively paediatric approach to assess children's understanding and reflect their development in healthcare practice.

Enacting health and illness

Adults are often called upon to make decisions for children. We also limit children's ability to make choices and act on them, often in the name of their best interest and safety. This section explores how these limits are enacted in the healthcare arena, asking whether children can, and should be permitted to, make choices that enact their agency and identity in more potent ways than we currently allow.

In hospital settings, the autonomy of the ill person can be significantly restricted. For example, their diet, visiting hours and activities may be monitored to ensure that they do not interfere with their medical treatment. Although, broadly speaking, consent is sought for procedures, when the ill person becomes a patient this in itself often undermines agency, autonomy and freedom. Patients cannot do everything they wish, may have restricted mobility and although they ultimately consent to or decline their course of treatment, that decision is made under conditions of at least partial ignorance: they usually do not have the relevant medical knowledge. Decisions can also be made under conditions of epistemic deficiency, as a result of pain, distress or the lack of sufficient time to probe the decision with a health professional.

In addition to restricted autonomy, ill children are also more vulnerable to epistemic injustice (Fricker 2007; Carel and Kidd 2014; Kidd and Carel 2016; Carel and Gyorffy 2014; Blease, Carel, and Geraghty 2017). Epistemic injustice is a term that describes how people from particular social groups (e.g. women, immigrants or, in our case, children) are treated as epistemically inferior, their credibility is unduly deflated and their experiences are not listened to or taken seriously. There are two types of epistemic injustice: testimonial injustice, in which the ill child's testimony is minimised, not taken into account, ignored or simply not solicited. The case of Victoria Climbié is a case of extreme testimonial injustice. Despite multiple admissions to hospital with horrific injuries, and despite being an older child capable of such reports, her testimony was never sought, as the Laming inquiry established (Laming 2003).

Hermeneutical injustice occurs when society as a whole lacks an interpretative framework to understand particular experiences. A contemporary example is the experience of transgender people. Western society can be seen as currently in the process of developing a language with which to recognise, interpret and fairly treat the experience of trans people. Prior to this process there was no framework within which to articulate such experiences, other than through the language of deviancy which devalued and erased the legitimacy of trans concerns and interests.

We suggest that children are susceptible to both types of epistemic injustice, and that ill children are doubly at risk of epistemic injustice, first because of epistemic biases and paternalistic views we may hold about children (that they cannot distinguish fact from fiction, or that their memories are flawed) and second because of stereotypes and biases we hold about ill persons (that they are confused or emotionally compromised so they cannot 'think straight').

Similarly, children who are also patients are doubly susceptible to limitations to their autonomy and agency. We first consider them as limited epistemic agents because of their age and developmental stage, and ask parents to make decisions on their behalf. Insofar as they are minors, the parents are their legal guardians and, hence, make such decisions for them (Carel and Gyorffy 2014). We then expose them to further restrictions to autonomy that arise from their status as patients. This may be seen as a 'double whammy' that needs guarding against in order to ensure that autonomy is preserved wherever possible and that children are partners in the decision-making process insofar as practical.

In the case of epistemic injustice, difficult decisions need to be made by paediatricians and family physicians, who need to decide how much a child is capable of understanding and how effective the parents are in making decisions for their children. Often epistemic judgements of children's contribution to the epistemic process of decision-making are skewed against the children, but with further consideration, this epistemic distortion can be corrected. The need to speak to the child away from family members was a powerful recommendation made by the enquiry into Climbié's murder.

Health professionals also need to be vigilant to family and community pressure put on children to take a particular decision about their medical treatment. A fictional case is described in Ian McEwan's novel, *The Children Act*, which tells the story of a 17-year-old boy who is a Jehovah's Witness, who is pressurised into refusing a life-saving blood transfusion, ultimately leading to his death.

Child protection cases are ones in which the parents' preferences and decision-making and the children's welfare radically break apart. However, from our clinical experience, such cases are rarely black and white. One common scenario is demonstrated by a three-month-old baby failing to gain weight adequately at home. No medical cause could be found, and she gained weight during every admission to hospital and lost weight when discharged again. The parents were adamant that they were following the same feeding regime at home and felt that the medical team was 'pointing the finger' at them.

Clearly the infant could not communicate its situation, so when they wished to go home the best interest of the child had to be determined by the paediatrician. Children and parents are allowed to take risks with informed consent and discharge against medical advice in some situations, but where there are safeguarding concerns this often has to be overruled by the medical team. In this case, the parents complied with medical advice to stay in and additional family support was sought in the form of a social worker, health visitor and mental health services for parents.

How can we overcome epistemic injustice when communicating with ill children? First, we need to be perpetually vigilant to the possibility that we might overlook or misunderstand the intended meaning of a child's testimony. Second, we need to be mindful of the importance of distinguishing between characteristics that are genuine descriptors of a particular age group and potentially harmful biases. Third, we should not always assume that when two interpretative frameworks clash, the adult interpretation should automatically trump the child's. Fourth, we need to remember that children will always be at a hermeneutical disadvantage within an adult-governed healthcare system. Adults who wish to understand the ill child will need to enter into their interpretative framework and understand their testimonies from within it (Carel and Gyorffy 2014).

Another set of cases in which parental and children's interests may diverge, sometimes radically, is the case of children with complex conditions. In many cases children who are very ill need to be ventilated in order to prevent them from dying. But when a physician decides to ventilate, they need to ask: what is the purpose of the ventilation if, overall, the child is very ill and on a downward course? Often the parents are not ready to accept that ventilation is not the right course of action. But the physician knows that putting a critically ill child on a ventilator means that they will stay on it or die. And so, the decision implies leaving the child in intensive care for the remainder of their life.

Here is a particular case of this kind. A baby was suffering with a severe form of degenerative neurological condition, which meant she would progressively deteriorate and die over a period of weeks. The baby already required respiratory support. She was not able to communicate pain or discomfort effectively, but nursing staff providing her care felt she was suffering considerably. Sadly, the parents were separated and had opposing views on how much she was suffering and, therefore, how much medical support should be given to keep her alive. In the end it came down to the medical team's assessment of what was in her best interests. One parent was overruled, and the baby's comfort was prioritised over prolonging her life. Respiratory support was not escalated, allowing her to pass away.

The parents' situation in many cases is complex and they are embroiled in a web of intense, often conflicting, emotions and thoughts. They do not want to witness their child's distress, and sometimes they understand that allowing a severely ill and suffering child with no prospect of improvement to die is in that child's best interests. But they also desperately do not want the child to die. Parents often feel ambivalent in other ways, too: the child requires treatment, but it is hard for the parents to see their child in pain or distress. The case of the severely ill baby Charlie Gard expresses the emotional bind the parents are in and how much delicacy is needed in order to support them but not collude in unnecessary treatment that will prolong the suffering of a young child.[1]

There are cases where older children and adolescents differ in their views from their parents. How does the health professional negotiate such discussions? Take, for example, diabetes. Like cystic fibrosis patients, children with insulin-dependent diabetes who have to inject themselves before every meal can become wayward about their self-care, typically in their teenage years. Many of these children have been diagnosed at a young age, at a time when education about managing their diabetes was largely directed at parents. They are involved, but remain dependent on adult understanding and motivation to maintain good control of their condition. Good paediatric diabetes care engages the child in understanding their condition early and reiterates educational messages, increasing the complexity of the content as the child develops and can understand and take on more responsibility.

Even so, it appears that despite best efforts the messages do not always get through, as exemplified by a 17-year-old diabetic of 12 years who recently told his team, 'you mean I have to take insulin every time I eat carbohydrates?'. This same boy had lost the motivation to follow his proper insulin regime during his teens and, despite being on an insulin pump,[2] had very poor control of his blood sugar levels, putting him at increased risk of kidney, heart and circulation problems and blindness. Fear of these complications of diabetes rarely seems to motivate this group of patients, though it usually highly motivates parents. As a result, self-care in managing chronic conditions is the cause of much conflict.

Adults need to take into account the quality of life issues important to the teen, like being nagged, having to inject in front of friends, not being able to eat what their friends eat and having to miss lessons because of low blood sugar levels. This needs to be balanced against parental and professional concerns about future health and fear of fatal hypoglycaemic events.

In this particular case, the team were concerned that the young person was not using the insulin pump safely. Life-threatening complications can occur if blood glucose levels are not monitored regularly throughout the day and this boy was not monitoring his levels at all some days. The mother, who heavily supported his care, wanted the son to continue using his pump as she perceived it to have the potential to provide the best diabetes control and was concerned he would not be given a pump in the adult service if he was not using it correctly now. The diabetic son was frightened of returning to having his insulin as multiple injections but was persuaded to take a 'pump holiday' to experience the difference now that he was older. In fact, he chose to give the pump back because he could not improve his adherence while on it and found injections less problematic than he remembered and overall less stressful. By demonstrating to his mother his level of understanding and current lack of motivation to change, the mother was also eventually convinced that this was the safer course of action.

Children are particularly vulnerable when they transition from paediatric to adult services. Increasingly transition is being understood to be an important area of paediatric care, particularly for those with chronic conditions like diabetes. The newer transition programs being introduced have educational goals tailored to age and stage covering different topics (such as issues around driving, alcohol and sex with diabetes) and that also gradually transfer the responsibility to the child to deliver their own care with support rather than passively receiving it.

One case of a newly diagnosed diabetic who was nearly 18 years old showed how difficult it can be when this gradual education and transition does not happen. The young person came from a disadvantaged background. Neither he nor his family would engage with health professionals, to the point of him being at real risk of serious illness (diabetic ketoacidosis) or even death. Social services were reluctant to get involved because he was nearly 18. Through perseverance the team managed to demonstrate that there may be an element of undiagnosed autistic spectrum traits contributing to his lack of engagement, meaning that he was not only still a minor but potentially also a vulnerable adult whose capacity to understand his health needs was limited. As a result, child protection proceedings were started to force the family to provide basic health support, and increased social care and health input was funded. Taken at face value, this young man was nearly 18, but saying that 'it's his choice' would fail to fully appreciate his needs, abilities and experiences.

To conclude, when it comes to decision-making, we suggest that adult carers for an ill child should be aware of epistemic injustice and the risks it poses to information gathering and deliberation. Was the child's point of view taken seriously enough? Was their testimony heard respectfully and empathically? Will it play a role in the clinical process and in the decision reached? We also suggest that more attention is given to the nature of the conflict between parental, medical and the child's views and to ways in which epistemic balance can be restored to the child's preference.

Situatedness: illness in the family

Children usually live in families (or with carers) and these families are seen by health professionals and treated as a basic unit within which the child lives, for better and for worse. Working with families and interfacing with several people who are all interlinked is different to working with an individual adult who may or may not have a family. This creates an additional layer of complexity to all aspects of care: from the type of interaction and communication in the clinic through decision-making to compliance, the health professional communicates with one or more adults, who may themselves be experiencing significant distress over the child's health, and may have varying degrees of understanding and different levels of competence both as parents and as those administering treatment to the child at home. A further pressing complication stems from the fact that the parents are the child's custodians; they have a relationship that limits the freedom of choice of the child and that is not present in the case of treating adults who live in families.

Understanding the child and their needs is only one aspect of the clinician's task, as the clinician will also need to understand the different relationships at play, hierarchies within the family structure and the specific cultural and social assumptions of different family members. Consider the case of Lea Lee, a Hmong child living in an immigrant community in California in the 1980s. Lea suffered from severe epilepsy, which was considered life-threatening by her physicians, but seen as a series of spiritual events by her family.

The parents, who did not speak English and came from Hmong culture, believed that the medication the doctors were giving their daughter was causing her illness, and that the illness needed to be treated by spiritual means. They believed that the root cause of her condition was a door being slammed by her sister, which led Lea's spirit to startle and leave her body.

The parents withheld her medication, causing Lea severe seizures which led to frequent hospitalisations. After some months, the physicians decided that the parental noncompliance with Lea's treatment amounted to child abuse and asked the court to place Lea in foster care. This increased the parental suspicion that the medical establishment was trying to harm their family, which caused a worsening of the relationship between the family and healthcare professionals. After a further year, Lea was returned to her family's care, where medication was again not given correctly or withheld altogether, leading to Lea's final catastrophic seizure which left her braindead.

The unfolding of this tragic story is documented in Ann Fadiman's *The Spirit Catches You and You Fall Down*, in which deep-seated spiritual beliefs are seen as the cause of Lea's tragic fate. This is an extreme case in which cultural differences about the cause and, hence, treatment of a condition led to a complete breakdown in the partnership between health professionals and the family.

Fadiman's book includes significant remorse from the clinicians who viewed the parents as an impediment to the correct medical treatment of Lea. This perspective was not helpful in ultimately achieving good care for her. Tools like cultural mediation, good translators and cultural experts, and more time to talk to parents may have ameliorated some of the difficulties the family and medical team experienced.

Other less extreme examples include accepting gendered status hierarchies within a family, although they run counter to an egalitarian ethos, where, for example, a health professional may be able to talk only to the father or grandfather as they are the decision makers, or where talking to the mother would be culturally inappropriate, despite the fact that this reduces the woman's ability to contribute to decision-making.

Family dynamics commonly affect how children display symptoms. Often families are unaware that they are colluding in the evolution of unhelpful behaviours. One 11-year-old girl was admitted to the paediatric ward with stomach pain and vomiting. As the medical team found no cause for her vomiting and suspected her of fabricating 'vomit', she started refusing to eat. When a nasogastric tube was placed to feed her so she did not starve, she developed pain in her legs and became 'too weak to walk'. She would 'collapse' when asked to stand, but never actually fell down, being able to hold herself with bent knees (a manoeuvre that requires considerably more strength than standing with locked knees) until a bed or wheelchair were brought close enough to sit on.

All along her parents were both supportive and very anxious about the underlying cause of her symptoms. They were understandably protective and resisted the possibility that some of her symptoms might not have a physical basis. Ultimately, they were inadvertently colluding with her somatic complaints. It took a prolonged admission (three months) and many investigations to demonstrate that there was no physiological cause for her symptoms and that she needed a firmer program of rehabilitation. Ultimately, her family were amenable to medical advice but their understandable initial responses to her distress probably prolonged her illness overall.

We finally consider children's experience of a family member's illness or disability (see ch. 23). Illness in the family may impact on children disproportionately. Child carers are not uncommon, and the responsibility may affect their education, well-being and ability to socialise with people their age. One of us looked after a family in which the mother developed primary progressive multiple sclerosis when her son was seven. Five years later she and the boy's father separated, and they shared his upbringing through his adolescence as she became more disabled. Although her son inevitably took on a carer role, good home care input and support from family therapists and their general practice buffered the impact of this situation on the boy.

Children who are not carers may still need to fend for themselves, as adult attention is diverted from them to the health problem: the ill family member may be incapacitated in various ways and other adults in the family may have less time because they have become carers. Children may be negatively impacted by the illness even if it is not acute or life-limiting. Their activities may be constrained and they may harbour deep anxiety about the illness. A health problem that occurs in the family is bound to affect all members of the family, even very young children who may seem oblivious to it.

To conclude, the role of family members, and in particular the parents, is considerably more significant in the case of child patients. The dynamics are more complex and the differing goals of child, family and medical team, require more consideration. The health professional requires specialised training and attentiveness to the needs of the child and the differences, whether subtle or significant, between the child's and the parents/carers' perspective and interests. Particular attention to cultural interpretations and to the expectations of the family is critical.

Conclusion

This chapter provided an overview of the intersection of two vulnerable groups: children and ill people. In considering children as ill persons, we took a phenomenological approach that anchors itself in an appreciation of the embodied nature of children, their constantly changing bodies and body schemas, and the situatedness of being an ill child or of living in a family where there is illness. The chapter advanced four claims:

1. Children have bodies that constantly change. This affects their illness experiences and their understanding of other processes in light of this, such as the process of illness and the process of receiving healthcare.
2. We make decisions for children and limit their ability to make choices and act on them, often in the name of their best interests and safety. As children grow and mature, they ought to be afforded more decision-making capacities, but this can lead to complex situations which require subtlety and close attunement from the health professional.
3. We should guard against epistemic injustice in children who are also patients, as they are doubly susceptible to different sorts of epistemic bias and silencing.
4. Children live in families and these families are seen by health professionals as a basic unit with which they work. Working with families and interfacing with several people who are

interlinked creates unique complexities and challenges, and requires psychological, cultural and social sensitivity.

We hope that the chapter laid out some of the philosophical foundations and medical challenges that characterise the field without reducing one to the other, or in other words, allowing the clinical empirical experience to illuminate the philosophical categories and vice versa.[3]

Notes

1 https://www.theguardian.com/uk-news/commentisfree/2017/aug/04/it-was-our-agonising-job-as-charlie-gard-care-team-to-say-enough
2 An insulin pump is a wearable, pager-sized device that delivers insulin continuously through a tiny tube that stays inserted just under the skin, allowing the patient to give themselves extra insulin when they eat without having to have a new injection every meal. It is a more flexible and finely tuned treatment for the motivated individual.
3 This chapter was co-authored by a philosopher (HC), a GP/family physician (GF) and a paediatrician (GG). The case studies presented here come from GF and GG's clinical experience, and from HC's shadowing work. Details have been altered or removed to avoid identification. HC is grateful to the Wellcome Trust for a Senior Investigator Award for the Life of Breath project (www.lifeofbreath.org; grant number 103340), which supported this research.

References

Blease, C., Carel, H., and Geraghty, A. 2017. "Epistemic Injustice in Healthcare Encounters: Evidence from Chronic Fatigue Syndrome," *Journal of Medical Ethics* 43(8): 549–557.
Carel, H. 2013. "Bodily Doubt," *Journal of Consciousness Studies* 20(7–8): 178–197.
Carel, H. 2016. *Phenomenology of Illness*. Oxford: Oxford University Press.
Carel, H., and Gyorffy, G. 2014. "Seen But Not Heard: Children and Epistemic Injustice," *The Lancet* 384(9950): 1256–1257.
Carel, H., and Kidd, I. J. 2014. "Epistemic Injustice in Healthcare: A Philosophical Analysis," *Medicine, Healthcare and Philosophy* 17(4): 529–540.
Crichton, P., Carel, H., and Kidd, I. J. 2017. "Epistemic Injustice in Psychiatry," *BJPsych Bulletin* 41(2): 65–70.
Fadiman, A. 1997. *The Spirit Catches You and You Fall Down*. New York, NY: Farrar, Straus and Giroux.
Fricker, M. 2007. *Epistemic Injustice: Power and the Ethics of Knowing*. Oxford: Oxford University Press.
Goffman, E. 1963. *Stigma: Notes on the Management of Spoiled Identity*. New York, NY: Prentice Hall.
Gopnik, A. 2009. *The Philosophical Baby*. London: The Bodley Head.
Jaser, S. S. 2010. "Psychological Problems in Adolescents with Diabetes," *Adolescent Medicine: State of the Art Reviews* 21(1): 138–151.
Kidd, I. J., and Carel, H. 2016. "Epistemic Injustice and Illness," *Journal of Applied Philosophy* 3(2): 172–190.
Laming, W. H. 2003. *The Victoria Climbié Inquiry*. Retrieved from https://www.gov.uk/government/uploads/system/uploads/attachment_data/file/273183/5730.pdf (last accessed 20 March 2018).
MacIntyre, A. 1999. *Dependent Rational Animals: Why Human Beings Need the Virtues*. London: Duckworth.
McEwan, I. 2015. *The Children Act*. London: Vintage.
Modi, A. C., and Quittner, A. L. 2006. "Barriers to Treatment Adherence for Children with Cystic Fibrosis and Asthma: What Gets in the Way?," *Journal of Paediatric Psychology* 31(8): 846–858.
Toombs, S. K. 1987. "The Meaning of Illness: A Phenomenological Approach to the Patient–Physician Relationship," *Journal of Medicine and Philosophy* 12: 219–240.

34
CHILDREN AND THE RIGHT TO VOTE

Ludvig Beckman

Introduction

The history of democracy is strongly associated with the gradual extension of suffrage and the inclusion of previously excluded groups and individuals in the realm of political rights. Democratization in this sense applies to young people and children, no less than to other groups, and is indicated by the decline of the mean voting-rights age every decade since the introduction of universal suffrage (Hamilton 2012; Cultice 1992).[1] Sixty years ago, no European democracy allowed 18-year-olds to vote; today, no European nation denies people aged 18 the vote. The tendency is to lower the age of voting further. Voting from the age of 16 is now allowed in several countries, including Austria, Argentina and Brazil. The general question raised by these developments concerns what the final destination should be: what is the appropriate voting-rights age in a democracy?

But this may not be the right question at all, as it assumes both that children can justifiably be excluded from political rights and that the reasons for excluding them are approximated by a uniformly applied voting age. Unless there are good reasons why both assumptions should be accepted, the question "what is the appropriate voting age?" does not appear. In this chapter, I focus on the reasons for these background beliefs.

One reason why children's political rights matter is that children's well-being matters. Public policy and law might of course be responsive to the perceived interests of children even though they are disenfranchised. Yet, our society is arguably adult-based, viewing children primarily as future adults, disregarding the wants of children *qua* children (Cohen 2005; Campiglio 2009). Given that these tendencies are disruptive to the well-being of children, there is reason to consider ways to include children as actual participants in the political process. The argument lends further support from the observation that the median voter in many developed countries is growing increasingly old. The political inclusion of children would mitigate against the rise of the "gerontocracy" (Berry 2012).

A second reason to care about the political inclusion of children is that it contributes instrumentally to the democratic process. It might do so in several ways, by, for example, bolstering civic virtue and knowledge or by increasing turnout rates in elections. It might also be argued that to exclude children would be undemocratic. Advocates of democracy easily slide from affirming the political rights of people or citizens, as general categories, to the exclusive recognition of adult's political rights (Schrag 2004). Children represent a "test case" for theories of democracy as it requires us to re-examine the boundaries of the democratic people.

In what follows, the first section deals with the meaning of political competence and the problem of regulating the age of voting. The subsequent sections examine the relationship between the value and meaning of democracy, on the one hand, and the inclusion of children, on the other.

Political competence and the regulatory problem

Throughout the course of history, education, intelligence and virtue have regularly been invoked as conditions for political rights. Along with prejudices of class, gender and race, the belief that only the competent should be granted the vote served to justify the exclusion of workers, women, racial and ethnic minorities and others (Smiley 1999: 376f.; Grover 2011: 108f.). Yet, the fact that children remain excluded from the vote indicates that knowledge, or what I will refer to as "political competence", remains a requirement for political rights in contemporary democracies.[2] According to Robert Dahl (1989: 126), the place of children in democracy teaches us "that we cannot get around the principle of competence".[3]

The elements of political competence are varied, including cognitive, moral or social skills, and knowledge in politics, economics and much else. Exactly what should be required for the vote is debated; the exclusion of children is explained by the inability of children to hold consistent political beliefs (Chan and Clayton 2006: 542), because they have less developed logical capacities (Purdy 1994: 229), because they cannot reflect on justice and a sense of one's own interests (Christiano 2009: 130; Dahl 1989; Weale 2007: 63) or because they are unable to "take the vote seriously" in the sense of adequately grasping its functions in a democratic society (Schrag 1975).

There is arguably broad agreement that the capacity to choose and to understand the nature of voting should be conditions for the right to vote. The reason why few protest the exclusion of infants is arguably that they lack the ability to use it in a meaningful way. However, the capacity to vote defined as the ability to cast a ballot and to understand what elections are for is distinct from the capacity to vote well by moral standards (Schrag 1975: 452; Hamilton 2012: 1450; Cook 2013: 450; Fowler 2014: 97). A person may be able to choose and understand the purpose of elections and still be unable to make good decisions. If the capacity to vote is sufficient for the right to vote, many children younger than 18 should likely be enfranchised. If the capacity to vote *well* is required, the conclusion might be that many people above 18 should be disenfranchised (Fowler 2014: 98).

Limitations in the moral and cognitive capacities of infants and very young children are obvious. Neurological research is invoked to support claims to the effect that cognitive capacities remain underdeveloped until late adolescence (Chan and Clayton 2006). Neurologists acknowledge that "teens are fundamentally different from adults when it comes to impulsivity, planfulness, sensitivity to peer influence". Yet, they insist that "chronological age" tells us little about "neurological or behavior maturity" of specific individuals (Johnson and Giedd 2015: 1725, 1731).

The relevance of neurological findings for determining the voting age in general is accordingly unclear; "there is no neurological evidence that indicates that 16- and 17-year-olds lack the requisite neurological maturation necessary for citizenship or for responsible voting" (Hart and Atkins 2011: 222; Hamilton 2012: 64; see also New Zealand's Royal Commission on Democracy 1986: 235).

Imperfections in the moral capacity of the voter are important to the extent that the right to vote is premised on a sense of justice and sensitivity to the interest of others. Children are traditionally depicted as selfish and egocentric; their exclusion from political rights is from that standpoint instrumental to the protection of justice and the interests of others. It turns out, however, that children are not by nature selfish. Advancements in child psychology indicate that other-regarding preferences and egalitarian choices dominate selfish preferences and behavior already by the age of seven or eight (Fehr, Bernhard and Rockenbach 2008). Worries that children are unable to appreciate the significance of civil rights and democratic institutions are similarly moderated by the observation that such concepts are "fairly well established by middle childhood" (Helwig and Turiel 2010: 577).

Claims to the effect that children should be denied political rights due to lack of political competence are not all the same, however. There are three distinct positions where the adult members of the demos either have no-duties to include children, claim-rights to the exclusion of children or duties to exclude children.

The view that adults have no-duties to include children is reflected in Christiano's (2009) claim that rights to inclusion are conditioned by minimum competence. The competent do not violate any rights of the incompetent by denying them rights to vote. Alternatively, adults have rights to the exclusion of children. This view lends support from the putative "right to a competent electorate" (Brennan 2011). Given such a right and that children lack competence, it follows that others have rights to the exclusion of children. The final alternative is that adults have duties to exclude children following the right of children not to be included. This position is grounded in the claim that political participation is harmful in the absence of moral and psychological maturity (Beckman 2009). To the extent that rights not to participate in harmful activities exist and to the extent that children are morally and psychologically immature, it follows that children have rights not participate in politics.

The regulatory problem

The age of voting either represents a problem of coordination or of optimization. Coordination problems are premised on the disutility of disorder. The justification for legal norms that resolve problems of coordination is that they protect us from the costs of anarchy (Endicott 2011: 29; Hardin 2013). In case the voting age is required in order to resolve a problem of coordination, it matters less what the exact voting age is, as long as there is one. The purpose of the age of voting is to secure stability in the organization of general elections and not to distribute some good on the basis of each person's capacity to use it wisely.

However, if the voting age is designed to secure political competence, the "accuracy" of the imposed voting age looms larger. A legal rule is accurate if and only if it applies to those people, and only to those people, to whom it should apply following some independent standard (Tucker 2012). Hence, the legal voting age is accurate if and only if it includes those people, and only those people, that are politically competent and if it excludes those people, and only those people, that are not. Accurate legal-voting-age rules are difficult to achieve. Any voting age is likely to exclude some competent while also including some incompetents.

Optimizing the vote age confronts two separate problems. The *validity* of the legally defined voting age depends on the extent to which it is justified by standards of competence. Whereas the right to vote is a discontinuous property, that a person is either entitled to or not, political competence is a graded property (Rehfeld 2011: 150). The problem is illustrated by the fact that people are generally as competent when they turn 18 as on the day before. But if the right to vote is awarded on the day people turn 18 on the basis of presumed political competence, it must either be true that they should also have been awarded the vote on the day before or denied the vote on the day they turned 18 (Cohen 1982: 151).

The distinct problem of *generality* follows from the fact that the age of voting applies equally to each person of the same age despite the fact that competence is possessed in unequal measure by each person of the same age. Because of variation in the pace of political maturity, any voting age is bound to be inaccurate in relation to some individuals. An extension of this point is that reasons for the exclusion of children apply equally to some adults (Schrag 2004: 369; Lecce 2009: 133; Tremmel 2015: 133). If the purpose is to exclude incompetent voters, the question is why only incompetent children should be excluded. The problems of validity and generality mean that no uniform voting age can be deduced from the aim of optimizing political competence among the members of the electorate.

Some of these problems are avoidable by treating votes as divisible goods. Thus, Rehfeld (2011) proposes that votes are divided into fractions that are distributed in proportion to the average maturity of distinct ages. For example, children aged 12 would have 1/7 of a vote, children aged 13 would have 2/7 of a vote, and so on. Rehfeld's formula reduced the problem of validity but offers no remedy to the problem of generality. By treating the members of the same age group equally, despite them differing in maturity, the implication is that unequally competent children are granted equal fractions of votes.[4]

The regulatory problem is mediated by dropping the notion of a voting age altogether. A specific proposal is that children should be tested for political competence by the same standards used to assess people with mental disabilities (Munn 2012; Hurme and Appelbaum 2007). However, the introduction of invidious testing authorizes public officials to decide the political rights of individuals. The record of abuse and wrongful discrimination following from the practice of testing for political competence is depressing (Schrag 1975: 453).[5] The regulation of the vote represents a constitutional problem just as much as a regulatory problem since it concerns how to best secure interests in protection against the abuse of public power.

Weighing the values of securing political competence and protecting people against abuses of public power, the notion of a legally imposed voting age may no longer seem so bad. Though any voting age is bound to be both over-inclusive (granting the vote to some incompetents) and over-exclusive (denying the vote to some competent), it provides protection against the arbitrary exercises of public power. The optimal voting age depends on where the balance should be struck between over-inclusion and over-exclusion. One view is that the state should always give priority to the costs of over-exclusion on the assumption that "erring on the side of generosity" represents the lesser evil (Goodin 1985).

However, a conclusive argument requires an all-things-considered evaluation of the reasons for and against the exclusion of children. So far, I have considered the meaning of political competence and the regulatory and constitutional problems involved. This is just one part of the story, however. In addition, we should consider the significance of voting rights in a democratic system and the potential benefits of extending the vote to children.

Democratic participation

In this and the following sections, I examine reasons for extending the vote to children that appeal either to the democratic value of children's participation, the meaning of membership in the democratic people or to the imperative of treating children as equals.

It is a common perception that the lowering of the voting-rights age is called for in order to encourage electoral participation and thereby improve the workings of democracy (Folkes 2004; Lecce 2009). In addition, the lowering of the voting-rights age is thought to stimulate children to learn the habits of voting earlier in life and to become more politically engaged.

Franklin (2004: 213) has argued that first-time electoral participation should ideally take place in circumstances where young voters can be habituated to vote. The age of 18 is particularly bad in this regard, as 18-year-olds are weakly connected to workplaces and parents, where voting habits are stronger. Moving the voting age either up or down is preferable as it allows first-time voting to take place in a more socially supportive environment.

Evidence that the lowering of the voting age boost turnout rates is scant, however. The results following field experiments are disappointing as they indicate that 16-year-olds are less likely to vote than their slightly older counterparts (Wagner, Johann, and Kritzinger 2012). The experience from the Norwegian trial with voting from 16 in some regions is similarly inconclusive (Godli 2015).

Lowering the voting-rights age is also proposed as a means towards *social* justice. The idea is that intergenerational justice requires increasing redistribution to the young and that this would follow if young people were increasingly present among the electorate (Van Parijs 1998: 299). The argument is based on children being disadvantaged relative to other age groups. The extent to which this is true is not clear, however. Some believe that poverty rates among young people and children exceed poverty rates among the old, whereas others insist that there is "no evidence that social expenditure has been shifting in favor of the elderly at the expense of children" (Bradshaw and Holmes 2011; see also Hollanders and Koster 2010).

It is indisputable, however, that the age of the median voter is climbing and that the political incentives to care for children's interests are weaker as long as they are unable to make their voices heard in elections (Henirichs 2002; van Parijs 1998: 296). Enfranchising the young is accordingly instrumental to *political* justice between different age groups. When the voting age in Austria was lowered to 16, the former Chancellor Alfred Gusenbauer explained the reform as "a means to react to the population aging and caring for the youth" (quoted in Campiglio 2009).

Extending voting rights to children in order to increase either turnout, social or political justice represent instrumental approaches to political rights. Rights are instrumentally justified if they are considered "justified by their ability to produce a different outcome" (Cruft 2010: 444). The instrumental case for the right to vote of children accordingly depends on assessments of the outcomes produced by granting children the vote. It is not clear, nevertheless, that the enfranchisement of young people is effective in shifting the political incentives of governments. Clearly, this is the case only if the number of young voters added to the electorate is large enough to be practically significant and if the political preferences of the newly added voters differ sufficiently from the adult population.[6]

More fundamentally, there is reason to question whether ideals of distribution or participation ever provide sufficient grounds for excluding or including people from the vote. The best distribution of goods or the best level of participation in politics are issues that people are bound to disagree about. Arguably, the point of democratic institutions is exactly to offer a framework for the peaceful resolution of such disagreement. But to accept this picture of democratic institutions is also to reject the argument that some people's right to vote are justified because they make some desired level of distribution or participation either more or less desirable. This argument must be rejected since the desirability of distributions or participations can only be the outcome of the exercise of political rights, not a prior standard by which the scope of such rights are defined (Waldron 1999). Others will, of course, disagree with Waldron's position. Like Kolodny, they might argue that inclusive political rights for all is at least partly justified by instrumental considerations to the effect that such institutions offer superior protection against domination and inequality.

The democratic people

Though "democracy" can be variously defined, it is not an empty vessel to be filled with just any content. It is accordingly possible that the inclusion of children is required by a suitable interpretation of the concept of democracy. The upshot is that the ideal of democracy might be inseparable from certain views on inclusion. For example, the point can be made that you will not have *democracy* unless women, workers and ethnic minorities are granted the vote. Could an analogous claim be made in support of including children?

Consider the argument that children should be granted voting rights for the reason that democracy requires the inclusion of every member of the people and because children, evidently, are members of the people. Though the inference is valid, the premise that democracy requires the inclusion of every member of the people is one that should be defended and not assumed. The relevant question is whether democratic voting requires the inclusion of every member of the people, not whether children are members of the people.

Alternatively, it can be argued that democracy requires the inclusion of children because children are citizens and because democracies should include citizens (Nolan 2010). However, citizenship is a legal category of political origins and there is no reason why the members of classes so created should equal the demos as defined by the democratic ideal.

The members of the demos are more plausibly settled by appeal to either the all-affected or the all-subjected principle (Goodin 2007; Beckman 2009). According to the first, everyone affected by law and policy should be included in the demos. According to the second, everyone subject to the laws should be included in the demos. Both principles provide support for the inclusion of children. The all-affected principle makes the case for children's vote obvious as they are directly affected by numerous policies, particularly those concerned with education and health. Children are affected also by the economy, crime rates and other societal phenomena that largely depend on public decisions.

The implications of the all-subjected principle are less determinate. The principle holds that inclusion is conditional on being a subject, defined in terms of either legal duties or coercive threats, or both (Beckman 2014b). One reading is that children, just like other residents in the jurisdiction of the state, are subject to legal duties and coercive threats and, therefore, fall within the purview of the all-subjected principle (Hamilton 2012: 30ff). Another reading is that the age of criminal responsibility is decisive as coercive threats are premised on legal sanctions that, in turn, are imposed only on people above the age of criminal responsibility. An observation in this regard is that the age of criminal responsibility is set below the age of voting almost everywhere (Cipriani 2013). Thus, children are held responsible for their actions by the criminal law, though they are considered insufficiently responsible for political participation. The consequent argument is that "criminal and participatory responsivities" should be rendered "more symmetrical" (Lau 2012; Munn 2012).

The claim that children should be enfranchised because they are members of the demos can be resisted in two ways. The first is to concede that extending political rights to children is more democratic but to deny that this constitutes a reason for extending the vote. From the fact that the inclusion of children is "more democratic" it does not follow that we have moral reasons to include children (Beckman 2009).

The second is to deny that either the quality of being affected or being subjected are sufficient for inclusion. Following Ben Saunders, democratic rights apply only to *agents* with the capacity to make decisions, excluding "patients" such as "animals, very young children, and the severely mentally handicapped" from democratic status (Saunders 2011: 286). An objection against this claim is that the distinction between agents and patients offers no explanation for why the inclusion of patients would be either undemocratic or morally objectionable. From the claim that agents subject to political authority are morally entitled to political rights, it does not follow that we have duties to exclude patients subject to political authority.

Democratic equality

Democracy is strongly associated with the belief in the equal moral worth of every person. A plain argument in favor of children's political rights is, accordingly, to point at the equal moral worth of children. Children ought to enjoy the same rights as adults, including political rights, since their moral status is the same. The claim is that of "equal rights for children!" (Holt 1975; Cohen 1982).

While it is correct that children's moral status is equal to that of adults, the inference that children must, therefore, be granted the same rights as adults is mistaken. Equal rights are an instance of equal treatment. But, as is often noted, equal treatment is not generally required for treatment as an equal (Dworkin 1977; Wall 2007: 424). This point is directly relevant to the rights of children. Equal rights for children are equivalent to the equal treatment of children. What matters though is that children are treated *as equals*. The point is that equal moral status neither precludes unequal treatment nor unequal rights, since other considerations than moral status are relevant in determining moral obligations towards children – such as, for example, greater vulnerability or need (Brennan and Noogle 1997: 8).

It might still be argued that unequal voting rights disadvantages children and that differential treatment to the disadvantage of another constitutes wrongful discrimination. Exclusion on the basis of age is arguably analogous to exclusions on the basis of either gender or race. Just as a person's age is unchosen, a person's sex or physical appearance are largely unchosen attributes. If differential treatment based on unchosen attributes is wrong, it is clearly wrong to treat people differently merely because of their age (Nunn 2002).

In reply, it can be observed that age is a very different basis for differential treatment than either race or gender. Though age is not chosen, it is a temporary condition that applies to everyone. This observation forms the basis of the view that unequal treatment at different ages is justified if we treat people as equals with respect to lives as wholes (Lippert-Rasmussen 2014: 160; Fowler 2014). Disenfranchisement at some point in time is compensated for by enfranchisement at some other point in time.

However, complete life neutrality is not fully adequate as justification for the exclusion of children from the vote. If unequal rights between the young and old is compensated for by equal rights throughout the life span of both young and old, it follows that the voting age could be set at any point and that it would even be plausible with a maximum voting age. Denying the right to vote for people below the age of 45 would be as plausible as denying the right to vote for people below the age of 12, and to disenfranchise the old would be as plausible as to disenfranchise the young (Lopez-Guerra 2014: 70; Gosseries 2014: 69). The fact that the young and old are granted the same bundle of rights during their lives as a whole is mitigating the problem but does not solve it. The value of equal rights between complete lives does not obliterate the value of equal rights between the young and old (McKerlie 2001).

A more powerful version of the argument from equal moral worth is that each person is owed symbolic affirmation of equal status. The point is not that equal rights deductively follow from the principle of equal moral worth. The point is that equal moral worth requires that equal status be manifested by political institutions (Beitz 1990: 110). A person who is denied political rights on the same terms as others is denied public recognition of equal status and is thus treated with "insult, dishonor, or denigration" (Waldron 1999: 237).

Chan and Clayton (2006: 554) object that equal status is imperiled only if rights already enjoyed are denied. There is no insult in the refusal to grant rights not previously enjoyed. Since children have not previously been entitled to vote, not extending the vote to children does not violate their status as equals. But the premise of this argument is bogus. The past exclusion of workers, women and minorities suggests that the refusal to grant a person political rights on equal terms to others does constitute harm to equal status. A person can for good reason be insulted by being denied a right, just as a person can for good reason be insulted by being deprived of a right.

Nevertheless, equal status does not require equal rights in all cases. To deny newborn infants the vote is not an insult to their status as equals, the reason being that newborn infants are not harmed in any identifiable sense from disenfranchisement. The premise is that entitlement to public recognition is conditioned by the capacity of being harmed in the absence of such recognition (Lopez-Guerra 2014: 71ff.). In so far as children do not have the capacity to understand the value of voting or what elections are all about, it seems that children's sense of equal status is not hurt by exclusion from the polling booth. Hence, children are disadvantaged by disenfranchisement only if they *do* have the capacity to participate in political life (Cook 2013). The premise of this argument is, of course, that equal political rights are necessary, not just sufficient, for recognition of equal status. Wall (2007: 429) questions this point by suggesting that a society that grants each member "equal civil liberties and a fair share of wealth" while at the same time *denying* them equal political rights would still recognize the equal status of all.

Discussions on the inclusiveness of democratic suffrage usually begin with the assumption that children are either wronged or harmed by exclusion. However, we might start from the opposite position and instead ask whether children are either wronged or harmed *by inclusion*. The backdrop for this question is that to grant children the same rights as adults is sometimes "bad for them" (Archard 2003: 16). The reason why children are denied the same rights as adults is not that children are unable to perform adult activities in a competent way, but that such activities are bad for children. The badness of children voting can be explained by analogy to the badness of children working. The justification is, in both cases, paternalistic. The reason why children have no moral right to take employment is not that children are particularly bad workers but that to work is bad for them. By analogy, the reason why children do not have moral rights to vote is not that they lack political competence, but that political participation is bad for them (Beckman 2009: 116f.). Against this view, it has been objected that it remains unclear that voting does, in fact, harm children (Lopez-Guerra 2014: 74). The objection is a valid one. It remains to be substantiated what the social and psychological consequences of enfranchisement are and if they are inimical to a good childhood.

Conclusions

The political status of children in a democracy raises questions about the nature of political competence, the problem of regulating the vote and the meaning and value of democracy. The regulatory aspect of the problem is often overlooked, though it is potentially decisive. The constitutional importance of securing that the vote is distributed non-arbitrarily will often provide strong reasons against optimizing the fit between the political competence of individuals and the legal criteria for political rights.

The democratic aspects of the problem point towards political participation, membership in the people and equal moral status as potential reasons for extending the vote below the current voting age. With respect to each of them, the discussion is ongoing and future research will determine the valence of each respective argument. The political status of children in democracy depends on the relationship between lowering the voting age, on the one hand, and electoral turnout and intergenerational justice, on the other. But it also depends on the extent to which such considerations are at all pertinent to questions regarding membership in the demos. Alternatively, the political status of children depends on whether the demos is best understood by reference to subjection to law or affectedness by public decisions, and if agential status is necessary for democratic inclusion. The political status of children also raises questions about the legitimacy of discrimination by age and whether children benefit or not from being either included or excluded. Children and the right to vote is, consequently, intimately related to central themes in the study of democracy.

Notes

1 With the exception that the mean voting age increased immediately following the removal of class-based restrictions in the early 20th century. The Soviet Union was the first European country to introduce the voting age of 18 in 1936, with many Eastern European countries following suit after the Second World War. Eighteen became the standard voting age in Western Europe in the 1960s and 1970s. See, generally, Cultice (1992).
2 Following Smiley (1999: 372), "political knowledge" is preferable to "political competence" as it does not signal the need to *judge* particular individuals. But since children are, in fact, judged incompetent to vote, the expression "political competence" is for the same reason the more appropriate.
3 Political competence is also pertinent to the exclusion of the mentally disabled. See Beckman (2014a).
4 Extra votes for parents is sometimes proposed (Campiglio 2009: 222; Rutherford 1998: 1503). However, extra votes for parents does not grant children the vote and is, in fact, premised on their exclusion.
5 For a more optimistic appraisal of competence testing and voting for children, see Cook (2013), Grover (2011: 58) and Wall (2014).
6 Following one version of the instrumental argument, the voting-rights age should be lowered "as a means to discipline fiscal policy" (Bertocchi, Lancia, and Russo 2011).

References

Archard, D. 2003. *Children, Family and the State*. Burlington: Ashgate.
Beckman, L. 2014a. "The Accuracy of Electoral Regulations: The Case of the Right to Vote by People with Cognitive Impairments," *Social Policy and Society* 13: 221–233.
Beckman, L. 2014b. "The Subjects of Collectively Binding Decisions: Democratic Inclusion and Extraterritorial Law," *Ratio Juris* 27: 252–270.
Beckman, L. 2009. *The Frontiers of Democracy: The Right to Vote and Its Limits*. Basingstoke: Palgrave Macmillan.
Beitz, C. 1990. *Political Equality*. Princeton, NJ: Princeton University Press.
Berry, C. 2012. *The Rise of Gerontocracy? Addressing the Intergenerational Democratic Deficit*. London: Intergenerational Foundation.
Bertocchi, G., Lancia, F., and Russo, A. 2011. *Youth Enfranchisement*, February 14. Retrieved from https://papers.ssrn.com/sol3/papers.cfm?abstract_id=3042645 (last accessed 20 March 2018).
Bradshaw, J., and Holmes, J. 2011. *An Analysis of Generational Equity Over Recent Decades in the OECD and UK*. Amsterdam: AIAS, GINI Discussion Paper 11.
Brennan, J. 2011. "The Right to a Competent Electorate," *The Philosophical Quarterly* 61: 700–724.
Brennan, S., and Noogle, R. 1997. "The Moral Status of Children: Children's Rights, Parents' Rights, and Family," *Social Theory and Practice* 23: 1–26.
Campiglio, L. 2009. "Children's Right to Vote: The Missing Link in Modern Democracies," *Sociological Studies of Children and Youth* 12: 221–247.
Chan, T. W., and Clayton, M. 2006. "Should the Voting Age be Lowered to Sixteen? Normative and Empirical Considerations," *Political Studies* 54: 533–558.
Christiano, T. 2009. *The Constitution of Equality*. Oxford: Oxford University Press.
Cipriani, D. 2013. *Children's Rights and the Minimum Age of Criminal Responsibility: A Global Perspective*. Farnham: Ashgate.
Cohen, E. F. 2005. "Neither Seen nor Heard: Children's Citizenship in Contemporary Democracies," *Citizenship Studies* 9: 221–240.
Cohen, H. 1982. "Ending the Double Standard: Equal Rights for Children," *Philosophy, Children, and the Family, Child Nurturance* 1: 149–158.
Cook, P. 2013. "Against a Minimum Voting Age," *Critical Review of International Social and Political Philosophy* 16: 439–458.

Cruft, R. 2010. "On the Non-Instrumental Value of Basic Rights," *Journal of Moral Philosophy* 7: 441–461.
Cultice, W. 1992. *Youth's Battle for the Ballot: A History of Voting Age in America*. New York, NY: Greenwood Press.
Dahl, R. 1989. *Democracy and Its Critics*. New Haven, CT: Harvard University Press.
Dworkin, R. 1977. *Taking Rights Seriously*. London: Duckworth.
Endicott, T. 2011. "The Value of Vagueness," in A. Marmor and S. Soames (eds.), *Philosophical Foundations of Language in the Law*. Oxford: Oxford University Press.
Fehr, E., Bernhard, H., and Rockenbach, B. 2008. "Egalitarianism in Young Children," *Nature* 454: 1079–1083.
Folkes, A. 2004. "The Case for Votes at 16," *Representation* 41: 52–56.
Fowler, T. 2014. "Status of Child Citizens," *Politics Philosophy Economics* 13: 93–11.
Franklin, M. N. 2004. *Voter Turnout and the Dynamics of Electoral Competition in Established Democracies since 1945*. Cambridge: Cambridge University Press.
Godli, P. H. 2015. "Giving 16-Year-Olds the Vote. Experiences from Norway," in J. Tremmel, A. Mason, P. Haakenstad Godli, and I. Dimitrijosk (eds.), *Youth Quotas and other Efficient Forms of Youth Participation in Ageing Societies*. Dordrecht: Springer.
Goodin, R. E. 1985. "Erring on the Side of Kindness in Social Welfare Policy," *Policy Sciences* 18: 141–156.
Goodin, R. E. 2007. "Enfranchising All Affected Interests, and its Alternatives," *Philosophy and Public Affairs* 35: 40–68.
Gosseries, A. 2014. "What Makes Age Discrimination Special? A Philosophical Look at the ECJ Case Law," *Netherlands Journal of Legal Philosophy* 43: 59–80.
Grover S. 2011. *Young People's Human Rights and The Politics of Voting Age*. Dordrecht: Springer.
Hamilton, V. E. 2012. "Democratic Inclusion, Cognitive Development, and the Age of Electoral Majority," *Brooklyn Law Review* 77: 1449–1516.
Hardin, R. 2013. "Why a Constitution?," in D. J. Galligan and M. Wersteeg (eds.), *Social and Political Foundations of Constitutions*. Cambridge: Cambridge University Press.
Hart, D., and Atkins, R. 2011. "American Sixteen- and Seventeen-Year-Olds Are Ready to Vote," *The ANNALS of the American Academy of Political and Social Science* 633: 201–222.
Helwig, C. C., and Turiel, E. 2010. "Children's Social and Moral Reasoning," in P. K. Smith and C. H. Hart (eds.), *The Wiley-Blackwell Handbook of Childhood Social Development*. Oxford: Wiley-Blackwell.
Hinrichs, K. 2002. "Do the Old Exploit the Young? Is Enfranchising Children a Good Idea?," *European Journal of Sociology* 43: 35–58.
Hollanders, D. A., and Koster, F. 2010. *The Graying of the Median Voter: Aging and the Politics of the Welfare State in OECD Countries*. Amsterdam, University of Amsterdam, AIAS Working Paper 10/98.
Holt, J. 1975. *Escape from Childhood: The Needs and Rights of Children*. Harmondsworth: Penguin.
Hurme, S. B., and Appelbaum, P. S. 2007. "Defining and Assessing Capacity to Vote: The Effect of Mental Impairment on the Rights of Voters," *McGeorge Law Review* 38: 931–1014.
Johnson, S. B., and Giedd, J. N. 2015. "Normal Brain Development and Child/Adolescent Policy," in J. Clausen and N. Levy (eds.), *Handbook of Neuroethics*. Berlin: Springer.
Lau, J. C. 2012. "Two Arguments for Child Enfranchisement," *Political Studies* 60: 860–876.
Lecce, S. 2009. "Should Democracy Grow Up? Children and Voting Rights," *Intergenerational Justice Review* 9: 133–39.
Lippert-Rasmussen, K. 2014. *Born Free and Equal?* Oxford: Oxford University Press.
Lopez-Guerra, C. 2014. *Democracy and Disenfranchisement. The Morality of Electoral Exclusions*. Oxford: Oxford University Press.
McKerlie, D. 2001 "Justice between the Young and the Old," *Philosophy & Public Affairs* 30: 152–177.
Munn, N. J. 2012. "Capacity Testing the Youth: A Proposal for Broader Enfranchisement," *Journal of Youth Studies* 15: 1048–1062.
Nolan, A. 2010. "The Child as 'Democratic Citizen': Challenging the 'Participation Gap'," *Public Law* Winter: 767–782.
Nunn, K. B. 2002. "The Child as Other: Race and Differential Treatment in the Juvenile Justice System," *DePaul Law Review* 51: 679–714.
Purdy, L. M. 1994. "Why Children Shouldn't Have Equal Rights," *International Journal of Children's Rights* 2: 223–241.
Rehfeld, A. 2011. "The Child as Democratic Citizen," *The ANNALS of the American Academy of Political and Social Science* 633: 141–166.
Report of The Royal Commission on the Electoral System, *Towards A Better Democracy*, 1986.

Rutherford, J. 1998. "One Child, One Vote; Proxies for Parents," *Minnesota Law Review* 82: 1463–1525.
Saunders, B. 2011. "Defining the Demos," *Politics Philosophy Economics* 11: 280–301.
Schrag, F. 1975. "The Child's Status in the Democratic State," *Political Theory* 3: 441–457.
Schrag, F. 2004. "Children and Democracy: Theory and Policy," *Politics. Philosophy and Economics* 3: 365–379.
Smiley, M. 1999. "Democratic Citizenship: A Question of Competence?," in S. L. Elkin and K. E. Soltan (eds.), *Citizen Competence and Democratic Institutions*. University Park, PA: Pennsylvania University Press.
Tremmel, J. 2015. "Democracy or Epistocracy? Age as a Criterion of Voter Eligibility," in J. Tremmel, A. Mason, P. Haakenstad Godli, and I. Dimitrijosk (eds.), *Youth Quotas and other Efficient Forms of Youth Participation in Ageing Societies*. Dordrecht: Springer.
Tucker, A. 2012. "Scarce Justice: The Accuracy, Scope and Depth of Justice," *Politics, Philosophy and Economics* 11: 76–96.
Van Parijs, P. 1998. "The Disfranchisement of the Elderly, and Other Attempts to Secure Intergenerational Justice," *Philosophy & Public Affairs* 27: 292–333.
Wagner, M., Johann, D., and Kritzinger, S. 2012. "Voting at 16: Turnout and the Quality of Choice," *Electoral Studies* 31: 372–383.
Waldron, J. 1999. *Law and Disagreement*. Cambridge: Cambridge University Press.
Wall, J. 2014. "Why Children and Youth Should Have the Right to Vote: An Argument for Proxy-claim Suffrage," *Children, Youth and Environments* 24: 108–123.
Wall, S. 2007. "Democracy and Equality," *The Philosophical Quarterly* 57: 416–438.
Weale, A. 2007. *Democracy*. London: Palgrave.

35
CHILDREN, CRIME AND PUNISHMENT

Christopher Bennett

Introduction

This chapter looks at some of the distinctive issues that criminal justice raises for the philosophy of childhood: how the philosophies of children and criminal justice inform one another (second section); how criminal justice marks the social environment in which children grow up (third section); and children's involvement in the criminal process (fourth section). To start with, however, we look at three case studies that illustrate the diversity and complexity of the ways in which children interact with the criminal justice system.

Children in criminal justice: some themes and examples

(i) On 7th April 2016, a court in Hartlepool, UK, sentenced two girls who had been 13 and 14 at the time of their crime to "at least 15 years" for the murder of Angela Wrightson, a vulnerable alcoholic who was in the habit of inviting strangers into her house in the hope of conversation.[1] The young people, who had a history of having lived in care homes, and who were described by their defence lawyer as having been involved with drugs and alcohol, and as having been "out of control," were convicted of a "gratuitous," "degrading" and "cowardly" attack that lasted nine hours – during which the pair communicated with friends via Facebook and Snapchat – and inflicted over 100 injuries on Wrightson. When the case was reported, it inevitably drew parallels with the abduction and murder of toddler James Bulger by Robert Thompson and John Venables, aged 10 and 11 at the time of the attacks, in 1993.

(ii) Ta-Nehisi Coates's memoir of "growing up black" in the US is written as a letter to his son in the wake of the decision of a grand jury not to indict white policeman Darren Brown for having shot and killed black teenager Michael Brown in Ferguson, Missouri, in August 2014 (Coates 2015). In the memoir, Coates describes what he calls "the Dream" of "those who think they are white."[2] "The Dream," conveyed by endless television programmes, is part hope and part belief about the nature of US society. It gives a picture of a world where children "did not regularly fear for their bodies," where "little white boys" had "complete collections of football cards, and their only want was a popular girlfriend and their only worry was poison oak" (Coates 2015: 20). Part of the Dream concerns the benevolent role of criminal justice agencies in upholding the security of "our" way of life against those who would threaten "us." By contrast:

> To be black in the Baltimore of my youth was to be naked before the elements of the world, before all the guns, fists, knives, crack, rape and disease. The nakedness is not an error, nor pathology. The nakedness is the correct and intended result of policy, the predictable upshot of people forced for centuries to live under fear. The law did not protect us. And now, in your time, the law has become an excuse for stopping and frisking you, which is to say, for furthering the assault on your body. But a society that protects some people through a safety net of schools, government-backed home loans and ancestral wealth but can only protect you with the club of criminal justice has either failed at enforcing its good intentions or has succeeded at something much darker.
>
> *(Coates 2015: 18)*

(iii) In 2007 a 15-year-old boy from Lisburn, Northern Ireland, was caught and charged with stealing £165 from a ballet school run by Gwen Gibson's daughter.[3] Because of changes in the youth justice system introduced under Northern Ireland's Good Friday Agreement, the victim and offender were given the opportunity to attend a Restorative Justice conference as an alternative to a formal prosecution. They agreed, Gwen Gibson taking the place of her daughter, who was "too traumatised" to attend. Before arriving, Gwen was very angry with the boy, since her daughter "had worked really hard to run her own business and didn't deserve this." She was also apprehensive: "I thought I was going to meet a hoodlum." But when she saw the boy – who was accompanied by his Care Manager, Probation Officer and a police officer – she was surprised: "He looked really scared." The boy lived in care, and had an unhappy relationship with his family. She started to feel some compassion for him. During the meeting, the boy made it clear that he was sorry and ashamed for what he had done. Gwen continued to write to the boy periodically after the meeting.

The case studies raise a number of themes that will be intertwined in what follows, and which it will be helpful to highlight at the outset. Firstly – raised by the Angela Wrightson murder – there is a question of the moral significance of crime. I take it that many – though by no means all – crimes are serious moral wrongs. But what kind of response does such wrongdoing require from the state? Some favour a purely forward-looking response that seeks to learn lessons from such events in order to minimise their likelihood in the future. For others, such an ameliorative response should be combined with the backward-looking insistence that those who do such terrible things have to be held to account. This fault line between those approaches that are purely forward-looking and those that acknowledge some backward-looking element is one on which anyone thinking about the issues of this chapter will need to take a position.

Secondly, whatever one thinks is the aim of criminal justice, there are many ways in which it might be implemented – as the example of restorative justice shows – and many supplementary values and constraints that help to determine its most appropriate vehicle. Thirdly, it is normally thought that it can be fair or appropriate to subject an individual to criminal justice responses only if they possess certain cognitive or volitional capacities. So, an important question is whether (and if so when) children can be thought to have those capacities, and in what ways youth justice should be different from adult criminal justice. Fourthly, criminal justice is not just about punishment; other distinctive features of criminal justice impact the social world in which children grow up. As Coates points out, police may view children (and their parents) either as potential victims or potential threats; their victimisation may or may not be taken seriously, and their stories listened to; and these distinctions may function as an important marker of a child's place in society. Fifthly, criminal justice cannot be thought about in isolation from other issues of social justice. One aspect of this is whether there is a link between crime and poverty, and whether, if there is, childhood deprivation should be recognised as a mitigating factor. But it is also about the way in which the impact of crime varies with class and race; and the way in which the – explicit or implicit – social standing of various groups influences their treatment by state agencies including criminal justice agencies. Children, by virtue of their greater dependence on others, are likely to be particularly vulnerable to such wider patterns of injustice (see ch. 27).

The philosophy of criminal justice and the philosophy of childhood

Two underlying sets of debates will impinge on any discussion of these issues: one about the proper nature and ends of punishment; and one about the nature and value of childhood. Punishment is often defined as the deliberate imposition of a burden, for a perceived infraction, by a party in a position of authority, and with the intention of communicating some form of disapproval of the infraction (Duff 1986). Since it involves deliberate harming in some way, some people think that no form of punishment can ever be justified. If punishment *is* to be justified, it will have to be in terms of some overarching purpose that requires and vindicates such deliberate harming. The candidates on offer are typically thought to be *public protection* – which might require the *incapacitation* of the offender, or his punishment as a *deterrent* (to deter him or others from future offending), or his coerced *reform* or *moral education*; or *justice* (sometimes called *retribution*: "payment of debts" to the victim or society); or the *communication* or *expression* of moral censure; or a hybrid of two or more of these ends (Duff 2013a). Which of these ends, if any, we think are legitimate reasons for the state to punish will impinge on any discussion of the topic of this chapter. For instance, if we think about the age of responsibility, a retributive theory might insist that it is only with moral maturity that an agent can be asked to answer for her actions; a deterrent theory might look at what age punishment would start to be useful as a deterrent; whereas an incapacitative theory would ask at what age individuals start to pose a sufficiently weighty risk to the public to justify locking them away.

Our answers will also depend on what we think is distinctive about childhood (Schapiro 1999; Baggatini and MacLeod 2014; see also ch. 7, ch. 10). What are the features that characterise being a child, and in virtue of which we identify one person as a child and another not? What moral capacities do children possess, and at what ages? When is it reasonable to expect children to be morally aware? When does childhood begin and end? What are its distinctive stages, and when do they typically occur? Is the value of childhood exhausted by its character as a preparation for adulthood, or are their distinctive intrinsic goods of childhood in which children have an important interest (and which may ground rights against the state)? To take just one of the possible debates in this area, someone who thinks primarily in terms of the intrinsic goods of childhood may be less inclined to agree that periods of unhappiness or deprivation during childhood can be justified if they are causally necessary conditions of greater happiness, or improved moral orientation, in later life (Gheaus 2015).

Perhaps we can allow, in ecumenical spirit, that each of the grounds mentioned as reasons for punishment is an important function of the state. Perhaps we can also allow that, whatever intrinsic goods there are to childhood, an important difference between adults and children is that childhood is so strongly characterised by its developmental aspects. This is not to say that adults no longer develop, or that childhood does not have its intrinsic goods; but it is to say both that the rate of development and change in childhood is much greater than that in adulthood, and that responsibilities to protect and sustain that process of development are much more extensive and much more stringent. If this is correct then reasons to punish or not to punish that have to do with the personal development of the wrongdoer herself will be particularly important. Of the moral education theory of punishment, Jean Hampton says:

> Punishments are like electrified fences. At the very least they teach a person, via pain, that there is a "barrier" to the action she wants to do, and so, at the very least, they aim to deter. But because punishment "fences" are marking *moral* boundaries, the pain which these "fences" administer (or threaten to administer) conveys a larger message to beings who are able to reflect on the reasons for these barriers' existence: they convey that there is a barrier to these actions *because* they are morally wrong.
>
> (Hampton 1984: 212)

The success of Hampton's account depends on an empirical claim: that punishments actually *are* effective in conveying a message about moral boundaries (and, presumably, significantly more effective than non-punitive alternatives). That might be hard to prove. Nevertheless, if successful in this respect, her account is attractive in that it would show how punishment might have a place among other duties that states have to educate children and promote and protect their development. Punishment of children may start off simply aiming to deter by giving an incentive for desistance that even an amoral being can recognise. But as children start to develop moral understanding, they are able to start to understand their punishment in a different way, and a finely judged punishment can come to be a dramatic way of marking actions as unacceptable. Even when punishments fail to deter, a child may still register its expressive power. This is one way in which our thinking about punishment might be affected by the fact that children have special developmental interests and, in particular, interests in developing morally. But, equally, we might think that the special developmental interests of children require us to take even more seriously than we should in regard to adult offenders the need to minimise their liability to those sorts of custody regimes in which they are blocked from taking part in activities typical of their life-stage.

Criminal justice in the child's social environment

This chapter deals with the involvement of children in the formal criminal justice mechanisms of the state, and I am largely setting aside the topic of punishment within the family, and indeed the participation of children in our informal interpersonal practices of accountability more generally. However, it is worth noting that these formal mechanisms work – and presumably only could work – against the background of informal patterns of socialisation, including socialisation to do with learning to take responsibility, incur culpability and accept punishment (Braithwaite 1989). As children start to become self-conscious, they start to understand that they are expected to be able to account for their actions, explaining themselves to others and offering justifications. They come to realise that not being able to give a good account of oneself can make one an object of censure. They come to develop a capacity for a range of emotional perceptions and actions that have to do with wrongdoing, such as feeling guilt, shame, remorse, apologising and making amends (Taylor 1985; Walker 2006; Radzik 2009). They learn to see that such reactions can be both intrinsically merited by certain circumstances, and also practically necessary for re-acceptance and reconciliation. They also learn which wrongs – in which situations, and involving which types of people – will be ignored or condoned, and which need to be taken more seriously. And they learn something about the role of punishment: its forms; the conditions under which its justice can be disputed and in which it must be accepted; and the claims to authority that are effective in establishing rights to punish. A formal institution of criminal law enforcement works, not with Hobbesian beings from the state of nature, but with social beings who have had extensive experience of complex and nuanced social practices of accountability.

While all children are subject to practices of accountability, criminal justice is, for most, something of which they are aware (the possibility of crime and criminals) but the details of which remain dim. For some, however, engagement with criminal justice marks a major feature of their lives, and a major point at which the state's influence is felt. Furthermore, all children grow up in a social environment in which crime and punishment has a distinctive place.

For one thing, "crime" is a distinctive moral category, different from "harm" or "wrong." One can be a perpetrator or victim of harm or wrongdoing without being socially labelled as such, and without the state using coercion to require you to play a part in a pre-defined process. Furthermore, one can be the victim of serious harms, the agents of which are diffuse or collective, and where culpability is hard to pin down. By contrast, "crime" involves state action against discrete acts of wrongdoing – although a contested category, its focus on "public wrongs" seems a fixed point in debates (Duff 2013b). The paradigm case is that of the individual agent, and collective wrongs can be accommodated only with difficulty. This has two implications relevant to this chapter, and which show how "crime" features in the social environment. The first is that getting involved with criminal justice means getting involved with a coercive state process that has its own momentum, where the matter has been taken out of any individual's hands and to which one's input may be formally required, often on pain of sanction. The criminal justice system is a major and rather distinctive state bureaucracy. It has its own procedures and language, intimate to insiders but sometimes baffling to outsiders; its own physical environment, comprising the specialised arena of the courtroom, the cells and interrogation rooms of police stations, and the hidden security apparatus of prisons; its own set of roles, rituals and often costumes and uniforms; and its own internal social and personal connections, routines, tensions, competitions and pressures (Christie 1977; Rock 1993). Becoming involved in the criminal justice system, therefore, means, in part, to leave the life of everyday social interaction and to enter a new and unfamiliar social environment. If this experience can be disorientating for adults, it is an interesting question what it is like for children, whether they find it even more intimidating and oppressive or whether, more habituated to interacting with what is unfamiliar, they are better able to adapt to its strangeness. A number of jurisdictions have wrestled with the question of how to make criminal justice institutions more accommodating to children, perhaps with mixed results.

The second implication is that children are very often harmed in ways that do not have identifiable individual perpetrators, and which do not qualify as crimes. This is not just the claim that many harmful acts that could be criminalised are not; nor the claim that many crimes are never reported (though these points are undoubtedly also true). Rather, it is the claim that long-lasting harms that may affect children most of all, such as environmental pollution – which is sometimes referred to as the most serious form of child abuse (Ferguson et al. 2013; Canadian Association of Physicians for the Environment 2000) – are overlooked when attention is focused on particular acts of wrongdoing. This leads some to claim that the focus of criminal justice is partial, and that a society with a criminal justice system gives disproportionate importance to individual responsibility in comparison to diffuse collective harms. Hence the radical claim – deriving from Marx's claims about law as superstructure – that criminal justice, with its individualistic focus, is an ideologically motivated distraction from fundamental matters of social welfare (Marx 1968; Norrie 1991; Wacquant 2009). While crimes are often episodes of personal tragedy, they do not often have the wide effects that, for instance, the closing of a factory might, or the cutting of a welfare programme. This connects to an important issue about perceptions of crime and punishment, and their reality. Media reporting of crime might reasonably be said to be out of proportion to its social effect (Cohen and Young 1973). There seems little doubt that reporting of crime can feed into fear of crime, and perceptions of one's social environment as criminogenic (Hale 1996). It serves to keep crime in the public eye, ensuring that even quite young children worry about "criminals," and can lead to perceptions that fail to track real probabilities of victimisation. This is not to deny that crime occurs, and that it can be traumatic to be a victim of crime. Nevertheless, children grow up in a world in which perceptions of crime and its reality may diverge quite widely.

Assuming that there is some good reason for the individualistic focus of criminal justice (Hampton 1991), however, it is also important to note that social factors interact in systematic ways with its operation. There is a good deal of unevenness in the criminal justice system's treatment of children (as with adults), and whether a child is likely to be involved in the criminal justice system, either as a perpetrator or as a victim, and what her fate will be, varies with factors such as class, race and gender (Reiman and Leighton 2012; on the role of race, see Alexander 2010). Firstly, social conditions such as poverty or local culture mean that some children are under more pressure to engage in criminal activity than others; often this means that perpetrators in the criminal justice system are overwhelmingly drawn from already socially disadvantaged and vulnerable groups. Secondly, points at which discretion can enter the criminal process are also points at which bias can enter, and that bias will often favour children (and adults) from already powerful social groups. For instance, many legal procedures use terms like "reasonable" or "public interest" that admit of a wide range of interpretations, and which, therefore, only weakly constrain the decisions of particular officials. This provides room for conscious prejudice or implicit bias to influence decisions, and little scope for appeal, since it may be hard to prove that an unacceptable interpretation has been put on the terms in question. On the assumption that prejudices are at least sometimes systematically connected with the interests of the powerful, and operate to the disadvantage of the already vulnerable, discretion can be problematic for minorities (Delgado 1987). Thirdly, the more socially disadvantaged lack resources to pay for good lawyers, or good contacts within the system, or simply the tacit knowledge of how things work and who to call on. These are familiar ways in which bureaucracies, even when well-meaning, can systematically favour those who are already well off. What the solution is to this is highly controversial. One route is to opt for maximum transparency and accountability, to try to give bias nowhere to hide. Another is to argue for greater public participation in the justice system, with participants drawn from all social groups (Dzur 2015). It is, however, hard to see how genuine reform could work without some accompanying equalisation of social and economic status.

It is a theme of Coates's memoir that one of the major ways in which children can be indirectly involved in criminal justice is by being the child of someone convicted of an offence, or of the victim of an offence, or being a member of a community in which a high number of crimes are committed, or in which large numbers of adults are incarcerated (Condry, Kotova, and Minson 2016; Alexander 2010). When a parent is incarcerated, this means their effective loss to the child for the duration of custody. It is possible that this may also be a period of relief from the parent's criminal activities and their consequences on family life, but it also undoubtedly threatens the bond between child and parent and makes that emotional connection more difficult. Assuming that such a bond is important, and that continuity of care is developmentally important (Brighouse and Swift 2014), it seems hard to imagine that there would not be some developmental impact on the child. Children will often attempt to maintain some form of connection with the parent while they are inside. But there are numerous obstacles. Prisons are often concerned with security above all else, and this can make it hard for families to share spontaneous time together. This, in turn, can make it harder for offenders to retain links with their families, and some speculate that this reinforces tendencies to reoffending. There are prison regimes – for instance, in some Nordic countries – that make it possible for families to be together, including regimes that see prison more as a curfew than a round-the-clock security regime (Larson 2013). It seems likely that children's interests will, except in extreme cases, be best served by these more open modes of custody, and by taking dependent children into account at the point of sentencing (Minson, Nadin, and Earle 2015).

Children in the criminal process

Having looked at the diffuse effects of criminal justice on the child's social environment, this section focuses on children's involvement in various stages of the criminal process.

Children committing crimes

On the one hand, we view children as innocents, so that there is something particularly awful, even deformed, about a child who is capable of terrible crimes; on the other hand, we view children as wild and amoral, needing to be trained and cultivated. These two views might be traced back to views of human nature outside of society: are human beings "noble savages," naturally good but corrupted by society, whose childhood is a brief moment of purity, or is it precisely the process of socialisation that makes them distinctively human? On the first view, cases of terrible crimes may be seen as evidence of a defect deep in a child's pre-social nature – that they are more "savage" than "noble" – and the hope might simply be that the defect can be contained effectively enough that the child can later live amongst society; on the second view, the capacity of a child to commit terrible crimes would rather cast light on the patterns of socialisation to which she had been subjected, either locally, by her own family and community, or more broadly in terms of the attitudes and values that characterise our form of society. The latter view, in turn, raises the question of how effective patterns of socialisation require individuals and communities to feel that they have a stake in society, the social bases of self-respect and the bases of social hope (Rawls 1971; Young 1990: ch. 2).

Children as victims

Despite the widespread perception of "stranger danger," children are more likely to be victims of crimes committed by a person they know (Finkelhor and Ormrod 2000). An issue that has come increasingly to the fore in recent times is that of children as victims of sexual offences. This is clearly not a localised problem: the terms "child sex ring" and "grooming" have become familiar terms in media reports (Jay 2014). The level of domestic child sexual abuse is also gradually coming to light. Some of these challenges are distinctively modern. Social media platforms put children in touch with many people whose identities they cannot easily verify, and where the content of conversations is hard for concerned adults to monitor. This raises familiar ethical issues about balancing the desirability of privacy against the importance of preventing crimes (Ryberg 2007; Lever 2008).

Clearly, children are also sometimes at real danger from strangers. An implication of the quotation from Coates at the start of this chapter is that a society that abandons portions of its youth to gangs and gang warfare is a society culpable of neglect. However, it is not obvious what the solution is. The determination not to abandon communities to gangs, along with the fact that much gang-related behaviour is not specifically criminal, led the UK's Labour government to introduce new powers to impose Anti-Social Behaviour Orders (ASBOs). ASBOs could be imposed for non-criminal behaviour and were not subject to anything like the same standards of evidence as a criminal conviction. They could require individuals to refrain from entering certain areas, or from associating with certain people. Breaching an ASBO, however, was a criminal act, and one consequence of ASBOs was that many more young people ended up in the criminal justice system (Ashworth 2004). ASBOs have since been abolished, and are perhaps a lesson on how hard it is to use the coercive powers of the state to tackle the problem of gang culture and its associated violence.

The age of criminal responsibility

Children who commit seriously wrongful or harmful actions may be dealt with in a number of ways; formal prosecution is only one possibility. Children over the age of criminal responsibility are liable to be charged and required to appear in court should they commit a criminal offence (or be suspected of having done so). It is often the case that children attend different courts from adults, and that the regimes of punishment are different. The main philosophical question here concerns the capacities an agent has to have to make the distinctive apparatus of criminal prosecution appropriate, and at what age it is reasonable to think that a person will have developed those capacities (Weijers and Duff 2002; von Hirsch 2009; Ryberg 2014). The main candidates for the capacity in question would appear to be:

a) the capacity to know what one was doing;
b) the capacity to know that what one was doing was against the law;
c) the capacity to know that what one was doing was morally wrong; and
d) the capacity to have some insight into why what one was doing was morally wrong.

According to Duff's influential account, the criminal process is marked by moral communication (Duff 1986). If the criminal sanction is, ideally, an expression of moral disapproval that the offender is meant to understand and receive as such, then it may be only when children develop an imaginative ability to feel remorse that they can properly be held criminally responsible.

Children in court

Children appear in court as defendants and as witnesses. As I noted above, courts are not easy places for adults, let alone children. However, it is perhaps hard to see how courts could be dispensed with entirely as long as the criminal justice system keeps to principles such as the presumption of innocence; the standard of proof "beyond reasonable doubt"; the principle of publicity (whereby criminal justice procedures have to be transparent and conducted in full public view); the right of defendants to confront their accusers in court; and the principle of orality (whereby evidence has to be presented in court orally by a witness whose mode of delivery can be scrutinised by the other participants). Each of these principles has some prima facie liberal justification in limiting state power and protecting the rights of defendants (Ashworth and Redmayne 2010). And they seem to count against the immediately appealing ways to protect children from the rigours of courtrooms, such as allowing children to present written evidence, or pre-filmed evidence. Similarly, cross-examination is a highly intimidating process to have to go through, and yet it is hard to see what the alternative is if we don't want to abandon the principle that convictions should be decided on by evidence presented in open court. This is by no means to say that there are no alternatives; simply that it will not be a straightforward matter to find them.

Even if it is impossible to avoid children being called as witnesses in criminal cases, the importance of diversionary procedures that avoid their ending up as defendants in court is widely recognised. One such procedure is the possibility of restorative justice, as depicted in our third case study (Campbell et al. 2006). When restorative justice is available, a child who is prepared to admit to an offence can avoid trial by agreeing to meet with the victim. In this meeting it is hoped that a more natural, less formally structured conversation might be possible about the impact of the offending behaviour, and that the child may have the chance to offer an apology and amends. While there are some problems with restorative justice in this context as a form of "coercive offer" in which contrition becomes compulsory, the restorative justice procedure contrasts positively with conventional criminal justice in retaining a clear relation to ordinary interpersonal forms of moral repair, such as apology and forgiveness (Bennett 2006).

Punishing children

Even in liberal Western societies, children and young people are routinely subject to custodial sentences. Normally this will involve specialist youth custody centres rather than adult prisons. As with adult incarceration, such regimes raise the question of whether those who are sent to such places have lost or forfeited rights to liberty and welfare (Walker 1991), but they might take on a different cast: on the one hand, children may not be thought to have such strong rights to self-determination (see ch. 9, ch. 10); on the other, the impact of incarceration on a child's future life may be that much greater. There are also questions about the meaningfulness and comprehensibility of forms of punishment that may be particularly sharp where children are concerned. One desideratum of a punishment – though often neglected – is that the offender should be able to understand its connection to their wrongdoing. Punishment should not be such as to prevent the offender from coming to see it as an expression of appropriate remorse. Where this desideratum is met, it is at least open to the punishment to play a progressive and beneficial role in the offender's life. However, although offenders can come to accept custody and "doing time" as the conventional response that follows conviction, it is hard to see that they can make moral sense of it as a way of making amends. This seems particularly likely to be true of children, who have not yet become hardened to the way the system treats them. In contrast to conventional modes of punishment such as imprisonment, restorative justice holds out the possibility of a settlement based on an intuitive understanding of what one might have to do to make things right (Van Ness and Strong 2014). The basic forms of interpersonal accountability that a child might learn in the family, the playground or the street, are not excluded but given an outlet when a child ends up in a face-to-face interaction with the victim of their offence.

It is also important to note that many people who end up in the criminal justice system – children included – have drug and mental health problems, and for them the criminal justice system has to be a form of care and support as well as a vehicle for justice. There are well-known debates about whether rehabilitation can and should be coercively imposed, and objections to open-ended rehabilitative treatments (von Hirsch 1976). Nevertheless, it seems undeniable that rehabilitative treatment should have a role in any youth justice system in which children often end up precisely because they have been failed elsewhere in their lives.

Conclusion

This chapter has given a brief survey of some of the many ethical and philosophical issues raised by the impact of criminal justice on children. Much discussion of children in political theory concerns the nature and value of the family, or the state's duties regarding education (see ch. 31).

By contrast, the present discussion has suggested that, in order to get a rounded picture of the relations between state and child, we need also to look at the diverse ways in which children are affected by the presence in society of institutions concerned with the labelling, prevention, investigation, prosecution and punishment of crime.

Notes

1 http://www.theguardian.com/uk-news/2016/apr/07/angela-wrightson-girls-tortured-alcoholic-hartlepool-life-sentences
2 Coates takes the phrase "those who think they are white" from Baldwin (1998).
3 This story is taken from the website of the Forgiveness Project: http://theforgivenessproject.com/stories/gwen-gibson-northern-ireland/

References

Alexander, M. 2010. *The New Jim Crow: Mass Incarceration in the Age of Colorblindness*. New York, NY: The New Press.
Ashworth, A. 2004. "Social Control and 'Anti-Social Behaviour': the Subversion of Human Rights?," *Law Quarterly Review* 120: 263–291.
Ashworth, A., and Redmayne, M. 2010. *The Criminal Process*, 4th edn. Oxford: Oxford University Press.
Baggatini, A., and MacLeod, C. (eds.). 2014. *The Nature of Children's Well-Being: Theory and Practice*. Dordrecht: Springer.
Baldwin, J. 1998. "On Being 'White' … And Other Lies," in D. R. Roediger (ed.), *Black on White: Black Writers on What It Means to be White*. New York, NY: Schocken.
Bennett, C. 2006. "Taking the Sincerity Out of Saying Sorry: Restorative Justice as Ritual," *Journal of Applied Philosophy* 23: 127–143.
Braithwaite, J. 1989. *Crime, Shame and Reintegration*. Cambridge: Cambridge University Press.
Brighouse H., and Swift, A. 2014. *Family Values: The Ethics of Parent-Child Relationships*. Princeton, NJ: Princeton University Press.
Campbell, C., Devlin, R., O'Mahoney, D., Doak, J., Jackson, J., Corrigan, T., and McEvoy, K. 2006. *Evaluation of the Northern Ireland Youth Conference Service*. Belfast: Northern Ireland Office.
Canadian Association of Physicians for the Environment (CAPE). 2000. "We're Allowing Environmental Child Abuse." Retrieved from https://cape.ca/environmental-child-abuse/ (last accessed 19 March 2018).
Christie, N. 1977. "Conflicts as Property," *British Journal of Criminology* 17: 1–15.
Coates, T.-N. 2015. *Between the World and Me*. Melbourne: Text Publishing.
Cohen, S., and Young, J. (eds.). 1973. *The Manufacture of News: Social Problems, Deviance and the Mass Media*. London: Constable.
Condry, R., Kotova, A., and Minson, S. 2016. "Collateral Damage: The Families and Children of Prisoners," in Y. Jewkes, J. Bennett and B. Crewe (eds.), *The Handbook on Prisons*, 2nd edn. Abingdon: Routledge.
Delgado, R. 1987. "The Ethereal Scholar: Does Critical Legal Studies Have What Minorities Want?," *Harvard Civil Rights-Civil Liberties Law Review* 22: 301–322.
Duff, R. A. 1986. *Trials and Punishments*. Cambridge: Cambridge University Press.
Duff, R. A. 2013a. "Legal Punishment," *Stanford Encyclopedia of Philosophy*. Retrieved from http://plato.stanford.edu/entries/legal-punishment/ (last accessed 19 March 2018).
Duff, R. A. 2013b. "Theories of Criminal Law," *Stanford Encyclopedia of Philosophy*. Retrieved from http://plato.stanford.edu/entries/criminal-law/ (last accessed 19 March 2018).
Dzur, A. 2015. *Punishment, Participatory Democracy and the Jury*. Oxford: Oxford University Press.
Ferguson, K., Cassells, R. C., MacAllister, J. W., and Evans, G. W. 2013. "The Physical Environment and Child Development: an International Review," *International Journal of Psychology* 48: 437–468.
Finkelhor, D., and Ormrod, R. 2000. "Characteristics of Crimes Against Juveniles," *Office of Juvenile Justice and Delinquency Prevention Juvenile Justice Bulletin* (June). Washington, DC: US Department of Justice.
Gheaus, A. 2015. "Unfinished Adults and Defective Children: On the Nature and Value of Childhood," *Journal of Ethics and Social Philosophy* 9: 1–21.
Hale, C. 1996. "Fear of Crime: A Review of the Literature," *International Review of Victimology* 4: 79–150.
Hampton, J. 1984. "The Moral Education Theory of Punishment," *Philosophy and Public Affairs* 13: 208–238.

Hampton, J. 1991. "Correcting Harms Versus Righting Wrongs: The Role of Retribution," *UCLA Law Review* 39: 1659–1702.
Jay, A. 2014. *Independent Inquiry into Child Sexual Exploitation in Rotherham 1997–2013*. Retrieved from http://www.rotherham.gov.uk/downloads/file/1407/indepencse_in_rotherham (last accessed 19 March 2018).
Larson, D. 2013. "Why Scandinavian Prisons Are Superior," *The Atlantic*. Retrieved from http://www.theatlantic.com/international/archive/2013/09/why-scandinavian-prisons-are-superior/279949/ (last accessed 19 March 2018).
Lever, A. 2008. "Mrs Aremac and the Camera: A Response to Ryberg," *Res Publica* 14: 35–42.
Marx, K. 1968. "Preface to A Contribution to the Critique of Political Economy," in K. Marx and F. Engels (eds.), *Selected Works*. London: Lawrence and Wishart.
Minson S., Nadin, R., and Earle, J. 2015. "Sentencing of Mothers: Improving the Sentencing Process and Outcomes for Women with Dependent Children," *Prison Reform Trust Discussion Paper*. Retrieved from http://www.prisonreformtrust.org.uk/Portals/0/Documents/sentencing_mothers.pdf (last accessed 19 March 2018).
Norrie, A. 1991. *Law, Ideology and Punishment*. Dordrecht: Kluwer.
Radzik, L. 2009. *Making Amends: Atonement in Law and Morality*. Oxford: Oxford University Press.
Rawls, J. 1971. *A Theory of Justice*. Oxford: Oxford University Press.
Reiman, J., and Leighton, P. 2012. *The Rich Get Richer and the Poor Get Prison: Ideology, Class and Criminal Justice*, 10th ed. London: Routledge.
Rock, P. 1993. *The Social World of an English Crown Court: Witnesses and Professionals in the Crown Court Centre at Wood Green*. Oxford: Clarendon Press.
Ryberg, J. 2007. "Privacy Rights, Crime Prevention, CCTV, and the Life of Mrs Aremac," *Res Publica* 13: 127–143.
Ryberg J. 2014. "Punishing Adolescents: On Immaturity and Diminished Responsibility," *Neuroethics* 7: 327–336.
Schapiro, T. 1999. "What Is a Child?," *Ethics* 109: 715–738.
Taylor, G. 1985. *Pride, Shame and Guilt*. Oxford: Clarendon Press.
Van Ness, D., and Strong, K. H. 2014. *Restoring Justice*, 5th edn. London: Routledge.
von Hirsch, A. 1976. *Doing Justice: The Choice of Punishments*. Boston, MA: Northeastern University Press.
von Hirsch, A. 2009. "Reduced Penalties for Juveniles: the Normative Dimension," in A. von Hirsch, A. Ashworth, and J. V. Roberts (eds.), *Principled Sentencing: Readings on Theory and Policy*, 3rd edn. Oxford: Hart.
Wacquant, L. 2009. *Punishing the Poor: the Neo-Liberal Government of Social Insecurity*. Durham, NC: Duke University Press.
Walker, N. 1991. *Why Punish?* Oxford: Oxford University Press.
Walker, M. 2006. *Moral Repair*. Cambridge: Cambridge University Press.
Weijers I., and Duff, R. A. (eds.). 2002. *Punishing Juveniles: Principle and Critique*. Oxford: Hart.
Young, I. M. 1990. *Justice and the Politics of Difference*. Princeton, NJ: Princeton University Press.

36
CHILDREN AND WAR

Cécile Fabre

Introduction

Children are the main victims of war. They are deliberately targeted by combatants; they are used as shields; they are killed as collateral damage, for example when a bomb lands on their school; they are routinely raped and physically abused by soldiers; they are often forced to flee their homes, and suffer disproportionately from war-induced hunger, thirst and diseases; war leaves them orphans, resource-less and at the mercy of the economic-cum-sexual predatory practices of adults. At the same time, it is estimated that there are several dozens of thousands of child soldiers worldwide, some of whom commit atrocities.[1] Notwithstanding the crimes which they commit, and as we shall see throughout this paper, those children too are victims, precisely for that reason.

The victimisation of children is morally egregious – in some respects more egregious still than the victimisation of adults. My aim in this chapter is twofold: to provide strong philosophical support for this intuition, and to highlight some important ethical issues arising from children's involvement in and exposure to war. In the second section, I defend the view that killing children, whether intentionally or not, is morally worse, other things equal, than killing adults. In the third section, I tackle the difficult issues raised by children who actively participate in armed conflicts. I defend the standard prohibition on child enlistment. But I also argue that, once children have been enlisted, it is morally permissible to kill them in self- or other-defence if they commit wrongful killings.

Two preliminary remarks. First, we need a rough and ready definition of a child, as distinct from an adult. Countries differ with respect to majority thresholds, and apply different age thresholds for different activities (permission to have sex no earlier than 16, right to vote no earlier than 18, etc.) I follow international practice, notably the 1989 United Nations (UN) Convention on the Rights of the Child, and define a child, in the context of war, as a human being under the age of 18 unless his or her country of citizenship has set a different majority threshold for the purpose of enlistment. This is unavoidably arbitrary, but one has to start somewhere.

Second, there is more to say about children and war than I can do here. In particular, the post-war rehabilitation and re-incorporation of children into civilian life are crucially important issues. I focus on the role and status of children during the war partly for lack of space but also and largely because it is there, I think, that philosophy has the most to say.

Children as non-combatants

Some of the harms which befall children in war are inflicted deliberately; others are an unintentional, albeit foreseen, side effect of military operations. In this section, I first provide support for the claim that children may not be deliberately harmed but that they may be harmed as a foreseen though unintended side effect of military operations, subject to various constraints. I then consider whether it matters to our moral assessment of harming in war that victims are children rather than adults. Throughout, for ease of exposition, I tackle that question by reference to killing: unless otherwise specified, the conclusions I reach with respect to lethal harm also apply to the case of non-lethal harm.

Just war theory's central question is that of the grounds upon which, if any, human beings may be harmed in general, and killed in particular, in and because of war. Just war theorists all endorse in its most general form the principle of non-combatant immunity, whereby non-combatants, who as such do not threaten, or contribute to threatening, the enemy, are not legitimate targets in war. This is why prisoners of war, or soldiers who are *hors de combat*, may not be killed *deliberately*. This is also why civilians who do not take part in hostilities are not legitimate targets either. Just war theorists also endorse, again in its most general form, the view that unintentionally though foreseeably harming non-combatants in the course of a military mission is morally permissible, so long as the military mission stands a reasonable chance of succeeding at bringing about its stated ends, as it is a necessary means to bringing about those ends, and as the harms thus inflicted are not disproportionate to the goods thus realised. Thus, a tactical bomber pilot is not deemed to commit a war crime if he targets a munitions factory in the foreknowledge that some civilians will die in the bombing, so long as he does not intend their deaths. These requirements have long been subject to thorough scrutiny, notably in contemporary just war theory (Fabre 2009; Frowe and Long 2014; Lazar 2015; McMahan 2009; Walzer 1992). For my purposes here, however, it suffices to note, in the first instance, that the principle of non-combatant immunity straightforwardly supports a prohibition against deliberately killing children. Furthermore, the permission to inflict collateral harms on non-combatants extends to non-combating children.

At first glance, the latter claim might perhaps seem hasty. Suppose that we are waging a just war, in the course of which three scenarios present themselves. In the first scenario, the munitions factory is located near an adult-only club. In the second scenario, it is located near a primary school. In the third scenario, it is located near a small town populated with both adults and children. I suspect that some readers might lean towards the view that our pilot may proceed in *Adult Club*, but not in *Primary School* – indeed, not even in *Small Town*, on the grounds, precisely, that children live in this town who would be killed. However, objecting to bombing in *Small Town* is, in effect, to rule out most wars as unjust, since very few wars can successfully be fought without destroying civilian areas in which both adults and children live. Moreover, such bombings, and even in *Primary School*, *ex hypothesi* serve just ends, one of which is the protection of *other* children at the hands of unjust combatants. Narrowing the scope of the principle of collateral damage to the killing of adults and thus forbidding *all* instances of child killings does seem unduly restrictive, not least because it would, in effect, dictate in favour of banning any war in which our combatants might unintentionally kill children – in effect, most if not all wars – at the cost of rescuing children who would otherwise die at the hands of our enemies. Unless one thinks that killing is *always* morally worse than letting die, there must be occasions when going to war is morally justified overall, even if in so doing we end up killing children.

Still, the harming of children in war does elicit greater revulsion than the harming of adults. In war, age discrimination in favour of children is not regarded as morally controversial – on the contrary. Children's lives, it is often felt, matter more, other things equal, than adults' lives. For this reason, many would say that killing children is morally worse, *ceteris paribus*, than killing adults.[2]

So stated, the statement is ambiguous. It does not distinguish between the following three claims, all of which rest on the assumption that, in a given case, killing children and killing adults are both morally wrong:

(1) Death is worse *for the children who die* than it is *for the adults who die*, and killing a child is, thus, morally worse for that child than killing an adult is morally worse for that adult.
(2) The death of a child is worse than the death of an adult, and killing the child is, thus, morally worse than killing the adult, *from the point of view of other agents*, such as, for example, those individuals' nearest and dearest.
(3) The death of a child is worse than the death of an adult, and killing the child is morally worse than killing the adult, *from an impersonal point of view*.[3]

Let me question those views (without taking a firm stand on either of them): death might be worse for a 21-year-old than for a one-year-old – particularly death of which the former is aware of her impending fate. Likewise, a parent may find it far worse to lose his 21-year-old daughter than his one-year-old daughter, on the grounds that he has a fully developed relationship with the former, which he did not have with the latter. And yet from an impersonal point of view, the death of a child may matter more than the death of a young adult, for example because, assessed impersonally, it consists in the loss of more years of life overall.

When assessing the badness of death and the wrongness of killing, we must take those considerations into account; other factors are relevant too, such as the quality of the life that remains to be lived, the extent to which one has so far lived one's life well, the numbers of lives taken, and so on.[4] Reviewing *all* of those issues is beyond the scope of this section. My main focus is on one particular question: what difference, if any, does childhood *as such* make to the permissibility of killing in war?

Interestingly, neither the prohibition on the deliberate killing of non-combatants nor the permission to kill non-combatants unintentionally account for the relevance of childhood. In so far as the prohibition articulates in the context of war the more general principle that individuals who do not pose a threat of lethal harm ought not to be killed deliberately, it applies with the same stringency to all non-combatants, irrespective of their age. To the extent that an unarmed adult poses no greater threat to the enemy than an unarmed child, those two acts of deliberate killing are equally wrong at the bar of the principle. Likewise, the permission to kill non-combatants unintentionally does not in itself weigh more heavily in favour of the collateral killing of adults than on the side of the collateral killing of children.

To justify the relevance of childhood to the permissibility of killing in war, we must identify morally salient differences between innocent children and innocent adults which are pertinent to war. In the remainder of this section, I scrutinise four such differences, and show that they provide only partial support for the view that childhood *as such* is relevant.

First, adults are to some degree causally *responsible* for the war which their community wages on their behalf, indeed sometimes at their behest. They pay the taxes thanks to which the war can be waged, they elect representatives who vote for the war, they work in war-related jobs, and so on. This does not turn them into combatants; nor does this always warrant deliberately killing them. If the war which they help support is unjust, it does, however, warrant conferring lesser weight on their lives, when making targeting decisions, than on the lives of children who do not in any way participate in the war.

Second, most children are more *vulnerable* than most adults to the ills of war. They are less likely to know where to find guns to defend themselves from marauding enemy soldiers, less able physically to fight, less economically resourceful and more dependent, morally and materially, on any such help which adults are willing and able to give them.[5] But they are also less able than most adults to take evasive steps such as running quickly and for long, to hiding effectively, and so on. Their greater vulnerability than adult civilians makes it worse to kill them, and the younger the child, the morally worse the killing. However, by that token, it is morally worse to target a bedridden elderly adult than a robust 16-year-old. If the choice, then, is between bombing a military target which is located near a high school and one located near a nursing home, the vulnerability argument dictates against the latter and in favour of the former, *ceteris paribus*: of course, this is an extraordinarily invidious choice, but it might have to be made.

Third, even though not all children are more vulnerable to the ills of war than any adult, whatever age threshold we adopt as demarcating childhood from adulthood, all children by definition are *younger* than all adults. The point is blindingly obvious, yet highly relevant here. For it is appropriate, generally, to conceive of years of a worthwhile life as *distribuenda*, in so far as years of life afford opportunities to flourish. Suppose that there is only one liver for two patients in serious need of a transplant, and that one of the patients is a child while the other is an adult. Other things equal (such as the seriousness of the need and prospects for recovery), it is just, I think, to give the liver to the child rather than the adult: the latter has had more opportunities than the former to have a flourishing life. By implication, it would be more unjust to withhold the liver from the child than to withhold it from the adult. Those considerations apply not just to savings, but to killings as well, and support the view that killing children is worse than killing adults – both from the point of view of those children relative to the point of view of those adults, from the point of view of third parties such as relatives and from an impersonal point of view.

A final reason as to why killing children is generally worse than killing adults is this: killing children has very long lasting, *multigenerational effects*: the children who die today are not going to be the taxpayers, doctors, plumbers, engineers and teachers of tomorrow, upon whom the current generations and the not-yet-born will depend for their continuing social, economic and political existence. To be sure, not all of those children would grow up into those adults were we not to kill them. But some would, and the long-term harmful consequences of killing them – not for those children themselves, but for those who are left behind – ought to be taken into consideration.

Again, however, by that very same token, killing adults is worse than killing children in one important respect, numbers being roughly equal. Those adults are *today's* teachers, engineers, builders and doctors upon whom the still-alive here and now – notably children – depend. In some cases, in fact, leaving children without the protection of adults might be worse for those children than instant death at the ends of the enemy.[6]

With respect to multigenerational harms, thus, whether we should spare children to the detriment of adults or *vice versa* depends on two things. First, it depends on the extent to which having fewer years of life as a result of instant death is better or worse (from the person's point of view, her relatives' or the impersonal point of view) than having more years of a pain-filled life. Second, it depends on the extent to which one may or must give priority to the well-being here and now of current generations over their future well-being, the well-being of previous (co-existing) generations and the well-being of their successors. This is far too complex an issue to tackle within the scope of this paper. But it is worth highlighting, if only to draw attention to the fact that the question of whether or not children may justifiably be killed in war lies at the intersection of deeper and broader issues which are extensively studied independently of, but seldom in relation to, one another – to wit, the permissibility of killing in war, the distribution of years versus quality of life and intergenerational justice.

In summary, the fact that someone is a child does make some difference to the permissibility of killing her: the younger the child, the more difference it makes. However, none of the four considerations I have outlined in support of that claim (responsibility, vulnerability, years of life as a *distribuenda* and multigenerational effects) yield the strong view that killing a child is *always* morally worse than killing an adult. In any given case, were we in possession of all the relevant facts and able under fire to make fine-grained judgements about (*inter alia*) quality of life, degree of vulnerability, etc., we might have to conclude that killing a child is not as bad as killing an adult. Therein lies the difficulty. In practice, it is impossible to make such fine-grained judgments. When making targeting decisions, thus, belligerents run two different kinds of risk. On the one hand, they might decide to harm adults on the grounds that children have had fewer opportunities for a flourishing life, are generally more vulnerable, less responsible for the war and more important to their community's long-term future. In so doing, they run the risk of harming those adults to a much greater extent overall than the children would have been harmed had the converse decision been made. On the other hand, they might decide to harm children on the grounds that adults have a lesser chance of recovery, that the survival of adults here and now is in fact too important to the country's medium-term future, and so on. In so doing, they run the risks of harming children to a much greater extent than those adults would have been harmed had the converse decision been made. The question, then, is that of which risks are morally preferable. The issue of multigenerational harm seems to fare poorly as an action-guiding consideration: we simply do not and cannot know what might happen in 30 years from now if we kill x number of children versus y number of adults. By contrast, on balance, it is more likely that a given child is less responsible, more vulnerable and endowed with fewer years of a comparable life than a given adult. Under considerations of epistemic uncertainty, thus, responsibility, vulnerability and distributive justice seem to dictate in favour of sparing children as a matter of policy.

Children as participants in war

For all the suffering which they endure, some children are not *unambiguously* and *only* war victims: all too often they participate in it. They are used by adult soldiers in a variety of roles: messengers, cooks, sexual slaves, water carriers and, increasingly so, fighters thanks to the fact that lethal firearms are much lighter to carry than they used to be. They are plied with drinks and drugs, and are often forced to commit atrocities against their own families and neighbours as part of the 'enlisting process': taken together, their substance addiction and the reprisals to which they would be subject were they to return to their villages make them completely dependent on their commanding officers (Singer 2005).

The claim that sexually, physically and psychologically abusing children into becoming combatants is morally impermissible need not detain us here, so obviously true it is. I also assume that just as juvenile common criminals are both punished and rehabilitated once their sentence is served (or so is the aim), so should child soldiers who have committed war crimes, precisely because they are perpetrators as well as victims – though war crime trials may not be the most appropriate punitive channel for either. In this section, I tackle two ethical issues raised by the phenomenon of child soldiers: the ethics of non-abusively enlisting children into armed forces, and the ethics of killing child soldiers in war.

Let me turn to enlistment first. Children have always participated in wars. Until relatively recently, their incorporation into armed forces was a relatively normal phenomenon.

Yet, contemporary international *norms* – unlike contemporary *practices* – do not reflect the old consensus (Drumbl 2012: ch. 5). The Rome Statute of the International Criminal Court and the 2002 Optional Protocol to the 1989 UN Convention on the Rights of the Child stipulate that the incorporation of a child younger than 15 into the armed forces is a war crime, and urge signatories to ensure that youngsters aged 16–18 are neither conscripted nor, if voluntary enlisted, treated as direct participants into hostilities. The International Labour Organisation Minimum Age Convention is more demanding, stipulating as it does that the minimum age for employing someone in a dangerous occupation is 18. In practice, most countries permit enlistment at 17 or 18.[7]

What justification is there, then, for *not* permitting the enlistment of children? Consider voluntary enlistment. As a first cut, children (one might think) are simply incapable of making an informed, truly voluntary, un-coerced decision to expose themselves to the risks of joining the army. So stated, however, the argument is too quick. For a start, there are many dangerous things that children in the 16–18 age bracket, indeed younger, are morally permitted to do and/or that it is morally permissible to have them do (albeit subject to tighter constraints than adults face): having sex (with concomitant risks, from sex itself or resulting pregnancy, to life and health), embarking in dangerous sports such as rugby or American football, consenting to risky medical procedures (see ch. 12). The incapacity argument against military enlistment must capture what is specific about this particular decision such that, even if the risks to life and limbs are the same and/or similarly likely to eventuate, it is worse than inducing children into those practices/activities.

Enlistment clearly *is* harmful in many different ways. First, as the laws of war stand, members of armed forces are legitimate targets. As far as the morality of war is concerned, some argue that it matters not whether soldiers fight for an unjust cause: *qua* soldiers they are legitimate targets regardless (Walzer 1992); others maintain that they are legitimate targets only if they fight for an unjust cause (McMahan 2009). Either way, they *will* be so regarded, and that really is what matters. Second – and in these crucial respects enlistment differs from having sex and playing rugby – a child soldier participates in a lethal and often unjust enterprise. He, or she, is complicitous in acts of killing, indeed may well be led to commit such acts, with considerable costs to his or her moral integrity if those killings are unjust, and to his or her mental health whether or not the killings are just. Of course, in a given case, unwanted pregnancy resulting from consensual sex might turn out to be more harmful to a 16-year-old girl than spending a few years in a regiment without being deployed in a war zone. By and large, however, enlistment is psychologically and morally more risky than pregnancy, let alone sex itself and playing dangerous sports. To the extent that children are not capable of properly understanding and evaluating those risks, they are not capable of making a truly voluntary decision to enlist.

Admittedly, some children might in fact be able to do precisely that, particularly at the older end of the age scale. As a matter of public policy, however, the question is whether we should err on the side of protecting children who lack a claim to enjoy protection from the consequences of their bad decision, or on the side of not protecting those who do have such a claim. Under conditions of uncertainty and in the light of the potential damage which enlistment can cause to a child, it seems to me that we should err on the latter side, and thus reject child enlistment altogether. By the same token, of course, we should reject the enlistment of incapable adults.

Consider next child conscription. The incapacity argument and the worries about voluntariness which it articulates do not work against it. For if conscription in general is permissible, and if, thus, freedom from coercive enlistment is not a necessary condition for just enlistment, the fact that children cannot make a properly voluntary decision to enlist is irrelevant. Yet, conscripting children really does seem morally wrong. An argument against coercive child enlistment specifically must account for *that* intuition, whilst accommodating adult conscription. (Of course, conscription might be morally unjustified for reasons which apply to both children and adults equally. I want to assume for the sake of argument, however, that conscripting adults is morally permissible, and to show that the best justification for it does not licence the conscription of children.)

Conscription is best justified as follows (Rawls 1971: 380–81; Gewirth 1982: 251–53). Individuals are under moral duties to contribute their fair share to the provision of the public and non-excludable good of national defence. Conscription – in effect, the legal enforcement of that duty – ensures compliance (or no free-riding) and provides coordination. On that view, conscription is justified only if and to the extent that there is a moral obligation to take part in the war effort: it justifiably sweeps in its net only those who are under the relevant moral duties. However, and this is crucial, children are not under those duties. For a start, very young children lack the requisite capacity for rational and moral agency, are not responsive to reasons and, thus, are not bearers of duties in general. Moreover, up until the age of 18, children are not considered mature enough to enjoy the rights and privileges of citizenship, notably the right to vote (see chs. 9, 34). If they are not deemed capable of participating, even if only indirectly through electing representatives, in decisions to go to war, then it is hard to see how they could, nevertheless, be deemed to be under an obligation to fight in that war. Admittedly, some children, particularly on the older end of the scale, are in fact appropriately held under those duties. Here again, though, as a matter of public policy, the question is whether we should err on the side of protecting children who lack a claim not to be conscripted, or on the side of not protecting those who do have such a claim. For reasons adduced in connection with non-coerced enlistment, we should err on the latter side and thus ban child conscription altogether – as well as, by the same token, the conscription of adults who lack rational and moral agency.

So much, then, for child enlistment. Even though there are good reasons for not permitting it, the fact is that children do take an active part in war, as members of regular or, more often these days, irregular armed forces. Studies suggest that in recent and current conflicts, only a minority carry weapons and are deployed on frontlines (Drumbl 2012: ch. 3). But when those children are actually engaged in combat, they present their enemies – notably their adult enemies – with a dilemma which to some might seem insoluble, between defending themselves or their comrades by killing a child, and letting the child survive but risking death/serious harm to themselves or others. What, then, may or should they do?

On some accounts, an agent loses his right not to be killed only if he is morally responsible for subjecting someone to an unjustified lethal threat (e.g., Otsuka 1994). Children (it is said) lack the capacity for moral and rational agency, are therefore not morally responsible for the threat which they pose and therefore have not lost their right not to be killed (McMahan 2009: 200–1). Moreover, if, as it is plausible to aver, extreme duress exculpates an agent who kills an innocent person, a child who is told, for example, that his entire family will be massacred under his eyes unless he commits atrocities, is not responsible for so acting either, and thus has not lost his right not to be killed as a means to protect his intended victims.

On this picture, childhood is seen without much differentiation between its different ages as an innocent, morally untroubled state; and child soldiers in particular are seen as passive victims, necessarily coerced into fighting, without exercising control over their fate, at the mercy of the adults around them. But this is not how it is. For without wanting to deny that many child soldiers are indeed vulnerable in this way, some are not. In particular, child soldiers who actually fight on the front line tend to be teenagers, not young children; as teenagers, their capacity for rational and moral agency is closer to that of an adult (Drumbl 2012: ch. 2; Vaha 2011). Even if it is true that agents who are not morally responsible for their actions have not lost their right not to be killed, more children than we might be prepared to acknowledge are to some degree responsible for their actions and, thus, have lost their right not to be killed. To be sure, of those, most have been very badly abused. But then again, *by that point itself*, so have their adult comrades, and we do not say of those that they are not responsible for their actions.

Alternatively, one could accept this Western, post-17th-century conception of childhood (Ariès 1962; Archard 2004), and thus hold that (most) child soldiers are not morally responsible for their actions, yet maintain that they have lost their right not to be killed – simply in virtue of the fact that they subject some innocent third party to an unjustified lethal threat: they need not be in any way morally responsible for it (Frowe 2014; Quong 2009; Fabre 2012: 56–58). So long as a child poses just such a threat, he has lost his right not to be killed – even if he is acting under the influence of drugs, alcohol or both, even if he acts under extreme duress and however young he is (Gade 2011).

Crucially, the view that we are morally permitted to kill child soldiers is entirely compatible with the claim that we may not blame those children for so acting, and that we ought not to punish them *ex post* as we would punish morally responsible adults. It is also compatible with the claim that, given a choice between killing child soldiers and killing adult combatants, other things equal we certainly ought to opt for the latter; and things would have to be considerably unequal before we would be licenced to opt for the former. Finally, that view is also entirely compatible with yet another claim which I take to be correct: as a soldier defending myself from those children, I ought to incur greater risk to myself when confronting them than if they were morally culpable for their actions (McMahan 2006: 48–49.) For example, if I have a choice between killing five children but running a risk of being wounded in the process, and killing ten children at no risk to myself, I ought (other things equal) to do the former, not the latter.

Here is a difficult question. Assuming that I (a soldier) am morally permitted to kill enemy child soldiers who pose unjust lethal threats, am I also morally obliged to do so? If I desist, as some soldiers have been known to do (Coleman 2011), other innocent third parties will die at the hands of the children. This is particularly problematic when I am under a *prima facie* duty to protect those third parties – for example, my comrades-in-arms, or (in a war of humanitarian intervention or robust peacekeeping operations) innocent civilians, including children, caught into the crossfires. If I am under an independently justified duty to protect others from children's lethal actions, and if killing children who pose a wrongful lethal threat is morally permissible, then it seems that I ought to kill them (Zupan 2011).

Conclusion

In this paper, I have defended the intuitions that the killing of innocent children is generally worse than the killing of innocent adults, that child enlistment is morally objectionable, but that killing child soldiers is (sometimes) morally permissible. Childhood matters particularly in so far as it is indicative of lesser responsibility, greater vulnerability (see ch. 27) and fewer opportunities (measured in years yet to live) for a flourishing life. As we saw throughout, however, some of those considerations (notably lack of responsibility and vulnerability) also apply to adults who are similar to children in those ways. This is important, for however awful we find the suffering to which children are subject in war, whether they fight or not, there is no reason in principle to draw a thick red line between *all* adults on the one hand, and *all* children on the other hand. In practice, however, if we have to choose between killing adults and killing children under conditions of epistemic uncertainty, we have strong reasons to spare the latter at the expense, unfortunately, of the former.

I am aware that some of my lines of questioning/arguments may have appeared tasteless, repugnant even. It might have appeared repugnant, for example, to ask, as I did, how children's lives should be weighted towards adults' lives, or whether adult, fully grown soldiers are morally permitted to kill ten-year-old soldiers high on amphetamines. The taking of children's lives is morally horrible, period – and there comes a point where, confronted with this kind of awfulness, philosophising from the comfort of one's office seems a pointless enterprise. Still, civilian leaders, high-ranking officers at general headquarters and soldiers on the grounds do not have the luxury of not formulating judgments about what they ought to do when confronted with children, and cannot afford not to act on the basis of those judgments. If we believe, as we must, that those leaders and those ordinary soldiers are answerable to us, their fellow and civilian citizens, then the least that we can do is precisely to spend a few uncomfortable hours thinking about the issue.[8]

Notes

1 See, e.g., press reports at http://www.voanews.com/content/unicef-says-children-main-victims-of-war/2459908.html; https://www.warchild.org.uk/issues/child-soldiers?gclid=CKue8pG5rcgCFQic2wodQEYPYQ; https://childrenandarmedconflict.un.org/effects-of-conflict/six-grave-violations/killing-and-maiming/; http://www.unicef.org.uk/UNICEFs-Work/What-we-do/war-conflict/
2 The view I am describing here does not rely on the assumption that children have higher moral status than adults: it could be that they do have the same moral status, but that in some cases, a child ought to be given priority over an adult (as, in fact, I shall argue below). On the moral status of children, see ch. 6.
3 Note that I am *assuming* for the sake of argument that killing children and adults is morally wrong. This assumption is crucial, for it is not entailed by the claim that death is bad for those agents. (There is no reason to suppose that death is *not* bad for the morally culpable attacker whom one is permitted to kill.)
4 On the badness of death and related issues, see, *inter alia*, McMahan (2002: ch. 2); Nagel (1970); Bradley, Feldman, and Johansson (2012).
5 Some might worry that in so describing children and adults as more or less able to harm their attackers, I am turning them into combatants. I am not so sure: defending oneself or some other party as a one-off act does not make one a combatant.
6 I owe this point to Alejandro Chehtman.
7 http://www.child-soldiers.org/international_standards.php
8 I am very grateful to Gideon Calder, Alejandro Chehtman, Jurgen De Wispelaere, Anca Gheaus, and Patrick Tomlin for their helpful comments on earlier drafts.

References

Archard, D. 2004. *Children: Rights, and Childhood.* London: Routledge.
Ariès, P. 1962. *Centuries of Childhood.* Harmondsworth: Penguin.
Bradley, B., Feldman, F., and Johansson, J. (eds.). 2012. *The Oxford Handbook of the Philosophy of Death.* New York, NY: Oxford University Press.
Coleman, S. 2011 "The Child Soldier," *Journal of Military Ethics* 10: 316–316.
Drumbl, M. 2012. *Reimagining Child Soldiers in International Law and Policy.* Oxford: Oxford University Press.
Fabre, C. 2009. "Guns, Food, and Liability to Attack," *Ethics* 120: 36–63.
Fabre, C. 2012. *Cosmopolitan War.* Oxford: Oxford University Press.
Frowe, H. 2014. *Defensive Killing.* Oxford: Oxford University Press.
Frowe, H., and Long, G. (eds.). 2014. *How We Fight.* Oxford: Oxford University Press.
Gade, E. K. 2011. "The Child Soldier: The Question of Self-Defence," *Journal of Military Ethics* 10: 323–326.
Gewirth, A. 1982. *Human Rights.* Chicago, IL: University of Chicago Press.
Lazar, S. 2015. *Sparing Civilians.* Oxford: Oxford University Press.
McMahan, J. 2002. *The Ethics of Killing: Problems at the Margins of Life.* New York, NY: Oxford University Press.
McMahan, J. 2006. "Killing in War: A Reply to Walzer," *Philosophia* 34(1): 47–51.

McMahan, J. 2009. *Killing in War*. Oxford: Oxford University Press.
Nagel, T. 1970. "Death," *Noûs* 4(1): 73–80.
Otsuka, M. 1994. "Killing the Innocent in Self-Defense," *Philosophy & Public Affairs* 23: 74–94.
Quong, J. 2009. "Killing in Self-Defence," *Ethics* 119: 507–537.
Rawls, J. 1971. *A Theory of Justice*. Cambridge, MA: Harvard University Press.
Singer, P. W. 2005. *Children at War*. New York, NY: Pantheon Books.
Vaha, M. 2011. "Child Soldiers and Killing in Self-Defence: Challenging the 'Moral View' on Killing in War," *Journal of Military Ethics* 10: 36–52.
Walzer, M. 1992. *Just and Unjust Wars: A Moral Argument with Historical Illustrations*. New York, NY: Basic Books.
Zupan, D. 2011. "The Child Soldier: Negligent Response to a Threat," *Journal of Military Ethics* 20: 320–322.

INDEX

abstract concepts, language acquisition 28–31
abuse *see* child protection
adolescence: brain functioning 3, 33–40; cultural context 36–38, 39–41; health issues 379–380; historical construction 38–39; history, culture and neuroscience 39–40; and paternalism 127; pubertal development 376; sexuality 273–274; social context 37–38
adoption 5, 213, 221–222; characterisation of 213–215; claim for increased resources 215–216; and decision to procreate 155; legitimate expectations 218–220; licensing of parenting 203–204, 206, 209, 217–218, 220–221; protection of children 220–221; regulating the adoption triad 217–218; right to parent 163, 164–166; transracial 255–257
advantage: parental partiality 181–182; tensions with egalitarianism 185–188
age: consent 135–136, 138–143; criminal responsibility 402; meaning of "child" 113; sexuality of children 271–272, 274–275; voting rights of children 386–388; *see also* adolescence; babies; child development; young children
agency: disabilities 263–264; health issues 378–380; limits of paternalism 176; looked-after children 369–370; metric of justice 320–322; voting rights 389
Almond, Brenda 192
altruism, decision to procreate 151–152
animal abuse 285
animals: autonomy of 117; full moral status (FMS) 71–73; and rights 104
animals and children 6; capacity contract 282–284; citizenship 283–284, 287–288, 291; political inclusion 287–288; reimagining the future 288–291; shared social worlds 284–287
anticipatory autonomy rights 120

antinatalism 154–155, 215; *see also* decision to procreate
Anti-Social Behaviour Orders (ASBOs) 401–402
Archard, David: families 192–193; licensing of parenting 208, 209; looked-after children 367; parent–child relationship 2; paternalism 130; sexuality of children 274
A-rights 108–109
Aristotle: children's engagement with philosophy 55; well-being 91–92
Arneson, Richard 68, 320, 321
Arnheim, Rudolf 46, 50
art by children 3, 45; authenticity 47–48; children as artists 48–50; as a cipher 46; as a creative response to the world 46; distinctions between adult and child art 51; pedagogy and ontogeny 45–46; as a way of seeing 46–47
assent 142; *see also* consent
assisted reproductive technologies (ART) 214, 216
attention deficit hyperactivity disorder (ADHD) 35–36
autonomy 4, 112–113, 120–121; application to children 115–118; health issues 377–380; importance of children's status 118–120; meaning of 113–115; meaning of "child" 113; open future 107–109; paternalism 124–127, 131; and rights 102–104, 108, 109; schooling 353–354; vulnerability of children 312–313

babies: health issues 379; knowledge development 13–14; language acquisition in the womb 23–24; and rights 103, 104, 105; *see also* child development
Barnes, Elizabeth 262–263
Baudelaire, Charles 46, 47

Index

Bayne, Tim 154, 160
beliefs 16–17; *see also* knowledge in childhood; make believe
Benatar, David 154–155
benevolent interference 123–125, 127–128, 129–130; *see also* paternalism
best interests of children 1–2; child labour 298–299; decision to procreate 153–154; good parenting 172–174; paternalism 129–131; political neutrality 335–336; right to parent 176–177; taking children into care 364–368; *see also* well-being
biological parents: vs. adoption process 214, 218–220; family structure 191–192, 194–197; genetic endowments 182; good parenting 170–172; licensing 202, 204–211; looked-after children 369; reproductive technologies 194, 214; right to parent 162–163, 164–166
biologism 202, 207, 216
biology: adolescent brain functioning 3, 33–40; full moral status (FMS) 72–73; *see also* child development
Blake, William 46
Blustein, Jefferey 2
Boccaccio, Giovanni 46–47
Bou-Habib, Paul 188
brain functioning, adolescence 3, 33–40; *see also* knowledge in childhood
Brake, Elizabeth 193–194
Brennan, Samantha 94, 110, 322
Brighouse, Harry: decision to procreate 155; families 193; good parenting 174, 175; love 231; parental partiality 187–188; right to parent 163; value of children/childhood 81; vulnerability of children 309, 312; well-being 94, 97
Brown, Alexander 219
Brown, Michael, murder case 395–396

capability approach 319, 325, 343–344
capacity contract, animals and children 282–284
Caplan, Bryan 151–152, 154
care for parents *see* filial duties
carefreeness 96, 97, 98
carer relationships 193–194
care system *see* looked-after children
Carey, Susan 28
causal knowledge 15–16
childbirth, biological mother 197
child-centred theories, right to parent 160, 163, 164–166
child-child trade-offs 221
child development: art by children 45–46; and child labour 298–299; full moral status (FMS) 69–70; health issues 375–377; knowledge in childhood 13–17; language acquisition 23, 24–31; puberty 376; punishment 397–398; well-being 91
childhood, and moral status *see* moral status of childhood
childhood, nature of 3; *see also* value of children/childhood
child labour *see* labour, children in
"child", meaning of 113, 374, 406
child protection: adoption 220–221; and animals 285; health issues 378–380; licensing of parenting 202, 205–206, 208; and rights 105–107; taking children into care 364–368; victims of crime 401–402; *see also* state intervention
childrearing *see* parenting
children and parents *see* decision to procreate; parent–child relationship
children/childhood in philosophy 1–2
children in society *see* society and children
child rights *see* rights of children
child's best interests *see* best interests of children
child soldiers 410–413; *see also* war and children
Chomsky, Noam 24–25, 26
citizenship: animals and children 283–284, 287–288, 291; political neutrality 333–335; schooling 355–356; voting rights 389
Clayton, Matthew: autonomy 114–115, 120; metric of justice 324; right to parent 164
Coates, Ta-Nehisi's memoir 395–397, 400–401
coercion: age of consent 135; schooling 351–353
cognition: brain functioning in adolescence 3, 33–40; cognitive disabilities 267–268; moral status of childhood 69–75; political inclusion 385; *see also* knowledge in childhood; language acquisition
Cohen, G. A. 320–322
commonsense views, moral status of childhood 69–70
communication *see* language acquisition
competency: good parenting 176–177; licensing of parenting 203, 204–211; political inclusion 385–387
complementarity, value of children/childhood 87
Conly, Sarah 152
conscription in war 411–412
consent 134–135, 143; age and capacity 135–136, 138–143; and assent 142; medicine 137–138, 141–142; open future 143; paternalism 124, 125, 129, 130–131; political legitimacy 137–138; research 142–143; sex 137–141, 274, 278; weight of 137
consequentialist reasons, procreation 150–151, 152
constructivism, art by children 46
consumerism, schooling 352–353
contraception 276
Cook, Philip 197–198
co-parenting 197–198

417

costs of children 339, 348; adoption 216; sharing costs, case for 342–347; which costs and interests 340–342
courts, children in 402–403
Craig, Edward 18
Crawford, Jim 153–154
creativity 46; *see also* art by children; make believe
C-rights 108–109
criminal justice 8, 395, 403–404; age of consent 138; case studies of children 395–397; and childhood 397–398; children in the system 401–403; child's social environment 398–401
cultural context: adolescent brain 36–38, 39–41; decision to procreate 148, 149–150; education 253–254

deafness 261, 265, 267
decision making: adolescent brain 34–35; age of consent 135–136; autonomy 113–114; limits of paternalism 176; and paternalism 127–129; *see also* consent
decision to procreate 4, 147, 156; antinatalism and criticisms 154–155; cited reasons 149–150; evaluating reasons 150–151; the good of the child 153–154; more children 151–152; skepticism about the debate 147–149; virtue ethics 152–153; *see also* right to parent
democracy 384, 388–389; *see also* political inclusion
democratic equality 390–391
deontological reasons, procreation 150–151
dependency: disabilities 263–264; parent–child relationship 307–312; *see also* vulnerability of children
developmentalism 94–95
developmental psychology, art by children 45–46; *see also* child development
De Wispelaere, Jurgen 209–210
disabilities 6, 260, 268; definition of 261–263; dependency, vulnerability and agency 263–264; education 266–267; moral status of children with cognitive disabilities 267–268; parental love and care 264–265; parents' disabilities 265–266; sex education 278–279
disciplinary context, children/childhood in philosophy 1–2
discrimination: disabilities 261–263; gender and the family 227–228; gendered division of labour 230–232; licensing of parenting 204–211; prejudice against children 36–37, 61–62, 251–252; race 251–252; *see also* equality of opportunity
diversity, and sex education 277
division of labour, gender roles 230–232
division of moral labor 173–174
divorced parents 198
drawing *see* art by children
dual-interest accounts, right to parent 163–164, 165–166

Duff, Anthony 402
duties 2; adoption 216; and gender 233–234; good parenting 172–174; parental partiality 184–185; procreation 149; and rights 101–102, 103; right to parent 160–161; sharing costs of children 346–347; vulnerability of children 312–313; *see also* filial duties
Dworkin, Ronald 138, 319–320, 321

eco-gluttony 152
economic context: child labour 296–298; equality of opportunity 162; schooling as preparation 354–355; *see also* costs of children; public money
education 8; adolescent brain 35; and child labour 296–298, 299; disabled children 266–267; good parenting 173; meaning of 351–352; parental partiality 181, 182, 185–186; political neutrality 331–335; racial context 252–254; sex education 276–279; value of philosophy 59–60; *see also* knowledge in childhood; language acquisition; philosophy, children's engagement with; schooling
egalitarianism: impartiality 183–184; tensions with parental advantages 185–188
emotions, decision to procreate 147, 150
employment: animals and children 290–291; gender and the family 230–231, 232–233; *see also* labour, children in
Engster, Daniel 208–209
enlistment in war 410–411, 412
entity's own sake 67–68
environmentalism: animals and children 288–289; decision to procreate 152; overpopulation 340, 348
epigenetics 37–38, 194–195
epistemic injustice 61–62
epistemic openness 57–59
epistemology *see* knowledge in childhood
equality, democratic 390–391
equality, metric of justice 318–319
equality of opportunity: looked-after children 368–370; parental partiality 181–188; prejudice against children 36–37, 61–62, 251–252; right to parent 162; schooling 355–357; sharing costs of children 342–346; *see also* discrimination; justice towards children
evils, pity towards children 96–99
evolutionary psychology 15
explicit knowledge 20
externalities, schooling 354–355

fabricated illness case 381–382
fair life chances 368–370
fairness *see also* justice
families: children as necessary to 193–194; composition of 191–192, 198–199;

418

criminal justice system 400–401; form and function 192–193; genetics 191–192, 194–197; health issues 380–382; looked-after children 363, 363–364, 369; parental partiality 187–188; parents' relationship 197–198; political neutrality 336–337; right to parent 158–159, 161–162; *see also* gender and the family; parent–child relationship
Feinberg, Joel: autonomy 120; paternalism 125–126, 127–128; rights 103, 108
feminism: gender roles 230–231; toys and gender 226–227, 229–230
filial duties 5, 236, 243–244; case study 241–243; definitions and distinctions 236–238; disabled parents 266; friendship account 239–241, 243; and gender 233–234; gratitude account 238–239, 242–243; special goods account 241, 242–243
finances *see* costs of children; public money
Fineman, Martha 194, 198, 305
Fishkin, James 368–369
Fogg-Davis, Hawley 256–257
Folbre, Nancy 339
fostering, licensing of parenting 203–204, 206, 209
Fowler, Timothy 324–325
Frankfurt, Harry 114
freedom *see* autonomy; liberty
Freud, Sigmund 273
Fricker, Miranda 61
Friedrich, Daniel 215–216
friendship account, filial duties 239–241, 243
Frisch, Lawrence 208, 209
full moral status (FMS) 68–75; *see also* moral status of childhood
functional MRI (fMRI), adolescent brain 33–34
funding *see* costs of children; public money
future options: consent 143; for the good of a child 129–131; paternalism 131; rights of children 107–109

gamete donation 195–196
gang warfare 401–402
Gelman, Susan 28
gender and the family 5, 225–226, 234; child's gender 226–230; gender roles 230–233; good parenting 171–172; policy responses to unequal gender roles 231–233; rigid norms 233–234; sexuality of children 275
gender variant 225–230
genetic endowments 182
genetic procreation 164–166; *see also* biological parents
genetic relatedness 170–171, 194–197
genetics of race 250
gestational procreation 164–166
Gheaus, Anca 82–83, 84, 312, 323
Gibson, Gwen theft case 396
Gillick principle 137, 138, 141–142, 143

goals: autonomy 116–117; paternalism 126
Goodin, Robert 304, 309, 310, 311–312
good parenting 169–170, 177; competency 176–177; duties 172–174; genetic relatedness 170–171; limits of paternalism 175–176; love 174; number of parents 172; sexual orientation and gender 171–172; shaping children's convictions 175; who 170
goods: looked-after children 369; metric of justice 318–325, 322–325; parental partiality 182; schooling 352, 354–355; vulnerability of children 308–312; *see also* best interests of children
Gopnik, Alison 58–59
government *see* public money; state intervention
Gutmann, Amy 355
gratitude account, filial duties 238–239, 242–243

Hampton, Jean 398
Hancock, Justin 278
Hannan, Sarah 87, 96, 97–99, 306, 309
happiness: value of children/childhood 84; well-being of children 94–96; *see also* hedonism
hard paternalism 128
harm: child labour 295–298; criminal justice 399–400; political neutrality 335–336; taking children into care 364–368; vulnerability of children 305; war 407–408
Haslanger, Sally 256–257
healthcare 8; animals and children 283–284, 289; disabilities 261
health issues in children 373–374, 382–383; embodiment 374–377; enacting health and illness 377–380; situatedness 380–382; *see also* disabilities
hedonism: metric of justice 317, 324; value of children/childhood 84; well-being 92–94
Hekma, Gert 275–276
heterosexual acts, age of consent 140, 274
heterosexual parents 5; expectation to reproduce 148–150; gender roles 230–233; nuclear family model 191–192, 198
historical context: adolescence 37–40; art by children 45–50; autonomy of children 117; rights of children 105–106; sexuality of children 272–273
homophobia 171, 174, 274
homosexual acts, age of consent 140, 274; *see also* sexual orientation of children
homosexual parents 5; adoption 171–172; expectation to reproduce 148–150; gender roles 230–233; licensing of parenting 204; nuclear family model 191–192, 198
Hursthouse, Rosalind 152–153

identity construction: biological parents 196–197; disabilities 264; gender and the family 226, 228; racial understanding of children 251–255

illness *see* health issues in children
imagination, epistemic openness 57–58
impartiality 183–184; *see also* parental partiality
implicit knowledge 20
inclusive special education 267
independence 114–115; *see also* autonomy
indoctrination: animals and children 286; and good parenting 175
infants *see* babies
information, learning from others 18–19; *see also* knowledge in childhood
informed consent 141, 143; *see also* consent
innateness, language acquisition 23–24, 26, 27–28
innocence: art by children 46; sex education 276–277; sexuality of children 96, 97, 272–273; well-being 94, 96
instrumental value of children/childhood 80–82; *see also* value of children/childhood
interests *see* best interests of children
interest theory of rights 104–105
interference 123–125; *see also* parent–child relationship; paternalism; state intervention
intersex 225, 229
intimacy, parental partiality 185, 187–188
intrinsic value of children 80–81, 91; *see also* value of children/childhood

Jencks, Christopher 356–357
justice, metric of 317–320, 326; agency assumption 320–322; intrinsic goods of childhood 322–325
justice, sharing costs of children 341–342, 346–347
justice towards children 7; egalitarianism vs. parental partiality 183–184, 185–188; health issues 377–380; looked-after children 363–364, 368–370; schooling 356–357; voting rights 388; vulnerability 312–313; *see also* equality of opportunity; prejudice against children
just war theory 407

Kant, Immanuel: autonomy 113–114, 116, 120–121; moral status of childhood 67, 69, 70; rights 109; well-being 92–93
Keller, Simon 241
killing in war 408–410, 413
Kitchener, Richard 53–54, 56, 57
Kittay, Eva 265, 268, 305
knowledge in childhood 13, 19–20; child development 13–16; language 23–24; learning from others 18–19; nature of 16–17; *see also* language acquisition
Kolers, Avery 160
Kraut, Richard 94–95
Krishnamurthy, Meena 148

labour, children in 6–7, 294; benefiting children 298–299; exploitative nature 299–301; harm of 295–298; rights 105–106; value of domestic work 290–291
LaFollette, Hugh: adoption 217–218; autonomy 118; licensing of parenting 205–207, 209–210
Lakoff, George 30–31
language acquisition 3, 23, 31–32; abstract concepts 28–31; knowledge of 23–24; syntax 24–26; vocabulary development 26–28
Lareau, Annette 182
learning *see* education; knowledge in childhood
legal context: adoption 213–215, 216, 217, 217–218, 218–221; age of consent 135–136, 138–143; child's best interests 1; courts, children in 402–403; criminal responsibility 402; parental partiality 185–186; political inclusion 385–387; unequally gendered parenting 231–233; *see also* criminal justice
legal rights 101–102, 105
legitimacy, consent 138
Leland, R. J. 309
LGBT *see* sexual orientation of children; sexual orientation of parents
Liao, S. Matthew 109, 174
liberationism, rights of children 105–107
liberty: paternalism 123–125; and rights 107; value of children/childhood 84; *see also* autonomy
licensing of parenting 5, 202–203, 211; adoption 203–204, 206, 209, 217–218, 220–221; nature of 203; philosophical positions 204–211; *status quo* 203–204, 210–211
linguistic nativism 24–25, 26
Lipman, Matthew 56–57
Locke, John 138, 273
Lone, Jana Mohr 54–55, 56
looked-after children 362, 370; grounds for taking children in 364–366; moral and social significance 362–364; role of state 366–368; social justice 363–364, 368–370
love: disabled children 264–265; gender and the family 228–229, 231; good parenting 174; parental partiality 186–187
luck egalitarianism 7

MacIntyre, Alasdair 262
Macleod, Colin: metric of justice 320–321, 323; parental partiality 184–185; vulnerability of children 306, 307–308
magnetic resonance imaging (MRI), adolescent brain 33–34
Maier, Corinne 148
make believe 58–59
marriage in families 191–192, 193–194
maternal thinking 227
maternity leave 230, 232
Matisse, Henri 49–50
Matthews, Gareth 55, 60–61

McMahan, Jeff 81
Mead, Margaret 39
medical care *see* healthcare
medical consent 137–138, 141–142
Melson, Gail 284–285
Mental Capacity Act, 136
mental health, adolescent brain 35–36
metaphor, language acquisition 30–31
middle class parents 182
Midgley, Mary 56
military *see* war and children
Mill, John Stuart 123–126, 127
minimalism, adoption 218
moral concepts, language acquisition 29
morality: child labour 294–301; child soldiers 410–413; decision to procreate 152–155; filial duties 236; gamete donation 196; killing in war 408–410, 413; parental partiality 186–187; punishment 398; vulnerability of children 307–308, 310–312
moral philosophy: contemporary context 1–2; well-being 92–93
moral rights 101–102
moral status, children with cognitive disabilities 268
moral status of childhood 3–4, 67–68; autonomy 119; full moral status (FMS) 68–75; political inclusion 385–386; right to parent 160
Mullin, Amy 114, 116–117, 126
Music Box (film) 241–243

naïve psychology 14–15
Narveson, Jan 161–162
nativism, linguistic 24–25, 26
nature of childhood 3; *see also* value of children/childhood
negative rights 102
neglect: good parenting 173–174; licensing of parenting 204, 205–206, 208; right to parent 162–163; taking children into care 7–8, 364–368
neighbourhood effects, schooling 353, 354–355
neurodiversity 264
neuroeducation 35
neuroscience: adolescence and cultural context 39–41; adolescent brain functioning 33–36; teen brain in popular culture 36–37
neutrality: metric of justice 324–325; sharing costs of children 344–346; *see also* political neutrality
Noggle, Robert 110, 129–130
non-instrumental goods 96–98
non-utilitarianism, moral status of childhood 67–68
Nozick, Robert 238
nuclear family model 191–192, 198; *see also* families
Nussbaum, Martha 319

object permanence 14, 29
obligations *see* duties
O'Neill, Onora 1–2, 109, 110
ontogeny, art by children 45–46
open future: consent 143; rights of children 107–109
other-regard 124, 128–129
Overall, Christine 206, 207
overpopulation 340, 348

parental leave 230, 232
parental love *see* love
parental partiality 180–181, 188–189; advantage 181–182; impartiality and egalitarian justice 183–184; special duties 184–185; tensions between advantage and egalitarianism 185–188
parental rights *see* rights of parents
parent-centred theories, right to parent 160, 162–163, 164–166
parent–child relationship: contemporary context 1–2; decision to procreate 155; filial duties 236–237, 241; and rights 102, 107–110; value of children/childhood 81–82; vulnerability of children 307–312; *see also* families; parental partiality
parenting 4–6; costs of children 340–342; disabled children 264–265; disabled parents 265–266; health issues in children 378–382; number of parents 172; political neutrality 331–335, 336–337; schooling as coercion 353; teen brain in popular culture 37; *see also* decision to procreate; families; good parenting; licensing of parenting; rights of parents; state intervention
parenting styles 182
parent–parent relationship 197–198
paternalism 123–124, 131–132; autonomy 119; child's future autonomy 131; against a child's will 125–127; for the good of a child 129–131; good parenting 175–176; interference with a child 124–125; voluntariness 127–129; well-being in childhood 90
paternity leave 230–231, 232
Paul, L. A. 147–148
pedagogy, art by children 45–46
perfectionism: metric of justice 324–325; political neutrality 335–336
personal value of children/childhood 80; *see also* value of children/childhood
philosophical context, children/childhood 1–2
philosophy, children's engagement with 3, 61–62; ability of children 53–54; epistemic injustice 61–62; epistemic openness 57–59; philosophical thinking 54–57; value for children 59–61; wondering in childhood 53
physical abuse *see* child protection
Piaget, Jean 13–14, 18, 28

Picasso, Pablo 50
pity towards children 96–99
Plato: right to parent 161; sexuality 272; wonder 53
play (make believe) 58–59
policy *see* legal context
political engagement of children 8
political inclusion: animals and children 287–288; democracy 388–389; democratic equality 390–391; the regulatory problem 385–387; voting competence 385–386; voting rights 384–392
political legitimacy, consent 137–138
political neutrality 7, 328–329, 337; definition of 329–330; justifications 330–331; objections to 335–337; parents and teachers 331–335
political philosophy, contemporary context 1–2
poverty, child labour 296–298
power, parent–child relationship 310; *see also* vulnerability of children
pregnancy, language acquisition in the womb 23–24; *see also* decision to procreate
prejudice against children: epistemic injustice 61–62; race 251–252; teen brain in popular culture 36–37; *see also* discrimination; justice towards children
pretending (make believe) 58–59
Prilleltensky, Ora 266
primitivism 47–48
Prinz, Jesse 30
priority privilege, parents 307
privilege, parents 307
procreation *see* biological parents; decision to procreate
Progressive Era 105–107
pronatalism 148–151; *see also* decision to procreate
property rights 161–162
protection of children *see* child protection
proxytype theory 30
prudential value 90–91, 96–98
psychology, decision to procreate 150
puberty 376
public money: political neutrality 332–333, 336–337; schooling 351–352, 357–358; sharing costs of children 342–346
public space, animals and children 289
punishment, criminal justice 397–399, 403

Quine, W. V. O. 27
Quinn, Warren 72, 73

racial context 6, 249, 257–258; children's understanding 251–255; genetic relatedness 171; ontology of 249–250; transracial adoption 255–257
rape 139–140, 271–272
rationality: autonomy 113–115, 116; cognitive disabilities 267–268; decision to procreate 147; paternalism 126

Rawls, John: age of consent 138; metric of justice 318–319; parental partiality 186–187; political neutrality 330–331, 333–334; schooling 351
reading to children 188
recapitulation theory 38
Regan, Tom 67, 70–71
regulation *see* policy
Reich, Rob 114, 117, 118
relational vulnerability 309–312; *see also* vulnerability of children
religion: good parenting 175; medication case 381; political neutrality 328–329, 330, 332–333, 336–337; sexuality of children 272–273
reproductive technologies: vs. adoption process 214, 216, 217; biological parents 194
research, and consent 142–143
responsibilities *see* duties
Richards, Norvin 127, 130
rights in trust 103–104, 108
rights, nature of 102–105
rights of children 4, 101–102; age of consent 135–136; autonomy 119; critiques of 109–110; distinct to childhood 108–109; open future 107–109; political neutrality 7; protection vs. freedom 107; protection vs. liberation 105–107; sexual 274–275; sexual citizenship 275–276; voting 384–392
rights of parents 4–5; decision to procreate 149; definition 159; open future 107–109; *see also* consent; paternalism; right to parent
right to parent 158–161, 166; competency 176–177; conditions for holding 162–164; definition 159; licensing of parenting 203, 205–206, 209–210; a particular child 164–166; who 161–162; *see also* rights of parents
risk: adolescent brain 34–35, 38–39; child soldiers 411
Rousseau, Jean-Jacques 13, 46, 273
Ruddick, Sara 227
Rulli, Tina 155, 215–216

same-sex couples *see* homosexual parents
Satz, Debra 300
Saunders, Ben 389
Scarre, Geoffrey 127
Schapiro, Tamar: autonomy 113–114; paternalism 127; well-being 93
Schoeman, Ferdinand 109, 110
schooling 359–360; aims 353–357; challenges 352–353; challenges reconsidered 357–359; meaning of 351–352; *see also* education
self-determination theory 114
self-governance 114–115, 117, 119; *see also* autonomy
self-interest: decision to procreate 151–152, 153; political inclusion of children 385–386
self-ownership, right to parent 161–162

self-regard 124, 128–129
Sen, Amartya 318–320
sentences (language acquisition) 24–26
sexual acts 271–272
sexual consent 137–141, 271–272
sexual innocence 96, 97, 272–273, 276
sexuality of children 271–274, 279; consent 137–141, 274; rights 274–275; risk 411; sex education 276–279; sexual citizenship 275–276, 277
sexual orientation of children 6, 226–230; intersex 225, 229; sexual citizenship 275–276; transgender 225–230, 377–378
sexual orientation of parents 5, 171–172; expectation to reproduce 148–150; gender roles 230–233; nuclear family model 191–192, 198
sexual relationships, family structure 193–194
sexual reproduction *see* biological parents
shared parenting 197–198
single parents 172
Skelton, Anthony 324
social and emotional behavioural difficulties (SEBD) 267
social context: adolescent brain 37–38; animals and children 284–287, 289–290; criminal justice system 398–401; decision to procreate 148–149; disabilities 261–262; families 192–193; gender and the family 226–230; good parenting 170; learning from others 18–19; parental partiality 184–185; race 249, 250, 254–255, 256–257; sexual orientation of parents 171–172
social justice: looked-after children 363–364, 368–370; voting rights of children 388
social pronatalism 149–150
society and children 6–7; *see also* animals and children; disabilities; labour, children in; racial context; sexuality of children; vulnerability of children
soft paternalism 128
special education 267
special goods account, filial duties 241, 242–243
special goods of childhood 2
special relationship accounts, moral status 72–73
speciesism 285–287
species-membership accounts, moral status 72–73
Spelke, Elizabeth 28
spiritual beliefs, medication case 381; *see also* religion
state institutions *see* education; healthcare
state intervention 7–9; adoption 214–215, 218–221; grounds for taking children into care 364–366; political neutrality 329–335; role in care system 366–368; *see also* costs of children; criminal justice; justice, metric of; legal context; licensing of parenting; political inclusion; schooling; war and children
Steinbock, Bonnie 73
stereotype threat, race 254
"storm and stress" 39–40

"stranger danger" 401–402
strong humane justice (SHJ) 356–357
suffrage 384–392; *see also* political inclusion
Swift, Adam: decision to procreate 155; families 193; good parenting 174, 175; love 231; parental partiality 187–188; right to parent 163; value of children/childhood 81; vulnerability of children 309, 312; well-being 94, 97
syntax, language acquisition 24–26

tax money *see* public money
teachers, political neutrality 331–335; *see also* education
technology *see* reproductive technologies
"teen brain" 36–37; *see also* adolescence
Terlazzo, Roza 130–131
Tomasello, Michael 24–25, 30
toys, gender and the family 226–227, 229–230
transgender 225–230, 377–378

United Nations Convention of the Rights of the Child (UNCRC) 283
universities, parental partiality 185–186
usage-based theory 24–25
utilitarianism: moral status of childhood 67–68; well-being 92–93

value of children/childhood 3–4, 79–81, 88; art 46–47; complementarity 87; decision to procreate 151–152; instrumental value 80–82; intrinsic value 80–81; is childhood good for children 81, 82–85; well-being standards 85–87; *see also* well-being
VanDeVeer, Donald 130
Velleman, J. David: families 195–197; genetic relatedness 170–171; right to parent 165
very young children *see* young children
victims, children as: crime 401–402; war 406; *see also* child protection; vulnerability of children
virtue ethics, decision to procreate 152–153
vocabulary development 26–28; *see also* language acquisition
voluntariness, paternalism 127–129
Vopat, Mark 206–208
voting rights 384–392; *see also* political inclusion
vulnerability of children 7, 304; disabilities 263–264; epistemic openness 59; health issues 373, 380; implications and obligations 312–313; morality 307–308, 310–312; nature of 304–307; relational vulnerability 309–312; value of children/childhood 83, 85; war 409

Wall, John 59
war and children 8, 406, 413–414; non-combatants 407–410; participants 410–413
Weeks, Jeffrey 275
Weinstock, Daniel 80, 82, 87, 208, 209–210

welfare: metric of justice 317–325; sharing costs of children 342–346
well-being 90, 99; autonomy 119; childhood literature 94–96; health issues 378–380; hurdles 91–94; limits of paternalism 175–176; pity towards children 96–99; preliminaries 90–91; standards of in childhood vs. adulthood 85–87; *see also* best interests of children; child protection
Western world: adolescence 38–40; art by children 46–50; decision to procreate 148
Whelan, Elizabeth 147, 148
White, Educated, Industrialized, Rich and Democratic ("WEIRD") societies 39–40
Williamson, Timothy 17

will theory of rights 102–105
Wittgenstein, Ludwig 16
wondering in childhood 53; *see also* philosophy, children's engagement with
work *see* employment; labour, children in
working class parents 182
Wrightson, Angela murder case 395, 396
Wynn, Karen 29

young carers 266
young children: autonomy 116–117; health issues 376; and paternalism 127; and rights 103, 104, 105, 109; sexuality 273–274; *see also* babies
Young, Thomas 152